The Illustrated Encyclopedia of

COMBAT AIRCRAFT
OF
WORLD WAR II

The Illustrated Encyclopedia of

COMBAT AIRCRAFT OF WORLD WAR II

Bill Gunston

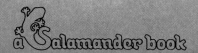

a Salamander book

Published by Salamander Books Limited
LONDON

A Salamander Book

Published by Salamander Books Ltd.,
Salamander House,
27 Old Gloucester Street,
London WC1N 3AF,
United Kingdom.

© Salamander Books Ltd. 1978

ISBN 0 86101 017 5

Distributed in Australia/New Zealand by
Summit Books, a division of Paul Hamlyn Pty Ltd.,
Sydney, Australia.

Credits

Editor: Ray Bonds

Designer: Steve Henderson

Colour drawings: © Pilot Press Ltd.;
Terry Hadler, and County Studios (© Salamander Books Ltd.).

Line drawings and cutaways: © Pilot Press Ltd.

Filmset by SX Composing Ltd., Rayleigh, Essex, England.

Colour reproduction by Web Offset Reproductions, 32 Paul
Street, London EC2, Metric Reproductions Ltd., Chelmsford,
Essex, and Paramount Litho Company, Basildon, Essex, England.

Two-tone colour reproduction by Adtype Ltd., 29 Clerkenwell
Road, London EC1, England.

Printed in Belgium by Henri Proost et Cie, Turnhout.

Editor's Acknowledgements

This book is not the first to be published on the subject, nor will
it be the last. But military aviation enthusiasts will quickly
recognize that this volume is unlikely ever to be surpassed for
sheer number of facts about and illustrations of combat aircraft
of World War II. In order to compile a book of this nature one
depends very heavily on the assistance of numerous institutions
and individuals all over the world. So many people have helped
to produce this volume that, while I thank all of them, there is not
the space to mention them all here. In particular, though, I am
indebted to Bill Gunston who, apart from displaying his sheer
professionalism and depth of knowledge in writing in excess of
150,000 words of data and description, also gave many useful
"leads" towards tracking down elusive contemporary
photographs of World War II aircraft; and to Pilot Press for
permitting us to reproduce their magnificent colour profile
drawings, three-view drawings and cutaways; and to the many
manufacturers who, though they could not hope to sell one more
of their current production aircraft by supplying photographs of
their wartime aeroplanes to a book publisher, nevertheless
scoured their archives on our behalf; and to all the museums,
institutions and individual aircraft enthusiasts who have
similarly strived to supply material for this most colourful
volume. I thank them all.

We decided to group the aircraft by country of origin, and present
them in alphabetical order of manufacturers' names. Where such
a strict order has, for space and technical reasons, threatened to
deprive a particular aircraft of its deserved coverage, we
"adjusted" the alphabet slightly. In particular, to overcome
production problems, the fold-outs showing the magnificent
Terry Hadler paintings, necessitated positioning the
Messerschmitt Bf 109 and Bf 110 between the Henschel Hs 126
and Hs 129, and likewise the Grumman F6F Hellcat and the
North American P-51 Mustang between the Martin Marauder
and the Martin Baltimore.

Ray Bonds

Contents

Introduction

To most Westerners the conflict called World War II means 1939-45, but it is not as simple as that. The Soviet Union and United States were drawn in in 1941, but Japan had been fighting continuously in China since 1937 and had been involved in sporadic but bloody battles with the Chinese and the Soviet Union since 1930. Forgotten areas such as Abyssinia and what is now Somalia had been invaded by Italy in 1936-37, and Tripolitania and Cyrenaica had suffered even earlier. Prosperous Sweden, on the other hand, never became embroiled at all, and it is without disrespect to that aeronautically important nation that its aircraft have been omitted from this volume.

For various reasons the aircraft that fought man's biggest and most diverse war have remained subjects of lasting interest to each new generation. It was indeed a war that had everything. In many places "eyeball" confrontations took place between fighter pilots who could see each other in the cockpit, and it all hinged on personal skill. In other places a rather different breed of men stalked the night sky, guided by fickle patterns of brightness on small cathode-ray tubes, until they could pump cannon shells into something that was just a little blacker than the sky background. Technical development was fantastic, and the pre-war air exercises and even participation in the Spanish Civil War were soon irrelevant to new operational circumstances.

At the start the war was one-sided. What most observers regard as the start of World War II took place 11 minutes ahead of schedule at 04.34 on 1 September 1939 when "Stukas" dive-bombed the Dirschau bridge over the Vistula. This set the scene. For 27 terrible days Poland was subjected to a rain of bombs put down with little opposition by everything from Hs 123 biplanes to trimotor Ju 52s. There was no need for advanced technology, and the campaign taught the Germans little (and even that was not heeded). Yet later the scene was to change dramatically. By 1942 the Luftwaffe hardly dared fly over Britain at all, and when the invasion forces were massing in 1944 the Luftwaffe could not even bring back pictures. By this time the Allies were conquering the Luftwaffe even over the heart of Germany, but the battle was being fought with new weapons. Radar pierced cloud and darkness—and often foolishly served as a beacon on which hostile fighters could home. New navigation aids guided aircraft to their targets, and back to friendly runways. Powerful warheads no longer fell unguided but could be steered by radio signals or electric signals transmitted through wires right up to the moment of impact. Cannon, rockets and recoilless guns had transformed air combat, while Germany had made giant strides with amazing "V-weapons" which actually did nothing to delay her eventual defeat.

In World War II more aircraft of more types were built than at any other time in history. Today, with our inflation on one hand and slashed defence budgets (except in the Soviet Union) on the other, we find it hard even to comprehend how single factories could roll out complex four-engined

bombers at the rate of 15 to 20 a day. In Germany in the final months there were a few of the most experienced pilots the world has ever seen, some of whom had flown more than a thousand combat missions. There were new fighters by the hundred, but hardly any suitable petrol. The new jets, with their diesel-oil fuel, usually had some supplies; but Allied air power had often wrecked their airfields and some of the Luftwaffe's jet units finished the war operating from public highways and hiding under the roadside trees.

There were countless other facets of this war that emerge from study of its aircraft. It was the first war in which air power at last extended everywhere, even into the middle of the wide North Atlantic. No longer could the U-boat lurk undetected, and the anti-submarine aircraft became so deadly that U-boats had to bristle with flak and try and fight

it out on the surface. Aircraft learned to destroy the heaviest tanks, to take out "hardened" (armoured) point targets and to pierce reinforced concrete 30 feet thick. For the first time supplies for large surface forces were flown in, and casualties flown out. Thousands of aircrew became familiar with the techniques of electronic warfare, including chaff, decoys, jamming and many other artful dodges that we are still trying to perfect 35 years later. It would be foolish to give the impression that they were days to which anyone would gladly return, but they were certainly great days—and nights—with great aircraft.

Bill Gunston

Commonwealth Boomerang

CA-12 to CA-19 Boomerang
(data for CA-12)

Origin: Commonwealth Aircraft Corporation, Australia.
Type: Single-seat fighter.
Engine: 1,200hp Pratt & Whitney R-1830-S3C4G Twin Wasp 14-cylinder two-row radial.
Dimensions: Span 36ft 3in (11m); length 25ft 6in (7·77m); height 11ft 6in (3·5m).
Weights: Empty 5,450lb (2474kg); loaded 7,600lb (3450kg).
Performance: Maximum speed 296mph (474km/h); service ceiling 29,000ft (8845m); range at 190mph (304km/h) 930 miles (1490km).
Armament: Normally, two 20mm Hispano cannon and four 0·303in Browning machine guns in wings.
History: First flight 29 May 1942; first delivery August 1942; final deliveries, early 1944.
User: Australia.

Development: When Australia suddenly found itself in the front line, in December 1941, it had no modern fighters save a few Buffaloes supplied to the RAF in Singapore. To try to produce a stop-gap quickly the Commonwealth Aircraft Corporation at Fishermen's Bend, Melbourne, decided to design and build their own. But the design team, under Wing Commander

Above: An echelon of four CA-13 Boomerangs of No 5 Squadron, Royal Australian Air Force. These tough and versatile aircraft served mainly in the New Guinea campaign.

Avia 534

534-III and -IV

Origin: A.S.P.R.L. "Avia", Czechoslovakia.
Type: Single-seat fighter.
Engine: 760/860hp Avia-built Hispano-Suiza 12 Ydrs 12-cylinder vee liquid-cooled.
Dimensions: Span 30ft 10in (9·4m); length 26ft 7in (8·1m); height 10ft 2in (3·1m).
Weights: Empty 3,218lb (1460kg); loaded 4,364lb (1980kg).
Performance: Maximum speed 249mph (400km/h); initial climb 2,953ft (900m)/min; service ceiling 34,770ft (10,600m); range 373 miles (600km).
Armament: Four 7·92mm Mk 30 (modified Vickers) machine guns.
History: First flight (B 34) late 1931; (B 534) August 1933; final delivery, not known but after 1938.
Users: Czechoslovakia (Army), Germany (Luftwaffe), Slovakia (CB, Insurgent AF).

Development: In 1930 the Avia works at Prague-Letnany, a subsidiary of the great Czech Skoda company, appointed a new chief designer, F. Nowotny. His first design was the B 34 fighter, which in 1932 was studied with a series of radial and vee engines and eventually gelled as the B 534.

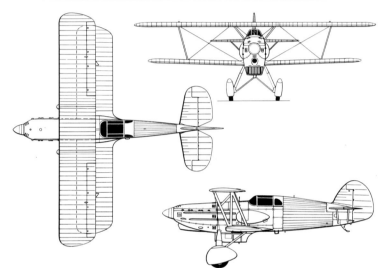

Above: Avia 534-IV with tailskid instead of wheel.

Letov S 328

S 328 and 528

Origin: Vojenska Tovarna na Letadla "Letov", Czechoslovakia.
Type: Two-seat reconnaissance bomber and utility.
Engine: (S 328) one 635hp Walter (Bristol licence) Pegasus II M2 nine-cylinder radial; (S 528) one 800hp Gnome-Rhône Mistral Major 14Krsd 14-cylinder two-row radial.
Dimensions: Span 44ft 11¼in (13·7m); length 33ft 11¾in (10·35m); (528) 34ft 1½in; height 10ft 11in (3·3m); (528) 11ft 2in.
Weights: (328) empty, 3,704lb (1680kg); loaded 5,820lb (2640kg).
Performance: Maximum speed 174mph (280km/h); (528) about 205mph (330km/h); initial climb 984ft (300m)/min; service ceiling 23,600ft (7200m); range 435 miles (700km), (328 with overload tank, about 795 miles, 1280km).
Armament: Four 7·92mm Ceska-Zbrojovka Mk 30 machine guns, two fixed in upper wing and two manually aimed from rear cockpit, with provision for two more Mk 30 fixed in lower wings; underwing bomb load of two 265lb (120kg) or six 110lb (50kg).
History: First flight (S 328F) February 1933; (S 528) 1935; final S 328 delivery, after March 1940.
Users: Bulgaria, Croatia, Czechoslovakia, Finland, Germany (Luftwaffe), Hungary, Slovakia and Soviet-managed Slovak Insurgent Combined Squadron.

Development: The S 328 saw an amazing amount of active service in various hands, and its similarity to the Swordfish shows what it might have accomplished had it carried a torpedo. It was designed by a team led by Alois Smolik, who had been chief designer ever since the Letov company evolved from the Czech Military Air Arsenal in 1918. The basic design was the S 28 of 1929, from which Smolik derived the S 228 supplied to Estonia. In 1933

Left: This Letov S 328 was one of about 100 assigned to combat duty with the Slovakian Air Force in the Polish campaign and on the Eastern Front against the Soviet Union. It is shown in 1941-43 markings, with yellow tactical theatre band. These machines equipped Nos 1 and 3 reconnaissance squadrons and No 2 liaison squadron, chiefly in tracking partisans in the Ukraine. Increasingly the Letovs and crews defected to the Soviet side, and on 29 August 1944 the Slovak Uprising led to a "free combined squadron".

Laurence J. Wackett, was severely restricted. The new fighter had to be based on the familiar North American trainer series, which since 1938 had served as the basis for the excellent Wirraway general-purpose combat machine and trainer, of which 755 were made by CAC by 1946. Moreover the only powerful engine available was the 1,200hp Twin Wasp, judged by 1942 to be much too low-powered for first-line fighters elsewhere. Despite these restrictions the resulting machine was tough, outstandingly manoeuvrable and by no means outclassed by the Japanese opposition. Wackett's team worked day and night to design the CA-12 in a matter of weeks and build and fly the prototype in a further 14 weeks. Testing and production went ahead together and, as there were no real snags, the first of 105 CA-12s were soon fighting in New Guinea. There followed 95 CA-13s with minor changes and 49 CA-19s, as well as a CA-14 with turbocharged engine and square tail. Boomerangs did not carry bombs but often marked targets for "heavies" and undertook close support with their guns.

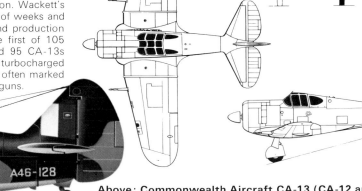

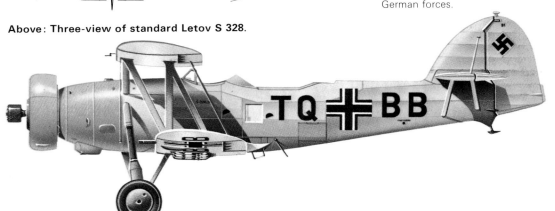

Above: Commonwealth Aircraft CA-13 (CA-12 and 19 similar).
Left: A CA-13 Boomerang of RAAF No 5 Sqn (actually the aircraft in the foreground in the formation photograph).

This was probably the finest fighter of its day, having outstanding speed and manoeuvrability, no vices and the heavy armament of four guns. Originally two were in the lower wing, as in Britain's Gloster Gladiator of two years later. Wing vibration when the guns were fired led to all four being put in the fuselage, with a bulge over the belt feed and case boxes. In 1935 the type went into large-scale production and at the time of the Munich crisis in September 1938 over 300 of the eventual total of 445 had been delivered, so the Czech Army was actually stronger in fighters than the Luftwaffe. Many of the aircraft were B 534-IIIs with enclosed cockpit and -IVs with more powerful 12Y engine. A batch of 35, designated Bk 534, were to have had a 20mm cannon firing through the propeller hub; only a few had the

Left: An Avia B 534-IV serving with the Slovakian Air Force on the Eastern Front in late 1941 (probably with the 11th Fighter Squadron). The Slovak tail insignia and yellow tactical theatre band are prominent. Like most Slovakian units, which included some equipped with the Do 17Z-2 bomber, these biplane fighters operated in the Ukraine, mainly on the Kiev sector.

big gun, most having a mere machine gun, with one more on each side. About 350 served with the Luftwaffe in 1939–41 as trainers and tugs for gliders and targets. Slovak Air Force fighter squadrons 11, 12 and 13 operated on the Russian front from July 1941, but morale was low and many Avias deserted to the Soviet side. Three aircraft survived to fight against the Germans in the Slovak revolt of 1944.

Finland ordered the S 328F. None were delivered to that customer, but the Czech government ordered the 328 for its own Army Air Force reconnaissance squadrons. Though there were small batches of 328N night fighters and 328V twin-float seaplanes, nearly all were reconnaissance bombers. They continued to come off the line long after flight testing of the 528, the intended successor, had shown superior performance. Only five 528s were built, but when German troops occupied Bohemia-Moravia in March 1939 more than 445 of the earlier type had been delivered. All were impressed into the Luftwaffe or the new Slovak Air Force, while production at Prague-Letnany continued, the final 30 being for the Bulgarian Air Force. More than 200 served in the Polish campaign and, from 1941, on the Russian Front, tracking partisans, night-fighting against Po-2 biplanes and even in close-support of ground forces. Many Slovak Letovs defected and in August 1944 surviving 328s in Czechoslovakia donned Red Stars as part of the Insurgent Combined Squadron which fought bitterly against the occupying German forces.

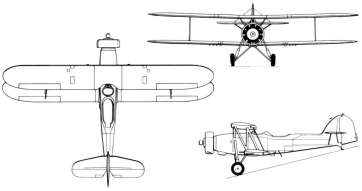

Above: Three-view of standard Letov S 328.

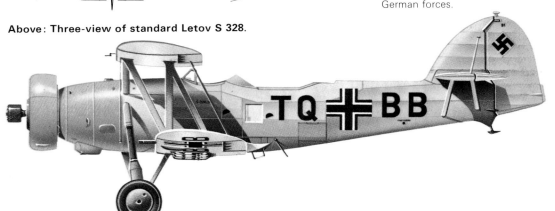

Left: This Letov S 328 was one of about 270 which were eventually assigned to the Luftwaffe A/B Schulen (pilot-training schools); this example was at the school at Olomouc, in Moravia. In winter 1942-43 many Letovs were withdrawn, with instructors, to serve in newly formed Störkampfstaffeln (night attack units). A few were used by the Bulgarian Air Force to patrol the Black Sea coastline. The Slovak examples that revolted in August 1944 adopted a Red Star or insurgent Slovak insignia.

Amiot 143

143M (B-5)

Origin: Avions Amiot (formerly SECM).
Type: Five-seat reconnaissance bomber.
Engines: Two 900hp Gnome-Rhône 14K Mistral Major 14-cylinder air-cooled radials.
Dimensions: Span 80ft 6in (24·53m); length 59ft 11in (18·25m); height 18ft 7¾in (5·65m).
Weights: Empty 13,448lb (6100kg); loaded 19,568lb (8876kg); maximum overload 21,385lb (9700kg).
Performance: Maximum speed 193mph (310km/h) at 13,120ft (4000m); maximum cruising speed 168mph (270km/h); normal range 746 miles (1200km); service ceiling 25,930ft (9000m).
Armament: Four 7·5mm MAC 1934 machine guns; up to 1,764lb (800kg) of bombs internally and same weight on external wing racks.
History: Prototype flew April 1931; production aircraft flew April 1935; first delivery July 1935.
User: France (Armée de l'Air).

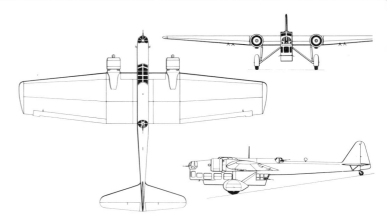

Above: Three-view of Amiot 143M of later production series with dorsal turret further forward and other minor changes.

Bloch MB.152C-1

MB-150 to 157 (data for 152)

Origin: SNCASO.
Type: Single-seat fighter.
Engine: 1,080hp Gnome-Rhône 14N-25 14-cylinder radial.
Dimensions: Span 34ft 6¾in (10·5m); length 29ft 10in (9·1m); height 13ft 0in (3·95m).
Weights: Empty 4,453lb (2020kg); loaded 5,842lb (2650kg).
Performance: Maximum speed 323mph (520km/h); climb to 16,400ft (5000m) in 6 minutes; service ceiling 32,800ft (10,000m); range 373 miles (600km).
Armament: Two 20mm Hispano 404 cannon (60-round drum) and two 7·5mm MAC 1934 machine guns (500 rounds each); alternatively four MAC 1934.
History: First flight (MB-150) October 1937; (MB-151) 18 August 1938; (MB-152) December 1938; (MB-155) 3 December 1939; (MB-157) March 1942.
Users: France (Armée de l'Air, Vichy AF), Greece, Romania.

Development: Like so many French aircraft of the time, the Bloch monoplane fighter story began badly, got into its stride just in time for the capitulation and eventually produced outstanding aircraft which were unable to be used. The prototype 150 was not only ugly but actually failed to fly, the frightened test pilot giving up on 17 July 1936. It was only after redesign with more power and larger wing that the aircraft finally left the ground. Bloch had been absorbed into the new nationalised industry as part of SNCASO and five of the new group's factories were put to work making 25. But the detail design was difficult to make, so the MB-151 was produced with the hope that 180 would be made each month from late 1938. Orders were also placed for the slightly more powerful MB-152, but by the start of World War II only 85 Blochs had been delivered and not one was fit for use; all lacked gunsights and most lacked propellers! Eventually, after overcoming desperate problems and shortages, 593 were delivered by the capitulation, equipping GC I/1, II/1, I/8, II/8, II/9, II/10, III/10 and III/9. The Germans impressed 173 surviving Bloch 151 and 152 fighters, passing 20 to Romania. The MB-155 had a 1,180hp engine and was used by Vichy France. The ultimate model was the superb MB-157, with 1,580hp 14R-4 engine and 441mph (710km/h) speed, never put into production. By this time the firm's founder had changed his name to Dassault.

Left: Bloch 152C-1 of GC II/1, in operational service when the Germans invaded France on 10 May 1940. On that date only two GC (Groupes de Chasse) were combat-ready despite the fact that well over 300 had been completed except for small but vital items. Total production was 140 MB.151 and 488 MB.152. Not especially good performers, they were at least tough. One 152C-1 landed on 15 May 1940 after a fight against 12 Bf 109s; it had 360 bullet holes.

Bloch 174

174 A3, 175 B3 and T

Origin: SNCASO.
Type: Three-seat reconnaissance, target marker and light bomber.
Engines: Two 1,140hp Gnome-Rhône 14N 14-cylinder radials.
Dimensions: Span 58ft 9½in (17·9m); length 40ft 1½in (12·23m); height 11ft 7¾in (3·59m).
Weights: Empty 12,346lb (5600kg); maximum 15,784lb (7160kg).
Performance: Maximum speed 329mph (529km/h) at 17,060ft (5200m); cruising speed 248mph (400km/h); climb to 26,250ft (8000m) 11min; service ceiling 36,090ft (11,000m); maximum range with 880lb (400kg) bomb load 800 miles (1,450km).
Armament: Two 7·5mm MAC 1934 fixed in wings, three fixed at different angles below and to the rear, and two manually aimed from rear cockpit; internal bay for eight 110lb (50kg) bombs, wing racks for light bombs or flares (175, three 441lb or equivalent).

History: First flight (170-01) 15 February 1938; (174-01) 5 January 1939; (first production 174 A3) 5 November 1939; first delivery to combat unit (GR II/33) 19 March 1940.
Users: France (Armée de l'Air, Aéronavale, Vichy AF), Germany (Luftwaffe).

Development: Under chief designer Henri Deplante the Bloch 170 was planned as a bomber and army co-operation machine in 1936–37. As a result of indecision by the Armée de l'Air this took three years to evolve into the Bloch 174 A3 reconnaissance and target-marking aircraft, with secondary capability as a bomber. By the time production of the 174 stopped in May 1940 a total of 50 had been delivered. The first sortie was flown in March 1940 by the famed Capitaine Antoine de Saint-Exupéry. As it had an insignificant bomb load the 174 made little impact on the Blitzkrieg – it was only in 1942, in Tunisia, that the survivors were fitted to conduct shallow dive-

Left: The excellent 174A3 suffered from its French industrial and political environment and none reached the Armée de l'Air until 19 March 1940. The first operational sortie took place on 29 March. Combat experience was outstanding, and the loss rate was even lower than for the equally fast Douglas DB-7. This example served with Vichy GR II/33 at Tunis El Aouina.

Development: Between the world wars French bombers were invariably aesthetic monstrosities. Fortunately few were built in numbers, but the 143, produced by SECM-Amiot and flown (as the 140) at Villacoublay in April 1931, had a long and varied operational career. Designed to a 1928 Multiplace de Combat specification, the 140 progressed through several stages to become the production 143, which entered service with GB 3/22 at Chartres in August 1935. The last of 138 was delivered in March 1937. At first the guns were all World War I Lewises, with drum magazines, but at the 41st aircraft they changed to the belt-fed MAC 1934 (though with only one gun at each rear position instead of two). The structure was all-metal, and the wing was so thick the engines could be reached in flight. Main wartime units were GB 34 at Dugny, GB 35 at Bron and GB 38 at Metz (which took the Amiots from GB 22). After leaflet raiding, operations began in earnest with the invasion of the Low Countries on 10 May, and in 197 night operations the rugged Amiots dropped 338,626lb (153 tonnes) of bombs for the loss of four aircraft. But in a desperate day assault on the Sedan bridges only one came back from GB I/38 and II/38. These lumbering bombers served Vichy France and then the Allies as transports in Tunisia until 1944.

Right: Before World War II the Amiots often flew in loose formation on day exercises; wartime missions were at night.

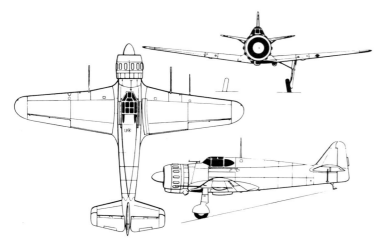

Above: Bloch 151C-1 with cannon armament (152 similar).

Right, upper: A Bloch 151C-1, outwardly almost identical to the slightly faster 152. Most 151s had four machine guns, but many had two cannon like the majority of the MB.152 type. Seven MB.151 fighters were sold to Greece and 30 served with Aéronavale (French Fleet Air Arm) squadrons AC 1 and AC 3.

Right: This line-up of MB.152 fighters probably formed part of GC I/1 or II/1, which were the first units to become operational. In May-June 1940 the Blochs gained 188 victories at the cost of 86 pilots killed, wounded or taken prisoner.

bombing with bombs of up to 500kg (1,102lb) — but the performance and handling were so outstanding and made such a difference to the casualty-rate among squadrons equipped with the type, that the Bloch 175 was hurriedly planned as a purpose-designed bomber. Altogether 25 Bloch 175 B3s were completed before France collapsed, with more than 200 on the production line, and had France been able to resist longer the 175 would have been a potent weapon. A few 174 and 175 aircraft saw service with the Luftwaffe, but most served Vichy France in North Africa and many survived the war. Indeed the torpedo-carrying 175T remained in production for the Aéronavale until 1950.

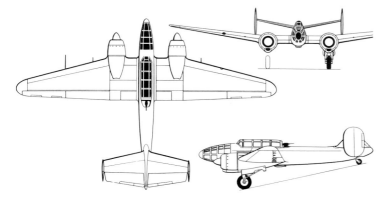

Above: Three-view of Bloch 174A3.

Above: A fully combat-ready Bloch 174A3, probably belonging to GR II/33 after the French Armistice. Later these aircraft were painted with the crimson/yellow stripes of the Vichy AF.

Breguet 690 family

Bre. 690, 691, 693

Origin: Soc. Louis Breguet.
Type: Two-seat light attack bomber.
Engines: Two 640/700hp Hispano-Suiza 14AB10/11 14-cylinder radials (693 two 680/700hp Gnome-Rhône 14M6/7 14-cylinder radials).
Dimensions: Span 50ft 4¾in (15·3m); length 33ft 7in (10·22m); height 10ft 3¾in (3·4m).
Weights: Empty 6,834lb (3100kg) (693: 6,636lb, 3010kg); maximum loaded 11,023lb (5000kg) (693: 10,800lb, 4900kg).
Performance: (Very similar for both) maximum speed 300mph (483km/h); time to climb to 13,120ft (4000m) 7 minutes; service ceiling 27,885ft (8500m); range 840 miles (1350km).
Armament: One 20mm Hispano 404 cannon with 60-round drum and two 7·5mm MAC 1934 machine guns (500 rounds each) all fixed firing forward (pilot could tilt all three 15° down for ground strafing); one MAC 1934 fixed firing obliquely down at rear (late-model 693 also had two more MAC 1934 oblique in nacelles); single MAC 1934 fed by 100-round drums on pivoted mount in rear cockpit; racks for eight 110lb (50kg) bombs in bomb bay.
History: First flight (Bre. 690) 23 March 1938; (Bre. 691) 22 March 1939; (Bre. 693) 25 October 1939; (Bre 695) 23 April 1940.
Users: France (Armée de l'Air), Italy (RA).

Development: In 1934 designers in seven countries began work on what were to become significant members of a new breed of fighter having two engines. These were hoped to be in no way inferior in performance to other, smaller, fighters and to be superior in navigation, long-range escort and ground attack. It was also considered they would be superior if fighting should ever be necessary at night. One of the best designs was Breguet's 690. It was finished in March 1937 but then had to wait almost a year for engines, because Breguet had not joined the newly nationalised French industry and Potez had priority for engines for the 630 family. But once it was able to fly it rivalled even the MS.406 single-seater, adopted as future Armée de l'Air fighter. With all haste, the Bre. 691 light attack version was put into production, all but the first 50 having imported Hamilton propellers because of a shortage of the Ratier type. At aircraft No 78 production switched to the Bre. 693, with more reliable G-R engines of even smaller diameter. By the capitulation 224 had been delivered, plus 50 Bre. 695 hastily put into production with the American P&W Twin Wasp Junior engine, which was lighter and more powerful but actually harmed flight performance, handling and pilot view. Breguet escadrilles fought valiantly, especially GBA I/54 and II/54. The Luftwaffe took engines from 693s to power Hs 129 and Me 323 aircraft, and some dozens of 693s served Italy in 1942–43.

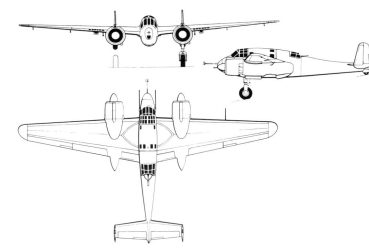

Above: Three-view of Breguet 691A-2.

Above: The various Breguet 690-family models were extremely similar externally. This unit, possibly GBA I/54, was equipped with the Bre.693 AB2 in the hectic spring of 1940.

Right: One of the first of the Breguet 690 family to be delivered was Bre.691 AB2 No 5, seen in manufacturer's finish prior to being ferried to Orléans-Bricy in October 1939.

Left: Another Hispano-engined Bre.691 pictured in operational trim with the 54e escadre, the only one to use this troublesome type. The Hispano engines had the oil cooler and carburettor ducts below and above, respectively.

Right: When the Germans occupied the whole of France in November 1942 they seized many Bre.693s and transferred them to the Italian Regia Aeronautica. Here they served until the Italian collapse in the autumn of 1943, chiefly as operational trainers.

Left: A late-production Bre.693 AB2 of GBA II/54, the most successful Breguet unit which was based at Roye in May 1940 but was later able to evacuate to Toulouse-Francazals. The Breguet 690 family proved extremely agile, tough and effective in operation, and so simple to maintain that combat strength was kept up despite frequent retreats.

Dewoitine D 520

D 520S

Origin: SNCA du Midi.
Type: Single-seat fighter.
Engine: One 910hp Hispano-Suiza 12Y-45 vee-12 liquid-cooled.
Dimensions: Span 33ft 5¾in (10·2m); length 28ft 8½in (8·75m); height 11ft 3in (3·4m).
Weights: Empty 4,630lb (2100kg); loaded 6,173lb (2800kg).
Performance: Maximum speed 329mph (530km/h); initial climb 2,362ft (720m)/min; service ceiling 36,090ft (11,000m); range 777 miles (1240km).
Armament: One 20mm Hispano-Suiza 404 cannon, with 60 rounds, firing through the propeller hub, and four 7·5mm MAC 1934 machine guns, each with 500 rounds, in wings.
History: First flight (520–01) 2 October 1938; (production, 520-2) 3 December 1939; service delivery 1 February 1940.
Users: Bulgaria, France, Italy (RA), Romania.

Development: Few people have ever disputed that this neat little fighter was the best produced in France prior to the Armistice; it was certainly the best to reach the squadrons. Unlike so many other hopeful types which just

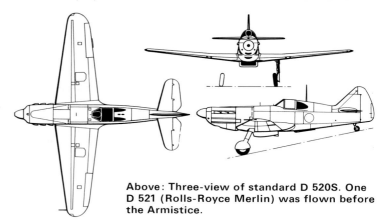

Above: Three-view of standard D 520S. One D 521 (Rolls-Royce Merlin) was flown before the Armistice.

Above: The white arrow and roundel surround show that this D 520S (No 147) was photographed in Vichy service.

failed to be ready in time, the D 520 made it — but only just. The great Marcel Doret did not help when, having made a splendid first test flight, he forgot about the retractable landing gear on 27 November 1938 and put the first prototype out of action. The new fighter was a direct development of the 500 series and though it was very small it was hoped to fit an engine of 1,300hp — but nothing suitable was available. The first prototype had an open cockpit and the second still had a curved windscreen, tailskid and two drum-fed machine guns, as did the first production machine. But the second was up to production standard. The Dewoitine plants had vanished into the nationalised SNCA du Midi under the law of 1936 and these were meant to deliver ten in September 1939 and 30 in October. Actually timing ran about three months late, but with the panic in 1940 industry went mad. In May 1940 101 were delivered and by June the output had reached ten per day, a figure seldom exceeded by any aircraft plant in history. GC I/3 was first to go into action, followed in late May by GC II/3, with III/3, III/6 and II/7 following before the capitulation. These groups were credited with 147 kills for the loss of 85 fighters and 44 pilots. Subsequently the Vichy government restored the D 520 to production, 740 being built in all. In 1942 the Luftwaffe seized 411, passing many to Italy, Romania and Bulgaria. But in 1944 GC I/8 was re-formed under Doret and, after painting out the German insignia, went into action against the last German pockets in southern France.

Farman F 222

F 221, 222 and 223 series

Origin: SNCA du Centre (until 1936 the Farman company).
Type: All, basically, five-seat heavy bombers.
Engines: (F 221) four 800hp Gnome-Rhône GR14Kbrs 14-cylinder two-row radials; (F 222) four 860hp GR14Kbrs; (F 222/2) four 950hp GR14N 11/15 or Kirs; (F 223) four 1,100hp Hispano-Suiza HS14Aa08/09 vee-12 liquid-cooled; NC 223.3, four 910hp HS12Y29; (NC 223.4) four 1,050hp HS12Y37.
Dimensions: Span (F 221, 222, 222/2) 118ft 1½in (36m); (F 223, NC 223) 110ft 2⅝in (33·5m); length (F 221–222/2) 70ft 8¾in (21·5m); (F 223, NC 223) 72ft 2in (22m); (NC 223.4) 77ft 1in (23·5m); height (all) 16ft 9in to 17ft 2¼in (5·22m).
Weights: Empty (F 222/2) 23,122lb (10,488kg); (NC 223.3) 23,258lb (10,550kg); (NC 223.4) 22,046lb (10,000kg); loaded (F 221) 39,242lb (17,800kg); (F 222/2) 41,226lb (18,700kg); (NC 223.3) 42,329lb (19,200kg); (NC 223.4) 52,911lb (24,000kg).
Performance: Maximum speed (F 221) 185mph (300km/h); (F 222/2) 199mph (320km/h); (NC 223.3) 248mph (400km/h) (264mph as un-armed prototype); (NC 223.4) 239mph (385km/h); service ceiling (F 221) 19,700ft (6000m); (F 222/2) 26,250ft (8000m); (NC 223.3 at maximum weight) 24,606ft (7500m); (NC 223.4 at maximum weight) 13,120ft (4000m); range with maximum bomb load (F 221) 745 miles (1200km); F 222/2) 1,240 miles (2000km); (NC 223.3) 1,490 miles (2400km); (NC 223.4) 3,107 miles (5000km).

Below: The third F 222/1, one of the first of the big Farmans to be delivered (to GB I/15, in 1936). The /1 differed in its nose and in having no outer-wing dihedral.

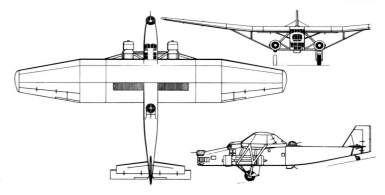

Above: Three-view of standard F 222/2.

Armament: (F 221) three manually aimed 7·5mm MAC 1934 machine guns in nose turret, dorsal and ventral positions; bomb load seldom carried; (F 222/2) same guns as 221; normal bomb load of 5,510lb with maximum internal capacity of 9,240lb (4190kg); (NC 223·3) one MAC 1934 manually aimed in nose, one 20mm Hispano 404 cannon in SAMM 200 dorsal turret, one 20mm Hispano 404 in SAMM 109 ventral turret; internal bomb load of 9,240lb. NC 223·4, one manually aimed 7·5mm Darne machine gun in entry door; internal bomb load of 4,410lb (eight 250kg bombs).
History: First flight (F 211) October 1931; (F 221) 1933; (F 222) June 1935; (F 222/2) October 1937; (NC 223) June 1937; (NC 223·3) October 1938; (NC 223·4) 15 March 1939.
User: France (Armée de l'Air, Aéronavale).

Development: This distinctive family formed the backbone of the Armée de l'Air heavy bomber force from 1935 until the collapse in 1940. It began with the F 210 of 1930, which set the pattern in having an angular box-like body, high-mounted wing and four engines slung on braced struts from the wing and fuselage in push/pull double nacelles. By way of the 220 came the 221, which served mainly as a 20-seat troop transport. The 222 introduced retractable landing gear, and the 36 F. 222/2 bombers of GBI/15 and II/15 served tirelessly in the dark months of 1940, often flying bombing missions by night over Germany and even Italy and as transports in North Africa until late 1944. The NC. 223.3, developed after nationalization, was a complete redesign and the most powerful and capable night bomber of 1938–40. The 223.4, a transatlantic mailplane, served with the Aéronavale as a heavy bomber, and in an epic 13hr 30min flight on 7–8 June 1940 one bombed Berlin.

Morane-Saulnier M.S.406

M.S.405, M.S.406C-1

Origin: Aeroplanes Morane-Saulnier; also assembled by SNCAO at St Nazaire-Bouguenais; variant built under licence by Dornier-Werke, Switzerland.

Type: Single-seat fighter.

Engine: One 860hp Hispano-Suiza 12Y-31 vee-12 liquid-cooled.

Dimensions: Span 34ft 9¾in (10·60m); length 26ft 9¼in (8·16m); height 9ft 3¾in (2·83m).

Weights: (406) empty 4,189lb (1900kg); loaded 5,364–5,445lb; maximum loaded 6,000lb (2722kg).

Performance: Maximum speed 302mph (485km/h); initial climb 2,789ft (850m)/min; service ceiling 30,840ft (9400m); range (without external tanks) 497 miles (800km).

Armament: One 20mm Hispano-Suiza HS-9 or 404 cannon with drum of 60 rounds, and two 7·5mm MAC 1934 in wings each with 300 rounds.

History: First flight (405) 8 August 1935; (production 405) 3 February

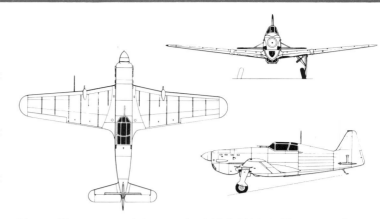

Above: Three-view of the standard M.S.406C-1. The unusual ventral radio aerial mast is shown retracted.

Right: Cutaway of a typical M.S.406C-1. All the 1,081 fighters of this type completed prior to the Armistice were essentially identical, and little different in engineering from the biplanes that preceded them.

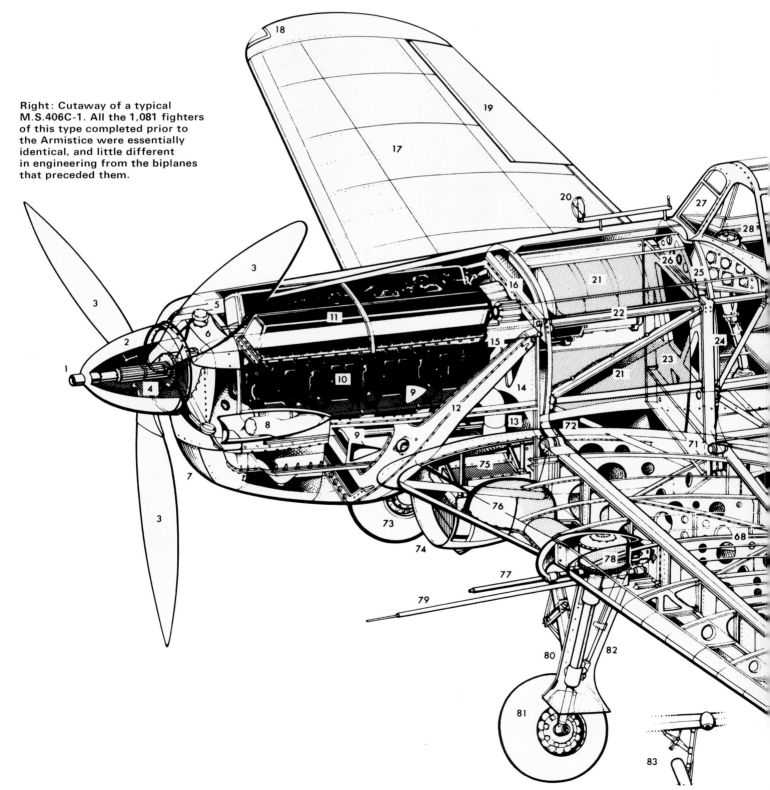

1938; (production 406) 29 January 1939; service delivery (406) 1 March 1939.

Users: Croatia, Finland, France, Germany, Turkey; ordered by China, Lithuania and Poland but for various reasons never in service with these countries.

Development: After their unbroken series of parasol monoplanes Morane-Saulnier built the M.S.405 secretly to meet a 1934 specification of the Armée de l'Air. Compared with other fighters at the start of World War II it was underpowered, lacking in performance and somewhat lacking in firepower. On the other hand its early start meant it was at least available, while other French fighters were mainly a vast collection of prototypes. Altogether 17 M.S.405 were built, most becoming prototypes of proposed future versions and ultimately giving rise to the Swiss D-3800 series of fighters which, unlike most 405s, did not have a retractable radiator.

continued on page 16 ▶

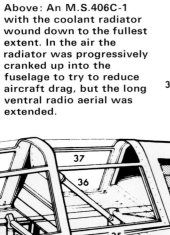

Above: An M.S.406C-1 with the coolant radiator wound down to the fullest extent. In the air the radiator was progressively cranked up into the fuselage to try to reduce aircraft drag, but the long ventral radio aerial was extended.

Morane-Saulnier 406 C1 cutaway drawing key:

1 Cannon muzzle
2 Propeller spinner
3 Chauvière 351M two-pitch propeller
4 Cannon barrel
5 Oil filler cap
6 Oil tank
7 Oil cooler
8 Coolant intake
9 Louvres
10 Exhaust ports
11 Hispano-Suiza 12Y-31 12-cylinder vee engine
12 Main engine support bearer
13 Supercharger
14 Fireproof bulkhead (with cannon cut-out)
15 Hispano-Suiza S7 cannon of 20-mm calibre
16 Cannon ammunition drum (60 rounds capacity)
17 "Plymax" stressed wing skinning
18 Starboard navigation light
19 Starboard aileron
20 Ring-and-bead auxiliary sight
21 Fuselage fuel tank (90·2 Imp gal/410 litres capacity)
22 Main upper longeron
23 Fuselage frame
24 Control column
25 Port instrument console
26 Main instrument console
27 Unarmoured windscreen
28 Reflector gunsight (OPL 31) mounting
29 Sliding cockpit canopy
30 Pilot's seat
31 Seat support frame
32 Provision for oxygen stowage
33 Control runs
34 Transmitter/receiver (Radio-Industrie 537)
35 Canopy track
36 Crash support bar
37 Aft cockpit glazing
38 Aerial mast
39 "Plymax" decking
40 Dorsal fabric (over wooden stringers)
41 Elektron formers
42 Main aft fuselage framework (Dural tubing)
43 Cross bracing
44 Fuselage/fin attachment frame
45 Tailskid bracing
46 Rear fuselage frame
47 Fin attachment point
48 Fin construction
49 Fin spar (Duralumin)
50 Balance
51 Rudder framework
52 Rudder post
53 Rudder hinge
54 Rudder tab
55 Tab cable
56 Tailplane strut
57 Elevator construction
58 Elevator balance
59 Tailplane structure
60 Tail skid
61 Ventral fabric
62 Hinged ventral aerial
63 Wing root fairing
64 Flap construction
65 Port aileron
66 Wingtip construction
67 Port navigation light
68 Wing ribs
69 Forward (main) wing spar
70 Aft wing spar
71 Rear spar/fuselage attachment point
72 Front spar/fuselage attachment points (two)
73 Starboard mainwheel
74 Retractable radiator
75 Radiator retraction links
76 Undercarriage well inner shell
77 Port 7,5-mm MAC 1934 machine gun
78 Ammunition drum (300 round capacity)
79 Pitot tube
80 Mainwheel leg
81 Port mainwheel (low-pressure tyre shown at ground angle)
82 Mainwheel leg fairing
83 Head-on view of canted mainwheel when under load

► An unusual feature was the fact that, except for the fabric-covered rear fuselage, most of the covering was Plymax (light alloy bonded to plywood). The M.S.406 was the 405 production version incorporating all the requested modifications. The production was shared out among the nationalised groups (Morane retaining only a small part of the work), with production lines at Bouguenais and Puteaux. By the time of the collapse in June 1940 no fewer than 1,081 had been completed, despite a desperate shortage of engines. In May 1940 the 406 equipped 19 of the 26 French combat-ready fighter groups. One who flew them said they were "free from vices, but too slow to catch German aircraft and too badly armed to shoot them down. Poorly protected, our own losses were high". The Vichy government fitted 32gal drop tanks to Moranes sent to Syria to fight the RAF. Many were used by Finland, fitted with skis and often with Soviet M-105P engines of higher power (the so-called LaGG-Morane).

Above: Comrades in arms, and neither adequate to face the Luftwaffe: an M.S.406C-1 escadrille visited by a Fairey Battle light bomber of the British Advanced Air Striking Force.

Left: M.S. 406C-1 of 1e Escadrille, GC I/2, based at Nîmes in the spring of 1940.

Below: New Moranes straight from Bouguennais are prepared for service at an Armée de l'Air unit in the autumn of 1939. The M.S.406 was as numerous as the Bf 109 in spring 1940.

Potez 63 series

630, 631, 633, 637 and 63·11

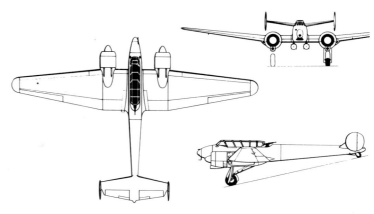

Origin: Avions Henri Potez.
Type: (630, 631) two- (sometimes three-) seat day and night fighter; (633) two-seat light attack bomber; (63.11) three-seat army co-operation and reconnaissance.
Engines: (630) two 725hp Hispano-Suiza 14AB 14-cylinder two-row radials; all other versions, two 700hp Gnome-Rhône 14M of same layout.
Dimensions: Span 52ft 6in (16m); length 36ft 4in (11·07m); (63·11 only) 36ft 1in; (11m); height 11ft 9¾in (3·6m).
Weights: Empty (630, 631, 633) typically 5,730lb (2600kg); (637) 6,390lb (2900kg); (63·11) 6,912lb (3205kg); maximum loaded (631) 8,235lb (3735kg); (633, 637) 9,285lb (4210kg); (63·11) 9,987lb (4530kg).
Performance: Maximum speed (630, 631, 633) 273mph (440km/h); (637) 267mph (430km/h); (63·11) 264mph (425km/h); initial climb (typical) 1,800ft (550m)/min; service ceiling (630, 631) 32,800ft (10,000m); (others, typical) 26,250ft (8000m).
Armament: See text.
History: First flight (Potez 63) 25 April 1936; (production 630) February 1938; (prototype 63·11) December 1938.
Users: France, Germany (Luftwaffe), Greece, Romania, Switzerland.

Development: Winner of a 1934 competition for a C3 (three-seat fighter) for the Armée de l'Air, the Potez 63 was a clean twin-finned machine powered by two of the new Hispano slim radials. It soon branched into a host of sub-variants, including many for foreign customers. The first 80 production aircraft were 630s, but they were soon grounded due to severe engine failure after only a few hours. The 631, however, was more successful and 208 were delivered (121 in May 1940 alone), equipping five fighter squadrons, two Aéronavale squadrons and many other units and shooting down 29 German aircraft (12 by the navy squadrons) in the Battle for

Above: Three-view of Potez 633, the unsuccessful attack bomber version which was widely exported but used as a combat aircraft by the Armée de l'Air on only one mission.

France. Most had two (some only one) 20mm Hispano 9 or 404 cannon, one or two 7·5mm MAC in the rear cockpit and, from February 1940, six MAC faired under the outer wings. The 633 had only two machine guns, one forward-firing and the other in the rear cockpit, and the profusion of export variants had several different kinds of gun. Maximum bomb load was 1,323lb (600kg), including 880lb (400kg) internal. Many 633s had a busy war, Greek examples fighting with the Allies and Romanian examples fighting the Russians. The 637 was used in numbers in May 1940 but was only a stop-gap for the 63·11, with glazed nose and humped rear canopy, which was used in large numbers by the Luftwaffe, Vichy French, Free French and others. Over 900 were built, bringing the total for the 63 family to more than 1,300.

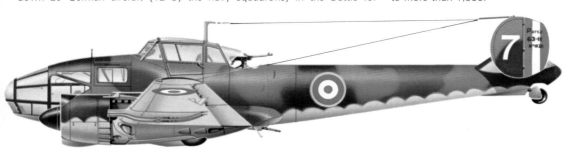

Left: Potez 63·11 No 831, shown as it was in 1943 when operating alongside other Allied air units in Tunisia. Large numbers of similar aircraft had fought against the RAF in several theatres, and more than 270 served with the Luftwaffe as advanced trainers and light utility transports. In 1942 many Vichy 63·11s were bartered with the Romanians for petrol.

SNCASE LeO 451

LeO 45, 451 B4 and derivatives

Origin: Soc Lioré et Olivier, Argenteuil, in 1937 nationalized as part of SNCASE; production see text.
Type: Medium bomber, later transport.
Engines: Two 1,140hp Gnome-Rhône 14N 48/49 14-cylinder radials.
Dimensions: Span 73ft 10¾in (22·52m); length 56ft 4in (17·17m); height 14ft 9¼in (4·50m).
Weights: Empty 17,225lb (7813kg); normal loaded 25,133lb (11,400kg); max 26,455lb (12,000kg).
Performance: Maximum speed 307mph (495km/h); service ceiling 29,530ft (9000m); range with 1,102lb (500kg) bomb load 1,430 miles (2300km).
Armament: One 20mm Hispano-Suiza 404 cannon in SAMM retractable dorsal turret, 7·5mm MAC 1934 in retractable ventral turret and MAC 1934 fixed in nose firing ahead; internal bay for up to 4,410lb (2000kg) of bombs.

Above: The Hispano is prominent on this LeO 451 of the Vichy Air Force (GB I/25, based at Tunis El Aouina) in mid-1942.

History: First flight 16 January 1937; service delivery 16 August 1939; final delivery 1943.
Users: France (Armée de l'Air, Vichy French and post-war AF), Germany (Luftwaffe), Italy (RA and CB), UK (RAF) and US (AAF).

Development: Beyond doubt the best bomber developed in France in the final years before the war, the LeO 45 was also available in substantial numbers. Despite chaotic conditions caused by nationalization of the airframe industry and widespread sabotage, production at Paris (Clichy and Levallois) and assembly at Villacoublay got into its stride by the spring of 1939. To provide the stipulated catwalk past the bomb bay small secondary bays were added in the inner wing and the main bay made even narrower than the slim fuselage. Production was dispersed to take in factories around Lyons, a second assembly-line at Ambérieu (Ain) and a third line at Marignane (Marseilles), and the evacuated Villacoublay plant was hastily moved to an underground works at Cravant near Auxerre in May 1940. The 451 B4 had been in action from the first day of war, and by May 1940 some 472 equipped eight Armée de l'Air groups. Missions could not have been more impossible, negating all the type's brilliant qualities, 47 being lost in the first 288 sorties (though on one mission the dorsal gunner destroyed two Bf 110s). Several sub-types served the Vichy forces and Luftwaffe, one Gruppe switching from Stalingrad to equip with the LeO 451T. Italy, the RAF and USAAF used the aircraft chiefly as a utility transport.

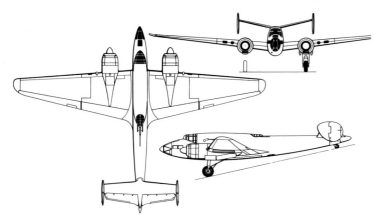

Above: Three-view of LeO 451 B4 with armament retracted.

Arado Ar 96

Ar 96A-1, Ar 96B-2 and Ar 396

Origin: Arado Flugzeugwerke; production almost entirely assigned to Ago Flugzeugwerke and to Avia and Letov in Czechoslovakia.
Type: Advanced trainer and multi-role tactical.
Engine: (96A) 240hp Argus As 10C inverted vee-8 aircooled; (B) 465hp As 410A-1 inverted vee-12 aircooled.
Dimensions: Span 36ft 1in (11·00m); length (A) 27ft 1in, (B) 29ft 11¼in (9.13m); height 8ft 6¼in (2·60m).
Weights: Empty (A) 1187lb, (B) 2,854lb (1295kg); maximum (A) 3,476lb (1577kg), (B) 3,747lb (1695kg).
Performance: Maximum speed (A, B) 205mph (330km/h); range (A) 560 miles (900km), (B) 615 miles (990km).
Armament: (A) none; (B) invariably one 7·92mm MG 17 above engine on right, sometimes 7·92mm MG 15 in rear cockpit and/or other guns in wing bulges and/or light bombs.
History: First flight 1938, (B) January 1940, final delivery (C.2B) 1948.
Users: Czechoslovakia (post-war), France (S.10), Germany, plus most other Axis air forces.

Development: Designed by Walter Blume, the Ar 96 was a typical Arado product, with distinctive tail and clean stressed-skin structure. It proved an ideal advanced trainer, and the Ar 96A entered Luftwaffe service in 1939. In 1940 much larger orders were placed for the 96B with more fuel and a larger engine, and this remained by far the most important advanced trainer of the Axis. The two-blade Argus propeller had a distinctive pitch-control windmill on the spinner, and there were five chief B sub-types of which a few could be used for gunnery and bombing training. The 96B towed light gliders, and even served in tactical roles on the Eastern front with various augmented armament. Total production by December 1944 was 11,546, and Letov built the C.2B version until 1948. The planned Ar 296 was developed into the 396, an all-wood replacement with 580hp As 411. Crude but effective, this was assigned to the French SIPA works, which after the liberation made large numbers as the S.11, followed by the metal S.12.

Right: The Ar 96B series was built in greater numbers than any other trainer in history except the American T-6 family, just topping the Vultee BT-13 Valiant family (11,537). The aircraft illustrated, probably Ar 96B-2 pilot trainers, do not bear the badge of an A/B Schule but by 1942 these were often omitted. All wartime Luftwaffe pilots knew the 96.

Arado Ar 196

Ar 196A-1 to A-5 (data for A-3)

Origin: Arado Flugzeugwerke GmbH.
Type: Two-seat maritime reconnaissance seaplane.
Engine: 960hp BMW 132K nine-cylinder radial.
Dimensions: Span 40ft 8in (12·4m); length 36ft 1in (11m); height 14ft 4½in (4·4m).
Weights: Empty 6,580lb (2990kg); loaded 8,223lb (3730kg).
Performance: Maximum speed 193mph (310km/h) at 13,120ft (4000m); initial climb 980ft (300m)/min; service ceiling 23,000ft (7020m); range 670 miles (1070km) at 158mph (253km/h).
Armament: Two MG FF 20mm cannon in wings outboard of propeller disc, one MG 17 7·92mm in top decking and twin MG 17 on pivoted mounting aimed by observer. Rack under each wing for 110lb (50kg) bomb.
History: First flight (196V1) May 1938; first operational service 1 August 1939.
Users: Bulgaria, Germany (Luftwaffe, Kriegsmarine), Romania.

Development: One of the very few float seaplanes to be used in World War II outside the Pacific area, the Ar 196 was designed as a replacement

Above: Built in small numbers in 1941, the Ar 196A-4 served on catapults of Kriegsmarine warships and preceded the A-3.

Below: By far the most numerous Ar 196 variant was the A-3, two of which are seen here flying on coastal patrol with 2/SAGr 128. This was formed in July 1943 at Brest and later moved to the south French coast where it ceased to exist.

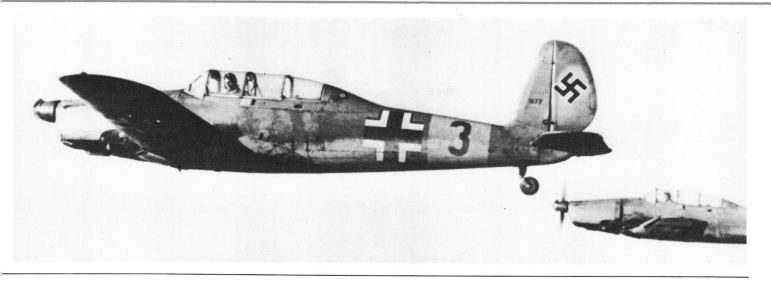

for the He 60 biplane on the catapults of all the German Navy's capital ships. Its duties were thus primarily reconnaissance and shadowing of surface vessels, but in comparison with such Allied types as the Curtiss Seagull and Fairey Seafox it had a much higher performance and eventually was given formidable armament. Four prototypes, powered by the 880hp BMW 132Dc engine (derived in Germany from the Pratt & Whitney Hornet), were flown in 1938, two with twin floats and the others with a large central float. The following year, 26 Ar 196A-1s were built, entering service in August aboard the battle cruisers *Gneisenau* and *Scharnhorst*, and at shore bases on the North Sea. In 1940 the Ar 196A-3 entered service, and this type made up the bulk of the 401 aircraft built. Though quite outclassed by the best fighters, the A-3 was a versatile multi-role aircraft which actually spent most of the war operating on sea patrols from coastal bases, mainly on the Bay of Biscay and islands in the Mediterranean. Batches were built by Vichy-France at Saint Nazaire and, in a slightly modified A-5 form, by Fokker at Amsterdam in 1943–44. About 50 served with co-belligerent Balkan air forces in the Adriatic and Black Sea. The type was never developed as an effective anti-submarine search and strike machine, despite its obvious potential.

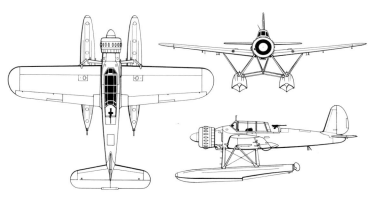

Above: Three-view of a typical Ar 196A-3.

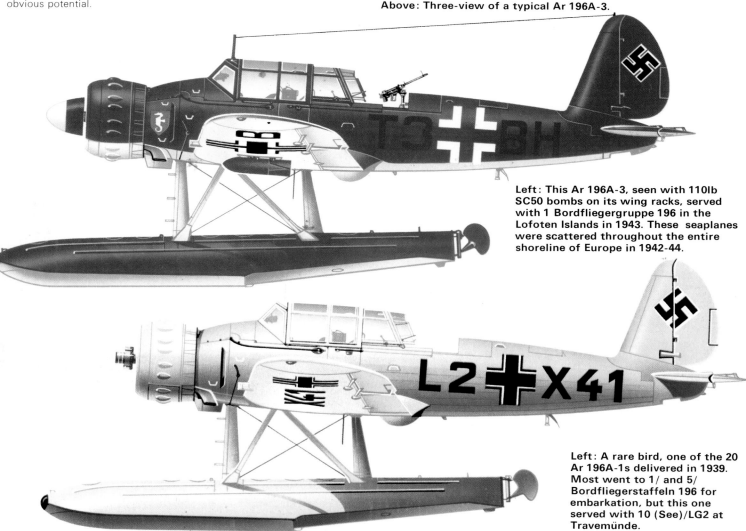

Left: This Ar 196A-3, seen with 110lb SC50 bombs on its wing racks, served with 1 Bordfliegergruppe 196 in the Lofoten Islands in 1943. These seaplanes were scattered throughout the entire shoreline of Europe in 1942-44.

Left: A rare bird, one of the 20 Ar 196A-1s delivered in 1939. Most went to 1/ and 5/ Bordfliegerstaffeln 196 for embarkation, but this one served with 10 (See)/LG2 at Travemünde.

Arado Ar 234 Blitz

Ar 234B-1 and B-2 Blitz

Origin: Arado Flugzeugwerke GmbH.
Type: Single-seat reconnaissance bomber.
Engines: Two 1,980lb (900kg) thrust Junkers Jumo 004B axial turbojets.
Dimensions: Span 46ft 3½in (14·2m); length 41ft 5½in (12·65m); height 14ft 1¼in (4·3m).
Weights: Empty 11,464lb (5200kg); loaded 18,541lb (8410kg); maximum with rocket takeoff boost 21,715lb (9850kg).
Performance: Maximum speed (clean) 461mph (742km/h); service ceiling 32,800ft (10,000m); range (clean) 1,013 miles (1630km), (with 3,300lb bomb load) 684 miles (1100km).
Armament: Two fixed MG 151 20mm cannon in rear fuselage, firing to rear and sighted by periscope; various combinations of bombs slung under fuselage and/or engines to maximum of 3,300lb (1500kg).
History: First flight (Ar 234V1) 15 June 1943, (Ar 234V9 with landing gear) March 1944, (Ar 234B-0 pre-production) 8 June 1944; operational delivery September 1944.
User: Germany (Luftwaffe).

Development: As the first jet reconnaissance bomber, the Ar 234 Blitz (meaning Lightning) spearheaded Germany's remarkably bold introduction of high-performance turbojet aircraft in 1944. Its design was begun under Walter Blume in 1941, after long studies in 1940 of an official specification for a jet-propelled reconnaissance aircraft with a range of 1,340 miles. The design was neat and simple, with two of the new axial engines slung under a high wing, and the single occupant in a pressurised cockpit forming the entire nose. But to achieve the required fuel capacity no wheels were fitted. When it flew on 15 June 1943 the first 234 took off from a three-wheel trolley and landed on retractable skids. After extensive trials with eight prototypes the ninth flew with conventional landing gear, leading through 20 pre-production models to the operational 234B-1, with ejection seat, autopilot and drop tanks under the engines. Main production centred on the 234B-2, made in many sub-variants, most of them able to carry a heavy bomb load. Service over the British Isles with the B-1 began in September 1944, followed by a growing force of B-2s which supported the Battle of the Bulge in the winter 1944–45. In March 1945 B-2s of III/KG76 repeatedly attacked the vital Remagen bridge across the Rhine with 2,205lb (1,000kg) bombs, causing its collapse. Though handicapped by fuel shortage these uninterceptable aircraft played a significant role on all European fronts in the closing months of the war, 210 being handed over excluding the many prototypes and later versions with four engines and an uncompleted example with a crescent-shaped wing.

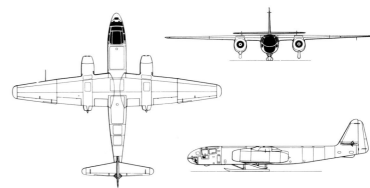

Above: Ar 234 V1 (first prototype) with skid landing gear.

Above: Take-off by the Ar 234 V9 (ninth prototype), first of the B-series with conventional landing gear. Other advanced features included pressure cabin, ejection seat and computer.

Blohm und Voss Bv 138

Bv 138A-1, B-1 and C-1 (data for C-1)

Origin: Hamburger Flugzeugbau GmbH.
Type: Six-crew reconnaissance flying boat.
Engines: Three 880hp Junkers Jumo 205D diesels with 12 opposed pistons in six cylinders.
Dimensions: Span 88ft 7in (27m); length 65ft 1½in (19·85m); height 19ft 4¼in (5·9m).
Weights: Empty 24,250lb (11,000kg); loaded 31,967lb (14,500kg); (rocket assist) 36,337lb (16,480kg).
Performance: Maximum speed 171mph (275km/h); climb to 10,000ft (3050m) in 24min; service ceiling 16,400ft (5000m); maximum range 2,500 miles (4023km).
Armament: 20mm MG 151 cannon in front and rear turrets; 13mm MG 131 in cockpit behind centre engine; four 331lb (150kg) depth charges or other stores under inner right wing.
History: First flight (Ha 138V-1) 15 July 1937; first delivery (A-1) January 1940; (C-1) 1941.
User: Germany (Luftwaffe).

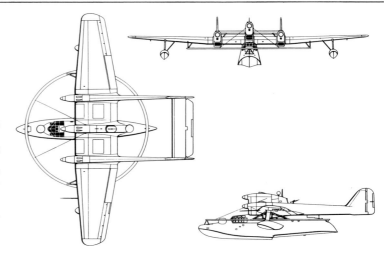

Above The Bv 138 MS minesweeper with degaussing ring.

Below: The definitive version was the Bv 138C, and examples served in many parts of Europe. This C-1 was operated by 3.(F)/SAGr 125, based at Constanza, Romania, on patrol over the Black Sea.

Right: Somewhere on the bitter Arctic convoy route this Bv 138C of SAGr 130 has made rendezvous with a U-boat—possibly to take on fuel oil for its diesels.

Below: The Ar 234 was the only jet bomber to be operational in World War II, and though it did not affect the course of the war its pinpricks were usually unstoppable. This B-2/P Blitz served with 9/KG 76 operating from Achmer in February 1945. It is seen with 1,102-lb (SC500) bombs hung under the nacelles, but the fuselage rack could carry a 3,086-pounder.

Below: In 1943 development began on a more powerful four-engined Ar 234C series. Some had twinned nacelles.

Development: Originally designated Ha 138, reflecting the fact that the aircraft subsidiary of the Blohm und Voss shipyard is (even today) Hamburger Flugzeugbau, the 138 was designed by Richard Vogt and took a long time to reach its final form. Major changes had to be made to the hull, wing, tail and tail booms, though none of the alterations were due to the unusual layout. The first 25 Bv 138A-1 boats were intended to be ocean reconnaissance platforms, but were not a success and ended up as transports in the Norwegian campaign and thereafter. They were underpowered with three

600hp Jumo 205 C diesel engines, the fuel oil being carried inside the tubular main spar of the wing. In late 1940 the Bv 138B-1 entered service with 880hp Jumo 205D engines, further modified tail and a 20mm turret at each end of the hull. After building 21, production was switched to the final Bv 138C-1, of which 227 were delivered in 1941–43. This had improved propellers, added a dorsal MG 131 and was greatly improved in equipment. Throughout 1942–45 the 138C gave good front-line service in the Arctic, the Baltic, the North Atlantic and Mediterranean.

Blohm und Voss
Bv 222 Wiking

Bv 222 prototypes, 222A and 222C

Origin: Hamburger Flugzeugbau GmbH.
Type: Strategic transport flying boat (see text).
Engines: (Most) six 1,000hp Bramo (BMW) Fafnir 323R nine-cylinder radials, (V7 and 222C) six 980hp Junkers Jumo 207C six-cylinder (12-piston) diesels.
Dimensions: Span 150ft 11in (46.00m); length 121ft 4½in (37.00m); height 35ft 9in (10.9m).
Weights: Empty (A) about 64,000lb (29,000kg), (C) 67,572lb (30,650kg); maximum (all) 108,030lb (49,000kg).
Performance: Maximum speed (all) 242mph (390km/h) without armament, 183mph (295km/h) with; maximum cruise at height 214mph (345km/h), (armed) 156mph (252km/h); maximum range at 152mph (245km/h) 3,790 miles (6100km); endurance 28hr.
Armament: Varied greatly from single 7.92mm MG 81 to five/six power turrets; (C) 13mm MG 131 manually aimed in bow, 20mm MG 151 in one or two dorsal turrets and two wing turrets (upper surface behind outer nacelles) plus various MG 131 or MG 81 from side windows.
History: First flight 7 September 1940; first service mission 10 July 1941.
User: Germany (Luftwaffe).

Development: Deutsche Luft Hansa ordered three of the large Bv 222 boats in 1937 for use on the North and South Atlantic. The prototype (222V-1) was civil, but after initial flight trials was modified into a freight transport for the Luftwaffe. There followed nine further aircraft, no two alike, V9 also being the first of four production 222C-0 transports with Jumo engines and improved armament, as well as FuG 200 Hohentwiel radar and FuG 216 rear warning. Only 13 were flown, and decision to drop the diesels led to a switch to the Fafnir, used in the majority of the prototypes,

Right: The last of the radial-engined A-series was the V8, seen here on the slipway with all engines running. It served only a few weeks with LTS See 222 before being shot down.

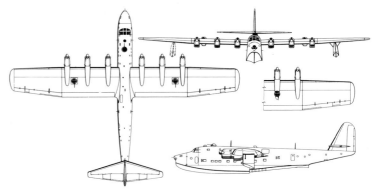

Above: Three-view of Bv 222C (V9); inset, right wing of V7.

from No 20, which with 14-19 were almost complete. From 1941 the Wikings shuttled from northern Norway to Africa bringing urgent stores. Despite their improving equipment, nearly all were shot down or destroyed at their moorings, but four survived to VE-day, one being scuttled by its crew and the others being flown to Britain and the USA for trials. The Wiking posed many development problems, and always seemed underpowered, but its basic qualities were good. From it derived the even bigger Bv 238, described at the end of the German section.

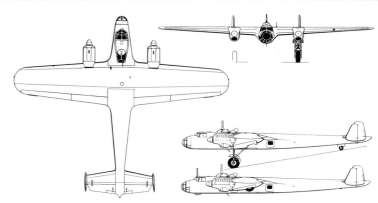

Dornier Do 17

Do 17E, F, K and P

Origin: Dornier-Werke GmbH.
Type: Three-seat medium bomber (17F, reconnaissance).
Engines: Two 750hp BMW VI 7.3 12-cylinder vee liquid-cooled; (17P) two 1,000hp BMW 132N nine-cylinder radials.
Dimensions: Span 59ft 0½in (18m); length (17E, F) 53ft 3¾in (16.25m); (17P) 52ft 9¾in (16.1m); height (17E, F) 14ft 2in (4.3m); (17P) 14ft 11in (4.57m).
Weights: Empty (17E, F) 9,921lb (4500kg); (17P) 10,140lb (4600kg); loaded (17E) 15,520lb (7050kg); (17F) 15,430lb (7000kg); (17P) 16,887lb (7660kg).
Performance: Maximum speed (17E, F) 220mph (355km/h); (17P) 249mph (400km/h); service ceiling (17E) 16,730ft (5100m); (17F) 19,685ft (6000m); (17P) 20,340ft (6200m); typical range (17E) 620 miles (1000km); (17F) 994 miles (1600km); (17P) 745 miles (1200km).
Armament: (17E) one 7.92mm MG 15 manually aimed from rear ventral hatch and one manually aimed to rear from dorsal position, with internal bomb load of 1,650lb (750kg); (17P) three MG 15s, one (normally fixed to fire ahead) in right windscreen, one in ventral hatch and one in dorsal position, with internal bomb load of 2,205lb (1000kg).
History: First flight (single-fin V1 prototype) autumn 1934; (Do 17E) 7 November 1936; (Do 17F) 10 November 1936; (Do 17P) late 1937.
Users: Germany (Luftwaffe), Jugoslavia, Soviet Union (2 aircraft only).

Development: Popularly dubbed "the flying pencil" in both Germany and Britain, the Do 17 was not planned as a bomber and secretly tested as a civil transport; its history was the other way round. Deutsche Luft Hansa decided its slender body left much too little room for the six passengers, but the Reichsluftfahrtministerium eventually decided the Do 17 was worth developing as a bomber. Numerous prototypes were built with different noses and engines and eventually the Do 17E-1 and the F-1 reconnaissance machine went into large-scale, and widely subcontracted, production for the embryo Luftwaffe. As early as March 1937 both were in combat service, with

Above: Three-view of the first major Luftwaffe versions, the Do 17F-1 (reconnaissance) and (bottom) Do 17E-1 bomber.

one Staffel of 17Fs being in Spain with the Legion Kondor (there to prove virtually immune to interception by the Republican forces). In the spring of 1937 a Do 17M prototype with powerful DB 600 engines walked away from all the fighter aircraft at the International Military Aircraft Competition at Zurich. This caused a great sensation and the first nation to buy the new bomber was Jugoslavia, receiving 20 from Germany plus a construction licence. The Jugoslav Do 17Kb-1 had a very early nose profile (the same, in fact, as the Zurich demonstrator) and Gnome-Rhône 14N radial engines. They had a 20mm Hispano cannon and three 7.92mm Brownings. About 70 were on strength when the Germans invaded Jugoslavia in April 1941, two escaping to Greece with cargoes of gold bullion. The several hundred E and F models formed the biggest portion of the Luftwaffe bomber and reconnaissance force up to 1939, but by the end of that year had been relegated to operational training. The later Do 17M-1 (Bramo Fafnir radials of 1,000hp) and Do 17P succeeded the E and F in production during 1937 and saw combat during World War II. They were the final types to retain the slender "flying pencil" shape and hemispherical nose-cap.

Left: A BMW-radial-engined Do 17P-1 reconnaissance model, serving with 4.(F)/14 "Münchausen" Staffel. In 1939 this was with Luftflotte IV in Austria, Silesia and Czechoslovakia.

DFS 230

DFS 230A-1, B-1, C-1, F-1

Origin: Deutsches Forschungsinstitut für Segelflugzeug; production by Gothaer Waggonfabrik and others.
Type: Assault glider.
Dimensions: Span (nearly all) 68ft 5½in (20·87m); length (A, B, C) 36ft 10½in (11·24m); height 8ft 11¾in (2·74m).
Weights: Empty (B-1) 1,896lb (860kg); maximum (A-1) 4,608lb (2090 kg), (B-1) 4,630lb (2100kg).
Performance: Normal towing speed 130mph (210km/h); dive limit speed 180mph (290km/h).
History: First flight, early 1937; service delivery (A-0) 1938, (A-1) 1939.
User: Germany, and possibly other Axis countries.

Development: Apparently no serious thought had been given to the use of gliders in war until Ernst Udet, later head of the Luftwaffe technical procurement department, visited DFS in 1933. He later placed an order for a military transport glider, the DFS 230, which was flown with conspicuous success by Hanna Reitsch in 1937. After demonstrations before senior officers the DFS 230 became the basis around which the new technique of glider-borne assault was developed. On 10 May 1940 it was put into effect with total success by 45 gliders, towed by Ju 52s to carefully planned pinpoint operations on bridges and forts in the Low Countries. The classic assault was on Fort Eben Emael, in Belgium, on the Albert Canal. The vast modern fortress was knocked out and held by 72 men who arrived silently within the outer walls at dawn. They held until the German Army arrived more than 24hr later, suffering total casualties of six men killed and 20 wounded. In Crete large forces of DFS 230 and other gliders suffered heavily, but took the island. Hundreds of 230s were used in North Africa and Italy, with progressively less effect, but went out in a blaze of glory when Otto Skorzeny's handpicked force stormed the mountain-top hotel where Mussolini was being held under armed guard and flew him out in a Storch. Most 230s were of the B-1 type with braking parachute; the C-1 had three solid fuel rockets in the nose to stop it in 30 metres, and the F-1 was an enlarged model seating 15. Nearly all were delivered before 1941, output being 1,022.

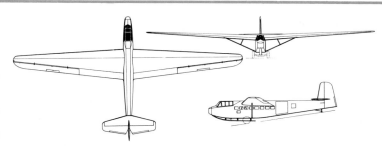

Above: Three-view of a typical DFS 230A-1 (wheels jettisoned).

Below: An operational DFS 230A-1 on tow, possibly during a combat mission. The tug was almost always the Ju 52/3m, and much research was done with close-coupled Starschlepp tows, used later in the war to tow heavy fuel tanks, bombs and even Fi 103 flying bombs.

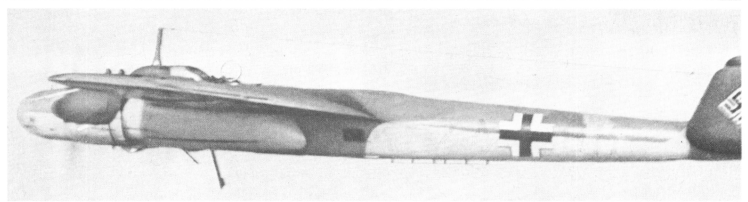

Above: In September 1939 the Do 17P-1 reconnaissance aircraft equipped 22 staffeln, but few were left a year later.

Below: Seen in the 1937 camouflage livery, this Do 17E-1 bomber had the benefit of combat experience in Spain.

Dornier Do 17Z and 215
Do 17Z-1 and -2 and Do 215A-1, B-1 and B-5

Origin: Dornier-Werke GmbH.
Type: Four-seat medium bomber and reconnaissance.
Engines: (Do 17Z-2) two 1,000hp Bramo Fafnir 323P nine-cylinder radials; (Do 215B-1) two 1,075hp Daimler-Benz DB 601A 12-cylinder inverted-vee liquid-cooled.
Dimensions: (Both) span 59ft 0½in (18m); length 51ft 9½in (15·79m); height 14ft 11½in (4·56m).
Weights: Empty (Do 17Z-2) 11,484lb (5210kg); (Do 215B-1) 12,730lb (5775kg); loaded (both) 19,841lb (9000kg).
Performance: Maximum speed (Do 17Z-2) 263mph (425km/h); (Do 215B-1) 280mph (450km/h); service ceiling (Do 17Z-2) 26,740ft (8150m); (Do 215B-1) 31,170ft (9500m); range with half bomb load (Do 17Z-2) 721 miles (1160km); (Do 215B-1) 932 miles (1500km).
Armament: Normally six 7·92mm Rheinmetall MG 15 machine guns, one fixed in nose, remainder on manually aimed mounts in front windscreen, two beam windows, and above and below at rear; internal bomb load up to 2205lb (1000kg).
History: First flight (Do 17S prototype) early 1938; (Do 17Z-2) early 1939; (Do 215V1 prototype) late 1938; first delivery (Do 17Z-1) January 1939, (Do 215A-1) December 1939; termination of production (Do 17Z series) July 1940, (Do 215 series) January 1941.
User: Germany (Luftwaffe).

Development: Whereas the slenderness of the first families of Do 17 bombers had earned them the nickname of "Flying Pencil", the Do 17S introduced a completely new front end with much deeper cabin and extensive window area all round. Such a change had been obvious from the inadequate defensive armament of the earlier models, revealed in the Spanish Civil War, and the penalty of increased weight and drag was to

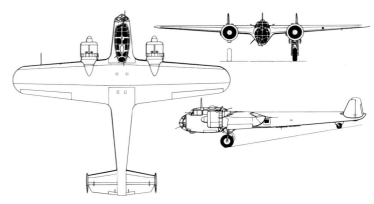

Above: Three-view of the Do 17Z-2.

some degree countered by a search for more powerful engines. The S prototype had DB 600 liquid-cooled engines, as did the Do 17U five-seat pathfinder, of which 12 were delivered to the nine Bomber Groups already using earlier Do 17s. The Do 17Z, powered by the Bramo radial engine, was at first underpowered and full bomb load had to await the more powerful Fafnir 323P of the 17Z-2. Between late 1939 and the summer of 1940 about 535 Do 17Z series bomber and reconnaissance machines were delivered and, though they suffered high attrition over Britain, they did much effective work and were the most popular and reliable of all Luftwaffe bombers of the early Blitzkrieg period. The Do 215 was the Do 17Z renumbered as an export version, with the more powerful DB 601 engine. The Do 215A-1 for Sweden became the Do 215B-0 and B-1 for the Luftwaffe and altogether 101 were put into service for bomber and reconnaissance roles; 12 were converted as Do 215B-5 night intruders, with a "solid" nose carrying two cannon and four machine guns, and operated by night over Britain before transfer to Sicily in October 1941.

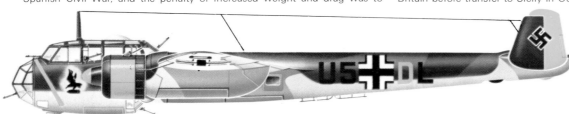

Left: The Z-2 bombers of III/KG 2 saw intense action in all campaigns up to 1941.

Below: Another Do 17Z-2 of KG 2 seen over the blue Aegean with an almost defenceless Greece ahead, in April 1941. Later, things got tougher.

Dornier Do 18

Do 18D, G, H, N

Origin: Dornier-Werke GmbH.
Type: D, G, reconnaissance and air/sea rescue; H, trainer, N, rescue.
Engines: (D) tandem push/pull Junkers Jumo 205C diesels, each rated at 600hp; (G, H, N) 700hp Jumo 205D.
Dimensions: Span 77ft 9in (23·7m); length 63ft 2in (19·25m); height 17ft 9in (5·45m).
Weights: (G-1) empty 12,900lb (5850kg); maximum 22,046lb (10,000 kg).
Performance: (G-1) Maximum speed at sea level 162mph (260km/h); typical cruise 106mph (170km/h); range 2,175 miles (3500km).
Armament: (D-1) typically one 7·92mm MG 15 manually aimed from bow and rear cockpits, with underwing racks for 1,102lb (500kg) load of weapons or stores on each side; (G-1) 13mm MG 131 in bow cockpit, 20mm MG 151 in power dorsal turret, same wing capacity; (H, N) none.
History: First flight (civil) 15 March 1935; (D) early 1938; final delivery, late 1939.
User: Germany (Luftwaffe, DLH).

Development: The Do 18, a pleasant and relatively harmless machine, was the first Luftwaffe type shot down by British aircraft in World War II; a flight of Skuas from *Ark Royal* caught three of the boats shadowing British warships on 26 September 1939 (and it is a fair reflection on the

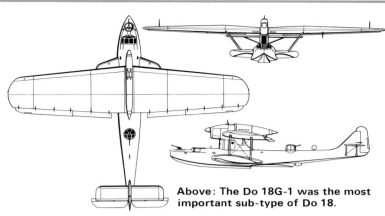

Above: The Do 18G-1 was the most important sub-type of Do 18.

Skua's capabilities as a fighter that two of the boats escaped). Only about 100 were delivered altogether, most being of the more powerful and better armed G version. Nearly all were confined to northern Europe and the Baltic/Atlantic areas. The N used to appear painted white, with prominent red crosses, though post-war evidence confirmed the belief that these sometimes were engaged in Elint (electronic intelligence) missions.

Below: One of the earlier variants was the Do 18D-1, one of which is seen on North Sea patrol (possibly with KüFlGr 106).

Dornier Do 24

Do 24T

Origin: Dornier-Werke GmbH; production by Weser, Aviolanda and Potez-CAMS (SNCAN); post-war, CASA, Spain.
Type: Reconnaissance flying boat (typical crew, six).
Engines: Three 1,000hp Bramo Fafnir 323R-2 nine-cylinder radials.
Dimensions: Span 88ft 7in (27m); length 72ft 2in (22m): height 17ft 10in (5·45m).
Weights: Empty 29,700lb (13,500kg); loaded 40,565lb (18,400kg).
Performance: Maximum speed 211mph (340km/h); service ceiling 19,360ft (5900m); maximum range 2,950 miles (4750km).
Armament: One 7·92mm MG 15 machine gun in bow turret, one MG 15 in tail turret and one 20mm MG 151/20 or 30mm MK 103 cannon in dorsal turret behind wing; underwing racks for 12 110lb (50kg) bombs or other stores.
History: First flight (Do 24V3) 3 July 1937; service delivery (Do 24K) November 1937; withdrawal from service (Spain) 1967.
Users: Germany, Netherlands, Spain, Sweden; post-war, France.

Below: The main Luftwaffe type was the Do 24T-1, this example being one of the 170 supplied from the Netherlands in 1941-44.

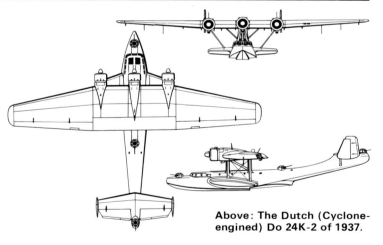

Above: The Dutch (Cyclone-engined) Do 24K-2 of 1937.

Development: This excellent trimotor flying boat was one of the very few aircraft of the Nazi period to be designed for a foreign government. The customer was the Netherlands and by 1940 a total of 11 had been built by Weserflugzeugbau and flown out to the Dutch East Indies naval air service (MLD). In addition, 26 more had been supplied by the Dutch de Schelde and Aviolanda companies, under a government-purchased licence. After the invasion of the Low Countries production was continued in Holland for the Luftwaffe, with the French Potez-CAMS factory at Sartrouville also assigned to Do 24 production in 1941. Production for the Luftwaffe amounted to 170 in Holland and 48 in France and the type was met all round the European coasts. One force-landed in Sweden in 1944, was impressed into RSAF service as the Tp 24 and not surrendered to the USSR until 1951. After VE-day the CAMS factory continued in production, making a further 20 aircraft to augment ex-Luftwaffe machines for a force of more than 60 in Aéronavale service until 1955. The remaining aircraft were sold to Spain to augment an original force of 12 purchased from Germany in 1944. Designated HR-5, the Do 24T-3 in Spain and the Spanish Mediterranean and Atlantic islands was the last type of large military flying boat operating in Europe. Since 1969 Dornier has been seeking markets for the proposed Do 24/72 development, powered by three 1,800hp Lycoming turboprops.

Dornier Do 217

Do 217E-2, K-2, M-1, J-2/N-2, P-1

Origin: Dornier-Werke GmbH.
Type: (E, K, M) four-seat bomber; (J, N) three-seat night fighter; (P) four-seat high-altitude reconnaissance.
Engines: (E-2, J-2) two 1,580hp BMW 801A or 801M 18-cylinder two-row radials; (K-2) two 1,700hp BMW 801D; (M-1, N-2) two 1,750hp Daimler-Benz DB 603A 12-cylinder inverted-vee liquid-cooled; (P-1) two 1,860hp DB 603B supercharged by DB 605T in the fuselage.

Dimensions: Span 62ft 4in (19m); (K-2) 81ft 4½in (24·8m); (P-1) 80ft 4in (24·4m); length 56ft 9¼in (17·3m); (E-2 with early dive brakes) 60ft 10½in (18·5m); (K-2 and M-1) 55ft 9in (17m); (J and N) 58ft 9in (17·9); (P) 58ft 11in (17·95m); height 16ft 5in (5m) (all versions same within 2in).
Weights: Empty (E-2) 19,522lb (8850kg); (M-1) 19,985 (9000kg); (K-2, J and N) all about 21,000lb (9450kg); (P) about 23,000lb (10,350kg); loaded (E-2) 33,070lb (15,000kg); (K-2, M-1) 36,817lb (16,570kg); (J and N) 30,203lb (13,590kg); (P) 35,200lb (15,840kg).
Performance: Maximum speed (E-2) 320mph (515km/h); (K-2) 333mph (533km/h); (M-1) 348mph (557km/h); (J and N) about 311mph (498km/h); (P) 488mph (781km/h); service ceiling (E-2) 24,610ft (7500m); (K-2) 29,530ft (9000m); (M-1) 24,140ft (7358m); (J and N) 27,560ft (8400m); (P) 53,000ft (16,154m); range with full bomb load, about 1,300 miles (2100km) for all versions.
Armament: (E-2) one fixed 15mm MG 151/15 in nose, one 13mm MG 131 in dorsal turret, one MG 131 manually aimed at lower rear, and three 7·92mm MG 15 manually aimed in nose and beam windows; maximum bomb load 8818lb (4000kg), including 3307lb (1500kg) external; (K-2)

Dornier Do 217K-1 cutaway drawing key:

1 Starboard rudder tab
2 Rudder controls
3 Rudder mass balance (lead insert)
4 Starboard tailfin
5 Leading-edge slot
6 Tailplane/tailfin attachment
7 Elevator
8 Elevator mass balance
9 Fixed tab
10 Trim tab
11 Tailplane construction
12 Elevator controls
13 Rear navigation light
14 Four aft-firing 7·9-mm MG 81 machine guns (*Rüstsatz* [field conversion set] 19)
15 Ammunition boxes
16 Tailplane trim control
17 Fuel emergency jettison
18 Mudguard
19 Tailwheel
20 Tailwheel doors
21 Tailwheel retraction mechanism
22 Tailplane carry-through
23 Fuselage skinning
24 Master compass
25 Dipole antenna
26 Anti-collision beacon
27 Elevator mass balance
28 Port tailfin
29 Leading-edge slot
30 Bomb bay division
31 Bomb bay hinge line
32 Bomb bay rear bulkhead entry/inspection hatch

33 Spherical oxygen cylinders
34 Starboard mainwheel
35 Mudguard
36 Mainwheel doors
37 Mainwheel retraction mechanism
38 Mainwheel well
39 FuG 25 (A-A recognition)
40 FuG 101 radio altimeter
41 Outer section split flaps
42 Starboard aileron
43 Aileron tab
44 Control lines
45 Rear spar
46 Braced wing ribs
47 Intermediate ribs
48 EGS 101 antenna
49 Starboard navigation light
50 Front spar
51 Leading-edge hot-air de-icing
52 Hot-air duct
53 Balloon-cable cutter in leading-edge
54 Starboard outer fuel tank (35 Imp gal/160l capacity)
55 Starboard oil tank (51·7 Imp gal/235l capacity)
56 Flame-damping exhaust pipes
57 Sliding-ring cooling air exit
58 BMW 801D 14-cylinder two-row radial engine
59 Annular oil cooler
60 VDM Three-blade metal propeller of 12·79ft (3·90m) diameter
61 Cooling fan
62 Cowling sliding nose-ring
63 Propeller boss
64 Starboard inner fuel tank (175 Imp gal/795l capacity)
65 Fuselage main fuel tank (231 Imp gal/1050l capacity)
66 Wing spar carry-through
67 Bomb bay top hinge line
68 Load-bearing beam
69 Bomb shackle
70 Bomb bay centre hinge line
71 Typical bomb load: two 2,205-lb (1000-kg) SC 1000 bombs
72 Forward bomb doors
73 13-mm MG 131 machine gun in ventral position (1,000 rounds)

74 Ammunition ejection chute
75 Ventral gunner's station
76 Armoured bulkhead
77 Cartridge collector box
78 Batteries (two 24-Volt)
79 Radio equipment
80 Dorsal gunner's seat support
81 Cabin hot-air
82 Dorsal gunner's station
83 Armoured turret ring
84 Aerial mast
85 Gun safety guard
86 Starboard beam-mounted 7·9-mm MG 81 machine gun (750 rounds)
87 13-mm MG 131 machine gun (500 rounds)
88 Electrically-operated dorsal turret
89 Revi gunsight
90 Angled side windows
91 Jettisonable decking
92 Bomb-aimer's folding seat
93 Navigator's table
94 Pilot's contoured seat
95 Rear-view gunsight
96 Upper instrument panel
97 Nose glazing
98 Control horns
99 Engine controls
100 One 13-mm MG 131 in strengthened nose glazing (alternatively twin 7·9-mm MG 81Z)
101 Balloon-cable cutter in nose horizontal frame

102 Cartridge ejection chute
103 Ammunition feed
104 Lotfe 7D bombsight
105 Bomb aimer's flat panel
106 Control column counterweight
107 Nose armour
108 Ventral gunner's quilt
109 Ammunition box (nose MG 131)
110 Cartridge collector box
111 Entry hatch
112 Entry hatch (open)
113 Entry ladder
114 Port mainwheel doors
115 Mudguard
116 Port mainwheel
117 Mainwheel leg cross struts
118 Port engine cowling
119 Landing light (swivelling)
120 Control linkage
121 Pitot head
122 Port navigation light
123 Port aileron
124 Aileron trim tab

Above: The sixth pre-production Do 217E-0 was used by BMW for engine development.

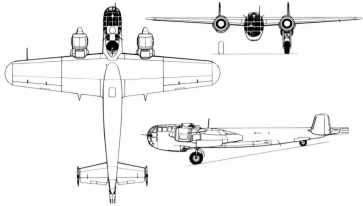

Above: The Do 217K-1 with new cockpit but original wing.

defensive armament similar to E-2, plus battery of four 7·92mm MG 81 fixed rearward-firing in tail and optional pair fixed rearward-firing in nacelles (all sighted and fired by pilot), and offensive load of two FX 1400 radio-controlled glide bombs and/or (K-3 version) two Hs 293 air-to-surface rocket guided missiles; (M-1) as E-2 except MG 15s replaced by larger number of MG 81; (J-2 and N-2) typically four 20mm MG FF cannon and four 7·92mm MG 17 in nose plus MG 131 for lower rear defence (N-2 often had later guns such as MG 151/20 in nose and MG 151/20 or MK 108 30mm in Schräge Musik upward-firing installation); (P) three pairs of MG 81 for defence, and two 1102lb bombs on underwing racks.

History: First flight (Do 217V1) August 1938; (pre-production Do 217A-0) October or November 1939; first delivery of E series, late 1940; termination of production, late 1943.

Users: Germany (Luftwaffe), (217 J) Italy (RA).

Development: Superficially a scaled-up Do 215, powered at first by the same DB 601 engines, the 217 was actually considerably larger and totally

continued on page 28 ▶

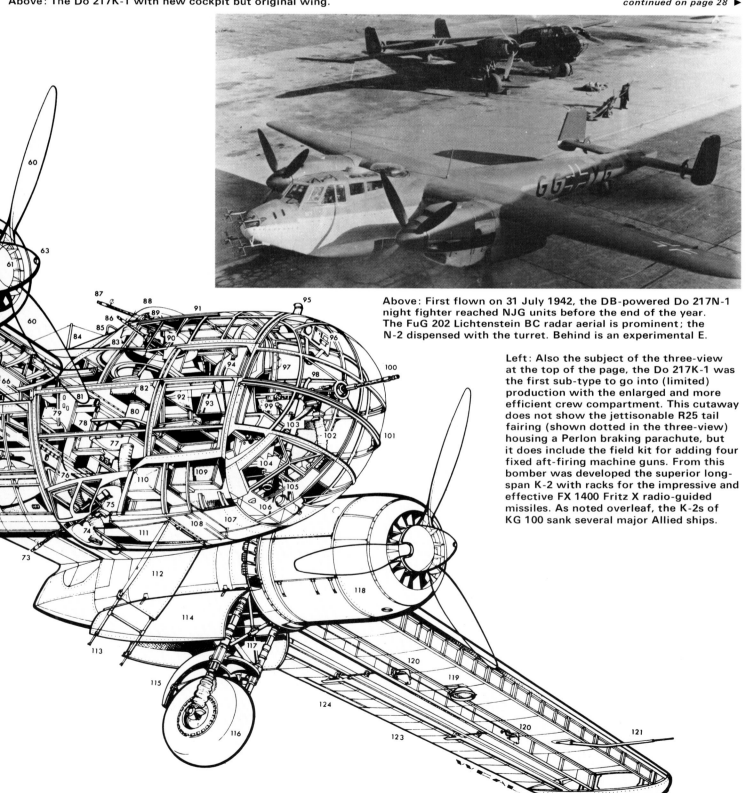

Above: First flown on 31 July 1942, the DB-powered Do 217N-1 night fighter reached NJG units before the end of the year. The FuG 202 Lichtenstein BC radar aerial is prominent; the N-2 dispensed with the turret. Behind is an experimental E.

Left: Also the subject of the three-view at the top of the page, the Do 217K-1 was the first sub-type to go into (limited) production with the enlarged and more efficient crew compartment. This cutaway does not show the jettisonable R25 tail fairing (shown dotted in the three-view) housing a Perlon braking parachute, but it does include the field kit for adding four fixed aft-firing machine guns. From this bomber was developed the superior long-span K-2 with racks for the impressive and effective FX 1400 Fritz X radio-guided missiles. As noted overleaf, the K-2s of KG 100 sank several major Allied ships.

▶ different in detail design. Much of Dornier's efforts in 1938–40 were devoted to finding more powerful engines and improving the flying qualities, and when the BMW 801 radial was available the 217 really got into its stride and carried a heavier bomb load than any other Luftwaffe bomber of the time. Early E models, used from late 1940, had no dorsal turret and featured a very long extension of the rear fuselage which opened into an unusual dive brake. This was soon abandoned, but the 217 blossomed out into a prolific family which soon included the 217J night fighter, often produced by converting E-type bombers, and the N which was likewise produced by converting the liquid-cooled M. Several series carried large air-to-surface missiles steered by radio command from a special crew station in the bomber. Long-span K-2s of III/KG 100 scored many successes with their

formidable missiles in the Mediterranean, their biggest bag being the Italian capital ship *Roma* as she steamed to the Allies after Italy's capitulation. The pressurised high-altitude P series had fantastic performance that would have put them out of reach of any Allied fighters had they been put into service in time. From 1943, Dornier devoted more effort to the technically difficult Do 317, which never went into service.

Below: This Do 217, Werk-Nr 4572, was the first of the K-2 family. Major structural stiffening allowed the span to be increased to about 81 ft 4½ in, enabling the aircraft to lift additional fuel and two of the Fritz X guided missiles which weighed 3,454lb each.

Dornier Do 335 Pfeil

Do 335A-1 and A-6

Origin: Dornier-Werke GmbH.
Type: (A-1) single-seat fighter, (A-6) two-seat night fighter.
Engines: Two 1,900hp Daimler-Benz DB 603G 12-cylinder inverted-vee liquid-cooled, in push/pull arrangement.
Dimensions: Span 45ft 4in (13·8m); length 45ft 6in (13·87m); height 16ft 4in (4m).
Weights: Empty (A-1) 16,314lb (7400kg); (A-6) 16,975lb (7700kg); maximum loaded (both) 25,800lb (11,700kg).
Performance: Maximum speed (A-1) 413mph (665km/h) sustained; 477mph (765km/h) emergency boost (A-6 about 40mph slower in each case); initial climb (A-1) 4,600ft (1400m)/min; service ceiling (A-1) 37,400ft (11,410m); (A-6) 33,400ft (10,190m); maximum range (both) 1,280 miles (2050km) clean, up to 2,330 miles (3750km) with drop tank.
Armament: Typical A-1, one 30mm MK 103 cannon firing through front propeller hub and two 15mm MG 151/15 above nose; underwing racks for light stores and centreline rack for 1,100lb (500kg) bomb; A-6 did not carry bomb and usually had 15mm guns replaced by 20mm MG 151/20s.
History: First flight (Do 335V1) autumn 1943; (production A-1) late November 1944.
User: Germany (Luftwaffe).

Development: Dornier took out a patent in 1937 for an aircraft powered by two engines, one behind the other, in the fuselage, driving tractor and pusher propellers. In 1939–40 Schempp-Hirth built the Gö 9 research aircraft to test the concept of a rear propeller driven by an extension shaft and in 1941 work began on the Do 231 fighter-bomber. This was replaced by the Do 335 and by first flight Dornier had orders for 14 prototypes, ten preproduction A-0s, 11 production A-1s and three dual-control trainer A-10 and A-12 with stepped tandem cockpits. At high speed the 335 was prone to unpleasant porpoising and snaking, but production continued on the A-1, the A-4 reconnaissance batch and the A-6 with FuG 220 radar operated by a rear-seat observer. Though heavy, the 335 was strong and very fast and was notable in having the first production type of ejection seat (for obvious reasons). By VE-day about 90 aircraft had been rolled out, more than 60 flown and about 20 delivered to combat units. Work was also well advanced on a number of versions of the Do 335B heavy fighter, with added 30mm MK 108 cannon in the wings (some having two-stage engines and long-span wings), the Do 435 with various very powerful engines, and the twinned Do 635 with two Do 335 fuselages linked by a new parallel centre-section. The 635, which was being designed and produced by Junkers as the 8-635, would have weighed 72,000lb as a reconnaissance aircraft, and flown 4,050 miles cruising at 398mph. Pfeil means "arrow".

Right: The only Pfeil in existence is this completely rebuilt exhibit. It was originally the second Do 335A-0, flying in late May 1944. In 1945 it was taken to the USA, languished at the Smithsonian's Silver Hill store, and 25 years later was returned to Germany and restored by Dornier at Oberpfaffenhofen.

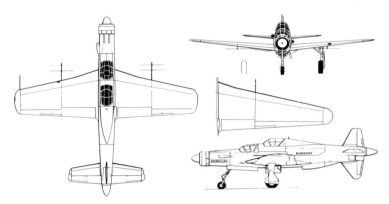

Above: Three-view of the Do 335A-6 two-seat night fighter with (inset) the long-span wing of B-8.

Below: The Do 335 V9, completed to full production standard and tested at Rechlin in May 1944.

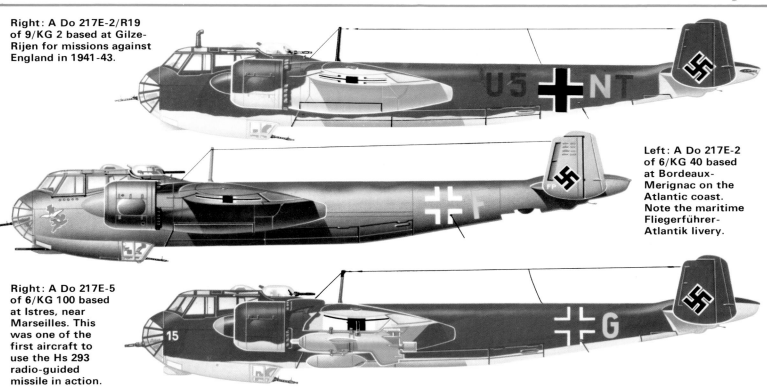

Right: A Do 217E-2/R19 of 9/KG 2 based at Gilze-Rijen for missions against England in 1941-43.

Left: A Do 217E-2 of 6/KG 40 based at Bordeaux-Merignac on the Atlantic coast. Note the maritime Fliegerführer-Atlantik livery.

Right: A Do 217E-5 of 6/KG 100 based at Istres, near Marseilles. This was one of the first aircraft to use the Hs 293 radio-guided missile in action.

Above: An earlier picture of the second A-0, the same machine as seen on the opposite page. It was used by EKdo 335.

Below: The Do 335 V3, like the second prototype, differed in many respects from the V1 flown in October 1943.

Fieseler Fi 156 Storch

Fi 156A, C, D, E, Fi 256

Origin: Gerhard Fieseler Werke GmbH, Kassel; production almost entirely by Morane-Saulnier, Puteaux, and Benes-Mraz, Czechoslovakia.
Type: STOL multi-role, see text.
Engine: (Almost all) 240hp Argus As 10C inverted-vee-8 aircooled; certain sub-types used other As 10 models of 260 or 270hp.
Dimensions: Span 46ft 9in (14·25m); length 32ft 5¾in (9·90m); height 9ft 10in (3·00m).
Weights: (Typical C) empty 2,050lb (930kg); maximum 2,910lb (1320kg).
Performance: Maximum speed 109mph (175km/h); minimum speed 32mph (51km/h); ground run (takeoff) 213ft (65m), (landing) 61ft (20m); range (max payload) 236 miles (380km), (max fuel) 600 miles (966km) at 60mph (97km/h).
History: First flight May 1936; service delivery, about May 1937; final delivery (France) 1949.
Users: Bulgaria, Croatia, Finland, France (1944 onwards), Germany, Hungary, Italy, Romania, Slovakia, Switzerland; captured specimens by most Allied air forces.

Development: Though only about 2,700 Storch (Stork) were built for the Axis, 2,549 of them during the war, it was used on every European front and for a vast range of duties. It beat two aeroplanes and a helicopter in a 1935 RLM competition for a STOL army co-op, casevac and liaison

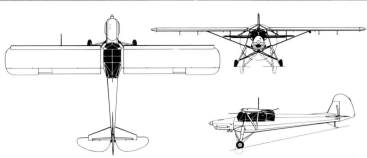

Above: Fi 156C-1, with in-flight landing-gear position dotted.

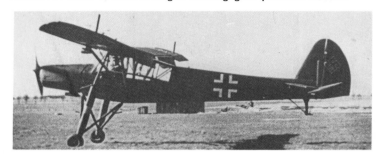

Focke-Wulf Fw 44

Fw 44A, B and C Stieglitz (Goldfinch)

Origin: Focke-Wulf Flugzeugbau, Bremen; licence-built in Argentina, Austria, Brazil, Bulgaria and Sweden.
Type: Primary trainer (also civil sporting aircraft).
Engine: (Fw 44A and C) 150hp Siemens Sh 14A seven-cylinder radial.
Dimensions: Span 29ft 6¼in (9·00m); length 23ft 11½in (7·30m); height 8ft 10¼in (2·70m).
Weights: Fw 44C empty 1,158lb (525kg); loaded (aerobatic) 1,698lb (770kg), (normal) 1,918lb (870kg).
Performance: Maximum speed 115mph (185km/h); range 419 miles (675km).
History: First flight September 1932; final delivery after 1938.
Users: Argentina, Austria, Bolivia, Brazil, Bulgaria, Chile, China, Colombia, Czechoslovakia, Finland, Germany (Luftwaffe and Luftdienst), Hungary, Romania, Sweden and Turkey.

Development: Designed under Kurt Tank in 1931 as the A44 (from the former Albatross-werke), the Fw 44 was the first really big success by Focke-Wulf and many thousands were made over a period of about a decade. At least 300 were exported prior to World War II, some of these being of the Fw 44B type with 120hp Argus As 8 inverted four-in-line engine. Of mixed construction, this trim tandem-seat biplane was delightful to fly and fully aerobatic. The cockpits had small fold-down side doors, bucket seats for a seat-type parachute and a folding rear seat for access to a baggage locker where a blind-flying hood could be clipped. In winter many Luftwaffe Stieglitz operated on skis. This popular machine equipped

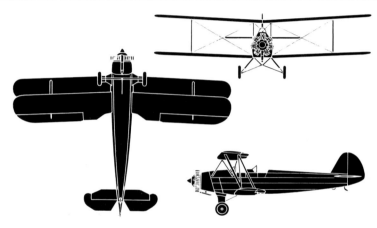

Above: Three-view of typical Fw 44C with wheeled landing gear.

at least ten of the regular Flugzeugführerschulen (FFS, pilot schools) and the officer candidate school at Fürstenfeldbruck, Munich.

Below: The Fw 44 was one of the mass-produced aircraft of the Luftwaffe, but unlike the Ar 66 and Go 145 it was not used as a tactical attacker by night. A curious feature of nearly all Focke-Wulfe aircraft of 1930-38 was the tail, with high tailplane ahead of the fin (and often with small auxiliary fins).

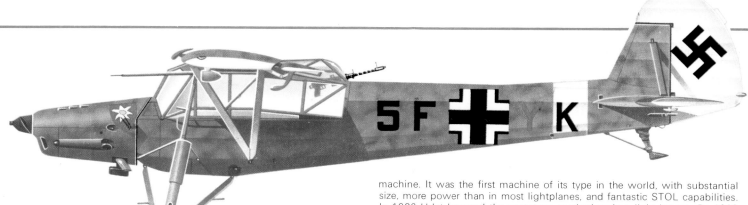

Above: A Fieseler Fi 156C-3/Trop operating in the North African theatre. Many were assigned as hacks to Luftwaffe units.

Left: One of the first production Fi 156C-1 Storch STOL aircraft making a tail-high full-flap landing (note full up-elevator). The Storch was large enough to fly many kinds of battlefield mission, and its only significant shortcoming was slow cruising speed (never more than 93mph). Feldmarschall Kesselring eventually switched to the faster Fw 189.

machine. It was the first machine of its type in the world, with substantial size, more power than in most lightplanes, and fantastic STOL capabilities. In 1936 Udet hovered the prototype motionless in a light breeze. By 1939 the main version, the 156C, was appearing in several forms, the C-1 being the standard staff aircraft flown by, or for, all leading staff officers. This was also the usual model issued to combat geschwader and other military formations, and it could mount a 7·92mm MG 15 at the upper rear of the large cabin. There was room for three (six in emergency), but most had only two seats. The side windows were wider than the rest of the fuselage, so that a small lower row could give vertical downwards vision. Another important series were the D sub-types with large side doors for a stretcher. Morane-Saulnier developed the wide five-seat Fi 256, but flew only two before the Germans departed. In 1944 Morane continued production, the post-war MS.500 Criquet having a Salmson radial. Mraz likewise kept building a version called K-65 Cap.

Focke-Wulf Fw 189 Uhu

Fw 189A-1, -2 and -3

Origin: Focke-Wulf Flugzeugbau GmbH; built under Focke-Wulf control by SNCASO, with outer wings from Breguet.

Type: Three-seat reconnaissance and close support.

Engines: Two 465hp Argus As 410A-1 12 cylinder inverted-vee air-cooled.

Dimensions: Span 60ft 4½in (18·4m); length 39ft 4½in (12m); height 10ft 2in (3·1m).

Weights: Empty 5,930lb (2690kg); loaded 8,708lb (3950kg).

Performance: Maximum speed 217mph (350km/h); climb to 13,120ft (4000m) in 8 min 20sec; service ceiling 23,950ft (7300m); range 416 miles (670km).

Armament: (A-2) one 7·92mm MG17 machine gun in each wing root, twin 7·92mm MG81 manually aimed in dorsal position and (usually) twin MG 81 in rear cone with limited field of fire; underwing racks for four 110lb (50kg) bombs.

History: First flight (Fw 189V1) July 1938; first delivery (pre-production Fw 189A-0) September 1940; final delivery August 1944.

User: Germany (Luftwaffe), Hungary, Slovakia.

Development: Today the diversity of aircraft layout makes us forget how odd this aircraft seemed. It looked strange to the customer also, but after outstandingly successful flight trials the 189 Uhu (Owl) was grudgingly bought in quantity as a standard reconnaissance aircraft. Though it flew in numbers well before the war — no two prototypes being alike — it was unknown by the Allies until it was disclosed in 1941 as "the Flying Eye" of the German armies. On the Eastern front it performed beyond all expectation, for it retained its superb handling (which made it far from a sitting duck to fighters) and also showed great toughness of structure and more than once returned to base with one tail shot off or removed by Soviet ramming attack. Attempts to produce special attack versions with small heavily armoured nacelles were not so successful, but 10 Fw 189B trainers were built with a conventional nacelle having side-by-side dual controls in a normal cockpit, with an observer above the trailing edge. The Fw 189A-3 was another dual-control version having the normal "glasshouse". Eventually the sole source became French factories with assembly at Bordeaux-Mérignac (today the Dassault Mirage plant), which halted as Allied armies approached. There were many different versions and several developments with more powerful engines, but the basic A-1, A-2 (better armament) and A-3 were the only types built in numbers, the total of these versions being 846.

Right: Close tactical work by a Uhu on the Eastern Front; the soldier is a member of a Luftwaffe ground reconnaissance unit.

Below: An Fw 189A-1 of 1.(H)/32 at Petsamo in northern Finland in December 1942. Aircooled engines never froze.

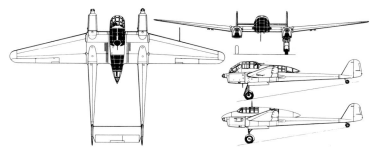

Above: Fw 189A-2 with additional side view (lower) of B-0.

Focke-Wulf Fw 190 and Ta 152

Fw 190A series, D series, F series, G series and Ta 152

Origin: Focke-Wulf Flugzeugbau GmbH; extremely dispersed manufacture and assembly, and part-subcontracted to Brandt (SNCA du Centre), France; also built in France post-war.
Type: Single-seat fighter bomber.
Engine: (A-8, F-8) one 1,700hp (2,100hp emergency boost) BMW 801Dg 18-cylinder two-row radial; (D-9) one 1,776hp (2,240hp emergency boost) Junkers Jumo 213A-1 12-cylinder inverted-vee liquid-cooled; (Ta 152H-1) one 1,880hp (2,250hp) Jumo 213E-1.
Dimensions: Span 34ft 5½in (10·49m); (Ta 152H-1) 47ft 6¾in (14·5m); length (A-8, F-8) 29ft 0in (8·84m); (D-9) 33ft 5¼in (10·2m); (Ta 152H-1) 35ft 5½in (10·8m); height 13ft 0in (3·96m); (D-9) 11ft 0¼in (3·35m); (Ta 152H-1) 11ft 8in (3·55m).

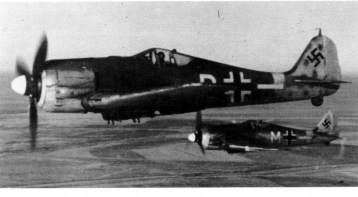

Above: A pair of Fw 190G-3 extended-range fighter-bombers flying over Romania, possibly in service with II/SG 10, in early 1944. By this time the Fw 190 was the most important Luftwaffe multi-role tactical aircraft on all fronts.

continued on page 34 ▶

Focke-Wulf Fw 190A-8 cutaway drawing key:

1 Pitot head
2 Starboard navigation light
3 Detachable wingtip
4 Pitot tube heater cable
5 Wing lower shell 'floating rib'
6 Aileron hinge
7 Wing lower shell stringers
8 Leading-edge ribs
9 Front spar
10 Outboard 'solid rib'
11 Wing upper shell stringers
12 Aileron trim tab
13 Aileron structure
14 Aileron control linkage
15 Ammunition box (125 rounds)
16 Starboard 20mm Mauser MG 151/20E cannon (sideways mounted)
17 Ammunition box rear suspension arm
18 Flap structure
19 Wing flap upper skinning
20 Flap setting indicator peep-hole
21 Rear spar
22 Inboard wing construction
23 Undercarriage indicator
24 Wing rib strengthening
25 Ammunition feed chute
26 Static and dynamic air pressure lines
27 Cannon barrel
28 Launch tube bracing struts
29 Launch tube carrier strut
30 Mortar launch tube (auxiliary underwing armament)
31 Launch tube internal guide rails
32 21cm (WfrGr.21) spin-stabilized Type 42 mortar shell
33 VDM three-blade constant-speed propeller propeller
34 Propeller boss
35 Propeller hub
36 Starboard undercarriage fairing
37 Starboard mainwheel
38 Oil warming chamber
39 Thermostat
40 Cooler armoured ring (6·5mm)
41 Oil tank drain valve
42 Annular oil tank (12·1 gal/55 litres)
43 Oil cooler
44 Twelve-blade engine cooling fan; 3·17 times propeller speed
45 Hydraulic-electric pitch control unit
46 Primer fuel line
47 Bosch magneto
48 Oil tank armour (5·5mm)
49 Supercharger air pressure pipes
50 BMW 801D-2 fourteen-cylinder radial engine
51 Cowling support ring
52 Cowling quick-release fasteners
53 Oil pump
54 Fuel pump (engine rear face)
55 Oil filter (starboard)
56 Wing root cannon synchronization gear
57 Gun troughs/cowling upper panel attachment
58 Engine mounting ring
59 Cockpit heating pipe
60 Exhaust pipes (cylinders 11–14)
61 MG 131 link and case chute
62 Engine bearer assembly
63 MG 131 ammunition boxes (400 rpg)
64 Fuel filter recess housing
65 MG 131 ammunition cooling pipes
66 MG 131 synchronization gear
67 Ammunition feed chute
68 Twin fuselage 13mm Rheinmetall MG 131 guns
69 Windscreen mounting frame
70 Emergency power fuse and distributor box
71 Rear-hinged gun access panel
72 Engine bearer/bulkhead attachment
73 Control column
74 Transformer
75 Aileron control torsion bar
76 Rubber pedals (EC pedal unit with hydraulic wheel-brake operation)
77 Fuselage/wing spar attachment
78 Adjustable rudder push rod
79 Fuel filler head
80 Cockpit floor support frame
81 Throttle lever
82 Pilot's seat back plate armour (8mm)
83 Seat guide rails
84 Side-section back armour (5mm)
85 Shoulder armour (5mm)
86 Oxygen supply valve
87 Steel frame turnover pylon
88 Windscreen spray pipes
89 Instrument panel shroud
90 30mm armoured glass quarterlights
91 50mm armoured glass windscreen
92 Revi 16B reflector gunsight
93 Canopy
94 Aerial attachment
95 Headrest
96 Head armour (12mm)
97 Head armour support strut
98 Explosive-charge canopy emergency jettison unit
99 Canopy channel slide
100 Auxiliary tank: fuel (25·3 gal/115 litres) or GM-1 (18·7 gal/85 litres)
101 FuG 16ZY radio transmitter-receiver
102 Handhold cover
103 Primer fuel filler cap
104 Autopilot steering unit (PKS 12)
105 FuG 16ZY power transformer
106 Entry step cover plate
107 Two tri-spherical oxygen bottles (starboard fuselage wall)
108 Auxiliary fuel tank filler point
109 FuG 25a transponder unit
110 Autopilot position integration unit
111 FuG 16ZY homer bearing converter
112 Elevator control cables
113 Rudder control DUZ-flexible rods
114 Fabric panel (Bulkhead 12)
115 Rudder differential unit
116 Aerial lead-in
117 Rear fuselage lift tube
118 Triangular stress frame
119 Tailplane trim unit
120 Tailplane attachment fitting
121 Tailwheel retraction guide tube
122 Retraction cable lower pulley
123 Starboard tailplane
124 Aerial
125 Starboard elevator
126 Elevator trim tab
127 Tailwheel shock strut guide
128 Fin construction
129 Retraction cable upper pulley
130 Aerial attachment stub
131 Rudder upper hinge
132 Rudder structure
133 Rudder trim tab
134 Tailwheel retraction mechanism access panel
135 Rudder attachment/actuation fittings
136 Rear navigation light
137 Extension spring
138 Elevator trim tab
139 Port elevator structure
140 Tailplane construction
141 Semi-retracting tailwheel
142 Forked wheel housing
143 Drag yoke
144 Tailwheel shock strut
145 Tailwheel locking linkage
146 Elevator actuation lever linkage
147 Angled frame spar
148 Elevator differential bellcrank
149 FuG 25a ventral aerial
150 Master compass sensing unit
151 FuG 16ZY fixed loop homing aerial
152 Radio compartment access hatch
153 Single tri-spherical oxygen bottle (port fuselage wall)
154 Retractable entry step
155 Wing-root fairing
156 Fuselage rear fuel tank (64·5 gal/293 litres)
157 Fuselage/rear spar attachment
158 Fuselage forward fuel tank (51 gal/232 litres)
159 Port wing root cannon ammunition box (250 rounds)
160 Ammunition feed chute
161 Wing root MG 151/20E cannon
162 Link and case chute
163 Cannon rear mount support bracket
164 Upper and lower wing shell stringers
165 Rear spar
166 Spar construction
167 Flap position indicator scale and peep-hole
168 Flap actuating electric motor
169 MG 151/20E cannon (sideways mounted)
170 Aileron transverse linkage
171 Ammunition box (125 rounds)
172 Ammunition box rear suspension arm
173 Aileron control linkage
174 Aileron control unit
175 Aileron trim tab

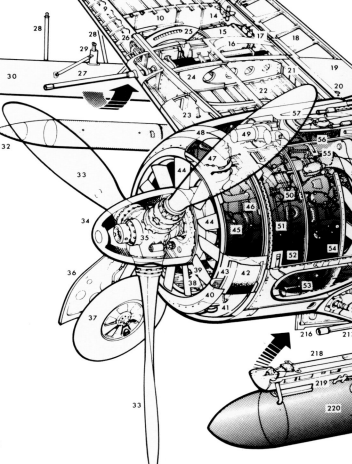

Left: Fw 190F-8 of SG 4 (former Stuka unit) at Köln-Wahn, December 1944.

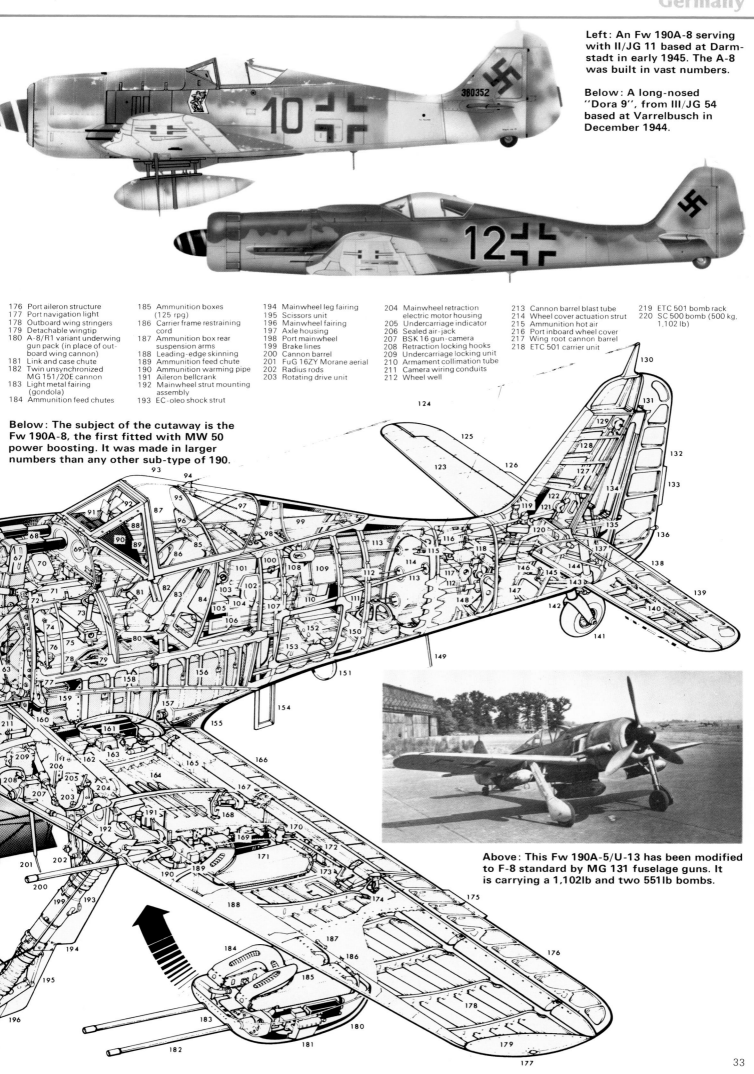

Left: An Fw 190A-8 serving with II/JG 11 based at Darmstadt in early 1945. The A-8 was built in vast numbers.

Below: A long-nosed "Dora 9", from III/JG 54 based at Varrelbusch in December 1944.

176 Port aileron structure
177 Port navigation light
178 Outboard wing stringers
179 Detachable wingtip
180 A-8/R1 variant underwing gun pack (in place of outboard wing cannon)
181 Link and case chute
182 Twin unsynchronized MG 151/20E cannon
183 Light metal fairing (gondola)
184 Ammunition feed chutes

185 Ammunition boxes (125 rpg)
186 Carrier frame restraining cord
187 Ammunition box rear suspension arms
188 Leading-edge skinning
189 Ammunition feed chute
190 Ammunition warming pipe
191 Aileron bellcrank
192 Mainwheel strut mounting assembly
193 EC-oleo shock strut

194 Mainwheel leg fairing
195 Scissors unit
196 Mainwheel fairing
197 Axle housing
198 Port mainwheel
199 Brake lines
200 Cannon barrel
201 FuG 16ZY Morane aerial
202 Radius rods
203 Rotating drive unit

204 Mainwheel retraction electric motor housing
205 Undercarriage indicator
206 Sealed air-jack
207 BSK 16 gun-camera
208 Retraction locking hooks
209 Undercarriage locking unit
210 Armament collimation tube
211 Camera wiring conduits
212 Wheel well

213 Cannon barrel blast tube
214 Wheel cover actuation strut
215 Ammunition hot air
216 Port inboard wheel cover
217 Wing root cannon barrel
218 ETC 501 carrier unit

219 ETC 501 bomb rack
220 SC 500 bomb (500 kg, 1,102 lb)

Below: The subject of the cutaway is the Fw 190A-8, the first fitted with MW 50 power boosting. It was made in larger numbers than any other sub-type of 190.

Above: This Fw 190A-5/U-13 has been modified to F-8 standard by MG 131 fuselage guns. It is carrying a 1,102lb and two 551lb bombs.

▶ **Weights:** Empty (A-8, F-8) 7,055lb (3200kg); (D-9) 7,720lb (3500kg); (Ta 152H-1) 7,940lb (3600kg); loaded (A-8, F-8) 10,800lb (4900kg); (D-9) 10,670lb (4840kg); (Ta 152H-1) 12,125lb (5500kg).
Performance: Maximum speed (with boost) (A-8, F-8) 408mph (653km/h); (D-9) 440mph (704km/h); (Ta 152H-1) 472mph (755km/h); initial climb (A-8, F-8) 2,350ft (720m)/min; (D-9, Ta 152) about 3,300ft (1000m)/min; service ceiling (A-8, F-8) 37,400ft (11,410m); (D-9) 32,810ft (10,000m); (Ta 152H-1) 49,215ft (15,000m); range on internal fuel (A-8, F-8 and D-9) about 560 miles (900km); (Ta 152H-1), 745 miles (1200km).
Armament: (A-8, F-8) two 13mm MG 131 above engine, two 20mm MG 151/20 in wing roots and two MG 151/20 or 30mm MK 108 in outer wings; (D-9) as above, or without outer MG 151/20s, with provision for 30mm MK 108 firing through propeller hub; (Ta 152H-1) one 30mm MK 108 and two inboard MG 151/20 (sometimes outboard MG 151/20s as well); bomb load (A-8, D-9) one 1,100lb (500kg) on centreline; (F-8) one 3,968lb (1800kg) on centreline; (Ta 152H-1) (some reconnaissance H-models unarmed).
History: First flight (Fw 190V1) June 1, 1939, (production Fw 190A-1) September 1940, (Fw 190D) late 1942.
Users: Croatia, Germany (Luftwaffe), Slovakia, Turkey; post-war, Argentina, France (Armée de l'Air, Aéronavale).

Development: Though flown well before World War II this trim little fighter was unknown to the Allies and caused a nasty surprise when first met over France in early 1941. Indeed, it was so far superior to the bigger and more sluggish Spitfire V that for the first time the RAF felt not only outnumbered but beaten technically. In June 1942 an Fw 190A-3 landed by mistake in England, and the Focke-Wulf was discovered to be even better than expected. It was faster than any Allied fighter in service, had far heavier armament (at that time the standard was two 7·92mm MG 17s over the engine, two of the previously unknown Mauser cannon inboard and two 20mm MG FF outboard), was immensely strong, had excellent power of manoeuvre and good pilot view. It was also an extremely small target, much lighter than any Allied fighter and had a stable widetrack landing gear (unlike the Bf 109). Altogether it gave Allied pilots and designers an inferiority complex. Though it never supplanted the 109, it was subsequently made in a profusion of different versions by many factories.

The A series included many fighter and fighter bomber versions, some having not only the increasingly heavy internal armament but also two or four 20mm cannon or two 30mm in underwing fairings. Most had an emergency power boost system, using MW 50 (methanol/water) or GM-1 (nitrous oxide) injection, or both. Some carried torpedoes, others were two-seaters, and a few had autopilots for bad weather and night interceptions. The F series were close-support attack aircraft, some having the Panzerblitz array of R4M rockets for tank-busting (also lethal against heavy bombers). There were over 40 other special armaments, and some versions had armoured leading edges for ramming Allied bombers. The G was another important series of multi-role fighter/dive bombers, but by 1943 the main effort was devoted to what the RAF called the "long-nosed 190", the 190D. This went into production in the autumn of 1944, after much development, as the Fw 190D-9 ("Dora 9"). This was once more the fastest fighter in the sky and the later D-models were redesignated Ta 152 in honour of the director of Focke-Wulf's design team, Dipl Ing Kurt Tank. The early 152C series were outstandingly formidable, but the long-span H sacrificed guns for speed and height. Tank himself easily outpaced a flight of P-51D Mustangs which surprised him on a test flight; but only ten of the H sub-type had flown when the war ended. Altogether 20,051 Fw 190s were delivered, plus a small number of Ta 152s (67, excluding development aircraft). It is curious that the Bf 109, a much older and less attractive design with many shortcomings, should have been made in greater quantity and flown by nearly all the Luftwaffe's aces.

In 1945 the Fw 190A-5 was put into production at an underground plant in France managed by SNCASO. By 1946 a total of 64 had been delivered.

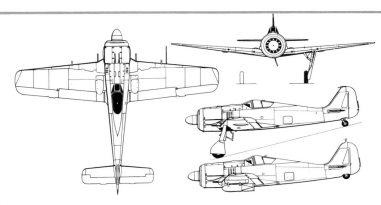

Above: Three-view of Fw 190A-3; lower side view, A-4/U-1.

Below: The culminating fighter in the whole family was the Ta 152H, a fabulous performer at high altitude. The fifth example is seen having its compass swung at Cottbus in 1945.

Above: The second production version of the Ta 152 was the C-series, without the long-span wing (photo shows Ta 152C V7, a Ta 152C-0/R11). This had a normal armament of one 30mm MK 108 and four MG 151 20mm, and flew in December 1944.

Below: A row of Fw 190A-4 fighters with pilots at cockpit readiness, on a French airfield in 1943. This mottled camouflage was unusual on fighter 190s at this time, though it was occasionally seen on Jabo 190s bombing English coasts.

Focke-Wulf Fw 200 Condor

Fw 200C-0 to C-8

Origin: Focke-Wulf Flugzeugbau GmbH, in partnership with Hamburger Flugzeugbau (Blohm und Voss).

Type: Maritime reconnaissance bomber and (C-6 to -8) missile launcher, many used as transports.

Engines: Usually four 1,200hp BMW-Bramo Fafnir 323R-2 nine-cylinder radials.

Dimensions: Span 107ft 9½in (30·855m); length 76ft 11½in (23·46m); height 20ft 8in (6·3m).

Weights: (C-3/U-4) empty 28,550lb (12,951kg); loaded 50,045lb (22,700kg).

Performance: Maximum speed (C-3) 224mph (360km/h); (C-8) 205mph (330km/h); initial climb, about 656ft (200m)/min; service ceiling 19,030ft (5800m); range with standard fuel, 2,206 miles (3550km).

Armament: Typical C-3/C-8, one forward dorsal turret with one 15mm MG 151/15 (or 20mm MG 151/20 or one 7·92mm MG 15), one 20mm MG 151/20 manually aimed at front of ventral gondola, three 7·92mm MG 15 manually aimed at rear of ventral gondola and two beam windows (beam guns sometimes being 13mm MG 131) and one 13mm MG 131 in aft dorsal position; maximum bomb load of 4,626lb (2100kg) carried in gondola and beneath outer wings (C-6, C-8, two Hs 293 guided missiles carried under outboard nacelles).

History: First flight (civil prototype) 27 July 1937; (Fw 200C-0) January 1940; final delivery (C-8) February 1944.

User: (Fw 200C series) Germany (Luftwaffe).

Development: Planned solely as a long-range commercial transport for the German airline Deutsche Luft Hansa, the prewar Fw-200 prototypes set up impressive record flights to New York and Tokyo and attracted export orders from Denmark, Brazil, Finland and Japan. Transport prototype and production versions were also used by Hitler and Himmler as VIP executive machines and several later variants were also converted as

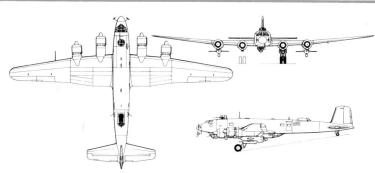

Above: The Fw 200C-8/U10, the final sub-type, with Hs 293s.

special transports. In 1938 the Japanese asked for one Condor converted for use as a long-range ocean reconnaissance machine. The resulting Fw 200V-10 prototype introduced a ventral gondola and led to the Fw 200C-0 as the prototype of a Luftwaffe aircraft which had never been requested or planned and yet which was to prove a most powerful instrument of war. Distinguished by long-chord cowlings, twin-wheel main gears (because of the increased gross weight) and a completely new armament and equipment fit, the C-0 led to the C-1, used operationally from June 1940 by KG 40 at Bordeaux-Mérignac. By September 1940 this unit alone had sunk over 90,000 tons of Allied shipping and for the next three years the C-series Condors were in Churchill's words, "the scourge of the Atlantic". But, though the Fw 200 family continued to grow in equipment and lethality, the Allies fought back with long-range Coastal Command aircraft, escort carriers and CAM (Catapult-Armed Merchantman) fighters and by mid-1944 surviving Condors were being forced into transport roles on other fronts. Total production was 276 and one of the fundamental failings of the Condor was structural weakness, catastrophic wing and fuselage failures occurring not only in the air but even on the ground, on take-off or landing.

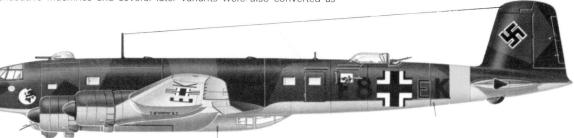

Left: An early Fw 200C-3 serving with KG 40 at Bordeaux-Mérignac and Cognac, west France, in the summer of 1941.

Below: A modified version was the Fw 200C-3/U2, whose bombing accuracy was increased by the Lotfe 7D sight.

Gotha Go 145

Go 145A, B and C

Origin: Gothaer Waggonfabrik AG, Gotha; production subcontracted to Ago, BFW (Messerschmitt) and Focke-Wulf; built under licence by CASA, Spain, and Demag, Turkey.
Type: Primary trainer, but see text.
Engine: 240hp Argus As 10C inverted-vee-8 aircooled.
Dimensions: Span 29ft 6¼in (9·00m); length 28ft 6½in (8·70m); height 9ft 6¼in (2·90m).
Weights: Empty (A) 1,940lb (880kg); maximum 3,043lb (1380kg).
Performance: Maximum speed 132mph (212km/h); typical range 404 miles (650km).
History: First flight February 1934; service delivery 1935; final delivery (Germany) not before 1943, (Spain) about 1945.
Users: Bulgaria, Croatia, Germany, Slovakia, Spain, Turkey (possibly others).

Development: The Go 145 is another of the many types of aircraft which made a giant contribution to World War II yet today are almost forgotten. This biplane trainer was not only manufactured in enormous numbers — at least 9,965 in Germany, plus more than 1,000 in Spain and Turkey — but it also became a combat type and stayed in the very forefront of battle from 1942 until the final collapse in 1945. The basic machine was wooden, with fabric covering, but it was so tractable and strong that, as well as equipping roughly half the elementary flying training schools for the Luftwaffe from 1936 onwards, the Go 145 was chosen to equip the night harassment squadrons on the Eastern Front (triggered by the maddening pinpricks of the Soviet Po-2). At first called Störkampfstaffeln, they were progressively expanded and upgraded, and Go 145 output was increased to meet the demand. In October 1943, after ten months, they were reclassified NSGr, the same as other night attack units, and many hundreds of 145s equipped six whole geschwader, plus the Ost-Flieger Gruppe. They carried various guns, light bombs, loudspeakers and even rockets. The only other sub-type in Luftwaffe use was the 145C gunnery trainer.

Below: A Go 145A flying dual at a Luftwaffe A/B Schule.

Gotha Go 242 and 244

Go 242A, B and C, Go 244B and Ka 430

Origin: Gothaer Waggonfabrik AG, Kassel; production subcontracted.
Type: Transport glider (244, transport aeroplane).
Engines: (244) two 700hp Gnome-Rhône 14M4/5 14-cylinder radials.
Dimensions: Span 80ft 4½in (24·50m); length 51ft 10in (15·81m); height (242) 14ft 4¼in (4·40m), (244) 15ft 5in (14·70m).
Weights: Empty (242A-2) 7,056lb (3200kg), (244B-2) 11,245lb (5100kg); maximum (242A-2) 15,655lb (7100kg), (244B-2) 17,198lb (7800kg).
Performance: Maximum speed (242 on tow) 149mph (240km/h), (244) 180mph (290km/h); maximum range at sea level (244) 373 miles (600km).
History: First flight (242) early 1941, (244) late 1941, (430) 1944.
User: Germany.

Development: This family of tactical transports was the only Gotha of World War II (other than the Go 145 designed much earlier). The 242 was a simple machine with nacelle of steel tube and fabric lifted and controlled by wooden wings and tail. It could carry 21 troops or light vehicles and stores loaded through the hinged rear fairing, took off on jettisonable wheels and landed on skids. The tug was usually the He 111, but the Bf 110 could cope on a good airfield; sometimes the He 111Z was used, and experiments were made with solid rocket ATO motors. Air bottles worked lift spoilers and flaps. Variants were A-1 (freight only), A-2 (troops), B-1 (nosewheel),

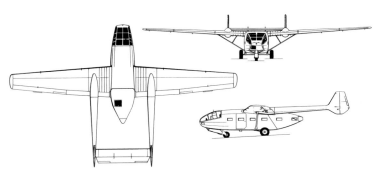

Above: Three-view of a typical Go 242B-1.

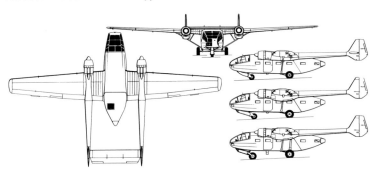

Above: Go 244B-1 (middle) with Go 244 V1 (top) and B-2 (lower).

B-2 (oleo landing gear), B-3 and -4 (paratroop), B-5 (dual trainer) and C-1 (flying boat). The number built was 1,528, in 1941-43, of which 133 were fitted with engines (almost always the French GR 14M, but sometimes the BMW 132Z or Russian M-25A) to become the Go 244. The 244B-1 to B-5 were conversions of the same 242 models, but they proved vulnerable in the Soviet Union and North Africa and were soon scrapped. The Ka 430, named for Gotha's lead designer Albert Kalkert, was a refined development with single tailboom. Experiments with the prototype included rocket braking.

Left: The Go 244B-1 was usually a conversion of the Go 242B-1 glider. The powered version was not a great success.

Heinkel He 51

He 51 A-1, B-2 and C-1

Origin: Ernst Heinkel AG; production see text.
Type: Single-seat fighter (B-2) reconnaissance seaplane; (C-1) land ground attack.
Engine: One 750hp BMW VI 7·3Z vee-12 water-cooled.
Dimensions: Span 36ft 1in (11m); length 27ft 6¾in (8·4m); (B-2) about 31ft; height 10ft 6in (3·2m); (B-2) about 11ft.
Weights: (A-1), empty 3,223lb (1462kg); loaded 4,189lb (1900kg).
Performance: Maximum speed (A-1) 205mph (330km/h); initial climb 1,969ft (600m)/min; service ceiling 24,610ft (7500m); range 242 miles (390km).
Armament: Standard, two 7·92mm Rheinmetall MG 17 synchronised above fuselage; (B-2) same plus underwing racks for up to six 22lb (10kg) bombs; (C-1) same plus underwing racks for four 110lb (50kg) bombs.
History: First flight (He 49a) November 1932; (He 49b) February 1933; (He 51A-0) May 1933; service delivery of A-1, July 1934.
Users: Germany, Spain.
Development: Gradually, as the likelihood of Allied legal action receded, Heinkel dared to build aircraft that openly contravened the Versailles Treaty. The most startling was the He 37, obviously a prototype fighter, which in 1928 achieved 194mph, or 20mph faster than the RAF Bulldog which was still a year away from service. Land and seaplane versions led to a succession of He 49 fighter prototypes in the 1930s and these in turn provided the basis for the refined He 51. After the Ar 65 this was the first fighter ordered into

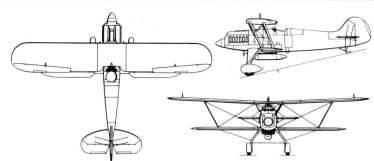

Above: Three-view of He 51C-1 (the B-1 was very similar).

production by the Reichsluftfahrtministerium for the reborn Luftwaffe. Though the initial order for He 51A-1s was only 75, Heinkel was unused to such an order and many were built under licence by Ago, Erla, Arado and Fieseler — which were also fast tooling for their own designs. In March 1935 the Luftwaffe was publicly announced, and JG1 "Richthofen" fighter squadron was combat-ready at Döberitz with its new Heinkels. In November 1936, 36 He 51A-1s went to Spain with the Legion Kondor, giving a sufficiently good showing for the Nationalists to buy at least 30 from Heinkel. There followed a total of 50 of various He 51B seaplane versions, the 38 B-2s being for service aboard cruisers. The final batch comprised 79 C-1 ground attack fighters, of which 28 served in Spain. The He 51 was still in active service in September 1939, operating in the close-support role in Poland, and remained as an advanced trainer until 1943.

Right: By the start of World War II most He 51 fighters had been assigned as advanced trainers to Jagdfliegerschulen (fighter-pilot schools). This He 51B-1 survived as late as 1942 at the main Balkan school A/B 123 at Agram (Zagreb). By then, Luftwaffe pilot training was disintegrating.

Heinkel He 59

He 59B, C, D, E and N

Origin: Ernst Heinkel AG, Marienehe; production subcontracted to Walter Bachmann AG, Ribnitz; also some built under licence (about 1935) by Arado Flugzeugwerke.
Type: See text.
Engines: Two 660hp BMW VI vee-12 water-cooled.
Dimensions: Span 77ft 9½in (23·70m); length (most) 57ft 1¾in (17·40m); height 23ft 3¾in (7·10m).
Weights: (C-2) empty 13,702lb (6215kg); maximum 19,842lb (9000kg).
Performance: Maximum speed (typical) 134mph (215km/h); extreme range with max fuel 1,087 miles (1750km).
Armament: Three or four 7·92mm MG 15 (later, MG 81) manually aimed from bow, dorsal and ventral positions; many sub-types carried at least one 20mm MG FF, and most B-2 having provision for 2,205lb (1000kg) of mines, bombs or other ordnance.
History: First flight (landplane second prototype) September 1931; service delivery (He 59A-0) August 1932; final delivery from new, probably 1936.
Users: Finland, Germany, Romania.

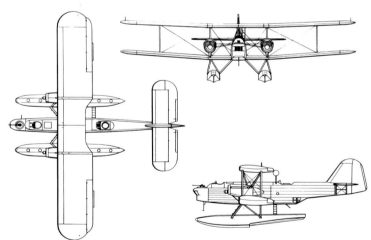

Above: The He 59B-2 reconnaissance and torpedo bomber.

Development: One of the first military aircraft built in Germany after the Versailles Treaty (which it openly contravened), the He 59 was destined to serve in an extraordinary variety of roles long after its antiquated appearance might have suggested it was obsolescent. In fact like many Axis warplanes it proved to be more and more useful, and though few were left by 1943 there were in that year at least 18 units operating different He 59 sub-types in mining, ground attack, rescue, transport, electronic warfare and psy-war missions. It was planned as a land or seaplane torpedo bomber, but in 1932 entered service mainly in the reconnaissance role. In the Kondor Legion in Spain it made heavy bombing attacks on Republican ports (often after a quiet gliding run-in at night), and in 1940 more than 180 were intensively used for all manner of missions — the most daring of which was the flying-in of ten He 59C-2 rescue transports to the Waal at Rotterdam to disgorge 60 troops who captured the city's main bridge. Most mining missions in 1939–43 were flown by B-2 or B-3 versions, but many were rebuilt as He 59N radio/radar trainers.

Left: This He 59N navigation trainer is typical of the oft-rebuilt He 59 seaplanes late in the war (when only a few survived). Some retained armament, while others served as trials platforms and trainers for airborne electronic systems.

Heinkel He 111

He 111 B series, E series, H series and P series

Origin: Ernst Heinkel AG; also built in France on German account by SNCASO; built under licence by Fabrica de Avione SET, Romania, and CASA, Spain.

Type: Four-seat or five-seat medium bomber (later, torpedo bomber, glider tug and missile launcher).

Engines: (He 111H-3) two 1,200hp Junkers Jumo 211D-2 12-cylinder inverted-vee liquid-cooled; (He 111P-2) two 1,100hp Daimler-Benz DB 601A-1 12-cylinder inverted-vee liquid-cooled.

Dimensions: (H-3) Span 74ft 1¾in (22·6m); length 53ft 9½in (16·4m); height 13ft 1½in (4m).

Weights: Empty (H-3) 17,000lb (7720kg); (P-2) 17,640lb (8000kg); maximum loaded (H-3) 30,865lb (14,000kg); (P-2) 29,762lb (13,500kg).

Performance: Maximum speed (H-3) 258mph (415km/h); (P-2) 242mph (390km/h) at 16,400ft (5000m) (at maximum weight, neither version could exceed 205mph, 330km/h); climb to 14,765ft (4500m) 30–35min at normal gross weight, 50min at maximum; service ceiling (both) around 25,590ft (7800m) at normal gross weight, under 16,400ft (5000m) at maximum; range with maximum bomb load (both) about 745 miles (1200km).

Armament: (P-2) 7·92mm Rheinmetall MG 15 machine gun on manual mountings in nosecap, open dorsal position and ventral gondola; (H-3) same, plus fixed forward-firing MG 15 or 17, two MG 15s in waist windows and (usually) 20mm MG FF cannon in front of ventral gondola and (sometimes)

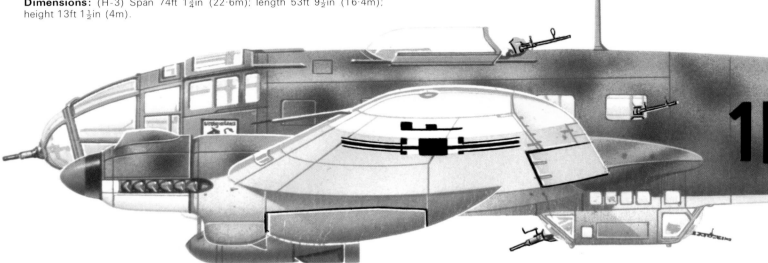

Heinkel He 111 H-3 cutaway drawing key:

1 Starboard navigation light
2 Starboard aileron
3 Lattice ribs
4 Front spar
5 Rear spar
6 Aileron tab
7 Starboard flap
8 Outboard fuel tank (220 gal/1,000 litres capacity)
9 Wing centre section/outer panel break line
10 Inboard fuel tank (154 gal/700 litres capacity) inboard of nacelle
11 Oil tank cooling louvres
12 Oil cooler air intake
13 Supercharger air intake
14 Three-blade VDM propeller
15 Airscrew pitch-change mechanism
16 Junkers Jumo 211D-1 12-cylinder inverted-vee liquid-cooled engine
17 Exhaust manifold
18 Nose-mounted 7·92mm MG 15 machine gun
19 Ikaria ball-and-socket gun mounting (offset to starboard)
20 Bomb sight housing (offset to starboard)
21 Starboard mainwheel
22 Rudder pedals
23 Bomb aimer's prone pad
24 Additional 7·92mm MG 15 machine gun (fitted by forward maintenance units)
25 Repeater compass
26 Bomb aimer's folding seat
27 Control wheel
28 Throttles
29 Pilot's seat
30 Retractable auxiliary windscreen (for use when pilot's seat in elevated position)
31 Sliding roof hatch
32 Forward fuselage bulkhead
33 Double-frame station
34 Port ESAC bomb bay (vertical stowage)
35 Fuselage windows (blanked)
36 Central gangway between bomb bays
37 Double-frame station
38 Direction finder
39 Dorsal gunner's (forward) sliding canopy
40 Dorsal 7·92mm MG 15 machine gun
41 Dorsal gunner's cradle seat
42 FuG 10 radio equipment
43 Fuselage window
44 Armoured bulkhead (8mm)
45 Aerial mast
46 Bomb flares
47 Unarmoured bulkhead
48 Rear fuselage access cut-out
49 Port 7·92mm beam MG 15 machine gun
50 Dinghy stowage
51 Fuselage frames
52 Stringers
53 Starboard tailplane
54 Aerial
55 Starboard elevator
56 Fin front spar
57 Fin structure
58 Rudder balance
59 Fin rear spar/rudder post
60 Rudder construction
61 Rudder tab
62 Tab actuator
63 Remotely-controlled 7·92 mm MG 17 machine gun in tailcone (fitted to some aircraft only)
64 Rear navigation light
65 Elevator tab
66 Elevator structure
67 Tailplane main spar
68 Tailplane front spar
69 Semi-retractable tailwheel
70 Tailwheel shock-absorber
71 Rudder control linkage
72 Fuselage/tail frame
73 Rudder control cables
74 Elevator push-pull control rods
75 Master compass
76 Observation window fairing
77 Glazed observation window in floor

Above: This colourful He 111H-3 served in the Zaporozhye region with Romania's Grupul 5, Corpul I.

Below: The subject of the cutaway drawing is the He 111H-3, a member of what became by far the most important He 111 family. Powered by the Jumo 211 engine (the final sub-type, a saboteur transport in 1944, had the 1,776hp Jumo 213) the H-series eventually ran to a unique 23 basic sub-models, each with its own variations.

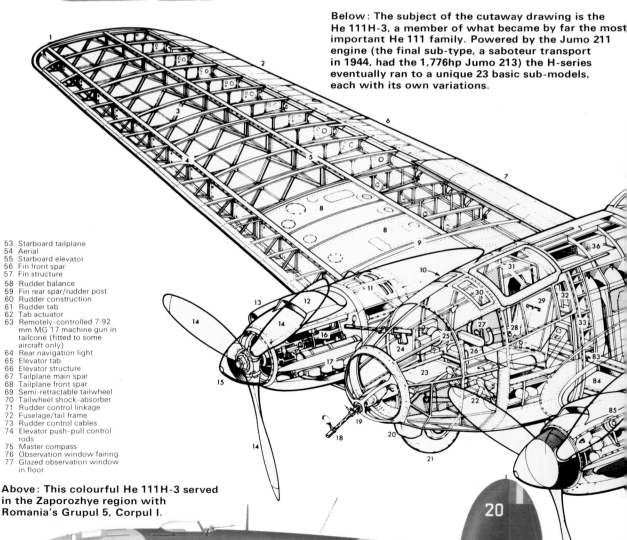

fixed rear-firing MG 17 in extreme tail; internal bomb load up to 4,410lb (2000kg) in vertical cells, stored nose-up; external bomb load (at expense of internal) one 4,410lb (2000kg) on H-3, one or two 1,102lb (500kg) on others; later marks carried one or two 1,686lb (765kg) torpedoes, Bv 246 glide missiles, Hs 293 rocket missiles, Fritz X radio-controlled glide bombs or one FZG-76 ("V-1") cruise missile.

continued on page 40 ▶

Below: Painted in North African camouflage, this He 111H-6 had by August 1943 been pushed back to Ottana, Sardinia. Serving with 2/KG 26, it has two forward-aimed MG FF 20mm cannon for attacks on shipping, heavy external racks (two 1,102lb are shown) and extra beam and tail guns.

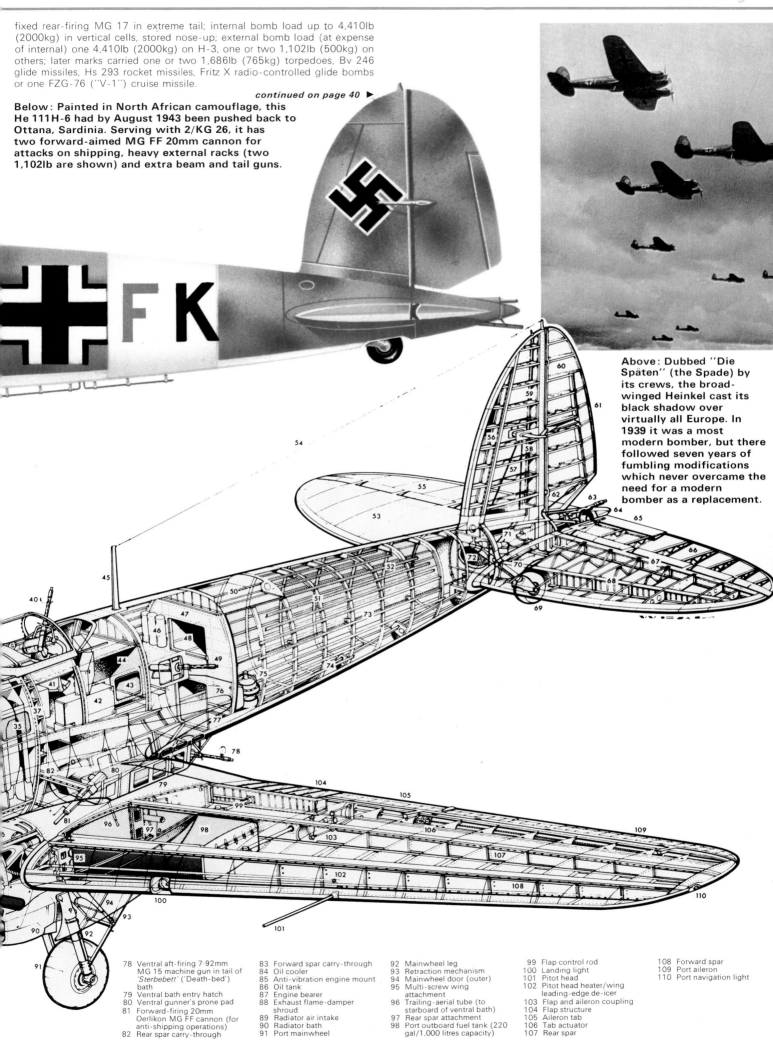

Above: Dubbed "Die Späten" (the Spade) by its crews, the broad-winged Heinkel cast its black shadow over virtually all Europe. In 1939 it was a most modern bomber, but there followed seven years of fumbling modifications which never overcame the need for a modern bomber as a replacement.

78 Ventral aft-firing 7·92mm MG 15 machine gun in tail of 'Sterbebett' ('Death-bed') bath
79 Ventral bath entry hatch
80 Ventral gunner's prone pad
81 Forward-firing 20mm Oerlikon MG FF cannon (for anti-shipping operations)
82 Rear spar carry-through
83 Forward spar carry-through
84 Oil cooler
85 Anti-vibration engine mount
86 Oil tank
87 Engine bearer
88 Exhaust flame-damper shroud
89 Radiator air intake
90 Radiator bath
91 Port mainwheel
92 Mainwheel leg
93 Retraction mechanism
94 Mainwheel door (outer)
95 Multi-screw wing attachment
96 Trailing-aerial tube (to starboard of ventral bath)
97 Rear spar attachment
98 Port outboard fuel tank (220 gal/1,000 litres capacity)
99 Flap control rod
100 Landing light
101 Pitot head
102 Pitot head heater/wing leading-edge de-icer
103 Flap and aileron coupling
104 Flap structure
105 Aileron tab
106 Tab actuator
107 Rear spar
108 Forward spar
109 Port aileron
110 Port navigation light

▶ **History:** First flight (He 111V1 prototype) 24 February 1935; (pre-production He 111B-0) August 1936; (production He 111B-1) 30 October 1936; (first He 111E series) January 1938; (first production He 111P-1) December 1938; (He 111H-1) January or February 1939; final delivery (He 111H-23) October 1944; (Spanish C.2111) late 1956.

Users: China, Germany (Luftwaffe, Luft Hansa), Hungary, Iraq, Romania, Spain, Turkey.

Development: A natural twin-engined outgrowth of the He 70, the first He 111 was a graceful machine with elliptical wings and tail, secretly flown as a bomber but revealed to the world a year later as a civil airliner. Powered by 660hp BMW VI engines, it had typical armament of three manually aimed machine guns but the useful bomb load of 2,200lb (1000kg) stowed nose-up in eight cells in the centre fuselage. In 1937 a number of generally similar machines secretly flew photo-reconnaissance missions over Britain, France and the Soviet Union, in the guise of airliners of Deutsche Luft Hansa. In the same year the He 111B-1 came into Luftwaffe service, with two 880hp Daimler-Benz DB 600C engines, while a vast new factory was built at Oranienburg solely to make later versions. In February 1937 operations began with the Legion Kondor in Spain, with considerable success, flight performance being improved in the B-2 by 950hp DB 600CG engines which were retained in the C series. The D was faster, with the 1,000hp Jumo 211A-1, also used in the He 111 F in which a new straight-edged wing was introduced. To a considerable degree the success of the early elliptical-winged He 111 bombers in Spain misled the Luftwaffe into considering that nothing could withstand the onslaught of their huge fleets of medium bombers. These aircraft — the trim Do 17, the broad-winged He 111 and the high-performance Ju 88 — were all extremely advanced by the standards of the mid-1930s when they were designed. They were faster than the single-seat fighters of that era and, so the argument went, therefore did not need much defensive armament. So the three machine guns carried by the first He 111 bombers in 1936 stayed unchanged until, in the Battle of Britain, the He 111 was hacked down with ease, its only defence being its toughness and ability to come back after being shot to pieces. The inevitable result was that more and more defensive guns were added, needing a fifth or even a sixth crew-member. Coupled with incessant growth in equipment and armour the result was deteriorating performance, so that the record-breaker of 1936–38 became the lumbering sitting duck of 1942–45. Yet the He 111 was built in ever-greater numbers, virtually all the later sub-types being

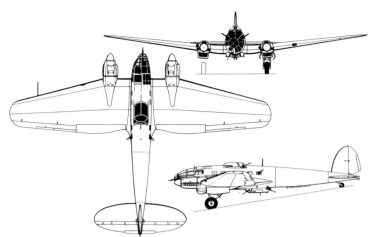

Above: A fairly late bomber variant, the He 111H-16.

members of the prolific H-series. Variations were legion, including versions with large barrage-balloon deflectors, several kinds of missiles (including a V-1 tucked under the left wing root), while a few were completed as saboteur transports. The most numerous version was the H-6, and the extraordinary He 111Z (Zwilling) glider tug of 1942 consisted of two H-6s joined by a common centre wing carrying a fifth engine. Right to the end of the war the RLM and German industry failed to find a replacement for the old "Spaten" (spade), and the total produced in Germany and Romania was at least 6,086 and possibly more than 7,000. Merlin-engined C.2111 versions continued in production in Spain until 1956.

Below: Luftwaffe armourers hand-pulled heavy bombs far more than did those of the RAF (though this may have been due to the fact that more RAF bombers operated from permanent bases). This 1,102lb SC500 is going to be hung externally as one of a pair under an He 111H-6 of KG 55 (not that in the picture). The photo was taken on the Eastern Front in June 1941.

Heinkel He 115

He 115A, B, C, D and E

Origin: Ernst Heinkel AG, Marienehe.
Type: Multi-role seaplane, see text.
Engines: Two BMW 132 nine-cylinder radials, (B-1) usually 865hp 132N, (C-1) usually 970hp 132K.
Dimensions: Span 73ft 1in (22·275m); length (typical) 56ft 9½in (17·30 m); height (typical) 21ft 7¾in (6·60m).
Weights: Empty (B-1) 14,748lb (6690kg); maximum 22,928lb (10,400kg).
Performance: Maximum speed (B, C, typical) 203mph (327km/h); maximum range (full weapons) 1,300 miles (2090km), (max fuel) 2,050 miles (3300km).
Armament: See text.
History: First flight (prototype) about October 1936; service delivery (115A-0) July 1937; final delivery about July 1944.
Users: Bulgaria, Finland, Germany, Norway, Sweden, UK (RAF).

Development: A wholly outstanding machine in all respects, the 115 was tough, beautiful to fly at speeds down to 75 knots, and carried a substantial load at relatively high speeds. In 1938 the prototype was specially streamlined to set class records, and the first Luftwaffe operational version, the A-1,

Above: A Weser-built He 115B-0 of 1939, one of the earliest versions for service use. Survivors were later re-equipped.

was sold to Norway and Sweden with small changes. Most A-models carried one LTF 5 or 6b torpedo or up to 2,205lb (1000kg) of mines or other stores, and the nose and rear cockpits each had a 7·92mm or 0·303in gun. By 1939 long-range B models were in production, which could carry the new 2,028lb (920kg) magnetic mine in addition to a 1,102lb (500kg) bomb load at a cruising speed of some 150mph. The B-2 had floats strengthened for ice or snow. In April 1940 the Norwegian aircraft were engaged in fierce combat and made many bombing missions on German forces before the four survivors set out for Scotland. One of these was fitted with eight wing machine guns and used by the RAF on secret agent-dropping between Malta and North Africa. Another Norse escapee was used in Finland. In 1940 production centred on the C series, with many variants, and often an MG 151 cannon in the nose. The single D had 1,600hp BMW 801 engines, and after being out of production 18 months a further 141 E-models were built in 1944 to bring the total past the 400 mark. Like the earlier versions the E-series were used for armed reconnaissance, minelaying, utility transport and casevac and even shallow dive bombing and torpedo bombing.

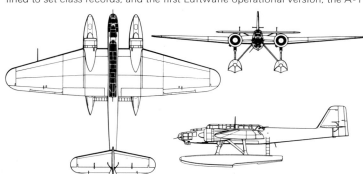

Left: Three-view of He 115B-1; later a nose cannon was added.

Heinkel He 177 Greif

He 177A-0 to A-5, He 277 and He 274

Origin: Ernst Heinkel AG; also built by Arado Flugzeugwerke.
Type: He 177, six-seat heavy bomber and missile carrier.
Engines: Two 2,950hp Daimler-Benz DB 610A-1/B-1, each comprising two inverted-vee-12 liquid-cooled engines geared to one propeller.
Dimensions: Span 103ft 1¾in (31·44m); length 72ft 2in (22m); height 21ft (6·4m).
Weights: Empty 37,038lb (16,800kg); loaded (A-5) 68,343lb (31,000kg).
Performance: Maximum speed (at 41,000lb, 18,615kg) 295mph (472 km/h); initial climb 853ft (260m)/min; service ceiling 26,500ft (7080m); range with FX or Hs 293 missiles (no bombs) about 3,107 miles (5000km).
Armament: (A-5/R2) one 7·92mm MG 81J manually aimed in nose, one 20mm MG 151 manually aimed at front of ventral gondola, one or two 13mm MG 131 in forward dorsal turret, one MG 131 in rear dorsal turret, one MG 151 manually aimed in tail and two MG 81 or one MG 131 manually aimed at rear of gondola; maximum internal bomb load 13,200lb (6000kg), seldom carried; external load, two Hs 293 guided missiles, FX 1400 guided bombs, mines or torpedoes (more if internal bay blanked off and racks added below it).
History: First flight (He 177V-1) 19 November 1939; (pre-production He 177A-0) November 1941; service delivery (A-1) March 1942; (A-5) February 1943; first flight (He 277V-1) December 1943; (He 274, alias AAS 01A) December 1945.
User: Germany (Luftwaffe).

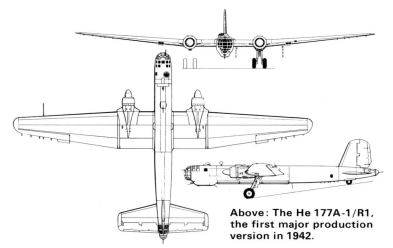

Above: The He 177A-1/R1, the first major production version in 1942.

Development: The Heinkel 177, Germany's biggest bomber programme in World War II, is remembered as possibly the most troublesome and unsatisfactory aircraft in military history, and it was only through dogged courage and persistence that large numbers were put into service. Much of the fault lay in the stupid 1938 requirement that the proposed heavy bomber and anti-ship aircraft should be capable of dive bombing. Certainly the wish to reduce drag by using coupled pairs of engines was mistaken, because no engines in bomber history have caught fire so often in normal cruising flight. Six of the eight prototypes crashed and many of the 35 pre-production A-0s (built mainly by Arado) were written off in take-off swings or in-flight fires. Arado built 130 A-1s, followed by 170 Heinkel-built A-3s and 826 A-5s with repositioned engines and longer fuselages. About 700 served on the Eastern Front, many having 50mm and 75mm guns for tank-busting; a few nervously bombed Britain in 400mph shallow dives, without any proper aiming of their bombs. So bothersome were these beasts that Goering forbade Heinkel to pester him any more with plans to use four separate engines, but Heinkel secretly flew the He 277, with four 1,750hp DB 603A, at Vienna, as the first of a major programme. The almost completely redesigned He 274 was a high-altitude bomber developed at the Farman factory at Suresnes, with four 1,850hp engines, a 145ft wing and twin fins. After the liberation it was readied for flight and flown at Orléans-Bricy.

Left: Main operational model was the A-5, of which 826 were built. This A-5/R2 has external racks for Fritz-X and Hs 293 guided missiles under its wings and on the centreline.

Heinkel He 162 Salamander

He 162A-2

Origin: Ernst Heinkel AG; first batch Vienna-Schwechat, production totally dispersed with underground assembly at Nordhausen (Mittelwerke), Bernberg (Junkers) and Rostock (Heinkel).
Type: Single-seat interceptor.
Engine: One 1,760lb (800kg) thrust BMW 003E-1 or E-2 Orkan single-shaft turbojet.
Dimensions: Span 23ft 7¾in (7·2m); length 29ft 8½in (9m); height 6ft 6½in (2–6m).
Weights: Empty 4,796lb (2180kg); loaded 5,940lb (2695kg).
Performance: Maximum speed 490mph (784km/h) at sea level, 522mph (835km/h) at 19,700ft (6000m); initial climb 4,200ft (1280m)/min; service ceiling 39,500ft (12,040m); range at full throttle 434 miles (695km) at altitude.
Armament: Early versions, two 30mm Rheinmetall MK 108 cannon with 50 rounds each; later production, two 20mm Mauser MG 151/20 with 120 rounds each.
History: First flight 6 December 1944; first delivery January 1945.
User: Germany (Luftwaffe).

Above: At one of the Heinkel plants an unpainted 162A-2 sits with canopy shattered in May 1945.

Development: Popularly called "Volksjäger" (People's Fighter), this incredible aircraft left behind so many conflicting impressions it is hard to believe the whole programme was started and finished in little more than six months. To appreciate the almost impossible nature of the programme, Germany was being pounded to rubble by fleets of Allied bombers that darkened the sky, and the aircraft industry and the Luftwaffe's fuel supplies were inexorably running down. Experienced aircrew had nearly all been killed, materials were in critically short supply and time had to be measured not in months but in days. So on 8 September 1944 the RLM issued a specification calling for a 750km/h jet fighter to be regarded as a piece of consumer goods and to be ready by 1 January 1945. Huge numbers of workers were organised to build it even before it was designed and Hitler Youth were hastily trained in primary gliders before being strapped into the new jet. Heinkel, which had built the world's first turbojet aircraft (He 178, flown 27 August 1939) and the first jet fighter (He 280 twin-jet, flown on its jet engines 2 April 1941) won a hasty competition with a tiny wooden machine with its engine perched on top and blasting between twin fins. Drawings were ready on 30 October 1944. The prototype flew in 37 days and plans were made for production to rise rapidly to 4,000 per month. Despite extreme difficulties, 300 of various sub-types had been completed by VE-day, with 800 more on the assembly lines. I/JG1 was operational at Leck, though without fuel. Despite many bad characteristics the 162 was a fighter of a futuristic kind, created in quantity far quicker than modern aircraft are even drawn on paper.

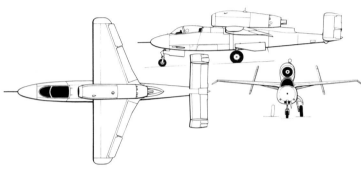

Above: Three-view of the mass-produced He 162A-2 Salamander.

Right: An He 162A-2 of I/JG 1 at Parchim for pilot conversion in March 1945.

Right: This He 162A-2 belonged to 2/JG 1 at Leck, where conditions were completely chaotic.

Right: A third He 162A-2, this time assigned to 3/JG-1 at Leck, a Gruppe that never converted to jets.

Right: Another He 162A-2 from 3/JG 1 at Leck. As they burned diesel oil the jets did have at least some fuel.

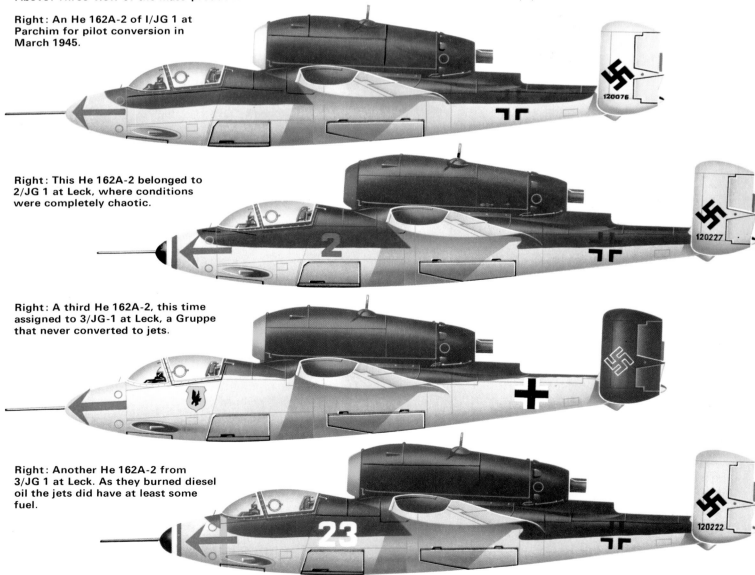

Heinkel He 219 Uhu

He 219A-0 to A-7, B and C series

Origin: Ernst Heinkel AG.
Type: A series, two-seat night fighter.
Engines: Usually two 1,900hp Daimler-Benz DB 603G inverted-vee-12 liquid-cooled; other engines, see text.
Dimensions: (A-series) span 60ft 2in or 60ft 8in (18·5m); length (with aerials) 50ft 11¾in (15·54m); height 13ft 5½in (4·1m).
Weights: (A-7) empty 24,692lb (11,200kg); loaded 33,730lb (15,200kg).
Performance: (A-7) maximum speed 416mph (670km/h); initial climb 1,804ft (550m)/min; service ceiling 41,660ft (12,700m); range 1,243 miles (2000km).
Armament: Varied, see text.
History: First flight (219V-1) 15 November 1942; service delivery (prototypes) May 1943; (production 219A-1) November 1943.
User: Germany (Luftwaffe).

Development: Ernst Heinkel was the pioneer of gas-turbine jet aircraft, flying the He 178 on 27 August 1939 and the He 280 twin-jet fighter as a glider on 22 September 1940 and with its engines on 2 April 1941 (before the purely experimental Gloster E.28/39). But Heinkel was unable to build the extremely promising He 280 in quantity, which was fortunate for the Allies. He had no spare capacity for the He 219 either, which had excited little official interest when submitted as the P.1060 project in August 1940 as a high-speed fighter, bomber and torpedo carrier. It was only when RAF night attacks began to hurt, at the end of 1941, that he was asked to produce the 219 as a night fighter (Uhu meaning Owl). The He 219V-1, with 1,750hp DB 603AS and two MG 151/20 cannon, plus an MG 131 in the rear cockpit, was fast and extremely manoeuvrable and the test pilots at Rechlin were thrilled by it. Successive prototypes had much heavier armament and radar and 100 were ordered from five factories in Germany, Poland and Austria. The order was soon trebled and Luftwaffe enthusiasm was such that even the early prototypes were sent to Venlo, Holland, to form a special trials unit. The first six night sorties resulted in the claimed destruction of 20 RAF bombers, six of them the previously almost immune Mosquitoes! More than 15 different versions of the 219 then appeared, immediately proving outstandingly formidable. The A-2/R1 had 603As, two MG 151/20 in the wing roots and two or four in a belly tray and two 30mm MK 108 firing upward at 65° in a Schräge Musik (Jazz Music) installation for destroying bombers by formating below them. The A-7/R1 had MK 108s in the wing roots and two of these big guns and two MG 151/20 in the tray, plus the Schräge Musik with 100 rounds per gun (the most lethal of all). Some versions had three seats, long-span wing and DB 603L turbocharged engines, or Jumo 213s or even the 2,500hp Jumo 222 with six banks of four cylinders. The B and C families would have been enlarged multi-role versions with rear turrets. Total A-type production was only 268, the officials at one time ignoring Luftwaffe enthusiasm by ordering production to be stopped!

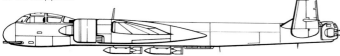

Above: The proposed He 219C-2 Jagdbomber with Jumo 222 engines.

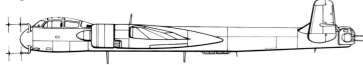

Above: The proposed He 219C-1 four-seat night fighter.

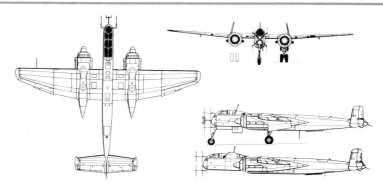

Above: Three-view of He 219A-5/R1; lower side view, the lengthened A-5/R4 with MG 131 in the rear cockpit for defence.

The He 219A-7/R4 had exceptional high-altitude equipment and performance, plus ejection seats, but armament was reduced to four MG 151/20, all firing ahead. This was relatively light.

Above: An He 219A-5/R2 just after capture of its airfield by the Allies. Splendid to fly, the 219 was a formidable machine.

Below: Another He 219A-5, this time fitted with not only SN-2 radar but also the older Lichtenstein C-1 in the centre.

Henschel Hs 123

Hs 123A-1

Origin: Henschel Flugzeugwerke AG.
Type: Single-seat dive bomber and close-support.
Engine: One 880hp BMW 132 Dc nine-cylinder radial.
Dimensions: Span 34ft 5½in (10·5m); length 27ft 4in (8·3m) height 10ft 6½in (3·2m).
Weights: Empty 3,316lb (1504kg); loaded 4,888lb (2217kg).
Performance: Maximum speed 214mph (345km/h); initial climb 2,950ft (900m)/min; service ceiling 29,530 ft (9000m); range 530 miles (850km).
Armament: Two 7·92mm Rheinmetall MG 17 machine guns ahead of pilot; underwing racks for four 110lb (50kg) bombs, or clusters of anti-personnel bombs or two 20mm MG FF cannon.
History: First flight, spring 1935 (public display given 8 May); first delivery (Spain) December 1936; final delivery, October 1938.
User: Germany (Luftwaffe).

Development: Though representing a class of aircraft generally considered obsolete by the start of World War II, this trim little biplane was kept

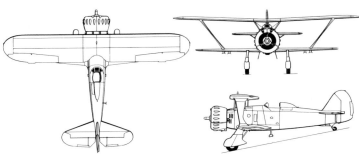

Above: Three-view of the Hs 123A-1.

hard at work until 1942, achieving results which in retrospect seem almost unbelievable. The prototype needed extensive modification to produce the A-1 production version, which was tested in the Spanish Civil War. Contrary to the staff-college theories then adhered to by the newly formed Luftwaffe, the Henschels were able to give close support to ground troops of a most real and immediate kind, strafing and bombing with great accuracy despite the lack of any radio link or even an established system of operation. Eventually the Luftwaffe realised that the concept of a close-support aircraft was valid. and a few Henschels were allowed to operate in this role, but all the effort and money was put into the Ju 87, and the Hs 123 was phased out of production before World War II. Yet in the Polish campaign these aircraft proved unbelievably useful, having the ability to make pinpoint attacks with guns and bombs and, by virtue of careful setting of the propeller speed, to make a demoralising noise. Moreover, it established an extraordinary reputation for returning to base even after direct hits by AA shells. As a result, though the whole force was incessantly threatened with disbandment or replacement by later types, the Hs 123 close-support unit II (Schlacht)/LG2 was sent intact to the Balkans in April 1941 and thence to the USSR. Here the old biplanes fought around the clock, proving far better adapted to the conditions than more modern types and continuing in front-line operations until, by the end of 1944, there were no more left.

Left: An Hs 123A-1 in front-line service, possibly with Schlacht/LG 2, in the campaign in France or the Balkans. By 1942 hardly any of the Henschels still wore their spats.

Henschel Hs 126

Hs 126A and B

Origin: Henschel Flugzeugwerke AG, Schönefeld.
Type: Army co-operation; later multi-role tactical.
Engine: One nine-cylinder radial, (A-O) 830hp Bramo Fafnir 323A, (A-1) 880hp BMW 132 Dc, (B) 900hp BMW Bramo Fafnir 323A-2 or Q-2.
Dimensions: Span 47ft 6¾in (14·50m); length 35ft 7¾in (10·85m); height 12ft 3¾in (3·75m).
Weights: Empty (B-1) 4,480lb (2032kg); maximum 7,209lb (3270kg).
Performance: Maximum speed 221mph (355km/h); service ceiling 27,070ft (8250m); maximum range at sea level 360 miles (580km).
Armament: One synchronized 7·92mm MG 17 and one manually aimed 7·92mm MG 15; light bombs or 110lb (50kg) bomb or extra tank.
History: First flight August 1936; service delivery (A-O) June 1937; final delivery January 1941.
Users: Bulgaria, Croatia, Greece, Germany, Spain.

Development: Developed in early 1936 from the disappointing Hs 122, the parasol-winged Hs 126 was a thoroughly sound machine very like the British Lysander in character though more conventional. The crew of two sat below and behind the wing in a capacious tandem cockpit, the pilot's portion being enclosed. Typical photographic, radio and light bombing equipment was carried, and the aircraft proved to have excellent STOL

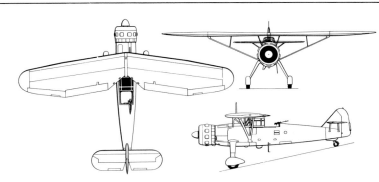

Above: Three-view of the Hs 126A (B-series, almost identical). By about 1941 nearly all the spats had been removed.

capability and ability to absorb much punishment. Altogether about 802 were delivered, maintaining the Aufklärungsstaffeln (recce squadrons) at a front-line strength of around 280 aircraft. By June 1941 virtually all were on the Eastern Front or in the Balkans or North Africa. A few survived until 1944–45 in operations against partisans in the Balkans, but most had been replaced by the Fw 189 and used for towing gliders. The 200-odd combat veterans served in Nachtschlacht (night ground attack) wings, often using a variety of armament schemes.

(See page 61 for Henschel Hs 129)

Left: This Hs 126A-1 was serving with 2.(H)/31 (Pz) from a base in Greece in April 1941. Like more than half the 126 strength, this machine was assigned to a Panzer corps, whose emblem it wears. Increasingly, the Fw 189 took over the front-line reconnaissance missions while the parasol-winged 126 was relegated to supply dropping, harrying partisans and general utility communications.

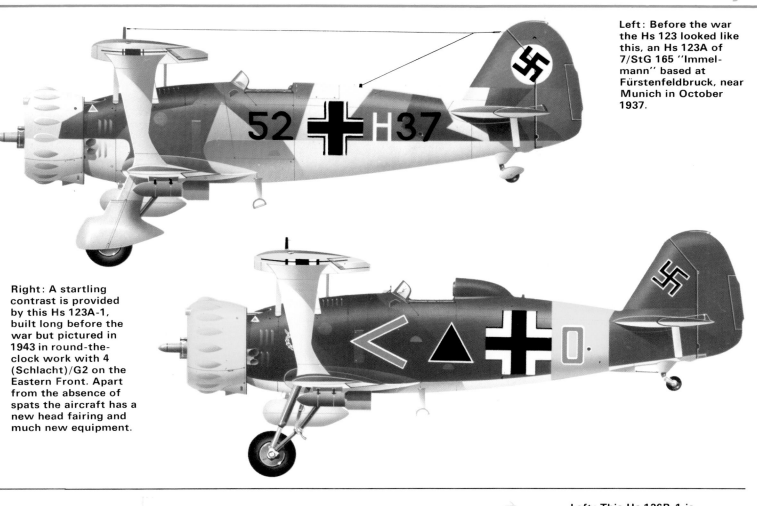

Left: Before the war the Hs 123 looked like this, an Hs 123A of 7/StG 165 ''Immelmann'' based at Fürstenfeldbruck, near Munich in October 1937.

Right: A startling contrast is provided by this Hs 123A-1, built long before the war but pictured in 1943 in round-the-clock work with 4 (Schlacht)/G2 on the Eastern Front. Apart from the absence of spats the aircraft has a new head fairing and much new equipment.

Left: This Hs 126B-1 is illustrated in winter camouflage whilst serving on the Don front with 3.(H)/21 in January 1943.

Below: This frame from a Luftwaffe ciné film shows an Hs 126B-1 serving with an Aufklärungsstaffel (recce squadron) during the assault on Greece in April 1941. It is flying over Athens.

Messerschmitt Bf 109

**Bf 109B, C, D, E, F, G, H and K series,
S-99 and 199, Ha-1109 and -1112**

Origin: Bayerische Flugzeugwerke, later (1938) renamed Messerschmitt AG; very widely subcontracted throughout German-controlled territory and built under licence by Dornier-Werke, Switzerland, and Hispano-Aviación, Spain (post-war, Avia, Czechoslovakia).

Type: Single-seat fighter (many, fighter bomber).

Engine: (B, C) one 635hp Junkers Jumo 210D inverted-vee-12 liquid-cooled; (D) 1,000hp Daimler-Benz DB 600Aa, same layout; (E) 1,100hp DB 601A, 1,200hp DB 601N or 1,300hp DB 601E; (F) DB 601E; (G) 1,475hp DB 605A-1, or other sub-type up to DB 605D rated 1,800hp with MW50 boost; (H-1) DB 601E; (K) usually 1,550hp DB 605ASCM/DCM rated 2,000hp with MW50 boost; (S-199) 1,350hp Jumo 211F; (HA-1109) 1,300hp Hispano-Suiza 12Z-89 upright vee-12 or (M1L) 1,400hp R-R Merlin 500-45.

Dimensions: Span (A to E) 32ft 4½in (9·87m); (others) 32ft 6½in (9·92m); length (B, C) 27ft 11in; (D, E, typical) 28ft 4in (8·64m); (F) 29ft 0½in; (G) 29ft 8in (9·04m); (K) 29ft 4in; (HA-1109-M1L) 29ft 11in; height (E) 7ft 5½in (2·28m); (others) 8ft 6in (2·59m).

Weights: Empty 3,483lb; (E) 4,189lb (1900kg) to 4,421lb; (F) around 4,330lb; (G) 5,880lb (2667kg) to 6,180lb (2800kg); (K, typical) 6,000lb; maximum loaded (B-1) 4,850lb; (E) 5,523lb (2505kg) to 5,875lb (2665kg); (F-3) 6,054lb; (G) usually 7,496lb (3400kg); (K) usually 7,439lb (3375kg).

Performance: Maximum speed (B-1) 292mph; (D) 323mph; (E) 348–354 mph (560–570km/h); (F-3) 390mph; (G) 353 to 428mph (569–690km/h), (K-4) 452mph (729km/h); initial climb (B-1) 2,200ft/min; (E) 3,100 to 3,280ft (1000m)/min; (G) 2,700 to 4,000ft/min; (K-4) 4,823ft (1470m)/min; service ceiling (B-1) 26,575ft; (E) 34,450ft (10.500m) to 36,090ft (11,000m); (F, G) around 38,000ft (11,600m); (K-4) 41,000ft (12,500m); range on internal fuel (all) 365–460 miles (typically, 700km).

Armament: (B) three 7·92mm Rheinmetall-Borsig MG 17 machine guns above engine and firing through propeller hub; (C) four MG 17, two above engine and two in wings, with fifth through propeller hub in C-2; (early E-1) four MG 17, plus four 50kg or one 250kg (551lb) bomb; (later E-1 and most other E) two MG 17 above engine, each with 1,000 rounds (or two MG 17 with 500 rounds, plus 20mm MG FF firing through propeller hub) and two MG FF in wings, each with 60-round drum; (F-1) two MG 17 and

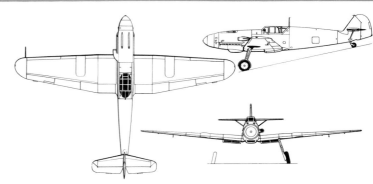

Above: Abandoned high-altitude variant, the Bf 109H of 1944.

Below: The original prototype, with British Kestrel engine.

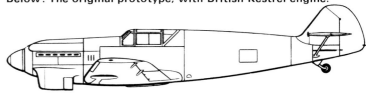

one MG FF; (F-2) two 15mm MG 151 and one MG FF; (F-4) two MG 151, one MG FF and one 20mm MG 151 in fairing under each wing; (G-1) two MG 17 or 13mm MG 131 over engine and one MG 151; (G-6) one 30mm MK 108, two MG 131 above engine and two MG 151 under wings; (K-4) two MG 151 above engine and one MK 108 or 103; (K-6) two MG 131 above engine, one MK 103 or 108 and two MK 108 under wings; (S-199) two MG 131 above engine and two MG 151 under wings; (HA-1109 series) two wing machine guns or 20mm Hispano 404. Many German G and K carried two 210mm rocket tubes under wings or various bomb loads.

History: First flight (Bf 109 V-1) early September 1935 (date is unrecorded); (production B-1) May 1937; (Bf 109E) January 1939; (Bf 109F prototype) July 1940; replacement in production by Bf 109G, May 1942.

Users: Bulgaria, Croatia, Finland, Germany (Luftwaffe), Hungary, Italy (ARSI), Japan, Jugoslavia, Romania, Slovakia, Slovak (CB Insurgent), Soviet Union (1940), Spain, Switzerland; (post-war) Czechoslovakia, Israel.

continued on page 49▶

Above: Taken from a German propaganda film of 1941, this photograph depicts a pair of Bf 109E-4/Trop fighters of I/JG 27 flying over the Cyrenaican (Libyan) desert, soon after the entry of the Afrika Korps. Finish is 78 Light Blue, 79 Sand Yellow and 80 Olive Green, with the white tail band denoting the Mediterranean theatre of operations.

Above: One of the last Bf 109E sub-types, this is an E-7, seen with a large dust filter on the engine air inlet. It was operating on the Leningrad front in 1942 with JG 5.

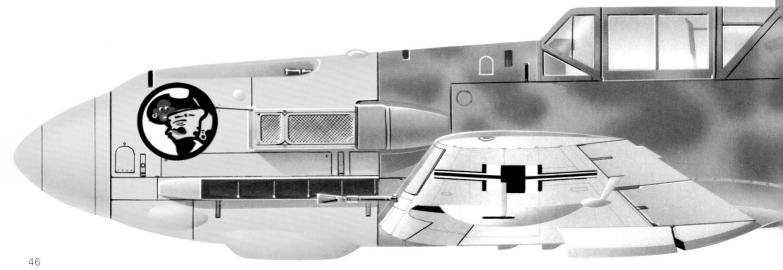

Above: The same I/JG 27 aircraft as seen at far left. This view from above flatters the camouflage capabilities of the 79/80 colour scheme against the North African terrain.

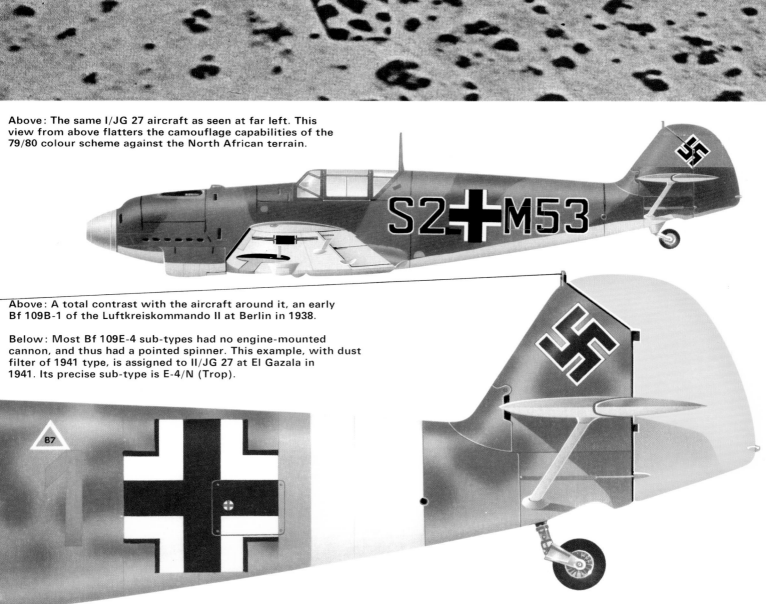

Above: A total contrast with the aircraft around it, an early Bf 109B-1 of the Luftkreiskommando II at Berlin in 1938.

Below: Most Bf 109E-4 sub-types had no engine-mounted cannon, and thus had a pointed spinner. This example, with dust filter of 1941 type, is assigned to II/JG 27 at El Gazala in 1941. Its precise sub-type is E-4/N (Trop).

Above: Bf 109G-2s of II (left) and III/JG 54 "Grunherz" (Green Heart) geschwader operating on the northern sector of the Eastern Front (probably at Silverskaya) in the summer of 1942. Relative merits of the Luftwaffe and Soviet fighters continue to be hotly debated.

Right: The Bf 109G-14/U4 introduced a wooden tail, previous improvements being the clear-view "Galland" hood and (five years late, and often incomplete) geared tabs on ailerons and/or elevators.

Messerschmitt Bf 109G-14/U4 cutaway drawing key:

1 Starboard navigation light
2 Starboard wingtip
3 Fixed trim tab
4 Starboard Frise-type aileron
5 Flush-riveted stressed wing-skinning
6 Handley Page leading-edge automatic slat
7 Slat control linkage
8 Slat equalizer rod
9 Aileron control linkage
10 Fabric-covered flap
11 Wheel fairing
12 Ammunition-feed fairing (both sides of fuselage)
13 Rheinmetall Borsig 13mm MG 131
14 Engine accessories
15 Starboard gun trough
16 Daimler-Benz DB 605AM twelve-cylinder inverted-vee liquid-cooled engine
17 Detachable cowling panel
18 Oil filler access
19 Oil tank
20 Propeller pitch-change mechanism
21 VDM electrically-operated constant-speed propeller
22 Spinner
23 Engine-mounted cannon muzzle
24 Blast tube
25 Propeller hub
26 Spinner back plate
27 Auxiliary cooling intakes
28 Coolant header tank
29 Anti-vibration rubber engine-mounting pads
30 Elektron forged engine bearer
31 Engine bearer support strut attachment
32 Plug leads
33 Exhaust manifold fairing strip
34 ejector exhausts
35 Cowling fasteners
36 Oil cooler
37 Oil cooler intake
38 Starboard mainwheel
39 Oil cooler outlet flap
40 Wing root fillet
41 Wing-fuselage fairing
42 Firewall/bulkhead
43 Supercharger air intake
44 Supercharger
45 20mm magazine
46 13mm ammunition feed
47 Engine bearer upper attachment
48 Ammunition feed fairing
49 MG 131 breeches
50 Instrument panel
51 20mm Mauser MG 151/20 cannon breech
52 Heel rests
53 Rudder pedals
54 Undercarriage emergency retraction cables
55 Fuselage frame
56 Wing/fuselage fairing
57 Undercarriage emergency retraction handwheel (outboard)
58 Tail trim handwheel (inboard)
59 Seat harness
60 Throttle lever
61 Control column
62 Cockpit ventilation inlet
63 Revi 16B reflector gunsight (folding)
64 Armoured windshield frame
65 Anti-glare gunsight screen
66 90mm armourglass wind-screen
67 'Galland'-type clear-vision hinged canopy
68 Framed armourglass head/back panel
69 Canopy contoured frame
70 Canopy hinges (starboard)
71 Canopy release catch
72 Pilot's bucket-type seat (8mm back armour)
73 Underfloor contoured fuel tank (88 gal/400 litres of 87 octane B4)
74 Fuselage frame
75 Circular access panel
76 Tail trimming cable conduit
77 Wireless leads
78 MW 50 (methanol water) tank (25 gal/114 litres capacity)
79 Handhold
80 Fuselage decking
81 Aerial mast
82 D/F loop
83 Oxygen cylinders (three)
84 Filler pipe
85 Wireless equipment packs (FuG 16zy communications and FuG 25a IFF)
86 Main fuel filler cap
88 Fuselage top keel (connector-stringer)
89 Aerial lead-in
90 Fuselage skin plating sections
91 'U' stringers
92 Fuselage frames (monocoque construction)
93 Tail trimming cables
94 Fin root fairing
95 Starboard fixed tailplane
96 Elevator balance
97 Starboard elevator
98 Geared elevator tab
99 All-wooden fin construction
100 Aerial attachment
101 Rudder upper hinge bracket
102 Rudder post
103 Fabric-covered wooden rudder structure
104 Geared rudder tab
105 Rear navigation light
106 Port elevator
107 Elevator geared tab
108 Tailplane structure
109 Rudder actuating linkage
110 Elevator control horn
111 Elevator connecting rod
112 Elevator control quadrant
113 Tailwheel leg cuff
114 Castoring non-retractable tailwheel
115 Lengthened tailwheel leg
116 Access panel
117 Tailwheel shock-strut
118 Lifting point
119 Rudder cable
120 Elevator cables
121 First-aid pack
122 Air bottles
123 Fuselage access panel
124 Bottom keel (connector stringer)
125 Ventral IFF aerial
126 Master compass
127 Elevator control linkage
128 Wing root fillet
129 Camber-changing flap
130 Ducted coolant radiator
131 Wing stringers
132 Wing rear pick-up point
133 Spar/fuselage upper pin joint (horizontal)

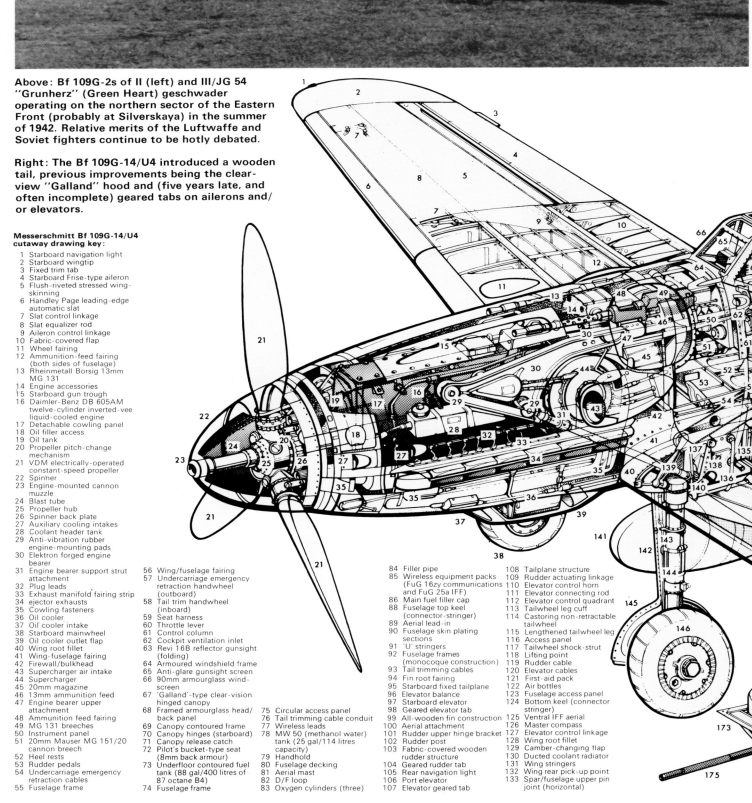

►**Development:** During World War II the general public in the Allied nations at first regarded the Messerschmitt as an inferior weapon compared with the Spitfire and other Allied fighters. Only in the fullness of time was it possible to appreciate that the Bf 109 was one of the greatest combat aircraft in history. First flown in 1935, it was a major participant in the Spanish Civil War and a thoroughly proven combat aircraft by the time of Munich (September 1938). Early versions were the Bf 109B, C and D, all of lower power than the definitive 109E. The E was in service in great quantity by the end of August 1939 when the invasion of Poland began. From then until 1941 it was by far the most important fighter in the Luftwaffe, and it was also supplied in quantity to numerous other countries (which are listed above). During the first year of World War II the "Emil", as the various E sub-types were called, made mincemeat of the many and varied types of fighter against which it was opposed, with the single exception of the Spitfire (which it greatly outnumbered). Its good points were small size, fast and cheap production, high acceleration, fast climb and dive, and good power of manoeuvre. Nearly all 109Es were also fitted with two or three 20mm cannon, with range and striking power greater than a battery of eight rifle-calibre guns. Drawbacks were the narrow landing gear, severe swing on take-off or landing, extremely poor lateral control at high speeds, and the fact that in combat the slats on the wings often opened in tight turns; while this prevented a stall, it snatched at the ailerons and threw the pilot off his aim. After 1942 the dominant version was the 109G ("Gustav") which made up over 70 per cent of the total received by the Luftwaffe. Though formidably armed and equipped, the vast swarms of "Gustavs"

were nothing like such good machines as the lighter E and F, demanding constant pilot attention, constant high power settings, and having landing characteristics described as "malicious". Only a few of the extended-span high-altitude H-series were built, but from October 1944 the standard production series was the K with clear-view "Galland hood", revised wooden tail and minor structural changes. After World War II the Czech Avia firm found their Bf 109 plant intact and began building the S-99; running out of DB 605 engines they installed the slow-revving Jumo, producing the S-199 with even worse torque and swing than the German versions (pilots called it "Mezek" meaning mule), but in 1948 managed to sell some to Israel. The Spanish Hispano Aviación flew its first licence-built 1109 in March 1945 and in 1953 switched to the Merlin engine to produce the 1109-M1L Buchón (Pigeon). Several Hispano and Merlin versions were built in Spain, some being tandem-seat trainers. When the last HA-1112 flew out of Seville in late 1956 it closed out 21 years of manufacture of this classic fighter, during which total output approached 35,000.

continued on page 50►

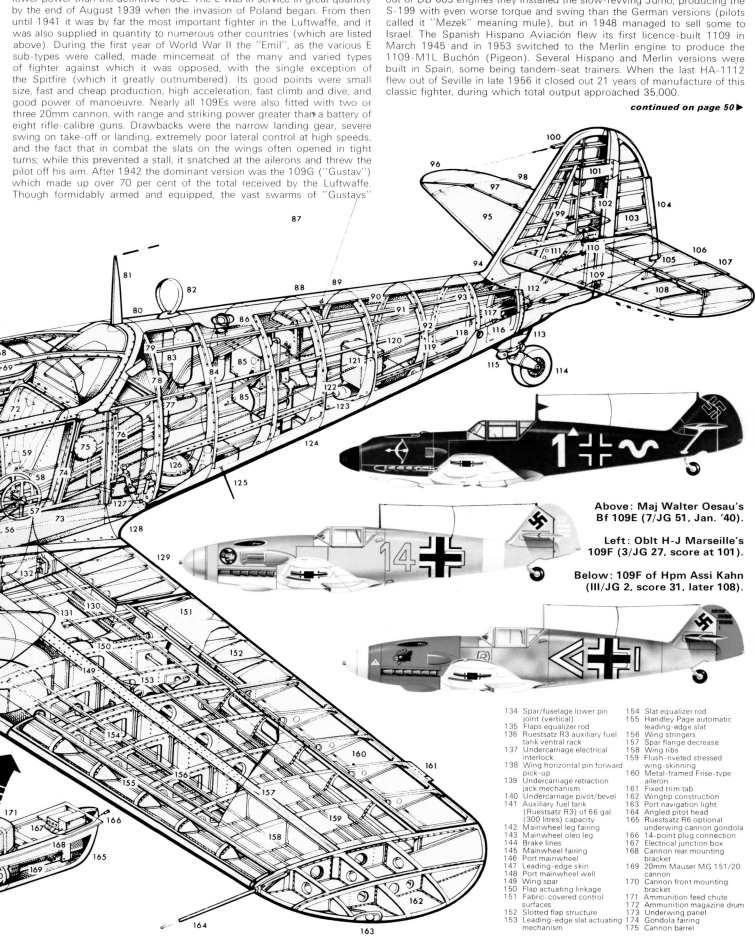

Above: Maj Walter Oesau's Bf 109E (7/JG 51, Jan. '40).

Left: Oblt H-J Marseille's 109F (3/JG 27, score at 101).

Below: 109F of Hpm Assi Kahn (III/JG 2, score 31, later 108).

134 Spar/fuselage lower pin joint (vertical)	154 Slat equalizer rod
135 Flaps equalizer rod	155 Handley Page automatic leading-edge slat
136 Ruestsatz R3 auxiliary fuel tank ventral rack	156 Wing stringers
137 Undercarriage electrical interlock	157 Spar flange decrease
138 Wing horizontal pin forward pick-up	158 Wing ribs
139 Undercarriage retraction jack mechanism	159 Flush-riveted stressed wing-skinning
140 Undercarriage pivot/bevel	160 Metal-framed Frise-type aileron
141 Auxiliary fuel tank (Ruestsatz R3) of 66 gal. (300 litres) capacity	161 Fixed trim tab
142 Mainwheel leg fairing	162 Wingtip construction
143 Mainwheel oleo leg	163 Port navigation light
144 Brake lines	164 Angled pitot head
145 Mainwheel fairing	165 Ruestsatz R6 optional underwing cannon gondola
146 Port mainwheel	166 14-point plug connection
147 Leading-edge skin	167 Electrical junction box
148 Port mainwheel well	168 Cannon rear mounting bracket
149 Wing spar	169 20mm Mauser MG 151/20 cannon
150 Flap actuating linkage	170 Cannon front mounting bracket
151 Fabric-covered control surfaces	171 Ammunition feed chute
152 Slotted flap structure	172 Ammunition magazine drum
153 Leading-edge slat actuating mechanism	173 Underwing panel
	174 Gondola fairing
	175 Cannon barrel

Messerschmitt Bf 109
▶ *continued*

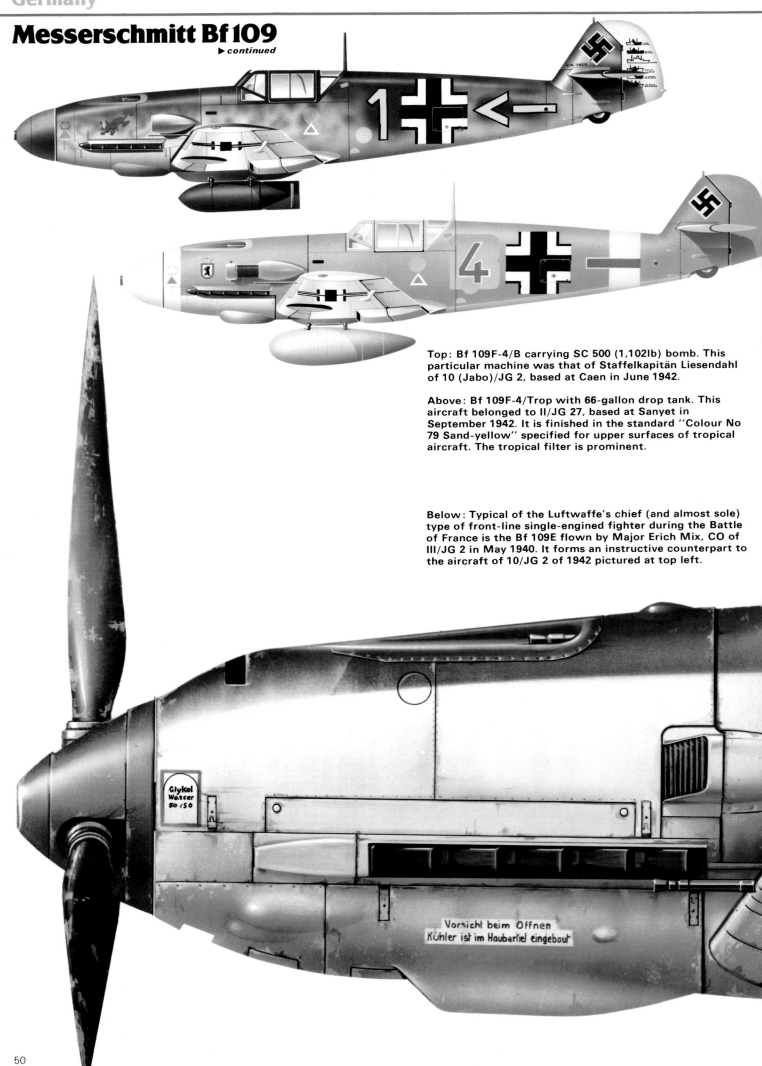

Top: Bf 109F-4/B carrying SC 500 (1,102lb) bomb. This particular machine was that of Staffelkapitän Liesendahl of 10 (Jabo)/JG 2, based at Caen in June 1942.

Above: Bf 109F-4/Trop with 66-gallon drop tank. This aircraft belonged to II/JG 27, based at Sanyet in September 1942. It is finished in the standard "Colour No 79 Sand-yellow" specified for upper surfaces of tropical aircraft. The tropical filter is prominent.

Below: Typical of the Luftwaffe's chief (and almost sole) type of front-line single-engined fighter during the Battle of France is the Bf 109E flown by Major Erich Mix, CO of III/JG 2 in May 1940. It forms an instructive counterpart to the aircraft of 10/JG 2 of 1942 pictured at top left.

W. Nr.

Nicht anfassen

Reifendruck 4,5 atü

Hier
anheben

Hier
aufbocken

Messerschmitt Bf110

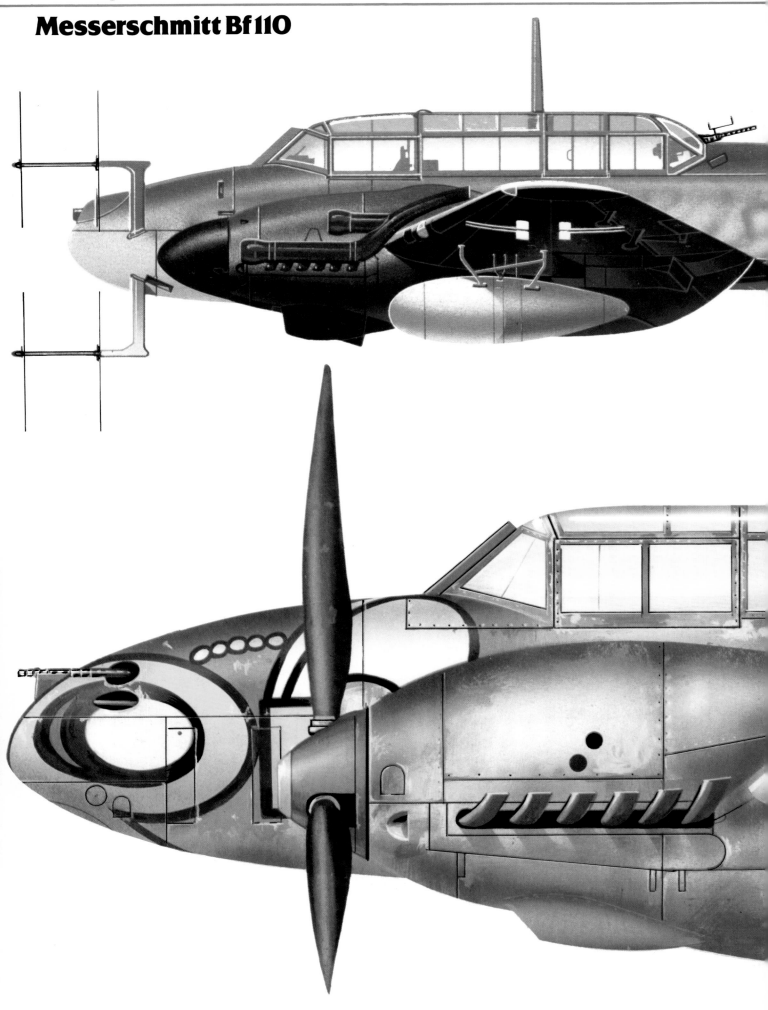

Below: A typical Luftwaffe night fighter of the late war period was this Bf 110G-4 of 7/NJG 4 based at many airfields in northwest Germany and at St Trond and Venlo in the Netherlands. Finished in 76 Light Blue all over, the upper surfaces were then given a sprayed mottle of 75 Grey-Violet.

3C + BR

Top: Bf 109F-5 of I(F)/122 based in Sardinia in 1943. This was a tactical reconnaissance aircraft, with vertical camera in the rear fuselage (and the engine-mounted cannon removed). Performance was not always high enough to escape interception, especially by two-stage-Merlin Spitfires.

Above: This Bf 109E of III/JG 52, based at Hopstadten in August 1940, has an unusual colour scheme with criss-crosses of 71 dark green sprayed on 02 grey. Underside is regulation 65 light blue.

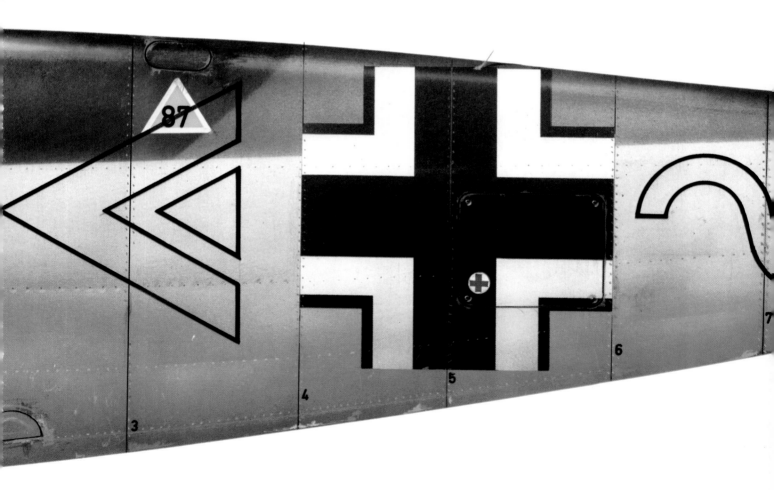

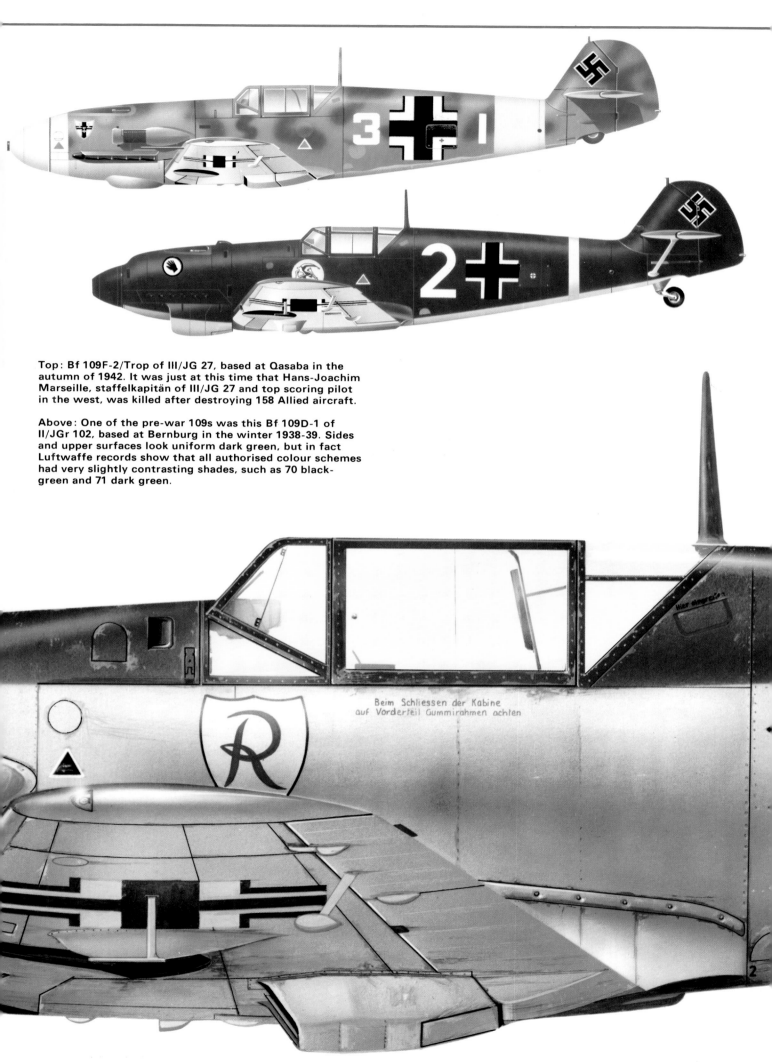

Top: Bf 109F-2/Trop of III/JG 27, based at Qasaba in the autumn of 1942. It was just at this time that Hans-Joachim Marseille, staffelkapitän of III/JG 27 and top scoring pilot in the west, was killed after destroying 158 Allied aircraft.

Above: One of the pre-war 109s was this Bf 109D-1 of II/JGr 102, based at Bernburg in the winter 1938-39. Sides and upper surfaces look uniform dark green, but in fact Luftwaffe records show that all authorised colour schemes had very slightly contrasting shades, such as 70 black-green and 71 dark green.

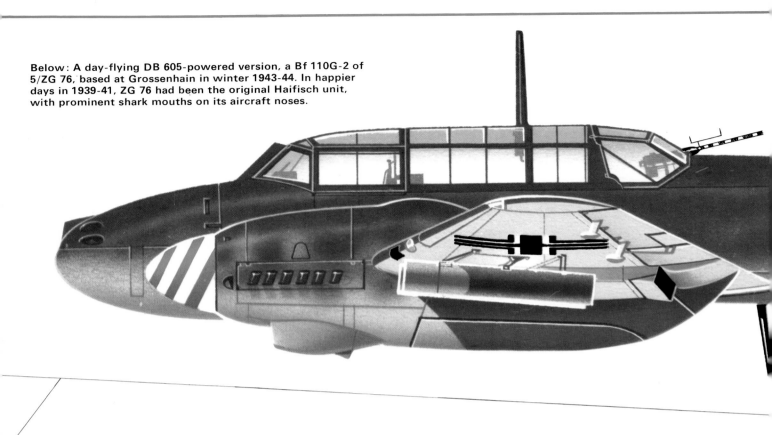

Below: A day-flying DB 605-powered version, a Bf 110G-2 of
5/ZG 76, based at Grossenhain in winter 1943-44. In happier
days in 1939-41, ZG 76 had been the original Haifisch unit,
with prominent shark mouths on its aircraft noses.

Below: Bf 110C-4/B, one of the earlier DB 601-powered models.
It is shown flying with SKG 1 (fast bomber geschwader 1) on
the Eastern Front, with that theatre's yellow tactical band.
SKG 1 retained the wasp motif it had used when it was ZG 1,
the original zerstörer geschwader. nicknamed Wespen (Wasp).

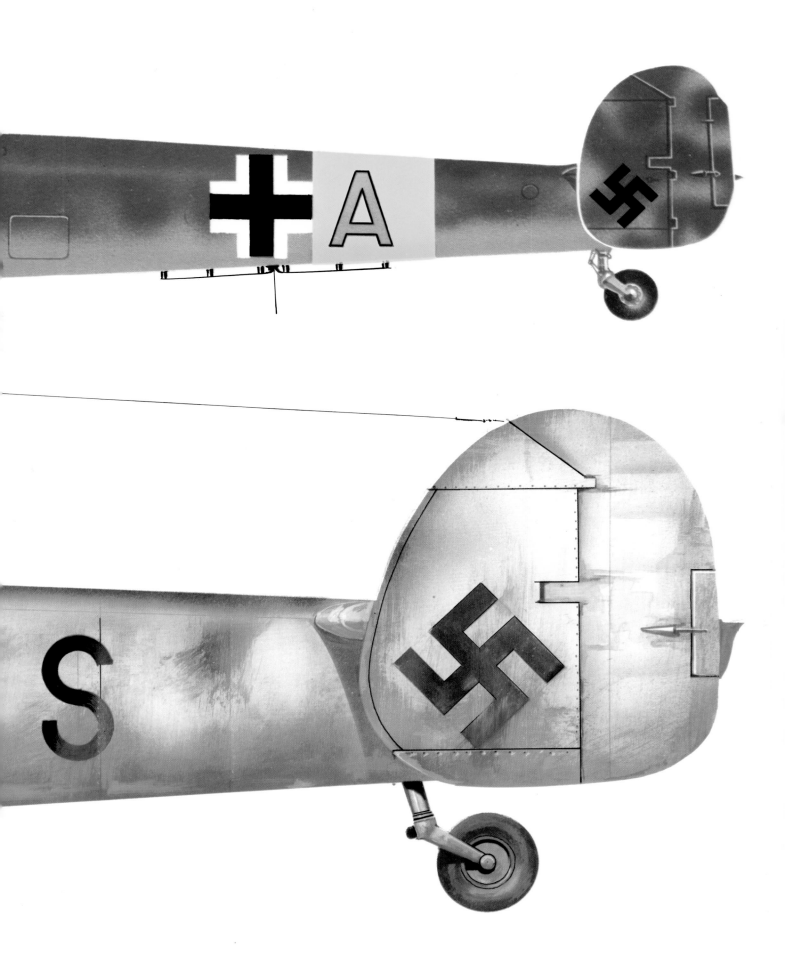

continued on page 58 ▶

Messerschmitt Bf 110 *continued*

Bf 110B series to H series
(data for Bf 110C-4/B)

Origin: Bayerische Flugzeugwerke, after 1938 Messerschmitt AG; widely dispersed manufacture.

Type: Two-seat day and night fighter (also used on occasion for ground attack and reconnaissance).

Engines: Two 1,100hp Daimler-Benz DB 601A; (later C-4s) 1,200hp DB 601N 12-cylinder inverted-vee liquid-cooled; (G, H) two 1,475hp DB 605B, same layout.

Dimensions: Span 53ft 4¾in (16·25m); length 39ft 8½in (12·1m); height 11ft 6in (3·5m).

Weights: Empty 9,920lb (4500kg); loaded 15,430lb (7000kg).

Performance: Maximum speed 349mph (562km/h) at 22,966ft (7000m); climb to 18,045ft (5500m), 8 minutes; service ceiling 32,800ft (10,000m); range 528 miles (850km) at 304mph (490km/h) at 16,400ft (5000m).

Armament: Two 20mm Oerlikon MG FF cannon and four Rheinmetall 7·92mm MG 17 machine guns fixed firing forward in nose, one 7·92mm MG 15 manually aimed machine gun in rear cockpit; C-4/B also fitted with racks under centre section for four 551lb (250kg) bombs. (G-4 night

continued on page 60▶

Above: Bf 110D of 8/ZG 26 climbing out of rugged territory in Sicily in 1942 to rendezvous with a bomber force for Malta.

Messerschmitt Bf 110G-4b/R3 cutaway drawing key:

1 The Hirschgeweih (Stag's Antlers) array for the FuG 220b Lichtenstein SN-2 radar
2 Single-pole type antenna for the FuG 212 Lichtenstein C-1 radar
3 Camera gun
4 Cannon muzzles
5 Cannon ports
6 Blast tubes
7 Starboard mainwheel
8 Armour plate (10-mm)
9 Twin 30-mm Rheinmetall Borsig MK 108 (Rüstsatz/Field Conversion Set 3) with 135 rpg
10 Armoured bulkhead
11 Supercharger intake
12 Position of nacelle-mounted instruments on day fighter model
13 Exhaust flame damper
14 Auxiliary tank
15 Three-blade VDM airscrew
16 Leading-edge automatic slat
17 Pitot tube
18 FuG 227/1 Flensburg homing aerial fitted to some aircraft by forward maintenance units (to home on Monica tail-warning radar emissions)
19 Stressed wing skinning
20 Starboard aileron
21 Trim tab
22 Slotted flap
23 Hinged canopy roof
24 Armoured glass windscreen (60-mm)
25 Instrument panel
26 Cockpit floor armour (4-mm)
27 Twin 20-mm Mauser MG 151 cannon with 300 rounds (port) and 350 rounds (starboard)
28 Pilot's seat
29 Control column
30 Pilot's back and head armour (8-mm)
31 Cannon magazine
32 Centre section carry-through
33 Radar operator's swivel seat
34 D/F loop
35 Aerial mast
36 Upward-firing cannon muzzles
37 Two 30-mm MK 108 cannon in schräge Musik (oblique music) installation firing obliquely upward (optional installation supplied as an Umrüst-Bausatz/Factory Conversion Set)
38 Ammunition drums
39 Aft cockpit bulkhead
40 FuG 10P HF R/T set
41 FuB1 2F airfield blind approach receiver
42 Handhold
43 Oxygen bottles
44 Aerials
45 Master compass
46 Starboard tailfin
47 Rudder balance
48 Rudder
49 Tab
50 Starboard elevator
51 Starboard tailplane
52 Variable-incidence tailplane
53 Elevator tab
54 Centre section fairing
55 Rear navigation light
56 Port elevator
57 Port tailfin
58 Rudder
59 Hinged tab
60 Tailwheel
61 Fuselage frames
62 Control lines
63 Dipole tuner
64 Batteries
65 Transformer
66 Slotted flap
67 Fuel tank of 57·3 Imp gal (260·5l) capacity
68 Oil tank of 7·7 Imp gal (35l) capacity
69 Ventral antenna
70 Coolant radiator
71 Radiator intake
72 Hinged intake fairing
73 Aileron tab
74 Aileron construction
75 Wingtip
76 Flensburg aerial (see 1
77 Port navigation light
78 Leading-edge automatic slat
79 Wing ribs
80 Mainspar
81 Underwing auxiliary fuel tank (66-Imp gal/300-l capacity)
82 Landing light
83 Undercarriage door
84 Mainwheel well
85 Supercharger intake
86 Undercarriage pivot point
87 Mainwheel leg
88 Mainwheel
89 Oil cooler
90 Oil cooler intake
91 VDM airscrew

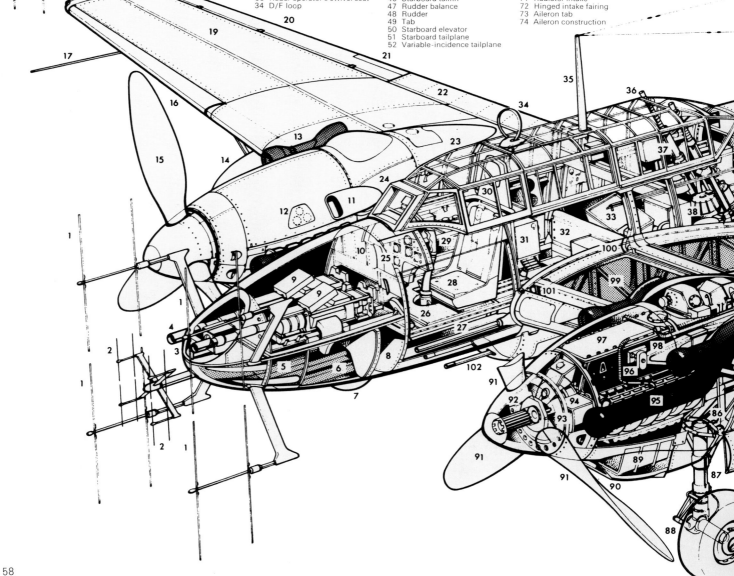

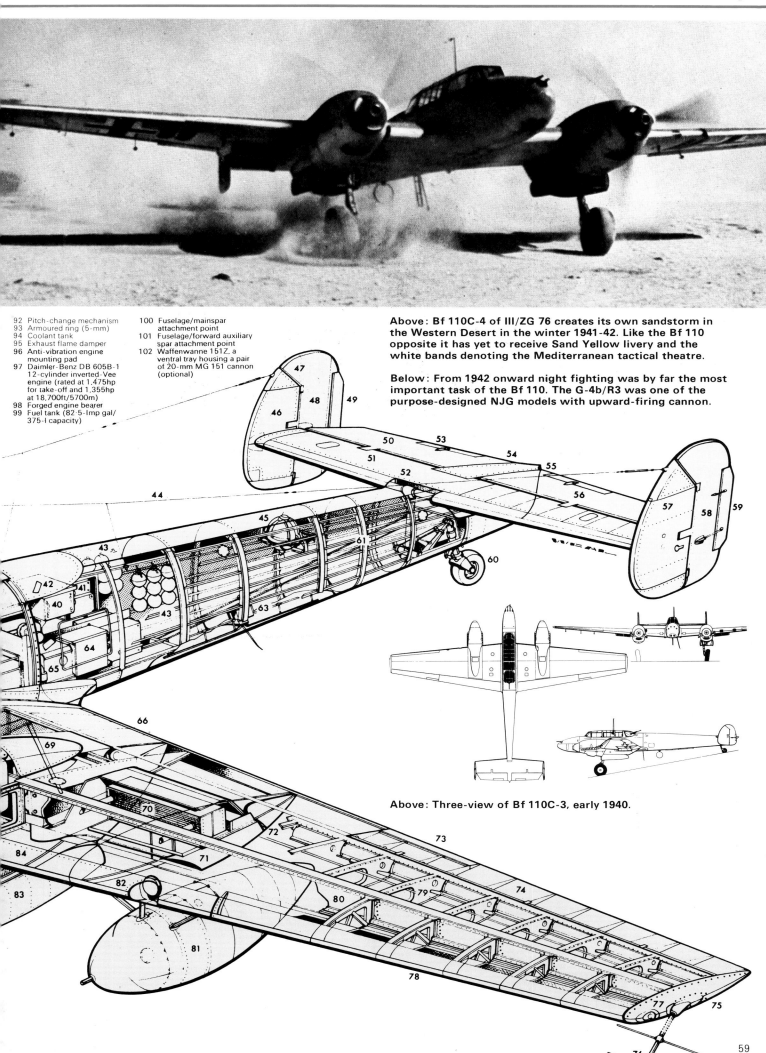

92 Pitch-change mechanism
93 Armoured ring (5-mm)
94 Coolant tank
95 Exhaust flame damper
96 Anti-vibration engine mounting pad
97 Daimler-Benz DB 605B-1 12-cylinder inverted-Vee engine (rated at 1,475hp for take-off and 1,355hp at 18,700ft/5700m)
98 Forged engine bearer
99 Fuel tank (82·5-Imp gal/ 375-l capacity)

100 Fuselage/mainspar attachment point
101 Fuselage/forward auxiliary spar attachment point
102 Waffenwanne 151Z, a ventral tray housing a pair of 20-mm MG 151 cannon (optional)

Above: Bf 110C-4 of III/ZG 76 creates its own sandstorm in the Western Desert in the winter 1941-42. Like the Bf 110 opposite it has yet to receive Sand Yellow livery and the white bands denoting the Mediterranean tactical theatre.

Below: From 1942 onward night fighting was by far the most important task of the Bf 110. The G-4b/R3 was one of the purpose-designed NJG models with upward-firing cannon.

Above: Three-view of Bf 110C-3, early 1940.

▶ fighter) two 30mm MK 108 and two 20mm MG 151 firing forward, and two MG 151 in Schräge Musik installation firing obliquely upwards (sometimes two 7·92mm MG 81 in rear cockpit).

History: First flight (Bf 110V1 prototype) 12 May 1936; (pre-production Bf 110C-0) February 1939; operational service with Bf 110C-1, April 1939; final run-down of production (Bf 110H-2 and H-4) February 1945.

User: Germany (Luftwaffe).

Development: As in five other countries at about the same time, the Reichsluftfahrtministerium decided in 1934 to issue a requirement for a new kind of fighter having two engines and exceptional range. Called a Zerstörer (destroyer), it was to be as capable as small single-seaters of fighting other aircraft, possibly making up in firepower for any lack in manoeuvrability. Its dominant quality was to be range, to escort bombers on raids penetrating deep into enemy heartlands. Powered by two of the new DB 600 engines, the prototype reached 316mph, considered an excellent speed, but it was heavy on the controls and unimpressive in power of manoeuvre. Too late to be tested in the Spanish Civil War, the production Bf 110B-1, which was the first to carry the two cannon, was itself supplanted by the C-series with the later DB 601 engine with direct fuel injection and greater power at all heights. By the start of World War II the Luftwaffe had 195 Bf 110C fighters, and in the Polish campaign these were impressive, operating mainly in the close-support role but demolishing any aerial opposition they encountered. It was the same story in the Blitzkrieg war through the Low Countries and France, when 350 of the big twins were used. Only when faced with RAF Fighter Command in the Battle of Britain did the Bf 110 suddenly prove a disaster. It was simply no match for the Spitfire or even the Hurricane, and soon the Bf 109 was having to escort the escort fighters! But production of DB 605-powered versions, packed with radar and night-fighting equipment, was actually trebled in 1943 and sustained in 1944, these G and H models playing a major part in the night battles over the Reich in 1943–45.

Above: An unidentified trio of what appear to be Bf 110Ds reveal little beyond the staffel colour of yellow seen on the tips of the spinners. They are probably from 9/ZG 26 newly assigned to the North African theatre.

Below: Bf 110G-2 of 12/NJG 3 (Stavanger, 1945); no radar.

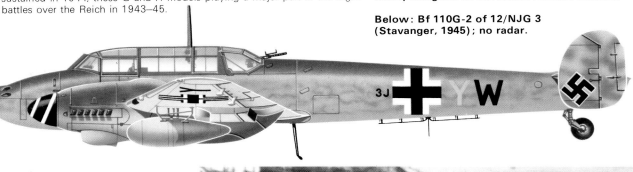

Below: A fine photo of two Bf 110D-1s of ZG26, soon after the Luftwaffe first went to Africa in 1941. Sand Yellow all over, with white theatre band.

Henschel Hs 129

Hs 129A and B series

Origin: Henschel Flugzeugwerke AG.
Type: Single-seat close support and ground attack.
Engines: (B-series) two 690hp Gnome-Rhône 14M 04/05 14-cylinder two-row radials.
Dimensions: Span 46ft 7in (14·2m); length 31ft 11¾in (9·75m); height 10ft 8in (3·25m).
Weights: (Typical B-1) empty 8,940lb (4060kg); loaded 11,265lb (5110kg).
Performance: (Typical B-1) maximum speed 253mph (408km/h); initial climb 1,390ft (425m)/min; service ceiling 29,530ft (9000m); range 547 miles (880km).
Armament: See text.
History: First flight (Hs 129V-1) early 1939; service delivery (129A-0) early 1941; first flight (129B) October 1941; service delivery (129B) late 1942.
Users: Germany (Luftwaffe), Hungary, Romania.

Development: Though there were numerous types of specialised close support and ground attack aircraft in World War I, this category was virtually ignored until the Spanish Civil War showed, again, that it is one of the most

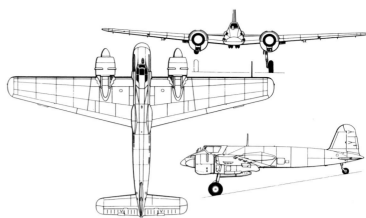

Above: Three-view of Hs 129B-1/R4 with bomb kit.

important of all. In 1938 the RLM issued a specification for such an aircraft — the whole purpose of the Luftwaffe being to support the Wehrmacht in Blitzkrieg-type battles — to back up the purpose-designed Ju 87 dive bomber. Henschel's Dipl-Ing F. Nicholaus designed a trim machine somewhat resembling the twin-engined fighters of the period but with more armour and less-powerful engines (two 495hp Argus As 410A-1 air-cooled inverted-vee-12s). The solo pilot sat in the extreme nose behind a windscreen 3in thick, with armour surrounding the cockpit. The triangular-section fuselage housed self-sealing tanks, guns in the sloping sides and a hardpoint for a bomb underneath. Test pilots at Rechlin damned the A-0 pre-production batch as grossly underpowered, but these aircraft were used on the Eastern Front by the Romanian Air Force. The redesigned B-series used the vast numbers of French 14M engines that were available and in production by the Vichy government for the Me 323. Altogether 841 B-series were built, and used with considerable effect on the Eastern Front but with less success in North Africa. The B-1/R1 had two 7·92mm MG 17 and two 20mm MG 151/20, plus two 110lb or 48 fragmentation bombs. The R2 had a 30mm MK 101 clipped underneath and was the first aircraft ever to use a 30mm gun in action. The R3 had a ventral box of four MG 17. The R4 carried up to 551lb of bombs. The R5 had a camera for vertical photography. The B-2 series changed the inbuilt MG 17s for MG 131s and other subtypes had many kinds of armament including the 37mm BK 3·7 and 75mm BK 7·5 with muzzle about eight feet ahead of the nose. The most novel armament, used against Russian armour with results that were often devastating, was a battery of six smooth-bore 75mm tubes firing recoilless shells down and to the rear with automatic triggering as the aircraft flew over metal objects.

Above: A Henschel Hs 129B-2/R2 of Schlachtgeschwader 9 on the Eastern Front, spring 1943 but still in winter colours.

Below: Another Hs 129B-2, in this case of 4 (Pz)/Sch.G 1, from the same period, with 70/71 oversprayed with white blobs.

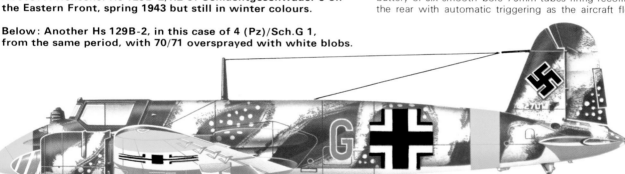

Below: A highly cleaned-up and somewhat falsified Hs 129B (sub-type obscured by changes including removal of the large pilot sight) in American charge long after World War II. Only two Hs 129s are thought to exist today.

Junkers Ju 52/3m
Ju 52/3m in many versions;
data for 3mg5e to 3mg14e

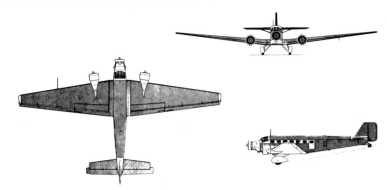

Origin: Junkers Flugzeug und Motorenwerke AG; also built in France on German account by a SNCASO/Breguet/Amiot group; built under licence by CASA, Spain.

Type: Passenger and freight transport (also bomber, reconnaissance, mine countermeasures, cas-evac and glider tug).

Engines: Three (one in Ju 52) of following types: 600hp BMW Hornet, 725hp BMW 132A, 830hp BMW 132T (standard on nearly all wartime versions), 925hp Bristol or PZL Pegasus, 750hp ENMASA Beta E-9C or 710hp Wright Cyclone (all nine-cylinder radials) or Jumo 5 diesel, Jumo 206 or BMW VI in-lines.

Dimensions: Span 95ft 11½in (29·25m); length 62ft (18·9m); height (landplane) 14ft 9in (4·5m).

Weights: Empty 12,346lb (5600kg); loaded 24,317lb (11,030kg).

Performance: Maximum speed 190mph (305km/h); initial climb 689ft (210m)/min; service ceiling 18,045ft (5500m); range 808 miles (1300km).

Armament: Usually none; in combat zones it was usual to mount one 13mm MG 131 manually aimed from open dorsal cockpit and two 7·92mm MG 15s manually aimed from beam windows.

History: First flight (Ju 52) 13 October 1930; (Ju 52/3m) May 1932; (Ju 52/3mg3e bomber) October 1934; final delivery (AAC.1) August 1947; (CASA 352-L) 1952.

Users: Argentina, Colombia, Ecuador, France, Germany (Luftwaffe, Kriegsmarine, Lufthansa), Hungary, Peru, Portugal, Slovakia, Spain, Sweden.

Development: One of the great aircraft of history, the Ju 52/3m was briefly preceded by the single-engined Ju 52 which had no military history. Most early Ju 52/3m versions were 15/17-passenger airliners which sold all over the world and also made up 75 per cent of the giant fleet of Lufthansa (reducing that airline's forced landings per million kilometres from 7 to only

Above: Three-view of typical pre-war civil Ju 52/3m.

1·5). In 1935 the 3mg3e bomber, with manually aimed MG 15s in a dorsal cockpit and ventral dustbin and bomb load of 3,307lb (1500kg) equipped the first bomber squadrons of the Luftwaffe. By 1936 about half the 450 built had been supplied to the Legion Kondor in Spain and to the Nationalist air force, but nearly all were equipped as troop transports, freighters and casualty-evacuation ambulances. These were the roles of most military versions, which were by far the most common transports on every front on which Nazi Germany fought. It is typical of the Nazi regime that, despite a wealth of later and more capable aircraft, the old "Auntie Ju" or "Iron Annie" was kept in full production throughout the war. Good STOL performance, with patented "double wing" flaps, robust construction, interchangeable wheel/ski/float landing gear and great reliability were the Ju 52's attributes. Total German output was 4,845. Many were built in France where 400 were completed as AAC.1s in 1947. The final 170 were built in Spain as CASA 352-Ls for the Spanish Air Force, which used them as T.2B multi-role transports until 1975.

Above: A typical early-wartime model, probably a Ju 52/3mg5e, which served with II/KGz.b.V 1 in southern Greece in May 1941.

Below: A Ju 52/3mg7e pictured crossing the Mediterranean in 1942. Rommel's Afrika Korps increasingly relied upon the "Tante Ju" (Auntie Ju), which suffered high attrition.

Junkers Ju 86

Ju 86D, E, G, K, P and R

Origin: Junkers Flugzeug und Motorenwerke AG; also built by Henschel, and built under licence by Saab, Sweden.
Type: (D, E, G and K) bomber; (P) bomber/reconnaissance; (R) reconnaissance.
Engines: (D) two 600hp Junkers Jumo 205C six opposed-piston cylinder diesels; (E, G) two 800 or 880hp BMW 132 nine-cylinder radials; (K) two 905hp Bristol Mercury XIX nine-cylinder radials; (P, R) two 1,000hp Jumo 207A-1 or 207B-3/V turbocharged opposed-piston diesels.
Dimensions: Span 73ft 10in (22·6m); (P) 84ft (25·6m); (R) 105ft (32m); length (typical) 58ft 8½in (17·9m); (G) 56ft 5in; (P, R) 54ft; height (all) 15ft 5in (4·7m).
Weights: Empty (E-1) 11,464lb (5200kg); (R-1) 14,771lb (6700kg); loaded (E-1) 18,080lb (8200kg); (R-1) 25,420lb (11,530kg).
Performance: Maximum speed (E-1) 202mph (325km/h); (R-1) 261mph (420km/h); initial climb (E) 918ft (280m)/min; service ceiling (E-1) 22,310ft (6800m); (R-1) 42,650ft (13,000m); range (E) 746 miles (1200m); (R-1) 980 miles (1577km).
Armament: (D, E, G, K) three 7·92mm MG 15 manually aimed from nose, dorsal and retractable ventral positions; internal bomb load of four 551lb (250kg) or 16 110lb (50kg) bombs; (P) single 7·92mm fixed MG 17, same bomb load; (R) usually none.
History: First flight (Ju 86V-1) 4 November 1934; (V-5 bomber prototype) January 1936; (production D-1) late 1936; (P-series prototype) February 1940.
Users: Bolivia, Chile, Germany (Luftwaffe, Lufthansa), Hungary, Portugal, South Africa, Spain, Sweden.

Development: Planned like the He 111 as both a civil airliner and a bomber, the Ju 86 was in 1934 one of the most advanced aircraft in Europe. The design team under Dipl-Ing Zindel finally abandoned corrugated skin and created a smooth and efficient machine with prominent double-wing flaps and outward-retracting main gears. The diesel-engined D-1 was quickly put into Luftwaffe service to replace the Do 23 and Ju 52 as the standard heavy bomber, but in Spain the various D-versions proved

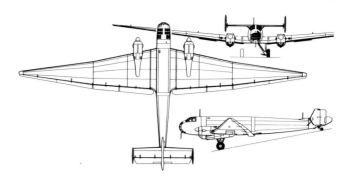

Above: Three-view of the ultimate extreme-altitude Ju 86, the Ju 86R-1. Their chief accomplishment was to trigger the development of numerous Allied high-altitude fighters.

vulnerable even to biplane fighters. The E-series bombers, with the powerful BMW radial, were faster and the fastest of all were the Swedish Bristol-engined Ks, of which 40 were built by Junkers (first delivery 18 December 1936) and 16 by Saab (last delivery 3 January 1941). Many D and E bombers were used against Poland, but that was their swan-song. By 1939 Junkers was working on a high-altitude version with turbocharged engines and a pressure cabin and this emerged as the P-1 bomber and P-2 bomber/reconnaissance which was operational over the Soviet Union gathering pictures before the German invasion of June 1941. The R series had a span increased even beyond that of the P and frequently operated over southern England in 1941–2 until — with extreme difficulty — solitary Spitfires managed to reach their altitude and effect an interception. Total military Ju 86 production was between 810 and 1,000. Junkers schemed many developed versions, some having four or six engines.

Below: One of the colourful Ju 86K-2 bombers of the Hungarian 3./I Bombázó Oszatály, based at Tapolca in 1938. Few were left when the Axis attacked the Soviet Union in 1941.

Below: The Ju 86G-1 was the only sub-type still in combat service with the Luftwaffe at the start of the Polish campaign in 1939.

Junkers Ju 87

Ju 87A, B and D series

Origin: Junkers Flugzeug und Motorenwerke AG; also built by Weser Flugzeugbau and SNCASO, France.
Type: Two-seat dive bomber and ground attack.

continued on page 66 ▶

Below: The cutaway drawing shows the Ju 87D-3, one of the more powerful and aerodynamically improved D-series that made up more than three-quarters of all production. The bombs shown, with Dienartstab fuzes, are among a great diversity of weapons and equipment that could be carried.

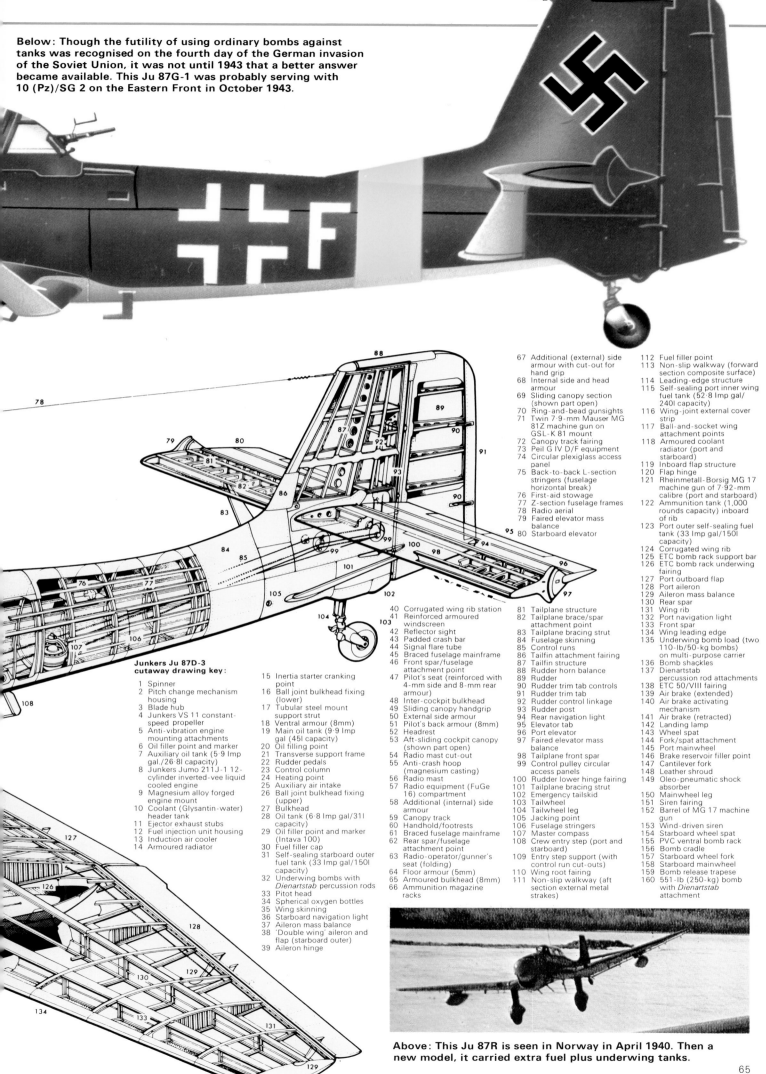

Below: Though the futility of using ordinary bombs against tanks was recognised on the fourth day of the German invasion of the Soviet Union, it was not until 1943 that a better answer became available. This Ju 87G-1 was probably serving with 10 (Pz)/SG 2 on the Eastern Front in October 1943.

Junkers Ju 87D-3 cutaway drawing key:

1 Spinner
2 Pitch change mechanism housing
3 Blade hub
4 Junkers VS 11 constant-speed propeller
5 Anti-vibration engine mounting attachments
6 Oil filler point and marker
7 Auxiliary oil tank (5·9 Imp gal./26·8l capacity)
8 Junkers Jumo 211J-1 12-cylinder inverted-vee liquid cooled engine
9 Magnesium alloy forged engine mount
10 Coolant (Glysantin-water) header tank
11 Ejector exhaust stubs
12 Fuel injection unit housing
13 Induction air cooler
14 Armoured radiator
15 Inertia starter cranking point
16 Ball joint bulkhead fixing (lower)
17 Tubular steel mount support strut
18 Ventral armour (8mm)
19 Main oil tank (9·9 Imp gal (45l capacity)
20 Oil filling point
21 Transverse support frame
22 Rudder pedals
23 Control column
24 Heating point
25 Auxiliary air intake
26 Ball joint bulkhead fixing (upper)
27 Bulkhead
28 Oil tank (6·8 Imp gal/31l capacity)
29 Oil filler point and marker (Intava 100)
30 Fuel filler cap
31 Self-sealing starboard outer fuel tank (33 Imp gal/150l capacity)
32 Underwing bombs with *Dienartstab* percussion rods
33 Pitot head
34 Spherical oxygen bottles
35 Wing skinning
36 Starboard navigation light
37 Aileron mass balance
38 'Double wing' aileron and flap (starboard outer)
39 Aileron hinge
40 Corrugated wing rib station
41 Reinforced armoured windscreen
42 Reflector sight
43 Padded crash bar
44 Signal flare tube
45 Braced fuselage mainframe
46 Front spar/fuselage attachment point
47 Pilot's seat (reinforced with 4-mm side and 8-mm rear armour)
48 Inter-cockpit bulkhead
49 Sliding canopy handgrip
50 External side armour
51 Pilot's back armour (8mm)
52 Headrest
53 Aft-sliding cockpit canopy (shown part open)
54 Radio mast cut-out
55 Anti-crash hoop (magnesium casting)
56 Radio mast
57 Radio equipment (FuGe 16) compartment
58 Additional (internal) side armour
59 Canopy track
60 Handhold/footrests
61 Braced fuselage mainframe
62 Rear spar/fuselage attachment point
63 Radio-operator/gunner's seat (folding)
64 Floor armour (5mm)
65 Armoured bulkhead (8mm)
66 Ammunition magazine racks
67 Additional (external) side armour with cut-out for hand grip
68 Internal side and head armour
69 Sliding canopy section (shown part open)
70 Ring-and-bead gunsights
71 Twin 7·9-mm Mauser MG 81Z machine gun on GSL-K 81 mount
72 Canopy track fairing
73 Peil G IV D/F equipment
74 Circular plexiglass access panel
75 Back-to-back L-section stringers (fuselage horizontal break)
76 First-aid stowage
77 Z-section fuselage frames
78 Radio aerial
79 Faired elevator mass balance
80 Starboard elevator
81 Tailplane structure
82 Tailplane brace/spar attachment point
83 Tailplane bracing strut
84 Fuselage skinning
85 Control runs
86 Tailfin attachment fairing
87 Tailfin structure
88 Rudder horn balance
89 Rudder
90 Rudder trim tab controls
91 Rudder trim tab
92 Rudder control linkage
93 Rudder post
94 Rear navigation light
95 Elevator tab
96 Port elevator
97 Faired elevator mass balance
98 Tailplane front spar
99 Control pulley circular access panels
100 Rudder lower hinge fairing
101 Tailplane bracing strut
102 Emergency tailskid
103 Tailwheel
104 Tailwheel leg
105 Jacking point
106 Fuselage stringers
107 Master compass
108 Crew entry step (port and starboard)
109 Entry step support (with control run cut-outs)
110 Wing root fairing
111 Non-slip walkway (aft section external metal strakes)
112 Fuel filler point
113 Non-slip walkway (forward section composite surface)
114 Leading-edge structure
115 Self-sealing port inner wing fuel tank (52·8 Imp gal/240l capacity)
116 Wing-joint external cover strip
117 Ball-and-socket wing attachment points
118 Armoured coolant radiator (port and starboard)
119 Inboard flap structure
120 Flap hinge
121 Rheinmetall-Borsig MG 17 machine gun of 7·92-mm calibre (port and starboard)
122 Ammunition tank (1,000 rounds capacity) inboard of rib
123 Port outer self-sealing fuel tank (33 Imp gal/150l capacity)
124 Corrugated wing rib
125 ETC bomb rack support bar
126 ETC bomb rack underwing fairing
127 Port outboard flap
128 Port aileron
129 Aileron mass balance
130 Rear spar
131 Wing rib
132 Port navigation light
133 Front spar
134 Wing leading edge
135 Underwing bomb load (two 110-lb/50-kg bombs) on multi-purpose carrier
136 Bomb shackles
137 Dienartstab percussion rod attachments
138 ETC 50/VIII fairing
139 Air brake (extended)
140 Air brake activating mechanism
141 Air brake (retracted)
142 Landing lamp
143 Wheel spat
144 Fork/spat attachment
145 Port mainwheel
146 Brake reservoir filler point
147 Cantilever fork
148 Leather shroud
149 Oleo-pneumatic shock absorber
150 Mainwheel leg
151 Siren fairing
152 Barrel of MG 17 machine gun
153 Wind-driven siren
154 Starboard wheel spat
155 PVC ventral bomb rack
156 Bomb cradle
157 Starboard wheel fork
158 Starboard mainwheel
159 Bomb release trapese
160 551-lb (250-kg) bomb with *Dienartstab* attachment

Above: This Ju 87R is seen in Norway in April 1940. Then a new model, it carried extra fuel plus underwing tanks.

▶**Engine:** (Ju 87B-1) one 1,100hp Junkers Jumo 211Da 12-cylinder inverted-vee liquid-cooled; (Ju 87D-1, D-5) 1,300hp Jumo 211J.
Dimensions: Span (Ju 87B-1, D-1) 45ft 3¼in (13·8m); (D-5) 50ft 0½in (15·25m); length 36ft 5in (11·1m); height 12ft 9in (3·9m).
Weights: Empty (B-1, D-1) about 6,080lb (2750kg); loaded (B-1) 9,371lb (4250kg); (D-1) 12,600lb (5720kg); (D-5) 14,500lb (6585kg).
Performance: Maximum speed (B-1) 242mph (390km/h); (D-1) 255mph (408km/h); (D-5) 250mph (402km/h); service ceiling (B-1) 26,250ft (8000m); (D-1, D-5) 24,000ft (7320m); range with maximum bomb load (B-1) 373 miles (600km); (D-1, D-5) 620 miles (1000km).
Armament: (Ju 87B-1) two 7·92mm Rheinmetall MG 17 machine guns in wings, one 7·92mm MG 15 manually aimed in rear cockpit, one 1,102lb (500kg) bomb on centreline and four 110lb (50kg) on wing racks; (D-1, D-5) two MG 17 in wings, twin 7·92mm MG 81 machine guns manually aimed in rear cockpit, one bomb of 3,968lb (1800kg) on centreline; (D-7) two 20mm MG 151/20 cannon in wings; (Ju 87G-1) two 37mm BK (Flak 18, or Flak 36) cannon in underwing pods; (D-4) two underwing WB81 weapon containers each housing six MG 81 guns.
History: First flight (Ju 87V1) late 1935; (pre-production Ju 87A-0) November 1936; (Ju 87B-1) August 1938; (Ju 87D-1) 1940; termination of production 1944.
Users: Bulgaria, Croatia, Germany (Luftwaffe), Hungary, Italy, Romania, Slovakia.

Development: Until at least 1942 the Ju 87 "Stuka" enjoyed a reputation that struck terror into those on the ground beneath it. First flown with a British R-R Kestrel engine and twin fins in 1935, it entered production in 1937 as the Ju 87A with large trousered landing gear and full equipment for dive bombing, including a heavy bomb crutch that swung the missile well clear of the fuselage before release. The spatted Ju 87B was the first aircraft in production with the Jumo 211 engine, almost twice as powerful as the Jumo 210 of the Ju 87A, and it had an automatic device (almost an auto-pilot) to ensure proper pull-out from the steep dive, as well as red lines at 60°, 75° and 80° painted on the pilot's side window. Experience in Spain had shown that pilots could black-out and lose control in the pull-out. Later a whole formation of Ju 87Bs in Spain was late pulling out over misty ground

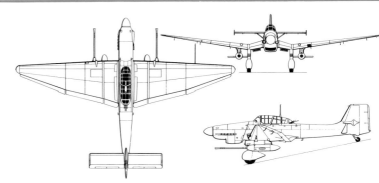

Above: The Ju 87G-1 anti-tank aircraft with two 37mm guns.

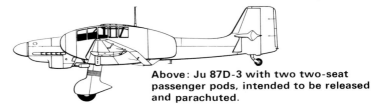

Above: Ju 87D-3 with two two-seat passenger pods, intended to be released and parachuted.

and many hit the ground. In Poland and the Low Countries the Ju 87 was terribly effective and it repeated its success in Greece, Crete and parts of the Russian front. But in the Battle of Britain its casualty rate was such that it was soon withdrawn, thereafter to attack ships and troops in areas where the Axis still enjoyed some air superiority. In 1942—45 its main work was close support on the Eastern front, attacking armour with big guns (Ju 87G-1) and even being used as a transport and glider tug. Total production, all by Junkers, is believed to have been 5,709.

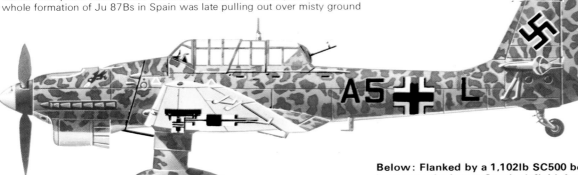

Left: A Ju 87B-2/Trop serving with III/StG 1 in Libya in 1941. The equipment of StG 1 had mostly been in action in Poland and the Low Countries, France and England since the start of the war.

Below: Flanked by a 1,102lb SC500 bomb, this Ju 87B "Stuka" is seen parked on a Greek airfield during the continuation of the Blitzkrieg campaign through the Balkans into north Africa. This was the last campaign in which the Ju 87 demolished its targets and encountered little opposition.

Junkers Ju 88

Many versions: data for Ju 88A-4, C-6, G-7, S-1

Origin: Junkers Flugzeug und Motorenwerke AG, dispersed among 14 plants with subcontract or assembly by ATG, Opel, Volkswagen and various French groups.

Type: Military aircraft designed as dive bomber but developed for level bombing, close support, night fighting, torpedo dropping, reconnaissance and as pilotless missile. Crew: two to six.

Engines: (A-4) two 1,340hp Junkers Jumo 211J 12-cylinder inverted-vee liquid-cooled; (C-6) same as A-4; (G-7) two 1,880hp Junkers Jumo 213E 12-cylinder inverted-vee liquid-cooled; (S-1) two 1,700hp BMW 801G 18-cylinder two-row radials.

Dimensions: Span 65ft 10½in (20·13m) (early versions 59ft 10¾in); length 47ft 2¼in (14·4m); (G-7, 54ft 1½in); height 15ft 11in (4·85m); (C-6) 16ft 7½in (5m).

Weights: Empty (A-4) 17,637lb (8000kg); (C-6b) 19,090lb (8660kg), (G-7b) 20,062lb (9100kg); (S-1) 18,300lb (8300kg); maximum loaded (A-4) 30,865lb (14,000kg); (C-6b) 27,500lb (12,485kg); (G-7b) 32,350lb (14,690kg); (S-1) 23,100lb (10,490kg).

Performance: Maximum speed (A-4) 269mph (433km/h); (C-6b) 300mph (480km/h); (G-7b) (no drop tank or flame-dampers) 402mph (643km/h); (S-1) 373mph (600km/h); initial climb (A-4) 1,312ft (400m)/min; (C-6b) about 985ft (300m)/min; (G-7b) 1,640ft (500m)/min; (S-1) 1,804ft (550m)/min; service ceiling (A-4) 26,900ft (8200m); (C-6b) 32,480ft (9900m); (G-7b) 28,870ft (8800m); (S-1) 36,090ft (11,000m); range (A-4) 1,112 miles (1790km); (C-6b) 1,243 miles (2000km); (G-7b) 1,430 miles (2300km); (S-1) 1,243 miles (2000km).

Armament: (A-4) two 7.92mm MG 81 (or one MG 81 and one 13mm MG 131) firing forward, twin MG 81 or one MG 131 upper rear, one or two MG 81 at rear of ventral gondola and (later aircraft) two MG 81 at front of gondola; (C-6b) three 20mm MG FF and three MG 17 in nose and two 20mm MG 151/20 firing obliquely upward in Schräge Musik installation; (G-7b) four MG 151/20 (200 rounds each) firing forward from ventral fairing, two MG 151/20 in Schräge Musik installation (200 rounds each) and defensive MG 131 (500 rounds) swivelling in rear roof; (S-1) one MG 131 (500 rounds) swivelling in rear roof; bomb loads (A-4) 1,100lb (500kg) internal and four external racks rated at 2,200lb (1000kg) (inners) and 1,100lb (500kg) (outers) to maximum total bomb load of 6,614lb (3000kg); (C-6b and G-7b, nil); (S-1) up to 4,410lb (2000kg) on external racks.

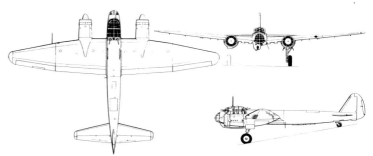

Above: Three-view of the first long-span version, the A-4.

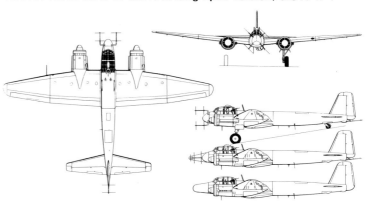

Above: Three-view of the Ju 88G-7a night fighter, with side elevations of G-7b (centre, FuG 218 Neptun) and -7c (FuG 240).

History: First flight (Ju 88V1) 21 December 1936; (first Ju 88A-1) 7 September 1939; (first fighter, Ju 88C-0) July 1939; (Ju 88C-6) mid-1942; (first G-series) early 1944; (S series) late 1943; final deliveries, only as factories were overrun by Allies.

Users: Bulgaria (briefly), Finland, Germany (Luftwaffe), Hungary, Italy, Romania. *continued on page 68▶*

Left: Ju 88A-4 of I/KG 54 "Totenkopf" (Death's Head) at Gerbini, April 1942; colours 78/79/80.

Below: Yet another A-4, this time belonging to one of the most famous units, I/KG 51 "Edelweiss". It was photographed on the Eastern Front in the summer of 1941, in 70/71/65 trim.

▶ **Development:** Probably no other aircraft in history has been developed in so many quite different forms for so many purposes — except, perhaps, for the Mosquito. Flown long before World War II as a civil prototype, after a rapid design process led by two temporarily hired Americans well-versed in modern stressed-skin construction, the first 88s were transformed into the heavier, slower and more capacious A-1 bombers which were just entering service as World War II began. The formidable bomb load and generally good performance were offset by inadequate defensive armament, and in the A-4 the span was increased, the bomb load and gun power substantially augmented and a basis laid for diverse further development. Though it would be fair to describe practically all the subsequent versions as a hodge-podge of lash-ups, the Ju 88 was structurally excellent, combined large internal fuel capacity with great load-carrying capability, and yet was never so degraded in performance as to become seriously vulnerable as were the Dornier and Heinkel bombers. Indeed, with the BMW radial and the Jumo 213 engines the later versions were almost as fast as the best contemporary fighters at all altitudes and could be aerobatted violently into the bargain. A basic design feature was that all the crew were huddled together, to improve combat morale; but in the Battle of Britain it was found this merely made it difficult to add proper defensive armament and in the later Ju 188 a much larger crew compartment was provided. Another distinctive feature was the large single struts of the main landing gear, sprung with stacks of chamfered rings of springy steel, and arranged to turn the big, soft-field wheels through 90° to lie flat in the rear of the nacelles. In 1940 to 1943 about 2,000 Ju 88 bombers were built each year, nearly all A-5 or A-4 versions. After splitting off completely new branches which led to the Ju 188 and 388, bomber development was directed to the streamlined S series of much higher performance, it having become accepted that the traditional Luftwaffe species of bomber was doomed if intercepted, no matter how many extra guns and crew it might carry. Indeed even the bomb and fuel loads were cut in most S sub-types, though the S-2 had fuel in the original bomb bay and large bulged bomb stowage (which defeated the objective of reducing drag). Final bomber versions included the P series of big-gun anti-armour and close-support machines, the Nbwe with flame-throwers and recoilless rocket projectors, and a large family of Mistel composite-aircraft combinations, in which the Ju 88 lower portion was a pilotless missile steered by the fighter originally mounted on top. Altogether bomber, reconnaissance and related 88s totalled 10,774, while frantic construction of night fighter versions in 1944–45 brought the total to at least 14,980. The Ju 88 night fighters (especially the properly designed G-series) were extremely formidable, bristling with radar and weapons and being responsible for destroying more Allied night bombers than all other fighters combined.

Above: One of the first Ju 88 combat missions starts engines: a long-span A-5 model, with yellow-staffel spinners and two SC 250 bombs hung externally.

Below: One of countless Ju 88 lash-ups was the P-1 anti-tank heavy-gun platform with 75mm PaK 40 with large muzzle brake.

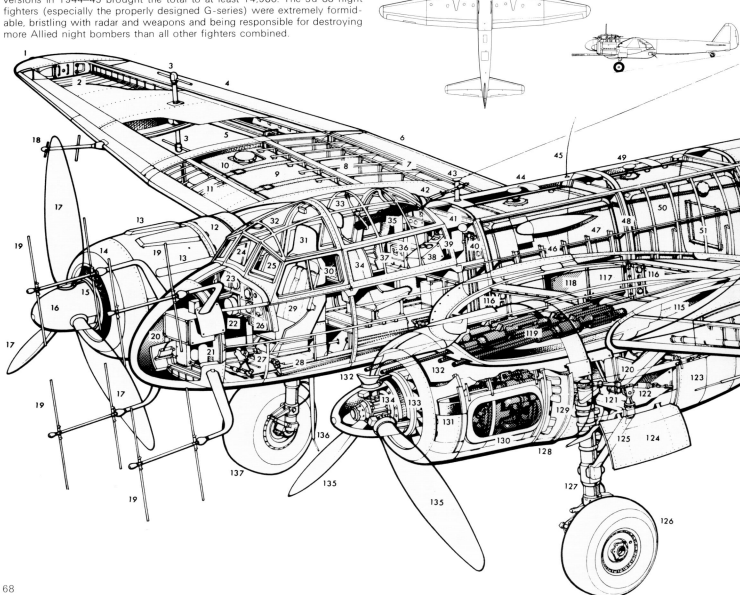

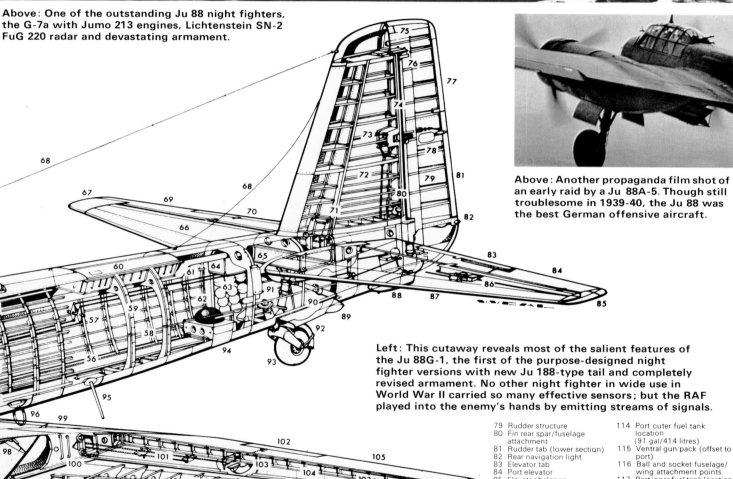

Above: One of the outstanding Ju 88 night fighters, the G-7a with Jumo 213 engines, Lichtenstein SN-2 FuG 220 radar and devastating armament.

Above: Another propaganda film shot of an early raid by a Ju 88A-5. Though still troublesome in 1939-40, the Ju 88 was the best German offensive aircraft.

Left: This cutaway reveals most of the salient features of the Ju 88G-1, the first of the purpose-designed night fighter versions with new Ju 188-type tail and completely revised armament. No other night fighter in wide use in World War II carried so many effective sensors; but the RAF played into the enemy's hands by emitting streams of signals.

Junkers Ju 88G-1 cutaway drawing key:

1 Starboard navigation light
2 Wingtip profile
3 FuG 227 Flensburg homing receiver aerial
4 Starboard aileron
5 Aileron control lines
6 Starboard flap
7 Flap-fairing strip
8 Wing ribs
9 Starboard outer fuel tank (91 gal/414 litres)
10 Fuel filler cap
11 Leading-edge structure
12 Annular exhaust slot
13 Cylinder head fairings
14 Adjustable nacelle nose ring
15 Twelve-blade cooling fan
16 Propeller boss
17 Three-blade variable-pitch VS 111 propeller
18 Leading-edge radar array
19 Lichtenstein SN-2 radar array
20 SN-2 radar
21 Bulkhead
22 Gyro compass
23 Instrument panel
24 Armoured-glass windscreen sections
25 Folding seat
26 Control column
27 Rudder pedal/brake cylinder
28 Control lines
29 Pilot's seat
30 Sliding window section
31 Headrest
32 Jettisonable canopy roof section
33 Gun restraint
34 Radio operator/gunner's seat
35 13mm MG 131 gun
36 Radio equipment
37 Ammunition box (500 rounds)
38 Lichtenstein SN-2 indicator box
39 FuG 227 Flensburg indicator box
40 Control linkage
41 Bulkhead
42 Armoured gun mounting
43 Aerial post/traverse check
44 Fuel filler cap
45 Whip aerial
46 Forward fuselage fuel tank (105 gal/480 litres)
47 Fuselage horizontal construction joint
48 Bulkhead
49 Fuel filler cap
50 Aft fuselage fuel tank (230 gal/1,046 litres)
51 Access hatch
52 Bulkhead
53 Control linkage access plate
54 Fuselage stringers
55 Upper longeron
56 Maintenance walkway
57 Control linkage
58 Fuselage horizontal construction joint
59 'Z'-section fuselage frames
60 Dinghy stowage
61 Fuel vent pipe
62 Master compass
63 Spherical oxygen bottles
64 Accumulator
65 Tailplane centre-section carry-through
66 Starboard tailplane
67 Elevator balance
68 Aerial
69 Starboard elevator
70 Elevator tab
71 Fin front spar/fuselage attachment
72 Fin structure
73 Rudder actuator
74 Rudder post
75 Rudder mass balance
76 Rudder upper hinge
77 Rudder tab (upper section)
78 Inspection/maintenance handhold
79 Rudder structure
80 Fin rear spar/fuselage attachment
81 Rudder tab (lower section)
82 Rear navigation light
83 Elevator tab
84 Port elevator
85 Elevator balance
86 Elevator tab actuator
87 Heated leading-edge
88 Tailbumper/fuel vent outlet
89 Tailwheel doors
90 Tailwheel retraction mechanism
91 Shock-absorber leg
92 Mudguard
93 Tailwheel
94 Access hatch
95 Fixed antenna
96 D/F loop
97 Lower longeron
98 Nacelle/flap fairing
99 Port flap
100 Wing centre/outer section attachment point
101 Aileron controls
102 Aileron tab (port only)
103 Aileron hinges
104 Rear spar
105 Port aileron
106 Port navigation light
107 FuG 101a radio altimeter aerial
108 Wing structure
109 Leading-edge radar array
110 Front spar
111 Pitot head
112 Landing lamp
113 Mainwheel well rear bulkhead
114 Port outer fuel tank location (91 gal/414 litres)
115 Ventral gun pack (offset to port)
116 Ball and socket fuselage/wing attachment points
117 Port inner fuel tank location (93·4 gal/425 litres)
118 Ammunition boxes (200 rpg)
119 Four Mauser MG 151 20mm cannon
120 Mainwheel leg retraction yoke
121 Leg pivot member
122 Mainwheel door actuating jack
123 Mainwheel door (rear section)
124 Mainwheel door (front section)
125 Leg support strut
126 Port mainwheel
127 Mainwheel leg
128 Annular exhaust slot
129 Exhaust stubs (internal)
130 BMW 801D engine (part-deleted to show gun pack)
131 Annular oil tank
132 Cannon muzzles (5 deg. downward angle)·
133 Twelve-blade cooling fan (3·17 times propeller speed)
134 Propeller mechanism
135 Three-blade variable-pitch VS 111 propeller
136 FuG 16ZY aerial
137 Starboard mainwheel

Junkers Ju 188

Ju 188A, D and E series, and Ju 388, J, K and L

Origin: Junkers Flugzeug und Motorenwerke AG; with subcontract manufacture of parts by various French companies.
Type: Five-seat bomber (D-2, reconnaissance).
Engines: (Ju 188A) two 1,776hp Junkers Jumo 213A 12-cylinder inverted-vee liquid-cooled; (Ju 188D) same as A; (Ju 188E) two 1,700hp BMW 801G-2 18-cylinder two-row radials.
Dimensions: Span 72ft 2in (22m); length 49ft 1in (14·96m); height 16ft 1in (4·9m).
Weights: Empty (188E-1) 21,825lb (9900kg); loaded (188A and D) 33,730lb (15,300kg); (188E-1) 31,967lb (14,500kg).
Performance: Maximum speed (188A) 325mph (420km/h) at 20,500ft (6250m); (188D) 350mph (560km/h) at 27,000ft (8235m); (188E) 315mph (494km/h) at 19,685ft (6000m); service ceiling (188A) 33,000ft (10,060m); (188D) 36,090ft (11,000m); (188E) 31,170ft (9500m); range with 3,300lb (1500kg) bomb load (188A and E) 1,550 miles (2480km).
Armament: (A, D-1 and E-1) one 20mm MG 151/20 cannon in nose, one MG 151/20 in dorsal turret, one 13mm MG 131 manually aimed at rear dorsal position and one MG 131 or twin 7·92mm MG 81 manually aimed at rear ventral position; 6,614lb (3000kg) bombs internally or two 2,200lb (1000kg) torpedoes under inner wings.
History: First flight (Ju 88B-0) early 1940; (Ju 88V27) September 1941; (Ju 188V1) December 1941; (Ju 188E-1) March 1942; (Ju 388L) May 1944.
User: Germany (Luftwaffe).

Development: In 1939 Junkers had the Jumo 213 engine in advanced development and, to go with it, the aircraft side of the company prepared an

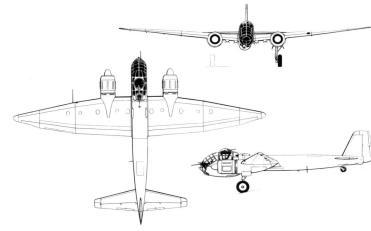

Above: Three-view of the Ju 188E-1 bomber, one of the versions with the BMW 801G-2 radial engine.

Below: Almost gaudy in 72/73 green shades oversprayed with 65 Light Blue, this Ju 188D-2 was operated by 1(F)/124 at Kirkenes, northern Norway, in 1944.

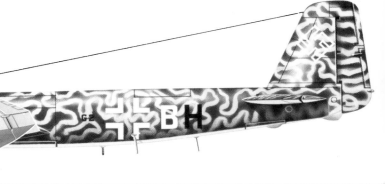

Junkers Ju 290

Ju 290A-1 to A-8 and B-1, B-2 and C

Origin: Junkers Flugzeug und Motorenwerke; design and development at Prague-Letnany, prototypes at Dessau and production at Bernberg.
Type: Long-range transport and reconnaissance bomber.
Engines: Four BMW 801 14-cylinder radials, (A) usually 1,700hp 801D, (B) 1,970hp 801E.
Dimensions: Span 137ft 9½in (42·00m); length 92ft 1in to 97ft 9in (A-5, 93ft 11½in, 28·64m); height 22ft 4¾in (6·83m).
Weights: Empty, not known (published figures cannot be correct); maximum (A-5) 99,141lb (44,970kg), (A-7) 101,413lb (45,400kg), (B-2) 111,332lb (50,500kg).
Performance: Maximum speed (all, without missiles) about 273mph (440km/h); maximum range (typical) 3,700 miles (5950km), (B-2) 4,970 miles (8000km).
Armament: See text.
History: First flight (rebuilt Ju 90V5) early 1939, (production 290A-0) October 1942; programme termination October 1944.
User: Germany (Luftwaffe).

Development: In 1936 Junkers considered the possibility of turning the Ju 89 strategic bomber into the Ju 90 airliner. With the death of Gen Wever the Ju 89 was cancelled and the Ju 90 became the pride of Deutsche Lufthansa. By 1937 the civil Ju 90S (Schwer = heavy) was in final design, with the powerful BMW 139 engine. By 1939 this had flown, with a new wing and BMW 801 engines, and via a string of development prototypes led to the Ju 290A-0 and A-1 transports first used at Stalingrad. The A-2 was an Atlantic patrol machine, with typical armament of five 20mm MG 151 (including two power turrets) and six 13mm MG 131. There were many other versions, and the A-7 introduced a bulbous glazed nose; armament of the A-8 series was ten MG 151 and one (or three) MG 131, the most powerful carried by any bomber of World War II. The B carried more fuel and pressurized crew compartments, and like some A versions had radar and could launch Hs 293 and other air/surface missiles. In 1944 three A-5 made round trips to Manchuria.

Right: Taken at the Junkers plant at Bernburg, the centre for Ju 290 development, this shows the first production A-7 (Werk-Nr 0186) being readied for flight in May 1944. The A-7 was the most advanced sub-type to reach production status; even so the initial batch of 25 was not completed.

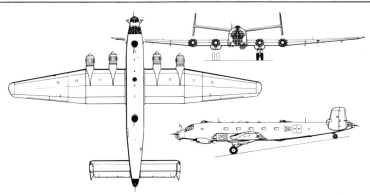

Above: One of the later sub-types was the Ju 290A-7, one of which is illustrated at the foot of the page.

Above: The Ju 90 V4, a development aircraft of 1937 (pre-290).

improved Ju 88 with a larger yet more streamlined crew compartment, more efficient pointed wings and large squarish tail. After protracted development this went into production as the Ju 188E-1, fitted with BMW 801s because the powerful Jumo was still not ready. The plant at Bernburg delivered 120 E-1s and a few radar-equipped turretless E-2s and reconnaissance F versions before, in mid-1943, finally getting into production with the A-1 version. Leipzig/Mockau built the A-2 with flame-damped exhaust for night operations and the A-3 torpedo bomber. The D was a fast reconnais-sance aircraft, and the Ju 188S was a family of high-speed machines, for various duties, capable of up to 435mph (696km/h). Numerous other versions, some with a remotely controlled twin-MG 131 tail turret, led to the even faster and higher-flying Ju 388 family of night fighters (J), recon-naissance (L) and bomber aircraft (K). Altogether about 1,100 Ju 188 and about 120 388s were delivered, while at the war's end the much larger and markedly different Ju 288 had been shelved and the Ju 488, a much enlarged four-engined 388, had been built at Toulouse. All these aircraft, and the even greater number of stillborn projects, were evidence of the increasingly urgent need to make up for the absence of properly conceived new designs by wringing the utmost development out of the obsolescent types with which the Luftwaffe had started the war.

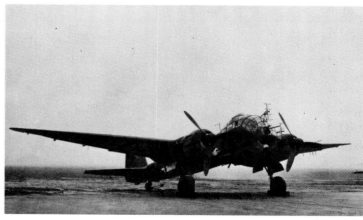

Above: Capable of carrying two advanced LT 1b or LT F5b torpedoes, and Hohentwiel radar, the Ju 188E-2 was one of the best anti-shipping aircraft of World War II.

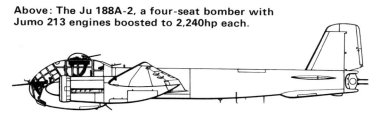

Above: The Ju 188A-2, a four-seat bomber with Jumo 213 engines boosted to 2,240hp each.

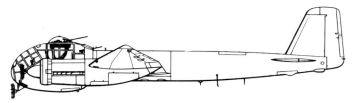

Above: Ju 188D-2 (shown in colour opposite).

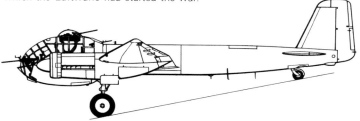

Above: The Ju 188C, with hydraulic tail barbette (abandoned).

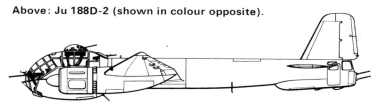

Above: Ju 188G-0 with wooden bomb pannier and manned turret.

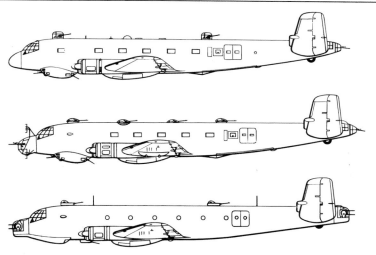

Above, from the top: Ju 290A-2, the first ocean patrol type; Ju 290A-8 with ten cannon; and the Ju 290B-1 heavy bomber.

Above: A rare air-to-air shot of the first Ju 290A-5 to be delivered to FAGr 5 ocean-reconnaissance geschwader in 1943.

Below: This picture of the first Ju 290A-3 (also used by 1/FAGr 5) shows the impressive size of these aircraft.

Messerschmitt Me 163 Komet

Me 163B-1

Origin: Messerschmitt AG.
Type Single-seat interceptor.
Engine: One 3,750lb (1700kg) thrust Walter HWK 509A-2 bi-propellant rocket burning concentrated hydrogen peroxide (T-stoff) and hydrazine/methanol (C-stoff).
Dimensions: Span 30ft 7in (9·3m); length 18ft 8in (5·69m); height 9ft 0in (2·74m).
Weights: Empty 4,191lb (1905kg); loaded 9,042lb (4110kg).
Performance: Maximum speed 596mph (960km/h) at 32,800ft (10,000m); initial climb 16,400ft (5000m)/min; service ceiling 54,000ft (16,500m); range depended greatly on flight profile but under 100km (62 miles); endurance 2½min from top of climb or eight min total.
Armament: Two 30mm MK 108 cannon in wing roots, each with 60 rounds.
History: First flight (Me 163V1) spring 1941 as glider, August 1941 under power; (Me 163B) August 1943; first operational unit (I/JG400) May 1944.
User: Germany (Luftwaffe).

Development: Of all aircraft engaged in World War II the Me 163 Komet (Comet) was the most radical and, indeed, futuristic. The concept of the short-endurance local-defence interceptor powered by a rocket engine was certainly valid and might have been more of a thorn in the Allies' side

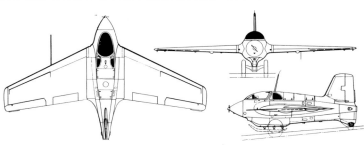

Above: Me 163B-1a showing takeoff trolley and landing skid.

than it was. Even the dramatically unconventional form of the Me 163, with no horizontal tail and an incredibly short fuselage, did not lead to great difficulty; in fact, the production fighter was widely held to have the best and safest characteristics of any aircraft in the Luftwaffe. But the swift strides into uncharted technology were bold in the extreme. It was partly to save weight and drag that the tailless configuration was adopted, and partly because the moving spirit behind the project was at first Dr Alex Lippisch,

Below: Purging the propellant pipes, with C-stoff generating steam clouds. On the ground the Komet was extremely dangerous!

Below: The prototype Me 163A V1 (first prototype), which languished 18 months as a glider before its rocket was fitted.

Messerschmitt Me 210 and 410 Hornisse

Me 210A, B and C series, Me 410A and B series

Origin: Messerschmitt AG.
Type: Two-seat tactical aircraft for fighter, attack and reconnaissance duties with specialised variants.
Engines: (Me 210, usual for production versions) two 1,395hp Daimler-Benz DB 601F inverted-vee-12 liquid-cooled; (Me 410A series, usual for production versions) two 1,750hp DB 603A of same layout; (Me 410B series) two 1,900hp DB 603G.
Dimensions: Span (210) 53ft 7¼in, later 53ft 7¾in (16·4m); (410) 53ft 7¾in; length (without 50mm gun, radar or other long fitment) (210) 40ft 3in (12·22m); (410) 40ft 10in or 40ft 11½in (12·45m); height (both) 14ft 0½in (4·3m).
Weights: Empty (210A) about 12,000lb (5440kg); (410A-1) 13,560lb (6150kg); maximum loaded (210A-1) 17,857lb (8100kg); (410A-1) 23,483lb (10,650kg).
Performance: Maximum speed (both, clean) 385mph (620km/h); initial climb (both) 2,133ft (650m)/min; service ceiling (210A-1) 22,967ft (7000m); (410A-1) 32,800ft (10,000m); range with full bomb load (210A-1) 1,491 miles (2400km); (410A-1) 1,447 miles (2330km).
Armament: Varied, but basic aircraft invariably defended by two remotely-controlled powered barbettes on sides of fuselage each housing one 13mm MG 131 and, if bomber version, provided with internal weapon bay housing two 1,102lb (500kg) bombs; external racks on nearly all (210 and 410) for two 1,102lb stores (exceptionally, two 2,204lb). Normal fixed forward-firing armament of two 20mm MG 151/20 and two 7·92mm MG 17. Me 410 versions had many kinds of bomber-destroyer armament, as described in the text.
History: First flight (Me 210V-1) 2 September 1939; (pre-production 210A-0) April 1941; final delivery (210) April 1942; first flight (310) 11 September 1943; (410V-1) probably December 1942.
User: Germany (Luftwaffe).

Development: Planned in 1937 as a valuable and more versatile successor to the Bf 110 twin-engined escort fighter, the Me 210 was little more than a flop and made hardly any contribution to the German war effort. After severe flight instability and landing-gear problems some progress was made in 1941 towards producing an acceptable machine which could be put into

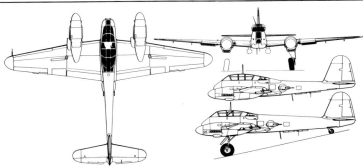

Above: Three-view of Me 210A-2 (upper side view, A-0).

Right: This Messerschmitt Me 410A-3 Hornisse was captured by the RAF at Trapani in Sicily in 1943. Previously operated by 2.(F)/122, it was one of the specialized photo-reconnaissance variants with a deepened forward fuselage without an internal weapons bay to allow the installation of two Rb 20/30, 50/30 or 75/30 cameras.

Below: Another A-3 showing the deep fuselage. Previous photo-reconnaissance versions of the Me 410 Hornisse had been mere lash-ups, with the cameras inadequately installed in the bomb bay and giving extremely poor results.

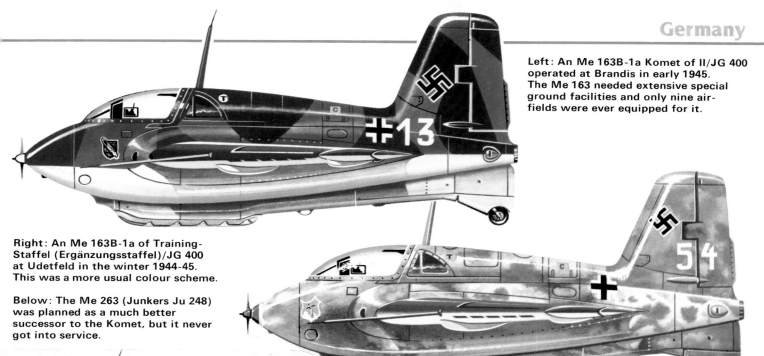

Left: An Me 163B-1a Komet of II/JG 400 operated at Brandis in early 1945. The Me 163 needed extensive special ground facilities and only nine air-fields were ever equipped for it.

Right: An Me 163B-1a of Training-Staffel (Ergänzungsstaffel)/JG 400 at Udetfeld in the winter 1944-45. This was a more usual colour scheme.

Below: The Me 263 (Junkers Ju 248) was planned as a much better successor to the Komet, but it never got into service.

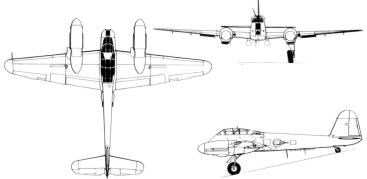

who liked tailless designs. Choice of two rocket propellants that reacted violently when they came into contact solved the problem of ignition in the combustion chamber but added an extremely large element of danger. Moreover, the 163 had no landing gear, taking off from a jettisoned trolley and landing on a sprung skid, and the landing impact often sloshed residual propellants together causing a violent explosion. Many aircraft were lost this way, and the original test pilot, glider champion Heini Dittmar, was badly injured when the skid failed to extend. Nevertheless by 1944 these bat-like specks were swooping on US bomber formations with devastating effect. Numerous improved versions were flying at VE day, but only 370 Komets had seen service and these had suffered high attrition through accidents.

Above: Three-view of Me 410A-1 Hornisse (Hornet).

production against the order for 1,000 placed "off the drawing board" in June 1939. Accidents were nevertheless frequent and manufacture was terminated at the 352nd aircraft. This major blow to the Luftwaffe and the company, which was reflected in an official demand for Willi Messerschmitt's resignation from the board, was partly salvaged by a further redesign and change to the DB 603 engine. The Me 310 was a high-altitude fighter-bomber with 58ft 9in wing and pressure cabin, but this was abandoned in favour of a less radical change designated 410. As with the 210, the reconnaissance 410s usually had cameras in the bomb bay and no MG 17s, while some attack or destroyer versions had four forward-firing MG 151 cannon, or two MG 151 and a 50mm BK 5 gun with 21 rounds. The Me 410A-2/U-2 was an important night fighter with SN-2 Lichtenstein radar and two MG 151 and two 30mm MK 108. Many of the 1,121 Me 410s carried Rüstsatz external packs housing two more MG 151, MK 108 or MK 103, and occasionally experienced pilots fitted as many as eight MG 151 all firing ahead. The 210mm rocket tube was a common fitment by 1944, some aircraft having a rotating pack of six tubes in the bomb bay.

Messerschmitt Me 262

Me 262A-1a Schwalbe, Me 262A-2 Sturmvogel, Me 262B-1a

Origin: Messerschmitt AG.
Type: (A-1a) single-seat fighter, (A-2a) single-seat bomber, (262B-1a) two-seat night fighter.
Engines: Two 1,980lb (900kg) thrust Junkers Jumo 004B single-shaft axial turbojets.
Dimensions: Span 40ft 11½in (12·5m); length 34ft 9½in (10·6m), (262B-1a, excluding radar aerials) 38ft 9in (11·8m); height 12ft 7in (3·8m).
Weights: Empty (A-1a, A-2a) 8,820lb (4000kg); (B-1a) 9,700lb (4400kg); loaded (A-1a, A-2a) 15,500lb (7045kg); (B-1a) 14,110lb (6400kg).
Performance: Maximum speed (A-1a) 540mph (870km/h); (A-2a, laden) 470mph (755km/h); (B-1a) 497mph (800km/h); initial climb (all) about 3,940ft (1200m)/min; service ceiling 37,565ft (11,500m); range on internal fuel, at altitude, about 650 miles (1050km).
Armament: (A-1a) four 30mm MK 108 cannon in nose, two with 100 rounds each, two with 80; (A-1a/U1) two 30mm MK 103, two MK 108 and two 20mm MG 151/20; (A-1b) as A-1a plus 24 spin-stabilised R4/M 50mm rockets; (B-1a) as A-1a; (B-2a) as A-1a plus two inclined MK 108 behind cockpit in Schräge Musik installation; (D) SG 500 Jagdfaust with 12 rifled mortar barrels inclined in nose; (E) 50mm MK 114 gun or 48 R4/M rockets; bomb load of two 1,100lb (500kg) bombs carried by A-2a.
History: First flight (262V1 on Jumo 210 piston engine) 4 April 1941; (262V3 on two Jumo 004-0 turbojets) 18 July 1942; (Me 262A-1a) 7 June 1944; first delivery (A-0 to Rechlin) May 1944; first experimental combat unit (EK 262) 30 June 1944; first regular squadron (8/ZG26) September 1944.
User: Germany (Luftwaffe).

Development: In the Me 262 the German aircraft industry created a potentially war-winning aircraft which could have restored to the Luftwaffe command of the skies over Germany. Compared with Allied fighters of its day, including the RAF Meteor I, which entered service a little earlier, it was much faster and packed a much heavier punch. Radar-equipped night fighter versions and sub-types designed to stand off from large bomber formations and blast them out of the sky were also developments against which the Allies had no answer. Yet for years the programme was held back by official disinterest, and by the personal insistence of Hitler that the world-beating jet should be used only as a bomber! It was in the autumn of 1938 that Messerschmitt was asked to study the design of a jet fighter, and the resulting Me 262 was remarkably unerring. First flown on a piston engine in the nose, it then flew on its twin turbojets and finally, in July 1943, the fifth development aircraft flew with a nosewheel. Despite numerous snags, production aircraft were being delivered in July 1944 and the rate of production was many times that of the British Meteor. On the other hand the

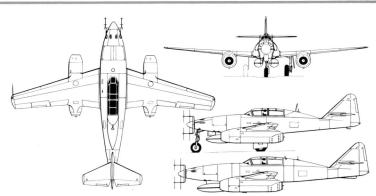

Above: Three-view of the Me 262B-1a night fighter; lower side view, the longer B-2a specially designed for this role.

Above: Starting the Jumo 004B engines of an A-1a of the Kommando Nowotny in late October 1944 (probably at Achmer). The Me 262 was potentially the greatest fighter of the war.

German axial engines were unreliable and casualties due to engine failure, fires or break-up were heavy. The MK 108 gun was also prone to jam, and the landing gear to collapse. Yet the 262 was a beautiful machine to handle and, while Allied jets either never reached squadrons or never engaged enemy aircraft, the 100 or so Me 262s that flew on operations and had fuel available destroyed far more than 100 Allied bombers and fighters. Even more remarkable, by VE-day total deliveries of this formidable aircraft reached 1,433.

Messerschmitt Me 321 and 323 Gigant

Me 321A and B, Me 323D and E

Origin: Messerschmitt AG.
Type: (321) heavy cargo glider; (323) heavy cargo transport.
Engines: (321) none; (323 production variants) six 1,140hp Gnome-Rhône 14N 48/49 14-cylinder two-row radials.
Dimensions: Span 180ft 5½in (55m); length 92ft 4¼in (28·15m); height (321B-1) 33ft 3½in (10·15m); (323) 31ft 6in (9·6m).
Weights: Empty (321B-1) 27,432lb (12,400kg); (323D-6) 60,260lb (27,330kg); (323E-1) 61,700lb (28,010kg); maximum loaded (321B-1) 75,852lb (34,400kg); (323D-6) 94,815lb (43,000kg); (323E-1) 99,208lb (45,000kg).
Performance: Maximum speed (321 on tow) 99mph (160km/h); (323D series) 177mph (285km/h); initial climb (321 towed by three Bf 110) 492ft (150m)/min; (323D series) 710ft (216m)/min; service ceiling (323D) about 13,100ft (4000m); range with "normal" payload (presumably not maximum) 684 miles (1100km).
Armament: See text.
History: First flight (321V-1) 7 March 1941; service delivery (321) about June 1941; final delivery (321) April 1942; first flight (323V-1) some reports claim April 1941 but others, much more plausible, state "autumn 1941"; service delivery (323D-1) May 1942; final delivery March 1944.
User: Germany (Luftwaffe).

Development: Following the dramatic vindication of the previously untried Blitzkrieg concept of airborne forces in May 1940 the Reichsluftfahrtministerium (RLM) asked Junkers and Heinkel to design huge transport gliders far bigger than the little DFS 230 used in the invasion of the Benelux countries. Junkers' Ju 322 Mammut was an expensive failure, but

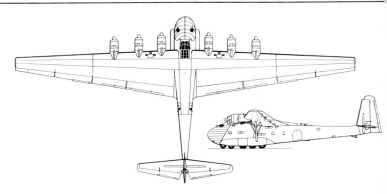

Above: Two-view of the Me 323D-1, the most numerous version.

Right: Man-handling an artillery piece, probably a 75mm Pak.40 anti-tank gun, up into the hold of an Me 323D-1.

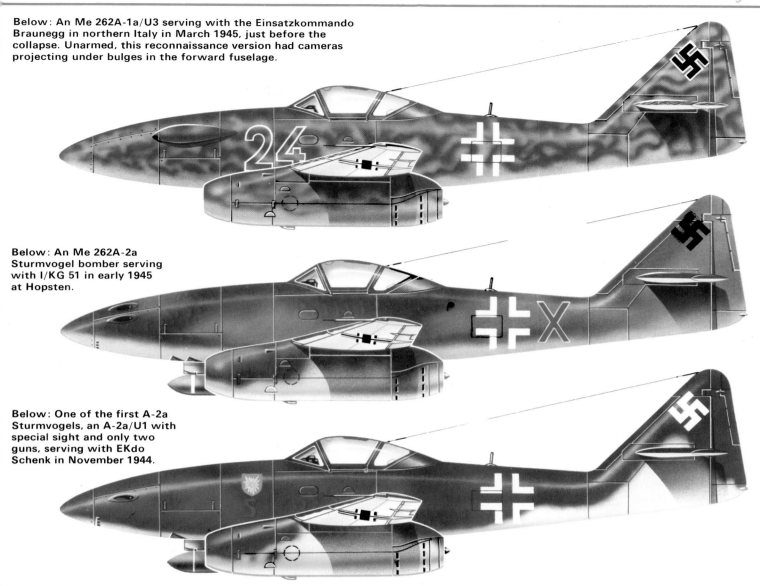

Below: An Me 262A-1a/U3 serving with the Einsatzkommando Braunegg in northern Italy in March 1945, just before the collapse. Unarmed, this reconnaissance version had cameras projecting under bulges in the forward fuselage.

Below: An Me 262A-2a Sturmvogel bomber serving with I/KG 51 in early 1945 at Hopsten.

Below: One of the first A-2a Sturmvogels, an A-2a/U1 with special sight and only two guns, serving with EKdo Schenk in November 1944.

the Me 321 Gigant went into production, despite the fact it was extremely tiring to fly on account of the very high control forces needed. Made chiefly of welded steel tube, with plywood or fabric covering, it carried the large payload of 48,500lb (22 tonnes), or a company of infantry. The 321A-1 had a single pilot but most of the 175 built were 321B-1 with a pair of crew who served as navigator and radio operator and manned two twin 7·92mm MG 15 machine guns in beam windows. Usual towing scheme was three Bf 110 in formation, but the specially built He 111Z was preferable and many units used various arrangements of take-off boost rockets. Dipl-Ing Degel then studied the powered 321C and D and eventually these became the 323V-1 with four engines (complete nacelles already in production at SNCASO for the Bloch 175) and 323V-2 with six. The six-engined Gigant

went into production, the D-1 having three-blade metal propellers and the D-2 two-blade wooden, each having five MG 15 in the nose and mounts for six MG 34 infantry m.g. in beam windows. Most later had five 13mm MG 131 added, but this did not stop Beaufighters shooting 14 into the sea as they ferried petrol to Rommel. Final versions in the run of 210 were the E-series with 1,340hp Jumo 211F, the E-1 having an MG 151 20mm turret above each centre-engine nacelle, and the 323G with 1,320hp Gnome-Rhône 14R.

Below: Takeoff of an Me 321A-1 Gigant under the lusty pull of a Heinkel He 111Z five-engined tug. The Z could handle the monster glider without the latter needing a.t.o. rockets.

Airspeed AS.51 Horsa

Horsa I and II

Origin: Airspeed (1934) Ltd (from January 1944 Airspeed Ltd).
Type: Assault glider.
Engine: None.
Dimensions: Span 88ft 0in (26·84m); length 67ft 0in (20·43m); height 19ft 6in (5·9m).
Weights: Empty 7,500lb (3402kg); loaded 15,250lb (6917kg).
Performance: Typical towing speed 127mph (204km/h); gliding speed 100mph (161km/h).
History: Prototype (DG597) flew 12 September 1941; first delivery (DP279) May 1942.
Users: Portugal, Turkey, UK (RAF), US (AAF).

Development: Germany's success with airborne assault in the Low Countries in May 1940 was so self-evident that the British decided to emulate and, if possible, improve on it. Urgent work went ahead with a number of types of training, troop-carrying and cargo glider and of these by far the most important was the Airspeed AS.51 Horsa, designed to specification X.26/40 as a multirole assault aircraft. It was the biggest glider that could reasonably be towed by available twin-engined tugs. At first training proceeded with Whitley V tugs, with Horsas camouflaged above and painted below with the diagonal black/yellow stripes first seen on target-towing aircraft. By 1943, the usual tug was the Albemarle and the operational gliders had black sides and undersurfaces. Very large orders were placed, not only with Airspeed at Christchurch but also with the Harris Lebus furniture firm, Austin Motor Co and Tata Industries of India. The Indian contract was cancelled but in Britain 3,655 Horsas were built and most saw action. In flight the Horsa creaked loudly and smelled of the wood from which it was made. The Mk I had towing brackets on the wings, necessitating a bifurcated

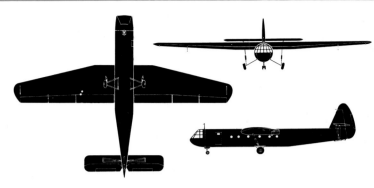

Above: Horsa I with landing gear in position.

rope. The Mk II had a single socket under the nose for a rope which by 1944 was often springy nylon. The rear fuselage could be jettisoned, and there was a large door on the left side; the whole nose of the Mk II could also swing open. With its huge flaps lowered by compressed air and air brakes above and below the wings, the Horsa could almost stand on its nose and swoop quietly into small fields, carrying up to 25 troops. Halifaxes towed two on a special mission to Norway in November 1942. The same type of tug was used in the invasion of Sicily. Hundreds of Horsas took nearly a quarter of the air-supplied loads in the Normandy invasion and, in March 1945, 440 carried the 6th Airborne Division across the Rhine. Many also served with the US Army.

Left: DP726 was one of a batch of 100 Horsa I gliders built by the Austin Motor Company. It is depicted in normal training configuration, but on an operational mission was designed to jettison the entire main landing gears and alight on a large sprung ash skid under the centre fuselage.

Airspeed Oxford

AS.10 (Oxford I, II) and AS.46 (III, V)

Origin: Airspeed (1934) Ltd, Portsmouth; also made at Christchurch and by de Havilland, Percival and Standard Motors.
Type: Advanced trainer; see text.
Engines: (I) two 355hp Armstrong Siddeley Cheetah IX seven-cylinder radial; (II) 375hp Cheetah X; (III) 425hp Cheetah XV; (IV) 300hp DH Gipsy Queen IV in-line; (V) 450hp Pratt & Whitney R-985-AN6 Wasp Junior nine-cylinder radial.
Dimensions: Span 53ft 4in (16·25m); length 34ft 6in (10·52m); height 11ft 1in (3·38m).
Weights: Empty, equipped (II) 5,380lb (2440kg), (V) 5,670lb (2575kg); maximum (II) 7,600lb (3450kg), (V) 8,000lb (3629kg).
Performance (without turret): Maximum speed (I, II) 188mph (301km/h), (V) 202mph (325km/h); initial climb (II) 1,480ft (450m)/min, (V) 2,000ft

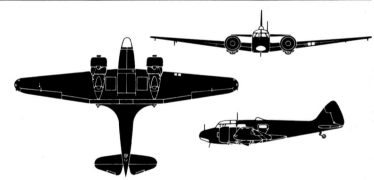

Above: Oxford II nav/radio trainer (but retaining bomb bay).

(610m)/min; service ceiling (typical) 20,000ft (6100m); range (typical) 550 miles (885km).
Armament: See text.
History: First flight 19 June 1937; service delivery November 1937; final delivery 14 July 1945.
Users (WWII): Australia, Canada, Egypt, France, New Zealand, Portugal, S Rhodesia, Turkey, UK (RAF, RN), USA (AAF).

Development: The "Ox-box" has never been one of the famed aircraft of history, yet its contribution to World War II was immense. Throughout the Commonwealth it was the chief vehicle in which were trained the scores of thousands of aircrew for the RAF and many other Allied air forces, and the number built (8,751) made it one of the major production programmes of all time. Built of wood, it was a trim machine which demanded precision of its pilots, and would never tolerate a sloppy landing. Early examples had an AW dorsal turret, and in 1940 a few carried additional guns. Nearly all had provision for bombing training, and other roles included training in navigation, photography, radio and twin-engine pilot conversion. Many hundreds served in communications, ambulance, AA co-operation and radio/radar calibration. The IV was an engine test-bed. The III and V had constant-speed propellers and higher performance.

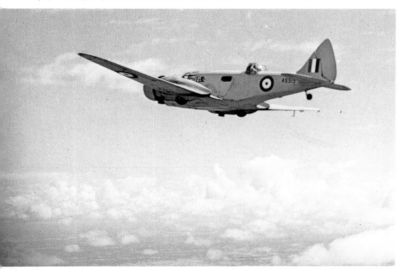

Left: AS515 was an Oxford I with turret. It is shown in use at an air-gunnery school in Canada.

Armstrong Whitworth A.W.38 Whitley

Whitley I to VIII (data for V)

Origin: Sir W. G. Armstrong Whitworth Aircraft.
Type: Five-seat heavy bomber.
Engines: Two 1,145hp Rolls-Royce Merlin X vee-12 liquid-cooled.
Dimensions: Span 84ft 0in (25·6m); length 70ft 6in (21·5m); height 15ft 0in (4·57m).
Weights: Empty 19,330lb (8768kg); maximum 33,500lb (15,196kg).
Performance: Maximum speed 222mph (357km/h); cruising speed, about 185mph (297km/h); initial climb 800ft (244m)/min; service ceiling from 17,600–21,000ft (5400–6400m); range with maximum bomb load 470 miles (756km); range with 3,000lb (1361kg) bombs 1,650 miles (2650km).
Armament: One 0·303 in Vickers K in nose turret; four 0·303 in Brownings in tail turret; up to 7,000lb (3175kg) bombs in cells in fuselage and inner wings.

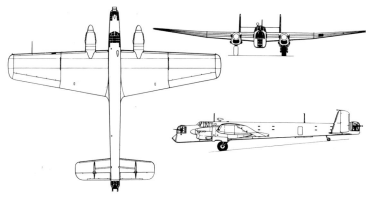

Above: Typical Whitley V with landing gear extended.

Left: This Whitley V served in the early part of the war with 102 Sqn. It took part in many leaflet raids, minelaying sorties and early missions to bomb targets in Germany and northern Italy.

History: First flight (prototype) 17 March 1936; first delivery (Mk I) January 1937; first flight (Mk V) December 1938; first delivery (Mk V) August 1939; production termination June 1943.
User: UK (RAF, BOAC).

Development: Designed to Specification B.3/34, this heavy bomber was at least an all-metal monoplane with retractable landing gear, but the original Mk I was still primitive. Its thick wing, which in the first batch had no dihedral, was set at a marked positive incidence, so that at normal cruising speeds the long slab-sided Whitley flew in a characteristic nose-down attitude. Powered by 795hp Armstrong Siddeley Tiger IX radials, the Mk I was soon replaced by the Mk II, and then by the III with the 920hp Tiger VIII. In 1938 production switched to the greatly improved Mk IV, with Merlin engines and a power-driven rear turret mounting four machine guns. The Mk IVA had a more powerful Merlin, and this was retained in the Mk V which was 15in longer and had straight-edged fins. AWA made 1,466 Whitley Vs, the last in June 1943, and also delivered 146 longer-range GR.VIII patrol aircraft with ASV radar for Coastal Command. Whitleys bore the brunt of long leaflet raids, starting on the first night of the war. On 19 March 1940 Whitleys dropped the first bombs to fall on Germany since 1918, and during the next two years these tough and capable aircraft made missions as far as Turin and Pilsen, often in terrible conditions, highlighting deficiencies in navigation and equipment the hard way. Coastal's first U-boat kill was U-206, sunk by a Whitley VII in November 1941. From 1942 the Whitley served mainly as a trainer for paratroops, as a glider tug and with 100 Group as a carrier of experimental or special-purpose radars and countermeasures. Total production was 1,737.

Below: Ground and aircrew investigate a last minute engine snag before the day air test that always preceded a mission.

Armstrong Whitworth A.W.41 Albemarle

Albemarle I to VI

Origin: "A. W. Hawksley".
Type: Four-crew special transport and glider tug.
Engines: Two 1,590hp Bristol Hercules XI 14-cylinder sleeve-valve radials.
Dimensions: Span 77ft 0in (23·47m); length 59ft 11in (18·25m); height 15ft 7in (4·75m).
Weights: Empty (GT.VI) 22,600lb (10,260kg); maximum 36,500lb (16,570kg).
Performance: Maximum speed 265mph (426km/h); initial climb 980ft (299m)/min; service ceiling 18,000ft (5490m); typical range 1,350 miles (2160km).
Armament: None except in Mk I/1 (Boulton Paul dorsal turret with four 0·303in Brownings and powered ventral turret with two 0·303in Brownings) and ST.I (manual dorsal installation with various guns).
History: First flight 20 March 1940; (production aircraft) December 1941; final delivery December 1944.
User: Soviet Union, UK (RAF).

Above: An Albemarle, probably an ST.II, on takeoff with Horsa I at the Heavy Glider Conversion Unit, Brize Norton.

Development: After Bristol had proposed the Type 155 bomber with a nosewheel landing gear (which at that time had not been used in Britain except experimentally) the Air Ministry issued Specification B.18/38 which was notable for its insistence on minimal use of light alloys, which were likely to be in short supply in event of war. Instead the design was to be made mainly of steel and wood, even though this would increase weight. Bristol dropped the 155, and the specification was met by the AW.41, first flown on 20 March 1940. Production was entirely subcontracted to firms outside the aircraft industry, and parts were brought to a plant at Gloucester for which Hawker Siddeley formed a company called A. W. Hawksley Ltd. Thus, not only did the Albemarle conserve strategic materials (with very small penalty, as it turned out) but it had no parent factory or design organization. Delivery began in October 1941, but only 32 were completed as bombers and these were converted as transports. Altogether 600 were delivered by the end of 1944, in many versions grouped into two main families: ST, or Special Transport, used all over Europe and North Africa; and GT, Glider Tug, used in Sicily, Normandy and at Arnhem. Glider towing needed high power at low airspeeds, and the Hercules overheated and poured oil smoke, but the Albemarle was otherwise pleasant to fly.

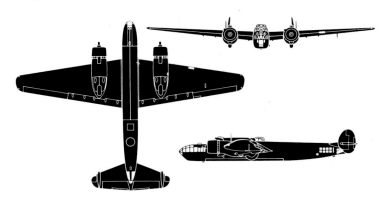

Above: The original Albemarle I Series I before conversion.

Avro 652M Anson

652A Anson I and later marks to T.22, USAAF AT-20

Origin: A. V. Roe Ltd, Chadderton, Bracebridge Heath, Newton Heath and Yeadon; in Canada by Federal Aircraft.
Type: Originally reconnaissance bomber, later crew trainer and multirole.
Engines: (I, X) two 355hp Armstrong Siddeley IX seven-cylinder radial; (II, III) 330hp Jacobs L-6MB (R-915) of same layout; (IV) 450hp Wright R-975-E3 Whirlwind; (V, VI) 450hp Pratt & Whitney R-985-AN14B Wasp Junior; (XI, XII) 420hp Cheetah XIX or XV.
Dimensions: Span 56ft 6in (17·22m); length (nearly all) 42ft 3in (12·88 m); height 13ft 1in (3·99m).
Weights: Empty, equipped (I) 5,375lb (2438kg), (V) 6,693lb (3036kg), (XII) 6,510lb (2953kg); maximum (I) 8,000lb (3629kg), (V) 9,460lb (4291kg), (XII) 9,900lb (4491kg).
Performance: (no turret): Maximum speed (I) 188mph (303km/h), (V) 190mph (306km/h), (XII) 175mph (282km/h); typical cruise 150mph (241km/h); typical range 700 miles (1127km).
Armament: See text.
History: First flight 24 March 1935; service delivery 6 March 1936; final delivery May 1952.

Users (WW2): Australia, Canada, Egypt, France, Greece, Iran, Ireland, Netherlands, UK (RAF, RN, ATA, BOAC), US (AAF).

Development: The abiding memory of "Faithful Annie" is of the most docile and reliable machine in the whole war. Yet when it was first delivered to 48 Sqn RAF Coastal Command it was very much a "hot ship". It was a monoplane, and it had retractable landing gear (laboriously cranked up and down by hand), and despite a large dorsal turret it was almost the fastest thing in the service. One attacked a U-boat only two days after the start of the war, and in June 1940 a close vic of three survived attacks by nine Bf 109Es, shooting down at least two of the German fighters despite having only a single drum-fed Lewis in each turret. Later many Mk I trainers had twin belt-fed Brownings in a Bristol turret, and virtually all Mk Is carried at least provision for bombing training. Altogether 6,704 Mk I were built, and thousands were used for general communications or converted into Mk X transports with smooth engine cowls and strong freight floors. DH Canada fitted some with American engines to produce the III and IV. Federal built 2,882 Ansons from 1941, most being Mk II (USAAF AT-20) but later batches being the V and VI with fuselages of Vidal moulded ply instead of steel tube and fabric. The XI and XII at last introduced hydraulic landing gear (on the Canadian machines from the start) and a much roomier fuselage, as well as constant-speed propellers and many other changes. These evolved into the modern stressed-skin C.19 and T.20, 21 and 22 for the post-war RAF. Total production was 11,020.

Below: Though the vast majority of Ansons were trainers, utility transports and hacks, this original Mk I is seen in 1942 still with 217 Sqn Coastal Command after six years.

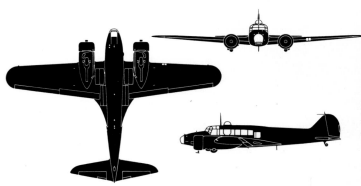

Above: Anson X with astro-dome (often absent).

Avro 679 Manchester

679 Manchester I and IA

Origin: A. V. Roe Ltd, Chadderton.
Type: Heavy bomber.
Engines: Two Rolls-Royce Vulture I 24-cylinder X-form, rated at 1,760hp but in fact derated to 1,480–1,500hp.
Dimensions: Span 90ft 1in (27·46m); length 70ft 0in (21·34m); height 19ft 6in (5·94m).
Weights: Empty 31,200lb (14,152kg); maximum 56,000lb but in fact never authorised above 50,000lb (22,680kg).
Performance: Maximum speed (typical) 250mph (402km/h); service ceiling (42,000lb) 19,500ft (5852m); range with maximum bomb load 1,200 miles (1930km).
Armament: Eight 0·303in Browning in power turrets in nose (2), mid-upper (2) and tail (4); internal fuselage bay accommodating bomb load up to 10,350lb (4695kg).
History: First flight 25 July 1939; service delivery November 1940; withdrawal from production November 1941.
User: UK (RAF).

Development: Rolls-Royce's decision in 1935 to produce a very powerful engine by fitting two sets of Peregrine cylinder-blocks to one crankcase (the lower pair being inverted, to give an X arrangement) prompted the Air Ministry to issue specification P.13/36 for a twin-engined heavy bomber of unprecedented capability. Handley Page changed to four Merlins (see Halifax) but Avro produced the Manchester with the Vulture engine. In most respects it was the best of all the new heavy bombers, but the engine was grossly down on power, and had to be derated further because of extreme unreliability. Originally the Manchester had two fins; in the production Mk I a fixed central fin was added, and the bulk of the 209 delivered had two larger fins (no central fin) and were designated IA. So hopeless was the engine situation that the plans to build Manchesters at Armstrong Whitworth and Fairey were cancelled, and Metropolitan-Vickers stopped at No 32. Avro went on until the vastly superior Lancaster could take over, the first batches of Lancasters having Manchester fuselages with a row of small windows along each side.

Above: L7516, ''S-Sugar'' of 207 Sqn, the first unit to receive the Manchester in November 1940. This aircraft was a Mk IA.

Below: Mk IA with two enlarged fins on increased-span tailplane.

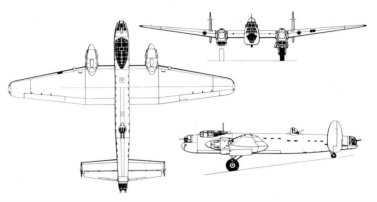

Avro 683 Lancaster

683 Lancaster I to MR.7 (data for I)

Origin: A. V. Roe Ltd; also Armstrong Whitworth, Austin Motors, Metropolitan-Vickers and Vickers-Armstrongs, UK, and Victory Aircraft, Canada.
Type: Seven-seat heavy bomber.
Engines: Four 1,460hp Rolls-Royce or Packard Merlin 20 or 22 (Mk II only: four 1,650hp Bristol Hercules VI, 14 cylinder two-row, sleeve-valve radials).
Dimensions: Span 102ft 0in (31·1m); length 69ft 4in (21·1m); height 19ft 7in (5·97m).
Weights: Empty 36,900lb (16,705kg); loaded 68,000lb (30,800kg); overload with 22,000lb bomb 70,000lb (31,750kg).

Performance: Maximum speed 287mph (462km/h) at 11,500ft (3500m); cruising speed 210mph (338km/h); climb at maximum weight to 20,000ft (6095m) 41 minutes; service ceiling 24,500ft (7467m); range with 14,000lb (6350kg) bombs 1,660 miles (2675km).
Armament: Nose and dorsal turrets (Mk II also ventral) with two 0·303in Brownings (some, including Mk VII, had Martin dorsal turret with two 0·5in), tail turret with four 0·303in Brownings, 33ft 0in (10·06m) bomb bay carrying normal load of 14,000lb (6350kg) or 22,000lb (9979kg) bomb with modification.
History: First flight 9 January 1941; service delivery (for test and training) September 1941; last delivery from new 2 February 1946.

continued on page 80 ▶

Below: An inspiring sight to anyone who remembers those great days—the final assembly line at A. V. Roe's Woodford plant in 1943 (Mk Is with serials in the batch JA672-JB748).

▶ **Users:** Australia, Canada, New Zealand, Poland, UK (RAF, BOAC).

Development: Undoubtedly one of the major influences on World War II, and one of the greatest aircraft of history, the "Lanc" came about because of the failure of its predecessor. In September 1936 the Air Staff issued specification P.13/36 for a twin-engined bomber of exceptional size and capability to be powered by two of the very powerful engines then under development: the Rolls-Royce Vulture 24-cylinder X engine was preferred. Handley Page switched to four Merlins with the Halifax, but A. V. Roe adhered to the big-twin formula and the first Type 679 Manchester flew on 25 July 1939. Altogether 209 Manchesters were delivered by November 1941, but the type was plagued by the poor performance and unreliability of its engine. Though it equipped eight Bomber Command squadrons, and parts of two others plus a flight in Coastal Command, the Manchester was withdrawn from service in June 1942 and survivors were scrapped.

Nevertheless the basic Manchester was clearly outstandingly good, and in 1940 the decision was taken to build a longer-span version with four Merlin engines. The first Lancaster (BT 308) flew as the Manchester III at the beginning of 1941. So outstanding was its performance that it went into immediate large-scale production, and Manchesters already on the line from L7527 onwards were completed as Lancasters (distinguished from later aircraft by their row of rectangular windows in the rear fuselage). Deliveries began in early 1942 to 44 Sqn at Waddington, and on 17 April 1942 a mixed force of 44 and 97 Sqns made a rather foolhardy daylight raid against the MAN plant at Augsburg, whereupon the new bomber's existence was revealed.

continued on page 82 ▶

Above: Late-war Lancs letting go thousand-pounders over a cloud-covered target in daylight, common from spring 1944.

Below: Cutaway drawing of a Lancaster III, similar to a Mk I except for Packard nameplates and US accessories on the engines. Usual night load was a 4,000-pounder plus incendiaries.

Avro Lancaster III cutaway drawing key:

1 Two 0·303in Browning machine guns
2 Frazer-Nash power-operated nose turret
3 Nose blister
4 Bomb-aimer's (optically flat) panel
5 Bomb-aimer's control panel
6 Side windows
7 External air temperature thermometer
8 Pitot head
9 Bomb-aimer's chest support
10 Fire extinguisher
11 Parachute emergency exit
12 F.24 camera
13 Glycol tank and step
14 Ventilator fairing
15 Bomb-door forward actuating jacks
16 Bomb-bay forward bulkhead
17 Control linkage
18 Rudder pedals
19 Instrument panel
20 Windscreen de-icer sprays
21 Windscreen
22 Dimmer switches
23 Flight-engineer's folding seat
24 Flight-engineer's control panel
25 Pilot's seat
26 Flight-deck floor level
27 Elevator and rudder control rods (underfloor)
28 Trim-tab control cables
29 Main floor/bomb-bay support longeron
30 Fire extinguisher
31 Communications radio and (if fitted) electronic jammers
32 Navigator's seat
33 Canopy vision blister
34 Pilot's head armour
35 Emergency escape hatch
36 D/F loop
37 Aerial mast support
38 Electrical services panel
39 Navigator's window
40 Navigator's desk
41 Aircraft and radio compass receiver
42 Wireless-operator's desk
43 Wireless-operator's seat
44 Wireless-operator's window
45 Front spar carry-through/ fuselage frame
46 Astrodome
47 Inboard section wing ribs
48 Spar join
49 Aerial mast
50 Starboard inner engine nacelle
51 Spinner
52 Three-blade de Havilland constant-speed propellers
53 Oil-cooler intake
54 Oil-cooler radiator
55 Carburettor air intake
56 Radiator shutter
57 Engine bearer frame
58 Exhaust flame-damper shroud
59 Packard-built Rolls-Royce Merlin 28 liquid-cooled engine
60 Nacelle/wing fairing
61 Fuel tank bearer ribs
62 Intermediate ribs
63 Leading-edge structure
64 Wing stringers
65 Wingtip skinning
66 Starboard navigation light
67 Starboard formation light
68 Aileron hinge fairings
69 Wing rear spar
70 Starboard aileron
71 Aileron balance tab

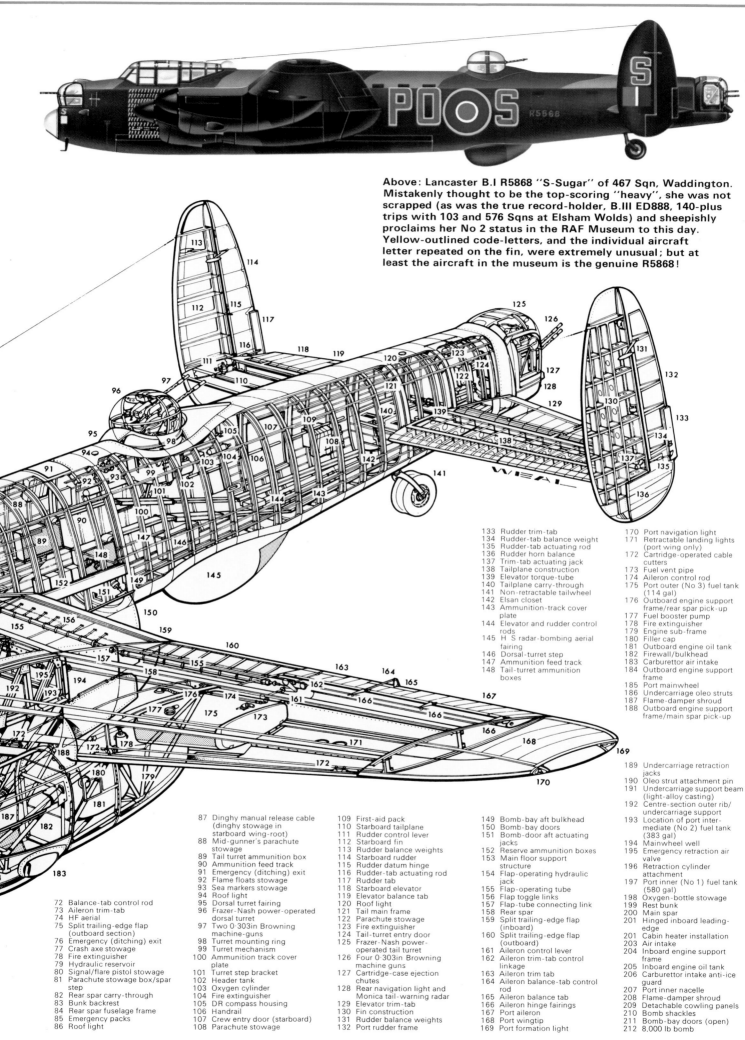

Above: Lancaster B.I R5868 "S-Sugar" of 467 Sqn, Waddington. Mistakenly thought to be the top-scoring "heavy", she was not scrapped (as was the true record-holder, B.III ED888, 140-plus trips with 103 and 576 Sqns at Elsham Wolds) and sheepishly proclaims her No 2 status in the RAF Museum to this day. Yellow-outlined code-letters, and the individual aircraft letter repeated on the fin, were extremely unusual; but at least the aircraft in the museum is the genuine R5868!

72 Balance-tab control rod
73 Aileron trim-tab
74 HF aerial
75 Split trailing-edge flap (outboard section)
76 Emergency (ditching) exit
77 Crash axe stowage
78 Fire extinguisher
79 Hydraulic reservoir
80 Signal/flare pistol stowage
81 Parachute stowage box/spar step
82 Rear spar carry-through
83 Bunk backrest
84 Rear spar fuselage frame
85 Emergency packs
86 Roof light
87 Dinghy manual release cable (dinghy stowage in starboard wing-root)
88 Mid-gunner's parachute stowage
89 Tail turret ammunition box
90 Ammunition feed track
91 Emergency (ditching) exit
92 Flame floats stowage
93 Sea markers stowage
94 Roof light
95 Dorsal turret fairing
96 Frazer-Nash power-operated dorsal turret
97 Two 0·303in Browning machine-guns
98 Turret mounting ring
99 Turret mechanism
100 Ammunition track cover plate
101 Turret step bracket
102 Header tank
103 Oxygen cylinder
104 Fire extinguisher
105 DR compass housing
106 Handrail
107 Crew entry door (starboard)
108 Parachute stowage
109 First-aid pack
110 Starboard tailplane
111 Rudder control lever
112 Starboard fin
113 Rudder balance weights
114 Starboard rudder
115 Rudder datum hinge
116 Rudder-tab actuating rod
117 Rudder tab
118 Starboard elevator
119 Elevator balance tab
120 Roof light
121 Tail main frame
122 Parachute stowage
123 Fire extinguisher
124 Tail-turret entry door
125 Frazer-Nash power-operated tail turret
126 Four 0·303in Browning machine guns
127 Cartridge-case ejection chutes
128 Rear navigation light and Monica tail-warning radar
129 Elevator trim-tab
130 Fin construction
131 Rudder balance weights
132 Port rudder frame
133 Rudder trim-tab
134 Rudder-tab balance weight
135 Rudder-tab actuating rod
136 Rudder horn balance
137 Trim-tab actuating jack
138 Tailplane construction
139 Elevator torque-tube
140 Tailplane carry-through
141 Non-retractable tailwheel
142 Elsan closet
143 Ammunition-track cover plate
144 Elevator and rudder control rods
145 H S radar-bombing aerial fairing
146 Dorsal-turret step
147 Ammunition feed track
148 Tail-turret ammunition boxes
149 Bomb-bay aft bulkhead
150 Bomb-bay doors
151 Bomb-door aft actuating jacks
152 Reserve ammunition boxes
153 Main floor support structure
154 Flap-operating hydraulic jack
155 Flap-operating tube
156 Flap toggle links
157 Flap-tube connecting link
158 Rear spar
159 Split trailing-edge flap (inboard)
160 Split trailing-edge flap (outboard)
161 Aileron control lever
162 Aileron trim-tab control linkage
163 Aileron control rod
164 Aileron balance-tab control rod
165 Aileron balance tab
166 Aileron hinge fairings
167 Port aileron
168 Port wingtip
169 Port formation light
170 Port navigation light
171 Retractable landing lights (port wing only)
172 Cartridge-operated cable cutters
173 Fuel vent pipe
174 Aileron control rod
175 Port outer (No 3) fuel tank (114 gal)
176 Outboard engine support frame/rear spar pick-up
177 Fuel booster pump
178 Fire extinguisher
179 Engine sub-frame
180 Filler cap
181 Outboard engine oil tank
182 Firewall/bulkhead
183 Carburettor air intake
184 Outboard engine support frame
185 Port mainwheel
186 Undercarriage oleo struts
187 Flame-damper shroud
188 Outboard engine support frame/main spar pick-up
189 Undercarriage retraction jacks
190 Oleo strut attachment pin
191 Undercarriage support beam (light-alloy casting)
192 Centre-section outer rib/undercarriage support
193 Location of port intermediate (No 2) fuel tank (383 gal)
194 Mainwheel well
195 Emergency retraction air valve
196 Retraction cylinder attachment
197 Port inner (No 1) fuel tank (580 gal)
198 Oxygen-bottle stowage
199 Rest bunk
200 Main spar
201 Hinged inboard leading-edge
201 Cabin heater installation
203 Air intake
204 Inboard engine support frame
205 Inboard engine oil tank
206 Carburettor intake anti-ice guard
207 Port inner nacelle
208 Flame-damper shroud
209 Detachable cowling panels
210 Bomb shackles
211 Bomb-bay doors (open)
212 8,000 lb bomb

▶ From then until the end of World War II Lancasters made 156,000 sorties in Europe and dropped 608,612 long tons of bombs. Total production, including 430 in Canada by Victory Aircraft, was 7,377. Of these 3,425 were Mk I and 3,039 the Mk III with US Packard-built engines. A batch of 300 was built as Mk IIs with the more powerful Bristol Hercules radial, some with bulged bomb bays and a ventral turret. The Mk I (Special) was equipped to carry the 12,000lb (5443kg) light-case bomb and the 12,000lb and 22,000lb (9979kg) Earthquake bombs, the H_2S radar blister under the rear fuselage being removed. The Mk I (FE) was equipped for Far East operations with Tiger Force. The aircraft of 617 (Dambusters) Sqn were equipped to spin and release the Wallis skipping drum bomb. The Mk VI had high-altitude Merlins and four-blade propellers and with turrets removed served 635 Sqn and 100 Grp as a countermeasure and radar spoof carrier. Other marks served as photo-reconnaissance and maritime reconnaissance and air/sea rescue aircraft, the last MR.7 leaving RAF front-line service in February 1954.

Lancasters took part in every major night attack on Germany. They soon showed their superiority by dropping 132 long tons of bombs for each aircraft lost, compared with 56 (later 86) for the Halifax and 41 for the Stirling. They carried a heavier load of bigger bombs than any other aircraft in the European theatre. The 12,000lb AP bomb was used to sink the *Tirpitz*, and the 22,000lb weapon finally shook down the stubborn viaduct at Bielefeld in March 1945. Around Caen, Lancasters were used en masse in the battlefield close-support role, and they finished the war dropping supplies to starving Europeans and ferrying home former prisoners of war.

Above: Incendiaries cascade from one of the highly secret B.Is of No 101 Sqn, from Ludford Magna, with Airborne Cigar electronic jamming equipment (note the two tall dorsal masts).

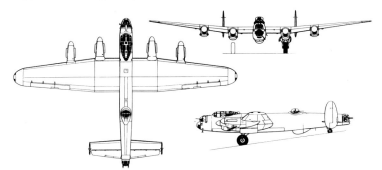

Left: Three-view of a typical Mk I or Mk III Lancaster.

Below: Colour photography was rare in Britain in World War II. This splendid picture was taken from beside the pilot of a Lanc of 50 Sqn at Swinderby (Press visit, 28 August 1942).

Blackburn Skua and Roc

Skua II, Roc I

Origin: The Blackburn Aircraft Company, Brough; Roc production assigned to Boulton Paul Aircraft, Wolverhampton.
Type: (S) two-seat carrier fighter/dive bomber; (R) two-seat carrier fighter.
Engine: 905hp Bristol Perseus XII nine-cylinder sleeve-valve radial.
Dimensions: Span (S) 46ft 2in (14·07m), (R) 46ft 0in (14·02m); length (S) 35ft 7in (10·85m), (R) 35ft 0in (10·67m); height 12ft 5in (3·79m).
Weights: Empty (S) 5,490lb (2490kg), (R) 6,121lb (2776kg); maximum (S) 8,228lb (3732kg), (R) 8,800lb (3992kg).
Performance: Maximum speed (S) 225mph (362km/h), (R) 196mph (315km/h); service ceiling 20,200ft (6157m); range (typical) 800 miles (1287km).
Armament: (S) four 0·303in Browning fixed in wings, one 0·303in Lewis or Vickers K in rear cockpit, 500lb (227kg) bomb on hinged arms under fuselage, light bombs under wings; (R) four 0·303in Browning in power dorsal turret, light bombs under wings.

History: First flight (S) 9 February 1937, (R) 23 December 1938; service delivery (S) November 1938, (R) April 1939.
User: UK (RN).

Development: The Skua was designed to a 1934 specification, O.27/34, for a naval dive bomber. Two prototypes powered by 840hp Mercury engines looked sleek against the Navy's fabric-covered biplanes, and eventually 190 were built to a later requirement (25/36), to enter service as the Fleet Air Arm's first monoplane and first with v-p propeller or retractable landing gear. During the first year of war the Skuas worked hard, and made many gallant attacks on German capital ships. On 26 September 1939 Skuas of 803 Sqn from *Ark Royal* shot down a Do 18, the first Luftwaffe aircraft destroyed by Britain. But the basic aircraft was underpowered, and by 1941 the Skua was becoming a target tug and trainer. Likewise the 136 turreted Rocs were even less capable of surviving, let alone acting as fighters. The 136 built, to O.30/35, never served on a carrier and were soon withdrawn. A few were seaplanes, with Shark-type floats.

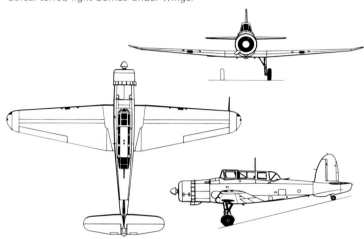

Above: Skua II showing four wing guns and upturned tips.

Right: Pre-war picture of a Skua making a practice bombing dive, with patented Zapp flaps fully depressed to limit speed.

Below: Though pleasant to fly, one wonders how the Roc, a 196mph fighter, could have been considered for combat duty.

Boulton Paul P.82 Defiant

Defiant I and II (data for I)

Origin: Boulton Paul Aircraft, Wolverhampton.
Type: Two-seat fighter.
Engine: I, 1,030hp Rolls-Royce Merlin III vee-12 liquid-cooled; II, 1,260hp Merlin 20.
Dimensions: Span 39ft 4in (12m); length 35ft 4in (10·75m); height 12ft 2in (3·7m).
Weights: Empty 6,000lb (2722kg); loaded 8,350lb (3787kg).
Performance: Maximum speed 303mph (488km/h); initial climb 1,900ft (579m)/min; service ceiling 30,500ft (9300m); range, probably about 500 miles (805km).
Armament: Hydraulically operated dorsal gun turret with four 0·303in Browning machine guns, each with 600 rounds.
History: First flight (prototype) 11 August 1937; (production Mk I) 30 July 1939; first delivery December 1939.
User: UK (RAF).

Development: By 1933 military staffs were intensely studying the enclosed gun turret, manually worked or power-driven, either to defend a bomber or to arm a fighter. A primitive form was seen on the Hawker Demon in 1936, while in France the *Multiplace de Combat* class of aircraft were huge fighters with turrets all over. The Defiant was a bold attempt to combine the performance of the new monoplanes with a powered enclosed turret carrying four 0·303in Brownings, each with 600 rounds. The gunner, behind the pilot, had a control column moved left/right for rotation, fore/aft for depression and elevation and with a safety/firing button on top. The Defiant itself was a clean and pleasant aircraft, but rather degraded in performance by carrying a crew of two and the heavy turret. No 264 Sqn went into action on 12 May 1940 in desperate fights over the Low Countries. On the 13th six escorted Battle bombers, and only one returned; it seemed the

Defiant was a failure against the Bf 109E. But seven days later remnants of 264 shot down "17 Messerschmitts without loss" and later on the same day destroyed eleven Ju 87s and 88s. Once the enemy were familiar with the Defiant it had had its day by daylight, but it did well in 1940–41 as a night fighter and was later fitted with radar. Most of the 1,064 built served as night fighters, target tugs and in air/sea rescue in Britain, the Middle East and Far East. Defiants carried the Mandrel jamming system to confuse German defences.

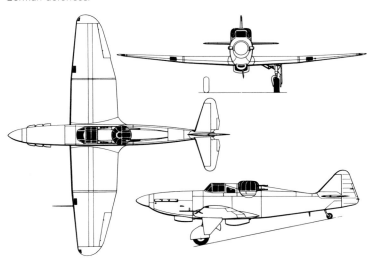

Above: Defiant I (II similar) with turret fairings raised.

Right: Defiant II of 125 Sqn on night operations in 1941-42 but lacking radar. Note fold-down radio masts.

Below: Fighter Command's 264 Sqn was the first recipient of the Defiant, and this photograph was taken during the working-up period in early 1940. In fact the concept of the sluggish two-seat fighter was faulty, and production of 1,060 (continued until February 1943) was a disgraceful error.

Bristol Type 156 Beaufighter

Beaufighter I to TF.X (data mainly Mk X)

Origin: Bristol Aeroplane Company, Filton and Weston-Super-Mare; also Department of Aircraft Production, Australia.

Type: Two-seat torpedo strike fighter (other marks, night fighters, target tugs).

Engines: Two 1,770hp Bristol Hercules XVII 14-cylinder sleeve-valve radials; (Mk II) 1,250hp R-R Merlin XX; (other marks) different Hercules; (one-offs had R-R Griffons and Wright GR-2600 Cyclones).

Dimensions: Span 57ft 10in (17·63m); length 41ft 8in (12·6m) (II, 42ft 9in); height 15ft 10in (4·84m).

Weights: Empty 15,600lb (7100kg) (I, II, 13,800lb; VI, XI, 14,900lb); loaded 25,400lb (11,530kg) (most other marks 21,000lb, 9525kg).

Performance: Maximum speed 312mph (502km/h) (fighter marks, 330mph, 528km/h); initial climb 1,850ft (564m)/min; service ceiling 26,500ft (8077m) (fighters, 30,000ft, 9144m); range 1,540 miles (2478km).

Armament: Four 20mm Hispano cannon fixed in underside of forward fuselage (initially hand loaded with 60-round drums, later with belt feed), and one 0·303in Vickers K aimed by observer (fighters, also six 0·303in Brownings, two fixed in outer left wing and four in right. One 1,605lb (728kg) torpedo on centreline or 2,127lb (954kg) and wing racks for eight rocket projectiles or two 1,000lb (454kg) bombs.

History: First flight (Type 156 prototype) 17 July 1939; (production Mk I) May 1940; service delivery 27 July 1940; first flight (Mk 21, Australia) 26 May 1944; last delivery from new (UK) September 1945, (Australia) October 1945.

Users: Australia, Canada, New Zealand, South Africa, UK (RAF), US (AAF); other countries post-war.

Development: During the critical years 1935–39 the most glaring gap in the RAF's armoury was the lack of any long-range fighter, any cannon-armed fighter and any fighter capable of effective bomber escort and night fighting. Leslie Frise and engine designer Fedden talked at length of the possibility of creating a single type out of the Blenheim and Beaufort families that could meet all demands, but no official requirement was forthcoming — other than the strange F.11/37 Specification for a fighter with a heavily armed cannon turret. Eventually the two Bristol leaders did the obvious thing: they proposed a new twin-Hercules two-seater carrying enough armament to blast anything in front of it out of the sky. By using the wing, tail, landing gear, systems and jigs of the Beaufort it could be put into production quickly. The Air Ministry was enthusiastic and the first of what was to be an historic war-winning aeroplane took the air only six months later. A snub-nosed battleship, it was immensely strong, surprisingly manoeuvrable and a great basis for development. Almost its only operational shortcoming was a tendency to swing on takeoff or landing, and instability at low speeds, which later addition of a large dorsal fin and dihedral tailplane did not fully cure.

continued on page 86 ▶

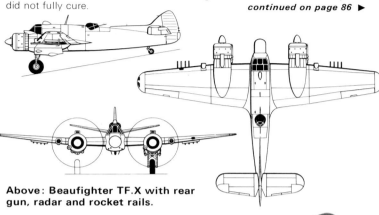

Above: Beaufighter TF.X with rear gun, radar and rocket rails.

Right: Seventh "Beau" built, a Mk IF of 25 Sqn at North Weald (before radar fitted).

Below: Typical Mk VIF, without AI.VIII radar, (probably) in Tunisia in 1942-43.

► Early models barely exceeded 300mph with low-power Hercules and, in the absence of Griffon engines, 450 were fitted with Merlins, but these were less powerful and accentuated instability. Speed was soon judged less important when the need for night fighters to beat the Blitz became urgent. Equipped with AI Mk IV radar the early deliveries to 25 and 29 Sqns were a major reason for the Luftwaffe giving up the Blitz on Britain. Eventually the "Beau" served on all fronts, having thimble-nose AI Mk VII in 1942, tor-

pedoes in 1943, rockets in 1944 and a spate of special installations in 1945. A total of 5,564 were built in England and 364 in Australia, the last fighter and torpedo versions serving with Coastal Command, the Far East Air Force and the RAAF until 1960. To the Luftwaffe it was a feared opponent even 500 miles out in the Atlantic; to the Japanese it was "Whispering death", so named because of the quietness of the sleeve-valve engines. It was sheer luck the "Beau" could be produced in time.

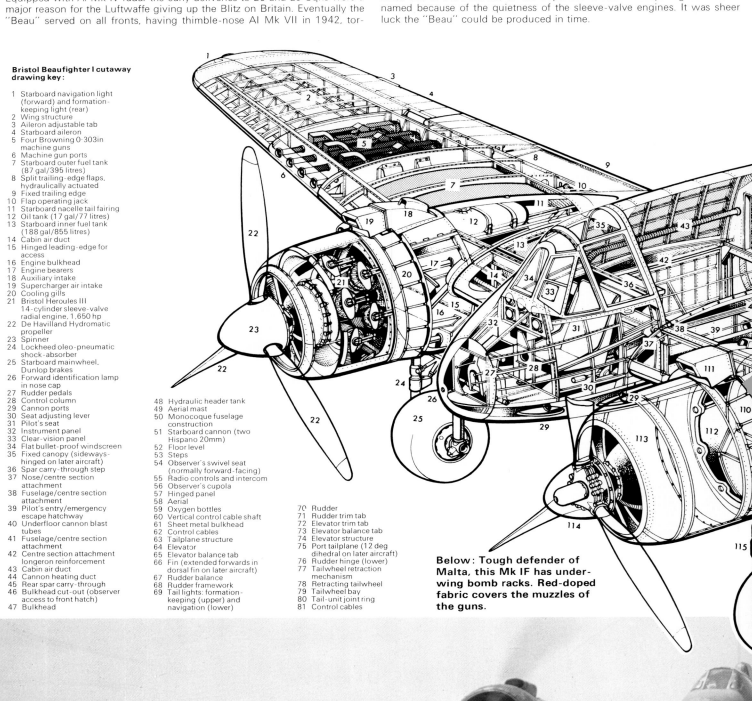

Bristol Beaufighter I cutaway drawing key:

1 Starboard navigation light (forward) and formation-keeping light (rear)
2 Wing structure
3 Aileron adjustable tab
4 Starboard aileron
5 Four Browning 0·303in machine guns
6 Machine gun ports
7 Starboard outer fuel tank (87 gal/395 litres)
8 Split trailing-edge flaps, hydraulically actuated
9 Fixed trailing edge
10 Flap operating jack
11 Starboard nacelle tail fairing
12 Oil tank (17 gal/77 litres)
13 Starboard inner fuel tank (188 gal/855 litres)
14 Cabin air duct
15 Hinged leading-edge for access
16 Engine bulkhead
17 Engine bearers
18 Auxiliary intake
19 Supercharger air intake
20 Cooling gills
21 Bristol Hercules III 14-cylinder sleeve-valve radial engine, 1,650 hp
22 De Havilland Hydromatic propeller
23 Spinner
24 Lockheed oleo-pneumatic shock-absorber
25 Starboard mainwheel, Dunlop brakes
26 Forward identification lamp in nose cap
27 Rudder pedals
28 Control column
29 Cannon ports
30 Seat adjusting lever
31 Pilot's seat
32 Instrument panel
33 Clear-vision panel
34 Flat bullet-proof windscreen
35 Fixed canopy (sideways-hinged on later aircraft)
36 Spar carry-through step
37 Nose/centre section attachment
38 Fuselage/centre section attachment
39 Pilot's entry/emergency escape hatchway
40 Underfloor cannon blast tubes
41 Fuselage/centre section attachment
42 Centre section attachment longeron reinforcement
43 Cabin air duct
44 Cannon heating duct
45 Rear spar carry-through
46 Bulkhead cut-out (observer access to front hatch)
47 Bulkhead

48 Hydraulic header tank
49 Aerial mast
50 Monocoque fuselage construction
51 Starboard cannon (two Hispano 20mm)
52 Floor level
53 Steps
54 Observer's swivel seat (normally forward-facing)
55 Radio controls and intercom
56 Observer's cupola
57 Hinged panel
58 Aerial
59 Oxygen bottles
60 Vertical control cable shaft
61 Sheet metal bulkhead
62 Control cables
63 Tailplane structure
64 Elevator
65 Elevator balance tab
66 Fin (extended forwards in dorsal fin on later aircraft)
67 Rudder balance
68 Rudder framework
69 Tail lights: formation-keeping (upper) and navigation (lower)

70 Rudder
71 Rudder trim tab
72 Elevator trim tab
73 Elevator balance tab
74 Elevator structure
75 Port tailplane (12 deg dihedral on later aircraft)
76 Rudder hinge (lower)
77 Tailwheel retraction mechanism
78 Retracting tailwheel
79 Tailwheel bay
80 Tail-unit joint ring
81 Control cables

Below: Tough defender of Malta, this Mk IF has underwing bomb racks. Red-doped fabric covers the muzzles of the guns.

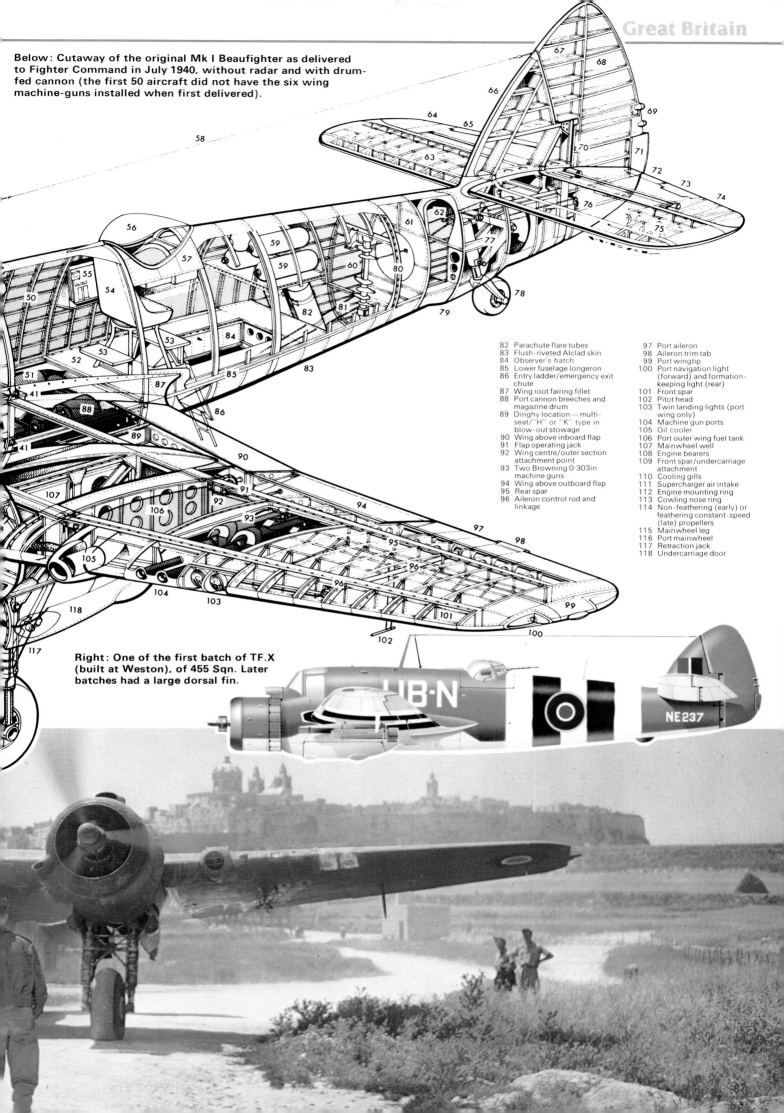

Below: Cutaway of the original Mk I Beaufighter as delivered to Fighter Command in July 1940, without radar and with drum-fed cannon (the first 50 aircraft did not have the six wing machine-guns installed when first delivered).

82 Parachute flare tubes
83 Flush-riveted Alclad skin
84 Observer's hatch
85 Lower fuselage longeron
86 Entry ladder/emergency exit chute
87 Wing root fairing fillet
88 Port cannon breeches and magazine drum
89 Dinghy location—multiseat/"H" or "K" type in blow-out stowage
90 Wing above inboard flap
91 Flap operating jack
92 Wing centre/outer section attachment point
93 Two Browning 0·303in machine guns
94 Wing above outboard flap
95 Rear spar
96 Aileron control rod and linkage

97 Port aileron
98 Aileron trim tab
99 Port wingtip
100 Port navigation light (forward) and formation-keeping light (rear)
101 Front spar
102 Pitot head
103 Twin landing lights (port wing only)
104 Machine gun ports
105 Oil cooler
106 Port outer wing fuel tank
107 Mainwheel well
108 Engine bearers
109 Front spar/undercarriage attachment
110 Cooling gills
111 Supercharger air intake
112 Engine mounting ring
113 Cowling nose ring
114 Non-feathering (early) or feathering constant-speed (late) propellers
115 Mainwheel leg
116 Port mainwheel
117 Retraction jack
118 Undercarriage door

Right: One of the first batch of TF.X (built at Weston), of 455 Sqn. Later batches had a large dorsal fin.

UB-N · NE237

Bristol Type 152 Beaufort

Beaufort I to VIII

Origin: Bristol Aeroplane Company; also made by Department of Aircraft Production, Fishermen's Bend, Australia.
Type: Four-seat torpedo bomber.
Engines: Two 1,130hp Bristol Taurus VI 14-cylinder sleeve-valve radials (most other marks, two 1,200hp Pratt & Whitney Twin Wasp).
Dimensions: Span 57ft 10in (17·63m); length 44ft 2in (13·46m); height 14ft 3in (4·34m).
Weights: Empty 13,107lb (5945kg); loaded 21,230lb (9629kg).
Performance: Maximum speed 260mph (418km/h) clean, 225mph (362km/h) with torpedo; service ceiling 16,500ft (5030m); range 1,600 miles (2575km).
Armament: Various, but typically two 0·303in Vickers K in dorsal turret and one fixed forward-firing in left wing, plus one 0·303in Browning in remote-control chin blister. Alternatively four 0·303in Brownings in wing, two Brownings manually aimed from beam windows and (Mk II) twin Brownings in dorsal turret (final 140 Australian Mk VIII, two 0·50in Brownings in dorsal turret). One 18in torpedo semi-external to left of centreline or bomb load of 2,000lb (907kg).

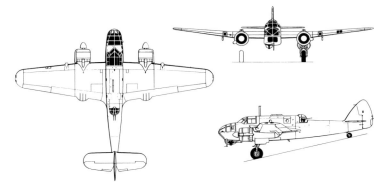

Above: Three-view of Beaufort I Series II with trailing-edge extensions and rearward-firing barbette under the nose.

Below: Australian-built Beaufort VIII with Twin Wasp engines and increased-area fin. All served in the southwest Pacific.

Right: Beauforts in torpedo practice with 217 Sqn, Coastal Command (in 1940, before the grey/white colour scheme was introduced).

Below: A Beaufort II, with Twin Wasp engines, snug in one of the blast pens built at Luqa from Malta's bombed buildings. The unit is probably 86 Sqn, which replaced 217 in Malta when the original squadron flew to Burma.

History: First flight 15 October 1938; first delivery October 1939; first flight of Australian aircraft (Mk V) August 1941; last delivery (Australia) August 1944.
Users: Australia, Turkey, UK.

Development: Derived from the Blenheim, the torpedo-carrying Beaufort was inevitably heavier because the Air Staff demanded a crew of four. Performance on Mercury engines was inadequate and, after studying an installation of the sleeve-valve Perseus, the choice fell on the Taurus, an extremely neat two-row engine only 46in in diameter. A clever installation was schemed for this but it overheated and various engine troubles held the programme back in the early days, but 22 and 42 Sqns of Coastal Command were fully operational by August 1940. As well as laying hundreds of mines they bombed the battlecruiser *Scharnhorst*, torpedoed the *Gneisenau* and sank numerous smaller ships. In 1939 plans were laid for Beaufort production in Australia and, because of the difficulty of supplying engines from Britain, the Australian Mks V-VIII had Twin Wasp engines, most of them made in Australia. A large batch of British Beauforts (Mk II) had this engine, but a Merlin-Beaufort was abandoned and from No 165 the Mk II reverted to later models of Taurus. The total built was 2,080, including 700 built in Australia for duty in the Southwest Pacific. Australian models had a bigger fin and progressed through four series with different equipment, ending with transport and trainer versions. The finest RAAF missions were against Japanese fleets at Normanby Island, in the Timor Sea and around New Guinea and the Solomons.

Below: One of the first Mk I Beauforts to be delivered to 42 Sqn in early 1940. It has an early dorsal turret and under-nose gun but lacks the trailing edge extension-plates.

Bristol Type 142 Blenheim

Types 142 M, 149 and 160 Blenheim/Bisley/ Bolingbroke (data for Blenheim IVL)

Origin: Bristol Aeroplane Company; also made by A. V. Roe, Rootes Securities and Canadian Vickers Ltd.

Type: Three-seat light bomber (IF, IVF, fighter versions).

Engines: Two 920hp Bristol Mercury XV (I, Bolingbroke I, II, 840hp Mercury VIII; Bolingbroke IV series, 750–920hp Twin Wasp Junior, Cyclone or Mercury XX; Blenheim V, 950hp Mercury XXX).

Dimensions: Span 56ft 4in (17·17m) (V, 56ft 1in); length 42ft 9in (13m) (I, 39ft 9in; Bolingbroke III, 46ft 3in; V, 43ft 11in); height 12ft 10in (3·91m) (Bolingbroke III, 18ft).

Weights: Empty 9,790lb (4441kg) (I, Bolingbroke III, 8,700lb; V, 11,000lb); loaded 14,400lb (6531kg) (I, 12,250lb; Bolingbrokes 13,400lb; V, 17,000lb).

Performance: Maximum speed 266mph (428km/h); (I) 285mph; (early IV) 295mph; (Bolingbrokes and V) 245–260mph; initial climb 1,500ft (457m)/min (others similar); service ceiling 31,500ft (9600m) (others similar except Bolingbroke III, 26,000ft); range 1,950 miles (3138km); (I) 1,125 miles; (Bolingbrokes) 1,800 miles; (V) 1,600 miles.

Armament: One 0·303in Vickers K in nose, two 0·303in Brownings in FN.54 chin turret and two 0·303in Brownings in dorsal turret; (I) single fixed Browning and single Vickers K in dorsal turret; (IF, IVF) four fixed Brownings under fuselage; bomb load 1,000lb (454kg) internal (non-standard aircraft had underwing 500lb racks).

History: First flight (Type 142) 12 April 1935; (142M Blenheim I) 25 June 1936; service delivery November 1936; termination of production (VD) June 1943; withdrawal from service (Finland) 1956.

Users: Canada, Finland, France, Greece, Jugoslavia, Lithuania, Portugal, Romania, Turkey, UK (RAF).

Development: It was the newspaper magnate Lord Rothermere who asked the Bristol company to build him a fast executive aircraft to carry a

Above: Almost certainly taken at Northolt shortly after the start of World War II, this line-up of 604 (County of Middlesex) Sqn shows the Mk IF fighter. Soon this acquired the world's first airborne radar and operated mainly by night.

Below: A standard Blenheim I bomber of 60 Sqn, at Lahore, India. By 1940, the year relevant to this colour scheme, many Blenheims were being shipped out of England or withdrawn from operations.

Below: A trio of Blenheim IV bombers of 139 Sqn. On 3 September 1939 one of these was the first Allied aircraft to cross the German frontier in World War II. Before long, however, the Blenheim was found to be extremely vulnerable to modern fighters.

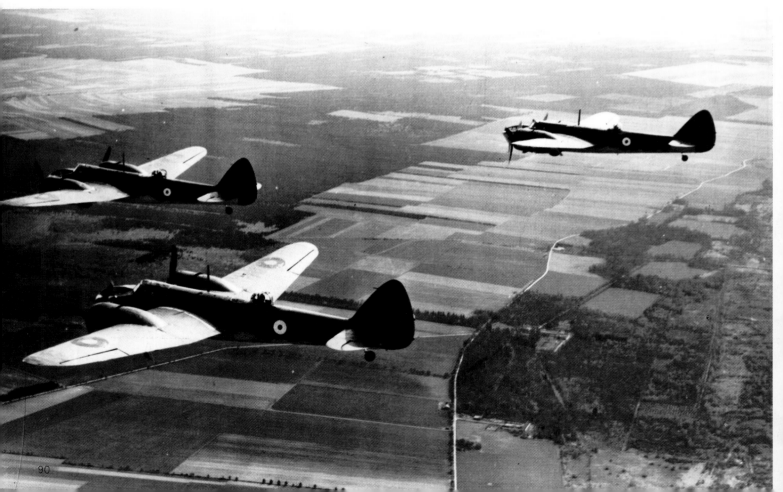

pilot and six passengers at 240mph, appreciably faster than any RAF fighter in 1934. The result was the Type 142, the first modern stressed-skin monoplane in Britain with retractable landing gear, flaps and, after a wait, imported American variable-pitch propellers. Its performance staggered even the designer, Barnwell, for on Air Ministry test it reached 307mph. The inevitable result was the Blenheim bomber, to produce which Barnwell designed a new fuselage with mid-wing and bomb bay beneath it. Pilot and nav/bomb-aimer sat in the neat glazed nose, and a part-retractable dorsal turret was added behind the wing. The Blenheim I was ordered in what were huge quantities to a company almost devoid of work. Ultimately 1,134 were built, many of which made gallant bombing raids early in the war and were then converted to IF fighter configuration (some having the AI Mk III, the first operational fighter radar in the world). The fast new bomber excited intense foreign interest and many were exported to Finland, Turkey, Jugoslavia, Lithuania, Romania and Greece. To provide a nav/bomb-aimer station ahead of the pilot the nose was then lengthened 3ft and this type was named Bolingbroke, a name retained for all the variety of Blenheims built in Canada (the Bolingbroke Mk III being a twin-float seaplane). A revised asymmetric nose was adopted for production in the speedy Mk IV, which later acquired a fighter gun pack (IVF) or a manual rear-firing chin gun (IVL), finally having a two-gun chin turret. Made by Bristol, Avro and Rootes, like the Mk I, the IV was the main combat version with the RAF, 3,297 being delivered and making many daylight missions in many theatres. The heavily armed and armoured two-seat Bisley attack aircraft did not go into production, but the three-seat equivalent did, as the Blenheim Mk V. Heavy and underpowered, the 902 VDs served in North Africa and the Far East.

Above: In the first two years of World War II British and other Allied aircraft were less effective against ships than such Luftwaffe aircraft as the Ju 87 and Ju 88. This Blenheim IV of 107 Sqn was photographed in June 1940 over a burning British ship off Bordeaux.

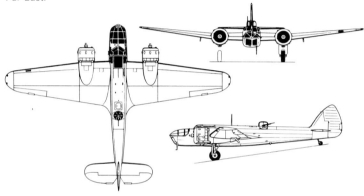

Above: Mk IV as originally delivered without under-nose gun.

Below: The "long-nosed" Blenheim IV, seen here in 1941, provided a proper station in the nose for the navigator/bomb-aimer. It carried more fuel than the Mk I, and needed more power.

De Havilland 82A Tiger Moth

D.H.82 and 82A Tiger Moth I and II, PT-24

Origin: The de Havilland Aircraft Co, Hatfield; most UK production by Morris Motors, Cowley, and overseas production by DH Australia, DH Canada and DH New Zealand, with 200 assembled in Bombay.
Type: Primary trainer.
Engine: (I) 120hp DH Gipsy III inverted four-in-line, (II) 130hp Gipsy Major I.
Dimensions: Span 29ft 4in (8·94m); length (landplane) 23ft 11in (7·29m); height (landplane) 8ft 9½in (2·68m).
Weights: Empty 1,100—1,200lb (525kg); maximum (most) 1,825lb (828kg).
Performance (landplane): Maximum speed 109mph (175km/h); service ceiling 13,600ft (4150m); range 300 miles (482km).
History: First flight 26 October 1931; final delivery March 1945.
Users: (Wartime) Australia, Canada, Egypt, Iran, Iraq, New Zealand, Portugal, S Africa, S Rhodesia, UK (RAF, RN), Uruguay, USA (USAAF).

Development: The original Moth of 1925 was developed into the Gipsy Moth and Genet Moth, both used as standard RAF elementary trainer and liaison aircraft, and then into the Tiger Moth with airframe of a different shape ideally suited for military training with seat-type parachute. Fully aerobatic, the Tiger was used for all ab initio pilot training and in a few cases (eg, in Iraq) carried armament. Total production amounted to 1,611 pre-war, 795 wartime at Hatfield, 3,210 by Morris, 1,520 in Canada, 1,085 in Australia and 344 in New Zealand. A few had floats, and many Canadian Tigers had heated enclosed cockpits and skis (USAAF designation PT-24). Nearly all Tigers were of the more powerful Mk II type, and in 1940 anti-spin strakes were added ahead of the tailplane roots. For a few weeks in 1940

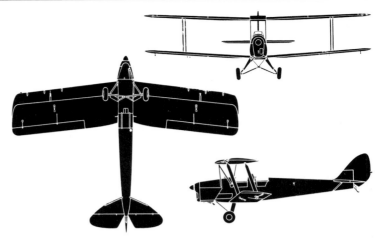

Above: Tiger Moth II (early series) with fuselage bomb rack.

a considerable number were flown by EFTS instructors on armed coastal patrol around Britain. Tigers continued in service in many air forces into the 1950s.

DE HAVILLAND QUEEN BEE (DH.82B)

First flown in 1935, this radio-controlled target was derived from the Tiger Moth by fitting a new all-wood fuselage with only the front cockpit. A few were seaplanes, and by 1944 Hatfield had built 320 and Scottish Aviation 60 for the RAF and Fleet Air Arm for use as targets for AA gunnery and in research programmes.

Left: This Tiger Moth II is typical of the early wartime aircraft, without extended tailplane-root strakes. In 1940 there was fear of German gas attack, and British service aircraft had a square or triangle of special paint, usually ahead of the fin (but sometimes on the fin itself) which changed colour in presence of gas.

Below: This later Mk II, with tailplane-root strakes, is being used for practice bombing in the post-1942 era—in the author's experience, most unusual. EM836, built by Morris Motors at Cowley, is fitted with a blind-flying hood over the rear cockpit and has a training-yellow side stripe.

De Havilland 98 Mosquito

D.H.98 Mosquito I to 43

Origin: The de Havilland Aircraft Company, Hatfield and Leavesden; also built by Airspeed, Percival Aircraft and Standard Motors (Canley); de Havilland Aircraft Pty, Australia; de Havilland Aircraft of Canada.

Type: Designed as high-speed day bomber, see text for subsequent variants.

Engines: (Mks II, III, IV and early VI) two 1,230hp Rolls-Royce Merlin 21 or (late FB.VI) 1,635hp Merlin 25; (Mk IX) 1,680hp Merlin 72; (Mk XVI) Merlin 72 or 1,710hp Merlin 73 or 77; (Mk 30) 1,710hp Merlin 76; (Mk 33) 1,640hp Merlin 25; (Mks 34, 35, 36) 1,690hp Merlin 113/114. Many other variants had corresponding Merlins made by Packard.

Dimensions: Span (except Mk XV) 54ft 2in (16·5m); length (most common) 40ft 6in (12·34m); (bombers) 40ft 9½in; (radar-equipped fighters and Mks 34–38) typically 41ft 9in; (Mk 39) 43ft 4in; height (most common) 15ft 3½in (4·66m).

Weights: Empty (Mks II–VI) about 14,100lb; (Mks VIII–30) about 15,200lb; (beyond Mk 30) about 15,900–16,800lb; maximum gross (Mks II and III) around 17,500lb; (Mks IV and VI) about 22,500lb; (later night fighters) about 20,500lb (but HF.XV only 17,395lb); (Mks IX, XVI and marks beyond 30) typically 25,000lb (11,340kg).

Performance: Maximum speed, from 300mph (TT.39 with M4 sleeve) to 370mph (595km/h) for early night fighters, 380mph (612km/h) for III, IV and VI, 410mph (660km/h) for IX, XVI and 30, and 425mph for 34 and 35; service ceiling, from 30,000ft (9144m) for low-rated naval versions to 34,500ft (10,520m) for most marks, to around 40,000ft (12,190m) for high-blown versions, with Mk XV reaching 44,000ft (13,410m); combat range, typically 1,860 miles (2990km), with naval TFs down at 1,260 miles and PR.34 up to 3,500 miles.

Armament: See text.

History: See text.

Users: Australia, Belgium, Canada, China, Czechoslovakia, France, Jugoslavia, New Zealand, Norway, Soviet Union, Turkey, UK (RAF, RN, BOAC), US (AAF).

continued on page 95 ▶

Right: An FB.VI, the most numerous single mark, attacking a ship in 1944. Cannon were used to help sight the eight rockets, which appear to have hit ideally below the waterline.

Below: A B.IV of 139 Sqn (the second user) at Marham, 1942.

Below: Almost certainly taken at Swanton Morley in early 1942, this scene shows quartets of 500-pounders— then all the ''Mossie'' could carry—going aboard a 105 Sqn B.IV.

De Havilland Mosquito B. Mk IV cutaway drawing key:

1 Starboard navigation light
2 Detachable wingtip
3 Starboard formation light
4 Resin lamp
5 Wing structure
6 Starboard aileron
7 Aileron trim tab
8 Aileron control linkage
9 Flap outer section
10 Flap jack inspection/access panel
11 Starboard outer fuel tanks, 24 Imp gals (109 l) outboard/34 Imp gals (155 l) inboard
12 Starboard inner fuel tanks, 65½ Imp gals (298 l) outboard/78 Imp gals (355 l) inboard
13 Nacelle fairing
14 Oil and coolant radiators (gun heating inboard)
15 Exhaust flame damping shroud
16 Starboard nacelle
17 Coolant pipe fairing
18 Propeller constant speed unit
19 Propeller hub
20 Spinner
21 Three-blade de Havilland hydromatic propeller
22 Navigation headlamp
23 Air thermometer
24 Bomb-aimer's windscreen de-icing jet
25 Bomb-aimer's heated (optically flat) window
26 Bombsight
27 Starboard mainwheel
28 Bomb selector switch panel
29 Bomb-aimer's writing tablet
30 Elbow rest
31 Nose compartment side windows
32 Fireman's axe
33 Camera leads stowage
34 Oxygen bayonet socket
35 Bomb-aimer's kneeling cushion
36 Fire-extinguisher (hand-held)
37 Very cartridge stowage (twelve)
38 Parachute stowage
39 Instrument panel
40 Distributor box
41 Windscreen de-icing jet
42 Folding navigation table (starboard wall)
43 Windscreen panels
44 Control column/brake lever
45 Throttle quadrant
46 Compass

47 Elevator and aileron control linkage
48 Rudder pedal assembly
49 Elevator trim handwheel
50 Wingroot radiator intake
51 Oil and coolant radiators (cabin heating inboard)
52 Intercomm equipment bay
53 Pilot's seat harness
54 Aft-vision canopy blister
55 Pilot's armoured headrest
56 Crash/emergency exit canopy section
57 Signal pistol discharge port
58 T.1154 transmitter
59 Forward spar wing attachment
60 Bulkhead No 2
61 HT power unit
62 Dinghy stowage
63 Hydraulic reservoir
64 Aerial mast
65 Bulkhead No 3
66 De-icing fluid reservoir
67 T.R.9F transmitter/receiver
68 Bulkhead No 4
69 Fuselage longerons
70 Flare chute
71 Bulkhead No 5
72 Fuselage sandwich skinning (ply/balsa/ply)
73 Spiral graining
74 Rudder control linkage
75 Bulkhead No 6
76 Fin attachment
77 Fin structure
78 Starboard tailplane
79 Elevator balance
80 Starboard elevator
81 Aerial attachment
82 Pitot head
83 Rudder balance
84 Rudder upper hinge
85 Rudder structure
86 Rudder trim tab
87 Rudder trim tab control linkage
88 Elevator internal mass balance
89 Tail cone
90 Rear navigation light
91 Elevator trim tab
92 Elevator trim tab control linkage
93 Port elevator
94 Tailplane structure
95 Elevator linkage
96 Tailplane spar support frame
97 Tailwheel retraction mechanism
98 Anti-shimmy (chined) tailwheel
99 Tailwheel leg
100 Bulkhead No 7
101 Rudder internal mass balance
102 Control cables

103 Ventral identification lamps (green/amber)
104 Fuselage lower longeron
105 Aft camera mounting boxes
106 F.24 camera
107 Camera heating cable stowage
108 Aft entry/access door
109 Oxygen bottles (port and starboard)
110 Bomb winch
111 Rear spar attachment
112 Centre-section fuel tanks (two), 68 Imp gals (309 l) each
113 Double wing upper skin (interleaved stringers)
114 Forward spar
115 Coolant header tank
116 Spinner

Top of page: Mosquito II night fighter of 23 Sqn, based at Luqa, Malta, in 1942. No. 23 was a pioneer NF squadron.

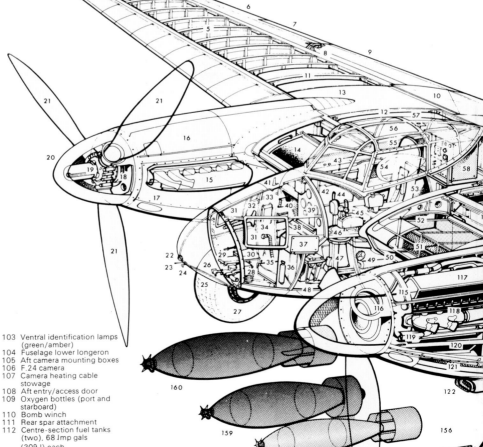

► **Development:** The de Havilland Aircraft Co planned the Mosquito in October 1938 as a high-speed unarmed day bomber, with the added attraction of wooden construction to ease the strain on Britain's hard-pressed materials suppliers. The Air Ministry showed no interest, suggesting instead the Hatfield plant should make wings for existing heavy bombers. In 1940, with extreme reluctance, it was agreed to allow the firm to proceed, the only role thought possible for an unarmed aircraft being reconnaissance. The first prototype, built secretly at Salisbury Hall by a team which grew from 12 in January 1940 to 30 in the summer, was flown painted yellow on 25 November 1940. From it stemmed 7,781 aircraft, built in Britain, Canada and Australia, of the following types;

PR.I Unarmed photo-reconnaissance, with span lengthened from 52ft 6in of prototype to 54ft 2in but still with short engine nacelles.

F.II Night fighter, with pilot and observer side by side, flat bullet-proof windscreen, extended nacelles (as in all subsequent aircraft, with flaps divided into inner and outer segments) and armament of four 20mm Hispano cannon with 300 rounds each under the floor and four 0·303in Brownings with 2,000 rounds each in the nose. First flew 15 May 1941; subsequently fitted with AI Mk IV or V radar or Turbinlight searchlight.

T.III Dual-control trainer, first flown January 1942 but produced mainly after the war (last delivery 1949).

B.IV Unarmed bomber, carrying four 500lb (227kg) bombs internally; first delivered to 105 Sqn at Swanton Morley November 1941, making first operational sortie (Cologne, the morning after the first 1,000-bomber night attack) on 31 May 1942. Some later fitted with bulged bomb bays for 4,000lb (1814kg) bomb.

FB.VI Fighter-bomber and intruder, by day or night; same guns as F.II but two 250lb (113kg) bombs in rear bay and two more (later two 500lb) on wing racks; alternatively, 50 or 100 gal drop tanks, mines, depth charges or eight 60lb rockets. Some fitted with AI radar. Total production 2,584, more than any other mark.

B.VII Canadian-built Mk IV, used in North America only.

PR.VIII Reconnaissance conversion of B.IV with high-blown Merlin 61.

Mk IX Important advance in bomber (B.IX) and reconnaissance (PR.IX) versions; high-blown two-stage engines, bulged bomb bay for 4,000lb bomb or extra fuel, much increased weight, paddle-blade propellers and new avionics (Rebecca, Boozer, Oboe or H_2S Mk VI).

NF.XII Conversion of F.II fitted with new thimble nose containing AI Mk VIII centimetric radar in place of Brownings.

NF.XIII Similar to Mk XII but built as new, with thimble or bull nose and same wing as Mk VI for drop tanks or other stores; flew August 1943.

NF.XV High-altitude fighter with wings extended to 59ft, pressurised cockpit, lightened structure, AI Mk VIII in nose and belly pack of four 0·303in Brownings to combat Ju 86P raiders.

Mk XVI Further major advance with two-stage Merlins, bulged bomb bay and pressurised cockpit. PR.XVI flew July 1943; B.XVI in January 1944, over 1,200 of latter being used for high-level nuisance raids with 4,000lb bombs.

NF.XVII Night fighter with new AI Mk X or SCR.720 (some with tail-looking scanner also); four 20mm each with 500 rounds.

FB.XVIII Dubbed Tse-Tse Fly, this multi-role Coastal Command fighter had low-blown engines and carried a 57mm six-pounder Molins gun with 25 rounds plus four Brownings, as well as eight 60lb rockets or bombs.

NF.XIX Mk XIII developed with AI.VIII or X or SCR.720 in bulged Universal Nose and low-blown Merlin 25s.

B.XX Canadian-built B.IV (USAAF designation F-8).

FB.21 to T.29, Canadian marks with Packard V-1650 (Merlin) engines, not all built.

NF.30 Night fighter with two-stage engines, paddle blades, AI Mk X and various sensing, spoofing or jamming avionics; based on Mk XIX.

PR.32 Extended-span reconnaissance version with Merlin 113/114.

Mk 33 First Royal Navy Sea Mosquito version, with power-folding wings, oleo main legs (in place of rubber in compression), low-blown engines driving four-blade propellers, arrester hook, four 20mm cannon, torpedo (or various bomb/rocket loads), American ASH radar and rocket JATO boost.

PR.34 Strategic reconnaissance version, with 113/114 engines, extra-bulged belly for 1,269 gal fuel (200gal drop tanks) and pressure cabin.

B.35 Equivalent bomber version, with PR and target-tug offshoots.

NF.36 Postwar fighter, with 113/114 engines and AI Mk X.

TF.37 Naval torpedo-fighter; basically Mk 33 with AI/ASV Mk XIII.

NF.38 Final fighter, mainly exported; AI Mk IX, forward cockpit.

TT.39 Complete rebuild by General Aircraft as specialised target tug.

FB.40 Australian-built Mk VI, with PR.40 as conversions.

PR.41 Australian-built derivative of PR.IX and Mk 40.

T.43 Australian trainer; all Australian production had Packard engines.

Facing page, lower: One of the first batch of Mk IV bomber Mosquitoes. Though slower than prototypes of later fighters, they were the fastest aircraft in service in 1941.

Left: Cutaway drawing of a typical Mk IV, the original bomber version that entered squadron service in November 1941, within a year of first flight. Subsequently the bomb load was doubled.

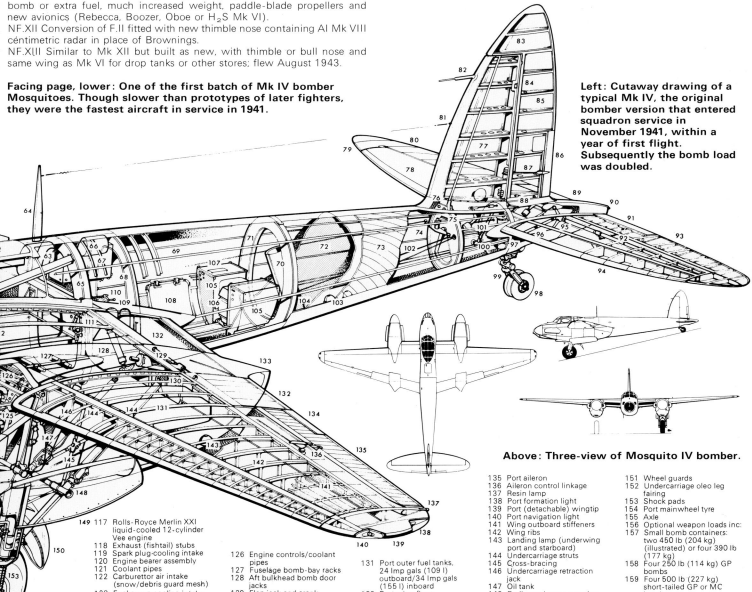

Above: Three-view of Mosquito IV bomber.

117	Rolls-Royce Merlin XXI liquid-cooled 12-cylinder Vee engine	135	Port aileron
118	Exhaust (fishtail) stubs	136	Aileron control linkage
119	Spark plug-cooling intake	137	Resin lamp
120	Engine bearer assembly	138	Port formation light
121	Coolant pipes	139	Port (detachable) wingtip
122	Carburettor air intake (snow/debris guard mesh)	140	Port navigation light
123	Fuel pump cooling intake	141	Wing outboard stiffeners
124	Flame-resistant insert panel	142	Wing ribs
125	Engine accessories	143	Landing lamp (underwing port and starboard)
126	Engine controls/coolant pipes	144	Undercarriage struts
127	Fuselage bomb-bay racks	145	Cross-bracing
128	Aft bulkhead bomb door jacks	146	Undercarriage retraction jack
129	Flap jack and crank	147	Oil tank
130	Undercarriage strut/rear spar attachment	148	Radius rod cross-member
131	Port outer fuel tanks, 24 Imp gals (109 l) outboard/34 Imp gals (155 l) inboard	149	Undercarriage doors
132	Port wing flaps	150	Mudguard
133	Nacelle aft fairing	151	Wheel guards
134	Aileron trim tab	152	Undercarriage oleo leg fairing
		153	Shock pads
		154	Port mainwheel tyre
		155	Axle
		156	Optional weapon loads inc:
		157	Small bomb containers: two 450 lb (204 kg) (illustrated) or four 390 lb (177 kg)
		158	Four 250 lb (114 kg) GP bombs
		159	Four 500 lb (227 kg) short-tailed GP or MC bombs, or
		160	Two 500 lb (227 kg) GP bombs

Fairey Albacore

Albacore I

Origin: Fairey Aviation Co, Hayes and Hamble.
Type: Carrier torpedo bomber.
Engine: 1,065hp Bristol Taurus II 14-cylinder sleeve-valve radial or 1,130hp Taurus XII.
Dimensions: Span 50ft 0in (15·24m); length 39ft 9½in (12·13m); height 15ft 3in (4·65m).
Weights: Empty 7,250lb (3289kg); maximum 10,600lb (4808kg).
Performance: Maximum speed 161mph (259km/h); service ceiling 20,700ft (6309m); range 930 miles (1497km).
Armament: Two 0·303in Vickers K manually aimed from rear cockpit, sometimes 0·303in Browning in lower right wing; 1,610lb (730kg) torpedo or up to 2,000lb (907kg) bombs.
History: First flight 12 December 1938; service delivery December 1939; combat service March 1940; final delivery May 1943.
User: Canada (RCAF), UK (RN).

Development: Planned as a successor to the Swordfish, the Albacore was designed to specification S.41/36. Though still a biplane, with wings braced with wire and covered with fabric, it had an all-metal monocoque fuselage and heated enclosed cabin. Pilot view was superb, and the "Applecore" was in fact very pleasant to fly. Fairey built 803, and though this was only a quarter of the number of Swordfish built (which stayed in production at Blackburn to the end of the war) the Albacore saw intense

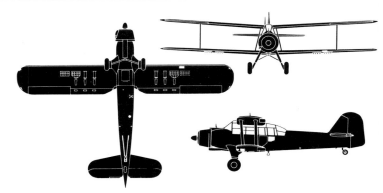

Above: Albacore I with multiple underwing stores racks.

Right: BF759, an Albacore I (the only mark, though there were many detail differences). It is apparently carrying mines on the wing racks, and the flaps are down.

action from the Arctic to Malaya. The first major torpedo attack was at Cape Matapan in March 1941; by 1942 there were 15 FAA squadrons, several of them shore-based in North Africa. Missions included target marking with flares, close support of troops with bombs, minelaying of European harbours and sinking flak-bristling E-boats from mast height. But it never became famous.

Fairey Barracuda

Type 100 Barracuda I, II, III and V

Origin: The Fairey Aviation Company; also built by Blackburn Aircraft, Boulton Paul Aircraft and Westland Aircraft.
Type: Three-seat (Mk V, two-seat) naval torpedo/dive bomber.
Engine: (I) one 1,260hp Rolls-Royce Merlin 30 vee-12 liquid-cooled; (II and III) one 1,640hp Merlin 32; (V) one 2,020hp R-R Griffon 37.
Dimensions: Span (I-III) 49ft 2in (15m); (V) 53ft 0in (16·15m); length (I-III) 39ft 9in (12·12m); (V) 41ft 1in (12·5m); height (I-III) 15ft 1in (4·6m); (V) 13ft 2in (4m).
Weights: Empty (I) 8,700lb (3946kg); (II, III) 9,407lb (4267kg); (V) 9,800lb (4445kg); loaded (I) 13,500lb (6125kg); (II, III) 14,100lb (6395kg); (V) 16,400lb (7450kg).
Performance: Maximum speed (I) 235mph; (II) 228mph (367km/h); (III) 239mph; (V) 264mph (422km/h); initial climb (I-III) 950ft (290m)/min; (V) 2,000ft (610m)/min; service ceiling (I) 18,400ft; (II) 16,600ft (5060m); (III) 20,000ft (6096m); (V) 24,000ft; range with full weapon load, (I, II) 524 miles (845km), (III) 686 miles (1104km); (V) 600 miles.
Armament: (I-III) two 0·303in Vickers K manually aimed in rear cockpit; (V) one fixed 0·50in Browning in wing, no rear guns; one 18in torpedo (1,610 or 1,620lb) or bomb load up to 2,000lb (907kg) under fuselage and wings (including mines or depth charges).
History: First flight 7 December 1940; production Mk I, 18 May 1942; service delivery, 10 January 1943; first Mk V (converted II) 16 November 1944; final delivery January 1946.
User: UK (RN).

Development: The Barracuda was designed to Specification S.24/37 to replace the Albacore, which in turn had been designed to replace the venerable Swordfish. The Albacore was withdrawn from production in 1943, after 800 had been built, while manufacture of Swordfish continued. The Barracuda, however, was in a different class and might have played a greater part in World War II had it not been so severely delayed. The first delay, from 1938–40, was due to abandonment of the proposed Rolls-Royce Exe engine, and the low-rated Merlin was only marginally powerful enough

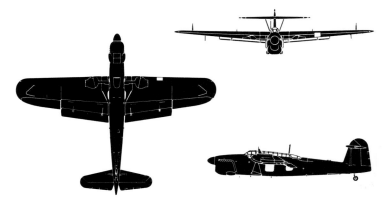

Above: Three-view of Barracuda II, without ASV radar.

as a substitute. Pressure of other programmes held back production two further years, but in May 1943 No 827 Sqn, Fleet Air Arm, was fully equipped and in April 1944 *Victorious* and *Furious* sent 42 aircraft to Kaafjord, Norway, to score 15 direct hits on the *Tirpitz* (for the loss of only two aircraft) in steep dive-bombing with armour-piercing bombs. Later the same month Barracudas were in heavy actions in the Dutch East Indies, and others were equipped to para-drop secret agents (from underwing nacelles) to occupied Europe. The II had more power and four-blade propeller, later receiving ASV.IIN radar, while the III had ASV.10 in an under-fuselage radome. Wartime output of "Barras" was: Fairey 1,131, Blackburn 700, Boulton Paul 692 and Westland 18 (mostly IIs). In 1945 production began on the much more powerful Mk V, later called TF.5, with redesigned structure and accommodation. Radar was housed in a left-wing pod, and later Mk Vs had a tall pointed tail and other changes, but only 30 were built and used mainly for training.

Below: A Barracuda II of a late batch fitted with ASV.IIN radar. Though curious in layout, and underpowered, the "Barra" proved effective in numerous difficult roles.

Fairey Battle

Battle I to IV (data for II)

Origin: The Fairey Aviation Company; and Avions Fairey, Belgium; shadow production by Austin Motors.
Type: Three-seat light bomber.
Engine: One 1,030hp Rolls-Royce Merlin II vee-12 liquid-cooled.
Dimensions: Span 54ft 0in (16·46m); length 42ft 1¾in (12·85m); height 15ft 6in (4·72m).
Weights: Empty 6,647lb (3015kg); loaded 10,792lb (4895kg).
Performance: Maximum speed 241mph (388km/h); initial climb 920ft (280m)/min; service ceiling 25,000ft (7620m); range with bomb load at economical setting 900 miles (1448km).
Armament: One 0·303in Browning fixed in right wing and one 0·303in Vickers K manually aimed in rear cockpit; bomb load up to 1,000lb (454kg) in four cells in inner wings.
History: First flight (prototype) 10 March 1936; production Mk I, June 1937; final delivery January 1941; withdrawal from service 1949.
User: Australia, Belgium, Canada, Poland, South Africa, Southern Rhodesia, Turkey, UK (RAF).

Development: The Battle will forever be remembered as a combat aeroplane which seemed marvellous when it appeared and yet which, within four years, was being hacked out of the sky in droves so that, ever afterward, aircrew think of the name with a shudder. There was nothing faulty about the aircraft; it was simply a sitting duck for modern fighters. Designed to Specification P.27/32 as a replacement for the biplane Hart and Hind, this clean cantilever stressed-skin monoplane epitomised modern design and carried twice the bomb load for twice the distance at 50 per cent higher speed. It was the first aircraft to go into production with the new Merlin engine, taking its mark number (I, II, III or IV) from that of the engine. Ordered in what were previously unheard-of quantities (155, then 500 and then 863 from a new Austin 'shadow factory'), production built up faster than for any other new British aircraft; 15 RAF bomber squadrons were equipped between May 1937 and May 1938. When World War II began, more than 1,000 were in service and others were exported to Poland, Turkey and Belgium (where 18 were built by Avions Fairey). On 2 September 1939 ten Battle squadrons flew to France as the major offensive element of the Advanced Air Striking Force. They were plunged into furious fighting from 10 May 1940 and suffered grievously. On the first day of the Blitzkrieg in the West two members of 12 Sqn won posthumous VCs and four days later, in an all-out attack on German pontoon bridges at Sedan, 71 Battles attacked and 31 returned. Within six months all Battles were being replaced in front-line units and the survivors of the 2,419 built were shipped to Canada or Australia as trainers (many with separate instructor/pupil cockpits) or used as target tugs or test beds.

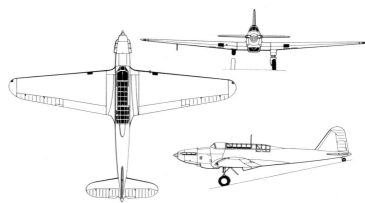

Above: Three-view of a standard Battle bomber (Mks I to IV).

Above: Flap position suggests this Battle has just landed. The yellow roundel ring was added to most Battles after the débacle in France, where the usual roundel was equal radii red, white and blue, often with striped rudder (not fin).

Below: One of the original batch of 150 Battle Is built at Stockport, seen with 106 Sqn in 1937 markings. Light series bomb carriers were usually under the wing.

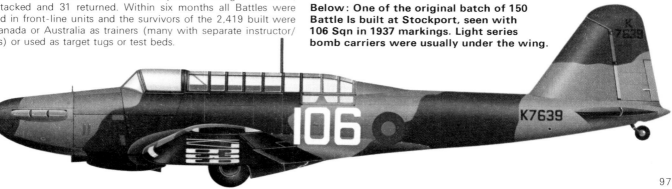

Fairey Firefly

Firefly I to 7 and U.8 to 10

Origin: The Fairey Aviation Company.
Type: Originally two-seat naval fighter; later, see text.
Engine: I, up to No 470, one 1,730hp Rolls-Royce Griffon IIB vee-12 liquid-cooled; from No 471, 1,990hp Griffon XII; Mks 4–7, 2,245hp Griffon 74.
Dimensions: Span (I-III) 44ft 6in (13·55m), (4-6) 41ft 2in (12·55m), (7) 44ft 6in (13·55m); length (I-III) 37ft 7in (11·4m); (4-6) 37ft 11in (11·56m); (7) 38ft 3in (11·65m); height (I-III) 13ft 7in (4·15m); (4-7) 14ft 4in (4·37m).
Weights: Empty (I) 9,750lb (4422kg); (4) 9,900lb (4491kg); (7) 11,016lb (4997kg); loaded (I) 14,020lb (6359kg); (4) 13,927lb (6317kg) clean, 16,096lb (7301kg) with external stores; (7) 13,970lb (6337kg).
Performance: Maximum speed (I) 316mph (509km/h); (4) 386mph (618km/h); initial climb (I) 1,700ft (518m)/min; (4) 2,050ft (625m)/min; service ceiling (I) 28,000ft (8534m); (4) 31,000ft (9450m); range on internal fuel (I) 580 miles (933km); (4) 760 miles (1223km).
Armament: (I) four fixed 20mm Hispano cannon in wings; underwing racks for up to 2,000lb (907kg) of weapons or other stores; (4 and 5) usually similar to I in most sub-types; (6) no guns, but underwing load increased to 3,000lb and varied; (7) no guns, but underwing load remained at 3,000lb and equipment changed.
History: First flight 22 December 1941; first production F.I 26 August

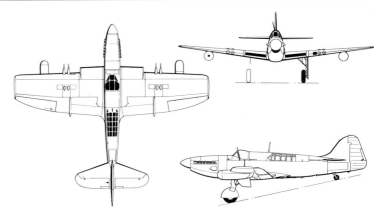

Above: Three-view of Fairey Firefly FR.5.

1942; production FR.4, 25 May 1945; final delivery of new aircraft May 1955.
User: UK (RN); other countries post-war.

Development: Before World War II Fairey designed a light bomber, P.4/34, from which evolved the Fulmar naval two-seat fighter to Specification O.8/38. A total of 600 of these slender carrier-based aircraft served during the war with various equipment and roles. The Firefly followed the same formula, but was much more powerful and useful. Designed to N.5/40 — a merger of N.8/39 and N.9/39 — it was a clean stressed-skin machine with folding elliptical wings housing the four cannon and with the trailing edge provided with patented Youngman flaps for use at low speeds and in cruise. Unlike the installation on the Barracuda, these flaps could be recessed into the wing. The pilot sat over the leading edge, with the observer behind the wing. The main wartime version was the Mk I, widely used from the end of 1943 in all theatres. Fairey and General Aircraft built 429 F.Is, 376 FR.Is with ASH radar and then 37 NF.2 night fighters. There followed the more powerful Mk III, from which derived the redesigned FR.4 with two-stage Griffon and wing-root radiators. There were 160 of these, 40 going to the Netherlands and the rest serving in Korea, with the 352 Mk 5s with folding wings. There were FR, NF and AS (anti-submarine) Mk 5s, and they were followed by the 133 specialised AS.6 versions with all role equipment tailored to anti-submarine operations. The 151 AS.7s rounded off production, this being a redesigned three-seater, with new tail and wings and distinctive beard radiator. More than 400 Fireflies were rebuilt in the 1950s as two-cockpit T.1s or armed T.2s, or as various remotely piloted drone versions (U.8, U.9, U.10). Some were converted as target tugs and for other civil duties.

Left: The wartime marks of Firefly had manually folded wings. These Firefly F.Is are being recovered after a Pacific mission.

Fairey Fulmar

Fulmar I and II

Origin: Fairey Aviation Co, Hayes.
Type: Carrier fighter bomber.
Engine: (I) 1,080hp Rolls-Royce Merlin VIII vee-12 liquid-cooled; (II) 1,300hp Merlin 30.
Dimensions: Span 46ft 4½in (14·14m); length 40ft 2in (12·24m); height 10ft 8in (3·25m).
Weights: Empty (II) 7,015lb (3182kg); normal loaded (II) 9,672lb (4387kg); maximum 10,200lb (4627kg).
Performance: Maximum speed (II) 272mph (440km/h); service ceiling (II) 27,200ft (8300m); range 780 miles (1255km).
Armament: Eight 0·303in Browning fixed in outer wings (some also 0·303in Vickers K manually aimed from rear cockpit), with underwing racks for two 250lb (113kg) bombs.
History: First flight 4 January 1940; service delivery 10 May 1940.
User: UK (RN).

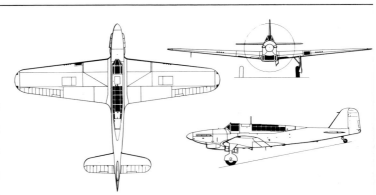

Above: Three-view of Fairey Fulmar I.

Development: Based on the P.4/34 light bomber first flown in January 1937, the Fulmar was designed by a team under Marcel O. Lobelle to meet the Admiralty's urgent need for a modern shipboard fighter. Specification O.8/38 was drawn up around the Fairey design, stipulating eight guns and a seat for a navigator. Development and clearance for service was amazingly rapid, and 806 Sqn equipped with the new fighter in July, reaching the Mediterranean aboard *Illustrious* in August 1940. Later 14 FAA squadrons used the Fulmar, most seeing intensive action in the Mediterranean or aboard CAM (catapult-armed merchant) ships in Atlantic convoys (a Fulmar was shot from a CAM ship as early as August 1941). Against the Regia Aeronautica the Fulmar did well, having adequate performance, good handling and fair endurance. After building 250 Mk I Fairey delivered 350 of the more powerful Mk II, the last in February 1943.

Left: N1854, the prototype Fulmar. This two-seat naval fighter was in service within weeks of its first taking the air.

Fairey Swordfish

Swordfish I-IV

Origin: The Fairey Aviation Company; later Blackburn Aircraft.

Type: Basic role, two-seat torpedo carrier and three-seat spotter reconnaissance; later many other duties.

Engine: (Mk I and early II) one 690hp Bristol Pegasus IIIM3 nine-cylinder radial; (later II onwards) 750hp Pegasus 30.

Dimensions: Span 45ft 6in (13·87m); length (landplane) 35ft 8in (10·87m); height 12ft 4in (3·76m).

Weights: Empty 4,700lb (2134kg); loaded 7,510lb (3410kg).

Performance: Maximum speed 138mph (222km/h); initial climb 1,220ft (372m)/min; service ceiling 19,250ft (5867m); range with full ordnance load 546 miles (879km).

Armament: One fixed 0·303in Vickers, one manually aimed 0·303in Browning or Vickers K in rear cockpit; crutch for 18in 1,610lb torpedo (or 1,500lb mine or 1,500lb of bombs). (Mk II-IV) underwing racks for eight 60lb rockets or other stores.

History: First flight (TSR.II) 17 April 1934; production Mk I December 1935; service delivery February 1936; final delivery June 1944.

User: UK (RN).

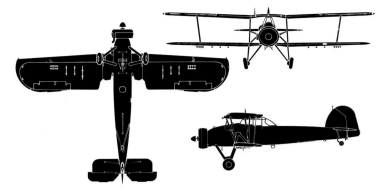

Above: Swordfish IV, the final mark with an enclosed cockpit.

Below: Probably taken in early 1942, this scene shows "Stringbags" huddled on the constricted deck of an escort carrier.

Development: One of the great combat aircraft of history, the well-loved "Stringbag" looked archaic even when new, yet outlasted the aircraft intended to replace it and served valiantly and successfully from countless carriers and rough airstrips from start to finish of World War II. Designed to Specification S.38/34, it derived from an earlier prototype which got into an uncontrollable spin. Designated TSR.II the revised aircraft had a longer, spin-proof body, necessitating sweeping back the upper wing slightly. All-metal, with fabric covering, pre-war Swordfish were often twin-float seaplanes, these usually serving in the three-seat spotter role. Most, however, equipped the Fleet Air Arm's 13 landplane torpedo squadrons and during World War II a further 13 were formed. Stories of this amazingly willing aircraft are legion. One aircraft made twelve minelaying sorties in 24 hours. Another torpedoed an enemy ship in a round trip taking ten hours. A handful based in Malta sank an average of 50,000 tons of enemy vessels (most very heavily armed with flak) every month in 1941-43. The highlight of the Swordfish's career was the attack on the Italian naval base of Taranto, on 10–11 November 1940, when two Swordfish were lost in exchange for the destruction of three battleships, a cruiser, two destroyers and other warships. The Mk II had metal-skinned lower wings for rocket-firing, the III had radar and the IV an enclosed cockpit. From 1940 all production and development was handled by Blackburn, which built 1,699 of the 2,391 delivered.

Right: One of the landplane Swordfish from the second production batch in 1935, pictured in wartime naval camouflage.

Below: No combat aircraft of World War II left a greater legacy of willing work. These paint-flaking Mk IIs, built by Blackburn, were on duty in 1944.

General Aircraft Hamilcar

G.A.L.49 Hamilcar and G.A.L.58 Hamilcar X

Origin: General Aircraft Ltd, Hanworth; production assigned to Birmingham Railway Carriage & Wagon Co, assisted by Co-operative Wholesale Society and AC Cars Ltd.
Type: Heavy assault glider.
Engines: None; (Mk X) two 965hp Bristol Mercury 31 nine-cylinder radial.
Dimensions: Span 110ft 0in (33·53m); length 68ft 0in (20·73m); height 20ft 3in (6·17m).
Weights: Empty 18,400lb (8346kg), (X) 25,510lb (11,571kg); maximum 36,000lb (16,330kg) (some, 37,000lb), (X) 47,000lb (21,319kg).
Performance: Tow limit speed 150mph (241km/h); maximum speed (glider in dive) 187mph (301km/h), (X) 145mph (232km/h); stalling speed 65mph (105km/h).
History: First flight 27 March 1942; service delivery early 1943; first flight (Mk X) February 1945.
User: UK (RAF).

Development: Designed to Specification X.27/40, the Hamilcar was the largest Allied glider to see action. It was planned to carry the vehicles and weapons that could not previously accompany airborne troops, typical loads being a 17-pounder gun and tug, the specially designed Tetrarch and Locust tanks, two Universal Carriers, or a wide range of scrapers, dozers and Bailey bridge gear. Built of wood, the Hamilcar was awesomely big. The two pilots climbed up the right side of the cavernous interior, emerged through a

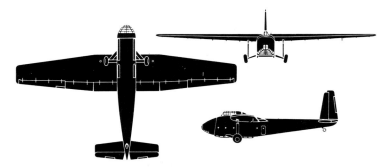

Above: Three-view of Hamilcar with practice landing gear.

Right: Flight near Dishforth, Yorkshire, of the prototype Hamilcar (with gear jettisoned) in 1942, towed by a Halifax II.

roof hatch 15ft (4·6m) above the ground and walked along a sloping and possibly icy roof to their tandem cockpits. Halifax and Stirling tugs pulled over 70 to Normandy in the small hours of D-day, and many more were used in the Market Garden and Rhine-crossing operations. Altogether GAL built 22 and the BRC&W group 390, with another 290 cancelled in early 1945. The Mk X, intended for the Far East, could operate as a conventional aircraft with 3½-ton load, and fly out of its destination field, or carry the full 9-ton load with a tug. Without payload the Mk X, of which only 22 were built by VJ-day, could fly 1,675 miles (2695km).

Gloster Gladiator

S.S.37 Gladiator I and II and Sea Gladiator

Origin: Gloster Aircraft Company.
Type: Single-seat fighter; (Sea Gladiator) carrier-based fighter.
Engine: One 840hp Bristol Mercury IX or IXS nine-cylinder radial; (Gladiator II) usually Mercury VIIIA of similar power.
Dimensions: Span 32ft 3in (9·85m); length 27ft 5in (8·38m); height 10ft 4in (3·17m).
Weights: Empty 3,450lb (1565kg), (Sea Gladiator) 3,745lb; loaded 4,750lb (2155kg), (Sea Gladiator) 5,420lb.
Performance: Maximum speed 253mph (407km/h), (Sea Gladiator) 245mph; initial climb 2,300ft (700m)/min; service ceiling 33,000ft (10,060m); range 440 miles (708km), (Sea Gladiator) 425 miles.
Armament: First 71 aircraft, two 0·303in Vickers in fuselage, one 0·303in Lewis under each lower wing; subsequent, four 0·303in Brownings in same locations, fuselage guns with 600 rounds and wing guns with 400.
History: First flight (S.S.37) September 1934; (Gladiator I) June 1936; (Sea Gladiator) 1938; service delivery March 1937; final delivery April 1940.
Users: Belgium, China, Egypt, Finland, Greece, Iraq, Ireland, Latvia, Lithuania, Norway, Portugal, South Africa, Sweden, UK (RAF, RN).

Development: Air Ministry Specification F.7/30 recognised that future fighters would have to be faster and better armed, but the delay in placing an order extended to a disgraceful 4½ years, by which time war clouds were distantly gathering and the fabric-covered biplane was swiftly to be judged obsolete. Folland's S.S.37 was built as a very late entrant, long after the competition to F.7/30 ought to have been settled. Though less radical than most contenders it was eventually judged best and, as the Gladiator, was at last ordered in July 1935. Features included neat single-bay wings, each of the four planes having small hydraulically depressed drag flaps; cantilever landing gear with Dowty internally sprung wheels; four guns; and, in the production aircraft, a sliding cockpit canopy. Most early production had the Watts wooden propeller, though performance was better with the three-blade metal Fairey-Reed type. The Mk II aircraft introduced desert filters, auto mixture control and electric starter from internal battery. The Sea Gladiator had full carrier equipment and a dinghy. Total production amounted to at least 767, including 480 for the RAF, 60 Sea Gladiators and

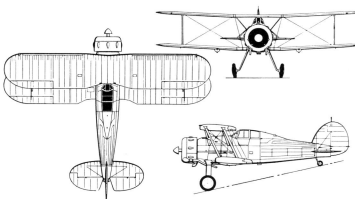

Above: Three-view of Gladiator I (II similar).

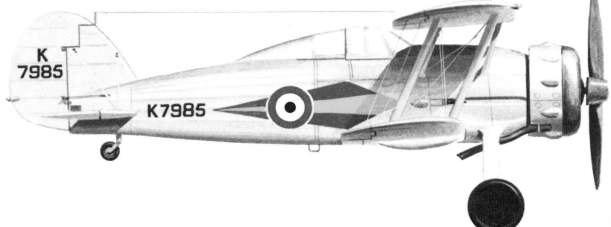

Right: This Gladiator I, seen in the markings of 73 Sqn in 1938, was one of the second production batch, in 1937. In the course of this batch the newly licensed Browning machine gun became available, but the propeller remained the original wooden two-blade type until 1939.

216 exported to 12 foreign countries. Gladiators of the Auxiliary Air Force intercepted the first bombing raid on Britain, over the Firth of Forth in September 1939, and these highly manoeuvrable biplanes were constantly in heroic action for the next three years. Aircraft from the torpedoed *Glorious* operated from a frozen lake in Norway and three Sea Gladiators defended Malta against the Regia Aeronautica from 11 June 1940.

Left: In 1937-40 the Gladiator was Britain's most exported aircraft and the small Gloster staff had to scheme numerous foreign armament and equipment fits. This example is one of a batch of 26 bought by Latvia, a country which relied on Britain for most of its military aircraft.

Below: The spirit of the RAF in the first months of war is captured exquisitely in this photograph of one of the then-new fighters beating up a car on the grass airfield (probably the CO's, because special-bodied coupés were not for junior pilots on a few shillings a day). This machine has the Fairey three-blade metal propeller later made standard.

Below: The Gladiator was the only effective fighter of the Norwegian Army Flying Service when the Luftwaffe invaded in April 1940. This ski-equipped example served with the Jageravdeling (fighter flight) at Oslo-Fornebu. It took on Bf 110s.

Gloster G-41 Meteor

G.41 Meteor I and II

Origin: Gloster Aircraft Company; (post-war, other builders).
Type: Single-seat fighter.
Engines: Two Rolls-Royce centrifugal turbojets (sub-types, see text).
Dimensions: Span 43ft 0in (13·1m); length 41ft 4in (12·6m); height 13ft 0in (3·96m).
Weights: Empty 8,140lb (3693kg); loaded 13,800lb (6260kg).
Performance: Maximum speed (I) 410mph (660km/h); initial climb (I) 2,155ft (657m)/min; service ceiling 40,000–44,000ft (12,192–13,410m); range on internal fuel about 1,000 miles at altitude (1610km).
Armament: Four 20mm Hispano cannon on sides of nose.
History: First flight (prototype) 5 March 1943; squadron delivery (F.I) 12 July 1944.
Users: UK (RAF), US (AAF, one, on exchange); (post-war, many air forces).

Development: Designed to Specification F.9/40 by George Carter, the Gloster G.41 was to have been named Thunderbolt, but when this name was given to the P-47 the Gloster twin-jet became the Meteor. The first Allied jet combat design, it was surprisingly large, with generous wing area.

Above: The sliding canopy identifies this as a Meteor III, in service with 2nd TAF squadrons in early 1945. From the 15th Mk III the engine switched to the new Derwent.

Handley Page Hampden

H.P.52 Hampden I and H.P.53 Hereford I

Origin: Handley Page Ltd; also built by English Electric Co. and Canadian Associated Aircraft.
Type: Four-seat bomber (Hampden, later torpedo bomber and minelayer).
Engines: (Hampden) two 1,000hp Bristol Pegasus XVIII nine-cylinder radials; (Hereford) two 1,000hp Napier Dagger VIII 24-cylinder H-type air-cooled.
Dimensions: Span 69ft 2in (21·98m); length 53ft 7in (16·33m); height 14ft 4in (4·37m).
Weights: Empty (Hampden) 11,780lb (5344kg); (Hereford) 11,700lb (5308kg); loaded (Hampden) 18,756lb (8508kg); (Hereford) 16,000lb (7257kg).
Performance: (Hampden) maximum speed 254mph (410km/h); initial climb 980ft (300m)/min; service ceiling 19,000ft (5790m); range with maximum bomb load 1,095 miles (1762km).
Armament: Originally, one offensive 0·303in Vickers fixed firing ahead, one 0·303in Lewis manually aimed from nose by nav/bomb aimer, one Lewis manually aimed by wireless operator from upper rear position and one Lewis manually aimed by lower rear gunner; bomb load of 4,000lb (1814kg). By January 1940 both rear positions had twin 0·303in Vickers K with

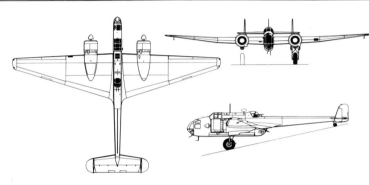

Above: Hampden I in 1940 with twin dorsal and ventral guns.

increased field of fire. Hard points for two 500lb bombs added below outer wings, provision for carrying mines or one 18in torpedo internally.
History: First flight (H.P.52 prototype) 21 June 1936; (production Hampden I) May 1938; (Hereford I) December 1939; termination of production March 1942.
Users: Canada, New Zealand, UK (RAF).

Development: On paper the Hampden, the last of the monoplane bombers to enter RAF service during the Expansion Scheme of 1936–38, was a truly outstanding aircraft. The makers considered it so fast and manoeuvrable they called it "a fighting bomber" and gave the pilot a fixed gun. They judged the three movable guns gave complete all-round defence without the penalties of heavy turrets and, while the Hampden was almost the equal of the big Whitley and Wellington in range with heavy bomb load, it was much faster than either; it was almost as fast as the Blenheim, but carried four times the load twice as far (on only fractionally greater power). Thanks to its well flapped and slatted wing it could land as slowly as 73mph. Designed to B.9/32, the prototype was angular but the production machine, to 30/36, looked very attractive and large orders were placed, eight squadrons being operational at the start of World War II. Hampdens were busy in September 1939 raiding German naval installations and ships (bombing German land was forbidden), until the daylight formations encountered enemy fighters. Then casualties were so heavy the Hampden was taken off operations and re-equipped with much better armament and armour — and, more to the point, used only at night. Despite cramp and near-impossibility of getting from one crew position to another, the "Flying Suitcase" had a successful career bombing invasion barges in the summer of 1940, bombing German heartlands, mine-laying and, finally, as a long-range torpedo bomber over the North Sea and northern Russia. Handley Page built 500, English Electric built 770 and Canadian Associated Aircraft 160. Short Brothers built 100 Herefords which never became operational; many were converted to Hampdens.

Above: Dorsal gunner's view of squadron playmates, probably in 1939. The Hampden was outstandingly manoeuvrable, but was found to be a death-trap in daylight against Bf 109s.

Below: A Hampden of 44 (Rhodesia) Sqn at Waddington, which in 1941-42 became the first unit to convert to the Lancaster. By this time the new roundels had narrow white and yellow rings.

Right: A Hampden I of 455 Sqn, Leuchars. The Hampden was perhaps the RAF bomber that most closely followed the philosophy of Luftwaffe bombers and yet, unlike the British aircraft, the Do 17Z, He 111 and Ju 88 had to continue in the thick of battle through lack of a replacement.

Though this made the early marks poor performers even on two engines, it proved beneficial in the long term, because marvellous engine development by Rolls-Royce transformed the Meteor into a multi-role aircraft with outstanding speed, acceleration and climb and, thanks to its ample proportions, it could be developed for such challenging roles as advanced dual training, long-range reconnaissance and two-seat night fighting. Initial development was protracted, not because of the revolutionary engines but because of the ailerons, tail and nosewheel. Several engines were used. First flight was with two Halford H.1, later called de Havilland Goblin; second, on 12 June 1943, was with Rolls-Royce Welland (W.2B/23); third, on 13 November 1943, was with Metrovick F.2 axials. The Welland, rated at 1,700lb, was chosen for the first batch of 16 Meteor Is, which entered service on 12 July 1944 with one flight of 616 Sqn, the pilots having previously converted. This was eight days before the first nine Me 262s of KG51 entered service. The first task of the new jet was to chase flying bombs, and even the Meteor I soon showed that it was formidable (though the guns jammed on the first encounter and F/O Dean finally succeeded by daringly tipping the missile over with his wing tip). The first major production version was the F.III, with 2,000lb Derwent 1s, extra tankage, sliding canopy and, on the last 15, longer nacelles. The Mk 4 introduced the redesigned Derwent 5 of 3,500lb thrust, with bigger nacelles on a wing whose tips were clipped to improve speed and rate of roll. In 1945 a Mk 4 set a world speed record at 606mph, raised the following year to 616mph. There were many post-war versions.

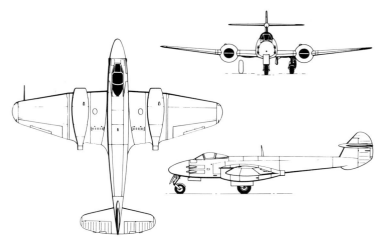

Above: Three-view of the Gloster Meteor F.III, with a sliding canopy, more power and more fuel.

Handley Page Halifax

H.P.57 Halifax I, H.P.59 Mk II Series 1A, III, H.P.61 Mk V, B.VI and VII, C.VIII and A.IX

Origin: Handley Page Ltd; also built by London Aircraft Production Group, English Electric Ltd, Rootes Securities (Speke) and Fairey Aviation Ltd (Stockport).

Type: Seven-seat heavy bomber; later ECM platform, special transport and glider tug, cargo transport and paratroop carrier.

Engines: Four Rolls-Royce Merlin vee-12 liquid-cooled or Bristol Hercules 14-cylinder two-row sleeve-valve radial (see text).

Dimensions: Span (I to early III) 98ft 10in (30·12m); (from later III) 104ft 2in (31·75m); length (I, II, III Srs 1) 70ft 1in (21·36m); (II Srs 1A onwards) 71ft 7in (21·82m); height 20ft 9in (6·32m).

Weights: Empty (I Srs 1) 33,860lb (15,359kg); (II Srs 1A) 35,270lb (16,000kg); (VI) 39,000lb (17,690kg); loaded (I) 55,000lb (24,948kg); (I Srs 1) 58,000lb (26,308kg); (I Srs 2) 60,000lb (27,216kg); (II) 60,000lb; (II Srs 1A) 63,000lb (28,576kg), (III) 65,000lb (29,484kg), (V) 60,000lb; (VI) 68,000lb (30,844kg); (VII, VIII, IX) 65,000lb.

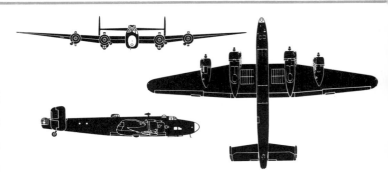

Above: Three-view of the extended-span Halifax B.III Series II (Mk VI similar). Most had H₂S radar fitted.

Left: A Halifax B.III Series II with extended wings and H₂S, serving with 640 Sqn at Leconfield, Yorkshire. Vivid tails were common among the multi-national Halifax units.

Below: An early Halifax II Series I with Boulton-Paul two-gun dorsal turret, on factory test.

Above: L9530 was one of the first production batch in 1940. Serving with 76 Sqn (MP-L) it had manual beam guns and prominent fuel-jettison pipes passing beneath the flaps. The photograph must have been taken from the right beam gun position of an accompanying Halifax, in mid-1941.

Performance: Maximum speed (I) 265mph (426km/h); (II) 270mph (435km/h); (III, VI) 312mph (501km/h); (V, VII, VIII, IX) 285mph (460 km/h); initial climb (typical) 750ft (229m)/min; service ceiling, typically (Merlin) 22,800ft (6950m); (Hercules) 24,000ft (7315m); range with maximum load (I) 980 miles (1577km); (II) 1,100 miles (1770km); (III, VI) 1,260 miles (2030km).
Armament: See text.
History: First flight (prototype) 25 October 1939; (production Mk I) 11 October 1940; squadron delivery 23 November 1940; first flight (production III) July 1943; final delivery 20 November 1946.
Users: Australia, Canada, France (FFL), New Zealand, UK (RAF, BOAC).

Development: Though it never attained the limelight and glamour of its partner, the Lancaster, the "Halibag" made almost as great a contribution to Allied victory in World War II, and it did so in a far greater diversity of roles. Planned as a twin-Vulture bomber to Specification P.13/36 with a gross weight of 26,300lb it grew to weigh 68,000lb as a formidable weapon platform and transport that suffered from no vices once it had progressed through a succession of early changes. By far the biggest change, in the summer of 1937, was to switch from two Vultures to four Merlins (a godsend, as it turned out) and the first 100 H.P.57s were ordered on 3 September 1937. This version, the Mk I, had a 22ft bomb bay and six bomb cells in the wing centre-section. Engines were 1,280hp Merlin X and defensive armament comprised two 0·303in Brownings in the nose turret, four in the tail turret and, usually, two in manual beam positions. The first squadron was No 35 at Linton on Ouse and the first mission Le Havre on the night of 11/12 March 1942. The I Srs 2 was stressed to 60,000lb and the Srs 3 had more fuel. The Mk II had 1,390hp Merlin XX and Hudson-type twin-0·303in dorsal turret instead of beam guns. On the II Srs 1 Special the front and dorsal turrets and engine flame dampers were all removed to improve performance. The II Srs 1A introduced what became the standard nose, a clear Perspex moulding with manually aimed 0·303in Vickers K, as well as the Defiant-type 4×0·303in dorsal turret and 1,390hp Merlin XXII. Later Srs 1A introduced larger fins which improved bombing accuracy; one of these, with radome under the rear fuselage, was the first aircraft to use H₂S ground-mapping radar on active service. In November 1942 the GR.II Srs 1A entered service with Coastal Command, with 0·5in nose gun, marine equipment and often four-blade propellers. The III overcame all the performance problems with 1,650hp Hercules and DH Hydromatic propellers, later IIIs having the wings extended to rounded tips giving better field length, climb, ceiling and range. The IV (turbocharged Hercules) was not built. The V was a II Srs 2A with Dowty landing gear and hydraulics (Messier on other marks), used as a bomber, Coastal GR, ASW and meteorological aircraft. The VI was the definitive bomber, with 1,800hp Hercules 100 and extra tankage and full tropical equipment. The VII was a VI using old Hercules XVI. The C.VIII was an unarmed transport with large quick-change 8,000lb cargo pannier in place of the bomb bay and 11 passenger seats; it led to the post-war Halton civil transport. The A.IX carried 16 paratroops and associated cargo. The III, V, VII and IX served throughout Europe towing gliders and in other special operations, including airdropping agents and arms to Resistance groups and carrying electronic countermeasures (ECM) with 100 Group. Total production amounted to 6,176, by H.P., English Electric, the London Aircraft Production Group (London Transport), Fairey and Rootes, at a peak rate of one per hour. Final mission was by a GR.VI from Gibraltar in March 1952, the Armée de l'Air phasing out its B.VI at about the same time.

Hawker Hurricane
Hurricane I to XII, Sea Hurricane IA to XIIA

Origin: Hawker Aircraft Ltd; also built by Gloster Aircraft, SABCA (Belgium) and Canadian Car & Foundry Inc.
Type: Single-seat fighter; later, fighter-bomber, tank buster and ship-based fighter.
Engine: One Rolls-Royce Merlin vee-12 liquid-cooled (see text for sub-types).
Dimensions: Span 40ft (12·19m); length 32ft (9·75m); (Mk I) 31ft 5in; (Sea Hurricanes) 32ft 3in; height 13ft 1in (4m).
Weights: Empty (I) 4,670lb (2118kg); (IIA) 5,150lb (2335kg); (IIC) 5,640lb (2558kg); (IID) 5,800lb (2631kg); (IV) 5,550lb (2515kg); (Sea H.IIC) 5,788lb (2625kg); loaded (I) 6,600lb (2994kg); (IIA) 8,050lb (3650kg); (IIC) 8,250lb (3742kg); (IID) 8,200lb (3719kg); (IV) 8,450lb (3832kg); (Sea H. IIC) 8,100lb (3674kg).
Performance: Maximum speed (I) 318mph (511km/h); (IIA, B, C) 345–335mph (560–540km/h); (IID) 286mph (460km/h); (IV) 330mph (531km/h); (Sea H. IIC) 342mph (550km/h); initial climb (I) 2,520ft (770m)/min; (IIA) 3,150ft (960m)/min; (rest, typical) 2,700ft (825m)/min; service ceiling (I) 36,000ft (10.973m); (IIA) 41,000ft (12,500m); (rest, typical) 34,000ft (10,365m); range (all, typical) 460 miles (740km), or with two 44 Imp gal drop tanks 950 miles (1530km).
Armament: (I) eight 0·303in Brownings, each with 333 rounds (Belgian model, four 0·5in FN-Brownings); (IIA) same, with provision for 12 guns and two 250lb bombs; (IIB) 12 Brownings and two 250 or 500lb bombs; (IIC) four 20mm Hispano cannon and bombs; (IID) two 40mm Vickers S guns and two 0·303in Brownings; (IV) universal wing with two Brownings and two Vickers S, two 500lb bombs, eight rockets, smoke installation or other stores.
History: First flight (prototype) 6 November 1935; (production Mk I) 12 October 1937; (II) 11 June 1940; (Canadian Mk X) January 1940; final delivery September 1944.
Users: (Wartime) Australia, Belgium, Canada, Czechoslovakia, Egypt, Finland, India, Iran, Iraq, Ireland, Jugoslavia, New Zealand, Poland, Portugal, Romania, South Africa, Soviet Union, Turkey, UK (RAF, RN).

continued on page 106 ▶

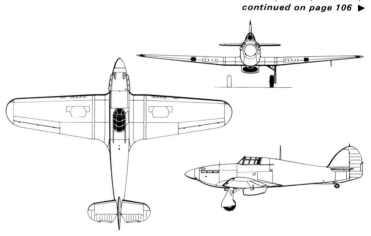

Above: Three-view of Hurricane I (with metal-skinned wings).

Below: The Hawker High-Speed Monoplane (F.36/34) prototype, flown in November 1935 a few weeks after the first Bf 109. Many detail changes were needed to yield the Hurricane.

▶**Development:** Until well into 1941 the Hurricane was by far the most numerous of the RAF's combat aircraft and it bore the brunt of the early combats with the Luftwaffe over France and Britain. Designed by Camm as a Fury Monoplane, with Goshawk engine and spatted landing gear, it was altered on the drawing board to have the more powerful PV.12 (Merlin) and inwards-retracting gear and, later, to have not four machine guns but the unprecedented total of eight. The Air Ministry wrote Specification F.36/34 around it and after tests with the prototype ordered the then-fantastic total of 600 in June 1936. In September 1939 the 497 delivered equipped 18 squadrons and by 7 August 1940 no fewer than 2,309 had been delivered, compared with 1,383 Spitfires, equipping 32 squadrons, compared with 18½ Spitfire squadrons. Gloster's output in 1940 was 130 per month. By this time the Hurricane I was in service with new metal-skinned wings, instead

continued on page 108 ▶

Above: Seen in post-war markings, this Hurricane (Langley-built IIC BD867) shows the constant-speed propeller that became standard in 1941.

Left: Hurricane I of 2e Escadrille "Le Chardon", Regiment I/2 at Diest, 1940. The Belgian aircraft had armament of four 0·5in FN-Brownings.

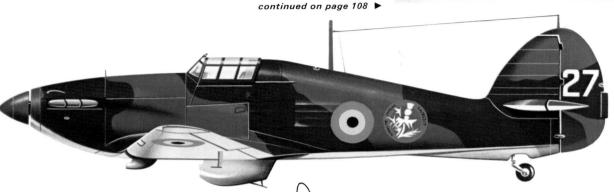

Hawker Hurricane Mk IIC cutaway drawing key:

1 Starboard navigation light
2 Starboard wingtip
3 Aluminium alloy aileron
4 Self-aligning ball-bearing aileron hinge
5 Aft wing spar
6 Aluminium alloy wing skinning (early Hurricanes, fabric)
7 Forward wing spar
8 Starboard landing light
9 Rotol or DH three-blade constant-speed propeller
10 Spinner
11 Propeller hub
12 Pitch-control mechanism
13 Spinner back plate
14 Cowling fairings
15 Coolant pipes
16 Rolls-Royce Merlin XX 12-cylinder engine, 1,185 hp
17 Cowling panel fasteners
18 'Fishtail' exhaust pipes
19 Electric generator
20 Engine forward mounting feet
21 Engine upper bearer tube
22 Engine forward mount
23 Engine lower bearer tubes
24 Starboard mainwheel fairing
25 Starboard mainwheel
26 Low pressure tyre
27 Brake drum (pneumatic brakes)
28 Hand-cranked inertia starter
29 Hydraulic system
30 Bearer joint
31 Auxiliary intake
32 Carburettor air intake
33 Wing root fillet
34 Engine oil drain collector/breather
35 Fuel pump drain
36 Engine aft bearers
37 Magneto
38 Two-stage supercharger
39 Cowling panel attachments
40 Engine tachometer
41 External bead sight
42 Removable aluminium alloy cowling panels
43 Engine coolant header tank
44 Engine firewall (armour-plated backing)
45 Fuselage (reserve) fuel tank (28 gal/127 litres)
46 Exhaust glare shield
47 Control column
48 Engine bearer attachment
49 Rudder pedals
50 Control linkage
51 Centre-section fuel tank (optional)
52 Oil system piping
53 Pneumatic system air cylinder
54 Wing centre-section/front spar girder construction
55 Engine bearer support strut
56 Oil tank (port wing root leading-edge)
57 Port undercarriage ram
58 Port undercarriage well
59 Wing centre-section girder frame
60 Pilot's oxygen cylinder
61 Elevator trim-tab control wheel
62 Radiator flap control lever
63 Entry footstep
64 Fuselage tubular framework
65 Landing lamp control lever
66 Oxygen supply cock
67 Throttle lever
68 Safety harness
69 Pilot's seat
70 Pilot's break-out exit panel
71 Map case
72 Instrument panel
73 Cockpit ventilation inlet
74 Reflector gunsight
75 Bullet-proof windscreen
76 Rear-view mirror
77 Rearward-sliding canopy
78 Canopy frames
79 Canopy handgrip
80 Perspex canopy panels
81 Head/back armour plate
82 Harness attachment
83 Aluminium alloy decking
84 Turnover reinforcement
85 Canopy track
86 Fuselage framework cross-bracing
87 Radio equipment (TR9D/TR133)
88 Support tray
89 Removable access panel
90 Aileron cable drum
91 Elevator control lever
92 Cable adjusters
93 Aluminium alloy wing/fuselage fillet
94 Ventral identification and formation-keeping lights
95 Footstep retraction guide and support rail
96 Radio equipment (R3002)
97 Upward-firing recognition apparatus
98 Handhold
99 Diagonal support
100 Fuselage fairing
101 Dorsal identification light
102 Aerial mast
103 Aerial lead-in
104 Recognition apparatus cover panel
105 Mast support
106 Wire-braced upper truss
107 Wooden fuselage fairing formers
108 Fabric covering
109 Radio antenna
110 All-metal tailplane structure
111 Static and dynamic elevator balance
112 Starboard elevator
113 Light-alloy leading-edge
114 Fabric covering
115 Fin structure
116 Diagonal bracing struts
117 Built-in static balance
118 Aerial stub
119 Fabric-covered rudder
120 Rudder structure
121 Rudder post
122 Rear navigation light
123 Balanced rudder trim tab
124 Wiring
125 Elevator trim tab
126 Fixed balance tab
127 Fabric-covered elevator
128 Tailplane rear spar
129 Tailplane front spar
130 Rudder lower hinge
131 Rudder operating lever
132 Connecting rod
133 Control pulleys
134 Elevator operating lever
135 Tailplane spar attachments
136 Aluminium alloy tailplane/fuselage fairing
137 Tailwheel shock-strut
138 Angled frame rear structure
139 Sternpost
140 Ventral fin
141 Dowty oleo-pneumatic fixed self-centering tailwheel
142 Fin framework
143 Handling-bar socket
144 Fabric covering
145 Swaged tube and steel gusset fitting and through-bolts
146 Upper tube/longeron
147 Rudder cables
148 Wooden stringers
149 Elevator cables
150 Aluminium alloy formers
151 Diagonal brace wires
152 Lower tube/longeron
153 Aluminium alloy former bottom section
154 Retractable entry footstep
155 Wing root fillet
156 Flap rod universal joint
157 Aileron cables
158 Fuselage/wing rear spar girder attachment
159 Main wing fuel tank (port and starboard: 33 gal/150 litres each)
160 Ventral Glycol radiator and oil cooler
161 Front spar wing fixings
162 Cannon forward mounting bracket
163 Cannon fairing
164 Recoil spring
165 Cannon barrels
166 Undercarriage retraction jack

Above: The cutaway drawing shows the very important Hurricane IIC, with more powerful engine and four 20mm cannon, which was the standard production sub-type in 1941.

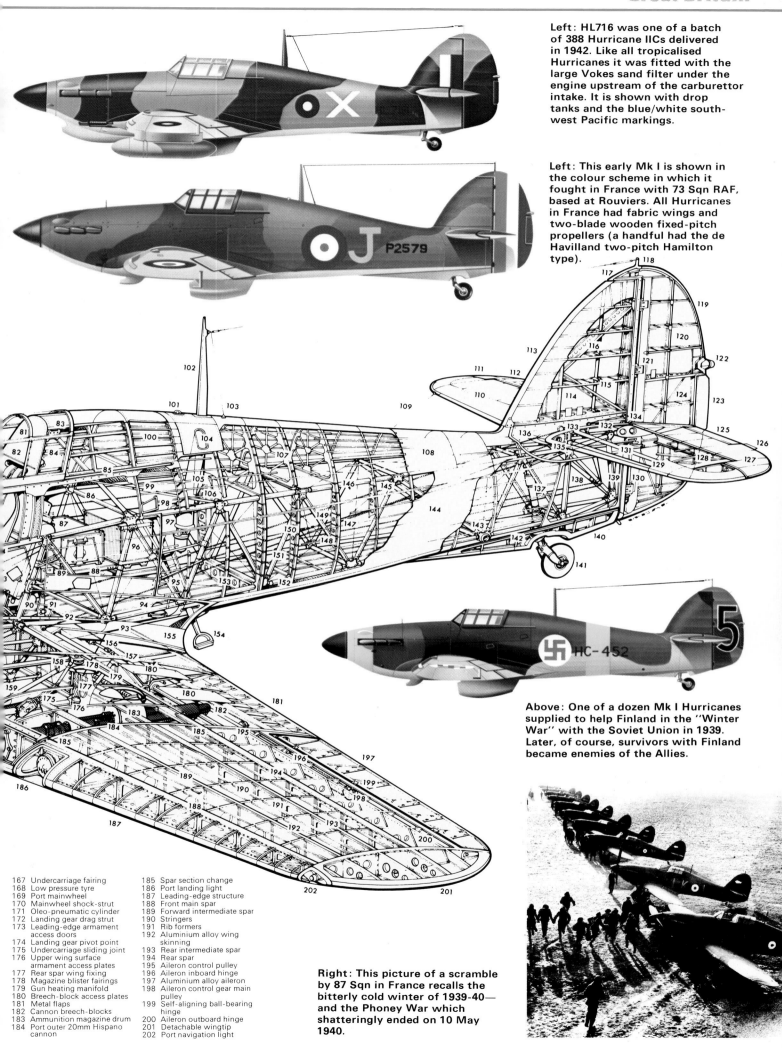

Left: HL716 was one of a batch of 388 Hurricane IICs delivered in 1942. Like all tropicalised Hurricanes it was fitted with the large Vokes sand filter under the engine upstream of the carburettor intake. It is shown with drop tanks and the blue/white south-west Pacific markings.

Left: This early Mk I is shown in the colour scheme in which it fought in France with 73 Sqn RAF, based at Rouviers. All Hurricanes in France had fabric wings and two-blade wooden fixed-pitch propellers (a handful had the de Havilland two-pitch Hamilton type).

Above: One of a dozen Mk I Hurricanes supplied to help Finland in the "Winter War" with the Soviet Union in 1939. Later, of course, survivors with Finland became enemies of the Allies.

167 Undercarriage fairing
168 Low pressure tyre
169 Port mainwheel
170 Mainwheel shock-strut
171 Oleo-pneumatic cylinder
172 Landing gear drag strut
173 Leading-edge armament access doors
174 Landing gear pivot point
175 Undercarriage sliding joint
176 Upper wing surface armament access plates
177 Rear spar wing fixing
178 Magazine blister fairings
179 Gun heating manifold
180 Breech-block access plates
181 Metal flaps
182 Cannon breech-blocks
183 Ammunition magazine drum
184 Port outer 20mm Hispano cannon

185 Spar section change
186 Port landing light
187 Leading-edge structure
188 Front main spar
189 Forward intermediate spar
190 Stringers
191 Rib formers
192 Aluminium alloy wing skinning
193 Rear intermediate spar
194 Rear spar
195 Aileron control pulley
196 Aileron inboard hinge
197 Aluminium alloy aileron
198 Aileron control gear main pulley
199 Self-aligning ball-bearing hinge
200 Aileron outboard hinge
201 Detachable wingtip
202 Port navigation light

Right: This picture of a scramble by 87 Sqn in France recalls the bitterly cold winter of 1939-40—and the Phoney War which shatteringly ended on 10 May 1940.

▶ of fabric, and three-blade variable pitch (later constant-speed) propeller instead of the wooden Watts two-blader. In the hectic days of 1940 the Hurricane was found to be an ideal bomber destroyer, with steady sighting and devastating cone of fire; turn radius was better than that of any other monoplane fighter, but the all-round performance of the Bf 109E was considerably higher. The more powerful Mk II replaced the 1,030hp Merlin II by the 1,280hp Merlin XX and introduced new armament and drop tanks. In North West Europe it became a ground-attack aircraft, and in North Africa a tank-buster with 40mm guns. While operating from merchant-ship catapults and carriers it took part in countless fleet-defence actions, the greatest being the defence of the August 1942 Malta convoy, when 70 Sea Hurricanes fought off more than 600 Axis attackers, destroying 39 for the loss of seven fighters. The Hurricane was increasingly transferred to the Far East, Africa and other theatres, and 2,952 were dispatched to the Soviet Union, some receiving skis. Hurricanes were used for many special trials of armament and novel flight techniques (one having a jettisonable biplane upper wing). Total production amounted to 12,780 in Britain and 1,451 in Canada (after 1941 with Packard Merlins) and many hundreds were exported both before and after World War II.

Right, upper: A Hawker test pilot wringing out a production Mk I Hurricane in the neighbourhood of Brooklands shortly before the outbreak of World War II. The aircraft is one of 24 for Jugoslavia, which in April 1941 fought the Luftwaffe.

Right, lower: Like the Bf 110, Beaufighter and many other aircraft of World War II, the Hurricane was fairly soon outclassed as a daytime dogfighter, yet remained in production almost to the end of the conflict because it was versatile and useful. The last of all was PZ865, a Mk IIC bomber delivered in September 1944 bearing the inscription "The Last of the Many" (as distinct from "The First of the Few").

Below: Idyllic study of a Hurricane I (one of a batch of 600 built by Gloster) in formation with two Spitfires from a batch of 1,000 Mk IIAs and IIBs built at Castle Bromwich. The photograph was taken in 1942 when hundreds of these former front-line machines were standard equipment at OTUs (Operational Training Units), advanced flying training schools and such mundane establishments as Ferry Pilot Pools and Maintenance Units. It was common to cruise with the hood open when there was little likelihood of meeting the enemy.

Hawker Typhoon

Typhoon IA and IB

Origin: Hawker Aircraft Ltd; built by Gloster Aircraft Company.
Type: Single-seat fighter bomber.
Engine: (Production IB) one 2,180hp Napier Sabre II, 24-cylinder flat-H sleeve-valve liquid-cooled.
Dimensions: Span 41ft 7in (12·67m); length 31ft 11in (9·73m); height 15ft 3½in (4·66m).
Weights: Empty 8,800lb (3992kg); loaded 13,250lb (6010kg).
Performance: Maximum speed 412mph (664km/h); initial climb 3,000ft (914m)/min; service ceiling 35,200ft (10,730m); range (with bombs) 510 miles (821km), (with drop tanks) 980 miles (1577km).
Armament: (IA) 12 0·303in Brownings (none delivered); (IB) four 20mm Hispano cannon in outer wings, and racks for eight rockets or two 500lb (227kg) (later 1,000lb, 454kg) bombs.
History: First flight (Tornado) October 1939; (Typhoon) 24 February 1940; (production Typhoon) 27 May 1941; final delivery November 1945.
Users: Canada, New Zealand, UK (RAF).

Development: The Typhoon's early life was almost total disaster. Though the concept of so big and powerful a combat aircraft was bold and significant, expressed in Specification F.18/37, the Griffon and Centaurus engines were ignored and reliance was placed on the complex and untried Vulture and Sabre. The former powered the R-type fighter, later named Tornado, which ground to a halt with abandonment of the Vulture in early 1941. The N-type (Napier), named Typhoon, was held back six months by the desperate need for Hurricanes. Eventually, after most painful development, production began at Gloster Aircraft in 1941 and Nos 56 and 609 Sqns at Duxford began to re-equip with the big bluff-looking machine in September of that year. But the Sabre was unreliable, rate of climb and performance at height were disappointing and the rear fuselage persisted in coming apart. There was much talk of scrapping the programme, but, fortunately for the Allies, the snags were gradually overcome. In November 1942 the Typhoon suddenly sprang to favour by demonstrating it could catch and destroy the fastest fighter-bombers in the Luftwaffe which were making low-level hit-and-run raids. In 1943 "Tiffy" squadrons shot-up and blasted everything that moved in northern France and the Low Countries, and in the summer of 1944 the hundreds of Typhoons — by now thoroughly proven and capable of round-the-clock operation from rough forward strips — formed the backbone of 2nd Tactical Air Force attack strength, sending millions of cannon shells, rockets and heavy bombs into German ground forces and in a single day knocking out 175 tanks in the Falaise gap. Gloster built 3,315 of the 3,330 Typhoons, the final 3,000-odd having a clear bubble hood instead of a heavy-framed cockpit with a car-type door on each side.

Above: One of the main run of Mk IB Typhoons with the neat and unobstructed sliding teardrop hood. User is 54 Sqn.

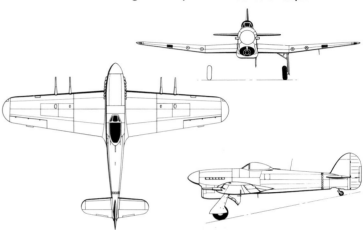

Above: Typhoon IB with sliding teardrop hood and whip aerial.

Left: A bombed-up Typhoon IB of 198 Sqn operating from Martragny, France, in July 1944.

Below: 175 Sqn servicing crew and an armourer with two 500-pounders tend one of the earlier Mk IB Typhoons with car-type doors and a rigid radio mast.

Hawker Tempest

Tempest V and VI

Origin: Hawker Aircraft Ltd; Mk II, Bristol Aeroplane Company.
Type: Single-seat fighter bomber.
Engine: (V) one 2,180hp Napier Sabre II 24-cylinder flat-H sleeve-valve liquid-cooled; (VI) one 2,340hp Sabre V.
Dimensions: Span 41ft (12·5m); length 33ft 8in (10·26m); height 16ft 1in (4·9m).
Weights: Empty 9,100lb (4128kg); loaded 13,500lb (6130kg).
Performance: Maximum speed (V) 427mph (688km/h); (VI) 438mph (704km/h); initial climb 3,000ft (914m)/min; service ceiling, about 37,000ft (11,280m); range (bombs, not tanks) 740 miles (1191km).
Armament: Four 20mm Hispano cannon in outer wings; underwing racks for eight rockets or up to 2,000lb (907kg) bombs.
History: First flight (prototype Mk V) 2 September 1942; (Mk I) 24 February 1943; (production V) 21 June 1943; (Mk II) 28 June 1943; (prototype VI) 9 May 1944; (production II) 4 October 1944.
Users: New Zealand, UK (RAF).

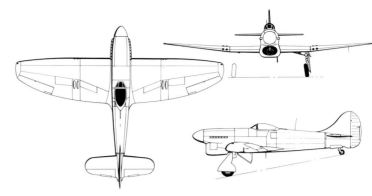

Above: Three-view of Hawker Tempest V (post-war, Mk 5).

Below: Test-flying a production Tempest V from the Hawker factory at Langley in 1944.

Development: The Typhoon was noted for its thick wing — occasional erratic flight behaviour at high speeds was traced to compressibility (local airflow exceeding the speed of sound), which had never before been encountered. In 1940 Hawker schemed a new laminar-flow wing with a root thickness five inches less and an elliptic planform rather like a Spitfire. This was used on the Typhoon II, ordered in November 1941 to Specification F.10/41, but there were so many changes the fighter was renamed Tempest. Fuel had to be moved from the thinner wing to the fuselage, making the latter longer, and a dorsal fin was added. The short-barrel Mk V guns were buried in the wing. Though the new airframe could take the promising Centaurus engine it was the Sabre-engined Mk V that was produced first, reaching the Newchurch Wing in time to destroy 638 out of the RAF's total of 1,771 flying bombs shot down in the summer of 1944. After building 800 Mk Vs Hawker turned out 142 of the more powerful Mk VI type with bigger radiator and oil coolers in the leading edge. After much delay, with production assigned first to Gloster and then to Bristol, the Centaurus-powered Mk II — much quieter and nicer to fly — entered service in November 1945, and thus missed the war. A few Mks 5 and 6 (post-war designations) were converted as target tugs.

Below: This Tempest was built as a Mk VI (note wing-root oil coolers) but was modified by Napier's team at Luton to have an annular radiator (at one time, a ducted spinner).

Miles Master and Martinet

M.9 Master I, M.19 Mk II, M.27 Mk III and M.25 Martinet

Origin: Phillips & Powis (Miles Aircraft) Ltd, Woodley, South Marston, Doncaster and Sheffield.

Type: Advanced trainer (see text).

Engine: (I) 715hp Rolls-Royce Kestrel 30 vee-12; (II) 870hp Bristol Mercury 20 nine-cylinder radial; (III) 825hp Pratt & Whitney R-1535-SB4G Twin Wasp Junior 14-cylinder two-row radial; (Martinet) 870hp Mercury 20 or 30.

Dimensions: Span (I) 39ft 0in (11·89m), (some I, all II, III) 35ft 7in or 35ft 9in (10·90m), (M'net) 39ft 1in (11·92m); length (I) 30ft 5in (9·27m), (II) 29ft 6in (8·99m), (III) 30ft 2in (9·20m), (M'net) 30ft 11in (9·425m); height (I) 10ft 0in (3·05m), (II, III) 9ft 3in (2·80m), (M'net) 11ft 7in (3·53m).

Weights: Empty (I) 4,308lb (1954kg), (II) 4,130lb (1873kg), (III) 4,210lb (1910kg), (M'net) 4,559lb (2068kg); maximum (I) 5,573lb (2528kg), (II) 5,312lb (2410kg), (III) 5,400lb (2449kg), (M'net) 6,750lb (3062kg).

Performance: Maximum speed (I) 226mph (364km/h), (II) 260mph (418km/h), (III) 231mph (372km/h), (M'net) 240mph (386km/h); service ceiling (typical) 27,500ft (8380m); range (typical) 500 miles (805km).

Armament: (Most, except Martinet) provision for 0·303in Browning in outer right wing, and for eight practice bombs.

History: First flight (Kestrel) 1937, (I) 1938, (production I) March 1939, (II) November 1939, (III) 1940, (Martinet) 24 April 1942.

Users: Ireland, Portugal, Turkey, UK (RAF).

Development: The brilliant Miles team produced the Kestrel as a private

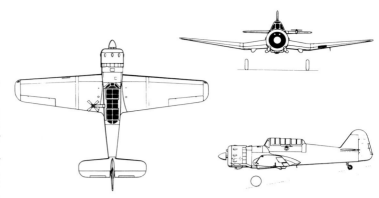

Above: Three-view of Miles M.25 Martinet I.

venture in 1937 to meet an obvious need. After the Air Ministry had spent 18 months trying to buy inferior machines it placed the biggest order for trainers in RAF history, and eventually 900 Master I were delivered. Though 70mph slower than the Kestrel they were ideal in preparing pilots for the new monoplane fighters. Kestrel stocks soon dwindled, and the fastest Master, the Mk II, was urgently planned — only to be held up a year while American engines were imported (for the Master III) in case there were too few Mercuries. Eventually 602 Mk III ran in parallel with 1,747 Mk II, several hundred II being converted in 1942 to tow Hotspur gliders (it involved cropping the bottom of the rudder). The slightly larger and heavier Martinet was the RAF's first purpose-designed tug; 1,724 were built, followed by 66 radio-controlled Queen Martinets. All the Master family were a delight to fly.

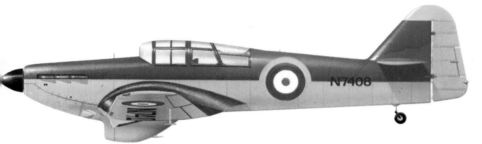

Left: N7408 was the first production Master I. Later the canopy was made taller, with framed, inclined windscreen.

Below: All production Masters had the instructor seated at the rear in a seat which could be elevated. By opening the roof hatch the instructor could then land safely, with good forward vision. This is a Mk III, with the 14-cylinder Twin Wasp Junior. The otherwise similar Mk II had a Mercury, of larger diameter. The airframe was mainly wooden.

Short S.25 Sunderland

Sunderland I, II, III and V (MR.5)

Origin: Short Brothers; also built by Blackburn Aircraft.
Type: Ocean patrol and anti-submarine flying boat with typical crew of 13.
Engines: (1) four 1,010hp Bristol Pegasus 22 nine-cylinder radials; (II, III) four 1,065hp Pegasus XVIII; (V) four 1,200hp Pratt & Whitney R-1830-90B Twin Wasp 14-cylinder two-row radials.
Dimensions: Span 112ft 9½in (34·39m); length 85ft 4in (26m); height 32ft 10½in (10·1m).
Weights: Empty (III) 34,500lb (15,663kg); (V) 37,000lb (16,783kg); maximum loaded (III) 58,000lb (26,308kg); (V) 60,000lb (27,216kg).
Performance: Maximum speed (III, V) 213mph (343km/h); initial climb (III) 720ft (220m)/min; (V) 840ft (256m)/min; service ceiling (typical) 17,400ft (5300m); maximum range (III, V) 2,900 miles (4670km).
Armament: (I) eight 0·303in Browning, two in nose turret, four in tail turret and two manually aimed from hatches behind each wing root; internal load of 2,000lb (907kg) of bombs, depth charges, mines and pyrotechnics wound out on rails under inner wing to release position inboard of inner engines; (II, III) as (I) but twin-0·303 in dorsal turret in place of manual guns; (V) as (II, III) with addition in some aircraft of four fixed 0·303in in nose; in many aircraft, also two manually aimed 0·5in Brownings from beam windows, usually in place of dorsal turret.

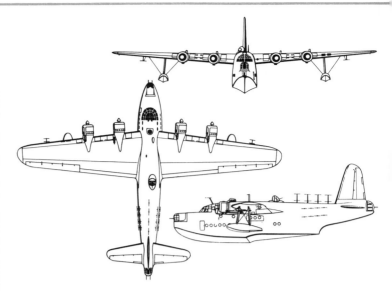

Above: Three-view of Sunderland III (with ASV radar).

Short S.29 Stirling

Stirling I to V

Origin: Short Brothers, Rochester and Belfast.
Type: (I–III) heavy bomber with crew of 7/8; (IV) glider tug and special transport; (V) strategic transport.
Engines: (I) four 1,595hp Bristol Hercules XI 14-cylinder sleeve-valve radials; (II) 1,600hp Wright R-2600-A5B Cyclone; (III, IV, V) 1,650hp Bristol Hercules XVI.
Dimensions: Span 99ft 1in (30·2m); length (except V) 87ft 3in (26·6m); (V) 90ft 6¾in (27·6m); height 22ft 9in (6·94m).
Weights: Empty (I) 44,000lb (19,950kg); (III) 46,900lb (21,273kg); (IV, V, typical) 43,200lb (19,600kg); maximum loaded (I) 59,400lb (26,943kg); (III, IV, V) 70,000lb (31,750kg).
Performance: Maximum speed (I–III) 270mph (435km/h); (IV, V) 280mph (451km/h); initial climb (typical) 800ft (244m)/min; service ceiling (I–III) 17,000ft (5182m); range (III) 590 miles (950km) with 14,000lb bombs or 2,010 miles (3235km) with 3,500lb; range (IV, V) 3,000 miles (4828km).
Armament: (I) two 0·303in Brownings in nose and dorsal turrets and

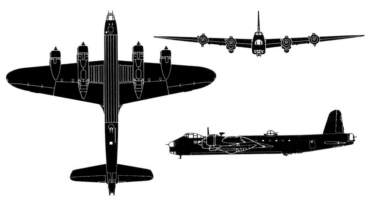

Above: Three-view of Stirling I with FN.64 ventral turret.

Below: One of an excellent series of colour photographs taken on a visit to 149 Sqn, one of the first users, in 1941. The immense landing gears gave trouble; the pilot's job was hard.

History: First flight 16 October 1937; service delivery May 1938; final delivery June 1946.
Users: Australia, Norway, South Africa, UK (RAF, BOAC); other countries post-war.

Development: Derived from the Imperial Airways Empire flying boat to meet Specification R.2/33, the Sunderland marked a vast improvement in fighting capability over previous biplane boats. From the outbreak of World War II these capacious, reliable and long-ranged boats were cease-lessly at work finding and sinking U-boats, rescuing seamen from sunken vessels and engaging in such fierce battles with enemy aircraft that the Sunderland became known to the Luftwaffe as "Flying Porcupine". Many times single Sunderlands fought off five or more hostile aircraft, and once a Sunderland shot down three of the eight Ju 88s that attacked it and drove off the others. The III introduced an improved planing bottom and, from 1940, all marks carried ASV radar, Leigh lights and an increasing amount of avionics. Altogether 739 were built, 240 by Blackburn at Dumbarton, the Mk III being by far the most numerous. After the war the MR.5 was used on the Berlin Airlift, in Korea, against terrorists in Malaya, on the North Greenland Expedition and by the French Navy and RNZAF. Last sortie was on 15 May 1959 from Singapore, from where Sunderlands had begun combat duty 21 years earlier.

Left: L2163 was one of the first Mk I Sunderlands, pictured here in 1939 sea-green/purple camouflage and large fin stripes.

four in tail turret, plus (early batches) two in remote control ventral turret; maximum bomb load 18,000lb (8165kg) in fuselage and inner wings; (II, III) as (I) but different dorsal turret; (IV) sole armament, tail turret; (V) none.
History: First flight 14 May 1939; (production Mk I) May 1940; final delivery (V) November 1945.
User: UK (RAF).

Development: Though extremely impressive, with vast length, un-precedented height and even two separate tailwheels, the Stirling was unpopular. Partly owing to short wing span it had a poor ceiling and sluggish manoeuvrability except at low level. Though it carried a heavy bomb load,

it could not carry bombs bigger than 2,000lb (the largest size when the design was completed in 1938). Operations began with daylight attacks in February 1941, soon switched to night, and by 1943 the Stirling was regarded mainly as a tug and transport and carrier of ECM jamming and spoofing devices for 100 Group. The RAF received 2,221 bomber versions, excluding the two Mk II conversions, and Short's new Belfast plant finally built 160 of the streamlined Mk V transports which carried 40 troops or heavy freight.

Left: Stirling I of 214 Sqn, based at Stradishall.

Below: Last-minute briefing for a Stirling crew before one of the early raids, which were in daylight. Note the tailwheels and original dorsal turret.

Supermarine Walrus and Sea Otter
Walrus I, II; Sea Otter ASR.II

Origin: Supermarine Aviation Works (Vickers) Ltd, Southampton; most W and all SO (except prototype) by Saro, East Cowes.
Type: Designed as shipboard reconnaissance (see text).
Engine: One Bristol nine-cylinder radial, (W I) 620hp Pegasus IIM2 pusher, (W II) 775hp Pegasus VI, (SO) 870hp Mercury 30 tractor.
Dimensions: Span (W) 45ft 10in (13·97m), (SO) 46ft 0in; length (W) 37ft 7in (11·45m); (SO) 39ft 4¾in (12·0m); height (land) (W) 15ft 3in (4·65m), (SO) 16ft 2in (4·90m).
Weights: Empty (W) 4,900lb (2223kg), (SO) 6,805lb (3087kg); maximum (W) 7,200lb (3266kg), (SO) 10,000lb (4536kg).
Performance: Maximum speed (W II) 135mph (217km/h), (SO) 150mph (241km/h); maximum range (W) 600 miles (966km), (SO) 725 miles (1170km).
History: First flight (Seagull I) 1922, (Seagull V) 21 June 1933, (Sea Otter) August 1938; final delivery (W) January 1944, (SO) July 1946.
Users: (W) Argentina, Australia, Egypt, Ireland, New Zealand, UK (RAF, RN); (SO) UK (RAF, RN).

Development: Supermarine built various Lion-engined Seagulls in the 1920s and produced the Pegasus-engined Seagull V for the RAAF. In 1935 the name Walrus was given to the Fleet Air Arm three-seater spotter carried by surface warships, with Lewis or Vickers K guns on two open ring mounts and up to 760lb (345kg) bombs or depth charges. Supermarine built 287, followed by 453 wooden-hulled Mk II by Saro. Nearly all served as ASR (air/sea rescue) amphibians, with crew of four; they rescued more than 5,000 aircrew around Britain and the bulk of more than 2,500 in the Mediterranean theatre. The Sea Otter had a fractionally better performance, and two dorsal hatches which when screwed upright formed wind-breaks for three Vickers K. It could get off the water with a much heavier overload, but deliveries did not begin until 5½ years after first flight. Saro built 290, used widely in the Far East. Both amphibians served as utility transports, Admirals' barges and in various electronic and other special roles.

Below: Air-to-air portrait of a Walrus in early-wartime camouflage. The Walrus was probably the oldest basic aircraft design to participate in the war; it proved extremely useful.

Above: A fine 1940 action-shot of a green/purple Walrus leaving the catapult of the battleship Warspite.

Below: Three-view of Walrus I with landing gear down.

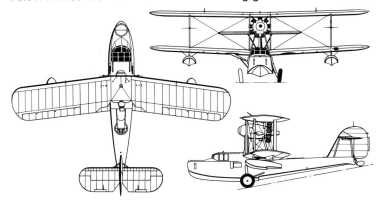

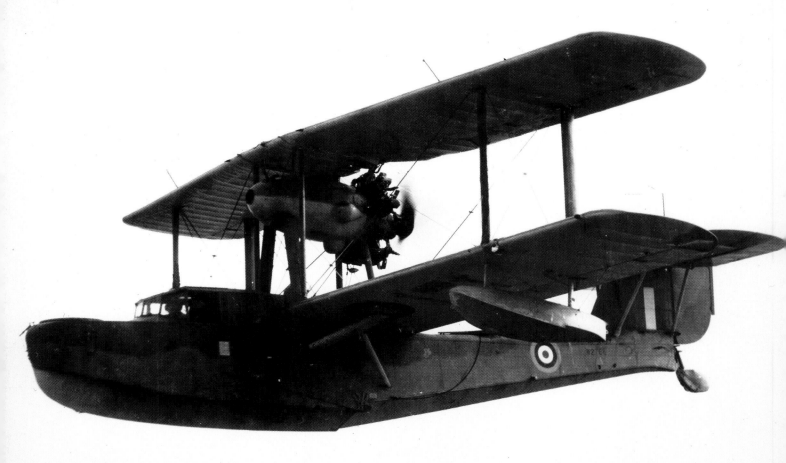

Supermarine Spitfire and Seafire

Mks I to 24 and Seafire I, III, XV, XVII and 45-47

Origin: Supermarine Aviation Works (Vickers) Ltd; also built by Vickers-Armstrongs, Castle Bromwich, and Westland Aircraft; (Seafire) Cunliffe-Owen Aircraft and Westland.

Type: Single-seat fighter, fighter-bomber or reconnaissance; (Seafire) carrier-based fighter.

Engine: One Rolls-Royce Merlin or Griffon vee-12 liquid-cooled (see text).

Dimensions: Span 36ft 10in (11·23m), clipped, 32ft 2in, or, more often, 32ft 7in (9·93m), extended, 40ft 2in (12·24m); length 29ft 11in (9·12m), later, with two-stage engine, typically 31ft 3½in (9·54m), Griffon engine, typically 32ft 8in (9·96m), final (eg Seafire 47) 34ft 4in (10·46m); height 11ft 5in (3·48m), with Griffon, typically 12ft 9in (3·89m).

Weights: Empty (Mk I) 4,810lb (2182kg); (IX) 5,610lb (2545kg); (XIV) 6,700lb (3040kg); (Sea.47) 7,625lb (3458kg); maximum loaded (I) 5,784lb (2624kg); (IX) 9,500lb (4310kg); (XIV) 10,280lb (4663kg); Sea.47) 12,750lb (5784kg).

Performance: Maximum speed (I) 355–362mph (580km/h); (IX) 408mph (657km/h); (XIV) 448mph (721km/h); (Sea.47) 451mph (724km/h); initial climb (I) 2,530ft (770m)/min; (IX) 4,100ft (1250m)/min; (XIV) 4,580ft (1396m)/min; (Sea.47) 4,800ft (1463m)/min; range on internal fuel (I) 395 miles (637km); (IX) 434 miles (700km); (XIV) 460 miles (740km); (Sea.47) 405 miles (652km).

Armament: See text.

History: First flight (prototype) 5 March 1936; (production Mk I) July 1938; final delivery (Mk 24) October 1947.

Users: (Wartime) Australia, Canada, Czechoslovakia, Egypt, France, Italy (CB), Jugoslavia, Netherlands, Norway, Poland, Portugal, South Africa, Soviet Union, Turkey, UK (RAF, RN), US (AAF).

Development: Possibly the most famous combat aircraft in history, the Spitfire was designed by the dying Reginald Mitchell to Specification F.37/34 using the new Rolls-Royce PV.12 engine later named Merlin. It was the first all-metal stressed-skin fighter to go into production in Britain. The following were main versions.

I Initial version, 450 ordered in June 1936 with 1,030hp Merlin II, two-blade fixed-pitch propeller and four 0·303in Browning guns. Later Mk IA with eight guns, bulged canopy and three-blade DH v-p propeller and Mk IB with two 20mm Hispano and four 0·303. Production: 1,566.

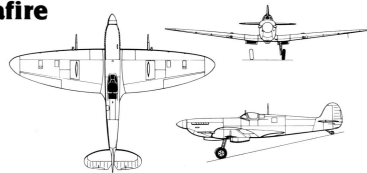

Above: Three-view of the mass-produced Spitfire IX.

II Mk I built at Castle Bromwich with 1,175hp Merlin· XII and Rotol propeller. Production: 750 IIA (eight 0·303), 170 IIB (two 20mm, four 0·303).

III Single experimental model; strengthened Mk I with many changes.

IV Confusing because Mk IV was first Griffon-engined, one built. Then unarmed Merlin photo-reconnaissance Mk IV delivered in quantity. Production: 229.

V Like PR.IV powered by 1,440hp Merlin 45, many detail changes, main fighter version 1941—42 in three forms: VA, eight 0·303; VB, two 20mm and four 0·303; VC "universal" wing with choice of guns plus two 250lb (113kg) bombs. All with centreline rack for 500lb (227kg) bomb or tank. Many with clipped wings and/or tropical filter under nose. Production: VA, 94; VB, 3,923; VC, 2,447.

VI High-altitude interim interceptor, 1,415hp Merlin 47, pressurised cockpit, two 20mm and four 0·303. Production: 100.

VII High-altitude, extended wing-tips, new 1,660hp Merlin 61 with two-stage supercharger (and symmetrical underwing radiators); retractable tailwheel, later broad and pointed rudder. Pressurised cockpit. Production: 140.

VIII Followed interim Mk IX, virtually unpressurised Mk VII in LF (low-altitude, clipped), F (standard) and HF (high-altitude, extended) versions. Production: 1,658. ***continued on page 116***▶

Below: Fine scramble picture of a section of 417 (RCAF) Sqn in Italy, early 1943. The aircraft are tropicalised Spitfire VCs, among the slowest variants ever to be used.

▶**IX** Urgent version to counter Fw 190, quick lash-up of V with Merlin 61; again LF, F and HF versions, plus IXE with two 20mm and two 0·5in. Production: 5,665.

X Pressurised photo-reconnaissance, Merlin 77, whole leading edge forming fuel tank. Production: 16.

XI As X but unpressurised, 1,760hp Merlin 63A or 1,655hp Merlin 70. Mainstay of Photo Reconnaissance Unit 1943–45. Production: 471.

XII Low altitude to counter Fw 190 hit-and-run bomber, 1,735hp Griffon III or IV, strengthened VC or VIII airframe, clipped. Production: 100.

XIII Low-level reconnaissance, low-rated 1,620hp Merlin 32, four 0·303. Production: 16.

XIV First with two-stage Griffon, 2,050hp Mk 65 with deep symmetric radiators and five-blade propeller, completely redesigned airframe with new fuselage, broad fin/rudder, inboard ailerons, retractable tailwheel. F.XIV, two 20mm and four 0·303; F.XIVE, two 20mm and two 0·5in; FR.XIVE, same guns, cut-down rear fuselage and teardrop hood, clipped wings, F.24 camera and extra fuel. Active in 1944, destroyed over 300 flying bombs. Production: 957.

XVI As Mk IX but 1,705hp Packard Merlin 266; LF.IXE, E-guns and clipped, many with teardrop hood, extra fuel. Production: 1,054.

XVIII Definitive wartime fighter derived from interim XIV, extra fuel, stronger, F and FR versions, some of latter even more fuel and tropical equipment. Production: 300.

continued on page 118 ▶

Above: No 92 Sqn was one of the first to receive the Spitfire VB, in March 1941. The Mk V was the most numerous of all (6,464).

Below: The VB is again the subject of this cutaway, which emphasises the basic simplicity of the structure and the relatively large size of the Hispano 20mm cannon, fed by 60-round drums. Structural heart of the wing was the single spar and strong D-box ahead of it.

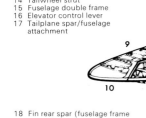

Supermarine Spitfire VB cutaway drawing key:

1 Aerial stub attachment
2 Rudder upper hinge
3 Fabric-covered rudder
4 Rudder tab
5 Sternpost
6 Rudder tab hinge
7 Rear navigation light
8 Starboard elevator tab
9 Starboard elevator structure
10 Elevator balance
11 Tailplane front spar
12 IFF aerial
13 Castoring non-retractable tailwheel
14 Tailwheel strut
15 Fuselage double frame
16 Elevator control lever
17 Tailplane spar/fuselage attachment
18 Fin rear spar (fuselage frame extension)
19 Fin front spar (fuselage frame extension)
20 Port elevator tab hinge
21 Port elevator
22 IFF aerial
23 Port tailplane
24 Rudder control lever
25 Cross shaft
26 Tailwheel oleo access plate
27 Tailwheel oleo shock-absorber
28 Fuselage angled frame
29 Battery compartment
30 Lower longeron
31 Elevator control cables
32 Fuselage construction
33 Rudder control cables
34 Radio compartment
35 Radio support tray
36 Flare chute
37 Oxygen bottle
38 Auxiliary long-range fuel tank (29 gal/132 litres)
39 Dorsal formation light
40 Aerial lead-in
41 HF aerial
42 Aerial mast
43 Cockpit aft glazing
44 Voltage regulator
45 Canopy track
46 Structural bulkhead
47 Headrest
48 Perspex canopy
49 Rear-view mirror
50 Entry flap (port)
51 Air bottles (alternative rear fuselage stowage)
52 Sutton harness
53 Pilot's seat (moulded Bakelite)
54 Datum longeron
55 Seat support frame
56 Wing root fillet
57 Seat adjustment lever
58 Rudder pedal frame
59 Elevator control connecting tube
60 Control column spade grip
61 Trim wheel
62 Reflector gunsight
63 External windscreen armour
64 Instrument panel
65 Main fuselage fuel tank (48 gal/218 litres)
66 Fuel tank/longeron attachment fittings
67 Rudder pedals
68 Rudder bar
69 Kingpost
70 Fuselage lower fuel tank (37 gal/168 litres)
71 Firewall/bulkhead
72 Engine bearer attachment
73 Steel tube bearers
74 Magneto
75 'Fishtail' exhaust manifold
76 Gun heating intensifier
77 Hydraulic tank
78 Fuel filler cap
79 Air compressor intake
80 Air compressor
81 Rolls-Royce Merlin 45 or 50 series 12-cylinder engine, 1,470 hp
82 Coolant piping
83 Port cannon magazine fairing
84 Flaps
85 Aileron control cables
86 Aileron push tube
87 Bellcrank
88 Aileron hinge
89 Port aileron
90 Machine-gun access panels
91 Port wingtip
92 Port navigation light
93 Leading-edge skinning
94 Machine-gun ports (protected)
95 Port wing cannon
96 Three-blade constant-speed propeller (Rotol or DH)
97 Spinner
98 Propeller hub
99 Coolant tank
100 Cowling fastening
101 Engine anti-vibration mounting pad
102 Engine accessories
103 Engine bearers
104 Main engine support member
105 Coolant pipe
106 Exposed oil tank
107 Port mainwheel
108 Mainwheel fairing
109 Carburettor air intake
110 Stub/spar attachment
111 Mainwheel leg pivot point
112 Main spar
113 Leading-edge ribs (diagonals deleted for clarity)
114 Mainwheel leg shock-absorber
115 Mainwheel fairing
116 Starboard mainwheel
117 Angled axle
118 Hispano 20mm cannon barrel support fairing
119 Spar cut-out
120 Mainwheel well
121 Gun heating pipe
122 Flap structure
123 Cannon magazine fairing
124 Cannon magazine drum (60 rounds)
125 Machine-gun support brackets
126 Gun access panels
127 Browning 0·303in machine-gun barrels
128 Machine-gun ports
129 Ammunition boxes (350 rpg)
130 Starboard aileron construction
131 Wing ribs
132 Single-tube outer spar section
133 Wingtip structure
134 Starboard navigation light

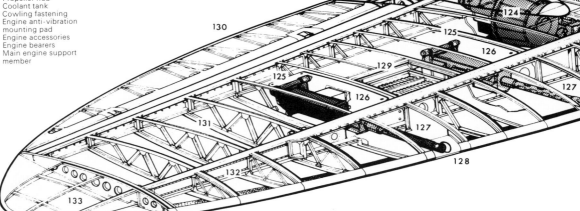

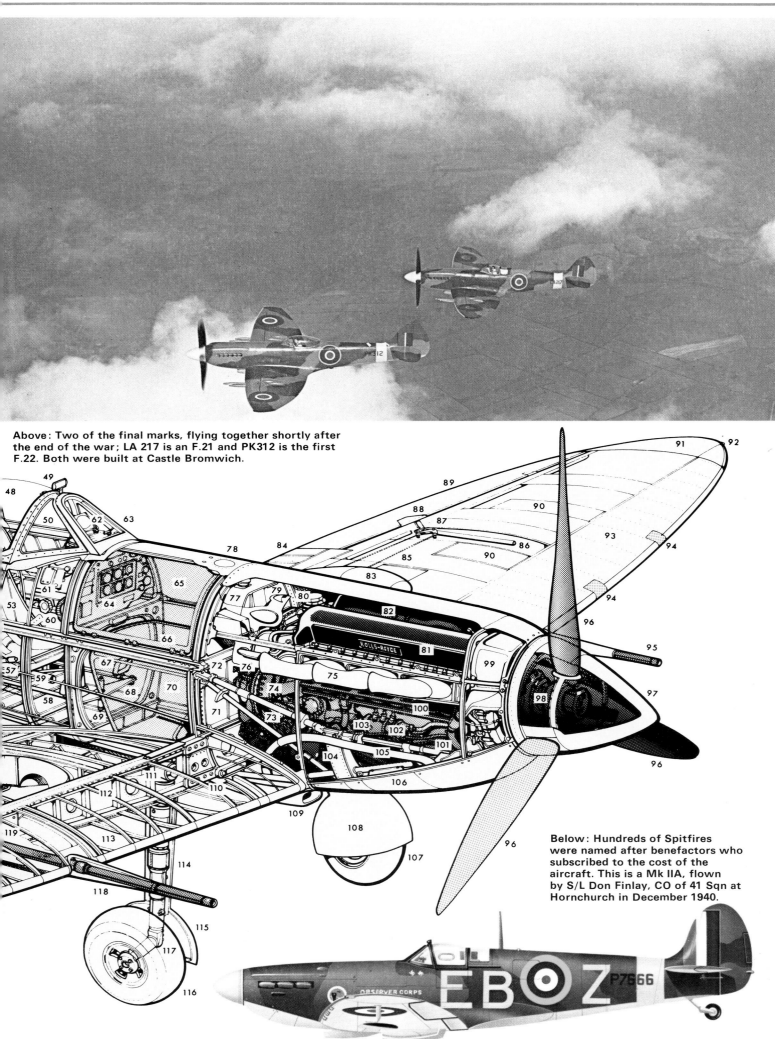

Above: Two of the final marks, flying together shortly after the end of the war; LA 217 is an F.21 and PK312 is the first F.22. Both were built at Castle Bromwich.

Below: Hundreds of Spitfires were named after benefactors who subscribed to the cost of the aircraft. This is a Mk IIA, flown by S/L Don Finlay, CO of 41 Sqn at Hornchurch in December 1940.

▶ **XIX** Final photo-reconnaissance, 2,050hp Griffon 65 and unpressurised, then Griffon 66 with pressure cabin and increased wing tankage; both option of deep slipper tank for 1,800 mile (2900km) range. Made last RAF Spitfire sortie, Malaya, 1 April 1954. Production: 225.

21 Post-war, redesigned aircraft with different structure and shape, 2,050hp Griffon 65 or 85, four 20mm and 1,000lb (454kg) bombs. Production: 122.

22 Bubble hood, 24-volt electrics, some with 2,375hp Griffon 65 and contraprop. Production: 278.

24 Redesigned tail, short-barrel cannon, zero-length rocket launchers. Production: 54. Total Spitfire production 20,334.

Seafire IB Navalised Spitfire VB, usually 1,415hp low-rated Merlin 46. Fixed wings but hook and slinging points. Conversions: 166.

IIC Catapult spools, strengthened landing gear, 1,645hp Merlin 32 and four-blade propeller. Various sub-types, Universal wing. Production: 262 Supermarine, 110 Westland.

III Manual double-fold wing, 1,585hp Merlin 55M, various versions. Production: 870 Westland, 350 Cunliffe-Owen.

XV (Later F.15) 1,850hp Griffon VI, four-blade, asymmetric radiators, cross between Seafire III and Spitfire XII. Production: 390.

XVII (F.17) Increased fuel, cut-down fuselage and bubble hood. Production: (cut by war's end): 232.

45 New aircraft entirely, corresponding to Spitfire 21; Griffon 61 (five-blade) or 85 (contraprop); fixed wing, four 20mm. Production: 50.

46 Bubble hood like Spitfire 22. Production: 24.

47 Navalised Spitfire 24, hydraulically folding wings, carb-air intake just behind propeller, increased fuel. Fought in Malaya and Korea. Production: 140. Total Seafires: 2,556.

Right: An unusual angle on a Spitfire VB rolling towards the photographic aircraft. There were no tabs on the ailerons, but there was one on each tail control surface.

Below: BL479 was yet another Spitfire VB, but a much later one than those in other illustrations. It had the LF (low-altitude fighter) clipped wing used on several other Merlin marks.

Vickers Vildebeest and Vincent

Vildebeest I to IV and Vincent (Types 267, 286 and 266)

Origin: Vickers (Aviation) Ltd.
Type: (Vildebeest) torpedo bomber with crew of three (IV, two); (Vincent) three-seat general purpose.
Engine: One 660hp Bristol Pegasus IIM3 nine-cylinder radial (Spanish CASA-built Vildebeest) 595hp Hispano 12Nbr; (Vildebeest IV) 825hp Bristol Perseus VIII nine-cylinder sleeve-valve radial.
Dimensions: Span 49ft (14·94m); length 36ft 8in (11·17m); (Vildebeest IV) 37ft 8in; height 17ft 9in (5·42m).
Weights: Empty 4,229lb (1918kg); (Vildebeest IV) 4,724lb; maximum loaded 8,100lb (3674kg); (Vildebeest IV) 8,500lb
Performance: Maximum speed 142mph (230km/h); (Vildebeest IV) 156mph; initial climb 765ft (233m)/min; service ceiling 17,000ft (5182m); range 1,250 miles (2000km).
Armament: One 0·303in Vickers fixed firing forward, one 0·303in Lewis manually aimed from rear cockpit; external bomb load of 1,000lb (454kg) or (Vildebeest) one 18in (457mm) torpedo.
History: First flight (Vildebeest) April 1928; service delivery (Vildebeest I) April 1933; (Vincent) late 1934; final delivery (Vildebeest IV) November 1937.
Users: UK (RAF); briefly Australia and New Zealand.

Development: Designed to replace the Horsley as the RAF's coastal-defence torpedo-bomber, the Vildebeest (originally Vildebeeste) appeared with an uncowled Jupiter engine and two widely separated cockpits, the pilot being just ahead of the rectangular slatted wings and having a superb view. The production Mk I had a third cockpit and early Pegasus engine. After building 176, Vickers delivered 18 Mk IV with the first sleeve-valve

Above: K4163 was a Vildebeest III. Large and surprisingly capable, the Vildebeest was not totally obsolete at the start of World War II and saw much valiant action.

engines ever cleared for service, fully cowled and driving three-blade Rotol propellers. In 1939 the Vildebeest was the RAF's only torpedo carrier, and in 1941 Nos 36 and 100 Sqns at Singapore fought alone to try to hold back the Japanese, the last two aircraft surviving until March 1942 in Sumatra. The later Vincent, of which 171 were built between 1934 and 1936, served throughout the Middle East and Africa until 1942. One of its main replacements was the aircraft described below.

Vickers Wellesley

Type 287, Wellesley I and II

Origin: Vickers (Aviation) Ltd.
Type: Two-seat general-purpose bomber.
Engine: One 925hp Bristol Pegasus XX nine-cylinder radial.
Dimensions: Span 74ft 7in (22·73m); length 39ft 3in (11·96m); height 12ft 4in (3·75m).
Weights: Empty 6,369lb (2889kg); maximum loaded (except record flight) 11,100lb (5035kg).
Performance: Maximum speed 228mph (369km/h); initial climb 1,200ft (366m)/min; service ceiling 33,000ft (10,060m); range with bomb load 1,110 miles (1786km).
Armament: One 0·303in belt-fed Vickers in right wing firing ahead, one Vickers K manually aimed from rear cockpit; four 500lb (227kg) or eight 250lb bombs in streamlined containers, originally fitted with bomb doors, under wings.
History: First flight 19 June 1935; service delivery April 1937; final delivery May 1938.
User: UK (RAF), possibly passed on to other Middle East countries.

Development: Vickers built a large biplane to meet the RAF G.4/31 specification, but it was so humdrum the company board decided at their own risk to build a monoplane using the radical geodetic (metal basketwork) construction developed for airships by their structural wizard B.N. (later Sir Barnes) Wallis. The result was so dramatically superior the Air Ministry lost its fear of monoplanes and bought 176 as the Wellesley. Distinguished by great span, high aspect ratio, extreme cruise efficiency and a most reliable engine (identical in size to the Jupiter but of virtually twice the power) it was natural to form a special Long-Range Development Flight. Three aircraft, with three seats, extra fuel and long-chord cowlings, took off from Ismailia, Egypt, on 5 November 1938; one landed at Koepang and the other two reached Darwin, 7,162 miles (11,525km) in 48 hours non-stop. In World War II Wellesleys were extremely active in East Africa, Egypt, the Middle East and surrounding sea areas until late 1942.

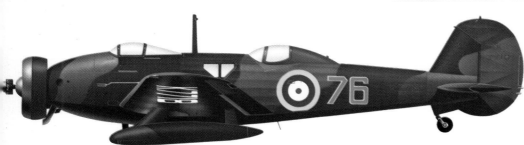

Above: The Wellesley saw most of its service in east and north-east Africa in 1940-42. This example, pictured in 1940, has the hood of the rear cockpit swung open and the gun ready for action. The containers housed the bombs.

Left: One of the very first Wellesleys to reach the RAF was this example delivered to 76 Sqn at RAF Finningley, Yorkshire, in April 1937.

119

Vickers-Armstrongs Wellington

Type 415 and 440, Wellington I to T.19

Origin: Vickers-Armstrongs (Aircraft) Ltd.
Type: Originally long-range bomber with crew of six; later, see text.
Engines: Variously two Bristol Pegasus nine-cylinder radials, two Rolls-Royce Merlin vee-12 liquid-cooled, two Pratt & Whitney Twin Wasp 14-cylinder two-row radials or two Bristol Hercules 14-cylinder two-row sleeve-valve radials; for details see text.
Dimensions: Span 86ft 2in (26·26m); (V, VI) 98ft 2in; length (most) 64ft 7in (19·68m), (some, 60ft 10in or, with Leigh light, 66ft); height 17ft 6in (5·33m), (some 17ft).
Weights: Empty (IC) 18,556lb (8417kg); (X) 26,325lb (11,940kg); maximum loaded (IC) 25,800lb (11,703kg); (III) 29,500lb (13,381kg); (X) 36,500lb (16,556kg).
Performance: Maximum speed (IC) 235mph (379km/h); (most other marks) 247–256mph (410km/h); (V, VI) 300mph (483km/h); initial climb (all, typical) 1,050ft (320m)/min; service ceiling (bomber versions,

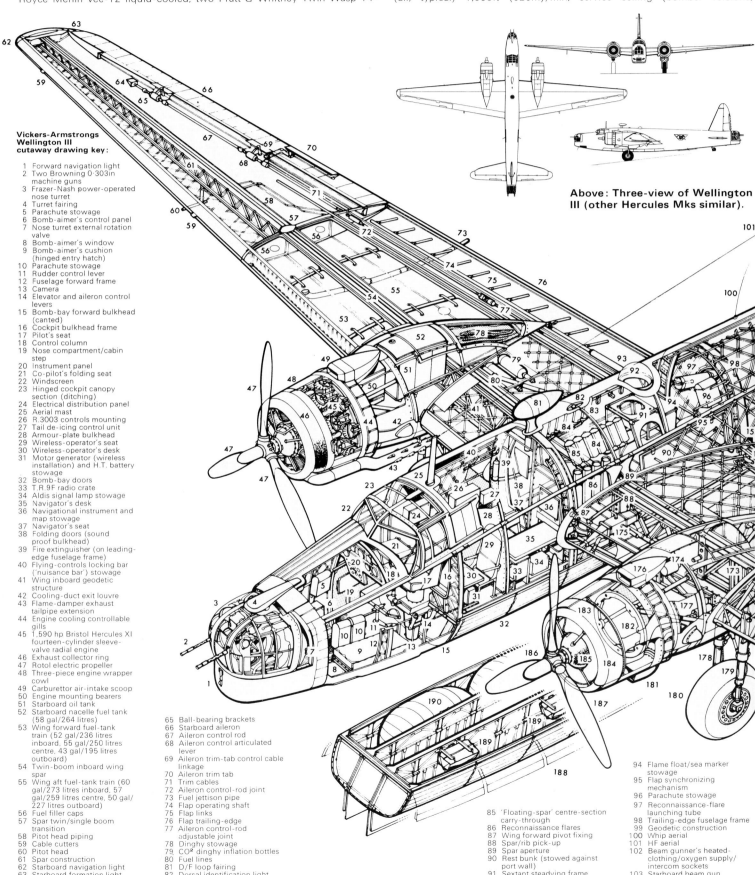

Above: Three-view of Wellington III (other Hercules Mks similar).

Vickers-Armstrongs Wellington III cutaway drawing key:

1 Forward navigation light
2 Two Browning 0·303in machine guns
3 Frazer-Nash power-operated nose turret
4 Turret fairing
5 Parachute stowage
6 Bomb-aimer's control panel
7 Nose turret external rotation valve
8 Bomb-aimer's window
9 Bomb-aimer's cushion (hinged entry hatch)
10 Parachute stowage
11 Rudder control lever
12 Fuselage forward frame
13 Camera
14 Elevator and aileron control levers
15 Bomb-bay forward bulkhead (canted)
16 Cockpit bulkhead frame
17 Pilot's seat
18 Control column
19 Nose compartment/cabin step
20 Instrument panel
21 Co-pilot's folding seat
22 Windscreen
23 Hinged cockpit canopy section (ditching)
24 Electrical distribution panel
25 Aerial mast
26 R.3003 controls mounting
27 Tail de-icing control unit
28 Armour-plate bulkhead
29 Wireless-operator's seat
30 Wireless-operator's desk
31 Motor generator (wireless installation) and H.T. battery stowage
32 Bomb-bay doors
33 T.R.9F radio crate
34 Aldis signal lamp stowage
35 Navigator's desk
36 Navigational instrument and map stowage
37 Navigator's seat
38 Folding doors (sound proof bulkhead)
39 Fire extinguisher (on leading-edge fuselage frame)
40 Flying-controls locking bar ('nuisance bar') stowage
41 Wing inboard geodetic structure
42 Cooling-duct exit louvre
43 Flame-damper exhaust tailpipe extension
44 Engine cooling controllable gills
45 1,590 hp Bristol Hercules XI fourteen-cylinder sleeve-valve radial engine
46 Exhaust collector ring
47 Rotol electric propeller
48 Three-piece engine wrapper cowl
49 Carburettor air-intake scoop
50 Engine mounting bearers
51 Starboard oil tank
52 Starboard nacelle fuel tank (58 gal/264 litres)
53 Wing forward fuel-tank train (52 gal/236 litres inboard, 55 gal/250 litres centre, 43 gal/195 litres outboard)
54 Twin-boom inboard wing spar
55 Wing aft fuel-tank train (60 gal/273 litres inboard, 57 gal/259 litres centre, 50 gal/227 litres outboard)
56 Fuel filler caps
57 Spar twin/single boom transition
58 Pitot head piping
59 Cable cutters
60 Pitot head
61 Spar construction
62 Starboard navigation light
63 Starboard formation light
64 Aileron control-rod stop bracket
65 Ball-bearing brackets
66 Starboard aileron
67 Aileron control rod
68 Aileron control articulated lever
69 Aileron trim-tab control cable linkage
70 Aileron trim tab
71 Trim cables
72 Aileron control-rod joint
73 Fuel jettison pipe
74 Flap operating shaft
75 Flap links
76 Flap trailing-edge
77 Aileron control-rod adjustable joint
78 Dinghy stowage
79 CO² dinghy inflation bottles
80 Fuel lines
81 D/F loop fairing
82 Dorsal identification light
83 Hand grips
84 Oxygen cylinders
85 'Floating-spar' centre-section carry-through
86 Reconnaissance flares
87 Wing forward pivot fixing
88 Spar/rib pick-up
89 Spar aperture
90 Rest bunk (stowed against port wall)
91 Sextant steadying frame
92 Astro-dome
93 Flap actuating cylinder
94 Flame float/sea marker stowage
95 Flap synchronizing mechanism
96 Parachute stowage
97 Reconnaissance-flare launching tube
98 Trailing-edge fuselage frame
99 Geodetic construction
100 Whip aerial
101 HF aerial
102 Beam gunner's heated-clothing/oxygen supply/intercom sockets
103 Starboard beam gun
104 Ammunition box
105 Gun mounting

typical) 22,000ft (6710m); (V, VI) 38,000ft (11,600m); range with weapon load of 1,500lb (680kg), typically 2,200 miles (3540km).

Armament: See text.

History: First flight (B.9/32) 15 June 1936; (production Mk I) 23 December 1937; service delivery (I) October 1938; final delivery (T.10) 13 October 1945.

Users: (Wartime) Australia, Czechoslovakia, France, New Zealand, Poland, UK (RAF). continued on page 122▶

Below: The subject of the cutaway is the most important "Wimpey", the Mk III, which continued to be a mainstay of Bomber Command after the entry to service of the more capable four-engined heavies.

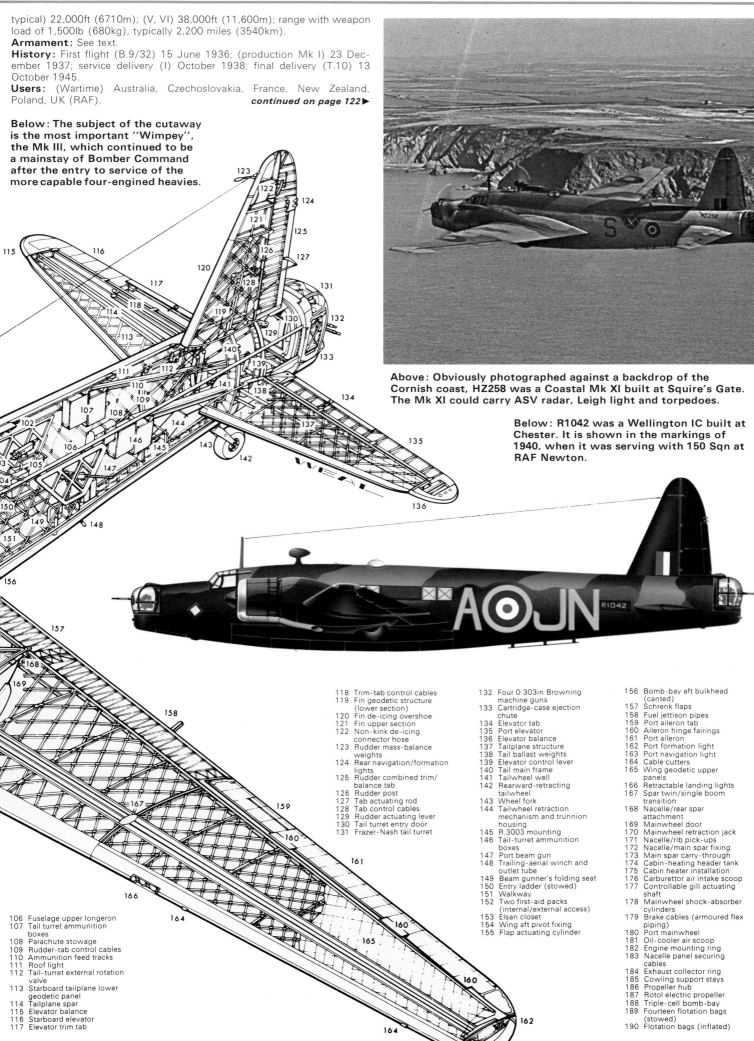

Above: Obviously photographed against a backdrop of the Cornish coast, HZ258 was a Coastal Mk XI built at Squire's Gate. The Mk XI could carry ASV radar, Leigh light and torpedoes.

Below: R1042 was a Wellington IC built at Chester. It is shown in the markings of 1940, when it was serving with 150 Sqn at RAF Newton.

106 Fuselage upper longeron
107 Tail turret ammunition boxes
108 Parachute stowage
109 Rudder-tab control cables
110 Ammunition feed tracks
111 Roof light
112 Tail-turret external rotation valve
113 Starboard tailplane lower geodetic panel
114 Tailplane spar
115 Elevator balance
116 Starboard elevator
117 Elevator trim tab
118 Trim-tab control cables
119 Fin geodetic structure (lower section)
120 Fin de-icing overshoe
121 Fin upper section
122 Non-kink de-icing connector hose
123 Rudder mass-balance weights
124 Rear navigation/formation lights
125 Rudder combined trim/balance tab
126 Rudder post
127 Tab actuating rod
128 Tab control cables
129 Rudder actuating lever
130 Tail turret entry door
131 Frazer-Nash tail turret
132 Four 0·303in Browning machine guns
133 Cartridge-case ejection chute
134 Elevator tab
135 Port elevator
136 Elevator balance
137 Tailplane structure
138 Tail ballast weights
139 Elevator control lever
140 Tail main frame
141 Tailwheel well
142 Rearward-retracting tailwheel
143 Wheel fork
144 Tailwheel retraction mechanism and trunnion housing
145 R.3003 mounting
146 Tail-turret ammunition boxes
147 Port beam gun
148 Trailing-aerial winch and outlet tube
149 Beam gunner's folding seat
150 Entry ladder (stowed)
151 Walkway
152 Two first-aid packs (internal/external access)
153 Elsan closet
154 Wing aft pivot fixing
155 Flap actuating cylinder
156 Bomb-bay aft bulkhead (canted)
157 Schrenk flaps
158 Fuel jettison pipes
159 Port aileron tab
160 Aileron hinge fairings
161 Port aileron
162 Port formation light
163 Port navigation light
164 Cable cutters
165 Wing geodetic upper panels
166 Retractable landing lights
167 Spar twin/single boom transition
168 Nacelle/rear spar attachment
169 Mainwheel door
170 Mainwheel retraction jack
171 Nacelle/rib pick-ups
172 Nacelle/main spar fixing
173 Main spar carry-through
174 Cabin-heating header tank
175 Cabin heater installation
176 Carburettor air intake scoop
177 Controllable gill actuating shaft
178 Mainwheel shock-absorber cylinders
179 Brake cables (armoured flex piping)
180 Port mainwheel
181 Oil-cooler air scoop
182 Engine mounting ring
183 Nacelle panel securing cables
184 Exhaust collector ring
185 Cowling support stays
186 Propeller hub
187 Rotol electric propeller
188 Triple-cell bomb-bay
189 Fourteen flotation bags (stowed)
190 Flotation bags (inflated)

▶ **Development:** It was natural that Vickers (Aviation), from October 1938 Vickers-Armstrongs (Aicraft), should have followed up the success of the Wellesley with a larger bomber using the geodetic form of construction. There were difficulties in applying it to wings, cut-out nacelles and fuselages with large bomb-doors and turrets, but the B.9/32 prototype was obviously efficient, and by September 1939 had been developed into Britain's most formidable bomber. The following were chief versions:

I Powered by 1,050hp Pegasus XVIII and originally with twin 0·303in Brownings in simple Vickers turrets at nose and tail; internal bomb load 4,500lb (2041kg). Built one-a-day at Weybridge, later a further 50 per month at Chester and, later still, about 30 a month at Squire's Gate, Blackpool. Mk IA had Nash and Thompson power turrets, and the main IC version had two beam guns (some earlier had a ventral barbette). Production: 180+ 183+ 2,685.

II Had 1,145hp Merlin X, otherwise as IC. Production: 400.

III Main Bomber Command type in 1941–2, with 1,375hp Hercules III or XI, and four-gun tail turret. Production: 1,519.

IV Flown by two Polish squadrons, powered by 1,200hp Twin Wasp R-1830-S3C4-G. Production: 220.

V Experimental pressurised high-altitude, turbocharged Hercules VIII. Three built, converted to VI.

VI Long-span pressurised, with 1,600hp Merlin R6SM engines, no guns and special equipment. Used by 109 Sqn and as Gee trainers. Production 63.

VII One only, Merlin engines, tested large 40mm Vickers S gun turret for P.92 fighter, later with twin fins.

VIII Conversion of IC as Coastal reconnaissance version, with ASV radar arrays, Leigh light in long nose, and two 18in torpedoes or anti-submarine weapons. Some, huge hoops for detonating magnetic mines.

IX Conversion of IC for special trooping.

X Standard bomber, similar to III but 1,675hp Hercules VI or XVI. Peak production rate per month in 1942 was Weybridge 70, Chester 130 and Blackpool 102. Production: 3,804.

XI Advanced Coastal version of X, no mast aerials but large chin radome, torpedoes, retractable Leigh light.

XII Similar to XI, with Leigh light ventral.

XIII Reverted to ASV Mk II with masts, and nose turret.

XIV Final Coastal, ASV.III chin radome, wing rocket rails, Leigh light in bomb bay.

Above: These early Mk I Wellingtons were photographed participating in exercises shortly before the outbreak of war.

XV, XVI Unarmed Transport Command conversions of IC.

Total production of this outstanding type amounted to 11,461. After World War II hundreds were converted for use as trainers, the main variant being the T.10 which remained in service until 1953. The T.19 was a specialised navigation trainer. The Vickers successor to the Wellington, the bigger Warwick, was inferior to four-engine machines, and was used mainly in Coastal and transport roles.

Below: A Polish corporal looks out of the right flight-deck window of a "Wimpey" with an obviously impressive ops record.

Vickers-Armstrongs Warwick

Type 462 (ASR.I), 460 (C.III), 473 (GR.V)

Origin: Vickers-Armstrongs Ltd, Weybridge.
Type: Designed as bomber (see text).
Engines: Two 18-cylinder radials, (I, III) 1,850hp Pratt & Whitney R-2800-S1A4G or -2SBG, (II, V) 2,520hp Bristol Centaurus VII sleeve-valve.
Dimensions: Span 96ft 8½in (29·48m); length (all) 72ft 5in to 72ft 11in (22·20m); height 18ft 6in (5·64m).
Weights: Empty (I) 28,154lb (12,701kg), (V) 31,230lb (14,226kg); maximum (I) 45,000lb (20,412kg), (III) 46,000lb (20,865kg), (V) 50,000lb (22,680kg).
Performance: Maximum speed (I) 224mph (360km/h), (III) 250mph (402km/h), (V) 295mph (475km/h); maximum range with full load (I) 2,300 miles (3700km), (III) 2,150 miles (3459km), (V) 3,052 miles (4911km).
History: First flight 13 August 1939, (production B.I) January 1942; service delivery (civil III) February 1943, (ASR.I) May 1943, (GR.V) June 1945.
User: UK (RAF, BOAC).

Development: Designed as a successor to the Wellington to B.1/35, the Warwick was potentially an outstanding aircraft, despite its geodetic/fabric construction, but its career was marred by continual indecision and by unavailability of properly developed engines. The Vultures used at first flight were hopeless, and eventually 16 B.I were delivered with Double Wasp R-2800 engines but used for research and trials. The ASR.I had the same engines and 369 were delivered càrrying Lindholme parachuted

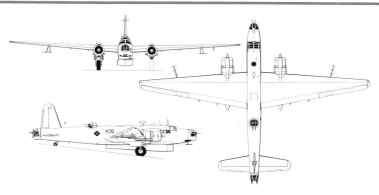

Above: Three-view of Warwick ASR.I with lifeboat and radar.

survival gear, a Mk I lifeboat and, later, ASV radar, a Mk II lifeboat and various armament including eight 0·303in in three turrets. The C.I was an unarmed transport, while the C.III had better nose and tail fairings and carried a freight pannier in the bomb bay. A vast improvement in stability came with a revised rudder and added dorsal fin, and in performance with a switch to Centaurus engines. The GR.II, 133 of which were built, served as a reconnaissance and multi-role machine in the UK and Mediterranean, but the completely redesigned GR.V just missed the war. With Leigh light instead of a dorsal turret, and 0·5in guns, this fine aircraft served in Coastal Command post-war. Though today mistakenly regarded as a near-failure, the 700-odd Warwicks worked hard during the war and among other things were the chief ASR landplanes, the chief carriers of mail, and as utility transports second only to the Dakota.

Below: Powered by Double Wasps, the Warwick C.III was a most useful and widely used transport, yet never in the limelight.

Westland Lysander

Lysander I, II, III and IIIA versions

Origin: Westland Aircraft Ltd; also built by National Steel Car Corporation, Malton, Toronto.
Type: Two-seat army co-operation; later, see text.
Engine: One Bristol nine-cylinder radial; (I) 890hp Mercury XII; (II) 905hp Perseus XII sleeve-valve; (III) 870hp Mercury XX or XXX.
Dimensions: Span 50ft (15·24m); length 30ft 6in (9·29m); height 11ft 6in (3·50m).
Weights: Empty (typical I) 4,044lb (1834kg); normal loaded (I) 5,833lb (2645kg); maximum loaded (I) 7,500lb (3402kg); (IIISCW) 10,000lb (4536kg).
Performance: Maximum speed (I, II) 237mph (381km/h); (IIISCW) 190mph (306km/h); initial climb (I) 1,900ft (580m)/min; service ceiling (I) 26,000ft (7925m); range (I) 600 miles (966km); (IIISCW) 1,400 miles (2253km).
Armament: When fitted, one 0·303in Browning, with 500 rounds, above each wheel spat (outside propeller disc) and one 0·303in Lewis or Vickers GO manually aimed from rear cockpit (IIIA, twin 0·303in Browning in rear

cockpit); bomb load up to two 250lb (113kg) on stub wings, or 16 20lb (9kg), four on fuselage carrier.
History: First flight 15 June 1936; service delivery June 1938; final delivery (Westland) January 1942, (Canada) late 1942.
Users: Canada, Egypt, Ireland, Turkey, UK (RAF, RN).

Development: One of the most distinctive military aircraft, the STOL Lysander was designed to A.39/34 as an army co-operation machine. When 16 Sqn at Old Sarum received the type in 1938 it practised sedate picking up of messages and spotting for artillery. When war came, however, the well-liked "Lizzie" blossomed forth as a remarkable multi-role aircraft. The first He 111 to be shot down in BEF territory (in November 1939) fell to a Lysander's modest armament, and in June 1940 some served as night fighters whilst others spent their time in fierce ground attack on the German army and making precision supply-drops to the defenders of Calais. During the rest of the war Lysanders served as target tugs, overseas close support, air/sea rescue and, memorably, in IIISCW form for dropping agents in Europe and recovering special passengers for Britain. The heavily loaded SCW had a belly tank, much special gear and a vital ladder to give access to the lofty cockpit. Production by Westland was 1,425, some of which were grotesque experimental versions; 325 more were built in Canada. In 1974, after years of work, a Californian restored one to flying condition.

Westland Whirlwind

Whirlwind I, IA

Origin: Westland Aircraft Ltd.
Type: Single-seat day fighter (later fighter-bomber).
Engines: Two 885hp Rolls-Royce Peregrine I vee-12 liquid-cooled.
Dimensions: Span 45ft (13·72m); length 32ft 9in (9·98m); height 11ft 7in (3·52m).
Weights: Empty (I) 7,840lb (3699kg); (IA) 8,310lb (3770kg); maximum loaded 10,270lb (4658kg); (IA) 11,388lb (5166kg).
Performance: Maximum speed (clean) 360mph (580km/h), (with bombs) 270mph (435km/h); initial climb (clean) 3,000ft (915m)/min; service ceiling (clean) 30,000ft (9144m); range, not recorded but about 800 miles (1290km).

Armament: Standard, four 20mm Hispano Mk I cannon in nose, each with 60-round drum; IA added underwing racks for bomb load up to 1,000lb (454kg).
History: First flight 11 October 1938; service delivery June 1940; final delivery December 1941.
User: UK (RAF).

Development: At the outbreak of World War II the gravest deficiency of the RAF was in the field of twin-engined high-performance machines for use as long-range escort or night fighters. This was precisely the mission of

Left: A Whirlwind I of 263 Sqn based at Exeter in 1941. One of only two squadrons to use the Whirlwind, 263 flew many Rhubarb offensive sweeps against the coastal areas of Europe within range, eventually carrying two 227kg (500lb) bombs. The Whirlwind was Britain's pioneer attempt to build a twin-engined fighter with cannon armament. The armament of four 20mm Hispanos was, for its time, devastating; but the Whirlwind was otherwise a poor aircraft because of its unreliable, low-powered engines. A batch of 200 were ordered, but the last 88 were cancelled.

Above: One of the few photographs of the extremely heavy and specially equipped Lysander IIISCW. This was the type used, from Tempsford and other airfields, to carry agents to enemy territory and, if possible, later bring them back.

Left: After 1940 nearly all Lysanders had their wheel spat covers left off to ease maintenance. This accentuated the utilitarian look of what had become a highly utilitarian STOL aircraft. Most remained in various kinds of operational service, but this example is seen with 54 Operational Training Unit. Light series bomb carriers can be seen attached to the stub wings (intended solely as bomb carriers) attached to the lower ends of the main legs. Pilots frequently flew with the canopy open, when on a warm day the "Lizzie" was one of the most pleasant aircraft in the sky. This example is a Mk III, with poppet-valve Mercury engine; the Perseus-engined machines were even smoother and quieter. Portions of a second aircraft (wheels below fuselage) may just be seen in the background.

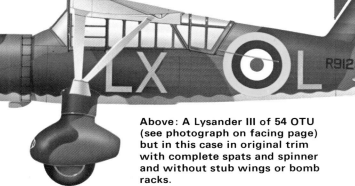

Above: A Lysander III of 54 OTU (see photograph on facing page) but in this case in original trim with complete spats and spinner and without stub wings or bomb racks.

Above: This strikingly striped machine is a target tug Lysander serving in Canada with the RCAF as part of the vast Empire Air Training Plan. One of 325 built at Malton by National Steel Car Corporation, it was in most respects identical to British-built Lysanders apart from having a proportion of North American equipment items. National Steel Car later became Victory Aircraft, building Lancasters and a York, and later Avro Canada and Hawker Siddeley Canada.

the Whirlwind, designed to a specification as early as F.37/35. It was a fine and pleasant machine, and in its slender nose was an unprecedented punch. Yet its development was delayed by engine troubles, the Peregrine being an unhappy outgrowth of the reliable Kestrel; another trouble was that, despite Fowler flaps, the landing speed was 80mph which was incompatible with short grass fields. Eventually only 263 and 137 Sqns used the type, which in combat showed much promise. In August 1941 No 263 escorted Blenheims to Cologne in daylight! Only 112 were built, ending their days as "Whirlibombers" on cross-Channel "Rhubarb" sorties strafing and bombing targets of opportunity.

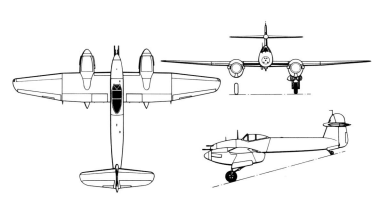

Above: Though instantly identifiable to almost every British schoolboy of the time, the Whirlwind was secret during most of its early career (though featured in Luftwaffe literature).

Left: Three-view of Whirlwind I, without bomb racks.

Fokker C.X

C.X

Origin: NV Fokker, Netherlands; licence built by Valtion Lentokonetehdas, Finland.

Type: Two-seat bomber and reconnaissance.

Engine: (Dutch) one 650hp Rolls-Royce Kestrel V vee-12 liquid-cooled; (Finnish) one licence-built 835hp Bristol Pegasus XXI nine-cylinder radial.

Dimensions: Span, 39ft 4in (12m); length (Kestrel) 30ft 2in (9·2m); (Pegasus) 29ft 9in (9·1m); height, 10ft 10in (3·3m).

Weights: Empty (both), about 3,086lb (1400kg); loaded (Kestrel) 4,960lb (2250kg); (Pegasus) 5,512lb (2500kg).

Performance: Maximum speed (Kestrel) 199mph (320km/h); (Pegasus) 211mph (340km/h); service ceiling (Kestrel) 27,230ft (8300m); (Pegasus) 27,560ft (8400m); range (Kestrel) 516 miles (830km), (Pegasus) 522 miles (840km).

Armament: Two 7·9mm machine guns fixed in top of front fuselage and third manually aimed from rear cockpit; underwing racks for two 385lb (175kg) or four 221lb (100kg) bombs.

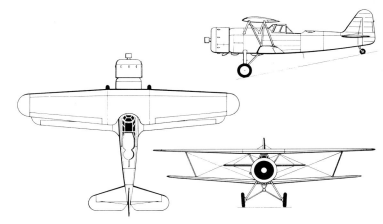

Above: Three-view of Finnish C.X with wheel landing gear.

Below: The State Aircraft Factory at Tammerfors stencilled the original company's name on the fins of the aircraft it built.

Left: This illustration of one of the special Pegasus-engined C.X bomber-reconnaissance aircraft made under licence in Finland shows the streamlined ski landing gears used in winter. Though by 1939 it represented an outmoded type the C.X was always popular with its crews.

History: First flight 1934; service delivery (Dutch) 1937; (Finnish) 1938.

Users: Finland, Netherlands.

Development: Derived from the C.V-E and planned as a successor, the C.X was a notably clean machine typical of good military design of the mid-1930s. By this time world-wide competition was very severe and Fokker could not achieve such widespread export success. The first orders were for ten for the Royal Netherlands East Indies Army, followed by 20 for the RNethAF (then called Luchtvaartafdeling, LVA), the last 15 having enclosed cockpits and tailwheels. Further small numbers were made in Holland, at least one having a 925hp Hispano-Suiza 12Y engine with 20mm cannon firing through the propeller hub. Fokker also developed a considerably more capable C.X for Finland, with the Pegasus radial. The Finnish State Aircraft Factory at Tampere went into licence-production with this version in 1938, the engine being made at Tammerfors. The Finnish C.X had an enclosed heated cockpit, rapid cold-weather starting and either wheel or ski landing gear. All available Dutch and Finnish C.X aircraft participated in World War II. None of the LVA machines survived the "Five Day War" of 10–15 May 1940, but the Finnish aircraft continued until at least 1944 under severe conditions and finally went into action not against the Russians but in helping them drive the Germans from Finnish territory in 1944–45.

Fokker D.XXI

D.XXI (D.21)

Origin: NV Fokker, Netherlands; licence-built by Valtion Lentokonetehdas, Finland; Haerens Flyvertroppernes Vaerkstader, Denmark; Spanish Republican Government plant.

Type: Single-seat fighter.

Engine: (Dutch) one 830hp Bristol Mercury VIII nine-cylinder radial; (Danish) 645hp Mercury VIS; (Finnish) 825hp Pratt & Whitney R-1535-SB4-G Twin Wasp Junior 14-cylinder two-row radial.

Dimensions: Span 36ft 1in (11m); length (Mercury) 26ft 11in (8·22m); (R-1535) 26ft 3in (8m); height 9ft 8in (2·94m).

Weights: Empty (Mercury) 3,180lb (1442kg); (R-1535) 3,380lb (1534kg); loaded (Mercury) 4,519lb (2050kg); (R-1535) 4,820lb (2186kg).

Performance: Maximum speed (Mercury VIII) 286mph (480km/h); (R-1535) 272mph (439km/h); climb to 9,842ft (3000m) 3·5min (Mercury); 4·5min (R-1535); service ceiling (Mercury) 36,090ft (11,000m); (R-1535) 32,000ft (9750m); range (Mercury) 590 miles (950km); (R-1353) 559 miles (900km).

Armament: (Dutch) four 7·9mm FN-Brownings, two in fuselage and two in wings; (Danish) two Madsen 7·9mm in wings and two Madsen 20mm cannon in underwing blisters; (Finnish) four 7·7mm machine guns in outer wings.

History: First flight, 27 March 1936; service delivery (Dutch) January 1938, (Finnish production) June 1938, (Danish production) 1939.

Users: Denmark, Finland, Netherlands.

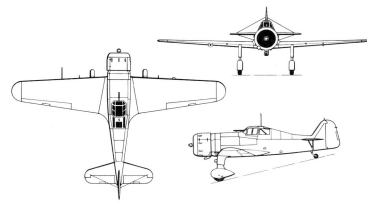

Above: Three-view of Dutch (LVA) model of D.XXI.

Fokker D.XXI came from a company with a great reputation all over the world, and though it was designed — by Ir. E. Schatzki, in 1935 — purely to meet the requirements of the Netherlands East Indies Army Air Service, it became the leading fighter of three major European nations and was planned as a standard type by a fourth. This was as well for Fokker, because the plans of the original customer were changed and a contract was never signed. Yet the little fighter was all one would expect: neat, tough and highly manoeuvrable, with good performance and heavy armament. It marked the transition between the fabric-covered biplane and the stressed-skin monoplane. The wing was wood, with bakelite/ply skin. The fuselage was welded steel tube, with detachable metal panels back to the cockpit and fabric on the rear fuselage and tail. Landing gear was fixed. The prototype flew at

Development: In the second half of the 1930s any sound warplane that was generally available could be sure of attracting widespread interest. The

Fokker G.I

G.Ia and G.Ib

Origin: NV Fokker, Netherlands.
Type: Three-seat (G.Ib, two-seat) heavy fighter and close-support.
Engines: (G.Ia) two 830hp Bristol Mercury VIII nine-cylinder radials; (G.Ib) two 750hp Pratt & Whitney R-1535-SB4-G Twin Wasp Junior 14-cylinder radials.
Dimensions: Span (G.Ia) 56ft 3¼in (17·2m); (G.Ib) 54ft 1½in (16·5m); length, (G.Ia) 37ft 8¾in (11·5m); (G.Ib) 33ft 9½in (10·3m); height 11ft 1¾in (3·4m).
Weights: Empty (G.Ia) 7,326lb (3323kg); (G.Ib) 6,930lb (3143kg); loaded, (G.Ia) 10,560lb (4790kg); (G.Ib) 10,520lb (4772kg).
Performance: Maximum speed (G.Ia) 295mph (475km/h); (G.Ib) 268mph (430km/h); time to climb to 19,680ft (6000m), (G.Ia) 8·9min; (G.Ib) 12·1min; service ceiling, (G.Ia) 30,500ft (9300m); (G.Ib) 28,535ft (8695m); range, (G.Ia) 945 miles (1520km); (G.Ib) 913 miles (1469km).
Armament: (G.Ia) row of eight 7·9mm FN-Browning machine guns fixed in nose, one similar gun manually aimed in tailcone; internal bomb bay for load of 880lb (400kg). (G.Ib) two 23mm Madsen cannon and two 7·9mm FN-Brownings in nose, otherwise same.
History: First flight, 16 March 1937; service delivery, May 1938.
Users: Denmark, Netherlands, Sweden.

Development: Appearance of the prototype G.I at the 1936 Paris Salon caused a sensation. The concept of a large twin-engined fighter was novel, and the devastating armament of the G.I caused it to be called "Le Faucheur" (the Grim Reaper). Nations practically queued to test-fly the Hispano-engined prototype and the first sale was 12 to Republican Spain in June 1937. Meanwhile the home LVA eventually signed for 36 of a much altered version with a third crew-member (radio operator) and Mercury engines in a larger airframe. Finland sought a licence, Sweden bought 18 and Denmark bought nine plus a licence. The Dutch placed an embargo on export of the Spanish aircraft, called G.Ib, and when Germany swept into Holland on 10 May 1940 these were still lined up at Schiphol. Guns were hastily taken from crashed or damaged aircraft and fitted to the Spanish machines which were thrown into the fight. The 23 combat-ready G.Ia fighters likewise fought until all were destroyed save one (in which, in

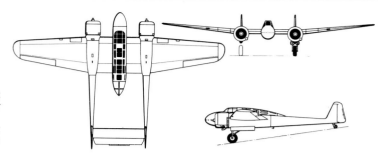

Above: Three-view of Dutch (LVA) G.Ia with eight machine guns.

1942, two senior Fokker pilots escaped to England). There were several non-standard G.Is, including one with a ventral observation cupola. All surviving or unfinished aircraft were impressed into the Luftwaffe and used as combat trainers and tugs.

Above: One of the first G.Ia three-seat fighters, pictured on flight test in early 1938. It was potentially an outstanding aircraft.

Left: The orange triangles identified neutral Holland after the start of World War II. This G.Ia was unable to fly on 10 May 1940 and was captured intact

Welschap on a Mercury VIS engine, and in May 1937 the home government ordered 36 with a more powerful Mercury, supplied from Bristol. There were many Fokker projects for developed D.XXIs with retractable landing gear and other engines, but the production aircraft was generally similar to the prototype. In the seventh (No 217) test pilot H. Leegstra set a Dutch height record at 37,250ft. Meanwhile production of a modified version was getting under way for Finland, which bought seven with a manufacturing licence. Denmark followed with an order for three and a manufacturing licence, and the fourth to adopt the D.XXI was Republican Spain. The latter set up a new plant and was about to start accepting deliveries when the area was overrun by Nationalist forces. The VL (Finnish

state factory) delivered 38 in 1938–39 and all of them participated very successfully in air battles against the Soviet forces from the start of the Soviet invasion on 30 November 1939. The D.XXI was put into accelerated production, but as all the Finnish-built Mercuries were needed for Blenheims the Finnish D.XXI was redesigned to take the heavier but less powerful Twin Wasp Junior, 55 of this type being built (one having retractable landing gear). The Danish Royal Army Aircraft Factory gradually delivered ten with low-rated Mercury and two cannon, eight being taken over during the German invasion in March 1940. Finally, on 10 May 1940 the 29 combat-ready aircraft in Holland fought round the clock until their ammunition ran out on the third day.

Right: Pleasing formation of the third and fifth Fokker D.XXI fighters escorting an early production Fokker T.V (T.5) heavy bomber. All were Bristol-engined.

Above: One of the last D.XXI fighters to be delivered, seen in its 1940 livery with prominent orange markings. KLM civil transports were orange all over

Fokker T.8W

T.8W

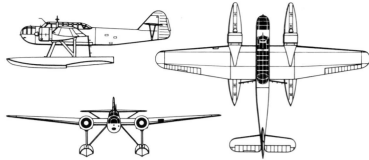

Origin: NV Fokker, Netherlands.
Type: Torpedo-bomber reconnaissance seaplane.
Engines: (T.8W, T.8W/G and T.8W/M) two 450hp Wright R-975-E3 nine-cylinder radials; (T.8W/C) two 890hp Bristol Mercury XI nine-cylinder radials.
Dimensions: Span (T.8W/G and /M) 59ft 1in (18m); (T.8W/C) 65ft 7½in (20m); length; (T.8W/G and /M) 42ft 7¾in (13m); (T.8W/C) 49ft 3in (15m); height (T.8W/G and /M) 16ft 4½in (4·95m); (T.8W/C) 17ft 8½in (5·4m).
Weights: Empty (T.8W/G) 7,055lb (3200kg); (T.8W/C) 9,700lb (4400kg); loaded; (T.8W/G) 11,030lb (5003kg); (T.8W/C) 15,432lb (7000kg).
Performance: Maximum speed (T.8W/G) 177mph (285km/h); (T.8W/C) 224mph (360km/h); service ceiling (T.8W/G) 22,310ft (6800m); (T.8W/C) 19,030ft (5800m); range (T.8W/G) 1,305 miles (2100km); (T.8W/C) 1,056 miles (1700km).
Armament: (T.8W/G and /M) three manually aimed 7·9mm FN-Brownings in nose, dorsal and ventral positions; one torpedo externally or bomb load of 1,323lb (600kg).
History: First flight (T.8W) 1938; (T.8W/C) late 1939.
Users: Finland (Navy), Germany (Luftwaffe), Netherlands (MLD), UK (RAF).

Development: The T.8W seaplane was designed to meet a 1937 specification by the MLD (Netherlands Naval AF, mainly in the East Indies). Five and then 14 were ordered, followed in 1940 by 12 T.8W/M. In May 1940 the T.8W was in service as the /G and as the /M with metal skinned rear fuselage, while the bigger /C was in production for Finland. In late May 1940 eight survivors of the frantic battle over Holland escaped to Britain, forming 320 Sqn of RAF Coastal Command until they ran out of spares in late 1940. Unfinished T.8Ws were completed for the Luftwaffe, one of the bigger C examples having land undercarriage.

Right: Pre-war formation of the first T.8W/G with a C.X biplane.

Below: The sixth T.8W/G in 1940 markings. Eight of these aircraft escaped to join the RAF, serialled AV958-965.

Above: Three-view of Fokker T.8W/G or /M.

Cant Z.501 Gabbiano

Z.501 and 501 bis Gabbiano (Gull)

Origin: CRDA Cantieri Riuniti dell' Adriatico, Monfalcone.
Type: Patrol flying boat.
Engine: 900hp Isotta-Fraschini Asso XIR2 C15 vee-12 liquid-cooled.
Dimensions: Span 73ft 9¾in (22·50m); length (most) 46ft 11in (14·30m); height 14ft 6in (4·42m).
Weights: Empty (typical) 8,488lb (3850kg); loaded 13,117lb (5950kg); max overload 15,542lb (7050kg).
Performance: Maximum speed 171mph (275km/h); normal range 1,490 miles (2400km); ultimate overload range 3,000 miles (4830km).
Armament: Two 7·7mm Breda-SAFAT manually aimed from engine nacelle and dorsal hull cockpit (early versions, third similar gun in bow position); racks on bracing struts for weapon load of 1,404lb (637kg).
History: First flight August 1934; service (military) delivery 1936; final delivery, probably late 1942.
User: Italy (RA, CB and ARSI); post-war Italian AF.

Above: A Z.501 Gabbiano of the 46th Squadriglia Ricognizione Marittima. Some examples had enclosed bow cockpits.

Development: It is curious that in World War II Italy should have used a wealth of float seaplanes but only one major type of flying boat. One of Ing Filippo Zappata's earliest designs, the Gabbiano set world class records for non-stop distance in 1934 and 1935, flying from Monfalcone to Eritrea and then to Somaliland. Several civil examples existed when production began for the Regia Aeronautica as a four/five-seat recon-naissance and attack machine, and by the entry into war in June 1940 no fewer than 202 were on strength. At first the 501 was active, but casualties in the face of the enemy were heavy, and attrition of the wooden aircraft severe, and as production slumped the operational force dwindled to about 40 at the September 1943 Armistice. About 19 served with the CB force and a few remained operational with the RSI. Several were still in service in 1950.

Cant Z.506B Airone

Z.506B Airone (Heron) serie I-XII and Z.506S

Origin: CRDA Cantieri Riuniti dell' Adriatico, Monfalcone; second-source production by Piaggio.
Type: Torpedo, bomber and reconnaissance seaplane, (S) air/sea rescue.
Engines: Three 750hp Alfa Romeo 126RC34 nine-cylinder radials.
Dimensions: Span 86ft 11¼in (26·50m); length 63ft 2in (19·25m); height 24ft 5½in (7·45m).
Weights: Empty 19,290lb (8750kg); max loaded 27,997lb (12,700kg).
Performance: Maximum speed 217mph (350km/h); typical endurance 6hr 26min; range with 2,094lb (950kg) weapon load 1,243 miles (2000km).
Armament: (Typical early series) ventral bay housing 1,764lb (800kg) torpedo or up to 2,205lb (1000kg) bombs or other weapons, with 7·7mm Breda-SAFAT manually aimed from rear, and retractable Breda M.1 dorsal turret with two 12·7mm Breda-SAFAT; (Serie XII) bomb load increased to 2,645lb (1200kg), dorsal turret changed to Delta E with one 12·7mm Scotti, and two 7·7mm Breda-SAFAT from beam windows.
History: First flight 1936; service delivery (civil) 1936, (military) December 1937; final delivery not known.
Users: Italy (Ala Littoria, RA, CB, ARSI and post-war AF), Germany (Luftwaffe), Poland.

Development: In 1936-37 civil Z.506 Airones set 16 world class records for speed, range and payload/height. The military version proved one of the finest marine aircraft ever built, and despite wooden construction was able to operate in Force 5 conditions and survive until at least 1959. Only one reached Poland, three days before the German assault. Italian examples served in Spain, and 95 were on strength in June 1940. In 1940-41

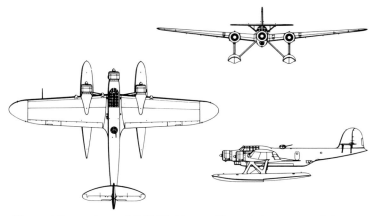

Above: Three-view of Z.506B Airone. Though less powerful than the Z.1007 landplane bomber (overleaf) the Airone was larger.

Airones were in hectic action in the Balkans, France and against the Allied navies, but by mid-1941 they were reassigned to coastal patrol, ASW and escort, with the Z.506S (Soccorso) converted for ASR operations. They had an outstanding record, and one achieved fame as the only aircraft ever hijacked by prisoners of war (the RAF took over and flew to Malta).

Below, left: On its beaching chassis the Airone stood high off the ground, a long ladder being needed to reach even the main entry door on the left side. Their tough utilitarian qualities kept these floatplanes flying up to and beyond the Italian surrender. One remained operational until 1956.

Below: About half the Airones of the Regia Aeronautica were painted dark olive (a green-brown) above and pale yellow green below, with the Mediterranean white theatre band. The ladder is not part of the aircraft.

Cant Z.1007 Alcione

Z.1007, 1007 bis and 1018

Origin: CRDA "Cant".
Type: Four/five-seat medium bomber.
Engines: Three 1,000hp Piaggio P.XIbis RC40 14-cylinder two-row radials.
Dimensions: Span 81ft 4in (24·8m); length 60ft 4in (18·4m); height 17ft 1½in (5·22m).
Weights: Empty 19,000lb (8630kg); loaded 28,260–30,029lb (12,840–13,620kg).
Performance: Maximum speed 280mph (448km/h); initial climb 1,550ft (472m)/min; service, ceiling 26,500ft (8100m); range 800 miles (1280km) with maximum bombs, 3,100 miles (4989km) with maximum fuel.
Armament: (First 25) four 7·7mm Breda-SAFAT machine guns in dorsal turret, two beam hatches and ventral position; (remainder) as before except dorsal and ventral guns 12·7mm Breda-SAFAT; internal bomb capacity 4,410lb (2000kg); alternatively two 1,000lb (454kg) torpedoes and four bombs up to 551lb (250kg) each on underwing racks.

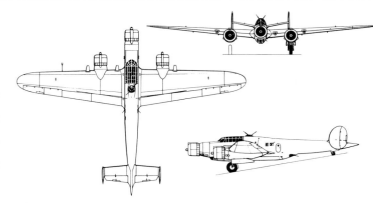

Above: Three-view of typical Z.1007bis (twin-finned version).

Left: A twin-finned Z.1007bis of 230a Squadriglia, 950 Gruppo.

Below: Part of a formation of Z.1007bis (single-fin model, no separate designation) winging their way to a target in the Balkans. Construction was almost entirely of wood.

History: First flight May 1937; (first production aircraft) 1939; entry to service 1939.
User: Italy (RA, CB, ARSI).

Development: A famous Italian naval yard, the Cantieri Monfalcone (Trieste), entered the aircraft construction business in 1923, forming a subsidiary called Cantieri Riuniti dell' Adriatico (always shortened to Cant). Their first products were seaplanes and flying boats and the most important of these was the three-engined Z.506B Airone (Heron) twin-float seaplane used in large numbers in World War II. Designer Filippo Zappata then produced a landplane bomber version, powered by three 840hp Isotta-Fraschini Asso inverted-vee liquid-cooled engines. Like the seaplane this new bomber, the Z.1007, was built entirely of wood. It received a generally favourable report from the Regia Aeronautica's test pilots and after modifications went into production, two other firms – Meridionali and Piaggio – later being brought in to increase rate of output. Nearly all the several hundred production Alciones (Kingfishers) were powered by the Piaggio radial engine, and this version, the Z.1007 bis, also had a longer fuselage, bigger wings and stronger landing gear. Almost·half also had twin tail fins.

Though easy meat for RAF fighters, Alciones were bravely operated throughout the Mediterranean, and many even served on the Russian front. Various developments culminated in the excellent twin-engined Z.1018 Leone (Lion), with metal airframe and 1,350hp engines, but few of these had been delivered when Italy surrendered in 1943.

Caproni Ca 133

Ca 101, 111 and 133 (data for 133)

Origin: Società Italiana Caproni.
Type: Colonial bomber and transport.
Engines: Three 450/460hp Piaggio P.VII RC14 Stella seven-cylinder radials.
Dimensions: Span 69ft 8in (21·3m); length 50ft 4⅝in (15·35m); height 13ft 1in (4m).
Weights: Empty 8,598lb (3900kg); loaded 14,330lb (6500kg).
Performance: Maximum speed 174mph (280km/h); initial climb 940ft (286m)/min; service ceiling 21,325ft (6500m); range 839 miles (1350km).
Armament: One or two 7·7mm or one 12·7mm machine gun on pivoted mounting in roof at trailing edge of wing; one machine gun in sliding hatchway in floor of rear fuselage; often one 7·7mm on each side in aft window-openings; bomb load (up to 2,200lb, 1000kg) carried in internal bay and on external racks under fuselage.
History: First flight (Ca 101) 1932; (Ca 111) 1933; (Ca 133) 1935; end of production, prior to 1938.
Users: Austria, Hungary, Italy (RA).

Development: As Mussolini restored "the lost colonies" and Italy forcibly built up an overseas empire, so did the need arise for "colonial" type aircraft similar to the British Wapiti and Vincent. Caproni produced the Ca 101 to meet this need, at least 200 being delivered in the early 1930s to serve as bomber, troop carrier, reconnaissance and ground attack machines and, most of all, to supply forward troops with urgent stores. Powered by three 235hp Alfa Romeo engines, it was made of robust welded steel tube with fabric covering. The Ca 111, powered by a single 950hp Isotta-Fraschini engine, gave even better service and survived the Albanian and Ethiopian campaigns to operate against Jugoslav partisans in World War II. The Ca 133 was the most important of all and many hundreds were built. When Italy entered the war in 1940 it equipped 14 Squadriglie di Bombardimento Terrestri (bomber squadrons), nearly all in East or North Africa. Though scorned by the RAF and easy meat on the ground or in the air, these versatile STOL machines worked hard and well and finished up as ambulances and transports in Libya, on the Russian Front and in Italy (on both sides after the 1943 surrender).

Left: A fully armed Ca 133 of Fliegerregiment 2 of the Austrian Air Force, one of several export customers. In the 1930s these versatile machines gave excellent service, but by the time Italy entered World War II they were outclassed. Their crews called them Vacca (cow) or Caprona (she-goat), which was a play on the name of the manufacturer. Two advanced models, the Ca 142 and 148, did not go into production.

Caproni Ca 135

Ca 135 and 135bis (data for 135bis)

Origin: Società Italiana Caproni.
Type: Five-seat medium bomber.
Engines: Two 1,000hp Piaggio P.XIbis RC40 14-cylinder two-row radials.
Dimensions: Span 61ft 8in (18·75m); length 47ft 1in (14·4m); height 11ft 2in (3·4m).
Weights: Empty 9,921lb (4500kg); loaded 18,740lb (8500kg).
Performance: Maximum speed 273mph (440km/h); initial climb 1,435ft (437m)/min; service ceiling 22,966ft (7000m); range with bomb load 746 miles (1200km).
Armament: Three Breda-SAFAT turrets, each mounting one 12·7mm or two 7·7mm guns, in nose, dorsal and ventral positions (dorsal and ventral retractable); bomb cells in fuselage and inner wings for up to 3,527lb (1600kg) weapon load.
History: First flight (135) 1 April 1935; (135bis) about November 1937.
Users: Hungary, Italy (RA).

Development: When the great Caproni combine took on Breda's designer Cesare Pallavicino it embarked on a series of modern aircraft of higher performance. The most important appeared to be the Ca 135 medium bomber, designed in the summer of 1934 to meet a Regia Aeronautica specification. A curious blend of wooden wings, light-alloy monocoque forward fuselage and steel tube plus fabric rear fuselage and tail, the prototype had two 800hp Isotta-Fraschini Asso engines but no guns. After over a year of testing the government ordered 14 as the Tipo Spagna to serve in the Spanish civil war. Peru bought six Tipo Peru, eventually purchasing 32. Yet the Ca 135 was not as good as the S.M.79 and Z.1007 by rival makers and the Regia Aeronautica kept delaying a decision. More powerful Fiat A.80 RC41 radials improved behaviour but at the expense of reliability and a good 135 did not appear until the Milan Aero Show in October 1937, when the Piaggio-engined 135bis was displayed. Though never adopted by the Regia Aeronautica it was frequently identified as having been used against Malta, Jugoslavia and Greece! The real raiders in these cases were probably BR.20s, but the 135 bis did find a customer: the Hungarian Air Force. Several hundred were operated by that service whilst attached to Luftflotte IV in the campaign on the Eastern Front in 1941–43.

Left: One of the colourful Ca 135bis bombers operated on the Eastern Front by the Hungarian Air Force (note tactical theatre marking of yellow bands). This example belonged to 4/III Bomb Group, but few of the Capronis lasted even until the end of 1942, and they were not entirely successful.

Caproni Ca 309-316

Ca 309 Ghibli (Desert Wind), 310 Libeccio (Southwest Wind), 311 and 311M, 312 and variants, 313, 314 and variants and 316

Origin: Cantieri Aeronautici Bergamaschi; production by various other Caproni companies, mainly at Castellamare and Taliedo.
Type: (309) colonial utility, (310) utility transport, (311) light bomber, (312) bomber and torpedo (312bis, 312IS, seaplanes), (313) bomber/torpedo bomber, (314) coastal patrol torpedo bomber, (316) catapult reconnaissance seaplane.
Engines: (309) two 185hp Alfa Romeo A.115 six-in-line; (310, 316) two 470hp Piaggio P.VII C.16 seven-cylinder radials; (311, 312) two 650hp Piaggio P.XVI RC35 nine-cylinder radials; (313, 314) two 650hp Isotta-Fraschini Delta RC35 inverted-vee-12.
Dimensions: Span (309-312) 53ft 1¼in (16·20m), (313) 52ft 10½in (16·11m), (314) 54ft 7½in (16·65m), (316) 52ft 2in (15·90m); length (309) 43ft 7½in (13·30m), (311, 313, 314) 38ft 8in (11·79m), (310, 312)
40ft 0½in (12·20m), (316) 42ft 3in (12·88m); height 10ft 8in to 13ft 3in (floatplanes about 16ft 9in) (3·26 to 4·04m, floatplanes 5·10m).
Weights: Empty (309) 3,850lb (1746kg), (others) about 7,050lb (3200kg); loaded (309) 6,067lb (2750kg), (others) 10,252–13,580lb (4650–6160kg).
Performance: Maximum speed (309) 158mph (254km/h), (others) 227–271mph (365–435km/h) except 316 only 204mph (328km/h).
Armament: See text.
History: First flight (309) 1936; main production 1938–42.
Users: Italy (civil, RA, CB, ARSI, post-war AF), Germany (Luftwaffe), Croatia, Hungary, Jugoslavia, Norway, Spain, Sweden.

Development: This diverse family had wooden wings, and fuselages of welded steel tube covered with fabric. The Ghibli was a light multi-role machine for African use, with radio, cameras, light bomb racks and two machine guns (one fixed, one in a dorsal position). The more powerful examples carried up to five 12·7mm and three 7·7mm guns with bomb/torpedo loads up to 1,764lb (800kg). Total production of all models was about 2,400.

Left: Another colourful Italian in foreign colours, in this case a Caproni Ca 310 Libeccio of the Norwegian Army Flying Service (Haerens Flyvevåben). This example was based at Sola airfield, Stavanger, in 1940, and was almost certainly destroyed on the ground within the first few hours of the German invasion of Scandinavia on 9 April 1940.

Above: A Caproni Ca 312 of the type with an unstepped nose. Most subsequent models reverted to a conventional windscreen.

Above: The Ca 310 Libeccio was the first of the family to have retractable landing gear. Later versions were more powerful.

Fiat B.R.20 Cicogna

B.R.20, 20M and 20 bis

Origin: Aeronautica d'Italia SA Fiat.
Type: Heavy bomber, with normal crew of five or six.
Engines: (B.R.20) two 1,000hp Fiat A.80 RC41 18-cylinder two-row radials; (B.R.20M) as B.R.20 or two 1,100hp A.80 RC20; (B.R.20bis) two 1,250hp A.82 RC32.
Dimensions: Span, 70ft 9in (21·56m); length, (B.R.20) 52ft 9in (16·2m); (B.R.20M, 20bis) 55ft 0in (16·78m); height 15ft 7in (4·75m).
Weights: Empty (all), about 14,770lb (6700kg); loaded (B.R.20) 22,046lb (10,000kg); (B.R.20M) 23,038lb (10,450kg).
Performance: Maximum speed, (B.R.20) 264mph (425km/h); (B.R.20M) 267mph (430km/h); (B.R.20bis) 292mph (470km/h); initial climb (all) about 902ft (275m)/min; service ceiling, (B.R.20, 20M) 22,145ft (6750m); (B.R.20bis) 26,246ft (8000m); range, (B.R.20, 20M) 1,243 miles (2000km); (B.R.20bis) 1,710 miles (2750km).
Armament: (B.R.20) four 7·7mm Breda-SAFAT machine guns in nose turret (one), dorsal turret (two) and manual ventral position; bomb load 3,527lb (1600kg); (B.R.20M) as B.R.20 except nose gun 12·7mm; (B.R.20bis) as B.R.20M with two extra 12·7mm guns manually aimed from lateral blisters; bomb load 5,511lb (2500kg).
History: First flight (prototype) 10 February 1936; service delivery, September 1936; first flight (B.R.20M) late 1939; first flight B.R.20bis, December 1941.
Users: Hungary, Italy (RA), Japan, Spain, Venezuela.

Development: Ing Rosatelli was responsible for a great series of B.R. (Bombardamento Rosatelli) designs from 1919 onwards. Most were powerful single-engined biplanes, but in the mid-1930s he very quickly produced the B.R.20, a large monoplane with stressed-skin construction and other modern refinements. Despite its relative complexity the original aircraft was put into production within six months of the first flight and by the end of 1936 the B.R.20-equipped 13° Stormo was probably the most advanced bomber squadron in the world. Fiat also built two civil B.R.20L record-breakers, and also offered the new bomber for export, soon gaining a valuable order for 85, not from the expected China but from Japan, which needed a powerful bomber to bridge the gap caused by a delay with the Army Ki-21. In June 1937 the B.R.20 figured prominently in the Aviazione Legionaria sent to fight for the Nationalists in Spain and, with the He 111, bore the brunt of their very successful bomber operations. Spain purchased a manufacturing licence, which was not taken up, and purchased at least 25 from Fiat. An additional number were brought by Venezuela. In 1940, when Italy entered World War II, some 250 had been delivered to the Regia Aeronautica, the last 60 being of the strengthened and much more shapely M (Modificato) type. In October 1940 two groups of 37 and 38 of the M model operated against England, but they were hacked down with ease and were recalled in January 1941. During 1942 the B.R.20 began to fade, becoming used for ocean patrol, operational training and bombing where opposition was light. A large force supported the Luftwaffe in Russia, where casualties were heavy. By the Armistice only 81 of all versions were left out of 606 built. The much improved B.R.20bis never even got into bulk production.

Left: One of the more uncommon Fiat B.R.20 Cicogna bombers was this example from a batch supplied to the Japanese Army in 1937. No fewer than 75 were delivered, seeing action in both the Chinese campaign and World War II. The aircraft illustrated served with the 1st Chutai, 12th Hikosentai. Japanese designation was Yi-shiki.

Fiat C.R.32

C.R.30, 32 and 32bis

Origin: Aeronautica d'Italia SA Fiat; built under licence by Hispano Aviaciòn, Spain.
Type: Single-seat fighter.
Engine: (C.R.30) one 600hp Fiat A.30 vee-12 water-cooled, (C.R.32) one 600hp Fiat A.30 RAbis.
Dimensions: Span (C.R.30) 34ft 5½in (10·45m); (C.R.32) 31ft 2in (9·5m); length (30) 25ft 8¼in (7·83m); (32) 24ft 5½in (7·45m); height (30) 8ft 7½in (2·62m); (32) 7ft 9in (2·4m).
Weights: Empty (both) about 3,100lb (1400kg); loaded (both) about 4,150lb (1900kg).
Performance: Maximum speed (30) 217mph (350km/h), (32) 233mph (375km/h); initial climb (both) 2,000ft (907m)/min; service ceiling (both) about 29,530ft (9000m); range (30) 528 miles (850km), (32) 466 miles (750km).
Armament: (C.R.30) two fixed Breda-SAFAT 7·7mm or 12·7mm machine guns above engine; (C.R.32) two 12·7mm; (C.R.32bis), two 12·7mm above engine and two 7·7mm above lower wings with provision for single 220lb (100kg) or two 110lb bombs.
History: First flight (C.R.30) 1932; (C.R.32) August 1933; final delivery, about October 1939.
Users: Argentina, China, Hungary, Italy (RA), Paraguay, Spain, Venezuela.

Development: In 1923 Ing Celestino Rosatelli supervised his first C.R. (Caccia Rosatelli) fighter. From it stemmed an unbroken line which reached its climax in the 1930s. The C.R.30 offered a considerable jump in performance, for it had much more power without increase in aircraft drag. The lusty Fiat vee-12 drove a metal propeller and was cooled by a prominent circular radiator in a duct in the chin position below the crankcase. The all-metal structure was notable for continuing the scheme of Warren (W-form) interplane bracing. The tail was also braced and the main gears had large wheel spats. The C.R.32 was a general refinement, built in larger numbers and forming the major part of the Regia Aeronautica fighter force in 1935–40. In August 1936 some were sent to form La Cucuracha squadron fighting for the Spanish Nationalist forces and this grew to become by far the largest of Franco's fighter units. Spain built many under licence as the Hispano HA-132-L Chirri, and more than 150 were exported by Fiat to China, Hungary and South American countries. The nimble little Fiats were compact, robust and highly manoeuvrable and gave impressive displays all over Europe in the hands of the Pattuglie Acrobatiche. Total Fiat output amounted to at least 1,212, the final 500 being mainly four-gun 32bis fighter-bombers and a few 32ter and 32quater versions with small modifications. The Regia Aeronautica did its best with the C.R.32 until 1942, finally using it for night tactical operations in Greece, Eritrea and Libya.

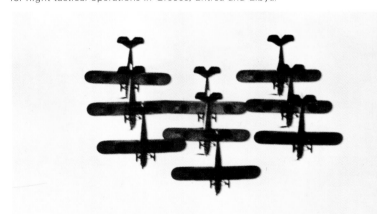

Above: The Fiat C.R.32 was the star performer at countless flying displays by Mussolini's flamboyant Regia Aeronautica in the mid-1930s. It was the mount chosen for the Pattuglie Acrobatiche.

Left: The C.R.32 used by a leading ace of the Spanish Nationalist (rebel) air force, Comandante Joaquín García Morato. The C.R.32 also equipped the leading unit of the Regia Aeronautica fighting in Spain, the La Cucuracha squadron. But by 1940 it was no longer capable of acting as a front-line dogfighter.

Fiat C.R.42 Falco

C.R.42, 42bis, 42ter, 42AS and 42N

Origin: Aeronautica d'Italia SA Fiat.
Type: Single-seat fighter.
Engine: One 840hp Fiat A.74 RC38 14-cylinder two-row radial.
Dimensions: Span 31ft 10in (9·7m); length 27ft 1¼in (8·25m); height 11ft 0in (3·35m).
Weights: Empty 3,790lb (1720kg); loaded 5,070lb (2300kg).
Performance: Maximum speed 267mph (430km/h); initial climb 2,400ft (732m)/min; service ceiling 34,450ft (10,500m); range 481 miles (775km).
Armament: (Early C.R.42) one 7·7mm and one 12·7mm Breda-SAFAT machine guns mounted above forward fuselage; (C.R.42bis) two 12·7mm; (C.R. 42ter) two 12·7mm and two more 12·7mm in fairings beneath lower wing; (C.R.42AS) two/four 12·7mm and underwing racks for two 220lb (100kg) bombs.
History: First flight (C.R.41) 1936; (C.R.42) January 1939; first service delivery, November 1939; termination of production, early 1942.
Users: Belgium, Finland, Hungary, Italy (RA), Sweden.

Above: Part of a formation of Fiat C.R.42 Falco fighters of the Regia Aeronautica's 62a Squadriglia. Though outstandingly manoeuvrable, the Falco lacked almost all other fighter qualities.

Left: This Falco belonged to the 95a Squadriglia, 10o Gruppo Caccia Terrestre, based at Echeloo, Belgium, in November 1940.

Development: In the mid-1930s the Fiat company made a firm move away from liquid-cooled vee engines and concentrated on air-cooled radials. Rosatelli prepared a fighter, the C.R.41, to take one of these, but only the prototype was built. Other nations were by this time (1936) giving up the open-cockpit, fabric-covered biplane in favour of the stressed-skin monoplane with retractable landing gear, but Rosatelli persisted with his C.R. family and developed the C.R.41 into the C.R.42. Though a robust, clean and very attractive design, it was really obsolete at the time of its first flight. Despite this — and perhaps confirming that Fiat knew the world market — the C.R.42 found ready acceptance. It went into large-scale production for the Regia Aeronautica and for Belgium (34, delivered January–May 1940), Hungary (at least 40, delivered December 1939–June 1940) and Sweden (72, delivered 1940–41). Total production, including the AS close support and N night fighter versions, amounted to 1,784. One group of 50 C.R.42bis provided the fighter element of the Corpo Aereo Italiano which operated from Belgium against England in October 1940–January 1941— with conspicuous lack of success. The rest persevered in the Mediterranean and North African areas, acting as both fighters and ground attack aircraft, a few being converted as dual trainers. One was built in 1940 as a twin-float seaplane and the final fling was a C.R.42B with 1,010hp DB 601A inverted-vee engine. The German power unit made it, at 323mph, the fastest biplane fighter but no production was attempted.

Fiat G.50 Freccia

G.50, 50bis, 50ter and 55 Centauro

Origin: Aeronautica d'Italia SA Fiat; also built by CMASA.
Type: Single-seat fighter.
Engine: (G.50, G.50bis) one 840hp Fiat A.74 RC38 14-cylinder two-row radial; (G.50ter) 1,000hp A.76 RC40S; (G.55) 1,475hp Daimler-Benz DB 605A inverted-vee-12 liquid-cooled.
Dimensions: Span, (G.50) 36ft 0in (10·97m); (G.55) 38ft 10½in (11·85m); length, (G.50) 25ft 7in (7·79m); (G.55) 30ft 9in (9.37m); height (G.50) 9ft 8in (2·9m); (G.55) 10ft 3¼in (3·15m).
Weights: Empty (G.50) 4,188lb (1900kg); (G.55) 6,393lb (2900kg); loaded (G.50) 5,966lb (2706kg); (G.55) 8,179lb (3710kg).
Performance: Maximum speed (G.50) 293mph (471km/h); (G.55) 385mph (620km/h); initial climb (G.50) 2,400ft (731m)/min; (G.55) 3,300ft (1000m)/min; service ceiling (G.50) 32,810ft (10,000m); (G.55) 42,650ft (13,000m); range (G.50) 621 miles (1000km); (G.55) 994 miles (1600km).
Armament: (G.50, G.50bis) two 12·7mm Breda-SAFAT machine guns above front fuselage; (G.55/0) as above, plus one 20mm Mauser MG 151 cannon firing through propeller hub; (G.55/I) as G.55/0 plus two 20mm MG 151 in outer wings.
History: First flight 26 February 1937; (G.50bis) September 1940; (G.55) 30 April 1942.
Users: Finland, Italy (RA, CB, ARSI), Spain.

Development: In 1935 the issue of a specification for an all-metal monoplane fighter for the Regia Aeronautica attracted at least six competing designs. Though the Macchi 200 was ultimately to become dominant, the initial winner was the Fiat G.50, the first major design by Ing Giuseppe Gabrielli (hence the designation). Its flight trials went smoothly, an order was placed in September 1937 for 45 and deliveries began early in 1938. About a dozen of the first production G.50s were sent to reinforce the Aviazione Legionaria in Spain, where their good qualities of speed and manoeuvrability were manifest. On the other hand pilots disliked having a sliding cockpit canopy, which was not easy to open quickly and interfered with vision, and in the next production batch of 200 an open cockpit was adopted. The poor armament was not changed, but fairings for the retracted

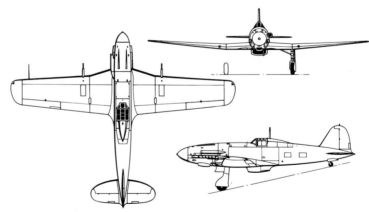

Above: Three-view of the G.55/I with three cannon.

wheels were added. Production from the CMASA plant at Marina di Pisa got under way in 1939, with deliveries replacing the C.R.32 in Regia Aeronautica fighter squadrons (not always to the pilots' delight), and a further 35 being flown to Finland in 1940 where they gave admirable service. The main production version was the G.50bis, with reprofiled fuselage giving improved pilot view, armour and self-sealing tanks. About 450 were built, mainly by CMASA. Other versions included the tandem-seat G.50B trainer, of which 139 were built; the G.50ter with more powerful engine; and prototypes of the G.50bis-A, with four 12·7mm guns and racks for two bombs, and of the DB 601A-powered G.50V. Few G.55 were built.

Below: G.50 of 1o Gruppo Sperimentale at Escalona, Spain, 1939.

Macchi M.C. 200 Saetta
M.C.200 (Serie I-XXI) and M.C.201

Origin: Aeronautica Macchi.
Type: Single-seat day fighter.
Engine: One 870hp Fiat A74RC38 14-cylinder two-row radial.
Dimensions: Span 34ft 8½in (10·58m); length 26ft 10½in (8·2m); height 11ft 6in (3·38m).
Weights: (Typical) empty 4,188lb (1900kg); (prototype) 3,902lb; (final production Serie XXI) 4,451lb; loaded 5,182lb (2350kg); (prototype) 4,850lb; (Serie XXI) 5,598lb.
Performance: Maximum speed 312mph (501km/h); initial climb 3,215ft (980m)/min; service ceiling 29,200ft (8900m); range 354 miles (570km).
Armament: Two 12·7mm Breda-SAFAT machine guns firing above engine cowling; later-Serie aircraft also had two 7·7mm in wings; M.C.200 C.B. (caccia bombardiere) had underwing racks for two bombs of up to 352lb (160kg) each, or two 33gal drop tanks.
History: First flight 24 December 1937; service delivery October 1939; final delivery, about December 1944.
User: Italy.

Development: Mario Castoldi's design team at Aeronautica Macchi, at Varese in the north Italian lakeland, was the source of the best fighters used by the Regia Aeronautica in World War II. Castoldi's staff had earlier gained great experience with high-speed aircraft with their record-breaking Schneider seaplanes, but their first monoplane fighter, the C.200, bore little evidence of this. Though a reasonably attractive stressed-skin monoplane, it had an engine of low power and the performance was correspondingly modest. Moreover it never had anything that other countries would have regarded as proper armament, though the pilot did have the advantage of

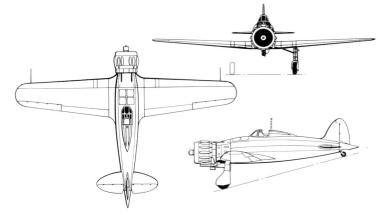

Above: Three-view of Macchi C.200 (late production serie).

cockpit indicators showing the number of rounds of ammunition unfired. Italian fighter pilots were by nature conservative; their protests caused the main production aircraft to have an open cockpit and fixed tailwheel, unlike the first batches, and combat equipment was simple in the extreme. Yet in combat with the lumbering Hurricane it proved effective, with outstanding dogfight performance and no vices. From late 1940 until Italy's surrender in September 1943 the C.200 saw more combat than any other Italian type, both around North Africa and Sicily and on the Eastern Front with the Corpo di Spedizone Italiano which claimed 88 Russian aircraft for the loss of 15 Saettas. The name Saetta, meaning lightning, refers to the lightning-bolts held by Jupiter, and is sometimes rendered as Arrow or Thunderbolt.

Left: A Macchi C.200 (or M.C.200 for Mario Castoldi) of a late serie in which the original sliding canopy had been replaced by a hinged hood open at the top. This one served the 90o Squadriglia, 10o Gruppo, 4o Stormo, based in Sicily in 1941.

Above: Takeoff of a section of Saettas of one of the late serie with wing guns but still an interim canopy.

Below: Contemporary colour photograph of Saettas parked amongst S.M.82 Canguru transports.

Above: An early-serie Saetta serving with the 81o Squadriglia, probably in 1940.

Below: A tactical base of the Regia Aeronautica, probably in southern Italy, with a Saetta and IMAM Meridionali Ro 37.

Macchi C.202 and 205

C.202 Folgore (Lightning), C.205V Veltro (Greyhound) and C.205N Orione (Orion)

Origin: Aeronautica Macchi; production also by SAI Ambrosini and Breda.
Type: Single-seat fighter (some, fighter bomber).
Engine: (202) 1,175hp Alfa Romeo RA1000 RC41-I (DB 601A-1) inverted-vee-12; (205) 1,475hp Fiat RA1050 RC58 Tifone (Typhoon) (DB 605A-1).
Dimensions: Span 34ft 8½in (10·58m) (205N, 36ft 11in, 11·25m); length 29ft 0½in (8·85m) (205N, 31ft 4in, 9·55m); height 9ft 11½in (3·04m) (205N, 10ft 8in, 3·25m).
Weights: Empty (202) 5,181lb (2350kg), (205V) 5,691lb (2581kg), (205N-2) 6,082lb (2759kg); loaded (202) 6,636lb (3010kg), (205V) 7,514lb (3408kg), (205N-2) 8,364lb (3794kg).
Performance: Maximum speed (202) 370mph (595km/h), (205V) 399mph (642km/h), (205N-2) 389mph (626km/h); service ceiling (all) about 36,000ft (11,000m).
Armament: See text.
History: First flight (202) 10 August 1940; service delivery (202) July 1941; final delivery, early 1944.
User: Italy (RA, CB, ARSI).

continued on page 136 ▶

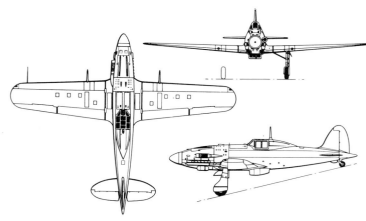

Above: Three-view of the Macchi C.205V Veltro.

Below: Wartime colour photograph of a Macchi C.202 Folgore taxiing out along a newly prepared taxiway. A ground-crewman rides on each wing, standard practice with poor-vision fighters.

Left: There were at least 25 authorised camouflage schemes used by Regia Aeronautica aircraft. This C.202 has one of the desert colour mixtures. Note the belly venturi.

Right: Another C.202 Folgore, fitted with the usual carburettor air-inlet sand filter. Note arms of the stormo and 73 Squadriglia.

Left: One of the C.205V Greyhounds to see active service. These aircraft were not outstanding in armament or performance, but beautiful to fly.

Right: Very few Macchi C.205N Oriones reached combat units. This example saw operational duty with the Aviazione Nazionale Repubblicana in December 1943.

Above: An M.C.202 Serie III. These were among the best fighters of the war, though available only in trivial numbers.

Above: The prototype M.C.205V Veltro, first Italian fighter with the DB 605 engine, flown on 19 April 1942.

▶**Development:** Essentially a re-engined Saetta, the MC202 was much more powerful and after quick and painless development went into production (first by Breda) in late 1940. Armament remained two 12·7mm Breda-SAFAT above the engine and two 7·7mm Breda-SAFAT in the wings, plus two bombs up to 353lb (160kg) or tanks. From the outset the cockpit was completely enclosed, opposition to this having finally withered. Up to Serie VIII many aircraft had no wing guns, while at least one Serie had two 20mm Mauser MG 151/20 in underwing fairings. About 1,500 were built by 1943, 392 by Macchi, achieving complete superiority over the Hurricane

and P-40. The more powerful 205 flew on 19 April 1942, but pathetic industrial performance (on engine as well as airframe) limited output to 262. The 205 Serie III dropped the 7·7mm wing guns in favour of MG 151/20s. The 205N was a total structural redesign instead of a converted 200, the first flying on 1 November 1942 with one MG 151/20 and four 12·7mm, two in the wing roots. It was an outstanding machine, retaining all the agility of earlier Macchi fighters, and the 205N-2 added powerful armament with two more MG 151/20 instead of the wing-root 12·7mm. None reached service.

Left: Serving with the 11th Squadriglia, this C.202 Folgore is painted in one of the predominantly green camouflage schemes.

Right: Pinnacle of the Macchi single-engined fighter designs to reach the squadrons, the C.205N-1 combined superb handling with improved firepower. This one joined the Co-Belligerent Air Force.

Piaggio P.108

P.108A, B, C, M and T

Origin: Società Anonima Piaggio & Cia.
Type: A, anti-shipping; B, bomber; C, civil; M, bomber; T, military transport.
Engines: Four 1,500hp Piaggio P.XII RC35 18-cylinder radials.

Dimensions: Span 104ft 11¾in (32·00m); length (B) 73ft 1½in (22·29m); height 19ft 8¼in (6·00m).
Weights: Empty (typical B) 36,375lb (16,500kg); max loaded 65,885lb (29,885kg).
Performance: Maximum speed (typical B) 267mph (430km/h); service ceiling 19,685ft (6000m); range with max bomb load 2,175 miles (3500km).
Armament: (B) eight 12·7mm Breda-SAFAT, two pairs in remote-sighted turrets above outer nacelles and four singles in nose and ventral turrets and waist positions; internal bay for three torpedoes or bomb load up to 7,716lb (3500kg).
History: First flight 1939; service delivery 1941; final delivery early 1944.
Users: Italy (RA, CB, ARSI), Germany (Luftwaffe).

Development: Derived from the P.50 of 1938, this large and powerful machine was the only Piaggio type to see much service in World War II, though 30 designs had been in use between the wars. The only model to see much use was the 108B (Bombardiere), of which 163 were built. Opening with night attacks on Gibraltar in early 1942, they later saw extensive service over North Africa, the Balkans, Soviet Union and Mediterranean (the Duce's son, Bruno Mussolini, was killed in one). The 16 C (Civile) aircraft were impressed as military transports, but the T (Trasporto) remained a prototype. The Luftwaffe took over the impressive 108A (Artiglieri) with 102mm gun in the forward fuselage. The M (Modificato) would have had a nose armament of one 20mm and four 7·7mm.

Left: A regular P.108B in operational service with the Regia Aeronautica. Though it made little impact on the war, the big Piaggio was, in fact, one of the heaviest and most powerful bombers of the entire conflict.

Savoia-Marchetti S.M.79 Sparviero

S.M.79-I, II and III, 79B and 79-JR

Origin: SIAI "Savoia-Marchetti"; built under licence (79-II) by Aeronautica Macchi and OM "Reggiane"; (79 JR) Industria Aeronautica Romana.
Type: 4/5-seat bomber, torpedo bomber and reconnaissance.
Engines: (I) three 780hp Alfa-Romeo 126 RC34 nine-cylinder radials; (II) three 1,000hp Piaggio P.XI RC40 14-cylinder two-row radials (one batch, 1,030hp Fiat A.80 RC41); (79B) two engines (many types); (79-JR) two 1,220hp Junker Jumo 211Da inverted-vee-12 liquid-cooled.
Dimensions: Span 69ft 6½in (21·2m); length (I) 51ft 10in; (II) 53ft 1¾in (16·2m); (B, -JR) 52ft 9in; height (II) 13ft 5½in (4·1m).

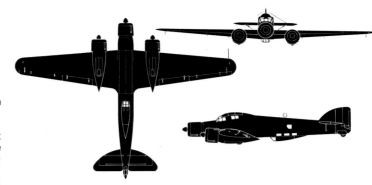

Above: Three-view of a typical S.M.79-II.

Left: A Savoia-Marchetti S.M.79-JR bomber of the 3rd Air Corps, Royal Air Forces of Romania, Eastern Front, 1943.

Below: S.M.79-II bombers of the Squadriglie Aerosiluranti (torpedo-bomber squadrons) with their weapons.

Weights: Empty (I) 14,990lb (6800kg); (II) 16,755lb (7600kg); (-JR) 15,860lb (7195kg); maximum loaded (I) 23,100lb (10,500kg); (II) 24,192lb (11,300kg); (-JR) 23,788lb (10,470kg).
Performance: Maximum speed (I) 267mph; (II) 270mph (434km/h); (B) 255mph; (-JR) 276mph; initial climb (typical) 1,150ft (350m)/min; service ceiling (all) 21,325–23,300ft (7000m); range with bomb load (not torpedoes), typical, 1,243 miles (2000km).
Armament: (Typical) one 12·7mm Breda-SAFAT fixed firing ahead from above cockpit, one 12·7mm manually aimed from open dorsal position, one 12·7mm manually aimed from rear of ventral gondola and one 7·7mm Lewis manually aimed from either beam window; internal bomb bay for up to 2,200lb (1000kg) or two 450mm torpedoes slung externally; (79B and -JR) no fixed gun, typically three/five 7·7mm guns and bomb load up to 2,640lb (1200kg).
History: First flight (civil prototype) late 1934; service delivery (I) late 1936; (II) October 1939; final delivery (III) early 1944.
Users: Brazil, Iraq, Italy (RA, CB, ARSI), Jugoslavia, Romania, Spain (Nationalist).

Development: Though often derided — as were most Italian arms in World War II — the S.M.79 Sparviero (Hawk) was a fine and robust bomber that unfailingly operated in the most difficult conditions with great reliability. The prototype, fitted with various engines and painted in civil or military liveries, set various world records in 1935–36, despite its mixed structure of steel tube, light alloy, wood and fabric. Built at unprecedented rate for the Regia Aeronautica, the 79-I established an excellent reputation with

the Aviación Legionaria in the Spanish civil war, while other Stormi laid the basis for great proficiency with torpedoes. Altogether about 1,200 of all versions served with the Regia Aeronautica, while just over 100 were exported. Most exports were twin-engined 79B versions, but the Romanian-built 79-JR was more powerful and served on the Russian front in 1941–44.

Below: Early S.M.79-I bombers of the Regia Aeronautica's 52o Squadriglia, photographed just before the war.

Reggiane Re 2000 series

Re 2000 Falco I (Falcon), 2001 Falco II, 2002 Ariete (Ram) and 2005 Sagittario (Archer)

Origin: Officine Meccaniche "Reggiane" SA; some Héjja built under licence by Mavag and Weiss Manfred, Hungary.
Type: Single-seat fighter.
Engine: (2000) one 1,025hp Piaggio P.XIbis RC40 14-cylinder two-row radial; (Héjja) 1,000hp WM K14; (2001) 1,175hp Alfa Romeo RA.1000 RC41 (DB 601) inverted-vee-12; (2002) 1,175hp Piaggio P.XIX RC45, (as P.XIbis); (2005) 1,475hp Fiat RA.1050 RC58 Tifone (Typhoon) (DB 605, as DB 601).
Dimensions: Span 36ft 1in (11m); length (2000) 26ft 2½in (7·95m); (2001–2) 26ft 10in; (2005) 28ft 7¾in; height (typical) 10ft 4in (3·15m).
Weight: Empty (2000) 4,200lb (1905kg); maximum loaded (2000) 5,722lb (2595kg); (2001) 7,231lb; (2002) 7,143lb; (2005) 7,848lb.
Performance: Maximum speed (2000–2) 329–337mph (say, 535km/h); (2005) 391mph (630km/h); initial climb (typical) 3,600ft (1100m)/min; service ceiling (2000) 36,745ft (11,200m); range (typical) 590 miles (950km).
Armament: See text.
History: First flight (2000) 1938; (2001) 1940; (2002) late 1941; (2005) September 1942.
Users: (Re 2000) Hungary, Italy (Navy), Sweden; (2001) Italy (RA and ARSI); (2002) Germany (Luftwaffe), Italy (ARSI); (2005) Germany (Luftwaffe), Italy (ARSI).

Development: A subsidiary of Caproni, the Reggiane company copied the Seversky P-35 to produce the nimble but lightly built Re 2000. Extremely manoeuvrable, it had two 12·7mm Breda-SAFAT on the top decking and could carry a 441lb (200kg) bomb. Almost all the 170 built served non-Italian forces, Sweden using 60 (as the J 20) and Hungary about 100 (as the Héjja) on the Eastern front. Production of the 2001 reached 252, in four series with two 12·7mm either alone or augmented by two 7·7mm or (in 150 CN2 night fighters) 20mm wing guns, plus a 1,410lb (640kg) bomb. About 50 2002 were built and only 48 of the excellent 2005 with three 20mm and two 12·7mm.

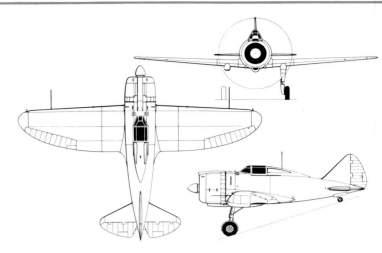

Above: Three-view of the Re 2000 Serie III.

Above: Very few radial-engined Reggiane fighters were delivered to the Regia Aeronautica. This appears to be an Re 2000-I.

Below: Almost certainly taken aboard the battleship Roma, this shows catapult trials of the Re 2000 Serie II.

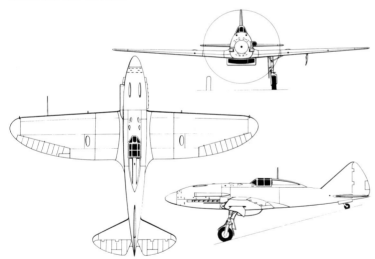

Above: Three-view of the Re 2005 Sagittario.

Below, right: Reggiane Re 2001 CN night fighters, serving with the Regia Aeronautica before the armistice of September 1943.

Below: MM 494, the first prototype Re 2005 Sagittario, flown in September 1942. Only about 48 were delivered.

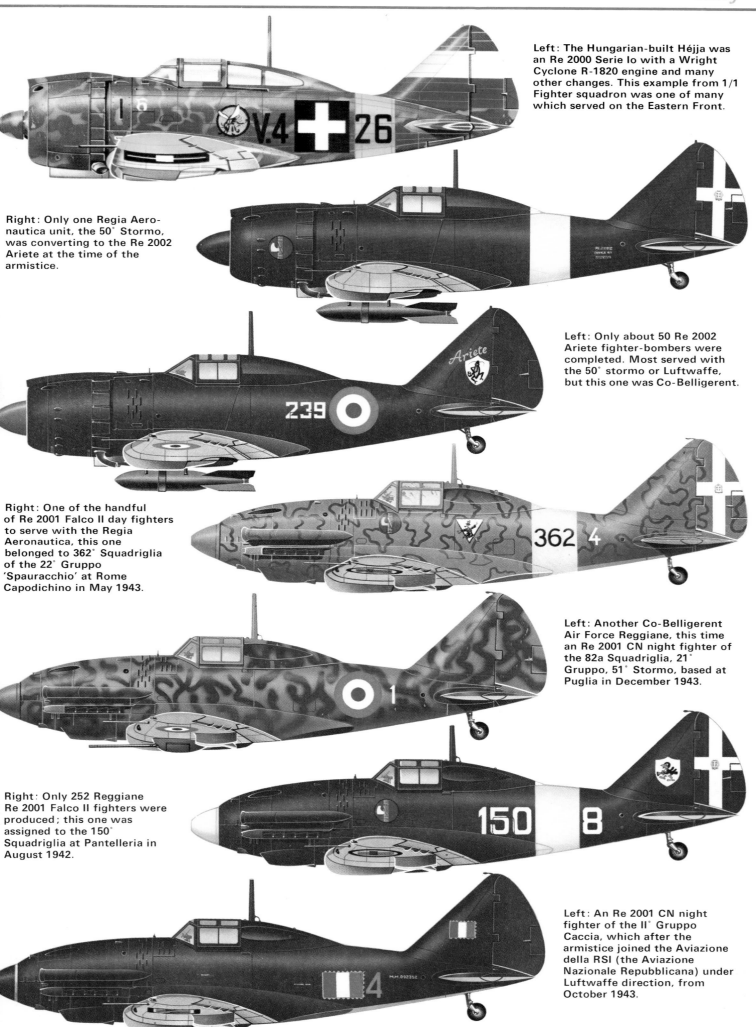

Left: The Hungarian-built Héjja was an Re 2000 Serie Io with a Wright Cyclone R-1820 engine and many other changes. This example from 1/1 Fighter squadron was one of many which served on the Eastern Front.

Right: Only one Regia Aeronautica unit, the 50° Stormo, was converting to the Re 2002 Ariete at the time of the armistice.

Left: Only about 50 Re 2002 Ariete fighter-bombers were completed. Most served with the 50° stormo or Luftwaffe, but this one was Co-Belligerent.

Right: One of the handful of Re 2001 Falco II day fighters to serve with the Regia Aeronautica, this one belonged to 362° Squadriglia of the 22° Gruppo 'Spauracchio' at Rome Capodichino in May 1943.

Left: Another Co-Belligerent Air Force Reggiane, this time an Re 2001 CN night fighter of the 82a Squadriglia, 21° Gruppo, 51° Stormo, based at Puglia in December 1943.

Right: Only 252 Reggiane Re 2001 Falco II fighters were produced; this one was assigned to the 150° Squadriglia at Pantelleria in August 1942.

Left: An Re 2001 CN night fighter of the II° Gruppo Caccia, which after the armistice joined the Aviazione della RSI (the Aviazione Nazionale Repubblicana) under Luftwaffe direction, from October 1943.

Savoia-Marchetti S.M.81 Pipistrello

S.M.81 Pipistrello (Bat) of many serie

Origin: SIAI "Savoia-Marchetti".
Type: Multi-role bomber, transport and utility.
Engines: (Most) three aircooled radials, usually 700hp Piaggio P.X nine-cylinder; others 580hp Alfa Romeo 125, 680hp Piaggio P.IX, 900hp Alfa Romeo 126 and 1,000hp Gnome-Rhône K-14; (81B, two engines, various).
Dimensions: Span 78ft 8¾in (24·00m); length (typical) 58ft 4¾in (17·80 m); height 14ft 7¼in (4·45m).
Weights: Empty (typical) 13,890lb (6300kg); max loaded 23,040lb (10,450kg).
Performance: Maximum speed 211mph (340km/h); typical range with bomb load 932 miles (1500km).

Below: Before Italy joined World War II many S.M.81 bombers had brightly painted upper surfaces (for forced landings).

Above: A pair of Pipistrello bombers, in silver or cream dope overall, on maritime reconnaissance duty. Note the large ventral gondola for the bomb aimer, a feature of several Italian aircraft.

Armament: Varied or absent, but usually two 7·7mm Breda-SAFAT in powered dorsal turret, two more in retractable ventral turret and two more aimed manually from beam windows; internal weapon bay for up to 2,205lb (1000kg) of bombs.
History: First flight 1935; service delivery, autumn 1935; final delivery, possibly 1941.
Users: Italy (RA, CB, ARSI, post-war AF), Spain.

Development: A military version of the very successful S.M.73 airliner, the S.M.81 was one of the world's best multi-role bomber/transport aircraft in 1935, but when Italy entered World War II in June 1940 (by which time about 100 were in service, plus about 40 in Spain) it was becoming obsolescent. Despite this its serviceability and popularity resulted in it appearing in every theatre in which Italy was engaged, from Eritrea to the Soviet Union. Until 1942 it was an important night bomber in the eastern Mediterranean, and it became the most important Italian transport in terms of numbers (though much inferior to the S.M.82 in capability). A few served with the post-war Aeronautica Militare until about 1951.

Savoia-Marchetti S.M.82 Canguru

S.M.82 Canguru (Kangaroo) of various serie

Origin: SIAI "Savoia-Marchetti".
Type: Heavy freight and troop transport.
Engines: Three 950hp Alfa Romeo 128RC21 nine-cylinder radials.
Dimensions: Span 96ft 9½in (29·50m); length 73ft 9¾in (22·50m); height 18ft 0½in (5·50m).
Weights: Empty 26,455lb (12,000kg); loaded 39,728lb (18,020kg).
Performance: Maximum speed 204mph (328km/h); range with unspecified payload at 137mph (220km/h) 2,467 miles (3970km).
Armament: Usually Breda-SAFAT retractable hydraulic turret with one or two 12·7mm, plus two to five 7·7mm manually aimed from side windows; large internal bomb bay seldom used except for overload fuel tanks.
History: First flight 1939; final delivery 1943.
Users: Germany (Luftwaffe), Italy (RA, CB, ARSI, post-war AF), UK (RAF), US (AAF).

Development: An enlarged development of the S.M.75 Marsupiale, the Canguru was the most capable transport in large-scale service with the Axis during most of the war, and because of its unique capability was used

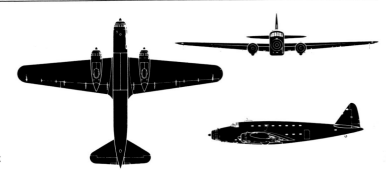

Above: Three-view of S.M.82 Canguru.

in substantial numbers even by the Luftwaffe. Though clearly underpowered, so that even with all three engines the rate of climb was pathetic (and near-zero at the seldom-used max overload weight of 20,000kg, 44,092lb), the Canguru was reliable and fully equipped with handling gear for aero engines and even dismantled fighters. Folding seats for 40 troops were provided (96 were once carried), and a normal fuel load was 15 to 18 drums of 40 Imp gal. The wing was wood, like most S.M. products, and the cavernous body steel tube and fabric. In September 1943 no fewer than 31 of these giants flew to join the Allies, and five were still in RAF foreign service in 1947.

Below: A Canguru loading torpedoes, without warheads. On the extreme right is an extremely rare bird, a Breda Ba 88 Lince (Lynx) twin-engined attack aircraft.

Below: The pot-bellied Canguru looked ungainly, and it was certainly underpowered, but it was probably the most capable transport in the whole armoury of the Axis powers.

Aichi D3A "Val"

D3A1 and D3A2

Origin: Aichi Tokei Denki KK.
Type: Two-seat carrier dive bomber.
Engine: 1,075hp Mitsubishi Kinsei 44 14-cylinder radial (D3A2, 1,200hp Kinsei 54).
Dimensions: Span 47ft 1½in (14·365m); (D3A2) 47ft 8in (14·53m); length 33ft 5½in (10·2m); (D3A2) 33ft 7in (10·25m); height 11ft (3·35m); (D3A2 same).
Weights: Empty 5,309lb (2408kg); (D3A2) 5,772lb (2618kg); loaded 8,047lb (3650kg); (D3A2) 8,378lb (3800kg).
Performance: Maximum speed 242mph (389km/h); (D3A2) 281mph (450km/h); service ceiling 31,170ft (9500m); (D3A2) 35,700ft (10,880m); range with bomb 1,131 miles (1820km); (D3A2) 969 miles (1560km).
Armament: Two fixed 7·7mm guns in wings, one pivoted in rear cockpit; centreline bomb of 551lb (250kg), plus two bombs under wings each of 66lb (30kg); (D3A2: wing bombs 132lb, 60kg).
History: First flight August 1936; (D3A2) probably 1941; termination of production 1944.
User: Imperial Japanese Navy.

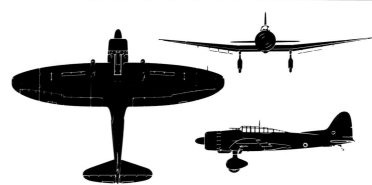

Above: Three-view of the cleaned-up Aichi D3A2.

Development: In World War II the proper designations of Japanese aircraft were difficult to remember and often unknown to the Allies, so each major type was allotted a codename. Even today "Aichi D3A" may mean little to a grizzled veteran to whom the name "Val" will evoke memories of terrifying dive-bombing attacks. Aichi began this design for the Imperial Navy in 1936, its shape showing the influence of Heinkel who were secretly advising the Navy at that time. A total of 478 D3A1, also called Model 11 or Type 99, were built by August 1942, when production switched to the D3A2, Model 22. The D3A1 was the dive bomber that attacked Pearl Harbor on 7 December 1941. In April 1942 Aichis confirmed their bomb-hitting accuracy of 80–82% by sinking the British carrier *Hermes* and heavy cruisers *Cornwall* and *Dorsetshire*. They were extremely strong and manoeuvrable, and until 1943 were effective dogfighters after releasing their bombs. But loss of skilled pilots in great battles of 1943–44, especially Midway and the Solomons, reduced bombing accuracy to 10% and the Aichis ceased to be the great threat they were in 1942. Production of the D3A2 was stopped in January 1944 at the 816th example of this cleaner and better-looking version. Some Aichis were converted as trainers or as overloaded Kamikaze aircraft. Nakajima developed a smaller version with retractable landing gear, the D3N1, but this was not adopted.

Above: Takeoff of a D3A1 from a Japanese carrier on 7 December 1941, en route for Pearl Harbor and World War II.

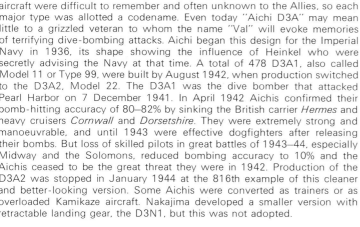

Right: The Aichi D3A1 was one of the world's best dive bombers at the time of its design in 1935. Also called Navy Dive Bomber Type 99 Model 11, it equipped Japanese carriers until the end of 1942.

Below: The later Val, the D3A2, or Type 99 Model 22, was a still better aircraft but never enjoyed Japanese air supremacy.

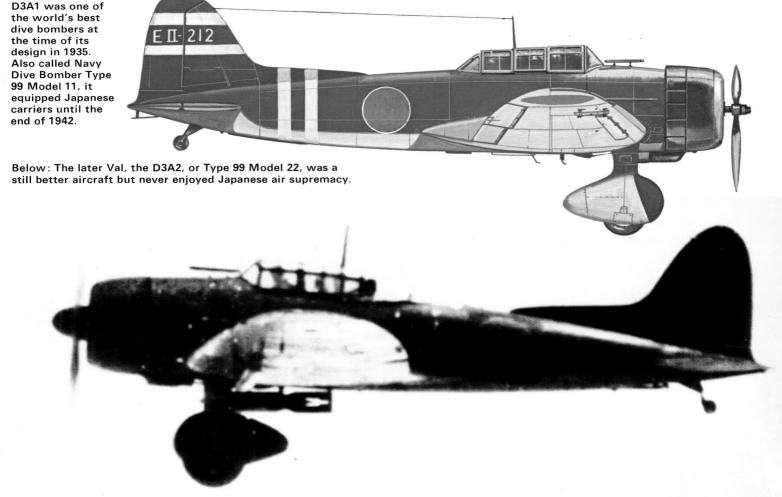

Aichi B7A Ryusei "Grace"

AM-23, 16-Shi Carrier Attack Bomber Ryusei (Shooting Star) (Allied code-name "Grace")

Origin: Aichi Kokuki KK; second-source production by Dai-Nijuichi Kaigun Kokusho (Sasebo Naval Air Arsenal).
Type: Two-seat carrier-based torpedo and dive bomber.
Engine: 1,825hp Nakajima NK9C Homare 12 18-cylinder radial.
Dimensions: Span 47ft 3in (14·40m); length 37ft 8½in (11·49m); height 13ft 4¼in (4·07m).
Weights: Empty 7,969lb (3614kg); loaded 12,568lb (5700kg).
Performance: Maximum speed 352mph (566km/h); service ceiling 29,365ft (8950m); range with full weapon load 1,150 miles (1850km); max range (overload) 1,889 miles (3040km).
Armament: Two 20mm Type 99 Model 2 in wings and single 7·92mm or 13mm gun aimed from rear cockpit; one 1,764lb (800kg) torpedo or similar weight of bombs.
History: First flight May 1942; service delivery May 1944; final delivery August 1945.
User: Japan (Imperial Navy).

Development: One of Japan's largest and most powerful carrier-based aircraft, the B7A was designed to a 1941 (16-Shi) specification for a fast and versatile aircraft to supplement and then replace the Nakajima B6N torpedo bomber and Yokosuka D4Y dive bomber. Though it did not carry

Above: A rare photograph of a fully operational B7A, complete with torpedo, apparently about to depart on a combat mission. Every operational flight was from land airstrips.

any more weapons than its predecessors, the B7A1 prototype proved to be greatly superior in performance, with speed and manoeuvrability at least as good as an A6M "Zero". Unfortunately the troublesome engine delayed development until Japan had lost command of the air, and by the time deliveries took place the last carriers were being sunk and home industry bombed to a standstill (the destruction of the Aichi Funakata plant by a May 1945 earthquake did not help). Only 114 aircraft flew, nine being B7A1 prototypes and the rest B7A2 production machines used from land bases.

Aichi E16A Zuiun "Paul"

AM-22, E16A1 Zuiun (Auspicious Cloud) (Allied code-name "Paul")

Origin: Aichi Kokuki KK; production transferred in 1944 to Nippon Hikoki KK.
Type: Two-seat reconnaissance seaplane.
Engine- 1,300hp Mitsubishi Kinsei 51 or 54 14-cylinder radial.
Dimensions: Span 42ft 0¼in (12·80m); length 35ft 6½in (10·84m); height 15ft 8½in (4·74m).
Weights: Empty 5,982lb (2713kg); loaded 8,379lb (3800kg); max overload 9,327lb (4230kg)
Performance: Maximum speed 278mph (448km/h); service ceiling 33,730ft (10,280m); range (normal) 600 miles (965km), (overload) 1,578 miles (2540km).
Armament: Two 20mm Type 99 cannon in wings and one 13mm Type 2 aimed from rear cockpit; one or two 551lb (250kg) bombs or other stores.
History: First flight May 1942; service delivery January 1944; final delivery August 1945.
User: Japan (Imperial Navy).

Development: This aircraft was designed to a 16-Shi (1941) specification for a much faster replacement for the E13A1, even though the latter was not then in service. The E16A1 had hydraulic dive brakes forming the fairings of the front float struts and could undertake steep diving attacks. Nevertheless, it was not as popular as its predecessor, and as the Allies enjoyed complete air superiority by 1944 it suffered heavily and seldom worked

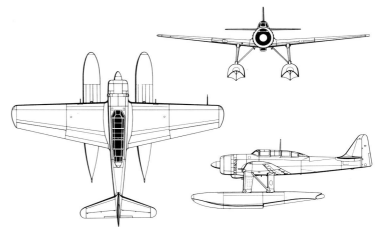

Above: Three-view of E16A1 Zuiun.

unhindered. Total production was only 256, Nippon Hikoki having mainly unskilled-student labour and being under heavy air attack. A single E16A2 flew with a 1,560hp Kinsei 62 engine.

Below: An excellent photograph of a production E16A1, which emphasizes the drag and weight penalty of the large float landing gear. Most crews preferred the old E13A1.

Aichi E13A "Jake"

E13A1, Navy Type 0 Reconnaissance Seaplane Model 11 (Allied code-name "Jake").

Origin: Aichi Tokei Denki KK; production also by Dai-Juichi Kaigun Kokusho (Hiro Naval Air Arsenal) and Kyushu Hikoki KK (Watanabe).
Type: Three-seat reconnaissance seaplane.
Engine: 1,080hp Mitsubishi Kinsei 43 14-cylinder radial.
Dimensions: Span 47ft 6¾in (14·50m); length 36ft 11¾in (11·27m); height 15ft 8in (4·79m).
Weights: Empty 5,825lb (2642kg); max loaded 8,048lb (3650kg).
Performance: Maximum speed 239mph (385km/h); service ceiling 26,100ft (7950m); maximum range 1,616 miles (2600km).
Armament: One 7·92mm Type 1 machine gun (based on German MG 15) aimed from rear cockpit, most late production in addition one 20mm Type 99 added as field modification firing down in limited arc from belly; four 132lb (60kg) bombs or depth charges — rarely, one 551lb (250kg).
History: First flight late 1938; service delivery 1941; final delivery August 1945.
User: Japan (Imperial Navy).

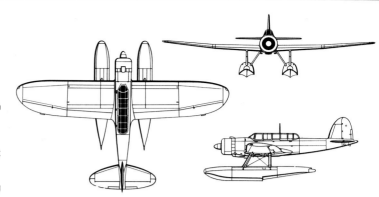

Above: Three-view of E13A1, without ventral cannon.

Below: A late-production E13A1 on its beaching chassis. Like the British Swordfish, it was more popular than its replacement.

Development: Though never famous, the E13A1 was made in larger numbers than any other Japanese floatplane, or marine aircraft of any type, and served on all fronts. Designed to a 1937 specification for a replacement for the Kawanishi E7K2, it was selected over rival aircraft from Kawanishi and Nakajima despite being larger and heavier. After various delays and changes Aichi got into production in December 1940. Operating from cruiser catapults and from seaplane tenders it made its debut in China in attacks on the Canton-Hangkow railway, and later reconnoitred Pearl Harbor before the attack of 7 December 1941. Despite poor armament this seaplane served in many roles including air/sea rescue and, in late 1944, Kamikaze attacks. By this time examples were being equipped with a cannon for strafing ships, improved radio and primitive MAD (magnetic anomaly detection) gear for finding submerged submarines. Production totalled 1,418.

Kawanishi H6K "Mavis"

H6K1 to H6K5, Navy Type 97 Large Flying Boat Models 1, 11, 22 and 23 (Allied code-name "Mavis")

Origin: Kawanishi Kokuki KK, Naruo.
Type: Long-range reconnaissance flying boat with crew of nine; (H6K3, H6K2-L and H6K4-L) transport.
Engines: Four Mitsubishi Kinsei 14-cylinder radials, (most) 1,000hp Kinsei 43, (H6K4 and 4-L) 1,070hp Kinsei 46, (H6K5) 1,300hp Kinsei 51 or 53.
Dimensions: Span 131ft 2¾in (40·00m); length 84ft 1in (25·63m); height 20ft 6¾in (6·27m).
Weights: Empty (H6K2) 22,796lb (10,340kg), (H6K5) 27,293lb (12,380 kg); normal loaded (1) 35,274lb (16,000kg), (5) 38,581lb (17,500kg); max loaded (1) as normal, (5) 50,706lb (23,000kg).
Performance: Maximum speed (1-4 typical) 207mph (333km/h), (5) 239mph (385km/h); range (most, normal) 2,690 miles (4330km), (5, normal) 3,107 miles (5000km), (5, max) 4,210 miles (6775km).
Armament: (1, 2, typical) hand-aimed 7·7mm Type 92 machine guns in bow and stern, plus a third in dorsal turret, (4, 5) 20mm Type 99 in tail turret and four or five 7·7mm Type 92 in nose, dorsal and beam blisters; (1, 2, 4, 5) two 1,764lb (800kg) torpedoes or total 2,205lb (1000kg) of bombs; (transport versions) no armament.

History: First flight 14 July 1936; service delivery January 1938; final delivery, mid-1943.
User: Japan (Imperial Navy).

Development: Obviously inspired by the Sikorsky S-42 but having a markedly superior performance, the H6K was an excellent machine and with an endurance of 26 hours made numerous outstanding missions. Until mid-1942 it was often engaged in bombing and torpedo attack, but lack of armour and self-sealing tanks caused even the H6K5 soon to revert to various auxiliary and (suffix L) transport roles. Altogether 215 of these graceful machines were delivered, the 2-L and 4-L transports normally seating up to 18 passengers and serving as the chief long-range Navy transports in the vast area held by the Japanese in the south-west Pacific. Several operated to airline-type schedules.

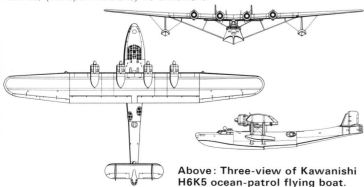

Above: Three-view of Kawanishi H6K5 ocean-patrol flying boat.

Right: One of a classic air-combat photographic sequence showing an H6K5 being shot down by Allied aircraft over the south-west Pacific. They usually flew alone.

Kawanishi H8K "Emily"

H8K1, H8K2; Type 2

Origin: Kawanishi Kokuki KK.
Type: Reconnaissance and attack flying boat.
Engines: Four Mitsubishi Kasei 14-cylinder two-row radials, (H8K1, Model 11) 1,530hp Kasei 12; (H8K2, Model 12) 1,850hp Kasei 22.
Dimensions: Span 124ft 8in (38m); length 92ft 3½in (28·1m); height 30ft 0¼in (9·15m).
Weights: Empty (H8K1) 34,000lb (15,440kg); (H8K2) 40,500lb (18,380 kg); loaded (H8K1) 68,343lb (31,000kg); (H8K2) 71,650lb (32,500kg).
Performance: Maximum speed (H8K1) 270mph (433km/h); (H8K2) 282mph (454km/h); initial climb 1,575ft (480m)/min; service ceiling 28,800ft (8770m); range, usually 3,000 miles (4800km), but overload reconnaissance range 4,474 miles (7200km).
Armament: Normally, five 20mm in power-driven nose, dorsal and tail

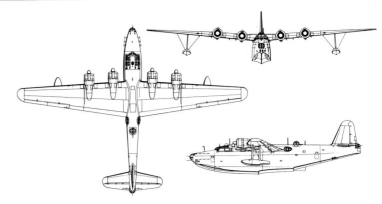

Above: Three-view of Kawanishi H8K2.

Kawanishi N1K1-J and 2-J Shiden "George"

N1K1-J and N1K2-J and variants

Origin: Kawanishi Kokuki KK; also built by Omura Kaigun Kokusho, Mitsubishi, Aichi, Showa and Dai-Juichi.
Type: Single-seat fighter.
Engine: One 1,990hp Nakajima Homare 21 18-cylinder two-row radial.
Dimensions: Span 39ft 3¼in (11·97m); length 29ft 1⅜in (8·885m); (N1K2-J) 30ft 8¼in (9·35m); height 13ft 3¾in (4·058m); (N1K2-J) 13ft (3·96m).
Weights: Empty 6,387lb (2897kg); (N1K2-J) 6,299lb (2657kg); maximum loaded 9,526lb (4321kg); (N1K2-J) 10,714lb (4860kg).
Performance: Maximum speed 362mph (583km/h); (N1K2-J) 369mph (594km/h); initial climb (both) 3,300ft (1000m)/min; service ceiling 39,698ft (12,100m); (N1K2-J) 35,400ft (10,760m); range 989 miles (1430km); (N1K2-J) 1,069 miles (1720km).
Armament: Originally two 20mm in wings and two 7·7mm above fuselage; after 20 aircraft, two extra 20mm added in underwing blisters; (N1K1-Ja) as before without 7·7mm; N1K2-J, four 20mm in wings, with more ammunition, plus two 550lb (250kg) bombs underwing or six rockets under fuselage; later prototypes, heavier armament.
History: First flight 24 July 1943; first flight (N1K2-J) 3 April 1944.
User: Japan (Imperial Navy).

Development: In September 1940 the JNAF issued a requirement for a high-speed seaplane naval fighter that did not need land airfields but could maintain air superiority during island invasions. The result was the formidable N1K1 Kyofu (mighty wind), produced by Kawanishi's Naruo plant and code-named "Rex" by the Allies. It was from this central-float seaplane that Kikuhara's team very quickly devised the N1K1-J landplane (Allied name: "George"). Though a hasty lash-up it was potentially one of

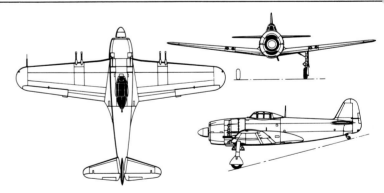

Above: Three-view of N1K2-J Shiden-Kai.

the best of all Japanese fighters. Its manoeuvrability, boosted by automatic combat flaps worked by a manometer (mercury U-tube) that measured angle of attack, was almost unbelievable. Drawbacks were the engine, plagued with snags, the poor view with the mid wing and the complex and weak landing gear (legacy from the mid-wing float-plane and big four-blade propeller). Naruo therefore produced the N1K2-J with low wing, new tail and drastically simpler airframe that could be built in half the man-hours. The unreliable engine still kept Shidens (the name meant violet lightning) mostly unserviceable, but they were potent and respected adversaries, encountered on all fronts from May 1944. Total production was 1,440. Huge production was planned from four companies and four Navy arsenals, but none produced more than ten aircraft, other than Kawanishi which delivered 543 1-Js and 362 2-Js from Naruo and 468 1-Js and 44 2-Js from Himeji. At Okinawa both versions were used in the Kamikaze role.

Right: Built from 23,000 fewer parts than the original mass-produced Shiden, the N1K2-J was an outstanding fighter in all respects, but appeared too late and in too-few numbers.

Above: A dramatic combat photograph taken, like that above right, from a USAAF B-26 Marauder. The latter's heavy armament defeated the cannon carried by the big flying boat.

Above: In this picture the "Emily", an H8K2, is going gently down towards the Pacific, whilst starting to burn. Even Allied fighter pilots treated this boat with respect, because most had an armament including five 20mm cannon.

Left: An H8K2 assigned to the Imperial Japanese Navy's Yokohama Air Corps. It was an outstanding aircraft.

Y-71

Left: An air-combat photograph of exceptional clarity for its time (1944). The H8K2 was the most powerful and most formidable long-range ocean patrol aircraft used by any of the combatants in World War II.

turrets and three 7·7mm manually aimed from beam and ventral rear windows; weapon load slung beneath inner wing, comprising two torpedoes or bombs to total weight of 4,410lb (2000kg); (H8K2-L) one 20mm and one 12·7mm, both manually aimed.

History: First flight late 1940; (production H8K1) August 1941.
User: Japan (Imperial Navy).

Development: Throughout the early part of the Pacific War the standard ocean patrol flying boat of the Imperial Japanese Navy was the Kawanishi H6K family (known to the Allies as "Mavis"). Though Kawanishi had a technical agreement with Short Brothers, the H6K looked like a Sikorsky S.42. It was an excellent aircraft, 217 being delivered including 36 transport

versions. The question of a replacement was a challenge and the JNAF published a specification in 1938 calling for 30 per cent higher speed and 50 per cent greater range. In the H8K, Kawanishi's design team, under Dr Kikuhara, created a flying boat which has served as the biggest single jump in the technology of such aircraft in all history. It was beyond dispute the best and most advanced flying boat in the world until many years after World War II. Its early trials were disastrous, because the great weight and narrow-beamed hull resulted in uncontrollable porpoising. The cure was found in adding a second step in the planing bottom, adjusting the powerful double-slotted Fowler flaps and adding a horizon mark on the large pitot post above the bows. Altogether the Kohnan plant built 17 H8K1, 114 H8K2 and 36 of the H8K2-L transport version (Allied name: "Emily"). They ranged alone on daring 24-hour missions and proved formidable. Their first sortie, in March 1942, was to have been a bombing raid on Oahu, Hawaii, with an intermediate refuelling from a submarine, but the target lay under dense low cloud. Later H8K2 versions carried radar and two had retractable stabilizing floats.

Kawasaki Ki-45 Toryu "Nick"

Ki-45 and 45A, Heavy Fighter Type 2, Kai B, C and D

Origin: Kawasaki Kokuki Kogyo.
Type: Originally long-range escort; later night fighter and attack.
Engines: Two 1,080hp Mitsubishi Ha-102 (Type 1) 14-cylinder two-row radials.
Dimensions: Span 49ft 3½in (15·02m); length (Kai C) 36ft 1in (11m); height 12ft 1½in (3·7m).
Weights: Empty (Kai A) 8,340lb (3790kg); (Kai C) 8,820lb (4000kg); loaded (all) 12,125lb (5500kg).
Performance: Maximum speed (all) 336mph (540km/h); initial climb 2,300ft (700m)/min; service ceiling 32,800ft (10,000m); range, widely conflicting reports, but best Japanese sources suggest 1,243 miles (2000km) with combat load for all versions.
Armament: (Ki-45-I and Kai-A) two 12·7mm fixed in nose and two 7·7mm manually aimed from rear cockpit; (Kai-B) same plus 37mm cannon in lower right forward fuselage (often with only one 12·7mm); (Kai-C) adapted for night fighting in May 1944, two 12·7mm installed at 30° between cockpits, with two 12·7mm and one 20mm or 37mm in nose; antiship versions, said to have carried 50mm or 75mm gun under nose, plus two 551lb (250kg) bombs under wings.
History: First flight (Ha-20 engine) January 1939; (Ha-25 engine) July 1940; (production Ki-45) September 1941.
User: Japan (Imperial Army).

Development: The first twin-engined fighter of the Imperial Japanese Army, the Ki-45 Toryu (dragon-slayer) was a long time in gestation. It was designed at Kawasaki's Gifu factory to meet a 1936 requirement issued in March 1937. Kawasaki had never used twin air-cooled engines and the Nakajima Ha-20B was an undeveloped engine which misbehaved; pilots disliked the hand-cranked landing gear. After trying contraprops, the choice fell on the Navy Ha-25 Sakae engine, but this in turn was replaced by the Ha-102 soon after production began in 1941. The Akashi plant began to

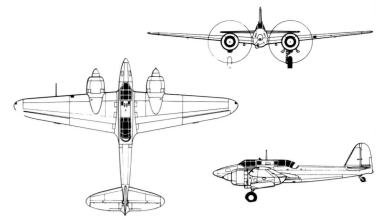

Above: Three-view of Kawasaki Ki-45 Kai-B with 37mm cannon; the Kai-C night fighter added two oblique upward-firing guns.

build the Ki-45 as a second source in late 1942, but combined output was only 1,698. Despite this modest total, and the fact that these aircraft were continually being modified, they were met on every Pacific front and known as "Nick". They were fairly fast and manoeuvrable but not really formidable until, on 27 May 1944, four Kai-B (modification B) made the first-ever suicide attack (on the north coast of New Guinea). By mid-1944 most Ki-45s had been modified to Kai-C configuration as night fighters, claiming seven victories over B-29s on the night of 15 June 1944. The two main Ki-45 bases at the close of the war were Hanoi and Anshan (Manchuria), from which aircraft made night interceptions and day Kamikaze attacks. The Ki-45 never operated in its design role of long-range escort.

Right: An early Ki-45, probably used as an engineering test aircraft since it does not bear the badge of a fighter training school. Engines are Ha-25s.

Left: One of the most colourful late-war examples was this Ki-45-Hei (Kai-C) based at Matsudo, Chiba Prefecture, in August 1945. It belongs to the 53rd Sentai (note badge on tail) and was assigned to the Shinten unit (anti-B-29).

Kawasaki Ki-48 "Lily"

Ki-48-I, -IIa, -IIb and -IIc (Allied code-name "Lily")

Origin: Kawasaki Kokuki Kogyo KK.
Type: Four-seat light bomber.
Engines: Two 14-cylinder radials, (-I) 980hp Nakajima Ha-25 (Army Type 99), (-II) 1,150hp Nakajima Ha-115 (Army Type 1).
Dimensions: Span 57ft 3¾in (17·47m); length (-I) 41ft 4in (12·60m), (-II) 41ft 10in (12·75m); height 12ft 5½in (3·80m).
Weights: Empty (-I) 8,928lb (4050kg), (-II) 10,030lb (4550kg); loaded (-I) 13,337lb (6050kg), (-II) 14,880lb (6750kg).
Performance: Maximum speed (-I) 298mph (480km/h), (-II) 314mph (505km/h); range (both, bomb load not specified) 1,491 miles (2400km).
Armament: (most) three 7·7mm Type 89 manually aimed from nose, dorsal and ventral positions, (-IIc) two Type 89 in nose, one ventral and manually aimed 12·7mm Type 1 dorsal; (all) internal bay for bomb load of

Above: The Ki-48-IIb was fitted with snow-fence type dive-bombing airbrakes above and below the wings.

up to 882lb (400kg), with normal load of 661lb (300kg) (-II capable of carrying 1,764lb, 800kg, but seldom used).
History: First flight July 1939; service delivery July or August 1940; final delivery October 1944.
User: Japan (Imperial Army).

Development: The Imperial Army's procurement organization tended to plan aircraft to meet existing, rather than future, threats. This straightforward bomber was requested in answer to the Soviet Union's SB-2. The latter was designed in 1933 and in action in Spain in 1936, but the Ki-48 (which was inferior in bomb load and only slightly faster) was a World War II machine. Entering service in China, it did well and proved popular, and it soon became the most important light bomber in the south-west Pacific with 557 -I built by June 1942. But its deficient performance and protection forced it to operate by night, which reduced the effectiveness of the small bomb load. The lengthened and more powerful -IIa had armour and protected tanks, and the -IIb had dive-bombing airbrakes; later examples of both had a dorsal fin. The -IIc had better armament, with provision also for machine guns fired from each side of the nose, but the Ki-48 was inherently obsolete and after a total of 1,977 of all versions production stopped in 1944. Many were used for suicide attacks and as test-beds for missiles and the Ne-00 turbojet (carried on a pylon under the bomb bay).

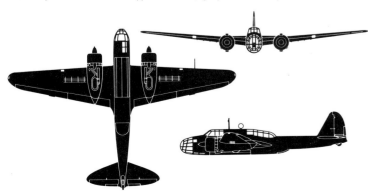

Above: Three-view of Ki-48-IIb (IIc similar).

Kawasaki Ki-102 "Randy"

Ki-102a, b and c
(Allied code-name "Randy")

Origin: Kawasaki Kokuki Kogyo KK.
Type: Two-seat (a) high-altitude fighter, (b) ground-attack aircraft or (c) night fighter.
Engines: Two 1,500hp Mitsubishi Ha-112 14-cylinder radials, (a, c) Ha-112-II Ru with turbochargers.
Dimensions: Span (a, b) 51ft 1in (15·57m), (c) 56ft 6¼in (17·23m); length (a, b) 37ft 6¾in (11·45m), (c) 42ft 9¾in (13·05m); height 12ft 1¾in (3·70m).
Weights: Empty (a) 11,354lb (5150kg), (b) 10,913lb (4950kg), (c) 11,464lb (5200kg); loaded (a) 15,763lb (7150kg), (b) 16,094lb (7300kg), (c) 16,755lb (7600kg).
Performance: Maximum speed (a, b) 360mph (580km/h), (c) 373mph (600km/h); service ceiling (a) 42,650ft (13,000m), (b) 32,800ft (10,000m),

Below: A standard Ki-102b after capture. This has the D/F loop acorn above the fuselage and the short-barrel 57mm gun.

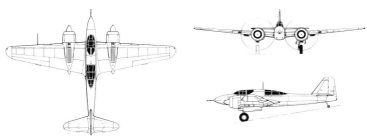

Above: Ki-102b with long-barrel 57mm and without D/F acorn.

(c) 44,295ft (13,500m); range (a, b) 1,243 miles (2000km), (c) 1,367 miles (2200km).
Armament: (a) one fixed 37mm Ho-203 in nose and two 20mm Ho-5 below, (b) one 57mm Ho-401 in nose, two Ho-5 below and manually aimed 12·7mm Ho-103 in rear cockpit, (c) two 30mm Ho-105 under fuselage and two 20mm Ho-5 mounted obliquely.
History: First flight March 1944; service delivery, about November 1944.
User: Japan (Imperial Army).

Development: In August 1942 the Ki-45 Toryu design team under Takeo Doi began work on a development designated Ki-96, three of these 3,000hp single-seat "heavy fighters" being built. In August 1943 approval was given for a further development with crew of two for use in the ground-attack role. Three prototypes and 20 pre-production Ki-102 were built, followed by 215 Ki-102b (Ki-102 Otsu) of which a few saw action in Okinawa. Some were used in the Igo-1-B air-to-ground missile programme. Two were rebuilt with pressure cabin as prototypes of the Ki-108, but the size of development task for this led to the Ki-102a being launched as a high-altitude fighter without pressure cabin. About 15 were delivered in July-August 1945 as the Ki-102 Ko. Right at the end of the war two Ki-102b were completely rebuilt as prototypes of the 102c night fighter with AI radar, greater span and length, new cockpit with rear-facing radar operator and different armament.

147

Kawasaki Ki-61 Hien "Tony"

Ki-61-I, II and III (Type 3 fighter) and Ki-100 (Type 5)

Origin: Kawasaki Kokuki Kogyo.
Type: Single-seat fighter.
Engine: (Ki-61-I) one 1,175hp Kawasaki Ha-40 inverted-vee 12 liquid-cooled; (Ki-61-II) one 1,450hp Kawasaki Ha-140 of same layout; (Ki-100) one 1,500hp Mitsubishi Ha-112-II 14-cylinder two-row radial.
Dimensions: Span 39ft 4½in (12m); length (-I) 29ft 4in (8·94m); (-II) 30ft 0½in (9·16m); (Ki-100) 28ft 11¼in (8·82m); height (all) 12ft 2in (3·7m).
Weights: Empty (-I) 5,798lb (2630kg); (-II) 6,294lb (2855kg); (Ki-100) 5,567lb (2525kg); loaded (-I) 7,650lb (3470kg); (-II) 8,433lb (3825kg); (Ki-100) 7,705lb (3495kg).
Performance: Maximum speed (-I) 348mph (560km/h); (-II) 379mph (610km/h); (Ki-100) 367mph (590km/h); initial climb (-I, -II) 2,200ft (675m)/min; (Ki-100) 3,280ft (1000m)/min; service ceiling (-I) 32,800ft (10,000m); (-II) 36,089ft (11,000m); (Ki-100) 37,729ft (11,500m); range (-I, -II) 990–1,100 miles (-I, 1800km, -II, 1600km); (Ki-100) 1,243 miles (2000km).
Armament: (Ki-61-Ia) two 20mm MG 151/20 in wings, two 7·7mm above engine; (-Id) same but wing guns 30mm; (-IIb) four 20mm Ho-5 in wings; (Ki-100) two Ho-5 in wings and two 12·7mm in fuselage, plus underwing racks for two 551lb (250kg) bombs.
History: First flight (Ki-60) March 1941; (Ki-61) December 1941; service delivery (Ki-61-I) August 1942; first flight (-II) August 1943; (Ki-100) 1 February 1945.

Right: A Ki-61-IIb bearing the markings of the 2nd Chutai's 244th Sentai (Tokyo defence area, 1945).

Below: An early prototype, with Ha-40 engine and original canopy. It was judged the best Army fighter of its day.

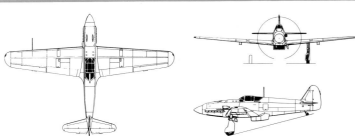

Above: Three-view of Ki-61 (interim aircraft with canopy having features of -I and -II and wing of -IIa).

User: Japan (Imperial Army).

Development: Kawasaki purchased a licence to build the German DB 601 engine in 1937 and the resulting revised and lightened engine emerged in 1940 as the Ha-40. Around this engine Kawasaki planned the Ki-60 and a lighter fighter designated Ki-61. Hien (the Japanese name meaning flying swallow). The latter was completed in December 1941 and flew well, reaching a speed of 368mph. During the first half of 1942 the prototype was extensively tested, performing very well against a captured P-40E and a Bf 109E sent to Japan by submarine. The submarine also brought 800 Mauser MG 151 cannon, and these were fitted to most early Ki-61s despite the unreliability of the supply of electrically fired ammunition. The Gifu

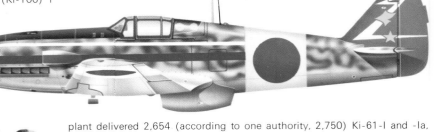

plant delivered 2,654 (according to one authority, 2,750) Ki-61-I and -Ia, the latter being redesigned for easier servicing and increased manoeuvrability. They went into action around New Guinea in April 1943, were called "Tony" by the Allies, and were the only Japanese fighters with a liquid-cooled engine. They were constantly in air combat, later moving to the Philippines and finally back to Japan. By 1944 the Ki-61-II was trickling off the assembly line with an unreliable engine that could not meet production demands. The II had a bigger wing and new canopy, but was soon replaced by the IIa with the old, proven, wing. Only 374 of all -II versions were built, and in early 1945 one of 275 engineless airframes was fitted with the Ha-112 radial. Despite the sudden lash-up conversion the result was a staggeringly fine fighter, easily the best ever produced in Japan. With desperate haste this conversion went into production as the Ki-100. One of the first Ki-100 units destroyed 14 Hellcats without loss to themselves in their first major battle over Okinawa and this easily flown and serviced machine fought supremely well against B-29s and Allied fighters to the end.

Kyushu K11W Shiragiku

K11W1 and W2 Shiragiku (White Chrysanthemum)

Origin: KK Watanabe Tekkosho (later Kyushu Hikoki KK).
Type: Trainer, transport and multi-role utility.
Engine: 515hp Hitachi GK2B Amakaze 21 nine-cylinder radial.
Dimensions: Span 49ft 1¾in (14·98m); length 33ft 7¼in (10·24m); height 12ft 10¾in (3·931m).
Weights: Empty (1) 3,697lb (1677kg); loaded (1) 5,829lb (2644kg), max overload (1) 6,173lb (2800kg).
Performance: Maximum speed 139mph (224km/h); range at 106mph (170km/h) as gunnery trainer 730 miles (1175km).
Armament: 7·7mm Type 92 manually aimed from rear cockpit, two 66lb (30kg) bombs on underwing racks (as Kamikaze, 551lb, 250kg, bomb under fuselage).
History: First flight, November 1942; service delivery, summer 1943; final delivery, August 1945.
User: Japan (Imperial Navy).

Development: Though one of the commonest aircraft in wartime Japan, the K11W never received an Allied code-name (though such names were allotted to 13 types never used by Japan at all and to 15 types which were pure fiction and never even existed). Obviously based on the North American O-47, this lumbering machine would probably have been better as a twin. In the capacious fuselage were cockpits for the pilot and radio-operator/gunner above the wing, and the instructor, navigator and bomb-aimer below. By VJ-day 798 had been built, a small number at the end of the war

being of the wooden K11W2 type used for transport and ASW. A derived version was the wooden Q3W1 Nankai (South Sea) two-seater with square-tipped wings and tail for ASW use carrying radar and MAD gear. It landed wheels-up in January 1945 and was abandoned.

Below: A standard K11W1 after capture. The main entry door is on the left side just behind the trailing edge. So slow a suicide attacker could hardly be effective.

Kyushu Q1W Tokai "Lorna"

Q1W1 and W2 Tokai (Eastern Sea) and Q1W1-K Tokai Ren (Eastern Sea Trainer) (Allied code-name "Lorna")

Origin: Kyushu Hikoki KK (previously Watanabe).
Type: Three-seat ASW aircraft, (-K) four-seat trainer.
Engines: Two 610hp Hitachi GK2C Amakaze 31 nine-cylinder radials.
Dimensions: Span 52ft 6in (16·00m); length 39ft 8¼in (12.09m); height 13ft 6¼in (4·118m).
Weights: Empty 6,839lb (3050kg); loaded 10,582lb (4800kg); max overload 11,755lb (5332kg).
Performance: Maximum speed 200mph (322km/h); normal range (315 Imp gal, 1430 litres) 814 miles (1310km), max range (715 Imp gal, 3240 litres) 2,013 miles (3240km).
Armament: 7·7mm Type 92 manually aimed from rear cockpit, external fuselage racks for two 551lb (250kg) depth bombs or other stores; provision in nose for two 20mm Type 99 cannon fixed firing ahead or inclined slightly down.
History: First flight September 1943; service delivery, late 1944; final delivery August 1945.
User: Japan (Imperial Navy).

Development: Like other countries, Japan was slow to develop aircraft designed specifically for the vital ASW role. KK Watanabe's design team under Nojiri were assigned to the task under a 17-Shi specification in 1942, but various delays (mainly associated with radar) kept the Q1W away from action until the last year of the war. A straightforward all-metal machine, with constant-speed propellers, the Q1W1 used its hydraulic slotted flaps at 90° to carry out steep diving attacks, and from the start it was pleasant to fly. The crew compartment resembled a Do 17Z or Ju 88, and the usual

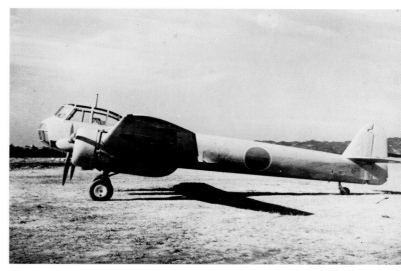

Above: One of the few surviving photographs of a Q1W1. This example was probably finished in pale sea grey, but others were dark olive and even dark blue. Japanese paint schemes were extremely diverse. Note white outline to Hinomaru.

mission was a low and slow search with naked eyes, though Type 3 ASV and MAD gear were carried. Most operations in 1945 were in Japanese territorial waters, the Korean strait and off Cheju Island, with no confirmed results. Even here many of the 153 built were shot down. The Q1W2 had a wood rear fuselage and the Q1W1-K was all-wood and used for electronic training.

Mitsubishi A5M "Claude"

A5M1 to A5M4

Origin: Mitsubishi Jukogyo KK; also built by Dai-Nijuichi KK and KK Watanabe Tekkosho.
Type: Single-seat carrier-based fighter.
Engine: One Nakajima Kotobuki (Jupiter) nine-cylinder radial; (1) 585hp 2-Kai-I; (2) 610hp 2-Kai-3; (4) 710hp Kotobuki 41 or (A5M4 Model 34) 3-Kai.
Dimensions: Span (2) 35ft 6in, (4) 36ft 1in (11·0m); length (2) 25ft 7in; (4) 24ft 9½in (7·55m); height 10ft 6in (3·2m).
Weights: Empty (2, typical) 2,400lb (1090kg); (4) 2,681lb (1216kg); maximum loaded (2) 3,545lb (1608kg); (4) 3,763lb (1708kg).
Performance: Maximum speed (2) 265mph (426km/h); (4) 273mph (440km/h); initial climb (2) 2,215ft (675m)/min; (4) 2,790ft (850m)/min; service ceiling (typical, all) 32,800ft (10,000m); range (2) 460 miles (740km); (4, auxiliary tank) 746 miles (1200km).
Armament: (All) two 7·7mm Type 89 machine guns firing on each side of upper cylinder of engine; racks for two 66lb (30kg) bombs under outer wings.
History: First flight 4 February 1935; service delivery 1936; final delivery December 1939.
User: Japan (Imperial Navy).

Development: One of the neatest little warplanes of its day, the A5M was the chief fighter of the Imperial Japanese Navy throughout the Sino-Japanese war and was numerically the most important at the time of Pearl Harbor. It was built to meet a 1934 specification calling for a speed of 218mph

Below, right: Two of the first A5Ms, probably from the small A5M1 batch, to reach the Chinese theatre in 1937. These turned the tables on the Chinese and achieved complete air supremacy.

Below: An A5M2b, with enclosed cockpit. Pilots disliked this feature, and subsequent versions reverted to an open cockpit.

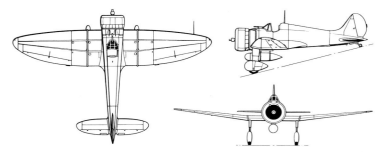

Above: Three-view of A5M4 with long-range tank.

and ability to reach 16,400ft in 6½ minutes, and beat these figures by a wide margin. Within days of first flight at Kagamigahara the Ka-14 prototype exceeded 279mph and reached 16,400ft in 5min 54sec, which the Japanese considered "far above the world level at that time". It was the Navy's first monoplane fighter, and one of the first all-metal stressed-skin machines built in Japan. The production A5M1, called Type 96 or S-96 and later given the Allied code name "Claude", abandoned the prototype's inverted-gull wing, originally chosen to try to improve pilot view, and also switched to a direct drive engine. The elliptical wing had split flaps, manoeuvrablity was superb and from their first combat mission on 18 September 1937, with the 2nd Combined Air Flotilla based at Shanghai, they acquitted themselves very well. During the conflict with the Soviet Union along the Manchukuo-Mongolian border throughout 1939 the A5M proved the biggest menace to the Russian aircraft, having earlier, on 2 December 1937, destroyed no fewer than ten I-16Bs of the Chinese in one dogfight over Nanking. Such results completely overcame the Naval pilots' earlier distrust of so speedy a monoplane and when the final A5M4 model entered service it was very popular. Mitsubishi built "about 800" (one source states 782), while Kyushu Aircraft (Watanabe) and the Sasebo naval dockyard (D-N) made 200 more. The final version was the A5M4-K dual trainer produced by conversion of fighters in 1941.

Mitsubishi A6M Zero-Sen "Zeke"

A6M1 to A6M8c and Nakajima A6M2-N

Origin: Mitsubishi Jukogyo KK; also built by Nakajima Hikoki KK.
Type: Single-seat carrier-based fighter, (A6M2-N) float seaplane.
Engine: (A6M1) one 780hp Mitsubishi MK2 Zuisei 13 14-cylinder two-row radial: (M2) 925hp Nakajima NK1C Sakae 12 of same layout; (M3) 1,130hp Sakae 21; (M5) as M3 with individual exhaust stacks; (M6c) Sakae 31 with same rated power but water/methanol boost to 1,210hp for emergency; (M8c) 1,560hp Mitsubishi Kinsei 62 of same layout.
Dimensions: Span (1, 2) 39ft 4½in (12·0m); (remainder) 36ft 1in (11·0m); length (all landplanes) 29ft 9in (9·06m); (A6M2-N) 33ft 2¾in (10·13m); height (1, 2) 9ft 7in (2·92m); (all later landplanes) 9ft 8in (2·98m); (A6M2-N) 14ft 1¼in (4·3m).
Weights: Empty (2) 3,704lb (1680kg); (3) 3,984lb (1807kg); (5) typically 3,920lb (1778kg); (6c) 4,175lb (1894kg); (8c) 4,740lb (2150kg); (A6M2-N) 3,968lb (1800kg); maximum loaded (2) 5,313lb (2410kg); (3) 5,828lb (2644kg); (5c) 6,050lb (2733kg; 2952kg as overload); (6c) as 5c; (8c) 6,944lb (3149kg); (A6M2-N) 5,423lb (2460kg).
Performance: Maximum speed (2) 316mph (509km/h); (3) 336mph (541km/h); (5c, 6c) 354mph (570km/h); (8c) 360mph (580km/h); (A6M2-N) 273mph (440km/h); initial climb (1, 2, 3) 4,500ft (1370m)/min; (5, 6c) 3,150ft (960m)/min; (2-N) not known; service ceiling (1, 2) 33,790ft (10,300m); (3) 36,250ft (11,050m); (5c, 6c) 37,500ft (11,500m); (8c) 39,370ft (12,000m); (A6M2-N) 32,800ft (10,000m); range with drop tank (2) 1,940 miles (3110km); (5) 1,200 miles (1920km).
Armament: (1, 2, 3 and 2-N) two 20mm Type 99 cannon each with 60-round drum fixed in outer wings, two 7·7mm Type 97 machine guns each

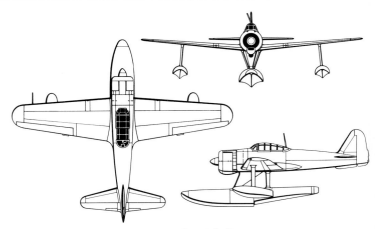

Above: Three-view of A6M2-N, by Nakajima.

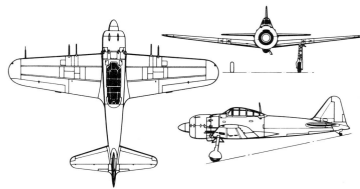

Above: Three-view of A6M5c, which introduced the final armament but was severely underpowered with unboosted engine.

Left: Nearly all these are the A6M5 Model 52 variant.

with 500 rounds above front fuselage, and wing racks for two 66lb (30kg) bombs; (5a) two 20mm Type 99 Mk 4 with belt of 85 rounds per gun, two 7·7mm in fuselage and wing racks for two 132lb (60kg) bombs; (5b) as 5a but one 7·7mm replaced by 12·7mm; (5c and all later versions) two 20mm Type 99 Mk 4 and two 13·2mm in wings, one 13·2mm (optional) in fuselage, plus wing racks for two 60kg.
History: First flight 1 April 1939; service delivery (A6M1) late July 1940; first flight (A6M2-N) December 1941; (A6M5) August 1943; (A6M2-K) January 1942.
User: Japan (Imperial Navy).

Development: The most famous of all Japanese combat aircraft possessed the unique distinction of being the first carrier-based fighter ever to outperform corresponding land-based machines; it was also a singularly unpleasant shock to US and British staff which had apparently never studied

Below: How a Japanese artist saw early-model A6M2 Model 21 Zero-Sens on a carrier flight deck (probably aboard Zuikaku before Pearl Harbor).

Below: The real thing: an A6M2 leaving for Pearl Harbor.

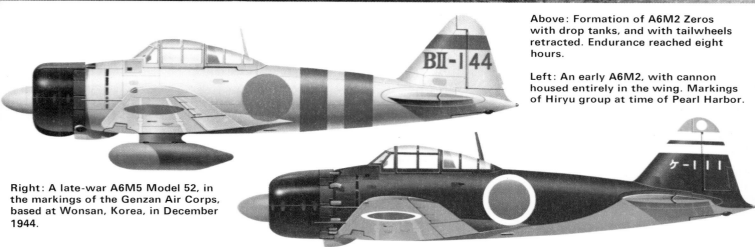

Above: Formation of A6M2 Zeros with drop tanks, and with tailwheels retracted. Endurance reached eight hours.

Left: An early A6M2, with cannon housed entirely in the wing. Markings of Hiryu group at time of Pearl Harbor.

Right: A late-war A6M5 Model 52, in the markings of the Genzan Air Corps, based at Wonsan, Korea, in December 1944.

Below: A neat stepped-up echelon of the A6M2-N floatplane version, which was outclassed as an air-combat fighter.

the behaviour of this fighter in China or even discovered its existence. It was designed by Mitsubishi to meet the severe demands of the 1937 Navy carrier-based fighter specification, seeking a successor to the A5M. Demands included a speed of 500km/h (311mph) and armament of two cannon and two machine guns. Under team leader Jiro Horikoshi the new fighter took shape as a clean, efficient but lightly built aircraft with outstanding manoeuvrability. With a more powerful engine it was accepted for production as the A6M2, though as it was put into production in 1940, the Japanese year 5700, it became popularly the Zero-Sen (Type 00 fighter), and to millions of its enemies was simply the "Zero" (though the official Allied code name was "Zeke"). Before official trials were completed two squadrons with 15 aircraft were sent to China in July 1940 for trials under operational conditions. They eliminated all opposition, as forcefully reported to Washington by Gen Claire Chennault, commander of the Flying Tigers volunteer force (his warning was obviously filed before being read). More than 400 had been delivered by the time the A6M2 and clipped-wing M3 appeared at Pearl Harbor. During the subsequent year it seemed that thousands of these fighters were in use, their unrivalled manoeuvrability being matched by unparalleled range with a small engine, 156gal internal fuel and drop tanks. So completely did the A6M sweep away Allied air power that the Japanese nation came to believe it was invincible. After the Battle of Midway the Allies slowly gained the ascendancy, and the A6M found itself outclassed by the F4U and F6F. Mitsubishi urgently tried to devise improved versions and the A6M5 was built in quantities far greater than any other Japanese combat aircraft. Improvements were mainly small and the combat-boosted Sakae 31 engine did not appear until the end of 1944. Only a few of the much more powerful A6M8c type

were produced, the main reason for this change of engine being destruction of the Nakajima factory. The final model was the A6M7 Kamikaze version, though hundreds of Zeros of many sub-types were converted for suicide attacks. Total production amounted to 10,937, of which 6,217 were built by Nakajima which also designed and built 327 of the attractive A6M2-N single-float seaplane fighter version (code name "Rufe") which operated throughout the Pacific war. The A6M2-K was one of several dual trainer versions.

Mitsubishi F1M "Pete"

F1M1, F1M2

Origin: Mitsubishi Jukogyo KK; also built by Dai-Nijuichi KK (Sasebo).
Type: Design role, reconnaissance (but see text).
Engine: (1) one 820hp Nakajima Hikari 1 nine-cylinder radial; (2) one 875hp Mitsubishi Zuisei 13 14-cylinder two-row radial.
Dimensions: Span 36ft 1in (11·0m); length 31ft 2in (9·5m); height 13ft 1½in (4·0m).
Weights: (2) empty 4,330lb (1964kg); normal loaded 5,620lb (2550kg); maximum overload 6,296lb (2856kg).
Performance: Maximum speed 230mph (370km/h); initial climb 1,969ft (600m)/min; service ceiling 30,970ft (9440m); range (normal weight) 276 miles (445km), (overload) 670 miles (1070km).
Armament: Two 7·7mm Type 89 fixed above engine, one manually aimed from rear cockpit; underwing racks for two 132lb (60kg) bombs or one 250kg (551lb).
History: First flight (F1M1 prototype) June 1936; (production F1M2) October 1939; service delivery 1941; final delivery March 1944.
User: Japan (Imperial Navy).

Development: At first glance a small observation biplane for catapulting from surface vessels might seem hardly to rank as much of a warplane, but in fact the F1M served throughout World War II in such roles as area-defence fighter, bomber, convoy escort, anti-submarine attack aircraft,

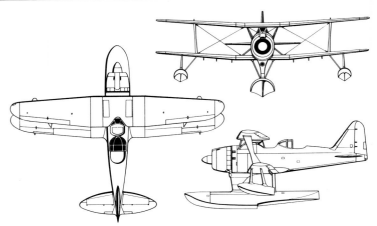

Above: Three-view of typical F1M2.

ocean patrol, rescue and even transport. It was in 1934 that the Imperial Japanese Navy issued a requirement for a new shipboard reconnaissance machine to succeed the Nakajima E8N (code name "Dave"). Mitsubishi's design team, led by Eitaro Sano, won over Aichi and Kawanishi rivals (using "Dave"-type floats) and notable features of the F1M1 were extreme attention to detail cleanliness and exceptional manoeuvrability at all speeds.

Mitsubishi G3M "Nell"

G3M1, G3M2 and G3M3; some rebuilt as L3Y

Origin: Mitsubishi Jukogyo KK, Nagoya; also built by Nakajima Hikoki KK at Koizumi.
Type: Long-range land-based bomber (L3Y, transport).
Engines: Two Mitsubishi Kinsei 14-cylinder two-row radials, (G3M1, L3Y1) 910hp Kinsei 3, (G3M2, L3Y2) 1,075hp Kinsei 42 or 45, (G3M3) 1,300hp Kinsei 51.
Dimensions: Span 82ft 0¼in (25·00m); length 53ft 11½in (16·45m); height 12ft 1in (3·685m).
Weights: Empty (1) 10,516lb (4770kg), (3) 11,551lb (5243kg); max loaded (1) 16,848lb (7642kg), (3) 17,637lb (8000kg).
Performance: Maximum speed (1) 216mph (348km/h), (2) 232mph (373km/h), (3) 258mph (415km/h); service ceiling (3) 33,730ft (10,280 m); maximum range (3) 3,871 miles (6228km).
Armament: (1 and 2) up to four 7·7mm Type 92 manually aimed from two retractable dorsal positions, ventral position and cockpit, (3) one 20mm Type 99 in dorsal fairing and three 7·7mm in side blisters, cockpit and ventral position; external bomb load or torpedo of 1,764lb (800kg).
History: First flight (Ka-15 prototype) July 1935; service delivery late 1936.
User: Imperial Japanese Navy.

Development: Derived from the Ka-9 of April 1934, the Ka-15 series of prototypes were among the first outstanding Japanese warplanes superior to Western types. Designed by a team under Prof Kiro Honjo, the Ka-15 was a smooth stressed-skin machine, with exceptional range. On 14 August 1937 the Kanoya air corps based on Taipei made the world's first trans-oceanic raid when a large force of G3M2 hit targets 1,250 miles away in China. Many other great raids were made, but the most famous action was the sinking of HMS *Prince of Wales* and *Repulse* (which thought they were out of range) on 10 December 1941. By 1943 most were in second-line service, though known to the Allies as "Nell". The L3Y transport conversion was code-named "Tina".

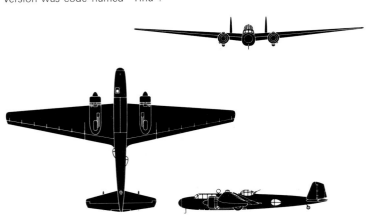

Above: Three-view of G3M3 Model 23 (G3M2 similar).

Above: Mitsubishi G3M2 bombers, probably of the Mihoro Kokutai, photographed whilst releasing their bombs in a stick. All aircraft in the picture are of the Model 22 sub-type with a large turtle-back dorsal gun position equipped with a 20mm cannon. The Mihoro Kokutai provided high-level bombers which sank the British capital ships *Prince of Wales* and *Repulse* on 10 December 1941.

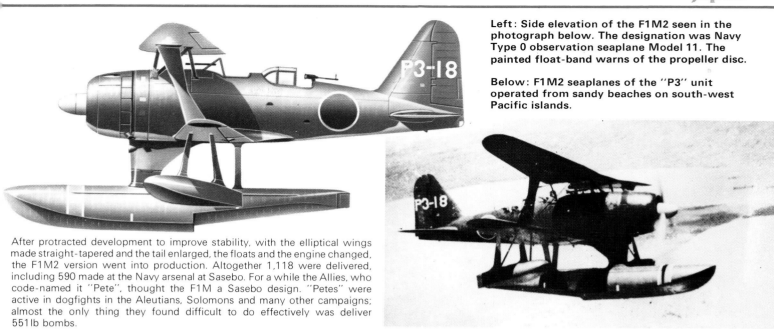

Left: Side elevation of the F1M2 seen in the photograph below. The designation was Navy Type 0 observation seaplane Model 11. The painted float-band warns of the propeller disc.

Below: F1M2 seaplanes of the "P3" unit operated from sandy beaches on south-west Pacific islands.

After protracted development to improve stability, with the elliptical wings made straight-tapered and the tail enlarged, the floats and the engine changed, the F1M2 version went into production. Altogether 1,118 were delivered, including 590 made at the Navy arsenal at Sasebo. For a while the Allies, who code-named it "Pete", thought the F1M a Sasebo design. "Petes" were active in dogfights in the Aleutians, Solomons and many other campaigns; almost the only thing they found difficult to do effectively was deliver 551lb bombs.

Mitsubishi G4M "Betty"

G4M1 to G4M3c and G6M

Origin: Mitsubishi Jukogyo KK.
Type: Land-based naval torpedo bomber and missile carrier.
Engines: (G4M1) two 1,530hp Mitsubishi Kasei 11 14-cylinder two-row radials; (subsequent versions) two Kasei 22 rated at 1,850hp with water/methanol injection.
Dimensions: Span 81ft 7¾in (24·89m); length (1) 65ft 6¼in; (later versions) 64ft 4¾in (19·63m); height (1) 16ft 1in; (later versions) 13ft 5¾in (4·11m).
Weights: Empty (1) 14,860lb (6741kg); (2) 17,623lb (7994kg); (3) 18,500lb (8391kg); loaded (1) 20,944lb (9500kg); (2, 3) 27,550lb (12,500kg); max overload (1) 28,350lb (12,860kg); (2, 3) 33,070lb (15,000kg).
Performance: Maximum speed (1) 265mph (428km/h); (2) 271mph (437km/h); (3) 283mph (455km/h); initial climb (1) 1,800ft (550m)/min; (2, 3) 1,380ft (420m)/min; service ceiling (all) about 30,000ft (9144m); range (with bombs at overload weight) (1) 3,132 miles (5040km); (2) 2,982 miles (4800km); (3) 2,262 miles (3640km).
Armament: (1) three manually aimed 7·7mm in nose, dorsal and ventral positions and 20mm manually aimed in tail; internal bomb load of 2,205lb (1000kg) or 1,764lb (800kg) torpedo externally; (2) as before but electric dorsal turret (one 7·7mm) and revised tail position with increased arc of fire; (2e, and, retro-actively, many earlier G4M2) one 7·7mm in nose, one 20mm in dorsal turret and manual 20mm in tail and two beam windows. (G4M2e) adapted to carry Ohka piloted missile.
History: First flight October 1939; service delivery April 1941; first flight (G4M2) November 1942.
User: Japan (Imperial Navy).

Development: Designed to an incredibly difficult 1938 Navy specification, the G4M family (Allied name, "Betty") was the Imperial Japanese Navy's premier heavy bomber in World War II; yet the insistence on the great range of 2,000 nautical miles (3706km) with full bomb load made the saving of weight take priority over defence and the aircraft was highly vulnerable and not very popular. The wing was of the same Mitsubishi 118 section as the Zero-Sen and boldly designed as an integral fuel tank to accommodate no less than 5,000 litres (1,100gal). The company kept recommending four engines and being overruled by the Navy, which, during the early flight-test stage, wasted more than a year, and 30 aircraft, in trying to make the design into the G6M bomber escort with crew of ten and 19 guns. Eventually the G4M1 was readied for service as a bomber and flew its first missions in South East China in May 1941. More than 250 operated in the Philippines and Malayan campaigns, but after the Solomons battle in August 1942 it began to be apparent that, once intercepted and hit, the unprotected

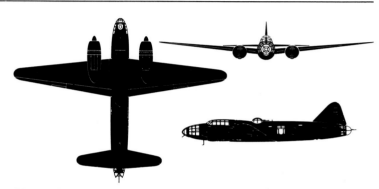

Above: Three-view of G4M2, without bulged weapon-bay doors.

bomber went up like a torch (hence the Allied nickname "one-shot lighter"). Total production reached the exceptional quantity of 2,479, most of them in the many sub-types of G4M2 with increased fuel capacity and power. Finally the trend of development was reversed with the G4M3 series with full protection and only 968gal fuel.

Above: Formation of variously coloured G4M1 bombers, probably operating over China in 1941 when the aircraft were new.

Left: A G4M2a of the 763rd Kokutai (Air Corps). This aircraft was found abandoned in the Philippines. Finish was dark green above and natural metal on underside.

Mitsubishi J2M Raiden "Jack"

J2M1 to J2M7

Origin: Mitsubishi Jukogyo KK; also small number (J2M5) built by Koza Kaigun Kokusho.

Type: Single-seat Navy land-based interceptor.

Engine: Most versions, one 1,820hp Mitsubishi MK4R-A Kasei 23a 14-cylinder two-row radial; (J2M5) 1,820hp MK4U-A Kasei 26a.

Dimensions: Span 35ft 5¼in (10·8m); length (most) 31ft 9¾in (9·70m); (J2M5) 32ft 7¾in (9·95m); height (most) 12ft 6in (3·81m); (J2M5) 12ft 11¼in (3·94m).

Weights: Empty (2) 5,572lb (2527kg); (3) 5,675lb (2574kg); (5) 6,259lb (2839kg); normal loaded (2) 7,257lb (3300kg); (3) 7,573lb (3435kg); (5) 7,676lb (3482kg); max overload (2, 3) 8,700lb (3946kg).

Performance: Maximum speed (2) 371mph (596km/h); (3) 380mph (612km/h); (5) 382mph (615km/h); initial climb (2, 3) 3,610ft (1100m)/min; (5) 3,030ft (925m)/min; range (2, 3 at normal gross) 655 miles (1055km); (2, 3 overload) 1,580 miles (2520km); (5, normal gross with 30min reserve) 345 miles (555km).

Armament: See text.

History: First flight (prototype) 20 March 1942; service delivery (J2M2) December 1943; first flight (J2M5) May 1944.

User: Japan (Imperial Navy).

Development: Though designed by a team led by the legendary Jiro Horikoshi, creator of the Zero-Sen, this utterly different little interceptor did little to enhance reputations, though there was nothing fundamentally faulty in its conception. It broke totally new ground, partly in being an interceptor for the Navy (previously the preserve of the Army) and partly in the reversal of design parameters. Instead of concentrating on combat manoeuvrability at all costs the J1M was designed solely for speed and fast climb. Manoeuvrability and even handling took second place. Unusual features in the basic design included a tiny laminar-flow wing fitted with combat flaps, a finely streamlined engine with propeller extension shaft and fan cooling, a very shallow enclosed canopy and a surprising number of forged parts in the stressed-skin airframe. Powered by a 1,460hp Kasei, the

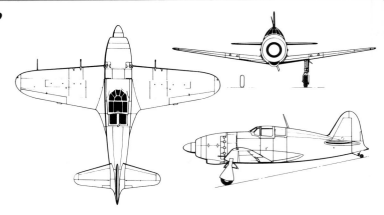

Above: Three-view of J2M3.

prototype Mitsubishi M-20, named Raiden (Thunderbolt), gave a great deal of trouble and was almost redesigned to produce the J2M2 with different engine, much deeper canopy, multi-stack exhaust and new four-blade propeller. Even then the Raiden suffered endless snags and crashes, but eventually 155 J2M2 were delivered with two 20mm Type 99 and two 7·7mm above the fuselage. Production then switched to the J2M3 with machine guns removed and the wing fitted with two Type 99 and two fast-firing Type 99-II. The J2M3a had four Type 99-II. Fitted with bulged canopy these models became the J2M6 and 6a. A few high-flying J2M4 turbocharged versions were built, with six cannon, the two added guns being in the top fuselage decking. Best of all was the J2M5 with only two (wing) cannon but a far better engine, and it proved formidable against high-flying B-29s. After VJ-day, when only 480 of all models had been built by Mitsubishi (one month's planned output!), the Allies (who called this fighter "Jack") spoke in glowing terms of its performance and handling.

Right: A J2M, probably a J2M3a Raiden 21a, of the 302nd Air Corps. This type had four Type 99-II cannon, faster-firing than the guns fitted to earlier models of this fighter.

Mitsubishi Ki-15 "Babs"

Ki-15-I, Ki-15-II, C5M, Karigane

Origin: Mitsubishi Jukogyo KK.

Type: Two-seat light attack bomber.

Engine: (I) one 750hp Nakajima Ha-8 nine-cylinder radial; (II) one 800hp Mitsubishi A.14 (later named Kinsei) 14-cylinder two-row radial.

Dimensions: Span 39ft 4¾in (12·0m); length (I) 27ft 11in (8·50m); height 9ft 10in (3·0m).

Weights: Empty (I) 3,968lb (1800kg); maximum loaded (I) 5,070lb (2300kg); (II) 6,834lb (3100kg).

Performance: Maximum speed (I) 280mph (450km/h); (II) about 298mph (480km/h); initial climb (both) about 1,640ft (500m)/min; service ceiling (I) 28,220ft (8600m); range with bomb load (both) about 1,100 miles (1800km).

Armament: One 7·7mm Type 89 (not always fitted) fixed in outer wing firing forward, and one manually aimed from rear cockpit; bomb load of up to 551lb (250kg) in (I) or 1,100lb (500kg) in (II) carried externally.

History: First flight (Karigane prototype) May 1936; (Ki-15-I) probably late 1936.

User: Imperial Japanese Army.

Development: This trim little machine stemmed from a private venture by the giant Mitsubishi company, inspired by the emergence in the United States of modern stressed-skin monoplanes (particularly the Northrop A-17). With company funds, but sponsored by the Asahi (Rising Sun) newspaper, a prototype was built to demonstrate the ability of the fast-growing Japanese industry to build modern aircraft. It was a time of intense nationalism and the resulting machine, named Karigane (Wild Goose) by Mitsubishi, was individually christened "Kamikaze" (Divine Wind) and prepared as an instrument of national publicity. Its greatest achievement was a notably trouble-free flight of 9,900 miles from Tokyo to London in April 1937. Others were built for similar purposes (one being "Asakaze" (Morning Wind) of the Asahi Press) and as fast mailplanes, while in 1938 a small batch was built with the 550hp Kotobuki (licence-built Bristol Jupiter) replaced by the much more powerful A.14 engine. In 1937 construction began of 437 military Ki-15 series for the Army and these were soon one of the first really modern types to go into action in the Sino-Japanese war, which had simmered for years and finally broke out in 1937. The Ki-15 was used for level bombing, close support and photo-reconnaissance, but was replaced by the Ki-30 (p. 156). In 1939 the Imperial Navy began to receive 50 of two C5M versions with different engines. Allied code name was "Babs".

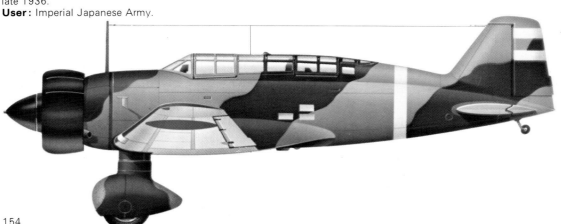

Left: A Mitsubishi Ki-15-I of the 1st Chutai, 15th Hikosentai, of the Imperial Army. When the second Sino-Japanese war broke out in 1937 the Ki-15 was one of the first types to go into action. It had a speed higher than that of any Chinese aircraft except the Soviet-supplied I-16.

Mitsubishi Ki-21 "Sally"

Ki-21-I, -IIa and -IIb

Origin: Mitsubishi Jukogyo KK; also built by Nakajima Hikoki KK.
Type: Seven-seat heavy bomber.
Engines: (I) two 850hp Nakajima Ha-5-Kai 14-cylinder two-row radials; (II) two 1,490hp Mitsubishi Ha-101 of same layout.
Dimensions: Span 73ft 9¾in (22·5m); length 52ft 6in (16·0m); height 15ft 11in (4·85m).
Weights: Empty (I) 10,341lb (4691kg); (II) 13,382lb (6070kg); maximum loaded (I) 16,517lb (7492kg); (II) 21,395lb (9710kg).
Performance: Maximum speed (I) 268mph (432km/h); (II) 297mph (478km/h); initial climb (I) 1,150ft (350m)/min; (II) 1,640ft (500m)/min; service ceiling (I) 28,220ft (8600m); (II) 32,800ft (10,000m); range with full bomb load (I) 1,678 miles (2700km); (II) 1,370 miles (2200km).
Armament: See text for defensive armament; internal bomb bay in fuselage for load of (I) 1,653lb (750kg) or (II) 2,205lb (1000kg).
History: First flight November 1936; service delivery 1937; first flight (Ki-21-II) mid-1940; final delivery September 1944.
User: Japan (Imperial Army).

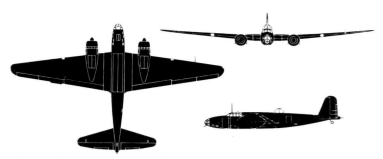

Above: Three-view of the Ki-21-IIb.

Development: In 1936 the Imperial Japanese Army issued a challenging specification for a new heavy bomber, demanding a crew of at least four, an endurance of five hours, a bomb load of 750kg and speed of 400km/h. Mitsubishi won over the Nakajima Ki-19 and built five prototypes powered by the company's own A.14 (Kinsei Ha-6) engine. The fields of fire of the three manually aimed 7·7mm machine guns were inadequate and the Army also requested a switch to the Ha-5 engine. With various modifications it was accepted as the Type 97 (also called OB-97; omoshi bakudanki meaning heavy bomber) and put into production not only by Mitsubishi but also, in 1938, by Nakajima. It rapidly became the premier Japanese Army heavy bomber and served throughout the "Chinese incident", the operational results being efficiently fed back to the procurement machine and the manufacturer. This led to the defensive armament being increased to five guns, one remotely controlled in the extreme 'tail, the crew being increased to seven. The bomb bay was enlarged, the flaps were increased in size and crew armour was dramatically augmented. The result was the Ki-21-Ib. Increase in fuel capacity and addition of a sixth (beam) gun resulted in the -Ic variant. In 1939 work began on the much more powerful -II, with increased-span tailplane. Several hundred of both versions were in use in December 1941 and they were met on all fronts in the Pacific war (being fairly easy meat for Hurricanes in Burma). Code-named "Sally" they faded from front-line service in 1943, though the -IIb with "glasshouse" replaced by a dorsal turret (one 12·7mm) improved defence when it entered service in 1942. Total production was 2,064 (351 by Nakajima), plus 500 transport versions (called MC-20, Ki-57 and "Topsy").

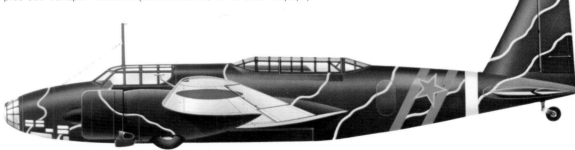

Above: After the Japanese lost air supremacy the Ki-21 had to hug the trees to evade Allied fighters. This Ki-21-IIb belonged to the 14th Sentai (Group).

Left: Ki-21-Ia of the 2nd Chutai, 60th Hikosentai

Below: A formation of Ki-21-IIa bombers. The nearest bears markings of the Hammamatsu Bomber School.

Mitsubishi Ki-30 "Ann"

Ki-30

Origin: Mitsubishi Jukogyo KK; also built by Tachikawa Dai-Ichi Rikugun Kokusho.
Type: Two-seat light bomber.
Engine: One 950hp Mitsubishi Ha-5 Zuisei 14-cylinder two-row radial.
Dimensions: Span 47ft 8¾in (14·55m); length 33ft 11in (10·34m) height 11ft 11¾in (3·65m).
Weights: Empty 4,915lb (2230kg); maximum loaded 7,324lb (3322kg).
Performance: Maximum speed 263mph (423km/h); initial climb 1,640ft (500m)/min; service ceiling 28,117ft (8570m); range (bomb load not stated) 1,056 miles (1700km).
Armament: One 7·7mm Type 89 machine gun fixed in wing (sometimes both wings) and one manually aimed from rear cockpit; internal bomb bay for three 220lb (100kg) or equivalent bomb load.
History: First flight February 1937; service delivery October 1938; final delivery 1941.

Users: Japan (Imperial Army), Thailand.

Development: With the Ki-32, Ki-27 fighter and Ki-21 heavy bomber, the Ki-30 was one of the important new stressed-skin monoplanes ordered by the Imperial Army under its modernisation plan of 1935. It was the first in Japan to have a modern two-row engine, as well as internal bomb bay, flaps and constant-speed propeller. It was notably smaller than the otherwise similar Fairey Battle produced in Britain. Unlike the British bomber the bomb bay was in the fuselage, resulting in a mid-wing and long landing gear (which was fixed). The pilot and observer/bomb aimer had a good view but were unable to communicate except by speaking tube. The Ki-30 was in service in numbers in time to be one of the major types in the Sino-Japanese war. In 1942 surviving aircraft played a large part in the advance to the Philippines, but then swiftly withdrew from first-line operations. Mitsubishi built 638 at Nagoya and 68 were completed at the Tachikawa Army Air Arsenal. In conformity with the Allied system of code-naming bombers after girls, the Ki-30 was dubbed "Ann". It was the ultimate development of the Karigane family of high-performance monoplanes.

Left: A Ki-30 light attack bomber of the 2nd Chutai (Squadron or Company) of the 10th Hikosentai (Group). The Ki-30 saw most of its action on the Asian mainland.

Right: Pilots and observers of a Ki-30 Chutai relax before a mission, probably in China in 1938. Like other Imperial Army aircraft of the period these bombers are either grey or in natural metal finish. Escorted on their short-range missions by Ki-27 fighters, the losses of Ki-30 units were at first commendably low.

Mitsubishi Ki-46 "Dinah"

Type 100 Models 1-4 (Ki-46-I to Ki-46-IVb)

Origin: Mitsubishi Jukogyo KK.
Type: Strategic reconnaissance (Ki-46-III-Kai, night fighter).
Engines: (I) two 870hp Mitsubishi Ha-26-I 14-cylinder two-row radials; (II) two 1,080hp Mitsubishi Ha-102 of same layout; (III) two 1,500hp Mitsubishi Ha-112-II of same layout; (IV) Ha-112-IIRu, same rated power but turbocharged.
Dimensions: Span 48ft 2¾in (14·7m); length (all except III-Kai) 36ft 1in (11·0m); (III-Kai) 37ft 8in (11·47m); height 12ft 8¾in (3·88m).
Weights: Empty (I) 7,450lb (3379kg); (II) 7,193lb (3263kg); (III) 8,446lb (3831kg); (IV) 8,840lb (4010kg); loaded (no overload permitted) (I) 10,630lb (4822kg); (II) 11,133lb (5050kg); (III) 12,620lb (5724kg); (IV) 13,007lb (5900kg); (III-Kai) 13,730lb (6227kg).
Performance: Maximum speed (I) 336mph (540km/h); (II) 375mph (604km/h); (III, III-Kai, IV) 391mph (630km/h); initial climb (I, II, III) about 1,970ft (600m)/min; (IV) 2,625ft (800m)/min; service ceiling (I, II, III) 34,500–36,000ft (10,500–11,000m); (IV) 38,000ft (11,500m); range (I) 1,305 miles (2100km); (II) 1,490 miles (2400km); (III) 2,485 miles (4000km); (III-Kai) 1,243 miles (2000km); (IV) not known, but at least 4000km.
Armament: (I, II) one 7·7mm manually aimed from rear cockpit; other types, none, except III-Kai, two 20mm Ho-5 cannon fixed in nose firing ahead and 37mm Ho-203 firing at elevation of 30° from top of fuselage.
History: First flight November 1939; (production II) March 1941; (III) December 1942; (III-Kai conversion) about September 1944.
User: Japan (Imperial Army).

Development: One of the most trouble-free and popular aircraft of the whole Pacific war, the Ki-46 "Shitei" (reconnaissance for HQ), code-named "Dinah" by the Allies, was one of only very few Japanese aircraft that could penetrate Allied airspace with some assurance it would survive. It was

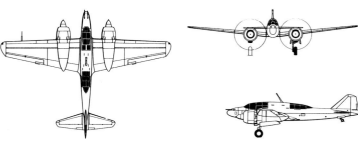

Above: Three-view of Ki-46-III-Kai.

also almost the only machine with the proven ability to operate at the flight levels of the B-29. In the first year of its use, which extended to every part of the Japanese war throughout the Pacific and China, much trouble was experienced from sparking-plug erosion and crew anoxia, both rectified by improved design and greater oxygen storage. Allied radar forced the Ki-46 to fly even faster and higher, leading to the almost perfectly streamlined Ki-46-III. These entered service in 1943, in which year many earlier versions were converted to Ki-46-II-Kai dual conversion trainers. Total production amounted to 1,742, all made by Mitsubishi at Nagoya and Toyama. Only four prototypes were finished of the turbocharged IVa, but many III models were hastily converted by the Army Tachikawa base into III-Kai night-fighters capable of intercepting B-29s. No radar was carried. At VJ-day Mitsubishi was trying to produce IIIc and IVb fighters and the IIIb ground-attack version.

Right: Action shot of an attack by Allied aircraft on a Japanese airstrip in the south-west Pacific. Parachute-retarded bombs have just missed three Ki-46-II.

Below: A Ki-46-II of the 18th Independent Reconnaissance Chutai (Dokuritsu Dai Shijugo Chutai).

Mitsubishi Ki-67 Hiryu "Peggy"

Ki-67-Ia, Ib and II and Ki-109

Origin: Mitsubishi Jukogyo KK; also built by Kawasaki and (assembly only) Nippon Kokusai Koku Kogyo KK, plus one by Tachikawa.
Type: Heavy bomber and torpedo dropper; Ki-109 heavy escort fighter.
Engines: Two 1,900hp Mitsubishi Ha-104 18-cylinder two-row radials.
Dimensions: Span 73ft 9¾in (22·5m); length 61ft 4¼in (18·7m); height 18ft 4½in (5·60m).
Weights: (Ib) empty 19,068lb (8649kg); loaded 30,346lb (13,765kg).
Performance: (Ib) Maximum speed 334mph (537km/h); initial climb 1,476ft (450m)/min; service ceiling 31,070ft (9470m); range with full bomb load 621 miles (1000km) plus 2hr reserve, also reported as total range 1,740 miles (2800km).
Armament: Standard on Ia, Ib, one 20mm Ho-5 in electric dorsal turret and single 12·7mm Type 1 manually aimed from nose, tail and two beam positions; internal bomb load 1,764lb (800kg); suicide attack 6,393lb (2900kg).
History: First flight "beginning of 1943"; service delivery April 1944; first flight (Ki-109) August 1944.
User: Japan (Imperial Army and Navy).

Development: Designed by a team led by Dr Hisanojo Ozawa to meet a February 1941 specification, this Army bomber not only met the demand for much higher speed but also proved to have the manoeuvrability of a fighter. It also lacked nothing in armour and fuel-tank protection, and was probably the best all-round bomber produced in Japan during World War II. With a crew of six/eight, it was often looped and shown to have excellent turning power, better than that of several Japanese fighters. Indeed the Ki-69 escort fighter version was developed in parallel with the bomber during 1942 but had to be shelved as delays to the bomber were becoming serious. These delays were due to inefficiency, material shortage and continual changes requested by the customer. By 1944 only 15 (all different) had been built, but production was then allowed to begin in earnest and by VJ-day the creditable total of 727 had been delivered, 606 by Mitsubishi and the rest by Kawasaki, Nippon and (one only) the Tachikawa arsenal. At first the Ki-67 Hiryu (Flying Dragon) was used as a torpedo bomber in the Philippine Sea battle, receiving the Allied name "Peggy". Later it operated against Iwo Jima, the Marianas and Okinawa and in the defence of Japan.

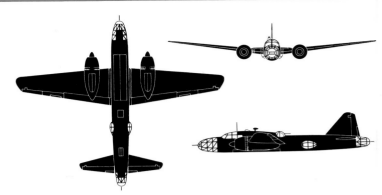

Above: Three-view of Ki-67-Ib.

There were only two versions used, the Ib having bulged waist blisters. Of many projected versions, of which the Ki-67-II with 2,500hp Ha-214 engines marked the biggest advance, only the Ki-109 reached the service trials stage. Armed with a 75mm gun with 15 hand-loaded rounds, plus a 12·7mm in the tail, this was meant to have 2,000hp turbocharged Ha-104 engines but none were available. With ordinary Ha-104s the Ki-109 could not get up to B-29 altitude!

Below: Air to-air photograph of a Ki-67-Ib of the 3rd Chutai of the 98th Sentai of the Imperial Army.

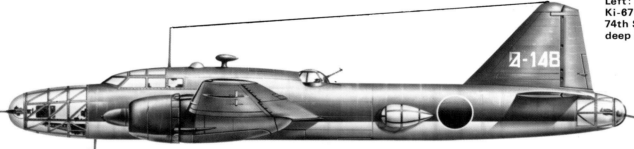

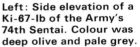

Left: Side elevation of a Ki-67-Ib of the Army's 74th Sentai. Colour was deep olive and pale grey.

Below: Though unit markings are not in evidence, this Ki-67-Ib is in full combat service. The Army loved it.

Nakajima B5N "Kate"

B5N1 and B5N2

Origin: Nakajima Hikoki KK; also built by Aichi Tokei Denki and Dai-Juichi Kaigun Kokusho (Hiro).
Type: (B5N1) three-seat carrier-based bomber; (2) torpedo bomber.
Engine: (B5N1 Model 11) one 770hp Nakajima Hikari 3 nine-cylinder radial; (B5N1 Model 12) 970 or 985hp Nakajima Sakae 11 14-cylinder two-row radial; (B5N2) 1,115hp Sakae 21.
Dimensions: Span 50ft 11in (15·52m); length (1) 33ft 11in; (2) 33ft 9½in (10·3m); height 12ft 1¾in (3·70m).
Weights: Empty (1) 4,645lb (2107kg); (2) 5,024lb (2279kg); normal loaded (1) 8,047lb (3650kg); (2) 8,378lb (3800kg); maximum loaded (2) 9,039lb (4100kg).
Performance: Maximum speed (1) 217mph (350km/h); (2) 235mph (378km/h); initial climb (both) 1,378ft (420m)/min; service ceiling (both) about 25,000ft (7640m); range (1) 683 miles (1100km); (2) normal gross, 609 miles (980km), overload (4100kg) 1,237 miles (1990km).
Armament: (1) one 7·7mm Type 89 manually aimed from rear cockpit; underwing racks for two 551lb (250kg) or six 132lb (60kg) bombs; (2) two 7·7mm manually aimed from rear cockpit; two 7·7mm fixed above forward fuselage; centreline rack for 1,764lb (800kg, 18in) torpedo or three 551lb bombs.
History: First flight January 1937; (production B5N1) later 1937; (B5N2) December 1939; final delivery, probably 1942.
User: Japan (Imperial Navy).

Development: Designed to meet a 1935 requirement, the B5N was judged ordinary and obsolescent in World War II, yet in its day it was advanced and bold. The Japanese keenly studied the stressed-skin aircraft of Northrop, Douglas and Clark, and swiftly copied new features. The B5N had not only a thoroughly modern structure but also variable-pitch propeller (not on RAF Hurricanes until mid-1940!), hydraulically retracting landing gear, Fowler flaps, NACA cowling, integral wing fuel tanks and, until judged troublesome, hydraulic wing-folding. The challenging specification demanded a speed of 330km/h (205mph), but the prototype beat this by

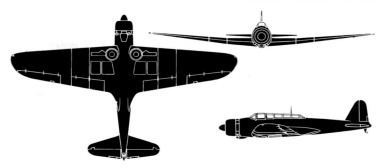

Above: Three-view of B5N1 Model 11.

23mph. The B5N1 went into production in time to serve in the Sino-Japanese war; a few of the rival fixed-gear Mitsubishi B5M were bought as an insurance. By 1940 some attack B5N were converted into B5N1-K trainers, but 103 bombed at Pearl Harbor. In the same attack 40 of the new B5N2 torpedo bombers took part, at least half finding their mark. Subsequently the B5N2 played the chief role in sinking the US carriers *Yorktown*, *Lexington*, *Wasp* and *Hornet*. They soldiered on into 1944 alongside their replacement the B6N. Total production was 1,149, including 200 by Aichi and 280 by Hiro Arsenal. Their Allied name was "Kate".

Right: These are early B5N1 models, and the absence of certain operational features suggests that they are probably of the B5N1-K trainer version. Operational B5Ns were usually painted, upper surfaces often being dark green.

Nakajima B6N Tenzan "Jill"

B6N1, B6N2

Origin: Nakajima Hikoki KK.
Type: Three-seat carrier-based torpedo bomber.
Engine: (B6N1) one 1,870hp Nakajima Mamori 11 14-cylinder two-row radial; (B6N2) 1,850hp Mitsubishi Kasei 25 of same layout.
Dimensions: Span 48ft 10¼in (14·894m); length 35ft 7½in (10·865m); height (1) 12ft 1¾in (3·7m); (2) 12ft 5½in (3·8m).
Weights: Empty 6,636lb (3010kg) (1, 2 almost identical); normal loaded 11,464lb (5200kg); maximum overload 12,456lb (5650kg).
Performance: Maximum speed (1) 289mph (465km/h); (2) 299mph (482km/h); initial climb (1) 1,720ft (525m)/min; (2) 1,885ft (575m)/min; service ceiling (1) 28,379ft (8650m); (2) 29,659ft (9040m); range (normal weight) (1) 907 miles (1460km); (2) 1,084 miles (1745km), (overload) (1) 2,312 miles (3720km); (2) 1,895 miles (3050km).
Armament: One 7·7mm Type 89 manually aimed from rear cockpit and one manually aimed by middle crew-member from rear ventral position, with fixed 7·7mm firing forward in left wing (often absent from B6N1); 1,764lb

Below: A formation of Nakajima B6N2 torpedo bombers, probably photographed by the radio-operator/gunner of another. Colours are dark green and pale grey, with black engine cowls.

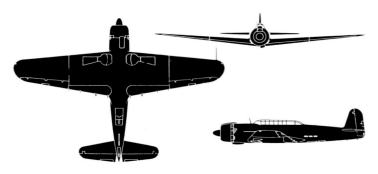

Above: Three-view of B6N2, without radar.

(800kg, 18in) torpedo carried offset to right of centreline, or six 220lb (100kg) bombs under fuselage.
History: First flight March 1942; service delivery (B6N1) early 1943; (B6N2) December 1943.
User: Japan (Imperial Navy).

Development: Named Tenzan (Heavenly Mountain) after a worshipped mountain in China, and code-named "Jill" by the Allies, the B6N was another conventional-looking aircraft which in fact was in many respects superior to the seemingly more advanced machines of the Allies (in this case the Grumman TBF and Fairey Barracuda). Designed as a replacement for B5N, Tenzan was slim and clean, with no internal weapon bay. The torpedo was offset, and to increase clearance on torpedo release the big oil cooler was offset in the other direction (to the left). The distinctive shape of the vertical tail was to minimise stowage length in the three-point attitude on carriers. Nakajima's big Mamori engine, driving a four-blade Hamilton-type propeller, suffered severe vibration and overheating, and though the B6N1 was kept in service it was replaced in production by the B6N2. The lower power of the proven Kasei was counteracted by the improved installation with less drag, and jet-thrust from the exhaust stubs. Tenzans went into action off Bougainville in the Marshalls campaign in June 1944. Subsequently they were heavily committed, many being later equipped with ASV radar for night attacks and ending in April-June 1945 with a hectic campaign of torpedo and suicide attacks off Okinawa and Kyushu. By this time the Imperial Navy had no operating carrier and hardly any skilled pilots.

Nakajima C6N Saiun "Myrt"

C6N1, 1-B and 1-S Saiun (Painted Cloud) (Allied code-name "Myrt")

Origin: Nakajima Hikoki KK, Koizuma and Haneda.
Type: Carrier-based strategic reconnaissance aircraft, (1-B) attack, (1-S) land-based night fighter.
Engine: 1,990hp Nakajima NK9H Homare 21 18-cylinder radial.
Dimensions: Span 41ft 0in (12·50m); length 36ft 1in (11·00m); height 13ft 0in (3·96m).
Weights: Empty 6,411lb (2908kg); loaded 9,921lb (4500kg); max overload 11,627lb (5274kg).
Performance: Maximum speed 378mph (609km/h); service ceiling 35,238ft (10,740m); range 1,914 miles (3080km); max range with overload fuel 3,300 miles (5310km).
Armament: (C6N1) one 7·92mm Type 2 manually aimed from rear cockpit; (1-B) forward-firing cannon and 1,764lb (800kg) torpedo; (1-S) two 20mm Type 99 cannon fixed obliquely in fuselage.
History: First flight 15 May 1943; service delivery July 1944; final delivery August 1945.
User: Japan (Imperial Navy).

Development: This outstandingly clean aircraft was an example of Japanese specialization defeated by circumstances. No other nation built a purpose-designed carrier-based reconnaissance aircraft in World War II, and the 17-Shi (spring 1942) specification was very challenging. The C6N was faintly like a Fw 190 stretched to seat a pilot, navigator/observer

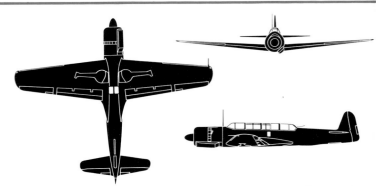

Above: Three-view of C6N1, showing tabbed Fowler flaps and ventral observation/camera windows.

and radio operator/gunner in tandem. As evidence of advanced design, the flaps were tabbed Fowlers, and the laminar-section wing (only slightly larger than a Zero's) also had drooping ailerons and slats, and was almost entirely given over to six integral tanks. The troublesome Homare was beautifully cowled and had thrust-giving ejector exhausts. Another feature that was new to Japan was thick-skinned structure, reducing the numbers of parts and cutting the number of rivets from 220,000 for a Zero to under 100,000. Altogether 463 of these speedy machines were built, but need for the C6N1-B was swept away by loss of the carrier force. Some Saiuns were converted as C6N1-S night fighters with crew of two and oblique cannon. There were many advanced prototypes and projected versions.

Nakajima J1N1 "Irving"

J1N1-C, J1N1-F, J1N1-S Gekko and J1N1-C-Kai

Origin: Nakajima Hikoki KK.
Type: (C, F) three-seat reconnaissance; (S, C-Kai) two-seat night fighter.
Engines: All operational versions, two 1,130hp Nakajima Sakae 21 14-cylinder two-row radials.
Dimensions: Span 55ft 8½in (16·98m); length (all, excluding nose guns or radar) 39ft 11½in (12·18m); height 14ft 11½in (4·562m).
Weights: Empty (C, S) 10,697lb (4852kg); loaded (C) 15,984lb (7250kg); (S) 15,212lb (6900kg); maximum overload (both) 16,594lb (7527kg).
Performance: Maximum speed (C, S) 315mph (507km/h); initial climb (C, S) 1,968ft (600m)/min; service ceiling 30,578ft (9320m); range (C, S, normal gross) 1,585 miles (2550km), (overload) 2,330 miles (3750km).
Armament: (J1N1-C) one 20mm Type 99 cannon and two 7·7mm Type 97 fixed in nose; (J1N1-S) four 20mm Type 99 Model 2 cannon fixed in rear cockpit, two firing obliquely upwards and two firing obliquely downwards; (J1N1-F) manual dorsal turret with single 20mm gun.
History: First flight May 1941; (production C) August 1942; service delivery (C) end of 1942; first flight (S) August 1943.
User: Japan (Imperial Navy).

Development: In 1938, before the Zero-Sen had flown, the Imperial Navy issued a specification for a twin-engined, long-range escort fighter, to reach a speed of 280 knots, and have a range of 1,300 nautical miles or 2,000 n.m. with extra fuel (the n.m. was the standard naval unit in Japan). Mitsubishi abandoned this project, but Nakajima's design team under K. Nakamura succeeded in producing a large prototype which proved to have remarkable manoeuvrability. Fitted with large fabric-covered ailerons, slotted flaps (opened 15° for combat) and leading-edge slats, it could dog-fight well with a Zero and the prototype was eventually developed to have

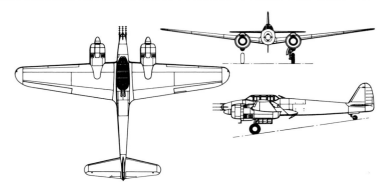

Above: Three-view of J1N1-S Gekko night fighter.

no flight limitations. But the Navy doubted the practicability of the complex scheme of two dorsal barbettes, each mounting two 7·7mm guns, remotely aimed in unison by the navigator. Eventually the Navy decided to buy the J1N1-C with these barbettes removed to serve as a three-seat photographic aircraft. (Some reports claim the failure as a fighter was due to lateral control problems, but Nakajima test pilots insist it was simply a matter of armament.) Soon after sorties began over the Solomons in the spring of 1943 the commander of the 251st Air Corps, Yasuna Kozono, hit on a way of intercepting Allied heavy night bombers. He had several aircraft modified as C-Kai night fighters with upper and lower pairs of oblique cannon. The armament proved effective, and most of the 477 J1N aircraft were built as J1N1-S Gekko (Moonlight) fighters with nose radar and a smoother cabin outline. They were good, robust aircraft, but unable to intercept the fast, high-flying B-29. Their Allied name was "Irving".

Below: The first prototype of the J1N1-C, the production version of the original reconnaissance aircraft.

Nakajima Ki-27 "Nate"

Ki-27a and -27b

Origin: Nakajima Hikoki KK; also built by Mansyu Hikoki Seizo KK.
Type: Single-seat interceptor fighter and light attack.
Engine: Prototype, one 650hp Nakajima Ha-1a (Jupiter-derived) nine-cylinder radial; 27a and 27b, one 710hp Ha-1b.
Dimensions: Span 37ft 0¾in (11·3m); length 24ft 8½in (7·53m); height 9ft 2¼in (2·8m).
Weights: Empty 2,403lb (1090kg); loaded 3,638lb (1650kg); (27b) up to 3,946lb.
Performance: Maximum speed 286mph (460km/h); initial climb 2,953ft (900m)/min; service ceiling, not recorded but about 34,400ft (10,500m); range 389 miles (625km).
Armament: Two 7·7mm Type 89 machine guns fixed in sides of fuselage, firing inside cowling; external racks for four 55lb (25kg) bombs.
History: First flight 15 October 1936; service delivery, early 1938; service delivery (Ki-27b) March 1939; final delivery July 1940.
User: Japan (Imperial Army) and Manchukuo.

Development: The Imperial Japanese Army's first low-wing monoplane fighter, the Ki-27 was in continuous production from 1937 to 1940 and was not only built in much larger quantities than other Japanese aircraft of its day but outnumbered almost every Japanese warplane of World War II. It was designed to meet a 1935 fighter requirement and competed against designs from Kawasaki and Mitsubishi. Though not the fastest, it was easily the most manoeuvrable; in fact it was probably the most manoeuvrable military aircraft of its day and possibly in all history, with plenty of engine power and (the Army having chosen the biggest of three possible sizes of wing) the extremely low loading of 17·9lb/ft². The loaded weight was roughly half that of contemporary Western fighters, and the penalty was paid in light construction and light armament. At the time Japanese pilots cared nothing for speed, fire-power or armour, but sacrificed everything for good visibility and manoeuvrability, and they resisted the introduction of later aircraft such as the Ki-43. Hundreds of Ki-27s fought Chinese and Soviet aircraft over Asia, scoring about 90 per cent of the claimed 1,252 Soviet aircraft (an exaggerated figure) shot down in 1939 after the Nomonhan Incident. Other Ki-27s served with the Manchurian air force, and at the time of Pearl Harbor they outnumbered all other Japanese fighters. Called "Nate" by the Allies, they continued in front-line use throughout the first year of the Pacific War. No fewer than 3,399 were built, 1,379 by the Manchurian (Mansyu Hikoki) company.

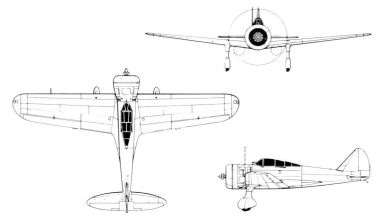

Above: Three-view of the Ki-27b.

Above: The Ki-27 was one of the most manoeuvrable fighters of all time. These two Ki-27b models bear on their rudders the badge of the Akeno Fighter Training School. Most World War II Army fighter pilots trained on Ki-27s.

Left: The colourful unit markings of this Ki-27b proclaim that it belongs to the 1st Chutai of the 1st Hikosentai, numerically the premier squadron of the Imperial Army.

Below: This early production Ki-27b – distinguished from the original Ki-27a model by the transparent glazing of the fairing behind the sliding main canopy, and various other details – was pictured in China in 1938-39. Hinomarus are seen on the wings apparently modified by transverse stripes, while a patriotic slogan adorns the fuselage.

Nakajima Ki-43 Hayabusa "Oscar"

Ki-43-I to Ic, IIa and b, IIIa and b

Origin: Nakajima Hikoki KK; also built by Tachikawa Hikoki KK and Tachikawa Dai-Ichi Rikugun (Arsenal).
Type: Single-seat interceptor fighter (from IIa, fighter-bomber).
Engine: (Ki-43-I series) one 975hp Nakajima Ha-25 (Ha-35/12) Sakae 14-cylinder two-row radial; (II) 1,105hp Ha-115 Sakae; (III) 1,250hp Ha-112 (Ha-33/42) Kasei of same layout.
Dimensions: Span (I) 37ft 10½in; (IIa) 37ft 6¼in (11·437m); (IIb and subsequent) 35ft 6¾in (10·83m); length (I) 28ft 11¾in (8·82m); (II, III) 29ft 3¼in (8·92m); height (all) 10ft 8¾in (3·273m).
Weights: empty (I) 4,354lb (1975kg); normal loaded (I) 5,824lb (2642kg); (II series) 5,825–5,874lb (typically 2655kg); (III) 6,283lb (2850kg).
Performance: Maximum speed (I) 308mph (515km/h); (II) 320mph (515km/h); (III) 363mph (585km/h); initial climb (typical II) 3,250ft (990m)/min; service ceiling (I) 38,500ft; (II, III) 36,800ft (11,215m); range (I) 746 miles (1200km); (II, III) internal fuel 1,060 miles (1700km), with two 45-gal drop tanks 1,864 miles (3000km).
Armament: (Ia) two 7·7mm Type 80 above engine; (Ib) one 12·7mm, one 7·7mm; (Ic) two 12·7mm; (all II series) two 12·7mm, each with 250 rounds, and wing racks for two 551lb (250kg) bombs; (IIIa) same; (IIIb) two 20mm Ho-5 cannon replacing 12·7mm in top decking, same bomb racks.
History: First flight January 1939; (production Ki-43-I) March 1941; (prototype IIa) February 1942; (prototype IIb) June 1942; (IIIa) December 1944.
Users: Japan (Imperial Army), Thailand; post-war, France (Indo-China) and Indonesia (against Dutch administration).

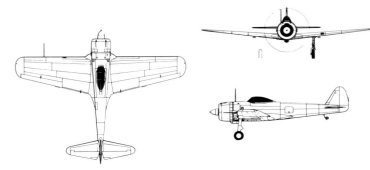

Above: Three-view of the Ki-43-IIa.

Development: Code-named "Oscar" by the Allies, the Ki-43 Hayabusa (Peregrine Falcon) was the most numerous of all Imperial Army warplanes and second only in numbers to the Zero-Sen. Compared with the famed Navy fighter it was smaller, lighter and much cheaper to produce. It was cast in the traditional Army mould in which everything was sacrificed for manoeuvrability, though the first prototype (designed by Hideo Itokawa to meet a 1938 Army contract which was simply awarded to Nakajima, without any industrial competition) was very heavy on the controls and disappointing. One prototype was even given fixed landing gear to save weight, but after many changes, and especially after adding a "combat manoeuvre flap" under the wings, the Ki-43 was turned into a dogfighter that could out-manoeuvre every aircraft ever ranged against it. After a few had carelessly got in the way of Allied fighters the more powerful II appeared with some armour, self-sealing tanks and slightly reduced span. The mass-produced clipped-wing IIb followed, serving in every Japanese battle. To the end,

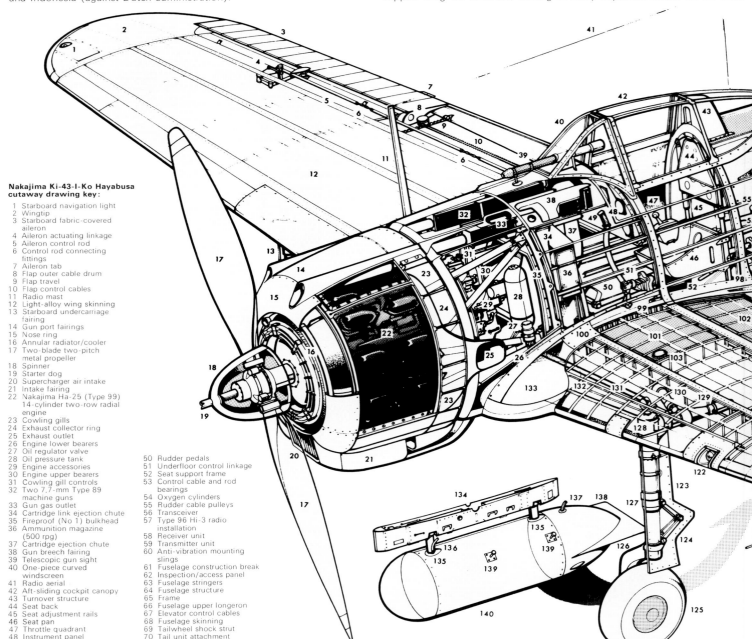

Nakajima Ki-43-I-Ko Hayabusa cutaway drawing key:

1. Starboard navigation light
2. Wingtip
3. Starboard fabric-covered aileron
4. Aileron actuating linkage
5. Aileron control rod
6. Control rod connecting fittings
7. Aileron tab
8. Flap outer cable drum
9. Flap travel
10. Flap control cables
11. Radio mast
12. Light-alloy wing skinning
13. Starboard undercarriage fairing
14. Gun port fairings
15. Nose ring
16. Annular radiator/cooler
17. Two-blade two-pitch metal propeller
18. Spinner
19. Starter dog
20. Supercharger air intake
21. Intake fairing
22. Nakajima Ha-25 (Type 99) 14-cylinder two-row radial engine
23. Cowling gills
24. Exhaust collector ring
25. Exhaust outlet
26. Engine lower bearers
27. Oil regulator valve
28. Oil pressure tank
29. Engine accessories
30. Engine upper bearers
31. Cowling gill controls
32. Two 7·7-mm Type 89 machine guns
33. Gun gas outlet
34. Cartridge link ejection chute
35. Fireproof (No 1) bulkhead
36. Ammunition magazine (500 rpg)
37. Cartridge ejection chute
38. Gun breech fairing
39. Telescopic gun sight
40. One-piece curved windscreen
41. Radio aerial
42. Aft-sliding cockpit canopy
43. Turnover structure
44. Seat back
45. Seat adjustment rails
46. Seat pan
47. Throttle quadrant
48. Instrument panel
49. Control column
50. Rudder pedals
51. Underfloor control linkage
52. Seat support frame
53. Control cable and rod bearings
54. Oxygen cylinders
55. Rudder cable pulleys
56. Transceiver
57. Type 96 Hi-3 radio installation
58. Receiver unit
59. Transmitter unit
60. Anti-vibration mounting slings
61. Fuselage construction break
62. Inspection/access panel
63. Fuselage stringers
64. Fuselage structure
65. Frame
66. Fuselage upper longeron
67. Elevator control cables
68. Fuselage skinning
69. Tailwheel shock strut
70. Tail unit attachment
71. Tailfin root fairing

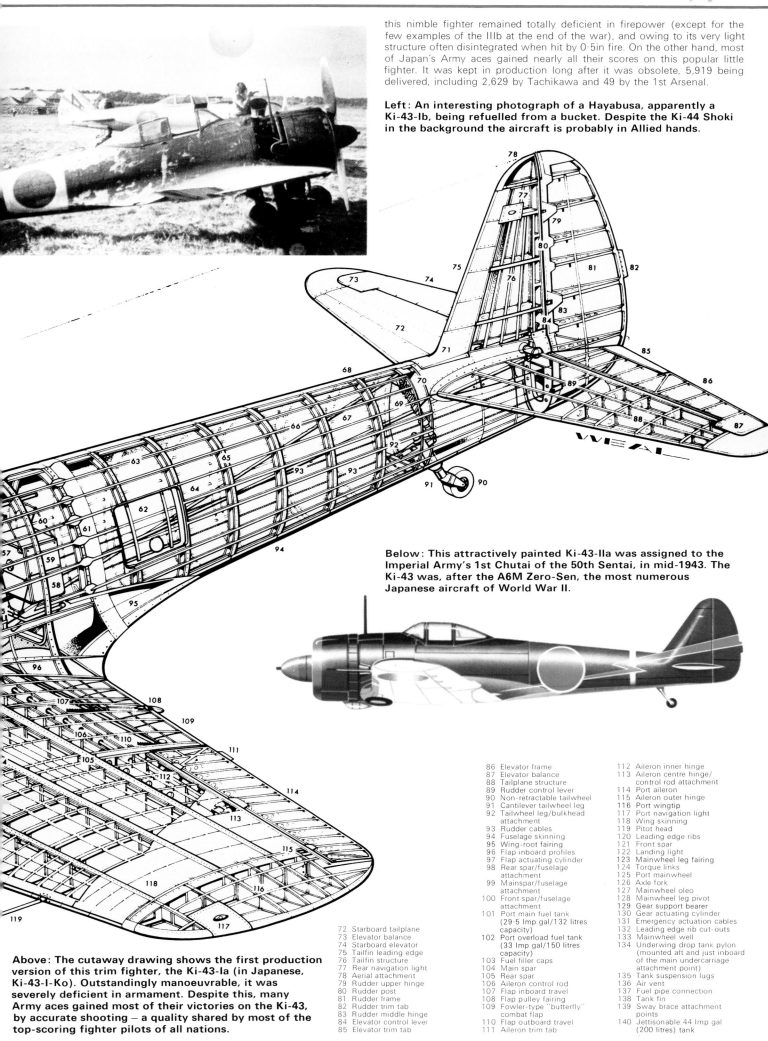

this nimble fighter remained totally deficient in firepower (except for the few examples of the IIb at the end of the war), and owing to its very light structure often disintegrated when hit by 0·5in fire. On the other hand, most of Japan's Army aces gained nearly all their scores on this popular little fighter. It was kept in production long after it was obsolete, 5,919 being delivered, including 2,629 by Tachikawa and 49 by the 1st Arsenal.

Left: An interesting photograph of a Hayabusa, apparently a Ki-43-Ib, being refuelled from a bucket. Despite the Ki-44 Shoki in the background the aircraft is probably in Allied hands.

Below: This attractively painted Ki-43-IIa was assigned to the Imperial Army's 1st Chutai of the 50th Sentai, in mid-1943. The Ki-43 was, after the A6M Zero-Sen, the most numerous Japanese aircraft of World War II.

Above: The cutaway drawing shows the first production version of this trim fighter, the Ki-43-Ia (in Japanese, Ki-43-I-Ko). Outstandingly manoeuvrable, it was severely deficient in armament. Despite this, many Army aces gained most of their victories on the Ki-43, by accurate shooting – a quality shared by most of the top-scoring fighter pilots of all nations.

72 Starboard tailplane
73 Elevator balance
74 Starboard elevator
75 Tailfin leading edge
76 Tailfin structure
77 Rear navigation light
78 Aerial attachment
79 Rudder upper hinge
80 Rudder post
81 Rudder frame
82 Rudder trim tab
83 Rudder middle hinge
84 Elevator control lever
85 Elevator trim tab

86 Elevator frame
87 Elevator balance
88 Tailplane structure
89 Rudder control lever
90 Non-retractable tailwheel
91 Cantilever tailwheel leg
92 Tailwheel leg/bulkhead attachment
93 Rudder cables
94 Fuselage skinning
95 Wing-root fairing
96 Flap inboard profiles
97 Flap actuating cylinder
98 Rear spar/fuselage attachment
99 Mainspar/fuselage attachment
100 Front spar/fuselage attachment
101 Port main fuel tank (29·5 Imp gal/132 litres capacity)
102 Port overload fuel tank (33 Imp gal/150 litres capacity)
103 Fuel filler caps
104 Main spar
105 Rear spar
106 Aileron control rod
107 Flap inboard travel
108 Flap pulley fairing
109 Fowler-type "butterfly" combat flap
110 Flap outboard travel
111 Aileron trim tab

112 Aileron inner hinge
113 Aileron centre hinge/control rod attachment
114 Port aileron
115 Aileron outer hinge
116 Port wingtip
117 Port navigation light
118 Wing skinning
119 Pitot head
120 Leading edge ribs
121 Front spar
122 Landing light
123 Mainwheel leg fairing
124 Torque links
125 Port mainwheel
126 Axle fork
127 Mainwheel oleo
128 Mainwheel leg pivot
129 Gear support bearer
130 Gear actuating cylinder
131 Emergency actuation cables
132 Leading edge rib cut-outs
133 Mainwheel well
134 Underwing drop tank pylon (mounted aft and just inboard of the main undercarriage attachment point)
135 Tank suspension lugs
136 Air vent
137 Fuel pipe connection
138 Tank fin
139 Sway brace attachment points
140 Jettisonable 44 Imp gal (200 litres) tank

Nakajima Ki-44 Shoki "Tojo"

Ki-44-Ia, b and c, IIa, b and c and III

Origin: Nakajima Hikoki KK.
Type: Single-seat interceptor fighter and (II onwards) fighter-bomber.
Engine: (Ia) one 1,260hp Nakajima Ha-41 14-cylinder two-row radial; (Ib and all subsequent) 1,520hp Nakajima Ha-109 of same layout.
Dimensions: Span 31ft (9·448m); length 28ft 8½in (8·75m); height 10ft 8in (3·248m).
Weights: Empty (Ia) 3,968lb (1800kg); (II, typical) 4,643lb (2106kg); normal loaded (no overload permitted) (Ia) 5,622lb (2550kg); (IIc) 6,107lb (2770kg); (III) 5,357lb (2430kg).
Performance: Maximum speed (Ia) 360mph (579km/h); (IIc) 376mph (605km/h); initial climb (IIc) 3,940ft (1200m)/min; service ceiling (IIc) 36,745ft (11,200m); range on internal fuel (typical) 560 miles (900km) (endurance, 2hr 20min).
Armament: (Ia) two 12·7mm Type I in wings and two 7·7mm Type 89 in fuselage; (Ib, IIa, IIb) four 12·7mm Type I, two in fuselage and two in wings, with (II series) wing racks for two 220lb (100kg) bombs; (IIc) two 12·7mm in fuselage, two 40mm Ho-301 low-velocity cannon; (III) two 12·7mm in

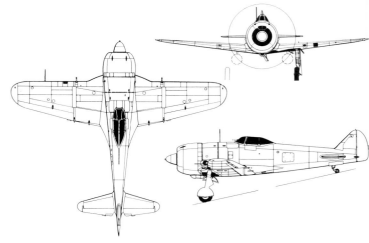

Above: Three-view of Ki-44-IIb.

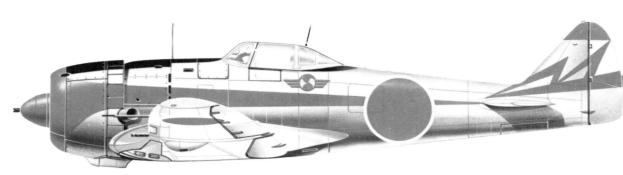

Left: A mainly unpainted Ki-44-IIb of the Shinten (Sky Shadow) experimental unit of the 47th Sentai, based at Narimasu, Tokyo, in summer of 1944.

Right: A Ki-44-Ic, the rare interim model of late 1942. Only 40 were built of all Dash-I models combined.

Nakajima Ki-49 Donryu "Helen"

Ki-49-I, IIa, IIb, III and Ki-58

Origin: Nakajima Hikoki KK; also built by Tachikawa Hikoki KK and (few) Mansyu Hikoki.
Type: Eight-seat heavy bomber; Ki-58, escort fighter.
Engines: (I) two 1,250hp Nakajima Ha-41 14-cylinder two-row radials; (II) two 1,450hp Nakajima Ha-109-II of same layout; (III) two 2,500hp Nakajima Ha-117 18-cylinder two-row radials.
Dimensions: Span 66ft 7¼in (20·3m); length 53ft 1¾in (16·2m); height 13ft 11½in (4·25m).
Weights: Empty (II) 15,653lb (7100kg); normal loaded 23,545lb

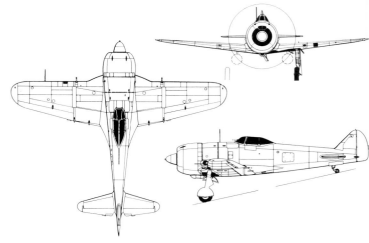

Above: Three-view of Ki-49-I (II has oil coolers under engines).

(10,680kg).
Performance: Maximum speed (II) 304mph (490km/h); initial climb 1,312ft (400m)/min; service ceiling 26,772ft (8160m); range with bomb load, 1,491 miles (2400km).
Armament: (I) one 20mm cannon manually aimed in dorsal position, single 7·7mm manually aimed at nose and tail; (IIa) as (I) plus extra 7·7mm in ventral and two beam positions (total five); (IIb) as IIa but with all 7·7mm replaced by 12·7mm, thus 20mm dorsal and single 12·7mm in nose, tail, ventral and two beam positions; all versions, internal bay for bomb load up to 2,205lb (1,000kg).
History: First flight August 1939; (production Ki-49-I) probably May 1940; (II) 1942; final delivery December 1944.
User: Japan (Imperial Army).

Above: Take-off by one of the few (129) Ki-49-I production aircraft. This example bears on its tail the badge of the Hammamatsu Heavy Bomber Training School (also see page 155).

Below: Side elevation of a Ki-49-IIb, of an unknown sentai operating in New Guinea in late 1943.

Development: Designed to a late 1938 specification aimed at replacing the Mitsubishi Ki-21, the Ki-49 was the first Japanese bomber to mount a 20mm cannon; but it was at first only slightly faster than the Ki-21, had a

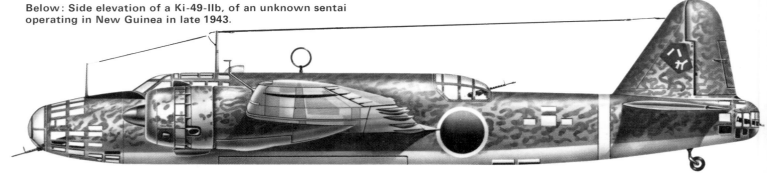

fuselage, two 20mm Ho-5 cannon in wings.
History: First flight (first of ten prototypes) August 1940; (production Ki-44-Ia) May 1942; (Ib, Ic) 1943; (IIb) December 1943.
User: Japan (Imperial Army).

Development: Marking a complete break with the traditional emphasis on manoeuvrability, the Ki-44 (code-named "Tojo" by the Allies) contrasted with the Ki-43 as did the J2M with the Zero-Sen. Suddenly the need was for greater speed and climb, even at the expense of poorer manoeuvrability and faster landing. In late 1940 a Ki-44 was tested against a Kawasaki Ki-60 and an imported Bf 109E, outflying both; but production was delayed until mid-1942 by the priority accorded the old Ki-43. Pilots did not like the speedy small-winged fighter, with poor view on take-off and such poor control that flick rolls and many other manoeuvres were banned. But gradually the fact that the Ki-44 could climb and dive as well as its enemies brought some measure of popularity, even though many inexperienced pilots were killed in accidents. Most Shokis (Demons) were -II series with retractable tailwheel and other changes, including a glazed teardrop canopy. The heavy cannon of the -IIc, firing caseless ammunition at 400 rounds per minute, were effective against Allied bombers. Probably the most successful mission ever flown in defending Japan was that of 19 February 1945 when a small force of Ki-44 (probably -IIc) climbed up to 120 B-29s and destroyed ten, two reportedly by suicide collisions. Total production was 1,233, including a few of the lightened -III series.

poor ceiling and never did achieve any advance in range and bomb load. The 1,160hp Nakajima Ha-5B engines of the prototype were replaced by the Ha-41, and 129 of the -I model were built at Ohta, after whose Donryu (Dragon Swallower) shrine the type was named. The production machine was the Type 100 heavy bomber, and the Allied code name was "Helen". Its first mission was a raid on Port Darwin from a New Guinea base on 19 February 1942. The main model was the better-armed -II series, of which 649 were built by Nakajima, 50 by Tachikawa and a few by Mansyu in Harbin, Manchuria. Though met in all parts of the Japanese war, the Ki-49 was not very effective; many were destroyed at Leyte Gulf, and by late 1944 all were being used either for non-combatant purposes or as suicide machines or, with ASV radar or magnetic-mine detectors, for ocean patrol. As it was a poor bomber three were converted as Ki-58 fighters with five 20mm cannon and three 12·7mm guns, while two were rebuilt as Ki-80 leadships for attack by fighter-bomber or suicide aircraft. The much more powerful III model was not ready by August 1945, though six were built.

Below: This photograph is probably the best surviving of any type of Donryu. The subject is the mass-produced Ki-49-IIb, and the unit possibly the 110th Hikosentai.

Nakajima Ki-84 Hayate "Frank"

Ki-84-I to Ic, and many projects

Origin: Nakajima Hikoki KK; also built by Mansyu Hikoki Seizo KK and (three Ki-106) Tachikawa Hikoki KK.
Type: Single-seat fighter-bomber.
Engine: In all production models, one 1,900hp Nakajima Homare Ha-45 Model 11 18-cylinder two-row radial.
Dimensions: Span 36ft 10½in (11·238m); length 32ft 6½in (9·92m); height 11ft 1¼in (3·385m).
Weights: Empty 5,864lb (2680kg); normal loaded 8,267lb (3750kg); maximum overload (seldom authorised) 9,150lb (4150kg).
Performance: Maximum speed 388mph (624km/h); initial climb 3,600ft (1100m)/min; service ceiling 34,450ft (10,500m); range on internal fuel 1,025 miles (1650km); range with 98-gal drop tanks, 1,815 miles (2920km).
Armament: (Ia) two 20mm Ho-5 in wings, each with 150 rounds, and two 12·7mm Type 103 in top of fuselage with 350 rounds; (Ib) four 20mm, each

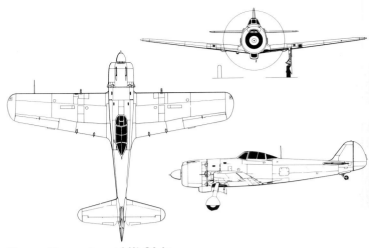

Above: Three-view of Ki-84-Ia.

Left: Most Hayates were camouflaged or painted in various green shades. This pretty specimen served with HQ Chutai, 29th Sentai, on Taiwan (Formosa) in the summer of 1945.

Right: A more regular paint scheme is seen on this Ki-84-Ia of the 1st Chutai, 73rd Sentai, based in the Philippine Islands in December 1944.

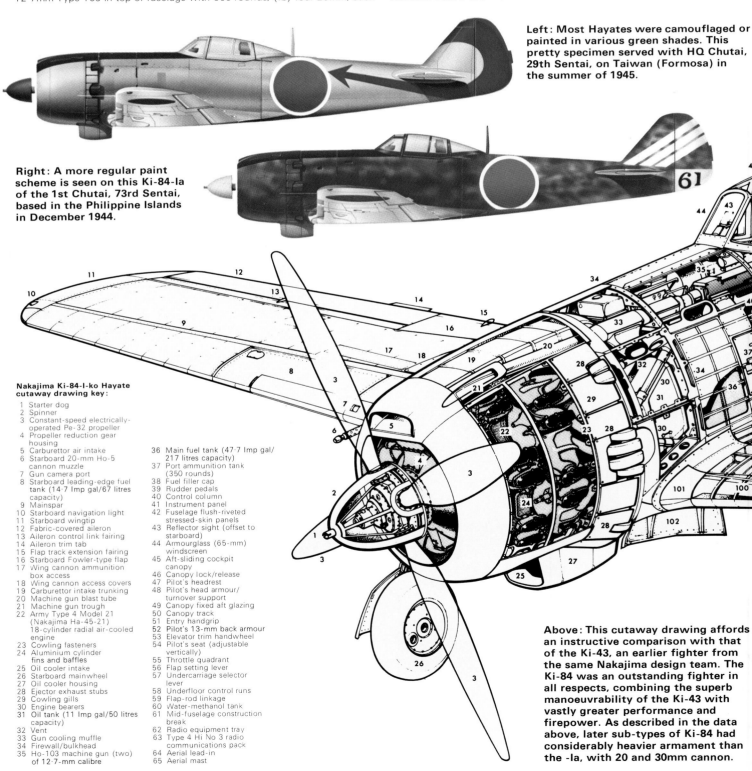

Nakajima Ki-84-I-ko Hayate cutaway drawing key:

1. Starter dog
2. Spinner
3. Constant-speed electrically-operated Pe-32 propeller
4. Propeller reduction gear housing
5. Carburettor air intake
6. Starboard 20-mm Ho-5 cannon muzzle
7. Gun camera port
8. Starboard leading-edge fuel tank (14·7 Imp gal/67 litres capacity)
9. Mainspar
10. Starboard navigation light
11. Starboard wingtip
12. Fabric-covered aileron
13. Aileron control link fairing
14. Aileron trim tab
15. Flap track extension fairing
16. Starboard Fowler-type flap
17. Wing cannon ammunition box access
18. Wing cannon access covers
19. Carburettor intake trunking
20. Machine gun blast tube
21. Machine gun trough
22. Army Type 4 Model 21 (Nakajima Ha-45-21) 18-cylinder radial air-cooled engine
23. Cowling fasteners
24. Aluminium cylinder fins and baffles
25. Oil cooler intake
26. Starboard mainwheel
27. Oil cooler housing
28. Ejector exhaust stubs
29. Cowling gills
30. Engine bearers
31. Oil tank (11 Imp gal/50 litres capacity)
32. Vent
33. Gun cooling muffle
34. Firewall/bulkhead
35. Ho-103 machine gun (two) of 12·7-mm calibre
36. Main fuel tank (47·7 Imp gal/217 litres capacity)
37. Port ammunition tank (350 rounds)
38. Fuel filler cap
39. Rudder pedals
40. Control column
41. Instrument panel
42. Fuselage flush-riveted stressed-skin panels
43. Reflector sight (offset to starboard)
44. Armourglass (65-mm) windscreen
45. Aft-sliding cockpit canopy
46. Canopy lock/release
47. Pilot's headrest
48. Pilot's head armour/turnover support
49. Canopy fixed aft glazing
50. Canopy track
51. Entry handgrip
52. Pilot's 13-mm back armour
53. Elevator trim handwheel
54. Pilot's seat (adjustable vertically)
55. Throttle quadrant
56. Flap setting lever
57. Undercarriage selector lever
58. Underfloor control runs
59. Flap-rod linkage
60. Water-methanol tank
61. Mid-fuselage construction break
62. Radio equipment tray
63. Type 4 Hi No 3 radio communications pack
64. Aerial lead-in
65. Aerial mast

Above: This cutaway drawing affords an instructive comparison with that of the Ki-43, an earlier fighter from the same Nakajima design team. The Ki-84 was an outstanding fighter in all respects, combining the superb manoeuvrability of the Ki-43 with vastly greater performance and firepower. As described in the data above, later sub-types of Ki-84 had considerably heavier armament than the -Ia, with 20 and 30mm cannon.

with 150 rounds, two in wings and two in fuselage; (Ic) two 20mm in fuselage and two 30mm Ho-105 cannon in wings; (all operational models) two racks under outer wings for tanks or bombs up to 551lb (250kg) each.

History: First flight March 1943; (production Ia) August 1943; service delivery April 1944.

User: Japan (Imperial Army).

continued on page 168 ▶

Left: An early Ki-84-Ia Hayate. The long landing gears were prone to structural failure, as a result of faulty heat-treatment of the steel legs, and the complex and closely cowled engine gave prolonged trouble; so did the hydraulics.

Below: The skull and crossbones insignia identify this Hayate, another Ki-84-Ia, as belonging to the 58th Shimbu-tai in Japan in August 1945.

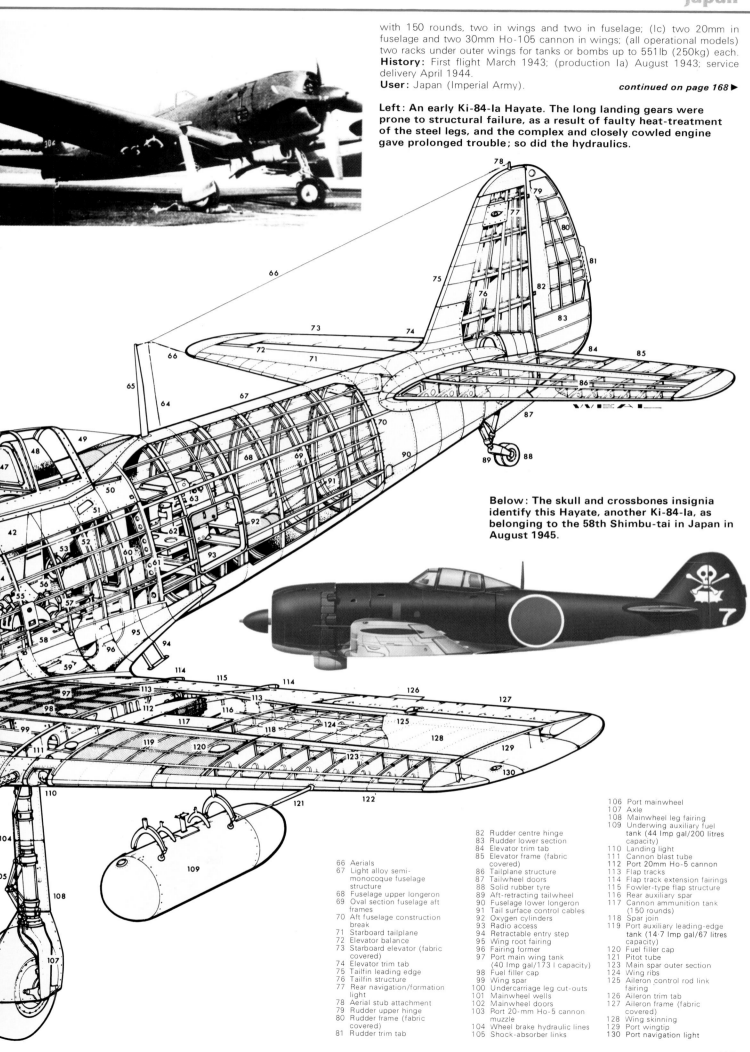

66 Aerials
67 Light alloy semi-monocoque fuselage structure
68 Fuselage upper longeron
69 Oval section fuselage aft frames
70 Aft fuselage construction break
71 Starboard tailplane
72 Elevator balance
73 Starboard elevator (fabric covered)
74 Elevator trim tab
75 Tailfin leading edge
76 Tailfin structure
77 Rear navigation/formation light
78 Aerial stub attachment
79 Rudder upper hinge
80 Rudder frame (fabric covered)
81 Rudder trim tab
82 Rudder centre hinge
83 Rudder lower section
84 Elevator trim tab
85 Elevator frame (fabric covered)
86 Tailplane structure
87 Tailwheel doors
88 Solid rubber tyre
89 Aft-retracting tailwheel
90 Fuselage lower longeron
91 Tail surface control cables
92 Oxygen cylinders
93 Radio access
94 Retractable entry step
95 Wing root fairing
96 Fairing former
97 Port main wing tank (40 Imp gal/173 l capacity)
98 Fuel filler cap
99 Wing spar
100 Undercarriage leg cut-outs
101 Mainwheel wells
102 Mainwheel doors
103 Port 20-mm Ho-5 cannon muzzle
104 Wheel brake hydraulic lines
105 Shock-absorber links
106 Port mainwheel
107 Axle
108 Mainwheel leg fairing
109 Underwing auxiliary fuel tank (44 Imp gal/200 litres capacity)
110 Landing light
111 Cannon blast tube
112 Port 20mm Ho-5 cannon
113 Flap tracks
114 Flap track extension fairings
115 Fowler-type flap structure
116 Rear auxiliary spar
117 Cannon ammunition tank (150 rounds)
118 Spar join
119 Port auxiliary leading-edge tank (14·7 Imp gal/67 litres capacity)
120 Fuel filler cap
121 Pitot tube
123 Main spar outer section
124 Wing ribs
125 Aileron control rod link fairing
126 Aileron trim tab
127 Aileron frame (fabric covered)
128 Wing skinning
129 Port wingtip
130 Port navigation light

► **Development:** Code-named "Frank" by the Allies, the Ki-84 of the Imperial Army was generally regarded as the best Japanese fighter of World War II. Yet it was not without its problems. Part of its fine all-round performance stemmed from the extremely advanced direct-injection engine, the first Army version of the Navy NK9A; yet this engine gave constant trouble and needed skilled maintenance. T. Koyama designed the Ki-84 to greater strength factors than any earlier Japanese warplane, yet poor heat-treatment of the high-strength steel meant that landing gears often simply snapped. Progressive deterioration in quality control meant that pilots never knew how particular aircraft would perform, whether the brakes would work or whether, in trying to intercept B-29s over Japan, they would even be able to climb high enough. Despite this, the Ki-84 was potentially superb, a captured -Ia out-climbing and outmanoeuvring a P-51H and P-47N! First batches went to China, where the 22nd Sentai flew rings round Gen Chennault's 14th Air Force. The unit then moved to the Philippines, where the rot set in, with accidents, shortages and extremely poor serviceability. Frequent bombing of the Musashi engine factory and extreme need to conserve raw material led to various projects and prototypes made of wood (Ki-84-II series and Ki-106) or steel (Ki-113) and advanced models with the 2,000hp Ha-45ru turbo charged engine, Ha-45/44 with two-stage three-speed blower and 2,500hp Ha-44/13. Total production of the Hayate (Hurricane) was 3,514 (2,689 at Ohta, 727 at Utsonomiya and 95 in Manchuria by Mansyu, which also flew the Ki-116 with smaller Ha-112 engine) and three at Tachikawa.

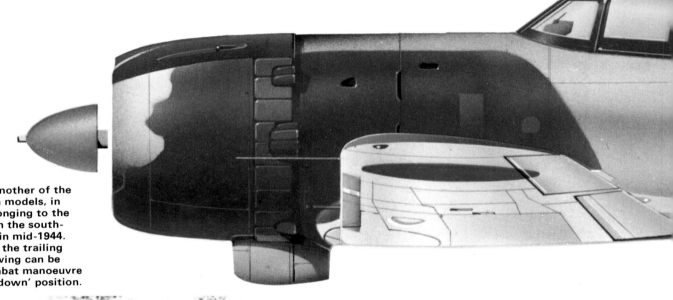

Below: Yet another of the early Ki-84-Ia models, in this case belonging to the 11th Sentai in the south-west Pacific in mid-1944. Just beneath the trailing edge of the wing can be seen the combat manoeuvre flaps in the 'down' position.

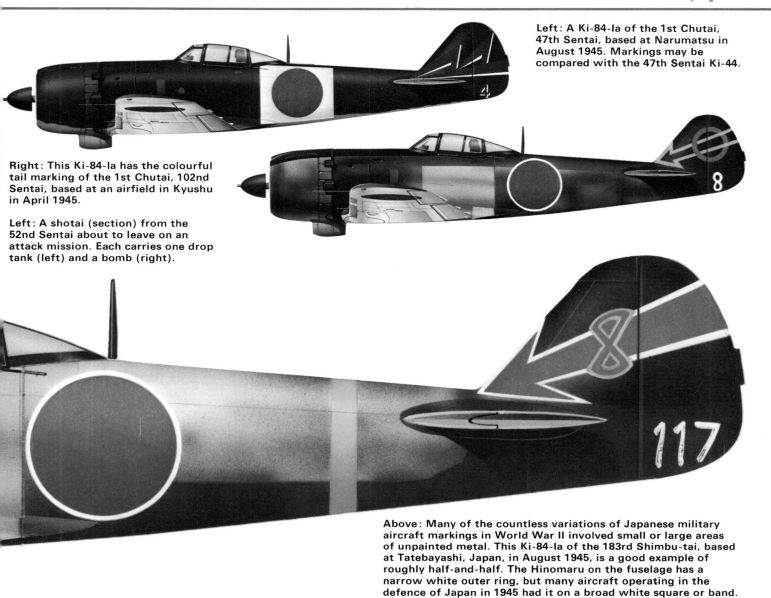

Left: A Ki-84-Ia of the 1st Chutai, 47th Sentai, based at Narumatsu in August 1945. Markings may be compared with the 47th Sentai Ki-44.

Right: This Ki-84-Ia has the colourful tail marking of the 1st Chutai, 102nd Sentai, based at an airfield in Kyushu in April 1945.

Left: A shotai (section) from the 52nd Sentai about to leave on an attack mission. Each carries one drop tank (left) and a bomb (right).

Above: Many of the countless variations of Japanese military aircraft markings in World War II involved small or large areas of unpainted metal. This Ki-84-Ia of the 183rd Shimbu-tai, based at Tatebayashi, Japan, in August 1945, is a good example of roughly half-and-half. The Hinomaru on the fuselage has a narrow white outer ring, but many aircraft operating in the defence of Japan in 1945 had it on a broad white square or band.

Nakajima Ki-115 Tsurugi

Ki-115 and various proposed developments (no Allied code-name published)

Origin: Designed by Aori Kunihiro assisted by Mitaka Research and Ota Manufacturing; prototype by Mitaki and production by Nakajima at Iwate and Ota.

Type: Single-seat suicide attack aircraft.

Engine: 1,150hp Nakajima Ha-35 Type 23 (Ha-115 Sakae) 14-cylinder radial.

Dimensions: Span 28ft 0½in (8·55m); length 28ft 2½in (8·60m); height 10ft 10in (3·30m).

Weights: Empty 3,616lb (1640kg); loaded 5,688lb (2580kg); max overload with 800kg bomb 6,349lb (2880kg).

Performance: Maximum speed 342mph (550km/h); range with 500kg bomb 746 miles (1200km).

Armament: Belly recess for bomb of 551lb (250kg), 1,102lb (500kg) or 1,764lb (800kg).

History: First flight March 1945.

User: Not delivered.

Development: As the concept of piloted suicide attacks had become firmly established during 1944 the Imperial Army recognised that it was inefficient to use a motley collection of unsuitable aircraft, and that an aircraft designed for such attack should be produced with extreme urgency. Nakajima was given the job on 20 January 1945, and the first aircraft emerged within three months. One might have expected the Ki-115 to be

wooden, but instead the small wing was all-metal stressed-skin, the fuselage was steel tube with skin panels mainly of thin mild steel, and the tail was wood/fabric. The landing gear was unsprung steel tube, and arranged to be jettisoned after take-off. Handling was atrocious, but improved when a new sprung landing gear and bolted-on wing flaps were fitted. By VJ-day Nakajima had built 22 and the Ota plant 82, all with wing fixtures for rockets (never fitted) to boost speed in the final dive. The Ki-115b was a development with larger wings and all-wood structure and the Toka a proposed Navy version. The significantly more effective Ki-230 was not built.

Right: The Ki-115 was possibly the cheapest manned combat aircraft of World War II, but it was also one of the least satisfactory. Few photographs exist of this hastily contrived and elusive machine, which, had it been started earlier, might have been a thorn in the side of the Allies. Unusually, this specimen appears to have a dark-painted fuselage.

Tachikawa Ki-36/ Ki-55 "Ida"

Ki-36 (Army Type 98 Direct Co-operation), Ki-55 (Army Type 99 trainer) (Allied code-name "Ida")

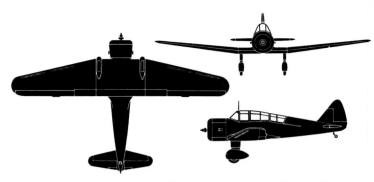

Origin: Tachikawa Hikoki KK, second-source production by Kawasaki.
Type: Ki-36, two-seat army co-operation; Ki-55, advanced trainer.
Engine: 510hp Hitachi Ha-13a (Army Type 98) nine-cylinder radial.
Dimensions: Span 38ft 8½in (11·80m); length 26ft 3in (8·00m); height 11ft 11¼in (3·64m).
Weights: Empty (36) 2,749lb (1247kg); loaded (36) 3,635lb (1649kg).

Above: Three-view showing Ki-36 spats but no belly windows.

Below: This Ki-36 "direct co-operation" aircraft could have been photographed on any front on which Japan fought from 1939 onwards. By 1943 most survivors were in China.

Performance: Maximum speed (36) 217mph (349km/h); range 767 miles (1235km).
Armament: Synchronized 7·7mm Type 89 on right above fuselage (36 and 55), one Type 89 manually aimed from rear cockpit (36 only) and underwing racks for ten 27·5lb (12·5kg) or 33lb (15kg) bombs (36 only).
History: First flight (36) 20 April 1938; service delivery, early 1939; final delivery January 1944.
Users: Japan (Imperial Army), Manchukuo and Thailand (puppet states); post-war, Indonesia insurgent AF.

Development: Though little known, these were among the most common Japanese aircraft of the World War II period. The Ki-36 was designed to meet a May 1937 specification for an army co-operation machine able to use forward airstrips and carry cameras, radio and light anti-personnel bombs. Both pilot and observer had a good view, the latter having windows in the floor. Early service in China was extremely successful, but against the Allies casualties were heavy and from 1943 the type was withdrawn to secondary areas, though in late 1944 some appeared with 1,102lb (500kg) bombs in the suicide role. Total production was 1,334. The Ki-55 trainer was simpler, with no combat gear, spats or belly windows. It was the chief wartime advanced trainer of the Japanese and satellite air forces, 1,389 being built.

Yokosuka D4Y Suisei "Judy"

D4Y1 and 1-C, D4Y2, 2-C and 2-S, D4Y3 and D4Y4

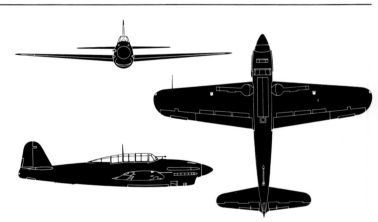

Origin: Dai-Ichi Kaigun Koku Gijitsusho, Yokosuka; production aircraft built by Aichi Kokuki KK and Dai-Juichi Kaigun Kokusho.
Type: Two-seat carrier dive bomber; (1-C, 2-C, reconnaissance; 2-S night fighter; D4Y4, single-seat Kamikaze).
Engines: (1) one 1,200hp Aichi Atsuta 21 inverted-vee-12 liquid-cooled (Daimler-Benz 601); (2) 1,400hp Atsuta 32; (3, 4) 1,560hp Mitsubishi Kinsei 62 14-cylinder two-row radial).
Dimensions: Span (1, 2) 37ft 8½in (11·493m); (3, 4) 37ft 9in (11·50m); length (all, despite engine change) 33ft 6½in (10·22m); height (1, 2) 12ft 1in (3·67m); (3, 4) 12ft 3¼in (3·74m).
Weights: Empty (1) 5,650lb (2565kg); (2) 5,840lb (2635kg); (3) 5,512lb (2501kg); (4) variable; maximum loaded (1) 9,615lb (4361kg); (2) 9,957lb (4353kg); (3) 10,267lb (4657kg); (4) 10,434lb (4733kg).
Performance: Maximum speed (1) 339mph (546km/h); (2) 360mph (580km/h); (3) 356mph (574km/h); initial climb (1) 1,970ft (600m)/min; (others) 2,700ft (820m)/min; service ceiling (typical) 34,500ft (10,500m); range (2) 749 miles (1205km); (3) 945 miles (1520km).
Armament: Normally, two 7·7mm Type 97 fixed above engine, one 7·7mm manually aimed from rear cockpit; internal bomb bay for single 551lb (250kg) bomb, plus one 66lb (30kg) bomb under each wing; (4) see text.
History: First flight November 1940; (production D4Y1) May 1941; service delivery, late 1941.
User: Japan (Imperial Navy).

Above: Three-view of D4Y1 (D4Y2 very similar).

Below: A D4Y3 Suisei Model 33, with two 72·6 Imp gal drop tanks. By the time this radial-engined model was delivered nearly all Suiseis had to be assigned to land-based units.

Development: Designed to a challenging specification of the Imperial Japanese Navy of 1937, which called for a long-range two-seat dive bomber as fast as the "Zero" fighter, the D4Y was one of the very few Japanese aircraft to go into production with a liquid-cooled engine. The supposed lower drag of such an engine had been one of the factors in meeting the requirement, but the Japanese version of the DB 601 had an unhappy history in carrier service. The first D4Y versions in combat were 1-C reconnaissance aircraft flying from the carrier *Soryu* during the Battle of Midway in June 1942. The carrier was sunk in that encounter, and soon most D4Y were being operated by unskilled crews from island airstrips. In 1943 the main problems with the aircraft — named Suisei (Comet), and called "Judy" by the Allies — were solved by switching to the smooth and reliable radial engine. During the final year of the war the D4Y4 appeared as a single-seat suicide attacker carrying 1,764lb (800kg) of explosives, while some dozens of Atsuta-engined examples were turned into 2-S night fighters with one or two 20mm cannon fixed obliquely behind the rear cockpit. Total production was 2,038.

Yokosuka P1Y1 Ginga "Frances"

P1Y1 Model 11, P1Y1-S, P1Y2 and 2-S

Origin: Design by Dai-Ichi Kaigun Koku Gijitsusho, but all construction by Nakajima Hikoki KK and Kawanishi Kokuki KK.
Type: Three-seat multi-role attack bomber; -S, two-seat night fighter.
Engines: (1) two 1,820hp Nakajima Ho-21 Homare 11 18-cylinder two-row radials; (2) 1,825hp Mitsubishi Kasei 25 14-cylinder two-row radials.
Dimensions: Span 65ft 7½in (20m); length 49ft 2½in (15m); height 14ft 1¼in (4·30m)
Weights: Empty (1) 14,748lb (6690kg); normal loaded (1) 23,148lb (10,500kg); maximum loaded (1) 29,762lb (13,500kg).
Performance: Maximum speed (1) 345mph (556km/h); (2) 354mph (570km/h); initial climb (1) 2,100ft (650m)/min; service ceiling 33,530ft (10,220m); range (1) 2,728 miles (4390km).
Armament: (1 and 2) one 20mm Type 99-II cannon manually aimed from nose, one 20mm or 12·7mm manually aimed from rear cockpit (a few aircraft had dorsal turret with two 20mm or 12·7mm); internal bay for two 551lb (250kg) bombs, plus small bombs beneath outer wings; as alternative, one 1,764lb (800kg) or 1,874lb (850kg) torpedo externally, or

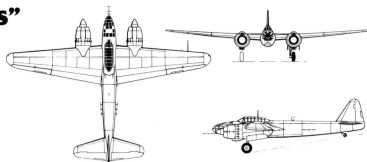

Above: Three-view of late-model P1Y1 with ASV search radar.

two 1,102lb (500kg) bombs inboard of engines; (1-S, 2-S) two 20mm fixed firing obliquely upward in centre fuselage, plus single 20mm aimed from rear cockpit, or powered dorsal turret with two 20mm.
History: First flight (Y-20 prototype) early 1943; (production P1Y1) August 1943; (prototype P1Y2-S) June 1944.
User: Japan (Imperial Navy).

Development: Similar to late-model Ju 88 aircraft in size, power and capability, this fine-looking aircraft was one of the best designed in Japan during World War II. The 1940 Navy specification called for a land-based aircraft capable of level and dive bombing, but by the time production began at the Nakajima factories at Koizumi and Fukushima it had already become a torpedo bomber, and it was to do much more before its brief career was over. At sea level it could outrun many Allied fighters and it was manoeuvrable and well protected; yet it carried 1,290gal of fuel and had greater range than any other aircraft in its class. Called Ginga (Milky Way), and christened "Frances" by the Allies, this machine would have been a menace had it not been crippled by lack of skilled crews, lack of fuel and lack of spares. Nevertheless Nakajima built 1,002, of which some were used as suicide aircraft while a few were converted into the P1Y1-S night fighter. Kawanishi had meanwhile developed a completely new version, the Kasei-engined P1Y2, and delivered 96 P1Y2-S night fighters called Kyokko (Aurora), which saw little action.

Below: This photograph appears to show an unpainted development aircraft. All P1Y1s were outstanding aircraft.

Yokosuka MXY-7 Ohka "Baka"

MXY-7 Model 11 and Model 22

Origin: Dai-Ichi Kaigun Koku Gijitsusho, Yokosuka; 600 Model 11 built by Dai-Ichi Kaigun Kokusho.
Type: Single-seat piloted missile for surface attack.
Engine: (11) one three-barrel Type 4 Model 20 rocket motor with sea-level thrust of 1,764lb (800kg); (22) TSU-11 jet engine, with piston-engined compressor, rated at 441lb (200kg) thrust.
Dimensions: Span (11) 16ft 4¾in (5m); (22) 13ft 6¼in (4·12m); length (11) 19ft 10¾in (6·07m); (22) 22ft 6¼in (6·88m); height (both) about 3ft 11¼in (1·20m).
Weights: Empty (no warhead) (11) 970lb (440kg); (22) 1,202lb (545kg); loaded (11) 4,718lb (2140kg); (22) 3,200lb (1450kg).
Performance: Maximum speed on level (11) 534mph (860km/h); (22) about 300mph (480km/h); final dive speed (both) 621mph (1000km/h); climb and ceiling, normally launched at about 27,000ft (8200m); range (11) 55 miles (88km).
Armament: (11) warhead containing 2,645lb (1200kg) of tri-nitroaminol; (22) warhead weight 1,323lb (600kg).
History: Start of design August 1944; start of quantity production (11) September 1944; service delivery, early October 1944.
User: Japan (Imperial Navy).

Development: Having accepted the principle of the Kamikaze suicide attack, the Imperial Navy was only logical in designing an aircraft for this duty instead of using inefficient and more vulnerable conventional machines having less devastating effect. Built partly of wood, Model 11 was carried aloft by a G4M ("Betty"), without bomb doors and specially modified for the task, and released about 50 miles from the target. The pilot then held a fast glide at about 290mph (466km/h), electrically igniting the rocket while pushing over into a steep final dive for the last 30 seconds of trajectory. Though nearly all these missiles failed to reach their objectives, the few that did wrought fearful havoc. Ohka (Cherry Blossom) was called "Baka" (Japanese for "fool") by the Allies, which was not very appropriate. Several manufacturers delivered 755, and 45 unpowered K-1 versions were delivered for training. The Model 22, of which some 50 were delivered, was underpowered. Not completed by VJ-day, the Model 33 would have had the Ne-20 turbojet; Models 43A and 43B were for launching from submarines and land catapults, respectively, but these too failed to see service.

Right: A genuine operational Model 11, complete with warhead and motor, found abandoned (probably on Okinawa). All Ohka variants carried a cherry blossom motif on the side of the fuselage (here partly obscured by the joint strap).

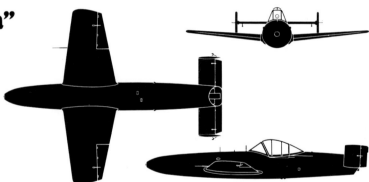

Above: Three-view of MXY-7 Model 11.

PZL P.11

P.11a, 11b and 11c

Origin: Panstwowe Zaklady Lotnicze, Poland.
Type: Single-seat fighter.
Engine: One Bristol-designed nine-cylinder radial; (11a) 500hp Skoda Mercury IVS2; (11b) 595hp IAR Gnome-Rhône K9 (Jupiter); (11c) 645hp PZL Mercury VIS2.
Dimensions: Span 35ft 2in (10·72m); length 24ft 9in or 24ft 9½in (7·55m); height 9ft 4in (2·85m).
Weights: Empty (11c) 2,524lb (1145kg); loaded 3,960lb (1795kg).
Performance: Maximum speed (11c) 242mph (390km/h); initial climb 2,625ft (800m)/min; service ceiling 36,090ft (11,000m); range (economic cruise, no combat) 503 miles (810km).
Armament: (11a) two 7·7mm (0·303in) Browning, each with 700 rounds, in sides of fuselage; (11c) two 7·7mm KM Wz 33 machine guns, each with 500 rounds, in sides of fuselage, and two more, each with 300 rounds, inside wing at junction of struts; provision for two 27lb (12·25kg) bombs.
History: First flight (P.11/I) August 1931; (production P.11a) June 1933.
Users: Bulgaria (P.24), Greece (P.24), Poland (P.11c), Romania (P.11b, P.24).

Development: Having hired brilliant young designer Zygmund Pulaski at its formation in 1928, the Polish PZL (National Aero Factory) set itself to

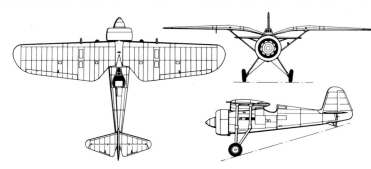

Above: Three-view of P.11c (with wing guns fitted).

building gull-winged monoplane fighters of outstanding quality. All the early production models were powered by Polish-built Jupiter engines, and large numbers of P.7a fighters formed the backbone of the young Polish Air Force. The P.11 was the natural successor, but when the prototype was about to fly Pulaski was killed in a crash and his place was taken by W. Jakimiuk (later designer for D. H. Canada and SNCASE). The first P.11 was powered by a Gnome-Rhône Jupiter and subsequent prototypes by a Mistral and Mercury from the same source, but after prolonged trials the P.11a went into production with the Polish-built Mercury IVS. In 1934 the fuselage was redesigned to improve pilot view by lowering the engine and raising the pilot (11c). A new tail and modified wings were introduced and provision was made for two wing guns and radio, but these were usually not available for fitting. The final production model was the export version of the 11a, the 11b, which was built in Romania as the IAR P.11f. Many further developments were planned, but the main fighter force defending Poland in September 1939 comprised 12 squadrons of P.11c, most with only two guns and operating with no warning system in chaotic conditions. They nevertheless destroyed 126 Luftwaffe aircraft for the loss of 114 of their own number. Final PZL fighter was the P.24 family, of which there were many variants produced entirely for export. Most had a 970hp Gnome-Rhône 14N engine, and two cannon and two machine guns.

Above: In 1935 the P.11c, examples of which are seen here in front-line Polish service, was one of the most formidable fighters in the world. By 1939 it was long overdue for replacement.

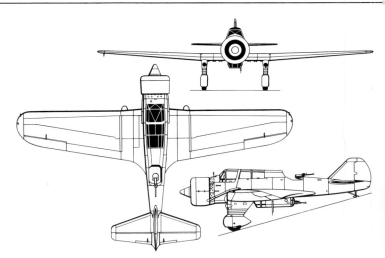

Above: This P.11c is depicted in the markings of No 113 Sqn, 1st Air Regiment, of the Polish Air Force. Popularly called Jedenatska (The Eleventh), it was virtually the only fighter available in Poland to oppose the much more formidable Bf 109 in September 1939. The planned replacement, the P.50 Jastrzab, was a single prototype (and that was shot down by Polish AA!).

PZL P.23 and 43 Karaś

P.23A and B, P.43A and B

Origin: Panstwowe Zaklady Lotnicze, Poland.
Type: Three-seat reconnaissance bomber.
Engine: (P.23A) one 580hp PZL (Bristol-licence) Pegasus II nine-cylinder radial; (P.23B) 680hp PZL Pegasus VIII; P.43A, 930hp Gnome-Rhône 14 Kfs 14-cylinder two-row radial; (P.43B) 980hp G-R 14N1.
Dimensions: Span 45ft 9in (13·95m); length (23) 31ft 9in (9·68m); (43) 32ft 10in; height 11ft 6in (3·5m).
Weights: Empty (23, typical) 4,250lb (1928kg); loaded (23) 6,918lb (3138kg); maximum overload 7,774lb (3526kg).
Performance: Maximum speed (23A) 198mph (320km/h); (23B) 217mph (350km/h); (43B) 227mph (365km/h); initial climb (typical) 985ft (300m)/min; service ceiling (typical) 24,600ft (7500m); range with bomb load, 410 miles (660km) (overload, 932 miles, 1500km).
Armament: (23) one 7·7mm Browning or KM Wz 33 firing forward, one on PZL hydraulically assisted mount in rear cockpit and third similarly mounted in rear ventral position; external bomb load of up to 1,543lb (700kg); (43) as 23 but with two forward-firing guns, one on each side of cowling.
History: First flight (P.23/I) August 1934; (production Karaś A) June 1936; (P.43A) 1937.
Users: Bulgaria, Poland, Romania.

Development: Designed by a team led by Stanisław Prauss, the P.23

Above: Three-view of P.23A (P.23B almost identical).

was hardly beautiful yet it provided the tactical attack capability of one of Europe's largest air forces in the late 1930s. By the outbreak of World War II, 14 of the bomber regiments of the Polish Air Force had been equipped with the Karaś (Carp); its successor, the greatly improved Sum, was about to enter service. When designed, in 1931–32, the Karaś was an outstandingly

PZL P.37 Łoś

P.37-I Łoś A and P.37-II Łoś B (Łoś = Elk).

Origin: Panstwowe Zaklady Lotnicze, Poland.
Type: Medium bomber.
Engines: Two PZL-built Bristol Pegasus nine-cylinder radials, (Łoś A) 875hp Pegasus XIIB, (B) 925hp Pegasus XX.
Dimensions: Span 58ft 8¾in (17·90m); length 42ft 4in (12·90m); height 16ft 8in (5·08m).
Weights: Empty 9,293lb (4213kg); normal loaded 18,739lb (8500kg); max overload 19,577lb (8880kg).
Performance: Maximum speed 273mph (440km/h); service ceiling 19,685ft (6000m); range with 3,880lb (1760kg) bomb load 1,616 miles (2600km).
Armament: Single manually aimed 7·7mm KM Wz.37 machine guns in nose, dorsal and ventral positions; internal (fuselage and wing) bays for bomb load of up to 5,688lb (2580kg).
History: First flight June 1936; service delivery, spring 1938.
Users: Poland, Romania.

Development: Designed by a team led by Jerzy Dabrowski in 1934, this bomber (extraordinarily efficient in its ratio of empty to gross weight) was the subject of unwarranted political criticism instigated by the Army ground forces. Nevertheless by the outbreak of war four squadrons, with nine Łoś B each, were operational with the Bomber Brigade and they proved extremely effective in the few days they were able to operate. About 100 had been delivered, and a dozen more were readied for combat during the Polish campaign, some 40 Łoś A and B finally escaping to Romania. There they were taken over and in 1941 used against the Soviet Union, a few still serving as target tugs in the late 1950s. By 1938 the dramatic performance of the Łoś resulted in intense international interest, and had war not supervened PZL would have fulfilled export contracts for at least five, and probably nine, countries.

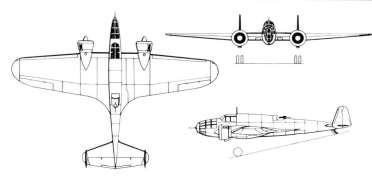

Above: Three-view of P.37 Łoś A (Łoś B outwardly identical).

Below left: Air and ground crews parade with their Łoś A bombers at the IIIrd Dyon (Conversion Unit) in late 1938.

Below: One of the first Łoś B bombers, pictured shortly before the German attack with a squadron of P.11c fighters.

modern aircraft, one of its radical features being the use of smooth skin of light-alloy/balsa sandwich construction. It carried a bomb load far heavier than any of its contemporaries and had no defence "blind spots", though its firepower was meagre. The more powerful P.43 was built for Bulgaria, 12 43A being followed by an order for 42 of the B model of which nearly all

were delivered by the start of World War II. Despite skill and heroism the Polish squadrons were soon overwhelmed, but a handful of Karaś managed to reach Romania, where they were refurbished, put into service with Romanian crews and used on the Bessarabian front in the invasion of the Soviet Union in 1941.

Below: Some of the 14 regiments equipped with the Karaś A are seen here at a large-scale review, probably in summer 1938.

Below: The P.23 Karaś was an outstandingly fine attack bomber in the mid-1930s; by 1939, like the P.11c, it was obsolescent.

Beriev MBR-2

Be-2, MBR-2 and -2bis

Origin: The design bureau of Georgei M. Beriev, Taganrog.
Type: Coastal patrol and utility flying boat.
Engine: (2) 680hp M-17B vee-12 water-cooled, (-2bis) 830hp AM-34N of same layout.
Dimensions: Span 62ft 4in (19·0m); length 44ft 3½in (13·5m); height about 14ft 9in (4·40m).
Weights: (2bis) empty, equipped, 7,024lb (3186kg); maximum 9,359lb (4245kg).
Performance: Maximum speed (2) 136mph (219km/h), (2bis) 154mph (248km/h); cruise (both) about 121mph (195km/h); max range with max fuel 932 miles (1500km), with bomb load 596 miles (959km).
Armament: 7·62mm ShKAS in bow cockpit and in manual dorsal turret, plus up to 661lb (300kg) bombs, depth charges or other stores under wings.
History: First flight 1931; service delivery, believed 1933; final delivery 1942.
User: Soviet Union (VVS-VMF).

Development: This remarkably small and quite ordinary machine had an active life considerably longer than 20 years, in the middle of which came World War II. Its great asset was a thoroughly good all-metal stressed-skin wing, though the hull was wood. Via a succession of intermediate models

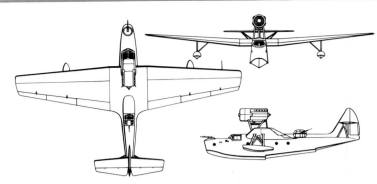

Above: Three-view of a typical MBR-2, there being few external differences between successive production batches.

it came to have an enclosed side-by-side cockpit, more fuel and much more powerful engine, increasing performance at high weights and resulting in a useful machine which could carry various weapons with a crew of five, or as many as eight passengers (there were civil versions, designated MP-1). Many of the 1,500+ built were equipped with fixed skis or wheels for use in the winter, while in the summer the MBR-2 was an excellent machine on water. Large numbers survived to serve on such duties as fisheries patrol long after 1945, even being assigned the NATO reporting name "Mote".

Below: The wooden hull stood up to harsh use remarkably well, though the paintwork often left something to be desired.

Below: Apparently the procedure was for the pilot to hand over to a marine pilot and ride to the slip in a towing launch.

Above: A wartime formation — it could be over the Black Sea, Baltic, Arctic or even in the Far East.

Ilyushin Il-2 Stormovik

BSh-2, TsKB-57, Il-2, Il-2M3 and Il-10

Origin: Design bureau of Sergei Ilyushin, Soviet Union.
Type: Single-seat or two-seat close support and attack.
Engine: (Il-2) one 1,300hp M-38 (from 1942) 1,750hp AM-38F; (Il-10) one 2,000hp AM-42; all engines vee-12 liquid-cooled.
Dimensions: Span (Il-2) 47ft 11in (14·6m); (Il-10) 45ft 7in (13·9m); length (Il-2) originally 38ft 2¾in, then 39ft 4½in (12m); (Il-10) 40ft 0¼in (12·2m); height (Il-2) 11ft 1¾in (3·4m); (Il-10) 11ft 5¾in (3·5m).
Weights: Empty (Il-2, typical) 7,165lb (3250kg); (Il-10) 7,495lb (3400kg); loaded (Il-2M3) 12,947lb (5872kg); (Il-10) 13,968lb (6336kg).
Performance: Maximum speed (Il-2) from 281mph clean to 231mph with 1,323lb bomb load; (Il-10) 311mph clean (500km/h); initial climb (Il-2, maximum bomb load) 490ft (150m)/min; service ceiling (all, with bomb load, typical) 21,325ft (6500m); range with bomb load (all, typical) 373 miles (600km).
Armament: (Original Il-2) two 20mm ShVAK and two 7·62mm ShKAS fixed in wing, underwing racks for eight 82mm rockets and four 220lb bombs; (Il-2M3) two 20mm VYa and/or two 37mm in wings, one manually aimed 12·7mm BS in added rear cockpit, bomb load of 1,323lb (600kg) including rockets and PTAB anti-armour bombs; (Il-10) two or four 20mm VYa or two or four 23mm NS 23, often with two 7·62mm ShKAS, dorsal turret with 20mm VYa, racks for up to 2,205lb (1000kg) of weapons.
History: First flight (BSh-2) 30 December 1939; (TsKB-57) 12 October 1940; (production Il-2) March 1941; (two-seat) September 1942; (Il-10) early 1944.
User: Soviet Union (FA).

Development: Especially when a second crew-member was added, the Stormovik (more accurately BSh, Bronirovanni Shtoormovik, armoured attacker) had a lot in common with the Fairey Battle. They were similar in shape, size, weight and general performance. But, while the underpowered and underarmed Battle was a deathtrap, hastily forgotten, the Soviet machine sustained what is believed to have been the biggest production run of any aircraft in history. Throughout World War II production from three large plants averaged about 1,200 per month and total Il-2 output exceeded 36,000. When the Il-10 is included the total of all versions reaches about 42,330. In fact, resemblance to the Battle was only skin-deep. The skin of

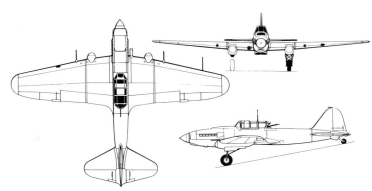

Above: Three-view of Il-2M3 with rear gun.

even the prototype BSh-2 was steel armour in all vital areas, the armour forming part of the structure and weighing over 1,540lb (15 per cent of gross weight). Vladimir Kokkinaki flew the prototype, finding it underpowered. With the AM-38 engine subsequent TsKB-57 prototypes did better and production began on a large scale in time for squadrons to have formed at the start of the German invasion. The single-seat Il-2 had a considerable fuel load and heavy armament which, for the first time, included effective ground-attack rockets. Produced in vast numbers in 1942, changes were called for which resulted in the M3 version with AM-38F engine, rear gun and heavier anti-tank armament. Operating in pairs at nought feet, or in sections of ten with escort at 1,000ft the Il-2s fought day and night along the Eastern Front and often shot down Bf 109s, besides (with new guns and special bombs) managing to defeat the thick armour of PzKW 5 Panther and PzKW 6 Tiger tanks. In the opinion of the Soviet Union, no other aircraft played so decisive a role in modern land warfare. By 1943 Ilyushin's bureau was designing the more streamlined Il-10, with wheels which turned to lie flush in the revised wing, all-stressed-skin structure, more power and improved armour and armament. Chosen over the rival Su-6, it went into production following the last Il-2s in June 1944 and was in service in large numbers by VE-day. Many remained in service in Communist forces until after the Korean war (1953).

Below: This Il-2M3 was presented by the people of Kustanai. The 'two-tone' Red Star was not uncommon.

Below: Manoeuvrable, incredibly tough and with devastating forward-firing armament, the Il-2 was no easy prey even for Luftwaffe fighters. These are rear-gunned models in 1944.

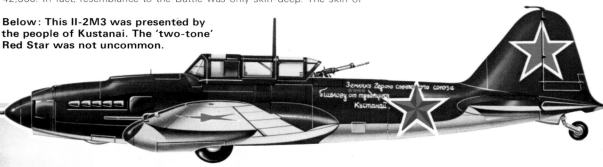

Lavochkin La-5 and La-7

La-5, -5FN, -7 and -7U

Origin: The design bureau of S. A. Lavochkin.
Type: Single-seat fighter (-7U, dual-control trainer).
Engine: (Original La-5) one 1,330hp Shvetsov M-82A or M-82F 14-cylinder two-row radial; (all other versions) one 1,700hp M-82FN.
Dimensions: Span 32ft 2in (9·8m); length 27ft 10¾in (8·46m); height 9ft 3in (2·84m).
Weights: Empty, no data; loaded (La-5) no data; (La-5FN) 7,406lb (3359kg); (La-7) 7,495lb (3400kg).
Performance: Maximum speed (La-5) 389mph (626km/h); (La-5FN) 403mph (650km/h); (La-7) 423mph (680km/h); initial climb (La-5FN) about 3,600ft (1100m)/min; (La-7) about 3,940ft (1200m)/min; service ceiling (La-5FN) 32,800ft (10,000m); (La-7) 34,448ft (10,500m); range (La-5) 398 miles (640km); (La-5FN) 475 miles (765km); (La-7) 392 miles (630km).
Armament: (La-5, -5FN) two 20mm ShVAK cannon, each with 200 rounds, above engine; optional underwing racks for light bombs up to total of 330lb (150kg); (La-7) three faster-firing ShVAK (one on right, two on left); underwing racks for six RS-82 rockets or two 220lb (100kg) bombs.
History: First flight (re-engined LaGG-3) January 1942; (production La-5) June 1942; (La-5FN) late 1942; (La-7) about June 1943.
User: Soviet Union.

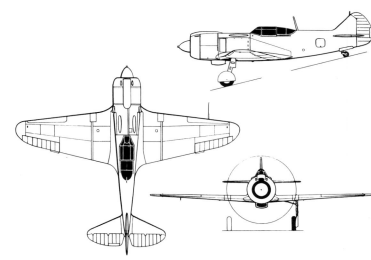

Above: Three-view of typical late-production La-5FN.

Below: The cutaway shows the simplicity, robustness and yet advanced design of this mass-produced fighter. Far better than the liquid-cooled LaGG-3 (p. 180) from which it stemmed, the La-5 had an advanced radial installation similar to that devised in Britain years later for the Tempest II and Sea Fury. Few fighters could stay with the La-5 at low level.

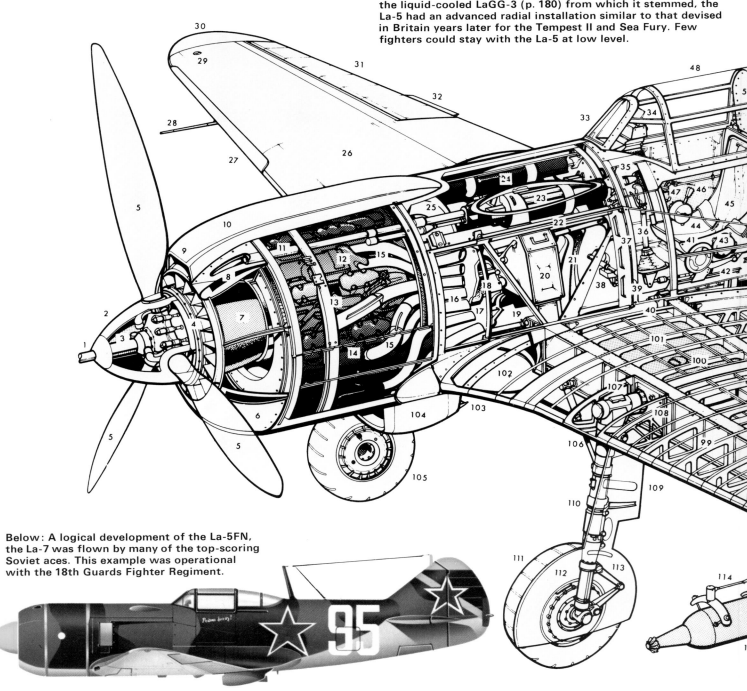

Below: A logical development of the La-5FN, the La-7 was flown by many of the top-scoring Soviet aces. This example was operational with the 18th Guards Fighter Regiment.

Development: Though the LaGG-3 was a serviceable fighter that used wood rather than scarce light alloys, it was the poorest performer of the new crop of combat aircraft with which the VVS-RKKA (Soviet Military Aviation Defence Forces) sought to halt the German invader. It was natural that urgent consideration should be given to ways of improving it and during 1941 Lavochkin's team converted one LaGG-3 to have an M-82 radial engine. Despite its fractionally greater installed drag (a matter of 1%) it offered speed increased from 353 to 373mph and, in particular, improved all-round performance at height. The liquid-cooled fighter was cancelled in May 1942, all production switching to the new machine, designated LaGG-5. But within a matter of weeks this in turn was replaced on the assembly line by a further improvement, tested as a prototype early in 1942, with a new fuselage

continued on page 178▶

Above: The La-7 had the same engine as the La-5FN but a considerably superior performance was gained by aerodynamic refinement. Total production of all Lavochkin 5/7/9/11 neared 37,000.

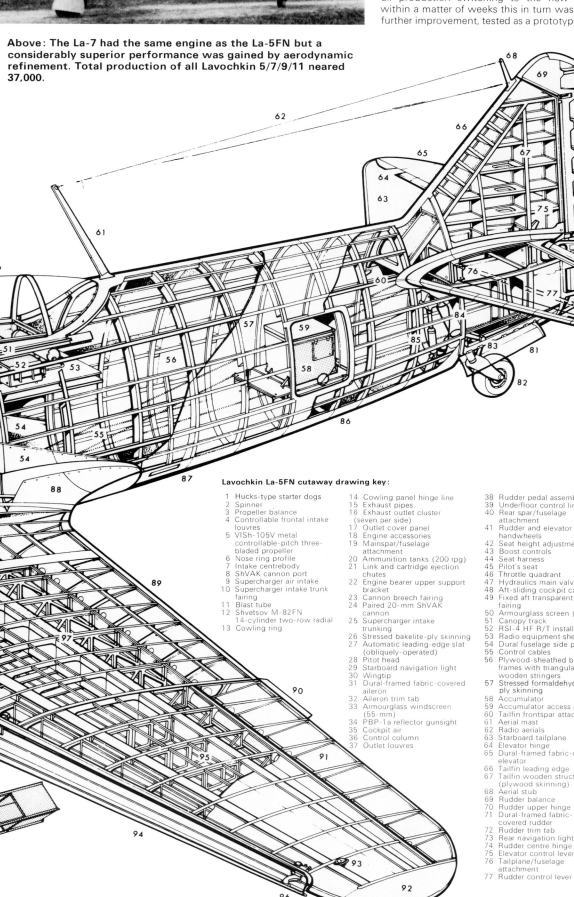

Lavochkin La-5FN cutaway drawing key:

1 Hucks-type starter dogs
2 Spinner
3 Propeller balance
4 Controllable frontal intake louvres
5 VISh-105V metal controllable-pitch three-bladed propeller
6 Nose ring profile
7 Intake centrebody
8 ShVAK cannon port
9 Supercharger air intake
10 Supercharger intake trunk fairing
11 Blast tube
12 Shvetsov M-82FN 14-cylinder two-row radial
13 Cowling ring
14 Cowling panel hinge line
15 Exhaust pipes
16 Exhaust outlet cluster (seven per side)
17 Outlet cover panel
18 Engine accessories
19 Mainspar/fuselage attachment
20 Ammunition tanks (200 rpg)
21 Link and cartridge ejection chutes
22 Engine bearer upper support bracket
23 Cannon breech fairing
24 Paired 20-mm ShVAK cannon
25 Supercharger intake trunking
26 Stressed bakelite-ply skinning
27 Automatic leading-edge slat (obliquely-operated)
28 Pitot head
29 Starboard navigation light
30 Wingtip
31 Dural-framed fabric-covered aileron
32 Aileron trim tab
33 Armourglass windscreen (55-mm)
34 PBP-1a reflector gunsight
35 Cockpit air
36 Control column
37 Outlet louvres
38 Rudder pedal assembly
39 Underfloor control linkage
40 Rear spar/fuselage attachment
41 Rudder and elevator trim handwheels
42 Seat height adjustment
43 Boost controls
44 Seat harness
45 Pilot's seat
46 Throttle quadrant
47 Hydraulics main valve
48 Aft-sliding cockpit canopy
49 Fixed aft transparent cockpit fairing
50 Armourglass screen (75-mm)
51 Canopy track
52 RSI-4 HF R/T installation
53 Radio equipment shelf
54 Dural fuselage side panels
55 Control cables
56 Plywood-sheathed birch frames with triangular-section wooden stringers
57 Stressed formaldehyde-ply skinning
58 Accumulator
59 Accumulator access panel
60 Tailfin frontspar attachment
61 Aerial mast
62 Radio aerials
63 Starboard tailplane
64 Elevator hinge
65 Dural-framed fabric-covered elevator
66 Tailfin leading edge
67 Tailfin wooden structure (plywood skinning)
68 Aerial stub
69 Rudder balance
70 Rudder upper hinge
71 Dural-framed fabric-covered rudder
72 Rudder trim tab
73 Rear navigation light
74 Rudder centre hinge
75 Elevator control lever
76 Tailplane/fuselage attachment
77 Rudder control lever
78 Elevator trim tab
79 Dural-framed fabric-covered elevator
80 Wooden two-spar tailplane structure (plywood skinning)
81 Tailwheel doors
82 Aft-retracting tailwheel (usually locked in extended position)
83 Tailwheel leg
84 Tailwheel shock strut
85 Retraction mechanism
86 Stressed bakelite-ply skinning
87 Retractable access step
88 Wing root fillet
89 Dural-skinned flap construction
90 Aileron tab
91 Dural-framed fabric-covered aileron
92 Wingtip
93 Port navigation light
94 Leading-edge automatic slat (obliquely operated)
95 Outboard ribs
96 Automatic slat actuating mechanism
97 Rear boxspar
98 Forward boxspar
99 Leading edge ribs
100 Fuel filler cap
101 Port fuel tank of three tank set (102 Imp gal/464 litres total capacity)
102 Mainwheel well
103 Oil cooler outlet flap
104 Engine oil cooler intake
105 Starboard mainwheel
106 Undercarriage hydraulic jack and ram
107 Undercarriage knuckle joint
108 Undercarriage/front spar attachment
109 Mainwheel leg fairing plate
110 Mainwheel oleo leg
111 Port mainwheel
112 Mainwheel fairing plate
113 Torque links
114 Underwing stores shackles
115 110-lb (50-kg) bomb

containing two 20mm guns and having a lower rear profile behind a canopy giving all-round vision. This was the La-5 which proved to be 28mph faster than a Bf 109G-2 at below 20,000ft. But the German fighter could outclimb it and efforts were made to reduce weight. The resulting La-5FN had an FN (boosted) engine, lighter wing with metal spars and overall weight 379lb (presumably on both empty and gross weight) less. Thousands of -5FNs participated in the huge battles around Kursk and throughout the Eastern front in 1943, demonstrating that Soviet fighters could be more than a match for their opponents. The La-5UTI was a dual trainer. Further refinement led to the harder-hitting La-7, with reduced weight (partly by reducing fuel capacity) and much reduced drag. The -7 and -7U trainer retained the slats and big ailerons that made the Lavochkin fighters such beautiful dog-fighters and were the choice of most of the Soviet aces (Ivan Kozhedub's aircraft is in the Central Soviet Air Force Museum).

Left: The FN (boosted engine) version could be identified by the extension of the carburettor inlet to the front of the cowl.

Below: La-5FN fighters of the 1st Czech (partisan) Fighter Regiment at Preborsk in 1943.

Ilyushin Il-4
TsKB-26, TsKB-30, DB-3 and DB-3F (Il-4)

Origin: Design bureau of Sergei Ilyushin, Soviet Union.
Type: Four-seat bomber and torpedo carrier.
Engines: Final standard, two 1,100hp M-88B 14-cylinder two-row radials.
Dimensions: Span 70ft 4¼in (21·44m); length 48ft 6½in (14·8m); height approximately 13ft 9in 4·2m).
Weights: About 13,230lb (6000kg); loaded 22,046lb (10,000kg).
Performance: Maximum speed 255mph (410km/h); initial climb 886ft (270m)/min; service ceiling 32,808ft (10,000m); range with 2,205lb of bombs 1,616 miles (2600km).
Armament: Three manually aimed machine guns, in nose, dorsal turret and periscopic ventral position, originally all 7·62mm ShKAS and from 1942 all 12·7mm BS; internal bomb bay for ten 220lb (100kg) bombs or equivalent, with alternative (or, for short ranges, additional) racks for up to three 1,102lb (500kg) or one 2,072lb (940kg) torpedo or one 2,205lb (1000kg) bomb, all under fuselage.
History: First flight (TsKB-26) 1935; (production DB-3) 1937; (DB-3F) 1939; final delivery 1944.
User: Soviet Union (DA, VMF).

Development: Though much less well-known around the world than such Western bombers as the B-17 and Lancaster, the Il-4 was one of the great bombers of World War II and saw service in enormous numbers in all roles from close support to strategic bombing of Berlin and low-level torpedo attacks. Originally known by its design bureau designation of TsKB-26 (often reported in the West as CKB-26), it was officially designated DB-3 (DB for Dalni Bombardirovshchik, long-range bomber) and went into production in early 1937. Powered by two 765hp M-85 engines, soon replaced by 960hp M-86, it was roughly in the class of the Hampden, with excellent speed, range, load and manoeuvrability but poor defensive armament (which was never changed, apart from increasing the calibre of the three guns). In 1939, when 1,528 had been delivered, production switched to the DB-3F with blunt nose turret replaced by a long pointed nose. In 1940, when over 2,000 were delivered, the designation was changed to Il-4, conforming with the new scheme in which aircraft were named for their designers (in this case Sergei Ilyushin). After the German

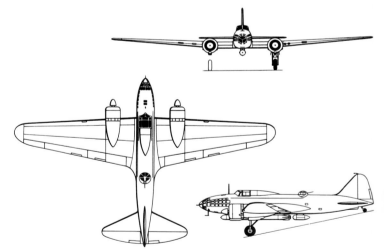

Above: Three-view of an Il-4 of the type used by the VVS-VMF for bombing and (as shown) torpedo attacks.

invasion desperate materials shortage nearly halted production but by 1942 new plants in Siberia were building huge numbers of Il-4s with a redesigned airframe incorporating the maximum amount of wood. More than 6,800 had been delivered when production was stopped in 1944. Il-4s bombed Berlin many times, the first time by a force of VVS-VMF (Soviet Navy) Il-4s on 8 August 1941. By 1943 reconnaissance and glider towing were additional duties for these hard-worked aircraft.

Right: These are Il-4 bombers of the regular air force type, not equipped for torpedo carrying (note absence of rear under-fuselage container). For many years Western students have wondered why the vast force of Soviet bombers accomplished so little in World War II. Today the answers are slowly seeping through; they accomplished much, still largely unknown.

Lavochkin La-11

La-9, La-11

Origin: The design bureau of S. A. Lavochkin.
Type: Single-seat fighter.
Engine: One 1,870hp Shvetsov ASh-82FNV 14-cylinder two-row radial.
Dimensions: Span (-9) 34ft 9½in (10·62m); (-11) 32ft 7½in (9·95m); length (-9) 29ft 6½in (9·0m); (-11) 28ft 3½in (8·6m); height (both) 9ft 8in (2·95m).
Weights: No data available, but gross weights were probably approximately (-9) 8,820lb (4000kg) and (-11) 9,040lb (4100kg).
Performance: Maximum speed (-9) 429mph (690km/h); (-11) 460mph (740km/h); initial climb (-9) 3,840ft (1170m)/min; (-11) 4,265ft (1300m)/min; service ceiling (both) 36,100ft (11,000m); range (-9) 373 miles (600km); (-11) 466 miles (750km).
Armament: (-9) four 20mm ShVAK symmetrically arranged around top decking; (-9bis) four 23mm NS23 in same positions; (-11) three NS23, two on left, one on right. No wing pylons normally fitted.
History: First flight (-9) early 1944; (-11) late 1944 or early 1945; service delivery (-11) summer of 1945.
User: Soviet Union; post-war, Soviet VVS-FA and PVO, Group of Soviet Forces in Germany and many satellite countries.

Development: These two excellent fighters were the result of natural development and refinement, taking advantage of the wealth of combat information that came to Lavochkin's bureau from the Eastern front in 1943–44. By this time the LaGG committee had broken up, and Lavochkin himself had become a Lt-General in the Aviation Engineering Corps, a Hero of Socialist Labour (for the La-5) and won a Stalin Prize of 100,000 roubles (for the La-7). He had the satisfaction of seeing production of the -7 outstrip that of all other aircraft except the Yak-3 in 1944 (13,300 in the year), despite the fact that by December it had been supplanted by the refined La-9. This had a revised structure incorporating much more metal stressed-skin than wood, with a taller fin and rudder and stubby wings strongly reminiscent

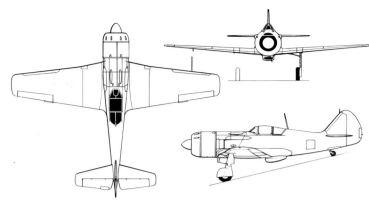

Above: Three-view of La-9.

of an Fw 190 or Bearcat. The cockpit was redesigned, and firing the guns caused quite a commotion with four large cannon all blasting ahead between the propeller blades. The switch to 23mm guns caused bulges to appear around the breeches of all four. Hundreds of La-9s were supplied to the Soviet Union's allies and friends and some were used for experiments with liquid rockets in the tail and/or pulsating athodyd engines (V-1 derived) under the wings. The final Lavochkin piston-engined fighter, the La-11, was a refined escort fighter with all-stressed-skin structure and much greater fuel capacity. It could be distinguished from the -9 by the oil cooler being moved from under the trailing edge to inside the cowling, under the engine. Many 11s were used by the Northern Air Force during the Korean War and they were important in Communist forces until 1960.

Right: Not strictly a World War II aircraft, the La-11 differed externally from the La-9 only in that the oil cooler was moved from the rear fuselage to the lower interior of the engine cowl.

Lavochkin LaGG-3

I-22, LaGG-1, I-301, LaGG-3

Origin: The design bureau of S. A. Lavochkin, in partnership with Gorbunov and Gudkov.

Type: Single-seat fighter.

Engine: (-1) one 1,050hp Klimov M-105P (VK-105P) vee-12 liquid-cooled; (-3) one 1,240hp M-105PF with improved propeller.

Dimensions: Span 32ft 2in (9·8m); length 29ft 1¼in (8·9m); height 8ft 10in (3·22m).

Weights: Empty (-1) 5,952lb (2700kg); (-3) 5,764lb (2620kg); maximum loaded (-1) 6,834lb (3100kg); (-3) 7,257lb (3300kg).

Performance: Maximum speed (-1) 373mph (600km/h); (-3) 348mph (560km/h); initial climb (both) 2,953ft (900m)/min; service ceiling (-1) 31,496ft (9600m); (-3) 29,527ft (9000m); range (both) 404 miles (650km).

Armament: Very varied; typically, one 20mm ShVAK firing through propeller hub, with 120 rounds, two 12·7mm BS above engine, each with 220 rounds, and underwing racks for six RS-82 rockets or various light bombs; LaGGs on Il-2 escort had three 12·7mm and two 7·62mm; some had a 23mm VIa cannon and various combinations of machine guns.

History: First flight (I-22) 30 March 1939; (production LaGG-1) late 1940; (production LaGG-3) 1941; final delivery June 1942.

User: Soviet Union.

Development: Semyon Alekseyevich Lavochkin headed a design committee which included V. P. Gorbunov and M. I. Gudkov in creating the very unusual I-22 fighter prototype of 1938–39. Though outwardly conventional, it was rare among the world's new crop of streamlined monoplane fighters not to have metal stressed-skin construction; instead it was built of wood, except for the control surfaces, which were light alloy with fabric covering, and the flaps which, to avoid damage, were all-metal. The ply skinning was both impregnated and bonded on with phenol-formaldehyde resin, which at the time seemed quaint but today is very widely used for this purpose. The result was a neat, clean and manoeuvrable fighter, which later showed outstanding robustness and resistance to combat damage. On the other hand it was inferior to other Russian fighters in all-round performance.

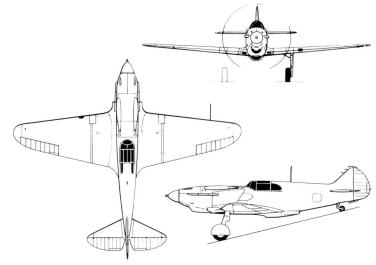

Above: Three-view of the LaGG-1, without slats, some hundreds of which were made even as the design was being changed.

Several hundred had been delivered, as the LaGG-1, when production was switched to the LaGG-3. This had a better engine, leading-edge slats, and improved armament options. By 1942 all LaGG fighters had internally balanced rudder, retractable tailwheel and wing fuel system for two 22gal drop tanks. Further development led to the switch to an air-cooled radial, from which stemmed all Lavochkin's later piston-engined fighters.

Below: Side elevation of a LaGG-3 that was operating with a fighter regiment on the Ukraine Front in the summer of 1942.

Below: A wintry scene as LaGG-3 fighters parade behind a banner bearing the omnipotent portrait of Lenin. These LaGGs have retractable ski landing gear. There are no gun bulges above the engine, as on aircraft with synchronised BS heavy machine guns. Note the dogs on the propeller shafts for a Hucks engine starter (of the type used by the RFC in World War I, but still useful).

Mikoyan MiG-3

MiG-1 (I-61), MiG-3, MiG-5 and MiG-7

Origin: The design bureau of Mikoyan and Gurevich.
Type: Single-seat fighter.
Engine: (-1) one 1,200hp Mikulin AM-35 vee-12 liquid-cooled; (-3) one 1,350hp AM-35A; (-5) one 1,600hp ASh-82A 14-cylinder radial; (-7) one 1,700hp VK-107A vee-12.
Dimensions: Span (all) 33ft 9½in (10·3m); length (-1, -3) 26ft 9in (8·15m); (-5) about 26ft; (-7) not known; height (-1, -3) reported as 8ft 7in (2·61m).
Weights: Empty (-1) 5,721lb (2595kg); (others) not known; maximum loaded (-1) given as 6,770lb and as 7,290lb; (-3) given as 7,390lb and 7,695lb (3490kg); (-5) normal loaded 7,055lb (3200kg); (-7) not known.
Performance: Maximum speed (-1) 390mph (628km/h); (-3) 398mph (640km/h), (also given as 407mph); (-5) over 400mph; (-7) probably over 440mph; initial climb (-1) 3,280ft (1000m)/min; (-3) 3,937ft (1200m)/min; (-5, -7) not known; service ceiling (-1, -3) 39,370ft (12,000m); (-5) not known; (-7) 42,650ft (13,000m); range (-1) 454 miles (730km); (-3) 776 miles (1250km); (-5, -7) not known.
Armament: (-1, -3) one 12·7mm BS and two 7·62mm ShKAS all in nose, later supplemented as field modification by underwing pods for two further unsynchronised BS; underwing rails for six RS-82 rockets or two bombs up to 220lb (100kg) each or two chemical containers; (-5) as above except four 7·62mm ShKAS disposed around cowling, no BS guns; (-7) not known but probably included 20mm ShVAK firing through propeller hub.
History: First flight (1—61) 5 April (also reported as March) 1940; (production MiG-1) September 1940; (MiG-3) about May 1941; final delivery (MiG-3) late 1941; first flight (-5) 1942; (MiG-7) 1943.
User: Soviet Union.

Development: There were probably several new Soviet fighter prototypes in 1938—40, but apart from the Yak-1 information is available on only one other, the I-61 designed by the new partnership of Artem I. Mikoyan and Mikhail I. Gurevich. Though handicapped by its long and heavy engine, which held the armament to a poor level, the mixed wood/metal fighter was a fair performer and went into production as the MiG-1, its only serious vice

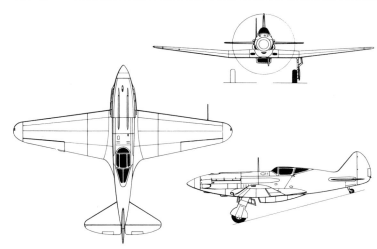

Above: Three-view of MiG-3. Nearly all were externally similar; none had any guns in the wings.

being an extreme tendency to swing on take-off and landing. In view of the amazing rapidity of its development this was an acceptable penalty and 2,100 are said to have been delivered before it was replaced in production by the refined MiG-3 with more powerful engine, new propeller, additional fuel tank, increased dihedral and sliding canopy. "Several thousand" are said to have been delivered, but despite adding extra guns they were no match for Luftwaffe fighters and by 1942 were being used for armed reconnaissance and close support. The MiG-5 was used in only small numbers, and few details are available of the all-metal high-altitude MiG-7 with pressurised cockpit.

Below: A MiG-3 of the 34th Fighter Aviation Regiment, Vnukovo (Moscow).

Below: Probably the best (almost the only) photograph taken of MiG-3s, possibly at Vnukovo (Moscow). White, scarlet and dark green are the ruling colours in this line-up; the green colour is for summer use.

Petlyakov Pe-2 and Pe-3

Pe-2, 2I, 2R, 2U and 3bis

Origin: The design bureau of V. M. Petlyakov.
Type: (2) attack bomber; (2I) interceptor fighter; (2R) reconnaissance; (2U) dual trainer; (3bis) fighter reconnaissance.
Engines: Two Klimov (Hispano-Suiza basic design) vee-12 liquid-cooled; (2, pre-1943) 1,100hp M-105R or RA; (2, 1943 onwards, 2R, 2U, 3bis) 1,260hp M-105PF; (2I) 1,600hp M-107A.
Dimensions: Span 56ft 3½in (17·2m); length 41ft 4¼in to 41ft 6in (12·6–12·66m); height 11ft 6in (3·5m).
Weights: Empty (typical) 12.900lb (5870kg); normal loaded 16,540–16,976lb (7700kg); maximum loaded (all versions) 18,780lb (8520kg).
Performance: Maximum speed (typical, 105R) 336mph (540km/h); (105PF) 360mph (580km/h); (107A) 408mph (655km/h); initial climb (typical) 1,430ft (436m)/min; service ceiling (except 2I) 28,870ft (8800 m); (2I) 36,100ft (11,000m); range with bomb load (105R) 746 miles (1200km); (105PF) 721 miles (1160km).
Armament: See text.
History: First flight (VI-100) 1939; (production Pe-2) June 1940; final delivery, probably January 1945.
User: Soviet Union (post-war, Czechoslovakia, Poland).

Below: A fine air-to-air scene. Comparable with the somewhat later Mosquito in performance, these are Pe-2FT models (FT meant front-line request, and specified extra upper and lower rear guns and added armour, needing the PF engine).

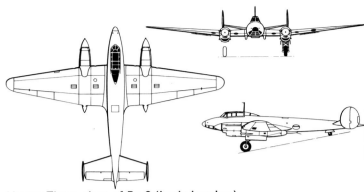

Above: Three-view of Pe-2 (basic bomber).

Development: Not until long after World War II did Western observers appreciate the importance of the Pe-2. Built throughout the war, it was one of the outstanding combat aircraft of the Allies and, by dint of continual improvement, remained in the front rank of tactical fighting along the entire Eastern front right up to the German surrender. It was planned by Vladimir M. Petlyakov's design team in 1938 as a high-altitude fighter designated

Right: The open bomb doors give a clue to the remarkable internal load of 6,615lb that could be carried by later models with the M-107 (VK-107) engine. There were many different types of nose and countless equipment and armament variations.

VI-100. When adapted to high-level bombing it kept the fighter's slim fuselage and this feature, coupled with intensive aerodynamic refinement, always made it fast enough to be difficult for German fighters to intercept it. Level bombing at height proved inaccurate, so dive brakes were added under the wings and the Pe-2 went into service in August 1940 as a multi-role dive and attack bomber, with crew of three and four 7·62mm ShKAS machine guns, two fixed firing ahead above the nose, one aimed from the upper rear position and one aimed from a retracting ventral mount with periscopic sight. Up to 2,205lb (1000kg) of bombs could be carried, either all externally or partly in the bomb bay and part in the rear of the long nacelles. The Pe-3bis fighter of 1941 had manoeuvre flaps instead of dive brakes, and additional fixed 20mm ShVAK and 12·7mm BS guns. During 1942 a 12·7mm power turret replaced the upper rear gun, the lower rear gun was made 12·7mm calibre and two 7·62mm beam guns were added. Extra armour, self-sealing tanks with cold exhaust-gas purging, detail drag-reduction and PF engines followed. The final versions had M-107 (VK-107) engines, various heavier armament and up to 6,615lb (3000kg) bomb load. Total production was just over 11,400.

From the basic three-seat low-level attack bomber, itself derived from a high-altitude fighter, stemmed numerous research or stillborn developments. One was the Pe-2VI high-altitude fighter, for which Dr M. N. Petrov's pressure cabin (planned for the original fighter) was resurrected. It had a heavy nose armament, but the high-flying threat (which was expected to include the Ju 288) never materialised. One of the leaders on the VI team was Myasishchev, who later accomplished important designs in his own right. Another fighter version, about two years later in timing than the Pe-3bis, was the Pe-2I with direct-injection M-107A engines and a speed comfortably in excess of 400mph. Other versions included the Pe-2R long-range low- and high-level reconnaissance aircraft, with a large camera installation instead of a bomb bay, and the Pe-2UT trainer with tandem dual controls. In 1943–45 a Pe-2R was also used for ground and flight rocket tests by the RD-1 nitric acid/kerosene engine, installed in the tail; 169 firings were made.

Above: These examples have the lower ventral gun but no D/F loop aerial under the nose. Other features of this sub-type include VHF radio, extra armour, additional fuel, rear radio mast and M-105 engines.

Petlyakov Pe-8

ANT-42, TB-7, Pe-8 (various sub-types)

Origin: The design bureau of A. N. Tupolev, with team headed by V. M. Petlyakov.

Type: Heavy bomber with normal crew of nine.

Engines: (Prototype) see text; (first production) four 1,300hp Mikulin AM-35A vee-12 liquid-cooled; (second production) four 1,475hp Charomski M-30B vee-12 diesels; (third production) four 1,630hp Shvetsov ASh-82FNV 14-cylinder two-row radials.

Dimensions: Span 131ft 0½in. (39·94m); length 73ft 8¾in (22·47m); height 20ft (6·1m).

Weights: Empty (first production) 37,480lb (17,000kg); (typical late production) about 40,000lb (18,000kg); maximum loaded (early) 63,052lb (28,600kg); (late, M-30B) 73,469lb (33,325kg); (ASh-82) 68,519lb (31,080kg).

Performance: Maximum speed (AM-35) 276mph (444km/h); (M-30B) 272mph (438km/h); (ASh-82) 280mph (451km/h); initial climb (typical) 853ft (260m)/min; service ceiling (AM-35, M-30B) about 22,966ft (7000m); (ASh-82) 29,035ft (8850m); range, see text.

Armament: (Typical) one 20mm ShVAK in dorsal and tail turrets, two 7·62mm ShKAS in nose turret and one 12·7mm BS manually aimed from rear of each inner nacelle; bomb load, see text.

History: First flight (ANT-42) 27 December 1936; (production TB-7) early 1939; (ASh-82 version) 1943; final delivery 1944.

User: Soviet Union (ADD).

Development: Despite the Soviet Union's great heritage of impressive heavy bombers the TB-7 was the only aircraft in this category in World War II and only a few hundred were built. This resulted from a Germanic concentration on twin-engined tactical machines rather than any short-coming in the Pe-8 and there was at no time any serious problem with propulsion, though the type of engine kept changing. The prototype, built

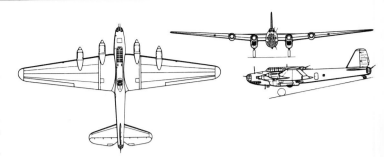

Above: Three-view of Pe-8 first series with AM-35 engines.

to a 1934 specification, had four 1,100hp M-105 engines supercharged by a large blower driven by an M-100 engine in the rear fuselage. Another had AM-34FRN engines, but the AM-35A was chosen for production at Kuznets in 1939, by which time the complex ACN-2 supercharging system had been abandoned. Performance at 8000m (26,250ft, double the maximum-speed height for earlier Soviet heavies) was outstanding and faster than the Bf 109B. In 1940, in line with the new Soviet designation system, the TB-7 was credited to Petlyakov, leader of the design team. Unfortunately he was killed in a crash two years later and most of the wartime development was managed by I. F. Nyezeval. Maximum bomb load was 8,818lb (4000kg), the range of 2,321 miles being raised to over 3,000 miles by the diesel engines substituted when AM-35 production ceased. The final radial-engined version could carry 11,600lb for 2,500 miles and many long missions were made into Hungary, Romania and East Germany the first major mission being on Berlin in mid-1941.

Right: The final Nyezeval-managed variant had direct-injection ASh-82FNV engines with slim inner nacelles, but not many were built owing to concentration on tactical bombers. The 4,410lb (2000kg) bomb was carried internally — but not very often.

Polikarpov I-15 and 153

TsKB-3, I-15, I-15bis, I-153

Origin: The design bureau of Nikolai N. Polikarpov.

Type: Single-seat fighter (15bis, 153, fighter-bomber).

Engine: (15) one 700hp Shvetsov M-25 (Wright Cyclone); (15bis) 750hp M-25B; (153) 1,000hp M-63, all nine-cylinder radials.

Dimensions: Span 29ft 11½in (9·13m); (bis) 33ft 6in; (153) 32ft 9¾in; length 20ft 7½in (6·29m); (bis) 20ft 9¼in; (153) 20ft 3in; height 9ft 7in (2·92m); (bis) 9ft 10in; (153) 9ft 3in.

Weights: Empty 2,597lb (1178kg); (bis) 2,880lb; (153) 3,168lb; maximum loaded 3,027–3,135lb (1370–1422kg); (bis) 4,189lb; (153) 4,431lb.

Performance: Maximum speed 224mph (360km/h); (bis) 230mph; (153) 267mph; initial climb (all) about 2,500ft (765m)/min; service ceiling 32,800ft (10,000m); (bis) 26,245ft; (153) 35,100ft; range 450 miles (720km); (bis) 280 miles; (153) 298 miles.

Armament: Four (sometimes two) 7·62mm DA or ShKAS in fuselage; (bis) as 15, plus two 110lb (50kg) or four 55lb bombs or six RS-82 rockets; (153) as 15bis but two 165lb bombs.

History: First flight (TsKB-3) October 1933; service delivery 1934; service delivery (bis) 1937; (153) 1939.

Users: China, Finland (captured Soviet), Soviet Union, Spain (Republican).

Development: One might jump to the conclusion that these Polikarpov biplanes were superseded by the I-16 monoplane (p. 186). In fact the I-16 flew before any of them, was in service first and, in 1939, was replaced in Mongolia by the more agile I-153! Polikarpov's bureau began work on the TsKB-3 in 1932, when the earlier I-5 was in full production. Unlike the

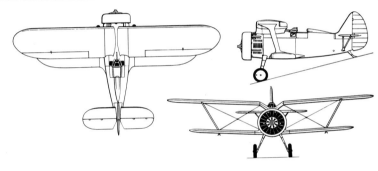

Above: Three-view of I-15 in original production form.

Right: Polikarpov's fighters, like all Soviet warplanes, had to live rough, with no protection save a camouflage net. Though a good picture of an I-153, the final retractable-undercarriage model of the biplanes, this photograph also shows the ubiquitous Hucks starter, based upon the Ford Model T chassis, which spu the front of the propeller shaft to start the engine.

Below left: The I-153 was one of the first carriers of rockets for air-to-ground use. Most carried six RS-82 missiles, but this aircraft has launch rails for eight of the weapons.

Below: This I-153, in winter finish, is carrying two large supply containers. Alternative loads on the same racks included 165lb (75kg) bombs or 22 Imp gal drop tanks.

I-5 the new fighter had a small lower wing and large upper gull wing curved down at the roots to meet the fuselage. As the I-15 the highly manoeuvrable fighter gained a world altitude record before serving in very large numbers (about 550) in Spain, where it was dubbed "Chato" (flat-nosed). It even served against the Finns and Luftwaffe, but by 1937 was being replaced by the I-15bis with continuous upper wing carried on struts. Over 300 of these served in Spain, and many were used as dive bombers against the Germans in 1941. The ultimate development was the powerful 153, with retractable landing gear, either wheels or skis folding to the rear. Some thousands served in the Far East, Spain, Finland and on the Eastern Front. Later sub-types had variable-pitch propellers and drop tanks well outboard under the lower wings.

Polikarpov I-16

I-16 Types 1, 4, 5, 10, 17, 18, 24, SPB and UTI

Origin: The design bureau of Nikolai N. Polikarpov.
Type: Single-seat fighter (except SPB dive bomber and UTI two-seat trainer).
Engine: (Type 1) one 480hp M-22 (modified Bristol Jupiter) nine-cylinder radial; (Type 4) 725hp M-25A (modified Wright Cyclone) of same layout; (Types 5, 10, 17) 775hp M-25B; (Types 18 and 24) 1,000hp Shvetsov M-62R (derived from M-25).
Dimensions: Span 29ft 6½in (9·00m); length (to Type 17) 19ft 11in (6·075 m); (18, 24 and UTI) 20ft 1¼in (6·125m); height (to 17) 8ft 1¼in (2·45m); (18, 24) 8ft 5in (2·56m).

continued on page 188 ▶

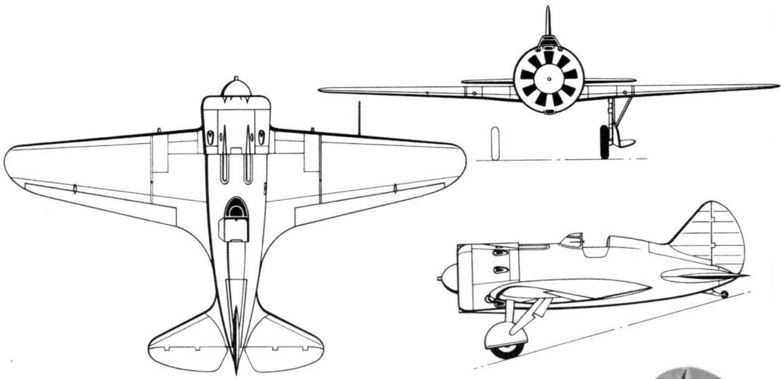

Above: Three-view of I-16 Type 24.

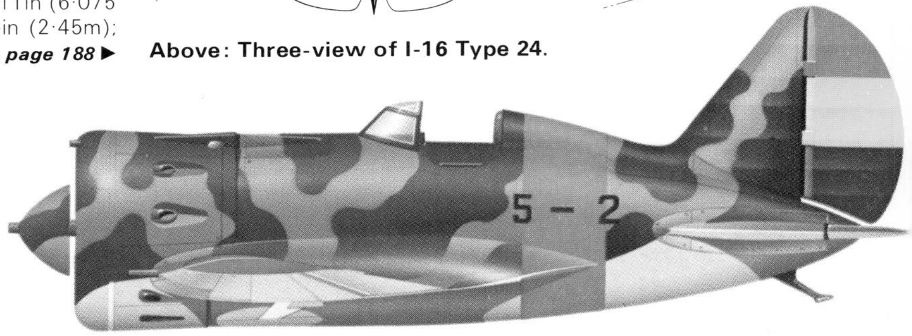

Above: I-16 Type 6 "Rata" of 4a Mosca Escuadrilla, Grupo núm 31, Spanish Republican AF.

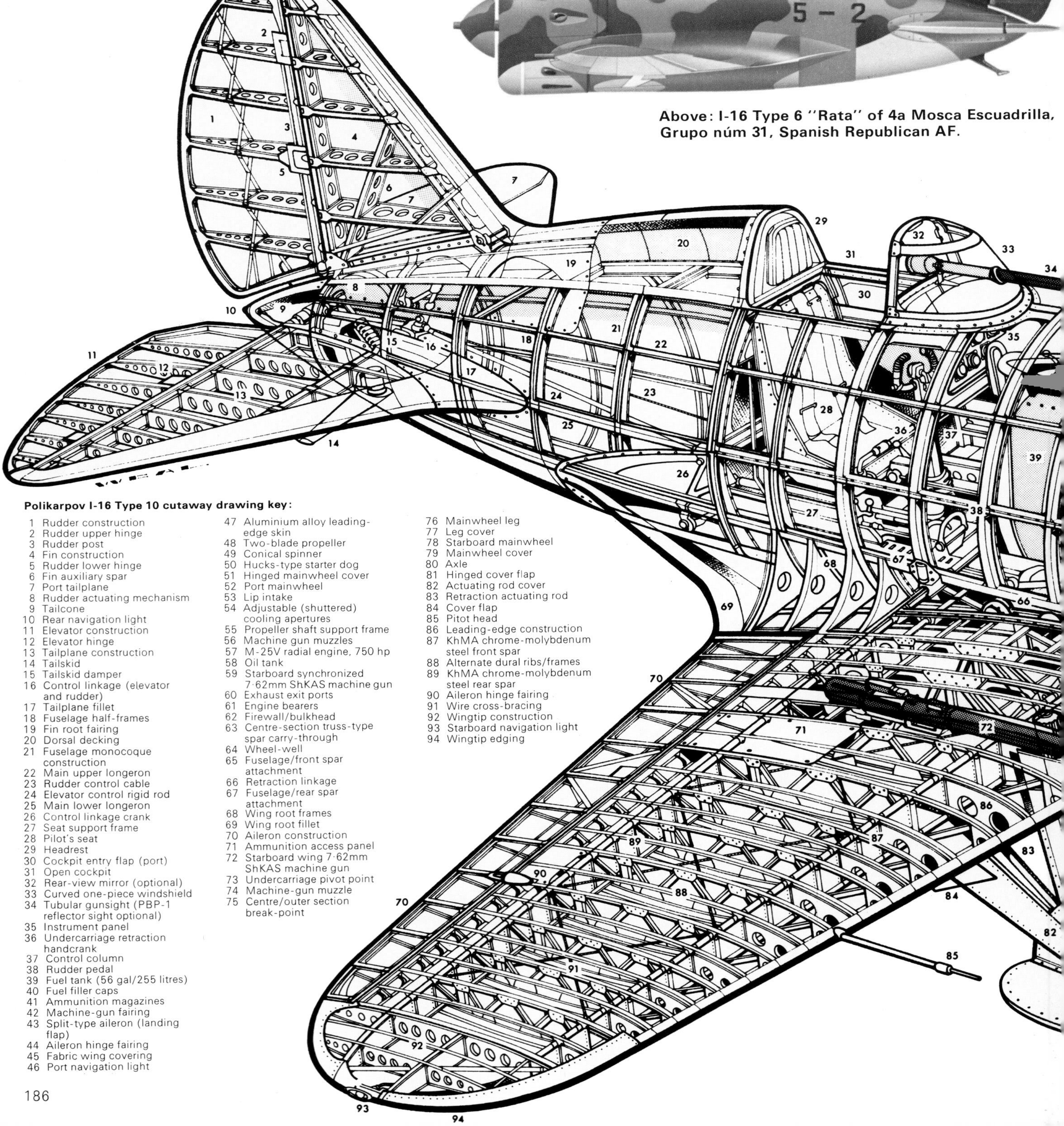

Polikarpov I-16 Type 10 cutaway drawing key:

 1 Rudder construction
 2 Rudder upper hinge
 3 Rudder post
 4 Fin construction
 5 Rudder lower hinge
 6 Fin auxiliary spar
 7 Port tailplane
 8 Rudder actuating mechanism
 9 Tailcone
10 Rear navigation light
11 Elevator construction
12 Elevator hinge
13 Tailplane construction
14 Tailskid
15 Tailskid damper
16 Control linkage (elevator and rudder)
17 Tailplane fillet
18 Fuselage half-frames
19 Fin root fairing
20 Dorsal decking
21 Fuselage monocoque construction
22 Main upper longeron
23 Rudder control cable
24 Elevator control rigid rod
25 Main lower longeron
26 Control linkage crank
27 Seat support frame
28 Pilot's seat
29 Headrest
30 Cockpit entry flap (port)
31 Open cockpit
32 Rear-view mirror (optional)
33 Curved one-piece windshield
34 Tubular gunsight (PBP-1 reflector sight optional)
35 Instrument panel
36 Undercarriage retraction handcrank
37 Control column
38 Rudder pedal
39 Fuel tank (56 gal/255 litres)
40 Fuel filler caps
41 Ammunition magazines
42 Machine-gun fairing
43 Split-type aileron (landing flap)
44 Aileron hinge fairing
45 Fabric wing covering
46 Port navigation light
47 Aluminium alloy leading-edge skin
48 Two-blade propeller
49 Conical spinner
50 Hucks-type starter dog
51 Hinged mainwheel cover
52 Port mainwheel
53 Lip intake
54 Adjustable (shuttered) cooling apertures
55 Propeller shaft support frame
56 Machine gun muzzles
57 M-25V radial engine, 750 hp
58 Oil tank
59 Starboard synchronized 7·62mm ShKAS machine gun
60 Exhaust exit ports
61 Engine bearers
62 Firewall/bulkhead
63 Centre-section truss-type spar carry-through
64 Wheel-well
65 Fuselage/front spar attachment
66 Retraction linkage
67 Fuselage/rear spar attachment
68 Wing root frames
69 Wing root fillet
70 Aileron construction
71 Ammunition access panel
72 Starboard wing 7·62mm ShKAS machine gun
73 Undercarriage pivot point
74 Machine-gun muzzle
75 Centre/outer section break-point
76 Mainwheel leg
77 Leg cover
78 Starboard mainwheel
79 Mainwheel cover
80 Axle
81 Hinged cover flap
82 Actuating rod cover
83 Retraction actuating rod
84 Cover flap
85 Pitot head
86 Leading-edge construction
87 KhMA chrome-molybdenum steel front spar
88 Alternate dural ribs/frames
89 KhMA chrome-molybdenum steel rear spar
90 Aileron hinge fairing
91 Wire cross-bracing
92 Wingtip construction
93 Starboard navigation light
94 Wingtip edging

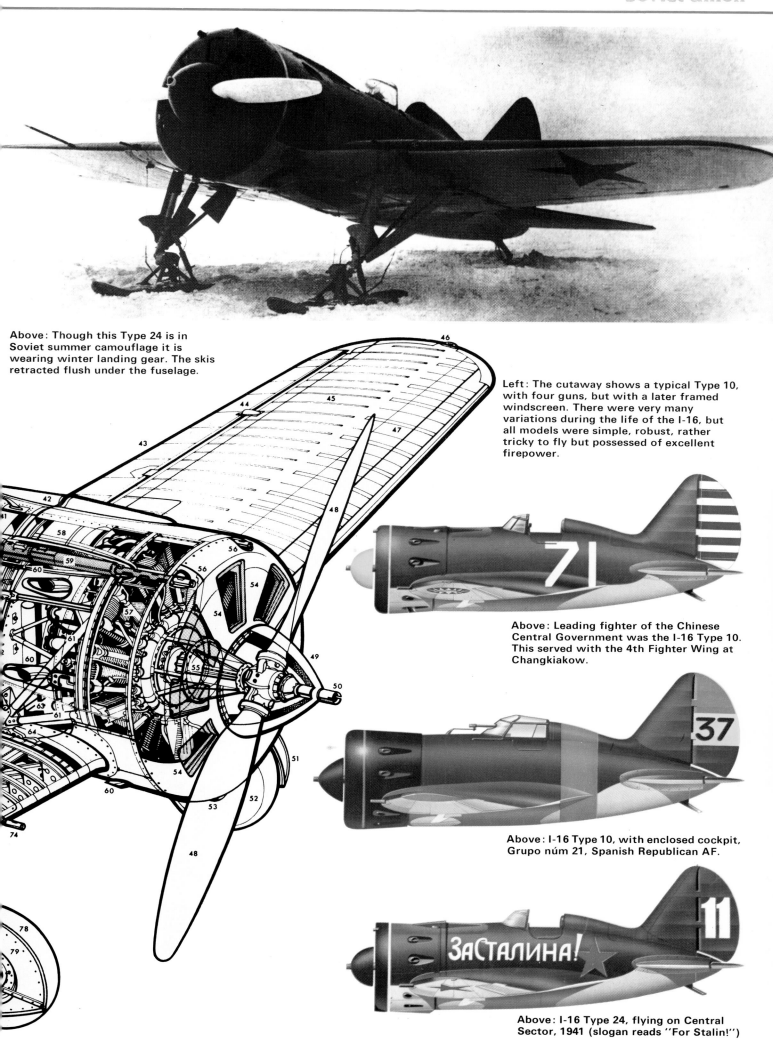

Above: Though this Type 24 is in Soviet summer camouflage it is wearing winter landing gear. The skis retracted flush under the fuselage.

Left: The cutaway shows a typical Type 10, with four guns, but with a later framed windscreen. There were very many variations during the life of the I-16, but all models were simple, robust, rather tricky to fly but possessed of excellent firepower.

Above: Leading fighter of the Chinese Central Government was the I-16 Type 10. This served with the 4th Fighter Wing at Changkiakow.

Above: I-16 Type 10, with enclosed cockpit, Grupo núm 21, Spanish Republican AF.

Above: I-16 Type 24, flying on Central Sector, 1941 (slogan reads "For Stalin!")

Weights: Empty (1) 2,200lb (998kg); (4, 5, 10) 2,791lb (1266kg); (18) 3,110lb (1410kg); (24) 3,285lb (1490kg); loaded (1) 2,965lb (1345kg); (4) 3,135lb (1422kg); (5) 3,660lb (1660kg); (10) 3,782lb (1715kg); (17) 3,990lb (1810kg); (18) 4,034lb (1830kg); (24) 4,215lb (1912kg) (24 overload, 4,546lb, 2062kg).

Performance: Maximum speed (1) 224mph (360km/h); (4–18) 280–288 mph (450–465km/h); (24) 326mph (525km/h); initial climb (4–24, typical) 2,790ft (850m)/min; service ceiling (typical) 29,500ft (9000m); range (1–18) 500 miles (800km); (24) 248 miles (400km), (with two 22gal drop tanks, 435 miles, 700km).

Armament: (1, 4, 5) two 7·62mm ShKAS machine guns in wings; (10) two ShKAS in wings, two in top decking of fuselage; (17) two ShKAS in top decking, two 20mm ShVAK cannon in wings; (18) as 10 or 17; (24) as 17; SPB, various guns plus external bomb load of 220lb (100kg). Many versions were later fitted with underwing rails for two RS-82 rockets.

Below, upper photograph: A trio of late-production I-16s with M-62 engines are seen in this shot from a propaganda film made on the Eastern Front in 1941. Despite frightful attrition in the opening week the Soviet fighter force always contested the sky with the slightly superior Bf 109E and 109F.

Bottom of page: This I-16 Type 10 is seen in Spanish service after the Republican defeat in 1939, in Nationalist markings. During the Civil War the Type 6 and Type 10 fighters were flown in Spain by Russian VVS pilots on a six-month tour.

History: First flight (I-16-1) 31 December 1933; production delivery (1) autumn 1934; (4) autumn 1935; final delivery (24) probably early 1942.
Users: China, Soviet Union, Spain (Republican).

Development: Possibly influenced by the Gee Bee racers of the United States, the TsKB-12, or I-16, was an extremely short and simple little fighter which — perhaps because of its slightly "homebuilt" appearance — was almost ignored by the West. Nobody outside the Soviet Union appeared to notice that this odd fighter, with wooden monocoque body and metal/fabric wing, was a cantilever monoplane with retractable landing gear and v-p propeller, which in its first mass-produced form was 60–75mph faster than contemporary fighters of other countries. It suddenly came into prominence when 475 were shipped to the Spanish Republicans, where its reliability, 1,800 rounds/min guns, manoeuvrability and fast climb and dive surprised its opponents, who called it the "Rata" (rat). A few old Type 10 remained in Spanish use until 1952. Hundreds of several types fought Japanese aircraft over China and Manchuria, where many I-16s were fitted with the new RS-82 rocket. The final, more powerful versions were built in far greater numbers than any others, about one in 30 being a UTI trainer with tandem open cockpits (and in some versions with fixed landing gear). Total production of this extremely important fighter is estimated at 7,000, of which probably 4,000 were engaged in combat duty against the German invader in 1941–43. Heroically flown against aircraft of much later design and often used for deliberate ramming attacks, the stumpy I-16 operated on wheels or skis long after it was obsolete yet today is recognised as one of the really significant combat aircraft of history.

Sukhoi Su-2

ANT-51, BB-1, Su-2

Origin: The design bureau of P. O. Sukhoi.
Type: Two-seat tactical attack bomber.
Engine: (Most) one 1,000hp Shvetsov M-88B 14-cylinder, two-row radial; (late batches) 1,520hp M-82 (ASh-82), same layout.
Dimensions: Span 46ft 11in (14·30m); length 33ft 7½in (10·25m); height, not known accurately.
Weights: Empty, typically 6,615lb (3000kg); maximum loaded 8,994–9,645lb (4375kg).
Performance: Maximum speed (M-88B) 283mph (455km/h); service ceiling 28,870ft (8800m); range with 882lb (400kg) bombs, 746 miles (1200km).
Armament: (Typical) four 7·62mm ShKAS machine guns fixed in wings, one in manual dorsal turret; internal bomb bay for load of 882lb (400kg), with underwing racks for additional bombs or RS-82 rockets (ten) to overload maximum of 1,323lb (600kg).
History: First flight (ANT-51) August 1937; (production BB-1) 1940; final delivery, probably 1943.
User: Soviet Union.

Development: Pavel Sukhoi, a young member of the great Tupolev design bureau, designed the ANT-51 in 1936–37 as a replacement for the disappointing R-10. The prototype achieved 250mph on its M-62 (Cyclone) engine and further prototypes with 950hp M-87 engines (derived from the Gnome-Rhône 14K) were more promising. Eventually the BB-1 was put into large-scale production, seeming to be a fine aircraft with docile handling, good armour, fair bomb load and adequate performance for its day. In early 1941 the more powerful M-88B was fitted and the designation changed from that of function to the new Soviet scheme naming the designer (thus, Su-2). Some 1,500 or more were in service with the Frontovaya Aviatsya (tactical air forces) when Germany invaded the Soviet Union in June 1941, and production went ahead rapidly with variants with or without the turret (and possibly including a single-seater). But losses were high, and even later substitution of the powerful M-82 engine made little difference. In late 1941 an Su-2 was flown with the 2,100hp M-90 engine, but neither this nor the completely redesigned (and much better) Su-6 was put into production.

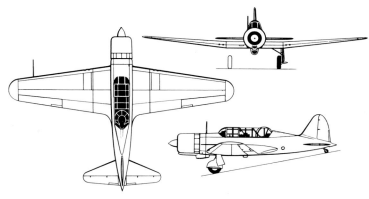

Above: Three-view of typical Su-2.

Above: Most Su-2 combat missions were desperate front-line sorties against the might of the German air and land forces. This Su-2 has landed for quick re-arming.

Left: This Su-2 was in use at a combat training unit at Sverdlovsk in late 1942.

Polikarpov Po-2

U-2, Po-2 (at least 14 sub-types), S-1 to -4, CSS-13

Origin: The design bureau of Nikolai N. Polikarpov.
Type: Originally primary trainer, see text.
Engine: Almost always, 110hp Shvetsov M-11 five-cylinder radial, or (after 1936) 125hp M-11D.
Dimensions: Span (varied ± 50mm, 2in) 37ft 5in (11·40m); length (varied ± 20mm, 0·79in) 26ft 8½in (8·14m); height (varied ± 100mm, 4in) 9ft 10in (3·00m).
Weights: Empty (typical) 1,350lb (612kg); maximum 1,900–2,340lb typical being 2,167lb (983kg).
Performance: Maximum speed (typical) 93mph (150km/h); min flying speed 40mph (65km/h); min field length 660ft (200m).
History: First flight 7 January 1928; service delivery 1928; final delivery (USSR) 1944, (Poland) 1954.
Users: (WWII) Soviet Union (all military arms, plus Aeroflot) and several other countries.

Development: Polikarpov created the U-2 as the Soviet Union's first mass-produced standard primary trainer. He had no idea that this simple little biplane was destined to become used for virtually every purpose for which a flying machine can be used. It remained in production 26 years, possibly ranks third among all aircraft in terms of numbers built, and quite unexpectedly became one of the weapons most disliked by the German invaders. In its first 13 years it was just a trainer and utility machine, production reaching about 13,500. From mid-1941 it blossomed into the U-2VS

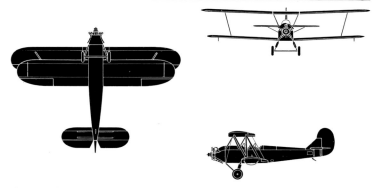

Above: Three-view of basic Po-2 without equipment or stores.

(military series), including the S (ambulance), P (seaplane), GN ("voice from the sky", psy-warfare), NAK (night artillery correction) and LNB (light night bomber) variants. Most had provision for a rear-cockpit ShKAS and sometimes other machine guns, and the LNB carried up to 551lb (250kg) of bombs, many switching to rockets by late 1943. Production in 1941–44 was at least 6,500, and Polikarpov said German troops believed his U-2 "could look over window sills to see if the enemy is inside". At least 100 regiments, each of 42 aircraft, used the U-2, many being honoured by the title Guards Regiments. They operated in intimate contact with the enemy, often below tree level or down the shattered streets of Berlin, right up to the surrender. Polikarpov died in 1944, and the beloved Kukuruznik (corn cutter) was redesignated Po-2 in his honour. It even received a NATO reporting name: "Mule". The CSS-13 ag/ambulance models were built in Poland in 1948–54.

Tupolev SB-2

ANT-40, SB-1, -2 and -2bis (ANT-41)

Origin: The design bureau of A. N. Tupolev.
Type: Medium bomber with usual crew of three.
Engines: Two vee-12 liquid-cooled; (early -2 versions) 750hp VK-100 (M-100) derived from Hispano-Suiza 12Y; (late -2 versions) 840hp M-100A; (-2bis versions) 1,100hp M-103.
Dimensions: Span 66ft 8½in (20·34m); length (with very few exceptions) 40ft 3¼in (12·29m); height 10ft 8in (3·28m).
Weights: Empty (early -2) 8,267lb (3750kg); (M-100A) typically 8,820lb (4000kg); (-2bis) about 10,800lb (4900kg); maximum loaded (early -2) 13,449lb (6100kg); (M-100A) 13,955lb (6330kg), (-2bis) normally 17,196lb (7800kg); overload 21,165lb (9600kg).
Performance: Maximum speed (early) 255mph (410km/h); (M-100A) 263mph (425km/h); (-2bis) 280mph (450km/h); initial climb (-2bis) 1,310ft (400m)/min; service ceiling (typical later version) 31,000–35,000ft (9500–10,500m); range with bomb load (typical -2) 746 miles (1200km); (-2bis, max fuel) 994 miles (1600km).
Armament: (Normal for all versions) four 7·62mm ShKAS machine guns, two manually aimed through vertical slits in nose, one from dorsal position and one from rear ventral position; internal bomb bay for six 220lb (100kg) or single 1,100lb (500kg).

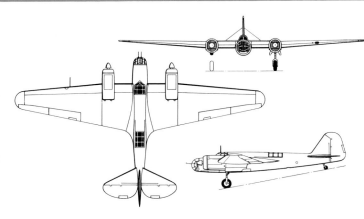

Above: Three-view of early SB-2 as used from 1936.

Left: First air force to use the SB-2 in action was the Spanish Republican AF (Grupo de Bombardeo núm 24 shown), which had over 200.

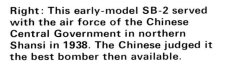

Right: This early-model SB-2 served with the air force of the Chinese Central Government in northern Shansi in 1938. The Chinese judged it the best bomber then available.

Left: Far more important were the later SB-2bis versions, with streamlined engine installations and many other changes including constant-speed propellers. The Germans found this example wrecked on the ground at Lvov in June 1941.

History: First flight (SB-1) 7 October 1934; service delivery (-2) early 1936; (-2bis) probably late 1938; final delivery, probably 1942.
Users: China, Soviet Union, Spain (Republican).

Development: Like the TB-3, the SB-2 was built in great numbers in the 1930s and bore a heavy burden in "the Great Patriotic War" from June 1941 until long after it was obsolescent. Though built to a 1933 specification it was actually much superior to Britain's later Blenheim and it was the Soviet Union's first stressed-skin bomber. The SB-1 prototype had M-25 radials, but performance was even better with the VK-100 in-lines and service in the Spanish civil war in 1936–39 initially found the Nationalists lacking any fighters able to catch the speedy, high-flying SB. In speed and rate of climb even the first service versions surpassed contemporary fighters and, despite a considerable increase in fuel capacity and weight, performance was improved with the more streamlined M-103, without the original bluff frontal radiators. Total production exceeded 6,000 of all versions, and the type served against Japan in 1938–39, in Finland and against German forces until 1943, the last two years mainly in the role of a night bomber.

Below: Pushing an early SB-2 into a wood for cover. In the first week after the invasion of the Soviet Union on 22 June 1941 more than two-thirds of the SB-2s were destroyed.

Tupolev TB-3

ANT-6, TB-3 Types 1932, 1934 and 1936

Origin: The design bureau of A. N. Tupolev.
Type: Heavy bomber with crew of ten (Type 1932) and later six.
Engines: Four vee-12 liquid-cooled: (1932) 730hp M-17; (1934) 900hp M-34R (derived from BMW VI); later 950–1,280hp M-34RN or RNF.
Dimensions: Span 132ft 10½in (40·5m); (1936) 137ft 1½in (41·8m); length (early) 81ft (24·69m); (1934 onward) 82ft 8¼in (25·21m); height, not available but about 18ft.
Weights: Empty, 22,000–26,450lb (11,000–12,000kg); maximum loaded (1932) 38,360lb (17,500kg); (1934) 41,021lb (18,606kg); (1936) 41,226lb (18,700kg), with overload of 54,020lb (24,500kg).
Performance: Maximum speed (M-17, 1932) 134mph (215km/h); (M-34R, 1934) 144mph (232km/h); (M-34RN, 1936) 179mph (288km/h); initial climb, not available; service ceiling (1932) 12,467ft (3800m); (1934) 15,090ft (4600m); (1936) 25,365ft (7750m); range with bomb load (typical of all) 1,550 miles (2500km).
Armament: (1932, 1934) five pairs of 7·62mm DA-2 machine guns in nose, two dorsal mountings and two underwing positions, all manually aimed; internal bomb cells for maximum load of 4,850lb (2200kg); (1936) five (later three or four) 7·62mm ShKAS manually aimed, by 1936 without wing positions; bomb load up to 12,790lb (5800kg) carried on 26 fuselage racks and 12 external racks under fuselage and wings.
History: First flight (ANT-6) 22 December 1930; (production TB-3) probably late 1931; (M-34 prototype) March 1933; final delivery, probably 1939.
Users: China, Soviet Union.

Development: Though seemingly archaic in appearance — and its basic design dated from 1926 — the TB-3 was a large and formidable aircraft with capabilities outstripping those of any other bomber in service in other

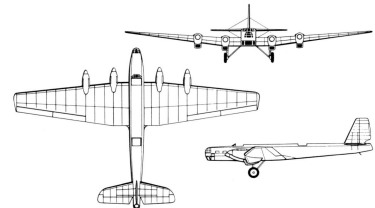

Above: Three-view of 1936 version with single mainwheels.

countries. Though not a stressed-skin design it was a cantilever monoplane with corrugated metal skin using Junkers technology and, thanks to generous stressing, had a considerable "stretching" capability that was put to good use during its long career. A leader in the Tupolev design team was young V. M. Petlyakov, later to produce bombers in his own right, but the aircraft was always known by its functional designation. The 1934 version had brakes on the tandem wire-spoked wheels, a tail turret in place of the underwing positions, and geared engines, which in 1935 were supercharged RN type. Altogether at least 800 of these fine machines were built, final models having smooth skin, single-wheel main gears and only three gunners in enclosed manual turrets. TB-3s saw much action against Japan, Poland, Finland and the German invader and served until 1944 as freight and paratroop transports.

Tupolev Tu-2

ANT-58, Tu-2 (many sub-variants), Tu-6

Origin: The design bureau of A. N. Tupolev.
Type: Attack bomber with normal crew of four.
Engines: Two 1,850hp Shvetsov ASh-82FN or FNV 14-cylinder two-row radials.
Dimensions: Span 61ft 10½in (18·86m); length 45ft 3¾in (13·8m); height 13ft 9½in (4·20m).
Weights: Empty 18,240lb (8273kg); maximum loaded 28,219lb (12,800kg).
Performance: Maximum speed 342mph (550km/h); initial climb 2,300ft (700m)/min; service ceiling 31,168ft (9500m); range with 3,307lb (1500kg) bombs 1,553 miles (2500km).
Armament: Typically three manually aimed 12·7mm Beresin BS, one in upper rear of crew compartment, one in rear dorsal position and one in rear ventral position, and two 20mm ShVAK, each with 200 rounds, fixed in

Above: Three-view of typical Tu-2.

Right: This Tu-2 served with an unidentified FA (Frontal Aviation) unit on the Berlin Front in April 1945. This superb bomber was designed by Tupolev in 1939 when he was in supposed disgrace (he had lately been imprisoned) for unspecified acts; unlike half the generals, he escaped with his life. For the first year it was called "Aircraft 301" to avoid mentioning Tupolev's name!

Below: Because of total preoccupation with the existing Pe-2, not many Tu-2 bombers saw action in World War II. This is a photograph dating from early 1945, when some 1,000 were in use.

wing roots for ground attack (later, often 23mm); internal bomb bay for maximum load of 5,000lb (2270kg), later 6,615lb (3000kg).
History: First flight (ANT-58) October 1940; (production Tu-2) August 1942; final delivery 1948.
User: (Wartime) Soviet Union.

Development: Though it was undoubtedly one of the outstanding designs of World War II, the Tu-2 had the misfortune to emerge into a Soviet Union teeming with the Pe-2, and the older and smaller machine continued to be produced at just ten times the rate of its supposed replacement (much the same happened with German bombers). It was formidable and reliable in service, extremely popular and hardly needed any major modification in the course of a career which extended right through the nervous Berlin Airlift (1948), Korea (1950–53, in North Korean service) and up to 1961 with several Communist nations. Known to NATO as "Bat", the post-war variants included a close-support type with 37mm cannon, a radar-equipped (night fighter?) variant and the high-altitude Tu-6 with long span and bigger tail.

Yakovlev Yak-1

Ya-26, I-26, Yak-1, Yak-7

Origin: The design bureau of A. S. Yakovlev.
Type: Single-seat fighter.
Engine: Initially, one 1,100hp VK-105PA (M-105PA) vee-12 liquid-cooled, derived from Hispano-Suiza 12Y; later, 1,260hp VK-105PF.
Dimensions: Span 32ft 9¾in (10m); length 27ft 9¾in (8.48m); height 8ft 8in (2.64m).
Weights: Empty (early I-26) 5,137lb (2375kg); maximum loaded 6,217lb (2890kg).
Performance: Maximum speed 373mph (600km/h), 310mph (500km/h) at sea level; initial climb 3,940ft (1200m)/min; service ceiling 32,800ft (10,000m); range, 582 miles (850km).
Armament: (I-26) one 20mm ShVAK cannon, with 120 rounds, firing through propeller hub and two 7.62mm ShKAS machine guns, each with 375 rounds, above engine. (Yak-1, late 1941) one 20mm ShVAK, with 140 rounds, one or two 12.7mm Beresin BS above engine, each with about 348 rounds, and underwing rails for six 25lb (12kg) RS-82 rockets. Some, wing racks for two 110lb or 220lb (50 or 100kg) bombs.
History: First flight March 1939; service delivery (pre-production) October 1940; (production) July 1941.
User: Soviet Union.

Development: In 1939 the Soviet government announced specifications for a new fighter. Surprisingly, the best of four rival prototypes was that from young Alexander S. Yakovlev, who had previously designed only

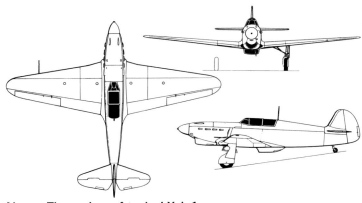

Above: Three-view of typical Yak-1

gliders and sporting machines. His Ya-26 earned him fame and riches, and in June 1941 was cleared for production as the chief Soviet fighter. At this time the designation was changed from I-26 to Yak-1, in conformity with the new policy of designation by design bureau rather than by function. In the same month the German hordes swept in from the West and the entire production line was moved 1,000 miles eastwards to Kamensk-Uralsk. Despite this there was a delay of only about six weeks, and about 500 Yak-1

Below: Newly completed Yak-1 fighters outside the original Yakovlev factory at Klimki, near Moscow, which was hurriedly evacuated in October 1941.

were in action by the end of 1941. With a wooden wing and steel-tube body it was a solid and easily maintained machine, with excellent handling. In parallel came the UTI-26 trainer, with tandem seats, which went into production as the Yak-7V. In late 1941 this was modified with lower rear fuselage to improve view and this in turn led to the Yak-7B fighter which in early 1942 supplanted the Yak-1 in production. Such was the start of the second-biggest aircraft-production programme in history, which by 1945 had delivered 37,000 fighters.

Below: Women flew all kinds of combat missions, and many became fighter aces. Behind is a 1941-series Yak-1 fighter

Left: The Yak-7B designation was applied to the Yak-1M after standardization of the PF engine and many minor improvements.

Left: One of the original Yak-1 family, in winter colour scheme. This had an all-wood wing and rifle-calibre fuselage guns. Each member of the Yak series merged into the next.

Below: This Yak-1M, with yellow-edged stars, proclaims "Collective workers of Shotovskovo village soviet, Ivanovskovo district, Zaporozhskoi oblast. Hero of the Soviet Union Guards Major Reshetov". The -1M was fitted with the new canopy but old engine and coolant radiator.

Yakovlev UT-2

AIR-10, Ya-10, UT-2

Origin: The design bureau of Alexander S. Yakovlev, at Khimki until September 1941, then evacuated to Siberia.
Type: Primary trainer and liaison.
Engine: (Pre-1936) 100hp Shvetsov M-11 five-cylinder radial, (most) 125hp M-11D, (some variants) 110hp M-11G.
Dimensions: Span 34ft 9½in (10·60m); length
Weights: Empty (typical)
Performance: Maximum speed (typical) 120mph (193km/h); cruise 100 mph (161km/h); range (typical maximum) 248 miles (400km).
History: First flight (AIR-10) 1935; service delivery (UT-2) 1936; final delivery, believed 1945.
User: (WWII) believed only Soviet Union.

Development: Yakovlev swiftly became the leading Soviet designer of light sporting aircraft and gliders, and it was natural that in 1934 he should produce the AIR-9 primary trainer. Later redesignated Ya-9, this was a simple steel-tube monoplane with plywood/fabric covering, powered by the ubiquitous M-11 radial. After exhaustive trials it emerged in 1935 as the slightly different AIR-10 (Ya-10), which went into mass-production in 1936. Thousands were used by Soviet flying clubs and schools, while the service version, designated UT-1 and UT-2 by the VVS, was painted olive drab or deep grey and usually had the prominent spats over the main gears removed. While the biplane U-2 did sterner duties the UT-2 served in World War II as the chief Soviet primary trainer, total production reaching 7,243. In 1947 it was succeeded in production by its direct descendant, the more powerful Yak-18, versions of which are still being built. The UT-2 received the NATO reporting name "Mink", but faded swiftly from Soviet bloc service after World War II.

Right: The military variants invariably had no spats, and were extremely simple aircraft. Ground crew on the wingtips may have been needed on very boggy airfields.

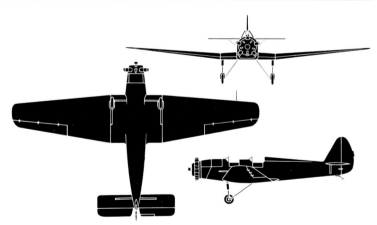

Above: Three-view of typical UT-2 military trainer.

Yakovlev Yak-3

Yak-1M and -3

Origin: The design bureau of A. S. Yakovlev.
Type: Single-seat fighter.
Engine: (-1M) one 1,260hp Klimov VK-105PF vee-12 liquid-cooled; (-3) 1,225hp VK-105PF-2; (final series) 1,650hp VK-107A.
Dimensions: Span 30ft 2¼in (9·20m); length 27ft 10¼in (8·50m); height 7ft 10in (2·39m).
Weights: Empty (VK-105) 4,960lb (2250kg); maximum loaded 5,864lb (2660kg).
Performance: Maximum speed (VK-105) 404mph (650km/h); (VK-107) 447mph (720km/h); initial climb (105) 4,265ft (1300m)/min; (107) 5,250ft (1600m)/min; service ceiling (105) 35,450ft (10,800m); range (105) 506 miles (815km).
Armament: One 20mm ShVAK, with 120 rounds, and two 12·7mm BS, each with 250 rounds.
History: First flight (-1M) 1942; (-3) spring 1943; service delivery (-3) about July 1943; (-3 with VK-107) not later than January 1944.
Users: Czech, French and Polish units, and Soviet Union.

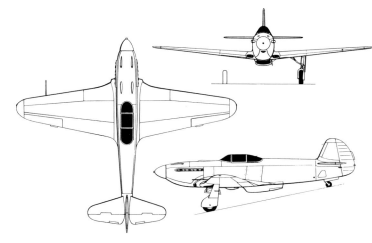

Above: Three-view of Yak-3 (some had hinged rudder-tab).

Development: As early as 1941 Yakovlev was considering means whereby he could wring the highest possible performance out of the basic Yak-1 design. As there was no immediate prospect of more power, and armament and equipment were already minimal, the only solution seemed to be to cut down the airframe, reduce weight and reduce drag. In the Yak-1M the wing was reduced in size, the oil cooler replaced by twin small coolers in the wing roots, the rear fuselage cut down and a simple clear-view canopy fitted, the coolant radiator duct redesigned and other detail changes made. The result was a fighter even more formidable in close combat than the -1 and -9 families, though it landed faster. The production -3 was further refined by a thick coat of hard-wearing wax polish, and after meeting the new fighter during the mighty Kursk battle in the summer of 1943 the Luftwaffe recognised it had met its match. Indeed by 1944 a general directive had gone out to Luftwaffe units on the Eastern Front to "avoid combat below 5000m with Yakovlev fighters lacking an oil cooler under the nose"! To show what the Yak-3 could do when bravely handled, despite its armament — which was trivial compared with that of the German fighters — on 14 July 1944 a force of 18 met 30 Luftwaffe fighters and destroyed 15 for the loss of one Yak-3. Small wonder that, offered all available Soviet, British or American fighters, the Normandie-Niemen Group changed from

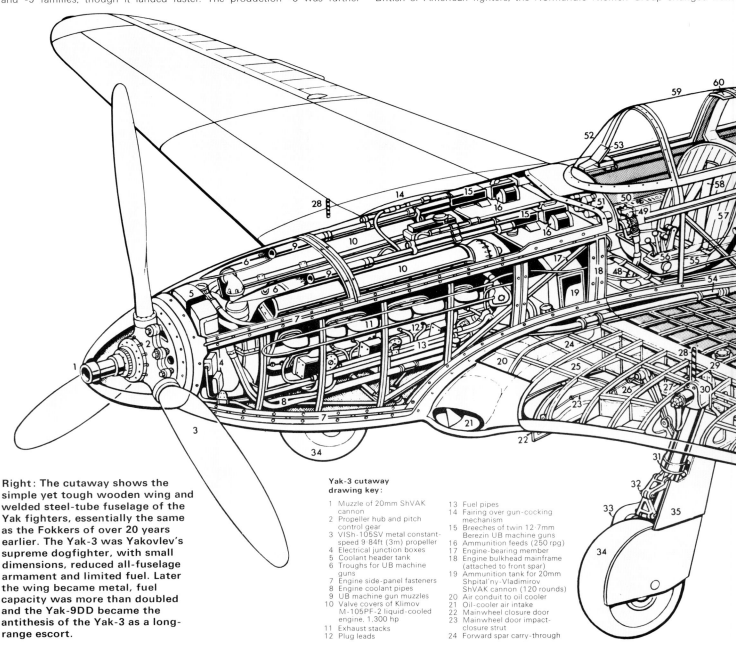

Right: The cutaway shows the simple yet tough wooden wing and welded steel-tube fuselage of the Yak fighters, essentially the same as the Fokkers of over 20 years earlier. The Yak-3 was Yakovlev's supreme dogfighter, with small dimensions, reduced all-fuselage armament and limited fuel. Later the wing became metal, fuel capacity was more than doubled and the Yak-9DD became the antithesis of the Yak-3 as a long-range escort.

Yak-3 cutaway drawing key:

1 Muzzle of 20mm ShVAK cannon
2 Propeller hub and pitch control gear
3 VISh-105SV metal constant-speed 9·84ft (3m) propeller
4 Electrical junction boxes
5 Coolant header tank
6 Troughs for UB machine guns
7 Engine side-panel fasteners
8 Engine coolant pipes
9 UB machine gun muzzles
10 Valve covers of Klimov M-105PF-2 liquid-cooled engine, 1,300 hp
11 Exhaust stacks
12 Plug leads
13 Fuel pipes
14 Fairing over gun-cocking mechanism
15 Breeches of twin 12·7mm Berezin UB machine guns
16 Ammunition feeds (250 rpg)
17 Engine-bearing member
18 Engine bulkhead mainframe (attached to front spar)
19 Ammunition tank for 20mm Shpital'ny-Vladimirov ShVAK cannon (120 rounds)
20 Air conduit to oil cooler
21 Oil-cooler air intake
22 Mainwheel closure door
23 Mainwheel door impact-closure strut
24 Forward spar carry-through

the Yak-9 to the Yak-3 and scored the last 99 of their 273 victories on these machines. It was natural that the more powerful VK-107 engine should have been fitted to the Yak-3, though the designation was not changed. After prolonged trials in early 1944 the Soviet test centre judged the 107-engined aircraft to be 60—70mph faster than either a Bf 109G or an Fw 190, but the re-engined aircraft was just too late to see action in World War II. As in the case of the Yak-1 and -9, there were various experimental conversions of the Yak-3, the best-known being the mixed-power Yak-3 ZhRD of early 1945, which reached at least 485mph (780km/h) on a VK-105 and a liquid-propellant rocket. A more radical installation was the Yak-7VRD with two large ramjets under the wings. Total production of the Yak-1, -3, -7 and -9 was not less than 37,000. These fighters may have been smaller and simpler than those of other nations in World War II but they served the Soviet Union well in its hour of great need. They conserved precious material, kept going under almost impossible airfield and maintenance conditions and consistently out-performed their enemies.

Right: As a point of comparison, this Yak-7B can be distinguished from the Yak-3 by the presence of the separate oil cooler under the engine, and slightly larger wing. The Yak-3 also had a lighter airframe.

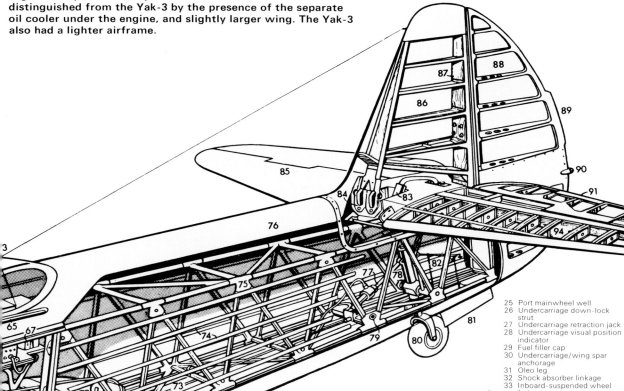

Above: The Yak-3 of Hero of the Soviet Union Sergei Luganskii, Central Sector, mid-1944.

47 Port inboard fuel tank
48 Control column base
49 Column hand grip (with gun triggers, selector buttons and brake lever)
50 Starboard instrument shelf (undercarriage air pressure cock, cooling flaps control lever, emergency undercarriage unlocking lever, fuel pressure and primer pump, starting air cock and oil dilution pump handle)
51 Instrument fascia panel (primary flying and engine instruments)
52 Single-piece moulded windscreen
53 PBP reflector gun sight
54 Engine coolant pipe to radiator
55 Bucket seat
56 Supercharger, propeller pitch and throttle levers
57 Armoured seat back
58 Seat harness
59 Sliding canopy
60 Head protection armour
61 Armourglass screen
62 Fixed aft-canopy fairing
63 Aerial attachment
64 Single-channel HF R/T

25 Port mainwheel well
26 Undercarriage down-lock strut
27 Undercarriage retraction jack
28 Undercarriage visual position indicator
29 Fuel filler cap
30 Undercarriage/wing spar anchorage
31 Oleo leg
32 Shock absorber linkage
33 Inboard-suspended wheel fork
34 Mainwheel low-pressure tyres

35 Two-piece undercarriage fairing plates
36 Wooden front spar
37 Plywood/fabric wing skinning
38 Wing structure (wooden ribs and stringers)
39 Pitot boom
40 Navigation light

aileron
42 Aileron trim tab
43 Aileron push rod
44 Inset split flap
45 Wooden rear spar
46 Port outboard fuel tank

65 Canopy track
66 Electrical equipment
67 Accumulator
68 Oxygen cylinder
69 Ventral coolant radiator
70 Radiator casing
71 Radiator aft fairing
72 Hydraulic reservoir
73 Control runs to tail
74 Wooden fuselage stringers
75 Welded steel-tube fuselage framework
76 Plywood/fabric fuselage skinning
77 Tailwheel retraction jack
78 Tailwheel oleo leg
79 Lifting point
80 Aft-retracting tailwheel
81 Tailwheel doors
82 Wheel-impact door-closure struts
83 Elevator mass balance
84 Fin/fuselage attachment
85 Elevator aerodynamic balance
86 Wooden fin structure (plywood covered)
87 Rudder post
88 Light-alloy rudder (fabric covered)
89 Rudder trim tab
90 Tail navigation light
91 Elevator trim tab
92 Light alloy elevator (fabric covered)
93 Wooden elevator spar
94 Wooden tailplane (plywood covered)

Yakovlev Yak-9

Yak-9, -9D, -9T, -9U and -9P

Origin: The design bureau of A. S. Yakovlev.
Type: Single-seat fighter (some, fighter-bomber).
Engine: (-9, D and T) one 1,260hp Klimov VK-105PF vee-12 liquid-cooled; (U, P) one 1,650hp VK-107A.
Dimensions: Span 32ft 9¾in (10m); length (-9, D, T) 28ft 0½in (8·54m); (U, P) 28ft 6½in (8·70m); height 8ft (2·44m).
Weights: Empty (T) 6,063lb (2750kg); (U) 5,100lb (2313kg); maximum loaded (T) 7,055lb (3200kg); (U) 6,988lb (3170kg).
Performance: Maximum speed (9) 373mph (600km/h); (D) 359mph (573km/h); (T) 367mph (590km/h); (U) 435mph (700km/h); (P) 416mph (670km/h); initial climb (typical, 9, D, T) 3,795ft (1150m)/min; (U, P) 4,920ft (1500m)/min; service ceiling (all) about 34,500ft (10,500m); range (most) 520–550 miles (840–890km); (D) 840 miles (1350km); (DD) 1,367 miles (2200km).
Armament: (Most) one 20mm ShVAK, with 100 rounds, and two 12·7mm BS, each with 250 rounds, plus two 220lb (100kg) bombs; (B) internal bay for 880lb (400kg) bomb load; (T) gun through propeller changed to 37mm NS-P37 with 32 rounds; (K) this changed for 45mm cannon; certain aircraft had 12·7mm BS firing through hub.
History: First flight (7DI) June 1942; (9M) about August 1942; (D, T) probably late 1943; (U) January 1944; (P) August 1945; final delivery (P) about 1946.
Users: (Wartime) France, Poland, Soviet Union.

Development: The Yak-7DI introduced light-alloy wing spars and evolved into the Yak-9, most-produced Soviet aircraft apart from the Il-2. Able to outfly the Bf 109G, which it met over Stalingrad in late 1942, the -9 was developed into the anti-tank -9T, bomber -9B, long-range -9D and very long-range -9DD. The DD escorted US heavy bombers, and once a large group flew from the Ukraine to Bari (southern Italy) to help Jugoslav partisans. The famed Free French Normandie-Niemen Group and both free Polish squadrons used various first-generation -9s. With a complete switch to stressed-skin structure and the VK-107 engine there was a dramatic jump in performance, the -9U entering service in the second half of 1944 and flying rings round the 109 and 190. The U could be identified by the smooth cowl, the oil coolers being in the wing root; the post-war -9P, encountered in Korea, had a DF loop under a transparent cover in the rear fuselage.

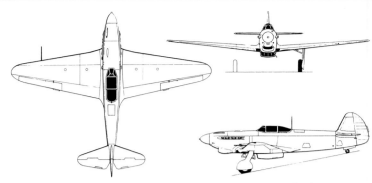

Above: Three-view of Yak-9D (single gun above engine).

Above: Sticking tailwheel doors were by no means peculiar to the Yak-9D, which with 143 Imp gal of fuel was used as an escort for USAAF heavy bombers shuttling to the Soviet Union. It entered service in 1943.

Left: Another early Yak-9, visually identified by the oil cooler under the engine. The Yak-9 introduced the metal wing, which increased fuel capacity.

Yermolaev Yer-2

DB-240, Yer-2 and -2bis

Origin: The design bureau of Vladimir G. Yermolaev, Voronezh (evacuated in September 1941).
Type: Long-range bomber.
Engines: (-2) two 1,100hp Klimov M-105 vee-12 liquid-cooled; (-2bis) two 1,475hp Charomskii ACh-30 (AM-30) vee-12 diesels.
Dimensions: Span (-2) 67ft 7in (20·60m); (-2bis) 78ft 8¾in (24·00m); length (-2bis) 54ft 1½in (16·50m); height 17ft 2in (5·23m).
Weights: Empty (-2bis) 17,196lb (7800kg); normal maximum (-2bis) 34,950lb (15,850kg), (overload) reported to be 40,962lb (18,580kg).
Performance: Maximum speed (-2bis) 261mph (420km/h); cruise 199mph (320km/h); service ceiling at max weight 23,470ft (7700m); max range with bomb load 3,107 miles (5000km).
Armament: Usually one (sometimes two) 20mm ShVAK in dorsal turret and two 12·7mm BS, all manually aimed; up to 11,023lb (5000kg) bombs internally.
History: First flight (DB-240) June 1940, (first production) about December 1940, (-2bis) 1942; final delivery, probably 1944.
User: Soviet Union.

Development: In 1938 Yermolaev's sleek Stahl-7 had been one of the first Soviet aircraft with stressed-skin construction. Its excellent long-range capability led to the DB-240 strategic bomber prototype, intended as a successor to Ilyushin's DB-3. Distinguished by its acutely cranked inverted-gull wing, it seated pilot and co-pilot/navigator in tandem under a canopy

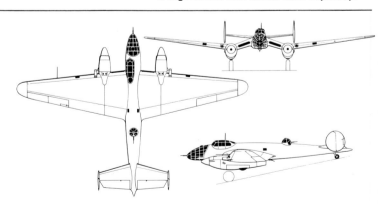

Above: Three-view of production-type Yer-2.

offset to the left, and had the usual three gun positions. Development was remarkably quick, and production was authorised in October 1940. On the night of 7 August 1941 four of the production Yer-2 bombers raided Berlin. In late 1940 one of the development prototypes was re-engined with Charomskii diesels, and (though this engine was troublesome) it later made a non-stop 2,864-mile flight from Moscow, dropping a 2,205lb (1000kg) bomb load on a range near Omsk. To match the increased power the aircraft was enlarged, and the flight deck rearranged for side-by-side pilots across the full width. Total production of this long-range aircraft was about 430, all but 128 being of the -2bis version. After the war Yermolaev flew a civil transport development to compete with the Ilyushin Il-12.

Bell P-39 Airacobra

P-39 to P39Q Airacobra (data for P-39L)

Origin: Bell Aircraft Corporation.
Type: Single-seat fighter.
Engine: 1,325hp Allison V-1710-63 vee-12 liquid-cooled.
Dimensions: Span 34ft 0in (10·37m); length 30ft 2in (9·2m); height (one prop-blade vertical) 11ft 10in (3·63m).
Weights: Empty 5,600lb (2540kg); loaded 7,780lb (3530kg).
Performance: Maximum speed 380mph (612km/h); initial climb 4,000ft (1220m)/min; service ceiling 35,000ft (10,670m); ferry range with drop tank at 160mph (256km/h) 1,475 miles (2360km).
Armament: One 37mm cannon with 30 rounds (twice as many as in first sub-types), two synchronised 0·5in Colt-Brownings and two or four 0·30in in outer wings.
History: First flight of XP-39 August 1939; (P-39F to M-sub-types, 1942); final batch (P-39Q) May 1944.
Users: France, Italy (CB), Portugal, Soviet Union, UK (RAF, briefly), US (AAF).

Development: First flown as a company prototype in 1939, this design by R. J. Woods and O. L. Woodson was unique in having a nosewheel-type landing gear and the engine behind the pilot. The propeller was driven by a long shaft under the pilot's seat and a reduction gearbox in the nose, the latter also containing a big 37mm cannon firing through the propeller hub. Other guns were also fitted in the nose, the first production aircraft, the P-39C of 1941, having two 0·30in and two 0·5in all synchronised to fire past the propeller. Britain ordered the unconventional fighter in 1940 and in June 1941 the first Airacobra I arrived, with the 37mm gun and 15 rounds having been replaced by a 20mm Hispano with 60. Two 0·303in Brownings

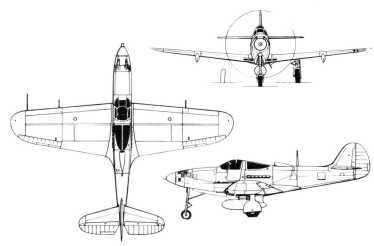

Above: Three-view of P-39Q with drop tank.

in the nose and four more in the wings completed the armament. No 601 Sqn did poorly with it and failed to keep the unusual aircraft serviceable, but the US Army Air Force used it in big numbers. Altogether 9,588 were built and used with fair success in the Mediterranean and Far East, some 5,000 being supplied to the Soviet Union, mainly through Iran. Biggest production version was the P-39Q, of which over 4,900 were built. The P-39 was succeeded in production in 1944 by the P-63 Kingcobra.

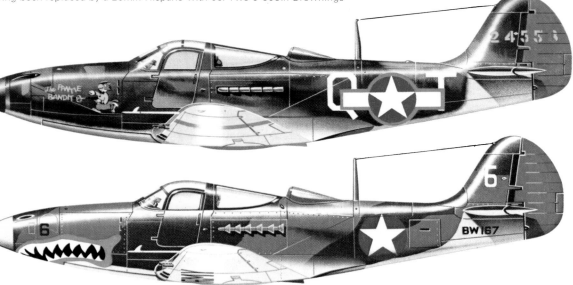

Left: The P-39L was an interim aircraft with Curtiss Electric propeller (data above apply). This one served with 91st FS, 81st FG.

Left: This Bell P-400 was a requisitioned British P-39, impressed into USAAC service still with the 20mm gun fitted, and with British serial number still showing.

Below: These are P-39Ds; the photograph was taken before mid-1942. The most numerous (Q) P-39 had no guns inside the wings.

Bell P-59 Airacomet

YP-59, P-59A and XF2L-1

Origin: Bell Aircraft Corporation.
Type: Single-seat jet fighter trainer.
Engines: Two 2,000lb (907kg) thrust General Electric J31-GE-3 turbojets.
Dimensions: Span 45ft 6in (13·87m); length 38ft 1½in (11·63m); height 12ft 0in (3·66m).
Weights: Empty 7,950lb (3610kg); loaded 12,700lb (5760kg).
Performance: Maximum speed 413mph (671km/h); service ceiling 46,200ft (14,080m); maximum range with two 125 Imp gal drop tanks 520 miles (837km) at 289mph (465km/h) at 20,000ft (6096m).
Armament: Usually none, but some YP-59A fitted with nose guns (eg one 37mm cannon and three 0·5in) and one rack under each wing for bomb as alternative to drop tank.
History: First flight (XP-59A) 1 October 1942; (production P-59A) 7 August 1944.
Users: US (AAF, Navy); (one UK in exchange for Meteor I).

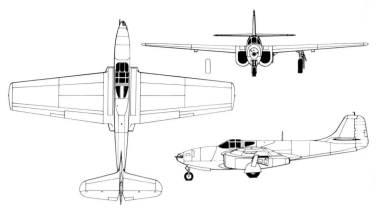

Above: Three-view of P-59A; P-59B was identical but had 55 Imp gal extra fuel capacity.

Development: In June 1941 the US government and General "Hap" Arnold of the Army Air Corps were told of Britain's development of the turbojet engine. On 5 September 1941 Bell Aircraft was requested to design a jet fighter and in the following month a Whittle turbojet, complete engineering drawings and a team from Power Jets Ltd arrived from Britain to hasten proceedings. The result was that Bell flew the first American jet in one year from the start of work. The Whittle-type centrifugal engines, Americanised and made by General Electric as the 1,100lb (500kg) thrust 1-A, were installed under the wing roots, close to the centreline and easily accessible (two were needed to fly an aircraft of useful size). Flight development went extremely smoothly, and 12 YP-59As for service trials were delivered in 1944. Total procurement amounted to 66 only, including three XF2L-1s for the US Navy, and the P-59A was classed as a fighter-trainer because it was clear it would not make an effective front-line fighter. But in comparison with the fast timescale it was a remarkable achievement, performance being very similar to that attained with the early Meteors.

Left: One of the first three XP-59 prototypes, seen on the desert at Muroc where Edwards AFB now fills the landscape.

Right: Rolling an XP-59A back to the apron after an early test. Elaborate precautions were taken to preserve secrecy, to the point of fitting a dummy propeller to the first XP-59A shipped to Muroc by rail in September 1942.

Bell P-63 Kingcobra

P-63A to E and RP-63

Origin: Bell Aircraft Corporation, Buffalo, NY.
Type: Single-seat fighter-bomber.
Engine: One Allison V-1710 vee-12 liquid-cooled, (A) 1,500hp (war emergency rating) V-1710-93, (C) 1,800hp V-1710-117.
Dimensions: Span 38ft 4in (11·68m); length 32ft 8in (9·96m); height 12ft 7in (3·84m).
Weights: Empty (A) 6,375lb (2892kg); maximum (A) 10,500lb (4763kg).
Performance: Maximum speed (all) 410mph (660km/h); typical range with three bombs 340 miles (547km); ferry range with three tanks 2,575 miles (4143km).
Armament: Usually one 37mm and four 0·5in, plus up to three 500lb (227kg) bombs.
History: First flight 7 December 1942; service delivery October 1943; final delivery early 1945.
Users: Brazil, France, Italy, Soviet Union, US (AAF).

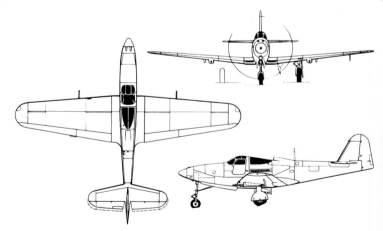

Above: Three-view of P-63A (all except D similar).

Development: Though it looked like a P-39 with a different tail, in fact the P-63 was a completely different design, greatly improved in the light of painful combat experience. It fully met a February 1941 Army requirement, but air war developed so fast that — though Bell did a competent job to a fast schedule — the P-63 was outclassed before it reached the squadrons. It never fought with the US forces, but 2,421 of the 3,303 built went to the Soviet Union where their tough airframes and good close-support capability made them popular. At least 300 went to the Free French, in both A and C variants (both of which had a wealth of sub-types). The D had a sliding bubble canopy and larger wing, and the E extra fuel. The only USAAF Kingcobras were 332 completed or modified as heavily armoured RP-63A or C manned target aircraft, shot at by live "frangible" (easily shattered) bullets. Each hit made a powerful lamp light at the tip of the spinner.

Left: A Kingcobra in USAAF markings, probably a P-63A-6 with bomb racks outboard of the wing guns.

Right: Bell's plant at Buffalo delivered well over 2,000 Kingcobras to the Soviet Union, where they stood up well to the harsh environment. Here are a few hundred at Buffalo.

Right: Side elevation of the 16th aircraft, strictly a P-59A but still without armament. Most early P-59 aircraft later were used for various trials programmes. One was shipped to England, where it was taken on charge as RJ362/G (called "Bell 27 Airacomet") in exchange for one of the first Meteors which was shipped to Muroc and checked out there by John Grierson.

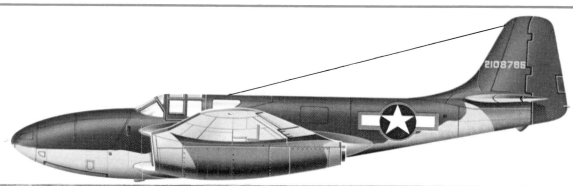

Boeing B-17 Fortress

Model 299, Y1B-17 and B-17 to B-17G (basic data for G)

Origin: Boeing Airplane Company, Seattle; also built by Vega Aircraft Corporation, Burbank, and Douglas Aircraft Company, Tulsa.
Type: High-altitude bomber, with crew of six to ten.
Engines: Four 1,200hp Wright R-1820-97 (B-17C to E, R-1820-65) Cyclone nine-cylinder radials with exhaust-driven turbochargers.
Dimensions: Span 103ft 9in (31·6m): length 74ft 9in (22·8m); (B-17B, C, D) 67ft 11in; (B-17E) 73ft 10in; height 19ft 1in (5·8m); (B-17B, C, D) 15ft 5in.
Weights: Empty 32,720–35,800lb (14,855–16,200kg); (B-17B, C, D) typically 31,150lb; maximum loaded 65,600lb (29,700kg) (B-17B, C, D) 44,200–46,650lb; (B-17E) 53,000lb.
Performance: Maximum speed 287mph (462km/h); (B-17C, D) 323mph; (B-17E) 317mph; cruising speed 182mph (293km/h); (B-17C, D) 250mph; (B-17E) 210mph; service ceiling 35,000ft (10,670m); range 1,100 miles (1,760km) with maximum bomb load (other versions up to 3,160 miles with reduced weapon load).
Armament: Twin 0·5in Brownings in chin, dorsal, ball and tail turrets, plus two in nose sockets, one in radio compartment and one in each waist position. Normal internal bomb load 6,000lb (2724kg), but maximum 12,800lb (5800kg).
History: First flight (299) 28 July 1935; (Y1B-17) January 1937; first delivery (B-17B) June 1939; final delivery April 1945.
Users: UK (RAF), US (AAC/AAF, Navy).

continued on page 202 ▶

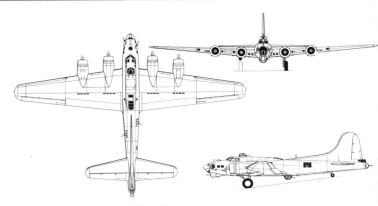

Above: Three-view of B-17G.

Below: The subject of the cutaway is the B-17F, the first model made in truly vast quantity (3,405) and second in importance only to the G of which 8,680 were made. Item 59 was often a 0.5in gun.

Boeing B-17F Fortress cutaway drawing key:

1 Rudder construction
2 Rudder tab
3 Rudder tab actuation
4 Tail gunner's station
5 Gunsight
6 Twin 0·5-in (12.7-mm) machine guns
7 Tail cone
8 Tail gunner's seat
9 Ammunition troughs
10 Elevator trim tab
11 Starboard elevator
12 Tailplane structure
13 Tailplane front spar
14 Tailplane/fuselage attachment
15 Control cables
16 Elevator control mechanism
17 Rudder control linkage
18 Rudder post

49 Support frame
50 Ball turret roof
51 Twin 0·5-in (12,7-mm) machine guns
52 Ventral ball turret
53 Wingroot fillet
54 Bulkhead
55 Radio operator's compartment
56 Camera access hatch
57 Radio compartment windows (port and starboard)
58 Ammunition boxes
59 Single 0·3-in (7,62-mm) dorsal machine gun
60 Radio compartment roof glazing
61 Radio compartment/bomb-bay bulkhead

19 Rudder centre hinge
20 Fin structure
21 Rudder upper hinge
22 Fin skinning
23 Aerial attachment
24 Aerials
25 Fin leading-edge de-icing boot
26 Port elevator
27 Port tailplane
28 Tailplane leading-edge de-icing boot
29 Dorsal fin structure
30 Fuselage frame
31 Tailwheel actuation
32 Toilet
33 Tailwheel (retracted) fairing
34 Fully-swivelling retractable tailwheel
35 Crew entry door
36 Control cables
37 Starboard waist hatch
38 Starboard waist 0·5-in (12,7-mm) machine gun
39 Gun support frame
40 Ammunition box
41 Ventral aerial
42 Waist gunners' positions
43 Port waist 0·5-in (12,7-mm) machine gun
44 Ceiling control cable runs
45 Dorsal aerial mast
46 Ball turret stanchion support
47 Ball turret stanchion
48 Ball turret actuation mechanism

62 Fire extinguisher
63 Radio operator's station (port side)
64 Handrail links
65 Bulkhead step
66 Wing rear spar/fuselage attachment
67 Wingroot profile
68 Bomb-bay central catwalk
69 Vertical bomb stowage racks (starboard installation shown)
70 Horizontal bomb stowage (port side shown)
71 Dinghy stowage
72 Twin 0·5-in (12.7-mm) machine guns
73 Dorsal turret
74 Port wing flaps
75 Cooling air slots
76 Aileron tab (port only)
77 Port aileron
78 Port navigation light
79 Wing skinning
80 Wing leading-edge de-icing boot
81 Port landing light
82 Wing corrugated inner skin (nine inter-rib cells)
83 Port outer wing fuel tank
84 No 1 engine nacelle
85 Cooling gills
86 Three-blade propellers
87 No 2 engine nacelle
88 Wing leading-edge de-icing boot

Above: A B-17G-25 of the 8th Air Force's 96th Bomb Group, based at Snetterton Heath, England.

89 Port mid-wing (self-sealing) fuel tanks
90 Flight deck upper glazing
91 Flight deck/bomb-bay bulkhead
92 Oxygen cylinders
93 Co-pilot's seat
94 Co-pilot's control column
95 Headrest/armour
96 Compass installation

97 Pilot's seat
98 Windscreen
99 Central control console pedestal
100 Side windows
101 Navigation equipment
102 Navigator's compartment upper window (subsequently replaced by ceiling astrodome)

103 Navigator's table
104 Side gun mounting
105 Enlarged cheek windows (flush)
106 Ammunition box
107 Bombardier's panel
108 Norden bombsight installation
109 Plexiglass frameless nose-cone

110 Single 0·5-in (12,7-mm) nose machine gun
111 Optically-flat bomb-aiming panel
112 Pitot head fairing (port and starboard)
113 D/F loop bullet fairing
114 Port mainwheel
115 Flight deck underfloor control linkage

297212

116 Wingroot/fuselage fairing
117 Wing front spar/fuselage attachment
118 Battery access panels (wingroot leading-edge)
119 No 3 engine nacelle spar bulkhead
120 Intercooler pressure duct
121 Mainwheel well
122 Oil tank (nacelle inboard wall)

123 Nacelle structure
124 Exhaust
125 Retracted mainwheel (semi-recessed)
126 Firewall
127 Cooling gills
128 Exhaust collector ring assembly
129 Three-blade propellers
130 Undercarriage retraction struts
131 Starboard mainwheel
132 Axle
133 Mainwheel oleo leg
134 Propeller reduction gear casing
135 1,000 hp Wright R-1820-65 radial engine
136 Exhaust collector ring
137 Engine upper bearers
138 Firewall
139 Engine lower bearers

140 Intercooler assembly
141 Oil tank (nacelle outboard wall)
142 Supercharger
143 Intake
144 Supercharger waste-gate
145 Starboard landing light
146 Supercharger intake
147 Intercooler intake
148 Ducting
149 No 4 engine nacelle spar bulkhead
150 Oil radiator intake
151 Main spar web structure
152 Mid-wing fuel tank rib cut-outs
153 Auxiliary mid spar
154 Rear spar
155 Landing flap profile
156 Cooling air slots
157 Starboard outer wing fuel tank (nine inter-rib cells)

158 Flap structure
159 Starboard aileron
160 Outboard wing ribs
161 Spar assembly
162 Wing leading-edge de-icing boot
163 Aileron control linkage
164 Wing corrugated inner skin
165 Wingtip structure
166 Starboard navigation light

Above: Olive-drab B-17Fs thunder aloft in 1942. Later the 8th AAF ''Forts'' were distinguished by unit insignia readable from a distance; and they were delivered unpainted, because the trail-streaming formations could be seen 100 miles away.

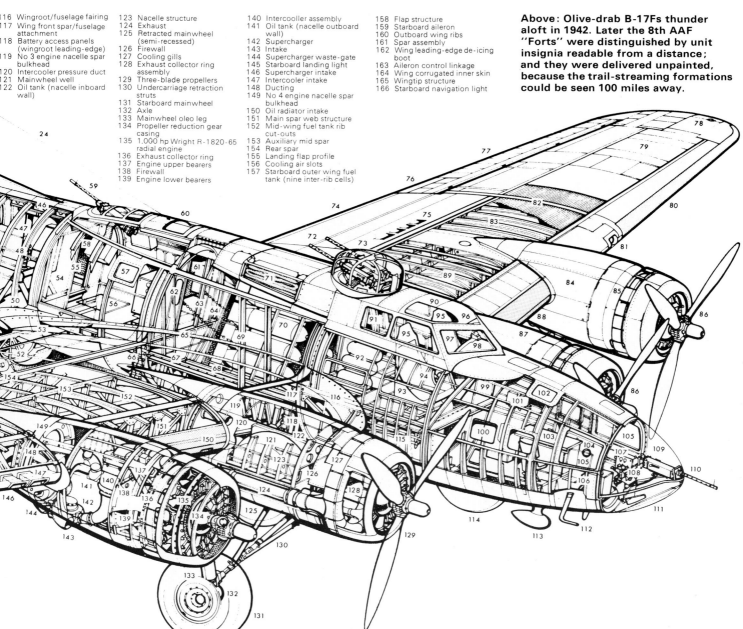

▶**Development:** In May 1934 the US Army Air Corps issued a specification for a multi-engined anti-shipping bomber to defend the nation against enemy fleets. The answer was expected to be similar to the Martin B-10, but Boeing proposed four engines in order to carry the same bomb load faster and higher. It was a huge financial risk for the Seattle company but the resulting Model 299 was a giant among combat aircraft, with four 750hp Pratt & Whitney Hornet engines, a crew of eight and stowage for eight 600lb (272kg) bombs internally.

Above: "Stop" waves a ground-crewman to the skipper of a red-tailed G-model on the green grass of a British base.

Left: Last-minute check before a mission by an RAF Coastal Command Fortress IIA (B-17E). Some 200 served from mid-1942.

The service-test batch of 13 Y1B-17 adopted the Wright Cyclone engine, later versions all being turbocharged for good high-altitude performance. The production B-17B introduced a new nose and bigger rudder and flaps, though the wing loading was conservative and an enduring characteristic of every "Fort" was sedate flying.

With the B-17C came a ventral bathtub, flush side guns, armour and self-sealing tanks. In return for combat data 20 were supplied to the RAF, which used them on a few high-altitude daylight raids with 90 Sqn of Bomber Command. It was found that the Norden sight tended to malfunction, the

Boeing B-29 Superfortress
Model 345, B-29 to -29C

Origin: Boeing Airplane Company, Seattle, Renton and Wichita; also built by Bell Aircraft, Marietta, and Glenn L. Martin Company, Omaha.
Type: High-altitude heavy bomber, with crew of 10–14.
Engines: Four 2,200hp Wright R-3350-23 Duplex Cyclone 18-cylinder radials each with two exhaust-driven turbochargers.
Dimensions: Span 141ft 3in (43·05m); length 99ft (30·2m); height 27ft 9in (8·46m).
Weights: Empty 74,500lb (33,795kg); loaded 135,000lb (61,240kg).
Performance: Maximum speed 357mph (575km/h) at 30,000ft (9144m); cruising speed 290mph (467km/h); climb to 25,000ft (7620m) in 43min; service ceiling 36,000ft (10,973m); range with 10,000lb (4540kg) bombs 3,250miles (5230km).
Armament: Four GE twin-0·50in turrets above and below, sighted from nose or three waist sighting stations; Bell tail turret, with own gunner, with one 20mm cannon and twin 0·50in; internal bomb load up to 20,000lb (9072kg). Carried first two nuclear bombs. With modification, carried two 22,000lb British bombs externally under inner wings.
History: First flight 21 September 1942; (pre-production YB-29) 26 June 1943); squadron delivery July 1943; first combat mission 5 June 1944; last delivery May 1946.
User: US (AAF, Navy).

Development and mass production of the B-29, the Boeing Model 345, was one of the biggest tasks in the history of aviation. It began with a March 1938 study for a new bomber with pressurised cabin and tricycle landing gear. This evolved into the 345 and in August 1940 money was voted for two prototypes. In January 1942 the Army Air Force ordered 14 YB-29s and 500 production aircraft. By February, while Boeing engineers worked night and day on the huge technical problems, a production organisa-tion was set up involving Boeing, Bell, North American and Fisher (General Motors). Martin came in later and by VJ-day more than 3,000 Superforts

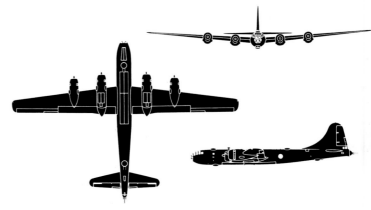

Above: Three-view of B-29 (two-gun forward dorsal turret).

had been delivered. This was a fantastic achievement because each represented five or six times the technical effort of any earlier bomber. In engine power, gross weight, wing loading, pressurisation, armament, air-borne systems and even basic structure the B-29 set a wholly new standard. First combat mission was flown by the 58th Bomb Wing on 5 June 1944, and by 1945 20 groups from the Marianas were sending 500 B-29s at a time to flatten and burn Japan's cities. (Three aircraft made emergency landings in Soviet territory, and Tupolev's design bureau put the design into produc-tion as the Tu-4 bomber and Tu-70 transport.) The -29C had all guns except those in the tail removed, increasing speed and altitude. After the war there were 19 variants of B-29, not including the Washington B.I supplied to help the RAF in 1950–58.

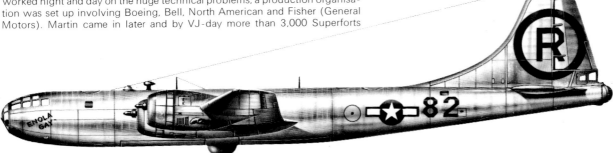

Left: One of the most famous Superforts was the unarmed "special" Enola Gay which on 6 August 1945 dropped the first atom bomb on Hiroshima.

Right: The first production B-29s were painted, but this was soon abandoned.

Browning guns to freeze at the high altitude and German fighters to attack from astern in a defensive blind spot. While surviving Fortress Is operated with Coastal and Middle East forces, the improved B-17D joined the US Army and bore the brunt of early fighting in the Pacific. But extensive combat experience led to the redesigned B-17E, with powered dorsal, ventral (ball) and tail turrets, a huge fin for high-altitude bombing accuracy and much more armour and equipment. This went into mass production by Boeing, Lockheed-Vega and Douglas-Tulsa. It was the first weapon of the US 8th Bomber Command in England and on 17 August 1942 began three gruelling years of day strategic bombing in Europe.

Soon the E gave way to the B-17F, of which 3,405 were built, with many detail improvements, including a long Plexiglas nose, paddle-blade propellers and provision for underwing racks. At the end of 1942 came the final bomber model, the B-17G, with chin turret and flush staggered waist guns. A total of 8,680 G models were made, Boeing's Seattle plant alone turning out 16 a day, and the total B-17 run amounted to 12,731. A few B-17Fs

Above: A sight to quicken the pulse! Sections of G-models from the 381st BG outward bound from Ridgewell, escorted by a lone P-51B Mustang. This group dropped 22,160 tons of bombs.

were converted to XB-40s, carrying extra defensive guns to help protect the main Bomb Groups, while at least 25 were turned into BQ-7 Aphrodite radio-controlled missiles loaded with 12,000lb of high explosive for use against U-boat shelters. Many F and G models were fitted with H_2X radar with the scanner retracting into the nose or rear fuselage, while other versions included the F-9 reconnaissance, XC-108 executive transport, CB-17 utility transport, PB-1W radar early-warning, PB-1G lifeboat-carrying air/sea rescue and QB-17 target drone. After the war came other photo, training, drone-director, search/rescue and research versions, including many used as engine and equipment testbeds. In 1970, 25 years after first flight, one of many civil Forts used for agricultural or forest-fire protection was re-engined with Dart turboprops!

Boeing Stearman
Model 75 Kaydet, PT-13, -17, -18, -27, N2S

Origin: Boeing Airplane Company (see text).
Type: Dual-control primary trainer.
Engine: 215hp Lycoming R-680-5 (PT-13, N2S-2, -5); 220hp Continental R-670-5 (PT-17, PT-27, N2S-1, -3, -4); 225hp Jacobs R-755 (PT-18) radials, R-680 having nine cylinders, others seven.
Dimensions: Span 32ft 2in (9·8m); length 25ft 0¼in (7·63m); height 9ft 2in (2·79m).
Weights: Empty about 1,936lb (878kg); loaded 2,717–2,810lb (1232–1275kg).
Performance: Maximum speed 120–126mph (193–203km/h); initial climb 840ft (256m)/min; service ceiling 11,200ft (3413m); range 440–505 miles (708–812km).
Armament: Only on Model 76D export versions, typically two 0·30in machine guns in lower wings and single 0·30in aimed by observer in rear cockpit. Optional racks for light bombs under fuselage.
History: First flight (Model 70) December 1933; (Model 75) early 1936; final delivery February 1945.
Users: US (AAC/AAF, Navy, Marines) and at least 25 other air forces.

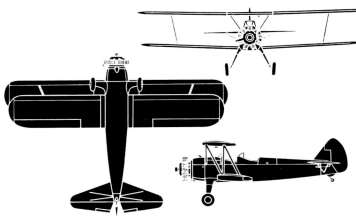

Above: Three-view of typical Boeing Stearman trainer.

Development: When the monopolistic United Aircraft and Transport combine was broken up by the government in 1934, the Stearman Aircraft Co remained a subsidiary of Boeing and in 1939 the Wichita plant lost the Stearman name entirely. Yet the family of trainers built by Boeing to Floyd Stearman's design have always been known by the designer's name rather than that of the maker. The Model 70 biplane trainer was conservative and, as it emerged when biplanes were fast disappearing from combat aviation, it might have been a failure — especially as Claude Ryan had a trim monoplane trainer competing for orders. Yet the result was the biggest production of any biplane in history prior to today's An-2, as the chief primary trainer in North America in World War II. The Model 70 flew on a 220hp Lycoming but the Navy, the first customer, bought 61 NS-1 primary trainers (Model 73) with surplus 225hp Wright Whirlwinds drawn from storage. By 1941 Boeing had delivered 17 similar aircraft and 78 Model 76s (with various engines) for export. But the main production type was the Model 75, ordered by the Army Air Corps after evaluating the first example in 1936. The first were PT-13s of various models, with Lycoming engines of 215 to 280hp, but the biggest family was the PT-17. The 300 built for the RCAF were named Kaydets, a name unofficially adopted for the entire series. A few Canadian PT-27 Kaydets and similar Navy N2S-5s had enclosed cockpits. Total production, including spares, was 10,346, of which several hundred are still flying, mainly as glider tugs and crop dusters.

Left: Primary trainers of the US Navy were doped all-yellow. Various types of NS and N2S Stearmans were the Navy's standard primary trainers of World War II.

Consolidated Vultee
Model 32 B-24 Liberator

For variants, see text
(data for B-24J Liberator B.VI)

Origin: Consolidated Vultee Aircraft Corporation; also built by Douglas, Ford and North American Aviation.
Type: Long-range bomber with normal crew of ten.
Engines: Four 1,200hp Pratt & Whitney R-1830-65 Twin Wasp 14-cylinder two-row radials.
Dimensions: Span 110ft 0in (33·5m); length 67ft 2in (20·47m); height 18ft 0in (5·49m).
Weights: Empty 37,000lb (16,783kg); loaded 65,000lb (29,484kg).
Performance: Maximum speed 290mph (467km/h); initial climb 900ft (274m)/min; service ceiling 28,000ft (8534m); range at 190mph (306km/h) with 5,000lb (2268kg) bomb load 2,200 miles (3540km).
Armament: Ten 0·50in Brownings arranged in four electrically operated turrets (Consolidated or Emerson in nose, Martin dorsal, Briggs-Sperry retractable ventral "ball" and Consolidated or Motor Products tail) with two guns each plus two singles in manual waist positions; two bomb bays with roll-up doors with vertical racks on each side of central catwalk for up to 8,000lb (3629kg); two 4,000lb (1814kg) bombs could be hung externally on inner-wing racks instead of internal load.
History: First flight (XB-24) 29 December 1939; first delivery (LB-30A) March 1941; first combat service (Liberator I) June 1941; first combat service with US Army (B-24C) November 1941; termination of production 31 May 1945; withdrawal from service (various smaller air forces) 1955–56.
Users: Australia, Brazil, Canada, China, Czechoslovakia, France, India, Italy (CB), New Zealand, Portugal, South Africa, Soviet Union, Turkey, UK (RAF, BOAC), US (AAF, Navy, Marines); other countries post-war.

Development: This distinctive aircraft was one of the most important in the history of aviation. Conceived five years after the B-17 it did not, in fact, notably improve on the older bomber's performance and in respect of engine-out performance and general stability and control it was inferior,

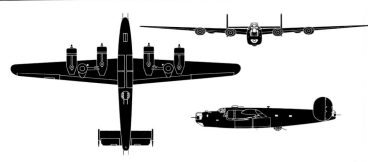

Above: Three-view of B-24H (B-24J similar except front turret).

being a handful for the average pilot. It was also by far the most complicated and expensive combat aircraft the world had seen — though in this it merely showed the way things were going to be in future. Yet it was built in bigger numbers than any other American aircraft in history, in more versions for more purposes than any other aircraft in history, and served on every front in World War II and with 15 Allied nations. In terms of industrial effort it transcended anything seen previously in any sphere of endeavour.

continued on page 206

Right: Best chronicled of all bombing missions by the USAAF is the Ploesti (Romania) refinery attack by B-24Ds of the 44th, 93rd, 98th and 389th Bomb Groups on 1 August 1943.

Below: Bombs rain down from B-24Hs of the 487th BG.

Brewster F2A Buffalo

F2A-1 (239), F2A-2 (339), F2A-3 and 439 Buffalo 1 (data for F2A-2)

Origin: Brewster Aircraft Company, Long Island City.
Type: Single-seat carrier or land-based fighter.
Engine: 1,100hp Wright R-1820-40 (G-205A) Cyclone nine-cylinder radial.
Dimensions: Span 35ft (10·67m); length 26ft 4in (8m); height 12ft 1in (3·7m).
Weights: Empty 4,630lb (2100kg); loaded 7,055lb (3200kg) (varied from 6,848–7,159lb).
Performance: Maximum speed 300mph (483km/h); initial climb 3,070ft (935m)/min; service ceiling 30,500ft (9300m); range 650–950 miles (1045–1530km).
Armament: Four machine guns, two in fuselage and two in wing, calibre of each pair being 0·30in, 0·303in or, mostly commonly, 0·50in.
History: First flight (XF2A-1) January 1938; first service delivery April 1939; termination of production 1942.
Users: Australia, Finland, Netherlands (E. Indies), New Zealand, UK (RAF), US (Navy, Marines).

Development: The Brewster company was established in 1810 to build carriages. In 1935 it plunged into planemaking and secured an order for a US Navy scout-bomber. It also entered a competition for a carrier-based monoplane fighter and won. Not surprisingly, it took almost two years — a long time in those days — to fly the first prototype. Yet one must give the

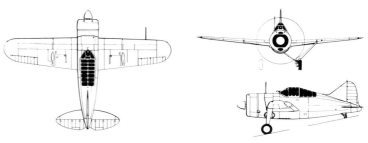

Above: Three-view of the F2A-3, the final sub-type ordered mainly to keep the Brewster factory busy during 1941.

team their due, for the F2A-1 was confirmed as the Navy's choice for its first monoplane fighter even after Grumman had flown the G.36 (Wildcat). In June 1938 a contract was placed for 54 of these tubby mid-wingers, then armed with one 0·50in and one 0·30in machine guns. Only 11 reached USS *Saratoga*; the rest went to Finland, where from February 1940 until the end of World War II they did extremely well. The US Navy bought 43 more powerful and more heavily armed F2A-2 (Model 339), and then 108 F2A-3 with armour and self-sealing tanks. Of these, 21 in the hands of the Marine Corps put up a heroic struggle in the first Battle of Midway. In 1939 bulk orders were placed by Belgium and Britain, and the RAF operated 170 delivered in 1941 to Singapore. Another 72 were bought by the Netherlands.

Above: A Brewster Model 239 (ex-F2A-1) of the Finnish Air Force. These fighters equipped Nos 24 and 26 Sqns of Air Regiment LeR 2, and were successful against various Soviet types.

Left: The wartime censor has deleted the code-letters of this RAF, RAAF or RNZAF squadron in Malaya (note Blenheim IV).

It had a curious layout, dictated by the slender Davis wing placed above the tall bomb bays. This wing was efficient in cruising flight, which combined with great fuel capacity to give the "Lib" longer range than any other landplane of its day. But it meant that the main gears were long, and they were retracted outwards by electric motors, nearly everything on board being electric. Early versions supplied to the RAF were judged not combat-ready, and they began the Atlantic Return Ferry Service as LB-30A transports. Better defences led to the RAF Liberator I, used by Coastal Command with ASV radar and a battery of fixed 20mm cannon. The RAF Liberator II (B-24C) introduced power turrets and served as a bomber in the Middle East. The first mass-produced version was the B-24D, with turbocharged engines in oval cowls, more fuel and armament and many detail changes; 2,738 served US Bomb Groups in Europe and the Pacific, and RAF Coastal Command closed the mid-Atlantic gap, previously beyond aircraft range, where U-boat packs lurked.

Biggest production of all centred on the B-24G, H and J (Navy PB4Y and RAF B.VI and GR.VI), of which 10,208 were built. These all had four turrets, and were made by Convair, North American, Ford and Douglas. Other variants included the L and M with different tail turrets, the N with single fin, the luridly painted CB-24 lead ships, the TB-24 trainer, F-7 photo-reconnaissance, C-109 fuel tanker and QB-24 drone. There was also a complete family of Liberator Transport versions, known as C-87 Liberator Express to the Army, RY-3 to the Navy and C.VII and C.IX to the RAF, many having the huge single fin also seen on the PB4Y-2 Privateer. Excluding one-offs such as the redesigned R2Y transport and 1,800 equivalent aircraft delivered as spares, total production of all versions was a staggering 19,203. Their achievements were in proportion.

Right: A B-24J-105 of the 392nd Bombardment Group of the 8th AAF, based at Wendling, England.

Below: The cutaway shows a B-24J, typical of the late B-24 models of which more were made than any other bomber in history.

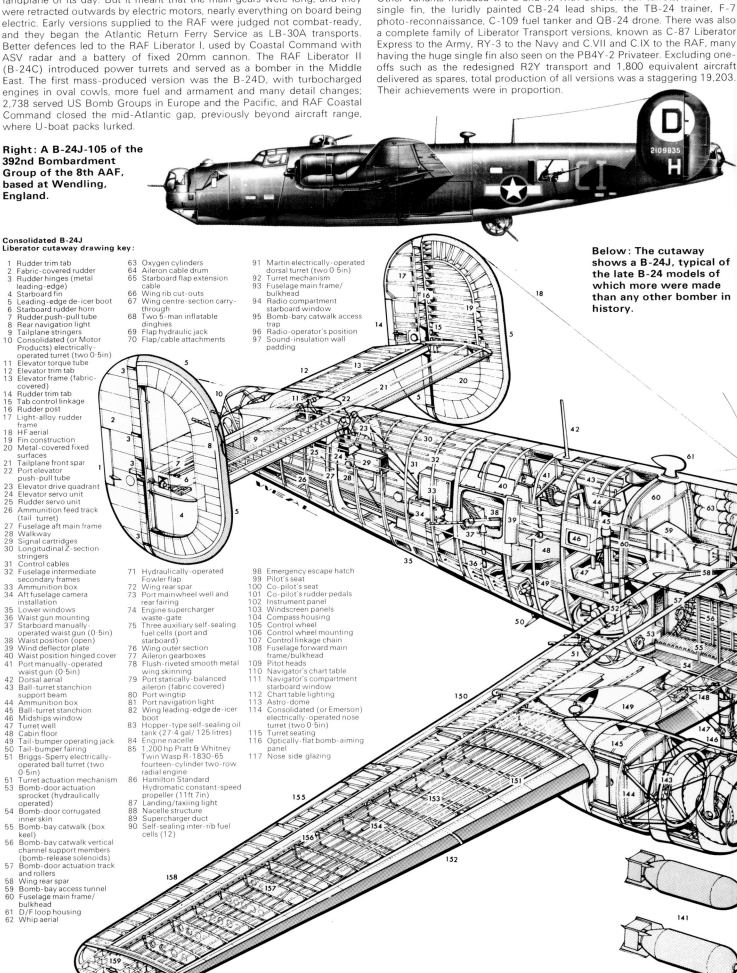

Consolidated B-24J Liberator cutaway drawing key:

1 Rudder trim tab
2 Fabric-covered rudder
3 Rudder hinges (metal leading-edge)
4 Starboard fin
5 Leading-edge de-icer boot
6 Starboard rudder horn
7 Rudder, push-pull tube
8 Rear navigation light
9 Tailplane stringers
10 Consolidated (or Motor Products) electrically-operated turret (two 0.5in)
11 Elevator torque tube
12 Elevator trim tab
13 Elevator frame (fabric-covered)
14 Rudder trim tab
15 Tab control linkage
16 Rudder post
17 Light-alloy rudder frame
18 HF aerial
19 Fin construction
20 Metal-covered fixed surfaces
21 Tailplane front spar
22 Port elevator push-pull tube
23 Elevator drive quadrant
24 Elevator servo unit
25 Rudder servo unit
26 Ammunition feed track (tail turret)
27 Fuselage aft main frame
28 Walkway
29 Signal cartridges
30 Longitudinal Z-section stringers
31 Control cables
32 Fuselage intermediate secondary frames
33 Ammunition box
34 Aft fuselage camera installation
35 Lower windows
36 Waist gun mounting
37 Starboard manually-operated waist gun (0.5in)
38 Waist position (open)
39 Wind deflector plate
40 Waist position hinged cover
41 Port manually-operated waist gun (0.5in)
42 Dorsal aerial
43 Ball-turret stanchion support beam
44 Ammunition box
45 Ball-turret stanchion
46 Midships window
47 Turret well
48 Cabin floor
49 Tail-bumper operating jack
50 Tail-bumper fairing
51 Briggs-Sperry electrically-operated ball turret (two 0.5in)
51 Turret actuation mechanism
53 Bomb-door actuation sprocket (hydraulically operated)
54 Bomb-door corrugated inner skin
55 Bomb-bay catwalk (box keel)
56 Bomb-bay catwalk vertical channel support members (bomb-release solenoids)
57 Bomb-door actuation track and rollers
58 Wing rear spar
59 Bomb-bay access tunnel
60 Fuselage main frame/bulkhead
61 D/F loop housing
62 Whip aerial

63 Oxygen cylinders
64 Aileron cable drum
65 Starboard flap extension cable
66 Wing rib cut-outs
67 Wing centre-section carry-through
68 Two 5-man inflatable dinghies
69 Flap hydraulic jack
70 Flap/cable attachments
71 Hydraulically-operated Fowler flap
72 Wing rear spar
73 Port mainwheel well and rear fairing
74 Engine supercharger waste-gate
75 Three auxiliary self-sealing fuel cells (port and starboard)
76 Wing outer section
77 Aileron gearboxes
78 Flush-riveted smooth metal wing skinning
79 Port statically-balanced aileron (fabric covered)
80 Port wingtip
81 Port navigation light
82 Wing leading-edge de-icer boot
83 Hopper-type self-sealing oil tank (27.4 gal/125 litres)
84 Engine nacelle
85 1,200 hp Pratt & Whitney Twin Wasp R-1830-65 fourteen-cylinder two-row radial engine
86 Hamilton Standard Hydromatic constant-speed propeller (11ft 7in)
87 Landing/taxiing light
88 Nacelle structure
89 Supercharger duct
90 Self-sealing inter-rib fuel cells (12)

91 Martin electrically-operated dorsal turret (two 0.5in)
92 Turret mechanism
93 Fuselage main frame/bulkhead
94 Radio compartment starboard window
95 Bomb-bary catwalk access trap
96 Radio-operator's position
97 Sound-insulation wall padding
98 Emergency escape hatch
99 Pilot's seat
100 Co-pilot's seat
101 Co-pilot's rudder pedals
102 Instrument panel
103 Windscreen panels
104 Compass housing
105 Control wheel
106 Control wheel mounting
107 Control linkage chain
108 Fuselage forward main frame/bulkhead
109 Pitot heads
110 Navigator's chart table
111 Navigator's compartment starboard window
112 Chart table lighting
113 Astro-dome
114 Consolidated (or Emerson) electrically-operated nose turret (two 0.5in)
115 Turret seating
116 Optically-flat bomb-aiming panel
117 Nose side glazing

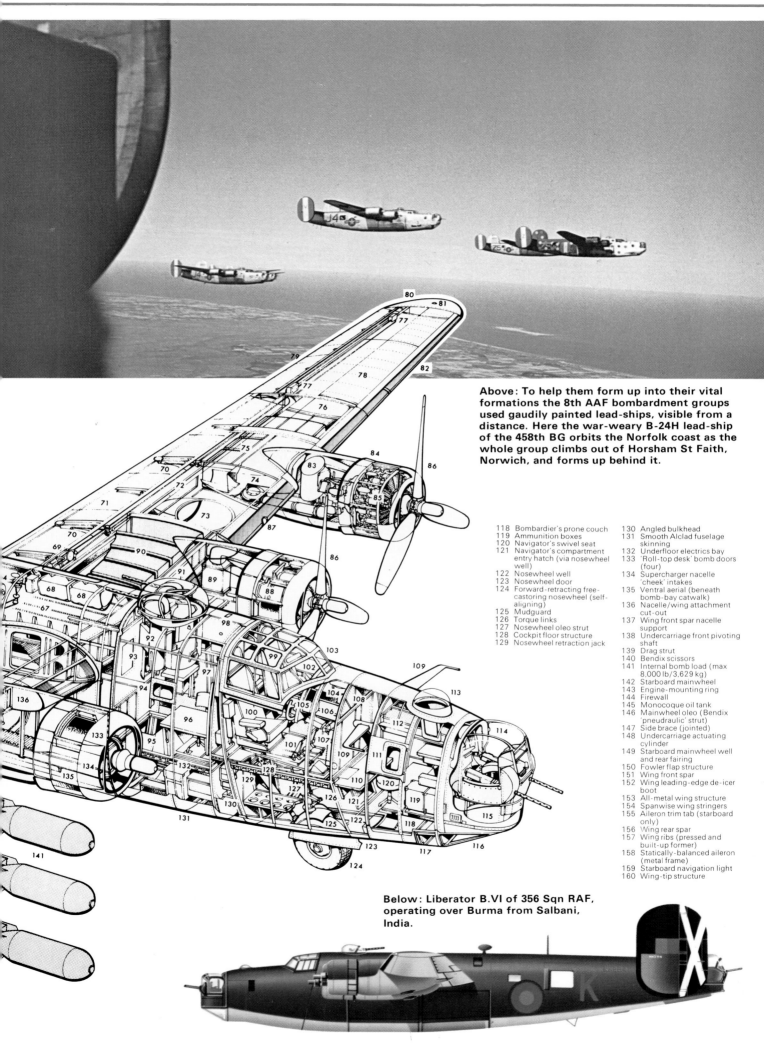

Above: To help them form up into their vital formations the 8th AAF bombardment groups used gaudily painted lead-ships, visible from a distance. Here the war-weary B-24H lead-ship of the 458th BG orbits the Norfolk coast as the whole group climbs out of Horsham St Faith, Norwich, and forms up behind it.

118 Bombardier's prone couch
119 Ammunition boxes
120 Navigator's swivel seat
121 Navigator's compartment entry hatch (via nosewheel well)
122 Nosewheel well
123 Nosewheel door
124 Forward-retracting free-castoring nosewheel (self-aligning)
125 Mudguard
126 Torque links
127 Nosewheel oleo strut
128 Cockpit floor structure
129 Nosewheel retraction jack

130 Angled bulkhead
131 Smooth Alclad fuselage skinning
132 Underfloor electrics bay
133 'Roll-top desk' bomb doors (four)
134 Supercharger nacelle 'cheek' intakes
135 Ventral aerial (beneath bomb-bay catwalk)
136 Nacelle/wing attachment cut-out
137 Wing front spar nacelle support
138 Undercarriage front pivoting shaft
139 Drag strut
140 Bendix scissors
141 Internal bomb load (max 8,000 lb/3,629 kg)
142 Starboard mainwheel
143 Engine-mounting ring
144 Firewall
145 Monocoque oil tank
146 Mainwheel oleo (Bendix 'pneudraulic' strut)
147 Side brace (jointed)
148 Undercarriage actuating cylinder
149 Starboard mainwheel well and rear fairing
150 Fowler flap structure
151 Wing front spar
152 Wing leading-edge de-icer boot
153 All-metal wing structure
154 Spanwise wing stringers
155 Aileron trim tab (starboard only)
156 Wing rear spar
157 Wing ribs (pressed and built-up former)
158 Statically-balanced aileron (metal frame)
159 Starboard navigation light
160 Wing-tip structure

Below: Liberator B.VI of 356 Sqn RAF, operating over Burma from Salbani, India.

Consolidated Vultee
Model 33 B-32 Dominator

XB-32, B-32 and TB-32

Origin: Consolidated Vultee Aircraft Corporation (Convair), Fort Worth, Texas; second-source production by Convair, San Diego.
Type: Long-range strategic bomber; (TB) crew trainer.
Engines: Four 2,300hp Wright R-3350-23 Duplex Cyclone 18-cylinder radials.
Dimensions: Span 135ft 0in (41·15m); length 83ft 1in (25·33m); height 32ft 9in (9·98m).
Weights: Empty 60,272lb (27,340kg); loaded 111,500lb (50,576kg); maximum 120,000lb (54,432kg).
Performance: Maximum speed 365mph (587km/h); service ceiling at normal loaded weight 35,000ft (10,670m); range (max bomb load) 800 miles (1287km), (max fuel) 3,800 miles (6115km).
Armament: (XB) two 20mm and 14 0·50in guns in seven remote-controlled turrets; (B) ten 0·50in in nose, two dorsal, ventral and tail turrets; max bomb load 20,000lb (9072kg) in tandem fuselage bays.
History: First flight (XB) 7 September 1942; service delivery (B) 1 November 1944.
User: USA (AAF).

Development: Ordered in September 1940, a month after the XB-29, the XB-32 was designed to the same Hemisphere Defense Weapon specification and followed similar advanced principles with pressurized cabins and remote-controlled turrets. Obviously related to the smaller B-24, the XB-32 had a slender wing passing above the capacious bomb bays, but the twin-wheel main gears folded into the large inner nacelles. There was a smoothly streamlined nose, like the XB-29, and twin fins. The second aircraft introduced a stepped pilot windscreen and the third a vast single fin like the final B-24 versions. Eventually the heavy and complex armament system was scrapped and replaced by simpler manned turrets, while in late 1943 the decision was taken to eliminate the troublesome pressurization and operate at 30,000ft or below. The B-32 was late and disappointing, though still a great performer. Large orders were placed at Fort Worth and San Diego, but only 115 had been delivered by VJ-day and a single squadron in the Marianas made two combat missions.

Right: It is a reflection on the development problems of the B-32 that roughly half the available photographs show aircraft lacking armament. This picture does depict a fully operational machine with a crew of eight including five gunners each in a powered turret. Propellers were 17ft Curtiss Electrics.

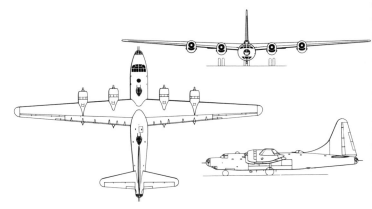

Above: Three-view of B-32 (TB-32 similar).

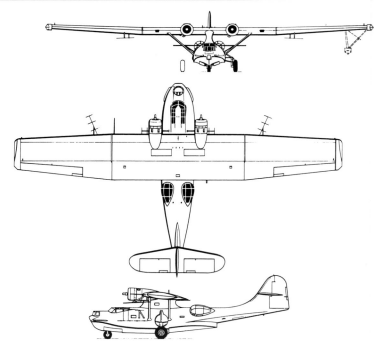

Consolidated Vultee
Model 28 PBY Catalina

PBY-1 to PBY-5A Catalina (data for -5)

Origin: Consolidated Vultee Aircraft Corporation; also made by Naval Aircraft Factory, Canadian Vickers, Boeing Canada, and Soviet Union (Taganrog).
Type: Maritime patrol flying boat with normal crew of seven.
Engines: Two 1,200hp Pratt & Whitney R-1830-92 Twin Wasp 14-cylinder two-row radials.
Dimensions: Span 104ft 0in (31·72m); length 63ft 11in (19·5m); height 18ft 10in (5·65m).
Weights: Empty 17,465lb (7974kg); loaded 34,000lb (15,436kg).
Performance: Maximum speed 196mph (314km/h); climb to 5,000ft (1525m) in 4min 30sec; service ceiling 18,200ft (5550m); range at 100mph (161km/h) 3,100 miles (4960km).
Armament: US Navy, typically one 0·30in or 0·50in Browning in nose, one 0·50in in each waist blister and one in "tunnel" in underside behind hull step; RAF typically six 0·303in Vickers K (sometimes Brownings) arranged one in nose, one in tunnel and pairs in blisters; wing racks for 2,000lb (907kg) of bombs and other stores.
History: First flight (XP3Y-1) 21 March 1935; first delivery (PBY-1) October 1936; (Model 28–5 Catalina) July 1939; final delivery, after December 1945.
Users: Australia, Brazil, Canada, Chile, Netherlands, New Zealand, Norway, Soviet Union, UK (RAF), US (AAF, Navy, Marines), Uruguay.

Development: Consolidated of Buffalo battled with Douglas of Santa Monica in 1933 to supply the US Navy with its first cantilever monoplane flying boat. Though the Douglas was good, its rival, designed by Isaac M. Laddon, was to be a classic aircraft and made in bigger numbers than any other flying boat before or since, by the new plant at San Diego. Its features included two 825hp Twin Wasps mounted close together on a wide clean wing, on the tips of which were to be found the retracted stabilising floats. The XP3Y-1, as it was called, clocked a speed of 184mph, which was high for a 1935 flying boat. The order for 60 was exceptional for those days, but

Above: Three-view of PBY-5A (Catalina IIA and III) with radar.

within a decade the total had topped 4,000. In 1938 three were bought by the Soviet Union, which urgently tooled up to build its own version, called GST, with M62 engines. In 1939 one was bought by the RAF, which soon placed large orders and called the boat Catalina, a name adopted in the USA in 1942. In December 1939 came the PBY-5A (OA-10) with retractable landing gear, which was named Canso by the RCAF. Many hundreds of both the boat and the amphibian were built by Canadian Vickers (as the PBV-1) and Boeing Canada (PB2B-1) and revised tall-fin

Consolidated Vultee PB4Y-2 Privateer

PB4Y-2 (P4Y-2) Privateer

Origin: Consolidated Vultee Aircraft Corporation.
Type: Maritime patrol bomber with normal crew of 11.
Engines: Four 1,200hp Pratt & Whitney R-1830-94 Twin Wasp 14-cylinder two-row radials.
Dimensions: Span 110ft 0in (33·5m); length 74ft 0in (22·6m); height 26ft 1in (7·9m).
Weights: Empty 41,000lb (18,600kg); loaded 65,000lb (29,484kg).
Performance: Maximum speed 247mph (399km/h); initial climb 800ft (244m)/min; service ceiling 19,500ft (5970m); range with maximum ordnance load 2,630 miles (4230km).
Armament: Consolidated nose and tail turrets, two Martin dorsal turrets and two Erco blister-type waist turrets each armed with two 0·50in Brownings; internal bomb bay similar to B-24 accommodating up to 6,000lb (2725kg) bombs, depth charges and other stores. In PB4Y-2B provision to launch and control two ASM-N-2 Bat air-to-surface missiles.
History: First flight (XPB4Y-2) 20 September 1943; first production delivery July 1944; final delivery September 1945.
Users: China, France, US (Navy).

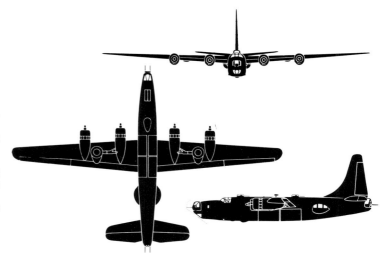

Above: Three-view of PB4Y-2 Privateer.

Development: In May 1943 the US Navy placed a contract with Convair (Consolidated Vultee Aircraft) for a long-range oversea patrol bomber derived from the B-24 Liberator. Three B-24Ds were taken off the San Diego line and largely rebuilt, with fuselages 7ft longer, with completely different interior arrangements, radically altered defensive armament and many airframe changes, such as hot-air de-icing and engine cowlings in the form of vertical ovals instead of flattened horizontal ones. The distinctive vertical tail was similar to that adopted on the final Liberator transport versions (C-87C, RY-3 and RAF C.IX) and much taller than that of the Liberator B-24N. The Navy bought a straight run of 739, of which 286 were delivered in 1944 and 453 in 1945. From the start performance was lower than that of Liberators of equal power because of the bigger and heavier airframe, extra equipment and emphasis on low-level missions. Over the ten years of service the Privateer — called P4Y from 1951 — grew more and more radar and secret countermeasures and finally made long electronic probing flights round (and probably over) the edges of the Soviet Union, at least one being shot down in the process. Over 80 served with the French Aéronavale and Chinese Nationalist Air Force.

Right: The resemblance to a B-24 is superficial; they were in fact totally different aircraft, apart from the basic wing.

Above: Depth-charge attack on a U-boat by an early RAF "Cat" in 1941. This was the year that a Catalina found the Bismarck.

Right: During World War II the PBY served all over the world. This busy mooring operation with the US Navy in 1942 probably took place in the Aleutians, though that is a mere guess from the scenery. Under the right wing are depth bombs.

versions were made at New Orleans (PBY-6A) and by the Naval Aircraft Factory at Philadelphia (PBN-1). The "Cat's" exploits are legion. One found the *Bismarck* in mid-Atlantic; one attacked a Japanese carrier in daylight after radioing: "Please inform next of kin"; in 1942 Patrol Squadron 12 started the Black Cat tradition of stealthy night devastation; and one had both ailerons ripped off by a storm but crossed the Atlantic and landed safely. Hundreds served in many countries for long after World War II.

Consolidated Vultee Model 29 PB2Y Coronado

PB2Y-1 to -5

Origin: Consolidated Aircraft (Consolidated Vultee, or Convair, from March 1943), San Diego, Calif.
Type: Ocean patrol, transport and ambulance flying boat.
Engines: Four 1,200hp Pratt & Whitney R-1830 Twin Wasp 14-cylinder radials (see text).
Dimensions: Span (floats up) 115ft 0in (35·05m); length (all, within 4in) 79ft 3in (24·16m); height 27ft 6in (8·38m).
Weights: Empty (-3) 40,935lb (18,568kg), (-3R) about 33,000lb (14,970kg); maximum (all) 68,000lb (30,845kg).
Performance: Maximum speed (typical) 223mph (359km/h); econ cruise 141mph (227km/h); range with max weapons (-3) 1,370 miles (2204km), (-5) 1,640 miles (2640km); max range (-3) 2,370 miles (3813km), (-5) 3,900 miles (6275km).
Armament: (Except transports) eight 0·5in guns in three power turrets and two manual beam windows; offensive load of up to 8,000lb (3629kg) internal plus 4,000lb (1814kg) external, including torpedoes.
History: First flight 17 December 1937; service delivery 31 December 1940; final delivery October 1943.
Users: UK (RAF), US (Navy).

Development: Few aircraft have been more extensively modified than the XPB2Y-1 in 1937–39, and the production PB2Y-2 of 1940 was again totally

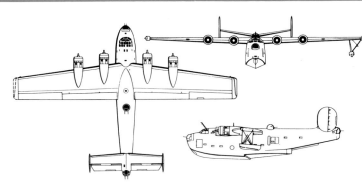

Above: Three-view of PB2Y-3.

different with a vast new hull which nevertheless did not stop it reaching 255mph. The main production run of 210 boats was designated PB2Y-3. The -3B served with RAF Transport Command, the -3R was stripped of military gear and had low-rated R-1830-92 engines giving better low-level performance carrying 44 passengers or 16,000lb cargo, the -5 had more than 60 per cent more fuel and -92 engines, and the -5H was an unarmed ambulance. The Coronado was trusty but rather sluggish, and often needed the takeoff rockets which it pioneered. Most combat-equipped -3 and -5 had ASV radar above the flight deck.

Right: A standard PB2Y-3. Many were converted into -3R transport or -5 radar platforms with extra fuel and low-blown engines.

Curtiss Hawk 75 (P-36 Mohawk), 81 (P-40 Tomahawk), and 87 (P-40 Warhawk, Kittyhawk)

A: Hawk 75A, P-36A, Mohawk IV
B: Hawk 81A, P-40C, Tomahawk IIB
C: Hawk 87D, P-40F, Kittyhawk II
D: Hawk 87M, P-40N, Kittyhawk IV

Origin: Curtiss-Wright Corporation.
Type: (A) single-seat fighter, (B) single-seat fighter, reconnaissance and ground attack; (C, D) single-seat fighter bomber.
Engine: (A) P-36A, 1,050hp Pratt & Whitney R-1830-13 Twin Wasp 14-cylinder two-row radial; Hawk 75A and Mohawk, 1,200hp Wright GR-1820-G205A Cyclone nine-cylinder radial; (B) 1,040hp Allison V-1710-33 vee-12 liquid-cooled; (C) 1,300hp Packard V-1650-1 (R-R Merlin) vee-12 liquid-cooled; (D) 1,200hp Allison V-1710-81, -99 or -115 vee-12 liquid-cooled.
Dimensions: Span 37ft 3½in (11·36m); length (A) 28ft 7in (8·7m), (B) 31ft 8½in (9·7m); (C) 31ft 2in (9·55m) or 33ft 4in (10·14m); (D) 33ft 4in (10·14m); height (A) 9ft 6in (2·89m), (B, C, D) 12ft 4in (3·75m).
Weights: Empty (A) 4,541lb (2060kg) (B) 5,812lb (2636kg), (C) 6,550lb (2974kg), (D) 6,700lb (3039kg); loaded (A) 6,662lb (3020kg), (B) 7,459lb (3393kg), (C) 8,720lb (3960kg), (D) 11,400lb (5008kg).
Performance: Maximum speed (A) 303mph (488km/h), (B) 345mph (555km/h), (C) 364mph (582km/h), (D) 343mph (552km/h); initial climb (A) 2,500ft (762m)/min, (B) 2,650ft (807m)/min, (C) 2,400ft (732m)/min, (D) 2,120ft (646m)/min; service ceiling (all) about 30,000ft (9144m); range on internal fuel (A) 680 miles (1,100km), (B) 730 miles (1175km), (C) 610 miles (976km), (D) 750 miles (1207km).

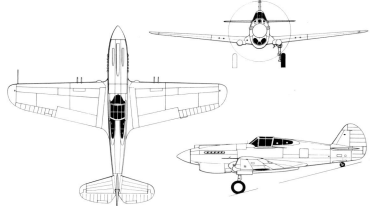

Above: Three-view of P-40C (Tomahawk similar).

Right: The middle-vintage Kittyhawks, roughly equivalent to the P-40D to N, were the most important fighter-bombers of the British Commonwealth air forces in the period from Alamein (October 1942) to the end of the war in northern Italy. Over 3,000 were in use, two of them being these Kittyhawk IIIs seen returning from a bombing mission in North Africa in early 1943. The ground-guidance "erk" had a rough ride.

Left: The Hawk 75C-1, equivalent to a P-36C or Mohawk, wrote a glorious chapter in Armée de l'Air service in 1939-40. Unlike many French programmes, the Hawk was delivered on time, and its crews were trained and capable in the nation's hour of need (but it had a hard time against the Bf 109E).

Left: This Tomahawk (British P-40C) is seen in the markings of No 349 (Belgian) Sqn, RAF, at Ikeja, West Africa, in early 1943.

Armament: (A) P-36A, one 0·50in and one 0·30in Brownings above engine; P-36C, as P-36A with two 0·30in in wings; Hawk 75A/Mohawk IV, six 0·303in (four in wings); (B) six 0·303in (four in wings); (C, D) six 0·50in in wings with 281 rounds per gun (early P-40N, only four); bomb load (A) underwing racks for total of 400lb (181kg); (B) nil; (C) one 500lb on centreline and 250lb (113kg) under each wing; (D) 500 or 600lb (272kg) on centreline and 500lb under each wing.

History: First flight (Model 75 prototype) May 1935; (first Y1P-36) January 1937; (first production P-36A) April 1938; (XP-40) October 1938; (P-40) January 1940; (P-40D) 1941; (P-40F) 1941; (P-40N) 1943; final delivery (P-40N-40 and P-40R) December 1944.

Users: Argentina, Australia, Belgium, Bolivia, Brazil, Canada, China,

Colombia, Egypt, Finland, France, Iraq, Italy (CB), Netherlands, New Zealand, Norway, Peru, Portugal, S. Africa, Soviet Union, Turkey, UK (RAF), US (AAC/AAF).

Development: In November 1934 Curtiss began the design of a completely new "Hawk" fighter with cantilever monoplane wing, backwards retracting landing gear (the wheels turning 90° to lie inside the wing) and all-metal stressed-skin construction. After being tested by the Army Air Corps this design was put into production as the P-36A, marking a major advance in speed though not in firepower. Successive types of P-36 and its export counterpart, the Hawk 75A, had different engines and additional guns and

continued on page 212▶

▶the Hawk 75A was bought in large numbers by many countries and made under licence in several. Biggest customer was the French Armée de l'Air, which began to receive the H75A in March 1939. Five groups – GC I/4, II/4, I/5, II/5 and III/2 – wrote a glorious chapter over France in May 1940, invariably outnumbered and usually outperformed, but destroying 311 of the Luftwaffe, more than the total H75A strength when France fell. The rest of the French orders were supplied to the RAF as Mohawks, serving mainly on the Burma front.

More than 1,300 radial-engined models were delivered, but the real story began with the decision in July 1937 to build the P-40, with the liquid-cooled Allison engine. This was a novel and untried engine in a land where aircraft engines had become universally air-cooled, and teething troubles were long and severe. Eventually, towards the end of 1940, the P-40B and RAF Tomahawk I were cleared for combat duty and the process of development began. The rest of the aircraft was almost unchanged and in comparison with the Bf109 or Spitfire the early P-40 showed up badly, except in the twin attributes of manoeuvrability and strong construction. Eventually the RAF, RAAF and SAAF took 885 of three marks of Tomahawk, used as low-level army co-operation machines in Britain and as ground

Left: Field maintenance on a P-40F Warhawk, probably in Tunisia or Sicily. This model had the Packard V-1650 (Merlin) with updraught carburettor (hence no duct above the cowling).

Below: The cutaway depicts the Hawk 75A-2 as used by the Armée de l'Air in 1940 and by Commonwealth air forces as various marks of Mohawk. The A-2 model, first ordered in January 1939, had two extra wing guns. Not all radial Hawks had the Twin Wasp; many used the single-row Cyclone.

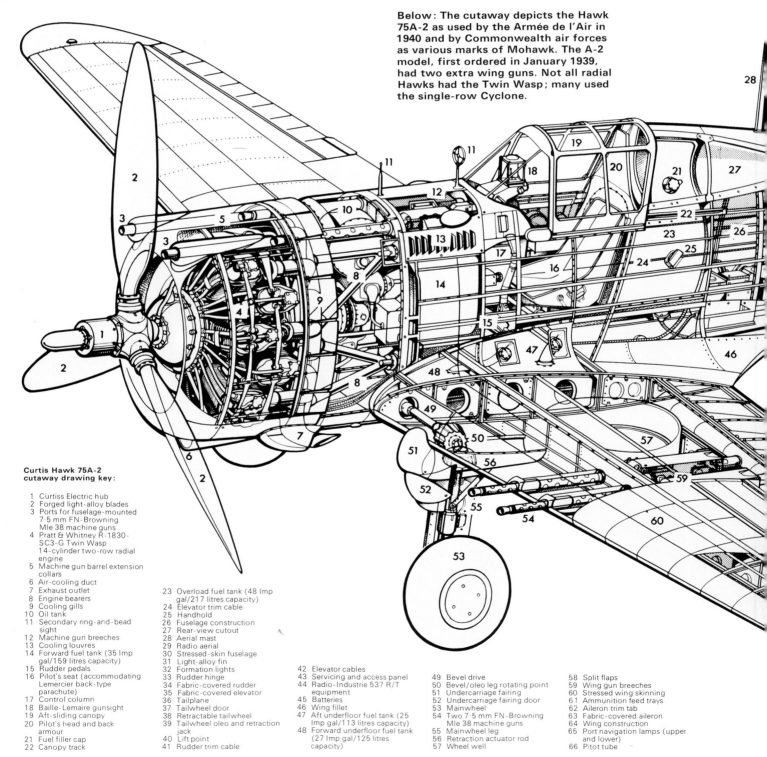

Curtis Hawk 75A-2 cutaway drawing key:

1 Curtiss Electric hub
2 Forged light-alloy blades
3 Ports for fuselage-mounted 7·5 mm FN-Browning Mle 38 machine guns
4 Pratt & Whitney R-1830-SC3-G Twin Wasp 14-cylinder two-row radial engine
5 Machine gun barrel extension collars
6 Air-cooling duct
7 Exhaust outlet
8 Engine bearers
9 Cooling gills
10 Oil tank
11 Secondary ring-and-bead sight
12 Machine gun breeches
13 Cooling louvres
14 Forward fuel tank (35 Imp gal/159 litres capacity)
15 Rudder pedals
16 Pilot's seat (accommodating Lemercier back-type parachute)
17 Control column
18 Baille-Lemaire gunsight
19 Aft-sliding canopy
20 Pilot's head and back armour
21 Fuel filler cap
22 Canopy track

23 Overload fuel tank (48 Imp gal/217 litres capacity)
24 Elevator trim cable
25 Handhold
26 Fuselage construction
27 Rear-view cutout
28 Aerial mast
29 Radio aerial
30 Stressed-skin fuselage
31 Light-alloy fin
32 Formation lights
33 Rudder hinge
34 Fabric-covered rudder
35 Fabric-covered elevator
36 Tailplane
37 Tailwheel door
38 Retractable tailwheel
39 Tailwheel oleo and retraction jack
40 Lift point
41 Rudder trim cable

42 Elevator cables
43 Servicing and access panel
44 Radio-Industrie 537 R/T equipment
45 Batteries
46 Wing fillet
47 Aft underfloor fuel tank (25 Imp gal/113 litres capacity)
48 Forward underfloor fuel tank (27 Imp gal/125 litres capacity)

49 Bevel drive
50 Bevel/oleo leg rotating point
51 Undercarriage fairing
52 Undercarriage fairing door
53 Mainwheel
54 Two 7·5 mm FN-Browning Mle 38 machine guns
55 Mainwheel leg
56 Retraction actuator rod
57 Wheel well

58 Split flaps
59 Wing gun breeches
60 Stressed wing skinning
61 Ammunition feed trays
62 Aileron trim tab
63 Fabric-covered aileron
64 Wing construction
65 Port navigation lamps (upper and lower)
66 Pitot tube

attack fighters in North Africa. Many hundreds of other P-40Bs and Cs were supplied to the US Army, Soviet Union, China and Turkey.

With the P-40D a new series of Allison engines allowed the nose to be shortened and the radiator was deepened, changing the appearance of the aircraft. The fuselage guns were finally thrown out and the standard armament became the much better one of six "fifties" in the wings. The RAF had ordered 560 of the improved fighters in 1940, and they were called Kittyhawk I. When the US Army bought it the name Warhawk was given to subsequent P-40 versions. The Merlin engine went into production in the USA in 1941 and gave rise to the P-40F; none of the 1,311 Merlin P-40s reached the RAF, most going to the Soviet Union, US Army and Free French. Most Fs introduced a longer fuselage to improve directional stability. Subsequent models had a dorsal fin as well and reverted to the Allison engine. Great efforts were made to reduce weight and improve performance, because the whole family was fundamentally outclassed by the other front-line fighters on both sides; but, predictably, weight kept rising. It reached its peak in the capable and well-equipped P-40N, of which no fewer than 4,219 were built. Some of the early Ns had all the weight-savings and could reach 378mph (608km/h), but they were exceptions. Altogether deliveries of P-40 versions to the US government amounted to 13,738. Though it was foolhardy to tangle with a crack enemy fighter in close combat the Hawk family were tough, nimble and extremely useful weapons, especially in close support of armies.

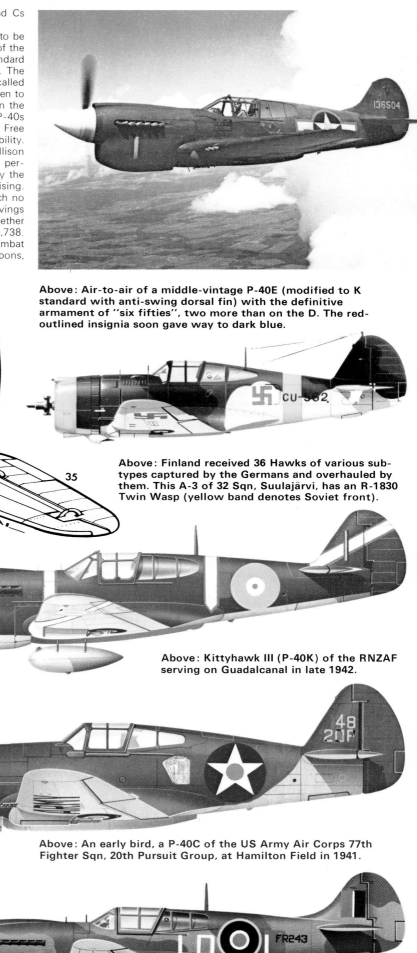

Above: Air-to-air of a middle-vintage P-40E (modified to K standard with anti-swing dorsal fin) with the definitive armament of "six fifties", two more than on the D. The red-outlined insignia soon gave way to dark blue.

Above: Finland received 36 Hawks of various sub-types captured by the Germans and overhauled by them. This A-3 of 32 Sqn, Suulajärvi, has an R-1830 Twin Wasp (yellow band denotes Soviet front).

Above: Kittyhawk III (P-40K) of the RNZAF serving on Guadalcanal in late 1942.

Above: An early bird, a P-40C of the US Army Air Corps 77th Fighter Sqn, 20th Pursuit Group, at Hamilton Field in 1941.

Above: Another long-fuselage Kittyhawk III, this time serving with 250 Sqn of the RAF in southern Italy in 1943-44.

Curtiss C-46 Commando

C-46A, D, E and F and R5C

Origin: Curtiss-Wright Corporation, Buffalo, NY; production at St Louis, Mo, and Louisville, Ky.
Type: Troop and cargo transport.
Engines: (A, D) two 2,000hp Pratt & Whitney R-2800-51 Double Wasp 18-cylinder radials, (E, F) 2,200hp R-2800-75.
Dimensions: Span 108ft 1in (32·92m); length 76ft 4in (23·27m); height 21ft 9in (6·63m).
Weights: Empty (A) 29,483lb (13,373kg); maximum (A) 50,000lb (22,680 kg).
Performance: Cruising speed (67 per cent) 227mph (365km/h), (econ) 193mph (31·1km/h); max range (no fuselage tanks) 1,600 miles (2575km), (max payload) 890 miles (1432km).
History: First flight 26 March 1940; service delivery (C-46) October 1941; final delivery 1945.
Users: (WWII) UK (BOAC), US (AAF, Navy).

Development: In 1936 Curtiss-Wright planned an exceptionally large and capable twin-engined airliner, of modern stressed-skin type, to try to recover its airline sales that had been swept away by the new monoplanes from Boeing, Lockheed and Douglas. In 1940 the CW-20 impressed not only airlines but also the US Army, and it was totally redesigned as a military transport. The sumptuous pressurized fuselage was replaced by an un-pressurized one with large doors and strong floor; twin fins became one, the R-2600 engines became more powerful R-2800s and the whole machine was tailored to quick production and troublefree service. By 1945 about 3,330 of these extremely useful aircraft had been delivered, almost all as

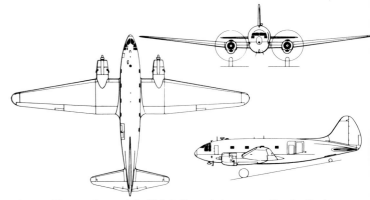

Above: Three-view of C-46A (all models generally similar).

various C-46 models but 160 being Navy R5C-1. Carrying up to 40 passengers or about 12,000lb (5440kg) of cargo, they were the mainliners of the "Hump" airlift to China, and by late 1944 were also numerous in Europe, taking part in the Rhine crossing. Though Curtiss never did achieve the civil sales they sought, the ex-wartime C-46 was destined to play a major role in outback nations right up to the present day, about 140 still being in daily use in Latin America.

Right: One of the first C-46As to be delivered to the US Army in 1941. Later blocks were unpainted and had numerous minor improvements. The RAF used a converted bomber, the Warwick, as a transport with half the capacity but the same engines.

Curtiss SB2C/A-25 Helldiver

SB2C-1 to -5 (data for -1)

Origin: Curtiss-Wright Corporation; also built by Fairchild and Canadian Car & Foundry (CanCar).
Type: Two-seat carrier-based dive bomber.
Engine: 1,700hp Wright R-2600-8 Cyclone 14-cylinder two-row radial.
Dimensions: Span 49ft 9in (15·2m); length 36ft 8in (11·2m); height 16ft 11in (5·1m).
Weights: Empty 11,000lb (4990kg); loaded 16,607lb (7550kg).
Performance: Maximum speed 281mph (452km/h); service ceiling 24,700ft (7530m); range 1,110 miles (1786km).
Armament: Two 20mm or four 0·50in guns in wings and two 0·30in or one 0·50in in rear cockpit; provision for 1,000lb (454kg) bomb load internally (later versions added wing racks).
History: First flight (XSB2C-1) 18 December 1940; (production SB2C-1) June 1942; termination of production 1945.
Users: US (AAF, Navy, Marines).

Development: During World War II, by far the most successful Allied dive bomber was the Helldiver, which perpetuated a Curtiss trade-name established with a biplane dive bomber used by the US Navy as the SBC series and, briefly, by the RAF as the Cleveland. The new monoplane was a totally different design, with very powerful engine, large folding wing and internal bomb bay. Yet development took a long time, partly because the prototype crashed but mainly because the US services asked for 880 further major design changes after the SB2C-1 had been frozen for production in November 1941. This was partly for Army/Navy/Marine Corps standardization, the Army/Marines aircraft being called A-25 Shrike or SB2C-1A. Eventually production rolled ahead at Curtiss, at Fairchild (who built SBFs) and Canadian Car & Foundry (who made SBWs). Altogether 7,200 Helldivers were delivered, roughly equally divided between the -1, -3, -4 and -5 subtypes. The -2 was a twin-float seaplane. From Rabaul in November 1943 Helldivers fought hard and effectively in every major action of the Pacific war.

Right: This Helldiver sub-type about to recover aboard its flat-top is probably a -3 (SB2C-3, SBF-3 or SBW-3). Total -3 production was 1,112, compared with 978 -1, 2,045 -4 and 970 -5.

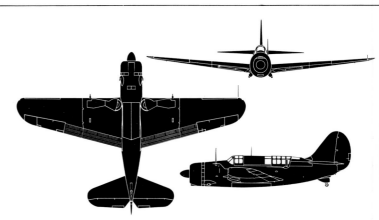

Above: Three-view of SB2C-4 (most sub-types generally similar).

Left: This SB2C-1 was assigned to squadron VB-8 (heavier-than-air bomber, No 8) of the US Navy, embarked aboard carriers in the Saipan campaign (indeed, it saw action in most Pacific battles).

Right: The 20mm cannon muzzle immediately outboard of the landing-gear leg proclaims this Helldiver to be a -3 or later model. On land airfields the high-pressure tyres and hard-rubber tailwheel could cause problems; this single engined aircraft had a gross weight similar to that of many twins.

Douglas DB-7 family
A-20, Boston, Havoc

A-20, Boston, Havoc, BD-2, F-3 and P-70

Origin: Douglas Aircraft Company; (Boston IIIA, Boeing Airplane Company).

Type: Two-seat fighter and intruder, three-seat bomber or two-seat reconnaissance aircraft.

Engines: Early DB-7 versions (Boston I, II, Havoc II) two 1,200hp Pratt & Whitney R-1830-S3C4-G Twin Wasp 14-cylinder two-row radials; all later versions, two 1,500, 1,600 or 1,700hp Wright GR-2600-A5B, -11, -23 or -29 Double Cyclone 14-cylinder two-row radials.

Dimensions: Span 61ft 4in (18·69m); length varied from 45ft 11in to 48ft 10in (A-20G, 48ft 4in, 14·74m); height 17ft 7in (5·36m).

Weights: Early Boston/Havoc, typically empty 11,400lb (5171kg), loaded 16,700lb (7574kg); (A-20G, typical of main production) empty 12,950lb (5874kg), loaded 27,200lb (12,340kg).

Performance: Maximum speed, slowest early versions 295mph (475km/h); fastest versions 351mph (565km/h); (A-20G) 342mph (549km/h); initial climb 1,200–2,000ft (366–610m)/min; service ceiling typically 25,300ft (7720m); range with maximum weapon load typically 1,000 miles (1,610km).

Armament: (Havoc I), eight 0·303in Brownings in nose, one 0·303in Vickers K manually aimed in rear cockpit; (Havoc II) twelve 0·303in in nose, (Havoc intruder), four 0·303in in nose, one Vickers K, and 1,000lb (454kg) bomb load; (A-20B) two fixed 0·5in Brownings on sides of nose, one 0·5in manually aimed dorsal, one 0·30in manually aimed ventral, 2,000lb (907kg) bomb load; (Boston III bomber) four fixed 0·303in on sides of nose, twin manually aimed 0·303in dorsal, twin manually aimed 0·303in ventral, 2,000lb (907kg) bomb load; (Boston III intruder) belly tray of four 20mm Hispano cannon, 2,000lb (907kg) bomb load; (A-20G) four 20mm and two 0·5in or six 0·5in in nose, dorsal turret with two 0·5in, manually aimed 0·5in ventral, 4,000lb (1814kg) bomb load. Many other schemes, early A-20s having fixed rearward firing 0·30in in each nacelle.

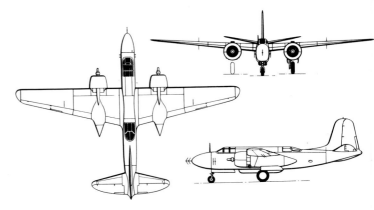

Above: Three-view of P-70 with four M-2 cannon and AI.IV radar.

History: First flight (Douglas 7B) 26 October 1938; (production DB-7) 17 August 1939; service delivery (France) 2 January 1940; termination of production September 1944.

Users: Australia, Brazil, Canada, France, Netherlands, New Zealand, South Africa, Soviet Union, UK (RAF), US (AAC/AAF, Navy).

Development: Designed by Jack Northrop and Ed Heinemann, the DB-7 family was one of the great combat aircraft of all time. Originally planned to meet a US Army Air Corps attack specification of 1938, it was dramatically altered and given more powerful Twin Wasp engines and a nosewheel-type landing gear (for the first time in a military aircraft). In February 1939 the French government ordered 100 of a further modified type, with deeper but narrower fuselage and other gross changes. This model, the DB-7, went into production at El Segundo and Santa Monica, with 1,764lb (800kg) bomb load and armament of six 7·5mm MAC 1934 machine guns. Delivery took place via Casablanca and about 100 reached the Armée de l'Air, beginning operations on 31 May 1940. Much faster than other bombers, the DB-7 was judged "hot", because it was a modern aircraft in an environment of small unpaved airfields and because it was very different, and more complex, than contemporary European machines. One unusual feature was the emergency control column in the rear gunner's cockpit for use if the pilot should be killed. A few DB-7s escaped to Britain, where most of the French order was diverted (increased to 270 by 1940), and over 100 were converted at Burtonwood, Lancs, into Havoc night fighters. Many Havocs had 2,700-million candlepower "Turbinlites" in the nose for finding enemy raiders by night, while 93 Sqn towed Long Aerial Mine charges on steel cables. In February 1942 the RAF began operations with the much more powerful Boston III; making daring daylight low-level raids over Europe, while production of the first US Army A-20s got into its stride. By far the most important model was the A-20G, with heavier bomb load, dorsal turret and devastating nose armament. Among many other important US Army versions were the P-70 night fighters and the transparent-nosed A-20J and K, often used as bombing lead ships by the 9th and 15th Air Forces (respectively in Northwest Europe and Italy). The RAF counterparts of the J and K were the Boston IV and V, of the 2nd Tactical Air Force and Desert AF (Italy). Total production of this hard-hitting aircraft was 7,385, of which 3,125 were supplied freely to the Soviet Union.

Above: There were many intruder sub-types. This is an early P-70A with the nose armament later fitted to some A-20G attack bombers: four 20mm M-2 cannon. This example has no radar.

Below: A-20G attack bomber, in 9th Air Force insignia, with twin-0·5in turret.

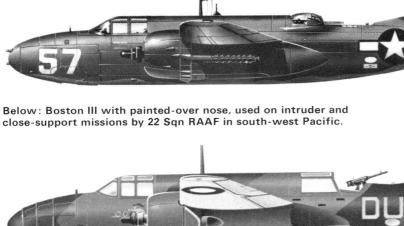

Below: Boston III with painted-over nose, used on intruder and close-support missions by 22 Sqn RAAF in south-west Pacific.

Below: This Havoc I, of 23 Sqn, RAF, based at Ford, Sussex, in 1940, is the oldest aircraft depicted on this spread. Visually distinguished by having the original smaller vertical tail, it has the lower-powered Twin Wasp engines without the night flame-suppressing exhaust later developed. This was a bomber-intruder; other Havoc Is had cannon instead.

Below: A Boston IIIA of 88 Sqn, RAF, operating with 2nd TAF in France, 1944.

Below: Skip-bombing by 5th Air Force A-20s on a Japanese freighter.

Above: A squadron of Boston III attack bombers of the RAF over North Africa.

Below: The A-20J and K were fitted with glazed noses as bombardier lead-ships.

Douglas A-26 Invader

A-26 (later B-26) and JD-1 Invader; rebuilt as B-26K, redesignated A-26A

Origin: Douglas Aircraft Company; (post-war B-26K) On Mark Engineering.
Type: Three-seat attack bomber; FA-26 reconnaissance, JD target tug.
Engines: Two 2,000hp Pratt & Whitney R-2800-27, -71 or -79 Double Wasp 18-cylinder two-row radials; On Mark B-26K, 2,500hp R-2800-103W.
Dimensions: Span 70ft (21·34m) (B-26K, 75ft, 22·86m, over tip tanks); length 50ft (15·24m); height 18ft 6in (5·64m).
Weights: Empty, typically 22,370lb (10,145kg); loaded, originally 27,000lb (12,247kg) with 32,000lb (14,515kg) maximum overload, later increased to 35,000lb (15,876kg) with 38,500lb (17,460kg) maximum overload.
Performance: Maximum speed 355mph (571km/h); initial climb 2,000ft (610m)/min; service ceiling 22,100ft (6736m); range with maximum bomb load 1,400 miles (2253km).
Armament: (A-26B) ten 0·5in Brownings, six fixed in nose and two each in dorsal and ventral turrets; internal bomb load of 4,000lb (1814kg), later supplemented by underwing load of up to 2,000lb (907kg); (A-26C) similar but only two 0·5in in nose; (B-26K, A-26A) various nose configurations with up to eight 0·5in or four 20mm, plus six 0·30in guns in wings and total ordnance load of 8,000lb (3629kg) in bomb bay and on eight outerwing pylons.
History: First flight (XA-26) 10 July 1942; service delivery December 1943; final delivery 2 January 1946; first flight of B-26K, February 1963.
Users: US (AAF, Navy).

Development: The Douglas Invader has a unique history. It was one of very few aircraft to be entirely conceived, designed, developed, produced in quantity and used in large numbers all during World War II. The whole programme was terminated after VJ-Day and anyone might have judged the aircraft finished. With new jets under development, Douglas made no effort to retain any design team on Invader development, neither did the Army Air Force show any interest. Yet this aircraft proved to be of vital importance in the Korean war and again in Vietnam and, by 1963, was urgently being manufactured for arduous front-line service. Some were in combat units 33 years after they were first delivered, a record no other kind of aircraft can equal. The design was prepared by Ed Heinemann at El Segundo as a natural successor to the DB-7 family, using the powerful new R-2800 engine. The Army Air Corps ordered three prototypes in May 1941, one with 75mm gun, one with four 20mm forward-firing cannon and four 0·5in guns in an upper turret, with radar nose, and the third as an attack bomber with optical sighting station in the nose and two defensive turrets. In the event it was the bomber that was bought first, designated A-26B. Much faster than other tactical bombers with the exception of the Mosquito, it was 700lb lighter than estimate, and capable of carrying twice the specified bomb load. It was the first bomber to use a NACA laminar-flow airfoil, double-slotted flaps and remote-control turrets (also a feature of the B-29). Combat missions with the 9th AF began on 19 November 1944 and these aircraft dropped over 18,000 tons of bombs on European targets. A total of 1,355 A-26Bs were delivered, the last 535 having -79 engines boosted by water injection. The A-26C, in service in January 1945, had a transparent nose, lead-ship navigational equipment and was often fitted with H₂S panoramic radar; production of this model was 1,091. In 1948 the B-26 Marauder was retired from service and the Invaders were redesignated B-26. Over 450 were used in Korea, and in Vietnam these fine

Above: Three-view of the much later B-26K.

aircraft were one of the most favoured platforms for night attack on the Ho Chi Minh trail and in other interdiction areas. Though top speed was depressed to about 350mph, the A-26A (as the rebuilt B-26K was called) could carry up to 11,000lb (4990kg) of armament and deliver it accurately and, with 2 hr over target, over a wide radius. In 1977 six air forces retained Invader squadrons.

Above: Just over 1,000 of these glazed-nose A-26C Invaders were delivered, with a bombardier and two 0·5in guns in the glazed nose for visual bombing at all levels and lead-ship duties with formations of "solid-nose" A-26B Invaders.

Below: The A-26B was the chief model used in both the European and Pacific theatres in World War II. The devastating nose armament could be augmented by locking the remote-control upper turret to fire dead ahead. The A-26 suffered the lowest loss rate of any bomber in the European theatre.

Douglas B-18 Bolo, Digby

B-18, B-18A Bolo and Digby I

Origin: Douglas Aircraft Company.
Type: Heavy bomber (later maritime patrol) aircraft, with normal crew of six.
Engines: Two 930hp Wright R-1820-45 or -53 Cyclone nine-cylinder radials.
Dimensions: Span 89ft 0in (27·3m); length 57ft 10in (17·63m); height 15ft 2in (4·62m).
Weights: Empty 19,700lb (8936kg); loaded 27,673lb (12,550kg).
Performance: Maximum speed 215mph (349km/h); service ceiling 23,900ft (7285m); range with maximum bomb load 1,180 miles (1900km).
Armament: Normally one 0·30in Browning machine gun in nose, dorsal and retractable ventral positions, all aimed manually; internal bomb load of up to 4,000lb (1814kg).
History: First flight (DB-1) October 1935; service delivery (B-18) 1937; (B-18A) 1939.
Users: Brazil, Canada, US (AAC/AAF).

Development: In 1934 the United States Army issued a requirement for a new bomber to replace the Martin B-10. Martin entered an improved B-10, Boeing the four-engined Model 299 and Douglas the DB-1 (Douglas Bomber 1). It was the last-named which won and nobody at the time expected that, whereas the Douglas would have a short career and soon be forgotten, the controversial Boeing giant would become perhaps the most famous bomber in history. Douglas were awarded an immediate contract for the unprecedented number (since 1918, at least) of 133 aircraft, designated B-18. Based on the DC-2 transport, the B-18 had a fat body bulged under the wing to accommodate an internal bomb bay. Orders were later placed for a further 217 modified aircraft designated B-18A, plus a

Above: A brave pre-war sight, a squadron of B-18 heavy bombers captured in one of the first air-to-air colour photographs.

further 20 for the Royal Canadian Air Force called Digby (after the British bomber airfield). In 1937–40 this family was the most important heavy warplane in North America, but after that it faded rapidly. No big orders were placed by France or Britain, as was the case with all the newer American bombers, and the B-17 gradually replaced the B-18 in US Army bombardment squadrons. In 1941 122 B-18As were converted as antisubmarine patrol aircraft, with a large nose radome and the first MAD installation projecting behind the tail, for use in the Caribbean and off the east coast of the United States. The Digbys were also used for maritime duties until 1943. A few B-18s were later converted for use as business aircraft and several even remain in various types of civilian use.

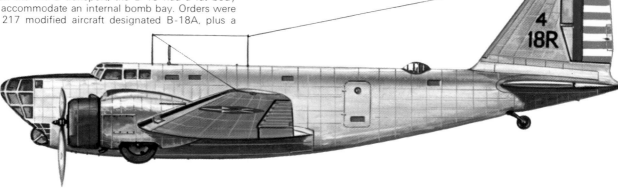

Right: The B-18A had a different nose, increased weight and other changes. Mainly assigned to the 5th and 11th Bombardment Groups, their cowls were coloured to denote the squadron.

Douglas DC-4 C-54 Skymaster

C-54A to J, R5D-1 to -6

Origin: Douglas Aircraft Company, Santa Monica.
Type: Strategic transport.
Engines: Four 1,350hp Pratt & Whitney R-2000-7 Twin Wasp 14-cylinder radials, (from late batches C-54D/R5D-3) R-2000-11, better altitude performance.
Dimensions: Span 117ft 6in (35·81m); length 93ft 11in (28·63m); height 27ft 6¼in (8·39m).
Weights: Empty (B) 38,200lb (17,328kg); maximum (B) 73,000lb (33,113kg).
Performance: Max cruise at optimum height 239mph (385km/h); max range with max useful load 1,500 miles (2414km); max range with max fuel 3,900 miles (6276km) at 190mph (306km/h).
History: First flight (prototype) 21 June 1938, (production C-54) 14 February 1942; final delivery (civil) post-war.
Users: (WWII) UK (RAF), US (AAF, Navy).

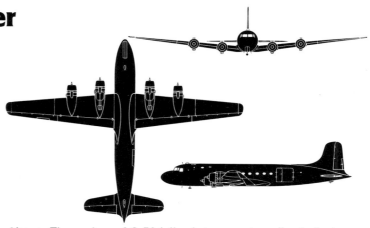

Above: Three-view of C-54 (all sub-types externally similar).

Development: The pre-war DC-4 did not prove a success, and eventually was sold to Japan (see Nakajima G5N), but in 1940 Douglas cut the DC-4 down in size and simplified it to produce a much better transport. In 1941 the production batch was taken over by the Army, and again altered for military use. Thus the first off the production line (there was no prototype of the new design) flew in olive drab. Ultimately 1,242 of these excellent machines were built, all having large freight doors and strong floors, about 44 removable seats, glider tow cleats and military gear throughout. The B had integral outer-wing tanks, the C was a VIP machine with electric hoist for President Roosevelt's wheelchair, and later marks (made mainly at Chicago) were convertible to several roles. Canadian Vickers bought a manufacturing licence, became Canadair in 1944 and finally built their DC-4s with Merlin engines. Post-war military versions took model sub-types up to C-54T, all rebuilds.

Right: Except for early production blocks, which were olive drab, all C-54s were delivered in shining metal finish, save only for the prominent black rubber de-icer boots on leading edges.

Douglas military DC-3 (C-47, Skytrain, Dakota)

C-47 and AC-47, R4D, C-53, Dakota, C-117, L2D and Li-2

Origin: Douglas Aircraft Company; built under licence by Showa and Nakajima, Japan, and (under direction of Lisunov bureau) Soviet Union.
Type: Utility transport (formerly also paratroop/glider tug): AC-47 air/ground weapon platform.
Engines: Usually two 1,200hp Pratt & Whitney R-1830-90D or -92 Twin Wasp 14-cylinder two-row radials; (C-117D) two 1,535hp Wright R-1820-80 Cyclone nine-cylinder radials; (Li-2) two 1,000hp M-62IR (Cyclone-derived) nine-cylinder radials; (L2D) two 1,050 or 1,300hp Mitsubishi Ki-43 or Ki-51 Kinsei 14-cylinder radials.
Dimensions: Span 95ft (28·96m); length 64ft 5½in (19·64m); height 16ft 11in (5·16m).
Weights: Empty, about 16,970lb (7700kg); loaded about 25,200lb (11,432kg); overload limit 33,000lb (14,969kg).
Performance: Maximum speed about 230mph (370km/h); initial climb, about 1,200ft (366m)/min; service ceiling 23,000ft (7000m); maximum range 2,125 miles (3420km).
Armament: (AC-47) usually three 7·62mm Miniguns; many other types of armament in other versions but none usually fitted.

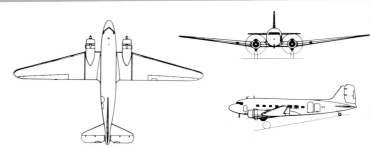

Above: Three-view of typical C-47 (all generally similar).

History: First flight (DST) 17 December 1935; first service delivery (C-41) October 1938.
Users: Australia, Bolivia, Brazil, China, France, Japan, New Zealand, South Africa, Soviet Union, UK (RAF, BOAC), US (AAC/AAF, Navy, Marines).

Development: When, in 1935, Douglas designer Arthur E. Raymond planned the Douglas Sleeper Transport (DST) as an enlarged and improved DC-2, he little thought that, as well as becoming the worldwide standard airliner of its day, it would be by far the most widely used military transport in history. During World War II there were numerous versions, some civil aircraft impressed into military use, some paratroopers and tugs and the vast majority utility C-47 versions with a strong cargo floor and large double doors. Oddities included a glider and a twin-float amphibian. US military production totalled 10,048 by June 1945, followed by small batches of redesigned Super DC-3 versions including the R4D-8 and C-117. Showa and Nakajima in Japan built about 571 of the L2D family and in the Soviet Union production of the Li-2 (with door on the right) is estimated to have exceeded 2,700. Many hundreds of these aircraft, most of them C-47s, remain in daily use in almost every air force (the RAF retired its last in 1970). Many serve as platforms for research projects and countermeasures and in Vietnam the AC-47 — called "Puff the Magic Dragon" — was developed in several versions to deliver suppressive fire against ground targets. Other important variants are the EC-47 series used for multi-spectral sensing and electronic reconnaissance.

Left: The C-47 in all versions was supremely reliable, and it had excellent wheelbrakes, but it needed two pilots to taxi safely in confined areas. Wheels-up landings were "a piece of cake".

Right: Old colour film plays tricks with shades, but there were two distinct olive shades for AAF transports, this C-47B Skytrain having the brown one. Engines were R-1830-90C.

Douglas SBD/A-24 Dauntless

SBD, A-24 Dauntless

Origin: Douglas Aircraft Company.
Type: Two-seat carrier-based (SBD) or land-based (A-24) dive bomber.
Engine: One 1,000hp Wright R-1820-32 or -52 or 1,200hp R-1820-60 or -66 Cyclone nine-cylinder radial.
Dimensions: Span 41ft 6in (12·65m); length 33ft (10·06m); height 12ft 11in (3·94m).
Weights: Empty, typically 6,535lb (2970kg); loaded 9,519–10,700lb (4320–4853kg).
Performance: (SBD-5): maximum speed 252mph (406km/h); initial climb 1,500ft (457m)/min; service ceiling 24,300ft (7400m): range (dive bomber) 456 miles (730km), (scout bomber) 773 miles (1240km).
Armament: One (later invariably two) 0·5in Browning machine guns fixed in nose, one (later two) 0·30in Brownings manually aimed from rear cockpit; one bomb or other store of up to 1,000lb (454kg) on swinging crutch under belly, outer-wing racks for two 100lb (45kg) bombs or, sometimes, two 250lb (113kg) bombs or depth charges.
History: First flight (XBT-1) July 1935; service delivery (XBT-1) 12 December 1935; (BT-1) 15 November 1937 to 19 October 1938; (XBT-2, Dauntless prototype) 23 July 1938; (SBD-1) 4 June 1940; termination of production 22 July 1944.
Users: Australia, Chile, France, Mexico, New Zealand, UK (RN, not operational), US (AAF, Navy, Marines).

Below: It is truly remarkable that the SBD, so similar to Britain's disastrous Battle, should have turned the whole tide of war in the Pacific. Note perforated dive brakes.

Development: In 1932 John K. Northrop set up his own company to specialise in the new technique of all-metal stressed-skin construction, though he retained close links with his former employer, Douglas Aircraft. His brilliant designer, Ed Heinemann, started in 1934 to develop a carrier-based dive-bomber for the new Navy carriers, basing the design on the established Northrop A-17A. The resulting Northrop BT-1 was ordered in quantity (54) in February 1936. It featured perforated split flaps and main gears folding backwards into large fairings. The last BT-1 was delivered in a greatly modified form, as the BT-2, with inward-retracting mainwheels, a 1,000hp Cyclone engine and many refinements. By this time Northrop had become the El Segundo division of Douglas and in consequence the production BT-2 was redesignated SBD-1. From June 1940 until four years later this was one of the most important US combat aircraft, indeed, in the first half of 1942 it saw more action than any other American type. After the 57 SBD-1s came 87 SBD-2s with greater fuel capacity, 584 SBD-3s with armour and self-sealing tanks (and 168 more for the Army with pneumatic tailwheel and no hook), 780 SBD-4 (24V electrics) plus 170 for the Army, 3,024 SBD-5s with 1,200hp engine (including 615 as Army A-24Bs) and 451 SBD-6 (1,350hp), to make the total 5,936. Dauntless sank more Japanese shipping than any other Allied weapon, stopped the Imperial Fleet at Midway and played a major role at the Coral Sea and Solomons actions.

Above: This squadron probably has the SBD-5 or -6, but differences between sub-types were mainly internal. ASV radar was introduced with the -4, together with radio navaids.

Below: Side elevation of an SBD-5, with 1,000lb GP bomb, assigned to shore-based VMSB-231, Marine Air Group 22.

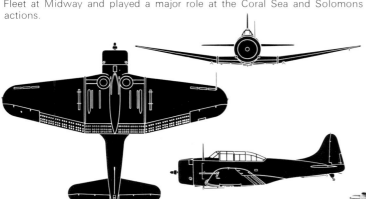

Above: Three-view typical of all SBD/A-24 variants.

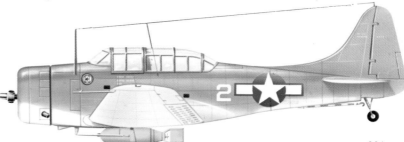

Douglas TBD Devastator

TBD-1 Devastator

Origin: Douglas Aircraft Company.
Type: Three-seat carrier-based torpedo bomber.
Engine: One 850hp Pratt & Whitney R-1830-64 Twin Wasp 14-cylinder two-row radial.
Dimensions: Span 50ft (15·24m); length 35ft 6in (10·82m); height 15ft 1in (4·6m).
Weights: Empty 7,195lb (3264kg); maximum loaded 10,194lb (4622kg).
Performance: Maximum speed 206mph (332km/h); initial climb at maximum weight 900ft (274m)/min; service ceiling 19,700ft (6000m); range with full weapon load 435 miles (700km).
Armament: One 0·30in Colt-Browning fixed on right side of nose, one 0·5in manually aimed in rear cockpit, single 21in (1,000lb 454kg) Bliss-Leavitt torpedo recessed into belly, light bomb racks under wings for total additional load of 500lb (227kg).
History: First flight (XTBD-1) January 1935; production delivery 25 June 1937.
User: US (Navy).

Development: In the early 1930s the US Navy ordered new aircraft carriers, the *Ranger, Yorktown* and *Enterprise*. Among their complement were to be squadrons of torpedo bombers and on 30 June 1934 orders were placed for two prototypes of rival designs. One was the Great Lakes XTBG-1, rather similar to the later British Swordfish. The other was the first cantilever monoplane designed for such a duty, the Douglas XTBD-1. The monoplane started with the drawback of being radically new, though the wing was very thick, the retracted main wheels protruded far enough for safe landings and the landing speed was only 59mph. The large canopy over the pilot, radio operator and gunner opened into six sections for "open cockpit" vision, and the all-round performance of the monoplane was superior. Despite competition from another monoplane contender, on 3 February 1936, the Douglas won the production order for 110 aircraft, then the largest peacetime order for aircraft placed by the US Navy. The production TBD had a taller canopy with crash pylon, power-folding wings and other changes. Altogether 129 were delivered, and over 100 were still the only carrier-based torpedo bombers in US service at the time of Pearl Harbor. Named Devastator, they immediately went into violent action, bombing and torpedoing almost on a round-the-clock basis. The middle crewmember aimed the torpedo, sighting through doors in the belly and from a prone position. In the Marshalls and Gilberts these aircraft proved formidable, but they were obsolescent and in the Battle of Midway 35 were shot down by flak and Zeros in a single action. The Devastator was soon afterwards replaced by the Avenger.

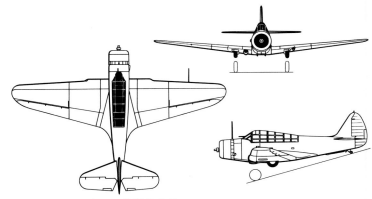

Above: Three-view of TBD-1 Devastator.

Above: In its day the TBD was an excellent aircraft, but that day was drawing swiftly to a close when the US Navy found itself at war on 7 December 1941. Its wing area was by then appropriate to aircraft of twice the weight and three times the power of the very early-series Twin Wasp engine.

Fairchild M-62 Cornell family

PT-19, -23 and -26, Cornell II

Origin: Fairchild Aircraft Division, Hagerstown, Maryland; built under licence by Aeronca, Howard, St Louis and Fleet (Canada).
Type: Primary trainer.
Engine: (19) 175hp Ranger 6-440C-2 inverted six-in-line aircooled, (23) 220hp Continental R-670-11 seven-cylinder radial, (26,Cornell II) 200hp Ranger L-440-7.
Dimensions: Span (19,23) 36ft 11¼in (11·26m), (26) 36ft 0in (10·97m); length (19,26) 27ft 11½in (8·52m), (23) 25ft 10¾in (7·90m); height 7ft 6in (2·29m).
Weights: Empty (23) 2,046lb (928kg), (26) 2,022lb (917kg); maximum (23) 2,747lb (1246kg), (26) 2,741lb (1243kg).
Performance: Maximum speed (typical) 126mph (203km/h); typical cruise 110mph (177km/h); typical range 430 miles (692km).
History: First flight (19) 1939; final delivery (23, 26) May 1944.
Users: (WWII) Argentina, Brazil, Canada, Chile, Colombia, Ecuador, Mexico, Norway, Paraguay, S Africa, S Rhodesia, UK (RAF), Uruguay, US (AAC/AAF).

Development: Fairchild's M-62 was a simple but quite large trainer with wooden wing (with manual flaps) and steel-tube/fabric fuselage. It immediately attracted export orders, usually with the Warner Super Scarab engine, but the US Army Air Corps adopted it in 1939 with the Ranger. The PT-19 was built by Fairchild and Aeronca, the radial-engined 23 in vast numbers by Howard, Aeronca and St Louis, and the 26 with enclosed cockpits by Fleet, for the Commonwealth Air Training Plan. Hundreds were used in S Rhodesia, where in 1946 the author supervised the destruction of 97 straight out of their crates. Total production was 7,250 in the USA and about 1,150 in Canada.

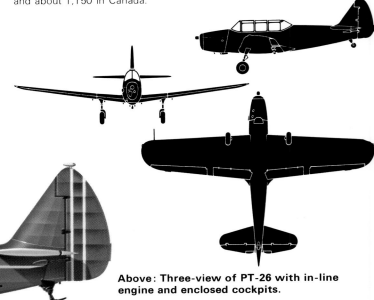

Above: Three-view of PT-26 with in-line engine and enclosed cockpits.

Left: Though little-used by US forces, the PT-26 variant was the most important to other Allies and served in vast numbers in the RAF and RCAF as the Cornell II. One batch equipped the "Little Norway" training school in Canada, with RNorAF insignia, cockpit heaters and often skis (here tail-ski only).

Grumman F4F/FM Wildcat

G-36, Martlet, F4F-1 to -4 and Eastern Aircraft FM-1 and -2

Origin: Grumman Aircraft Engineering Corporation; also built by Eastern Aircraft.

Type: Single-seat naval fighter.

Engine: (XF4F-2) one 1,050hp Pratt & Whitney R-1830-66 Twin Wasp 14-cylinder two-row radial; (G-36A, Martlet I (Wildcat I)) one 1,200hp Wright R-1820-G205A Cyclone nine-cylinder radial; (F4F-3) 1,200hp R-1830-76; (F4F-4 and FM-1 (Wildcat V)) R-1830-86; (FM-2 (Wildcat VI)) 1,350hp R-1820-56.

Dimensions: Span 38ft 0in (11·6m); length 28ft 9in to 28ft 11in (FM-2, 28ft 10in, 8·5m); height 11ft 11in (3·6m).

Weights: Empty (F4F-3) 4,425lb; (F4F-4) 4,649lb; (FM-2) 4,900lb (2226kg); loaded (F4F-3) 5,876lb; (F4F-4) 6,100lb rising to 7,952lb (3607kg) with final FM-1s; (FM-2) 7,412lb.

Performance: Maximum speed (F4F-3) 325mph (523km/h); (F4F-4, FM-1) 318mph (509km/h); (FM-2) 332mph (534km/h); initial climb, typically 2,000ft (610m)/min (3,300ft/min in early versions, 1,920 in main production and over 2,000 for FM-2); service ceiling, typically 35,000ft (10,670m) (more in light early versions); range, typically 900 miles (1448km).

Armament: (XF4F-2) two 0·5in Colt-Brownings in fuselage; (F4F-3) four 0·5in in outer wings; (F4F-4 and subsequent) six 0·5in in outer wings; (F4F-4, FM-1 and FM-2) underwing racks for two 250lb (113kg) bombs.

History: First flight (XF4F-2) 2 September 1937; (XF4F-3) 12 February 1939; production (G-36 and F4F-3) February 1940; (FM-2) March 1943; final delivery August 1945.

Users: France (FFL), Greece, UK (RN), US (Navy, Marines).

Development: Designed as a biplane to continue Grumman's very successful F3F series of single-seat carrier fighters, the XF4F-1 was re-planned on the drawing board in the summer of 1936 as a mid-wing monoplane. Though this machine, the XF4F-2, lost out to the Brewster F2A Buffalo, Grumman continued with the XF4F-3 with a more powerful engine and in early 1939 received a French Aéronavale order for 100, the US Navy following with 54 in August. The French aircraft were diverted to Britain and named Martlet I. Production built up with both Twin Wasp and Cyclone engines, folding wings being introduced with the F4F-4, of which Grumman delivered 1,169 plus 220 Martlet IVs for the Fleet Air Arm. Eastern Aircraft Division of General Motors very quickly tooled up and delivered 839 FM-1s and 311 Martlet Vs, the British name then being changed to the US name of Wildcat. Grumman switched to the Avenger, Hellcat and other types, but made F4F-7 reconnaissance versions, weighing 10,328lb and having a 24-hour endurance, as well as a floatplane version. Eastern took over the final mark, the powerful and effective FM-2, delivering 4,777 of this type (including 340 Wildcat VI) in 13 months. A Martlet I shot down a Ju 88 on Christmas Day 1940, and an F4F-3 of VMF-211 destroyed a Japanese bomber at Wake Island on 9 December 1941. Each event was the first of thousands of furious actions from which this quite old fighter emerged with a splendid reputation. Wildcats were especially valuable for their ability to operate from small escort carriers, the pioneer work having been done with British Martlets based in November 1940 on the 5,000 ton captured German vessel *Audacity* on which a flat deck had been built. Noted for their strength and manoeuvrability, Wildcats even sank Japanese submarines and a cruiser. *(See page 230 for Grumman F6F)*

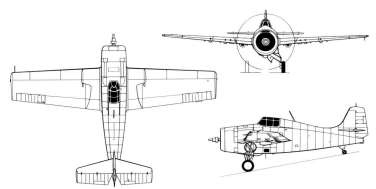

Above: Three-view of F4F-4 (most other versions similar).

Above: Part of a squadron of Eastern Aircraft FM-1 Wildcats over the Pacific. All FM models carried only four 0·5in guns.

Left: A US Navy F4F-4 (Twin Wasp and six guns) in 1944-45 colouring.

Below: A Royal Navy Wildcat V (with four guns, and in this case with the Cyclone cowled as in the later FM-2) pictured aboard a Fleet carrier of the Royal Navy.

Grumman F7F Tigercat

F7F-1 to -4N Tigercat

Origin: Grumman Aircraft Engineering Corporation.
Type: Single-seat or two-seat fighter bomber or night fighter (-4N for carrier operation).
Engines: Two Pratt & Whitney R-2800-22W or -34W Double Wasp 18-cylinder two-row radials each rated at 2,100hp (dry) or 2,400hp (water injection).
Dimensions: Span 51ft 6in (15·7m); length (most) 45ft 4in or 45ft 4½in (13·8m); (-3N, -4N) 46ft 10in (14·32m); height (-1, -2) 15ft 2in (4·6m); (-3, -4) 16ft 7in (5·06m).
Weights: Empty (-1) 13,100lb (5943kg); (-3N, -4N) 16,270lb (7379kg); loaded (-1) 22,560lb (10,235kg); (-2N) 26,194lb (11,880kg); (-3) 25,720lb; (-4N) 26,167lb.
Performance: Maximum speed (-1) 427mph (689km/h); (-2N) 421mph; (-3) 435mph; (-4N) 430mph; initial climb (-1) 4,530ft (1380m)/min; service ceiling (-1) 36,200ft; (-2N) 39,800ft (12,131m); (-3) 40,700ft; (-4N) 40,450ft; range on internal fuel (-1) 1,170 miles (1885km); (-2N) 960 miles; (-3) 1,200 miles; (-4N) 810 miles.
Armament: Basic (-1) four 0·5in Browning each with 300 rounds in the nose and four 20mm M-2 cannon each with 200 rounds in the wing roots;

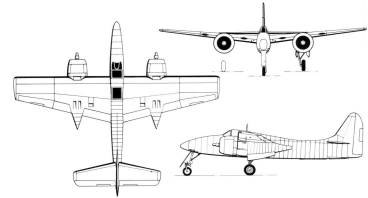

Above: Three-view of F7F-3 (most -3 had long NF or photo nose).

outer-wing pylons for six rockets or two 1,000 lb (454kg) bombs; alternatively, one 21in torpedo on fuselage centreline. (-3), nose guns only; (-2N, -3N, -4N) wing guns only.
History: First flight (XF7F-1) December 1943; first service delivery October 1944; final delivery, December 1946.

Grumman TBF/TBM Avenger

TBF and Eastern Aircraft TBM series

Origin: Grumman Aircraft Engineering Corporation; also built by Eastern Aircraft.
Type: Originally, three-seat torpedo bomber; later ASW (anti-submarine warfare) aircraft and AEW (airborne early warning) aircraft.
Engine: One 1,700hp Wright R-2600-8 or -20 Double Cyclone 14-cylinder two-row radial.
Dimensions: Span 54ft 2in (16·5m); length (to TBM-3) 40ft 0in (12·2m); (TBM-3E) 40ft 11½in (12·48m); height 16ft 5in (5m).
Weights: Empty (TBF-1) 10,100lb (4580kg); (TBM-3) 10,545lb (4787kg); loaded (TBF-1) 15,905lb (7214kg); (TBM-3) 18,250lb (8278kg); (TBM-3E) 17,895lb (8117kg).
Performance: Maximum speed (TBF-1) 278mph (445km/h); (TBM-3) 267mph (430km/h); initial climb (TBF-1) 1,075ft (376m)/min; service ceiling (TBF, TBM-1 to -3) about 23,400ft (7132m); (TBM-3E) 30,100ft; range with full weapon load, 1,010–1,215 miles (1600–1950km); ferry range, 2,530 miles (4072km).
Armament: (TBF-1, TBM-1) one 0·30in Browning in upper forward fuselage, one 0·5in in dorsal power turret and one 0·30in manually aimed in rear ventral position; internal bay for one 22in torpedo or 2,000lb (907kg) of bombs; (TBF-1C, TBM-1C, TBM-3) as above plus one 0·5in in each outer wing and underwing racks for eight 60lb (27kg) rockets. Most subsequent versions unarmed, or fitted for ASW weapons only.
History: First flight (XTBF-1) 1 August 1941; service delivery 30 January

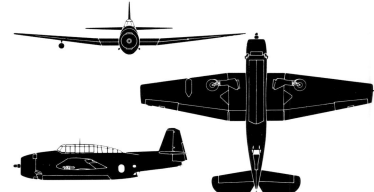

Above: Three-view of Eastern Aircraft TBM-3 (no turret).

1942; final delivery from new production, September 1945; final delivery of rebuild, August 1954.
Users: (wartime) New Zealand, UK (RN), US (Navy, Marines).

Development: Grumman's outstanding design and engineering staff, under W. T. (Bill) Schwendler, designed and developed this big and extremely useful torpedo bomber very quickly and it became one of the key aircraft in the Pacific war. Two prototypes were ordered on 8 April 1940 and large numbers were in action at the Battle of Midway just over two years later. From the start the TBF was robust and well equipped and one could not help comparing it with the British Barracuda which lacked power, self-defence and a weapon bay. Fortunately a proportion of deliveries went to the Fleet Air Arm, which originally considered the name Tarpon before

Below: A crowded flight deck somewhere in the Pacific in late 1942. Most of the picture is occupied by TBFs, but in the extreme foreground are F6F Hellcat fighters, while at the rear (wings spread) are a squadron of SBD Dauntless scout-bombers.

Users: UK (RN), US (Navy, Marines).

Development: Ordered on the same day as the F6F Hellcat prototypes in June 1941 the F7F was one of the boldest designs in the history of combat aircraft. During the preceding two years the US Navy had keenly studied air war in Europe and noted that the things that appeared to count were the obvious ones; engine power, armament and protective armour and self-sealing tanks. At a time when the average US Navy fighter had 1,000hp and two machine guns the Bureau of Aeronautics asked Grumman to build a fighter with more than 4,000hp and a weight of fire more than 200 times as great. The company had embarked on a venture along these lines in 1938 with the XF5F, which remained a one-off prototype that was judged not worth the cost and incompatible with Navy carriers. In contrast the F7F was planned on a basis of knowledge and though dramatically heavier and faster than any previous carrier aircraft it was matched with the deck of the large Midway class carriers then under construction. Most, however, were ordered for the Marine Corps for use from land. The F7F-1 of which 34 were built, were single seaters with APS-6 radar in a wing pod. The 66 F7F-2Ns followed, with nose radar in place of guns and the observer in place of the rear fuel tank. The -3 introduced the -34W engine and so had a larger tail; most of the 250 built were -3N night fighters or -3P photographic aircraft. The final models were strengthened -4s, cleared for carrier use, the whole batch being -4Ns. Tigercats arrived at a time when emphasis was rapidly switching to the jet.

Above: A rare bird, the single-seat F7F-3, which was virtually similar to the original F7F-1 but with more power and increased fuel capacity. Most -3s had a nose full of cameras or radar.

adopting the US Navy name. Of 2,293 Grumman-built aircraft delivered by December 1943, 402 went to the RN and 63 to the RNZAF. Eastern Aircraft, the second source, delivered 2,882 of the TBM-1 and -1C type, before switching to the slightly modified -3 in April 1944. Many -3s had no turret, all had strengthened wings for rockets or a radar pod, and no fewer than 4,664 were delivered by Eastern in 14 months. After 1945 development suddenly blossomed out into new versions, produced as conversions. The TBM-3E was packed with ASW search and attack equipment, the TBM-3W and -3W2 were grotesque "guppy" type early-warners with huge belly radar, the -3U was a tug and the -3R a COD (carrier on-board delivery) transport with seven passenger seats. The Fleet Air Arm put 100 TBM-3E anti-submarine versions into use as the Avenger AS.4 in 1953 and about 500 more post-war variants served with the USN, RCN, Aéronavale, Japan and Netherlands.

Right: Catapult takeoff with flap from a US Navy carrier.

Below: Air and ground crews of the Fleet Air Arm hustle before a bombing raid by Avenger IIs from a Pacific base in 1945.

Lockheed Model 414 (A-29, PBO) Hudson

Hudson I to VI, A-28, A-29, AT-18, C-63 and PBO-1

Origin: Lockheed Aircraft Corporation.
Type: Reconnaissance bomber and utility.
Engines: (Hudson I, II) two 1,100hp Wright GR-1820-G102A nine-cylinder radials; (Hudson III, A-29, PBO-1) two 1,200hp GR-1820-G205A, (Hudson IV, V, VI and A-28) two 1,200hp Pratt & Whitney R-1830-S3C3-G, S3C4-G or -67 14-cylinder two-row radials.
Dimensions: Span 65ft 6in (19·96m); length 44ft 4in (13·51m); height 11ft 10½in (3·62m).
Weights: Empty (I) 12,000lb (5443kg); (VI) 12,929lb (5864kg); maximum loaded (I) 18,500lb (8393kg); (VI) 22,360lb (10,142kg).
Performance: Maximum speed (I) 246mph (397km/h); (VI) 261mph (420km/h); initial climb 1,200ft (366m)/min; service ceiling 24,500ft (7468m); range (I) 1,960 miles (3150km); (VI) 2,160 miles (3475km).
Armament: (Typical RAF Hudson in GR role) seven 0·303in Brownings in nose (two, fixed), dorsal turret (two), beam windows and ventral hatch; internal bomb/depth charge load up to 750lb (341kg).
History: First flight (civil Model 14) 29 July 1937; (Hudson I) 10 December 1938; squadron delivery February 1939; USAAC and USN delivery, October 1941.
Users: Australia, Brazil, Canada, China, Netherlands, New Zealand, UK (RAF, BOAC), US (AAC/AAF, Navy).

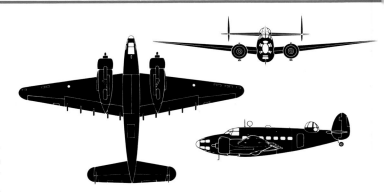

Above: Three-view of Hudson I (all Cyclone-powered similar).

Development: In 1938 the British Purchasing Commission was established in Washington to seek out US aircraft that could serve with the RAF and Royal Navy and help bolster British strength beyond the then-small capacity of the British aircraft industry. One of the urgent needs was for a modern long-range reconnaissance and navigation trainer aircraft and Lockheed Aircraft, at Burbank — just climbing out of the Depression — hastily built a mock-up of their Model 14 airliner to meet the requirement. An order for 200 aircraft, many times bigger than any previous order ever received by Lockheed, was fulfilled swiftly and efficiently. The order was many times multiplied and the versatile Hudson served with several RAF commands in many theatres of war. On 8 October 1939 a Hudson over Jutland shot down the first German aircraft claimed by the RAF in World War II. In February 1940 another discovered the prison ship *Altmark* in a Norwegian fjord and directed naval forces to the rescue. Over Dunkirk Hudsons acted as dog-fighters, in August 1941 one accepted the surrender of U-boat *U-570*, and from 1942 many made secret landings in France to deliver or collect agents or supplies. Hudsons of later marks carried ASV radar, rocket launchers and lifeboats. Total deliveries were 2,584 including about 490 armed versions for the US Army, 20 PBOs for the Navy and 300 AT-18 crew trainers. From this fine basic design stemmed the more powerful Vega Ventura bomber and ocean patrol aircraft and the PV-2 Harpoon at almost twice the weight of the Hudson I.

Above: This Cyclone-powered Hudson of the RAF is painted in post-1941 insignia but not in the expected dark sea grey and white of Coastal Command. Many served as transports.

Below: The Hudson was a useful utility transport, with plenty of room, high performance and long range. This Mk VI is being refuelled at an airfield in West Africa.

Below: Hudson GR.V (Twin Wasp engines) serving with 48 Sqn of RAF Coastal Command.

Lockheed P-38 Lightning

XP-38 to P-38M, F-4 and F-5, RP and TP conversions

Origin: Lockheed Aircraft Corporation.
Type: Single-seat long-range fighter (see text for variations).
Engines: Two Allison V-1710 vee-12 liquid-cooled; (YP-38) 1,150hp V-1710-27/29 (all P-38 engines handed with opposite propeller rotation, hence pairs of engine sub-type numbers); (P-38E to G) 1,325hp V-1710-49/52 or 51/55; (P-38H and J) 1,425hp V-1710-89/91; (P-38L and M) 1,600hp V-1710-111/113.
Dimensions: Span 52ft (15·86m); length 37ft 10in (11·53m); (F-5G, P-38M and certain "droop-snoot" conversions fractionally longer); height 12ft 10in (3·9m).
Weights: Empty, varied from 11,000lb (4990kg) in YP to average of 12,700lb (5766kg), with heaviest sub-types close to 14,000lb (6350kg); maximum loaded, (YP) 14,348lb (6508kg); (D) 15,500lb; (E) 15,482lb; (F) 18,000lb; (G) 19,800lb; (H) 20,300lb; (L, M) 21,600lb (9798kg).
Performance: Maximum speed (all) 391–414mph (630–666km/h); initial climb (all) about 2,850ft (870m)/min; service ceiling (up to G) 38,000–40,000ft; (H, J, L) 44,000ft (13,410m); range on internal fuel 350–460 miles (563–740km); range at 30,000ft with maximum fuel (late models) 2,260 miles (3650km).
Armament: See text.
History: First flight (XP-38) 27 January 1939; (YP-38) 16 September 1940; service delivery (USAAC P-38) 8 June 1941; (F-4) March 1942; (P-38F) September 1942; final delivery September 1945.
Users: France, UK (RAF, briefly), US (AAC/AAF).

Development: In February 1937 the US Army Air Corps issued a specification for a long-range interceptor (pursuit) and escort fighter, calling for a speed of 360mph at 20,000ft and endurance at this speed of one hour. Lockheed, which had never built a purely military design, jumped in with both feet and created a revolutionary fighter bristling with innovations and posing considerable technical risks. Powered by two untried Allison engines, with GEC turbochargers recessed into the tops of the tail booms, it had a tricycle landing gear, small central nacelle mounting a 23mm Madsen cannon and four 0·5in Brownings firing parallel directly ahead of the pilot, twin fins, Fowler flaps, cooling radiators on the flanks of the booms and induction intercoolers in the wing leading edges. This box of tricks ran into a ditch on its first taxi test, and two weeks after first flight undershot at Mitchell Field, NY, and was demolished. What made headlines, however, was that it had flown to New York in 7hr 2min, with two refuelling stops, demonstrating a performance which in 1939 seemed beyond belief. The enthusiasm of the Air Corps overcame the doubts and high cost and by 1941 the first YP-38 was being tested, with a 37mm Oldsmobile cannon, two 0·5s and two Colt 0·3s. Thirteen YPs were followed on the Burbank line by 20 P-38s, with one 37mm and four 0·5, plus armour and, in the 36 D models, self-sealing tanks. In March 1940 the British Purchasing Commission had ordered 143 of this type, with the 37mm replaced by a 20mm Hispano and far greater ammunition capacity. The State Department prohibited export of the F2 Allison engine and RAF aircraft, called Lightning I,

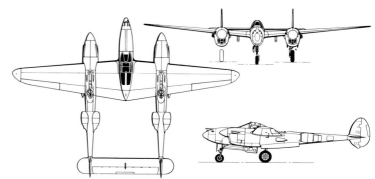

Above: Three-view of the mass-produced P-38J.

had early C15 engines without turbochargers, both having right-hand rotation (P-38s had propellers turning outward). The result was poor and the RAF rejected these machines, which were later brought up to US standard. The E model adopted the British name Lightning and the RAF Hispano gun. Within minutes of the US declaration of war, on 7 December 1941, an E shot down an Fw 200C near Iceland, and the P-38 was subsequently in the thick of fighting in North Africa, North West Europe and the Pacific. The F was the first to have inner-wing pylons for 1,000lb bombs, torpedoes, tanks or other stores. By late 1943 new G models were being flown to Europe across the North Atlantic, while in the Pacific 16 aircraft of the 339th Fighter Squadron destroyed Admiral Yamamoto's aircraft 550 miles from their base at Guadalcanal. The J had the intercoolers moved under the engines, changing the appearance, providing room for 55 extra gallons of fuel in the outer wings. Later J models had hydraulically boosted ailerons, but retained the wheel-type lateral control instead of a stick. The L, with higher war emergency power, could carry 4,000lb of bombs or ten rockets, and often formations would bomb under the direction of a lead-ship converted to droop-snoot configuration with a bombardier in the nose. Hundreds were built as F-4 or F-5 photographic aircraft, and the M was a two-seat night fighter with ASH radar pod under the nose. Lightnings towed gliders, operated on skis, acted as fast ambulances (carrying two stretcher cases) and were used for many special ECM missions. Total production was 9,942 and the P-38 made up for slightly inferior manoeuvrability by its range, reliability and multi-role effectiveness.

Above: The first sub-type to have inner-wing pylons was the P-38F.

Left: P-38F-5 from 347th FG, detached to the 13th Air Force at Guadalcanal.

Below: The deep engines of the much more numerous later models are seen in this unarmed photo F-5E.

United States of America

Lockheed PV-1/B-34 Ventura
Vega 37, Ventura I to V, B-34 Lexington, B-37, PV-1 and -3 and PV-2 Harpoon

Origin: Vega Aircraft Corporation, Burbank, California.
Type: Bomber and reconnaissance aircraft.
Engines: Two Pratt & Whitney R-2800 Double Wasp 18-cylinder radials, (Ventura I) 1,850hp R-2800-S1A4-G, (most others) 2,000hp R-2800-31.
Dimensions: Span 65ft 6in (19·96m), (H) 75ft 0in (22·86m); length 51ft 5in to 51ft 9in (15·77m); height 13ft 2in to 14ft 1in (4·29m).
Weights: Empty (PV-1, typical) 19,373lb (8788kg), (H) about 24,000lb (10,886kg); maximum (V) 31,077lb (14,097kg), (H) 40,000lb (18,144kg).
Performance: Maximum speed (V) 300mph (483km/h), (H) 282mph (454km/h); maximum range with max bomb load (all) about 900 miles (1448km).
Armament: See text.
History: First flight (RAF) 31 July 1941; service delivery (RAF) June 1942; final delivery (H) 1945.
Users: (WWII) Australia, Italy (CB), New Zealand, Portugal, South Africa, UK (RAF), US (AAF, Navy).

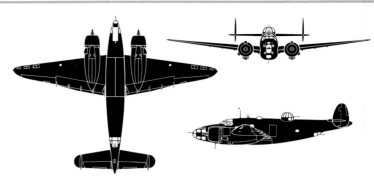

Above: Three-view of all Venturas (B-34 similar).

Development: Vega Aircraft, a 1940 subsidiary of Lockheed, was awarded a contract by the British Purchasing Commission in June 1940 for 875 of a new design of bomber derived from the Lockheed 18 airliner. Called Lockheed V-146, or Vega 37, it resembled a more powerful Hudson, with longer fuselage provided with a rear ventral position with two 0·303in Brownings. Two (later four) more were in the dorsal turret, and the nose had two fixed 0·5in and two manually aimed 0·303in. Bomb load was 2,500lb (1134kg). In October 1942 Bomber Command's No 21 Sqn swept into action with a gallant daylight attack on the Phillips works at Eindhoven, but the Ventura proved a mediocre bomber and deliveries stopped at about 300. The B-34 Lexington absorbed many of the unwanted machines, though the Army Air Force never used them operationally. The B-34B trainer, Ventura II and IIA were reconnaissance models (originally O-56), but the bulk of the 1,600 Venturas were Navy PV-1 patrol bombers with up to eight 0·5in, more fuel and ability to carry mines and torpedoes. About 380 similar aircraft served Commonwealth forces as Ventura V, surviving in South Africa to the 1970s. The PV-2 Harpoon was redesigned as a much better Navy bomber, with larger wings, new tail and up to ten 0·5in, rockets and 4,000lb (1814kg) of bombs or torpedoes. The 535 built saw brief service before being passed to Allies.

Left: Swinging the compass of a white PV-1 of the US Navy. Many of these multi-role aircraft carried Mk IV ASV radar.

Martin 167 Maryland
Model 167 Maryland I and II

Origin: The Glenn L. Martin Company.
Type: Three-seat reconnaissance bomber.
Engines: Two Pratt & Whitney Twin Wasp 14-cylinder two-row radials; (Maryland I) 1,050hp R-1830-S1C3-G; (II) 1,200hp R-1830-S3C4-G.
Dimensions: Span 61ft 4in (18·69m); length 46ft 8in (14·22m); height 10ft 1in (3·07m).
Weights: Empty 11,213lb (RAF Mk II); maximum loaded (I) 15,297lb; (II) 16,809lb (7694kg).
Performance: Maximum speed (prototype) 316mph; (I) 304mph; (II) 280mph (451km/h); initial climb 1,790ft (545m)/min; service ceiling (I) 29,500ft (8992m); (II) 26,000ft (7925m); range with bomb load 1,080 miles (1738km).
Armament: Four 0·303in Browning (France, 7·5mm MAC 1934) fixed in outer wings, two 0·303in Vickers K (France, MAC 1934) manually aimed

from dorsal turret and rear ventral position; internal bomb load of 2,000lb (907kg) (France 1,874lb, 850kg; Maryland I, 1,250lb, 567kg).
History: First flight 14 March 1939; (production 167F) 7 August 1939; service delivery (France) October 1939; final delivery 1941.
Users: France, South Africa, UK (RAF, RN).

Development: Designed as the US Army XA-22 attack bomber, the Martin 167 was not adopted but immediately attracted a big French order for the Armée de l'Air as the 167F, with Armée de l'Air designation 167A-3. Of 215 purchased, about 75 reached France before the June 1940 capitulation, squadrons GB I/62 and I/63 completing conversion and, despite being chosen for dangerous missions, suffering only 8 per cent casualties (the lowest of any French bomber type). Some survivors and undelivered aircraft went to the RAF, while most surviving French aircraft served the Vichy Air Force and operated against the Allies over Gibraltar, North Africa and Syria. The RAF accepted 75 ex-French machines and bought a further 150 with two-stage supercharged engines as the Maryland II, using all 225 as reconnaissance bombers in Cyrenaica, Malta and other Middle East areas. A few went to the Fleet Air Arm (one gave first warning of the departure of *Bismarck*) and four squadrons served with the South African AF. In basic arrangement rather like Luftwaffe bombers, the Maryland was quite fast, nice to fly, but cramped and inadequately armed.

Below: Martin 167A-3 of GB I/63, Armée de l'Air.

Below: AR702 was the first Maryland to be supplied to the RAF. Built to US standards, with single-stage Twin Wasps, this batch was ordered by France.

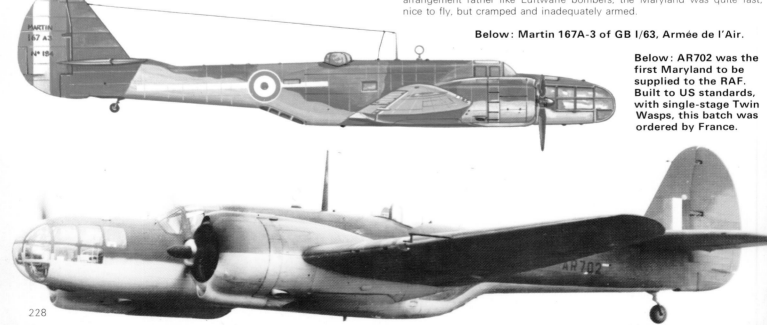

228

Martin 179 B-26 Marauder
Model 179, B-26A to G, Marauder I to III

Origin: The Glenn L. Martin Company.
Type: Five- to seven-seat medium bomber.
Engines: Two Pratt & Whitney Double Wasp 18-cylinder two-row radials; (B-26) 1,850hp R-2800-5; (A) 2,000hp R-2800-39; (B, C, D, E, F, G) 2,000hp R-2800-43.
Dimensions: Span (B-26, A and first 641 B-26B) 65ft (19·8m); (remainder) 71ft (21·64m); length (B-26) 56ft, (A, B) 58ft 3in (17·75m); (F, G) 56ft 6in (17·23m); height (up to E) 19ft 10in (6·04m); (remainder) 21ft 6in (6·55m).
Weights: Empty (early, typical) 23,000lb (10,433kg); (F, G) 25,300lb (11,490kg); maximum loaded (B-26) 32,000lb; (A) 33,022lb; (first 641 B) 34,000lb, then 37,000lb (16,783kg); (F) 38,000lb (G) 38,200lb (17,340kg).
Performance: Maximum speed (up to E, typical) 310mph (500km/h); (F, G) 280mph (451km/h); initial climb 1,000ft (305m)/min; service ceiling (up to E) 23,000ft (7000m); (F, G) 19,800ft (6040m); range with 3,000lb (1361kg) bomb load (typical) 1,150 miles (1850km).
Armament: (B-26, A) five 0·30in or 0·50in Browning in nose (1 or 2), power dorsal turret (2), tail (1, manual) and optional manual ventral hatch; (B to E) one 0·5in manually aimed in nose, twin-gun turret, two manually aimed 0·5in waist guns, one "tunnel gun" (usually 0·5in), two 0·5in in power tail turret and four 0·5in fixed as "package guns" on sides of forward fuselage; (F, G) same but without tunnel gun; some variations and trainer and Navy versions unarmed. Internal bomb load of 5,200lb (2359kg) up to 641st B, after which rear bay was disused (eliminated in F, G) to give maximum load of 4,000lb (1814kg). Early versions could carry two torpedoes.
History: First flight 25 November 1940; service delivery 25 February 1941; final delivery March 1945.
Users: France, South Africa, UK (RAF), US (AAF, Navy).

Development: With its background of leadership in bomber design, Martin pulled out all the stops to win the 1939 Medium Bomber competition of the US Army, and boldly chose a wing optimised for high-speed cruise efficiency rather than for landing. Though the Model 179 won the competition — 201 being ordered "off the drawing board" on 5 July 1939 — the actual hardware proved too much for inexperienced pilots to handle, with unprecedented wing loading. In fact there were no real problems, but the newness of the first B-26 versions, coupled with their reputation of being a

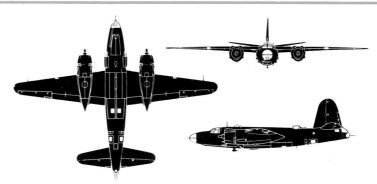

Above: Three-view of B-26C (Marauder III similar).

"widow maker", created a vicious circle of high casualties. Production B-26A models, with torpedo shackles between the bomb doors, were deployed to Australia the day after Pearl Harbor (8 December 1941), and later B models saw extensive South West Pacific service with the rear bomb bay used as a fuel tank (maximum bomb load 2,000lb). From the 641st B the wing and vertical tail were extended and on 14 May 1943 the Marauder began its career as the chief medium bomber of the 9th AF in the ETO (European Theatre of Operations). By VE-day the B-26 had set a record for the lowest loss-rate of any US Army bomber in Europe. About 522 also served with the RAF and South African AF in Italy. Total production amounted to 5,157 for the US Army (including Allied forces) plus a few dozen JM-1 and -2 target tug, reconnaissance and utility versions for the US Navy and about 200 AT-23 (later called TB-26) trainers. In 1948 the Marauder was withdrawn, and the B-26 designation passed to the Douglas Invader.

Right: This chrome-yellow beast is one of the early JM-1 target-towing and utility versions converted by the US Navy from early short-span bombers (pre-B-26B-10 block numbers). The Army Air Force counterpart was the TB-26B. The JM-1P was a photographic reconnaissance version.

Right: By far the most important user of the B-26 Marauder was the US 9th Army Air Force in the European theatre of operations. The aircraft illustrated was a B-26B-55 assigned to the 9th AAF 397th Bombardment Group (note invasion stripes).

Below: Students of the B-26 will know which outfit operated "Clark's Little Pill", leading a stream of C-models round a British taxiway. Tail numbers suggest the 323rd or 386th Bomb Groups of the 8th (not 9th) AAF.

Grumman F6F Hellcat

F6F-1 to -5 Hellcat

Origin: Grumman Aircraft Engineering Corporation.
Type: Single-seat naval fighter; later versions, fighter-bombers and night fighters.
Engine: Early production, one 2,000hp Pratt & Whitney R-2800-10 Double Wasp 18-cylinder two-row radial; from January 1944 (final F6F-3 batch) two-thirds equipped with 2,200hp (water-injection rating) R-2800-10W.
Dimensions: Span 42ft 10in (13·05m); length 33ft 7in (10·2m); height 13ft 1in (3·99m).
Weights: Empty (F6F-3) 9,042lb (4101kg); loaded (F6F-3) 12,186lb (5528kg) clean, 13,228lb (6000kg) maximum, (F6F-5N) 14,250lb (6443kg).
Performance: Maximum speed (F6F-3, -5, clean) 376mph (605km/h); (-5N) 366mph (590km/h); initial climb (typical) 3,240ft (990m)/min;

continued on page 232

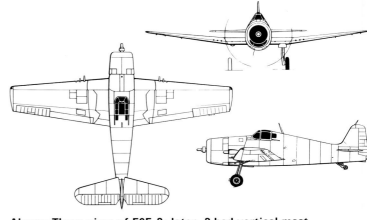

Above: Three-view of F6F-3; later -3 had vertical mast.

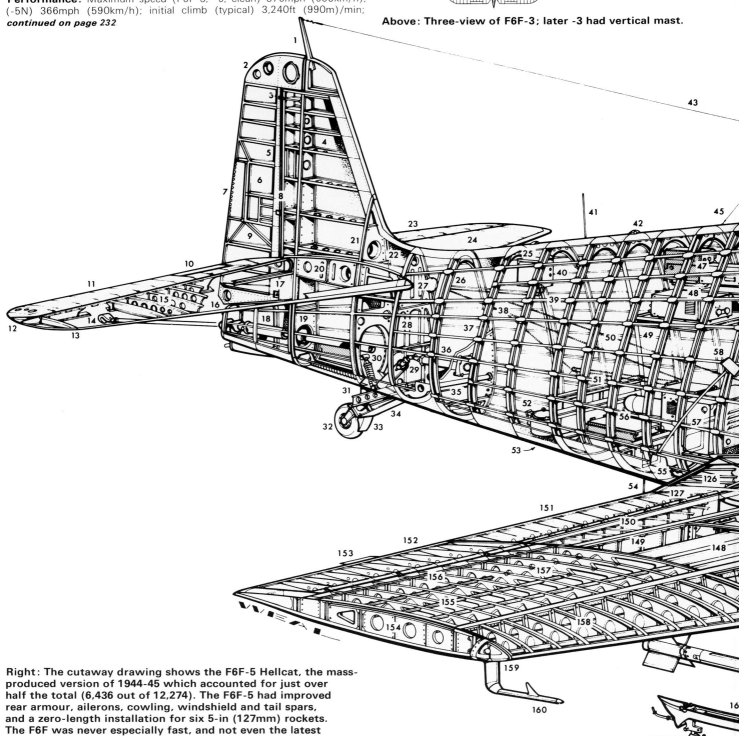

Right: The cutaway drawing shows the F6F-5 Hellcat, the mass-produced version of 1944-45 which accounted for just over half the total (6,436 out of 12,274). The F6F-5 had improved rear armour, ailerons, cowling, windshield and tail spars, and a zero-length installation for six 5-in (127mm) rockets. The F6F was never especially fast, and not even the latest versions had a teardrop clear-view canopy, but its big wing, tough structure and general fitness for harsh duty were outstanding.

Grumman F6F Hellcat cutaway drawing key:

1. Radio mast
2. Rudder balance
3. Rudder upper hinge
4. Aluminium alloy fin ribs
5. Rudder post
6. Rudder structure
7. Rudder trim tab
8. Rudder middle hinge
9. Diagonal stiffeners
10. Aluminium alloy elevator trim tab
11. Fabric-covered (and taped) elevator surfaces
12. Elevator balance
13. Flush riveted leading-edge strip
14. Arrester hook (extended)
15. Tailplane ribs
16. Tail navigation (running) light
17. Rudder lower hinge
18. Arrester hook (stowed)
19. Fin main-spar lower cut-out
20. Tailplane end rib
21. Fin forward spar
22. Fuselage/fin root fairing
23. Port elevator
24. Aluminium alloy-skinned tailplane
25. Section light
26. Fuselage aft frame
27. Control access
28. Bulkhead
29. Tailwheel hydraulic shock-absorber
30. Tailwheel centering mechanism
31. Tailwheel steel mounting arm
32. Rearward-retracting tailwheel (hard rubber tyre)
33. Fairing
34. Steel plate door fairing
35. Tricing sling support tube (for hoisting aboard carrier)
36. Hydraulic actuating cylinder
37. Flanged ring fuselage frames
38. Control cable runs
39. Fuselage longerons
40. Relay box
41. Dorsal rod antenna
42. Dorsal recognition light
43. Radio aerial
44. Radio mast
45. Aerial lead-in
46. Dorsal frame stiffeners
47. Junction box
48. Radio equipment (upper rack)
49. Radio shelf
50. Control cable runs
51. Transverse brace
52. Remote radio compass
53. Ventral recognition lights (3)
54. Ventral rod antenna
55. Destructor device
56. Accumulator
57. Radio equipment (lower rack)
58. Entry hand/footholds
59. Engine water injection tank
60. Canopy track
61. Water filler neck
62. Rear-view window
63. Rearward-sliding cockpit canopy (open)
64. Headrest
65. Pilot's head/shoulder armour
66. Canopy sill (reinforced)
67. Fire-extinguisher
68. Oxygen bottle (port fuselage wall)
69. Water tank mounting
70. Underfloor self-sealing fuel tank (60 US gal/227 litres)
71. Armoured bulkhead
72. Starboard console
73. Pilot's seat
74. Hydraulic handpump
75. Fuel filler cap and neck
76. Rudder pedals
77. Central console
78. Control column
79. Chart board (horizontal stowage)
80. Instrument panel
81. Panel coaming
82. Reflector gunsight
83. Rear-view mirror
84. Armoured glass windshield
85. Deflection plate (pilot forward protection)
86. Main bulkhead armour-plated upper section with hoisting sling attachments port and starboard
87. Aluminium alloy aileron trim tab
88. Fabric covered (and taped) aileron surfaces
89. Flush riveted outer wing skin
90. Aluminium alloy sheet wing tip (riveted to wing outer rib)
91. Port navigation (running) light
92. Formed leading-edge (approach/landing light and camera gun inboard)
93. Fixed cowling panel
94. Armour plate (oil tank forward protection)
95. Oil tank (19 US gal/72 litres)
96. Welded engine mount fittings
97. Fuselage forward bulkhead
98. Aileron control linkage
99. Engine accessories bay
100. Engine mounting frame (hydraulic fluid reservoir attached to port frames)
101. Controllable cooling gills
102. Cowling ring (removable servicing/access panels)
103. Pratt & Whitney R-2800-10W twin-row radial air-cooled engine
104. Nose ring profile
105. Reduction gear housing
106. Three-blade Hamilton Standard Hydromatic controllable pitch propeller
107. Propeller hub
108. Engine oil cooler (centre) and supercharger intercooler (outer sections) intakes
109. Oil cooler deflection plate under-protection
110. Oil cooler duct
111. Intercooler intake duct
112. Mainwheel fairing
113. Port mainwheel
114. Cooler outlet and fairing
115. Auxiliary tank support/attachment arms
116. Exhaust cluster
117. Supercharger housing
118. Exhaust outlet scoop
119. Wing front spar web
120. Wing front spar/fuselage attachment bolts
121. Undercarriage mounting/pivot point on front spar
122. Inter-spar self-sealing fuel tanks (port and starboard: 87·5 US gal/331 litres each)
123. Wing rear spar/fuselage attachment bolts
124. Structural end rib
125. Slotted wing flap profile
126. Wing flap centre-section
127. Wing fold line
128. Starboard wheel well (double-plate reinforced edges)
129. Gun bay
130. Removable diagonal brace strut
131. Three 0·5-in (12,7-mm) Colt Browning machine guns
132. Auxiliary tank aft support
133. Blast tubes
134. Folding wing joint (upper surface)
135. Machine-gun barrels
136. Fairing
137. Undercarriage actuating strut
138. Mainwheel leg oleo hydraulic shock strut
139. Auxiliary tank sling/brace
140. Long-range auxiliary fuel tank (jettisonable)
141. Mainwheel aluminium alloy fairing
142. Forged steel torque link
143. Low pressure balloon tyre
144. Cast magnesium wheel
145. Underwing 5-in (127mm) air-to-ground RPs
146. Mark V zero-length rocket launcher installation
147. Canted wing front spar
148. Inter-spar ammunition box bar (lower surface access)
149. Wing rear spar (normal to plane of wing)
150. Rear sub spar
151. Wing flap outer-section
152. Frise-type aileron
153. Aileron balance tab
154. Wing outer rib
155. Wing lateral stiffeners
156. Aileron spar
157. Wing outer-section ribs
158. Leading-edge rib cut-outs
159. Starboard navigation (running) light
160. Pitot head
161. Underwing stores pylon (mounted on fixed centre-section inboard of mainwheel leg)
162. Auxiliary fuel tank

231

service ceiling (-3) 37,500ft (11,430m); (-5N) 36,700ft (11,185m); range on internal fuel (typical) 1,090 miles (1755km).

Armament: Standard, six 0·5in Brownings in outer wings with 400 rounds each; a few -5N and -5 Hellcats had two 20mm and four 0·5in. Underwing attachments for six rockets, and centre-section pylons for 2,000lb of bombs.

History: First flight (R-2600) 26 June 1942; (same aircraft, R-2800) 30 July 1942; (production F6F-3) 4 October 1942; production delivery (F6F-3) 16 January 1943; final delivery November 1945.

Users: UK (RN), US (Navy, Marines).

Development: Though pugnacious rather than elegant, the Hellcat was a truly war-winning aircraft. It was designed and developed with great speed, mass-produced at a rate seldom equalled by any other single aircraft factory and used to such good effect that, from the very day of its appearance, the Allies were winning the air war in the Pacific. It began as the XF6F-1, a natural development of the F4F Wildcat with R-2600 Double Cyclone engine. Within a month the more powerful Double Wasp had been substituted and in the autumn of 1942 the production line took shape inside a completely new plant that was less advanced in construction than the Hellcats inside it! This line flowed at an extraordinary rate, helped by the essential rightness of the Hellcat and lack of major engineering changes during subsequent sub-types. Deliveries in the years 1942–45 inclusive were 10, 2,545, 6,139 and 3,578, a total of 12,272 (excluding two prototypes) of which 11,000 were delivered in exactly two years. These swarms of big, beefy fighters absolutely mastered the Japanese, destroying more than 6,000 hostile aircraft (4,947 by USN carrier squadrons, 209 by land-based USMC units and the rest by Allied Hellcat squadrons). The Fleet Air Arm, which originally chose the name Gannet, used Hellcats in Europe as well as throughout the Far East. Unusual features of the F6F were its 334 sq ft of square-tipped wing, with a distinct kink, and backward-retracting landing gear. The F6F-3N and -5N were night fighters with APS-6 radar on a wing pod; the -5K was a drone and the -5P a photographic reconnaissance version. After VJ-day hundreds were sold to many nations.

Above: F6F goes round again after getting a wave-off by the batsman — for obvious reasons, because the deck of this escort carrier is obstructed by another Hellcat.

Below: F6F-3 Hellcat pilots waiting to start their engines for a mission, aboard a US Navy carrier in the Pacific. The F6F-5 differed in having extra armour, better cowling and other details.

Above: A Hellcat takes off from USS Enterprise near the end of the war.

Right: Formation of US Navy Hellcats, probably from Fighter Squadron VF-8.

Below: A Naval photographer catches an F6F as it comes in to USS Yorktown.

continued on page 234 ▶

Gruman F6F Hellcat
▶ *continued*

Below: A much later aircraft was this F6F-5—albeit one from one of the first Dash-5 production blocks—showing the finish of Midnight Blue with national marking edged in Dark Blue instead of scarlet. On 10 October 1970 a similar Hellcat was fished out of the Pacific after 26 years on the ocean bottom. The guns fired perfectly.

Left: One of the first block of F6F-3 production aircraft, photographed in October 1942, less than three months after the first flight of the prototype. Developed far more rapidly than its great partner the F4U Corsair, the F6F had slightly lower performance but was extremely manoeuvrable, tough and eminently combat-worthy. It was top-scorer in the Pacific.

North American NA-73
P-51/A-36 Mustang

Far left: A P-51B from the final batches in the very first production block in early 1943, still in olive drab and with red-bordered insignia.

Left: Seated here on "Shangri-La", Capt Don Gentile (pronounced Jen-tilly) was top ace of the top P-51 group, the red-nosed 4th FG. He often fought beside his wing-man Godfrey; they destroyed 58 Luftwaffe aircraft with only eight guns between them.

Right, upper: One of the last of many Allied air forces to receive the P-51D in World War 2 was China. This one was repainted by the Peoples' Republic in 1949.

Right, lower: Another 4th FG aircraft, this time a P-51B-15 of the 334th Fighter Squadron.

Below: This was the P-51D flown by Lt Urban L. Drew of the 375th FS, 361st FG, based at Bottisham, Cambs, on the famous day (7 October 1944) when he shot down two Me 262 jets. Nothing could catch an alert 262 in full flight, but Drew flew to Achmer, the base of the élite Kommando Nowotny (which became operational three days earlier) and succeeded in bouncing the two jet fighters as they took off and climbed out.

U.S. ARMY P51D -5 NA
SERIAL NO. AAF 44-14164

Left: One of the first Hellcats to reach the US Navy was this F6F-3 used by VF-9 embarked aboard USS Yorktown in early 1943.

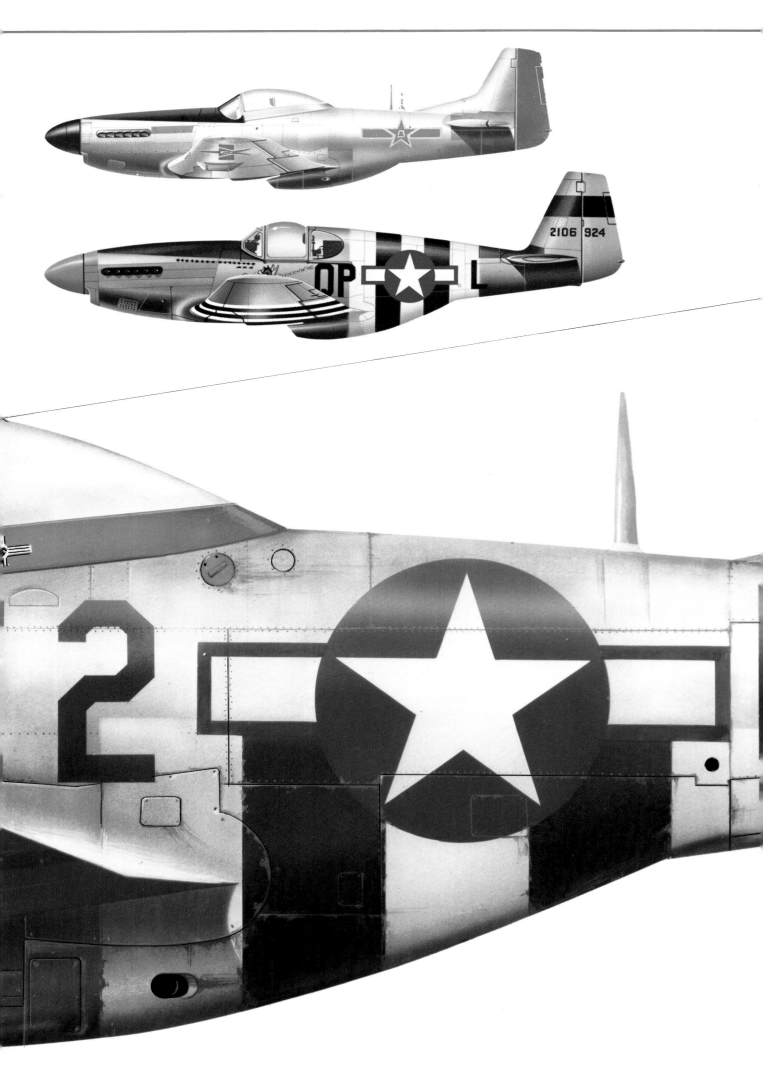

continued on page 242 ▶

North American NA-73 P-51/A-36 Mustang continued

P-51 to P-51L, A-36, F-6, Cavalier 750 to 2500, Piper Enforcer and F-82 Twin Mustang

Origin: North American Aviation Inc, Inglewood and Dallas; built under licence by Commonwealth Aircraft Corporation, Australia (and post-war by Cavalier and Piper).

Type: (P-51) single-seat fighter; (A-36) attack bomber; (F-6) reconnaissance; (post-war Cavalier and Piper models) Co-In; (F-82) night fighter.

Engine: (P-51, A, A-36, F-6A) one 1,150hp Allison V-1710-F3R or 1,125hp V-1710-81 vee-12 liquid-cooled; (P-51B, C, D and K, F-6C) one Packard V-1650 (licence-built R-R Merlin 61-series), originally 1,520hp V-1650-3 followed during P-51D run by 1,590hp V-1650-7; (P-51H) 2,218hp V-1650-9; (Cavalier) mainly V-1650-7; (Turbo-Mustang III) 1,740hp Rolls-Royce Dart 510 turboprop; (Enforcer) 2,535hp Lycoming T55-9 turboprop; (F-82F, G, H) two 2,300hp (wet rating) Allison V-1710-143/145.

Dimensions: Span 37ft 0½in (11·29m); (F-82) 51ft 3in (15·61m); length 32ft 2½in (9·81m); (P-51H) 33ft 4in; (F-82E) 39ft 1in (11·88m); height (P-51, A, A-36, F-6) 12ft 2in (3·72m); (other P-51) 13ft 8in (4·1m); (F-82) 13ft 10in (4·2m).

Weights: Empty (P-51 early V-1710 models, typical) 6,300lb (2858kg); (P-51D) 7,125lb (3230kg); (F-82E) 14,350lb (6509kg); maximum loaded (P-51 early) 8,600lb (3901kg); (P-51D) 11,600lb (5,206kg); (F-82E) 24,864lb (11,276kg).

Performance: Maximum speed (early P-51) 390mph (628km/h); (P-51D) 437mph (703km/h); (F-82, typical) 465mph (750km/h); initial climb (early) 2,600ft (792m)/min, (P-51D) 3,475ft (1060m)/min; service ceiling (early) 30,000ft (9144m); (P-51D) 41,900ft (12,770m), range with maximum fuel (early) 450 miles (724km); (P-51D) combat range 950 miles, operational range 1,300 miles with drop tanks and absolute range to dry tanks of 2,080 miles; (F-82E) 2,504 miles.

continued on page 244 ▶

North American P-51 Mustang cutaway drawing key:

1 Plastic (Phenol fibre) rudder trim tab
2 Rudder frame (fabric covered)
3 Rudder balance
4 Fin front spar
5 Fin structure
6 Access panel
7 Rudder trim-tab actuating drum
8 Rudder trim-tab control link
9 Rear navigation light
10 Rudder metal bottom section
11 Elevator plywood trim tab
12 Starboard elevator frame
13 Elevator balance weight
14 Starboard tailplane structure
15 Reinforced bracket (rear steering stresses)
16 Rudder operating horn forging
17 Elevator operating horns
18 Tab control turnbuckles
19 Fin front spar/fuselage attachment
20 Port elevator tab
21 Fabric-covered elevator
22 Elevator balance weight
23 Port tailplane
24 Tab control drum
25 Fin root fairing
26 Elevator cables
27 Tab control access panels
28 Tailwheel steering mechanism
29 Tailwheel retraction mechanism
30 Tailwheel leg assembly
31 Forward-retracting steerable tailwheel
32 Tailwheel doors
33 Lifting tube
34 Fuselage aft bulkhead/break point
35 Fuselage break point
36 Control cable pulley brackets
37 Fuselage frames
38 Oxygen bottles
39 Cooling-air exit flap actuating mechanism
40 Rudder cables
41 Fuselage lower longeron
42 Rear tunnel
43 Cooling-air exit flap
44 Coolant radiator assembly
45 Radio and equipment shelf
46 Power supply pack
47 Fuselage upper longeron
48 Radio bay aft bulkhead (plywood)
49 Fuselage stringers
50 SCR-695 radio transmitter-receiver (on upper sliding shelf)
51 Whip aerial
52 Junction box
53 Cockpit aft glazing
54 Canopy track
55 SCR-522 radio transmitter-receiver
56 Battery installation
57 Radiator/supercharger coolant pipes
58 Radiator forward air duct
59 Coolant header tank/radiator pipe
60 Coolant radiator ventral access cover
61 Oil-cooler air inlet door
62 Oil radiator
63 Oil pipes
64 Flap control linkage
65 Wing rear spar/fuselage attachment bracket
66 Crash pylon structure
67 Aileron control linkage
68 Hydraulic hand pump
69 Radio control boxes
70 Pilot's seat
71 Seat suspension frame
72 Pilot's head/back armour
73 Rearward-sliding clear-vision canopy
74 External rear-view mirror
75 Ring and bead gunsight
76 Bullet-proof windshield
77 Gyro gunsight
78 Engine controls
79 Signal-pistol discharge tube
80 Circuit-breaker panel
81 Oxygen regulator
82 Pilot's footrest and seat mounting bracket
83 Control linkage
84 Rudder pedal
85 Tailwheel lock control
86 Wing centre-section
87 Hydraulic reservoir
88 Port wing fuel tank filler point
89 Port Browning 0·5in guns
90 Ammunition feed chutes
91 Gun-bay access door (raised)
92 Ammunition box troughs
93 Aileron control cables
94 Flap lower skin (Alclad)
95 Aileron profile (internal aerodynamic balance diaphragm)
96 Aileron control drum and mounting bracket
97 Aileron trim-tab control drum
98 Aileron plastic (Phenol fibre) trim tab
99 Port aileron assembly
100 Wing skinning
101 Outer section sub-assembly
102 Port navigation light
103 Port wingtip
104 Leading-edge skin
105 Landing lamp
106 Weapons/stores pylon
107 500 lb (227 kg) bomb
108 Gun ports
109 Gun barrels
110 Detachable cowling panels
111 Firewall/integral armour
112 Oil tank
113 Oil pipes
114 Upper longeron/engine mount attachment
115 Oil-tank metal retaining straps
116 Carburettor
117 Engine bearer assembly
118 Cowling panel frames
119 Engine aftercooler
120 Engine leads
121 1,520 hp Packard V-1650 (R-R Merlin) twelve-cylinder liquid-cooled engine
122 Exhaust fairing panel
123 Stub exhausts
124 Magneto
125 Coolant pipes

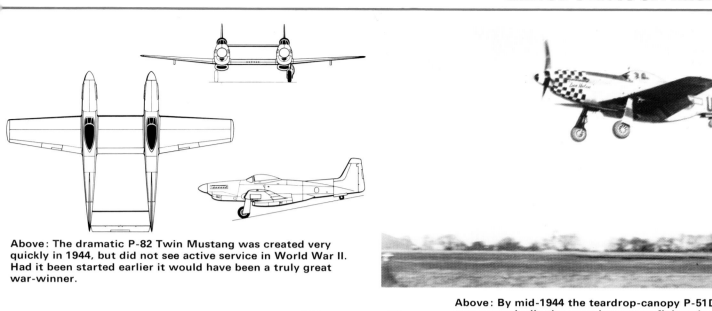

Above: The dramatic P-82 Twin Mustang was created very quickly in 1944, but did not see active service in World War II. Had it been started earlier it would have been a truly great war-winner.

Above: By mid-1944 the teardrop-canopy P-51D was numerically the most important fighter in the 8th Fighter Command in England. This one probably belonged to the 353rd FG, based at Raydon, with the checkerboard marking in black and yellow.

Left: The subject of the cutaway drawing is the P-51C. This was the interim sub-type with the V-1650 (Merlin) engine, a British-designed Malcolm bulged sliding canopy and other features not found in the P-51B, but the armament was still only four guns. In the meantime, North American Aviation had tested a beautiful streamlined bubble (teardrop) canopy on a modified P-51B with cut-down rear fuselage, and this led to the P-51D, with six guns.

126 Cowling forward frame
127 Coolant header tank
128 Armour plate
129 Propeller hub
130 Spinner
131 Hamilton Standard Hydromatic propeller
132 Carburettor air intake, integral with (133)
133 Engine-mount front-frame assembly
134 Intake trunk
135 Engine-mount reinforcing tie
136 Hand-crank starter
137 Carburettor trunk vibration-absorbing connection
138 Wing centre-section front bulkhead
139 Wing centre-section end rib
140 Starboard mainwheel well
141 Wing front spar/fuselage attachment bracket
142 Ventral air intake (radiator and oil cooler)
143 Starboard wing fuel tank
144 Fuel filler point
145 Mainwheel leg mount/pivot
146 Mainwheel leg rib cut-outs
147 Main gear fairing doors
148 Auxiliary fuel tank (plastic/pressed-paper composition, 90 gal/409 litres)
149 Auxiliary fuel tank (metal, 62·5 gal/284 litres)
150 27 in smooth-contour mainwheel
151 Axle fork
152 Towing lugs
153 Landing-gear fairing
154 Main-gear shock strut
155 Blast tubes
156 Wing front spar
157 Gun bay
158 Ammunition feed chutes
159 Ammunition boxes
160 Wing rear spar
161 Flap structure
162 Starboard aileron tab
163 Starboard aileron
164 Starboard aileron tab adjustment (ground setting)
165 Wing rib strengthening
166 Outboard section structure
167 Outer section single spar
168 Wingtip sub-assembly
169 Starboard navigation light
170 Detachable wingtip

▶**Armament:** (RAF Mustang I) four 0·303in in wings, two 0·5in in wings and two 0·5in in lower sides of nose; (Mustang IA and P-51) four 20mm Hispano in wings; (P-51A and B) four 0·5in in wings; (A-36A) six 0·5in in wings and wing racks for two 500lb (227kg) bombs; (all subsequent P-51 production models) six 0·5in Browning MG53-2 with 270 or 400 rounds each, and wing racks for tanks or two 1,000lb (454kg) bombs; (F-82, typical) six 0·5in in centre wing, six or eight pylons for tanks, radars or up to 4,000lb weapons.

History: First flight (NA-73X) 26 October 1940; (production RAF Mustang I) 1 May 1941; service delivery (RAF) October 1941; first flight (Merlin conversion) 13 October 1942; (P-51B) December 1942; final delivery (P-51H) November 1945; first flight (XP-82A) 15 April 1945; final delivery (F-82G) April 1949.

Users: (Wartime) Australia, Canada, China (and AVG), Netherlands, New Zealand, Poland, South Africa, Soviet Union, Sweden, UK (RAF), USA (AAC/AAF).

Development: In April 1940 the British Air Purchasing Commission concluded with "Dutch" Kindelberger, chairman of North American Aviation, an agreement for the design and development of a completely new fighter for the RAF. Designed, built and flown in 117 days, this silver prototype was the start of the most successful fighter programme in history. The RAF received 620 Mustang I, 150 IA and 50 II, while the US Army adopted the type with 500 A-36A and 310 P-51A. In 1942 the brilliant airframe was matched with the Merlin engine, yielding the superb P-51B, bulged-hood C (Mustang III) and teardrop-canopy D (Mustang IV), later C and all D models having six 0·5in guns and a dorsal fin. The final models were the K (different propeller) and better-shaped, lighter H, the fastest of all at 487mph. Total production was 15,586. Mustang and P-51 variants served mainly in Europe, their prime mission being the almost incredible one of flying all the way from British bases to targets of the 8th AF deep in Germany — Berlin or beyond — escorting heavies and gradually establishing Allied air superiority over the heart of Germany. After the war the Mustang proved popular with at least 55 nations, while in 1947–49 the US Air Force bought 272 examples of the appreciably longer Twin Mustang (two Allison-powered fuselages on a common wing), most of them radar night fighters which served in Korea. In 1945–48 Commonwealth Aircraft of

Above: A swarm of P-51D Mustangs, each with two 91·6-gal drop tanks, giving a range in excess of 2,000 miles. These examples served with the 15th Air Force in northern Italy.

Australia made under licence 200 Mustangs of four versions. In 1967 the P-51 was put back into production by Cavalier for the US Air Force and other customers, and the turboprop Turbo III and Enforcer versions were developed for the Pave Coin programme for Forward Air Control and light attack missions. Many of the new or remanufactured models of 1968–75 are two-seaters.

Below: A fine picture of Mustangs of the 8th Air Force 361st Fighter Group, based at Bottisham but soon headed for a base in France (St Dizier). Furthest from the camera is a P-51B.

Martin 187 Baltimore

Model 187, Baltimore I to V
(US Army A-30)

Origin: The Glenn L. Martin Company.
Type: Four-seat light bomber.
Engines: Two Wright Cyclone 14-cylinder two-row radials; (I, II) 1,600hp R-2600-A5B; (III, IV) 1,660hp R-2600-19; (V) 1,700hp R-2600-29.
Dimensions: Span 61ft 4in (18·69m); length 48ft 6in (14·78m); height 17ft 9in (5·41m).
Weights: Empty (III) 15,200lb (6895kg); maximum loaded (I) 22,958lb; (III) 23,000lb (10,433kg); (V) 27,850lb (12,632kg).
Performance: Maximum speed (I) 308mph; (III, IV) 302mph; (V) 320mph (515km/h); initial climb 1,500ft (457m)/min; service ceiling (typical) 24,000ft (7315m); range with 1,000lb bomb load (typical) 1,060 miles (1700km).
Armament: Four 0·303in Brownings fixed in outer wings; mid-upper position with manually aimed 0·303in Vickers K (I), twin Vickers (II), Boulton Paul turret with two or four 0·303in Browning (III), Martin turret with two 0·5in Browning (IV, V); rear ventral position with two 0·303in Vickers K; optional four or six fixed 0·303in guns firing directly to rear or obliquely downward. Internal bomb load up to 2,000lb (907kg).
History: First flight 14 June 1941; service delivery October 1941; final delivery May 1944.
Users: Australia, France, Italy, South Africa, Turkey, UK (RAF, RN).

Development: Martin received an RAF order in May 1940 for 400 improved Maryland bombers with deeper fuselages to allow intercommunication between crew members. In the course of design the more powerful R-2600 engine was adopted and the final aircraft marked an appreciable all-round improvement. The 400 were made up of 50 Mk I, 100 Mk II and 250 Mk III differing mainly in mid-upper armament. To facilitate Lend-Lease contracts, under which additional machines were ordered, the Model 187 was given the US Army designation A-30, but none were supplied for American use. After 281 Mk IIIA, identical to the III but on

Above: Ex-RAF Baltimore IV bombers flying over the Balkans with the Stormo Baltimore of the Italian Co-Belligerent AF. Seldom hitting the headlines, the Baltimore earned its keep.

US Lend-Lease account, and 294 Mk IV, production completed with 600 Mk V (A-30A), the total being 1,575 all for the RAF. Many were passed on to the South African AF, and a few to the Royal Navy, all being worked very hard in Cyrenaica, Tunisia, Sicily and Italy in bombing and close-support missions. In 1944 units of the co-belligerent Italian forces received ex-RAF machines and formed the Stormo Baltimore which was active over Jugoslavia and the Balkans.

Martin 162 PBM Mariner

Model 162, PBM-1 to 5A, Mariner GR.I

Origin: The Glenn L. Martin Company.
Type: Maritime patrol and anti-submarine flying boat with typical crew of nine.
Engines: (PBM-1) two 1,600hp Wright R-2600-6 Double Cyclone 14-cylinder two-row radials; (3C, 3S, 3R) 1,700hp R-2600-12; (3D) 1,900hp R-2600-22, (5, 5A) 2,100hp Pratt & Whitney R-2800-34 Double Wasp 18-cylinder two-row radials.
Dimensions: Span 118ft (36m); length (-1, 3S) 77ft 2in (23·5m); (3C) 80ft (24·38m); (5, 5A) 79ft 10in; height (-1) 24ft 6in; (remainder) 27ft 6in (8·4m).
Weights: Empty (-1) 26,600lb; (-3, typical) 32,328lb (14,690kg); (-5A)

34,000lb (15,422kg); maximum loaded (-1) 41,139lb; (3S) 56,000lb (25,400kg); (5) 60,000lb (27,216kg).
Performance: Maximum speed (all) about 205mph (330km/h); initial climb (typical) 800ft (244m)/min; service ceiling (-1) 22,400ft; (3S) 16,900ft; (5) 20,200ft (6160m); maximum range with military load (-1) 3,450 miles; (3C) 2,137 miles; (3S) 3,000 miles (4828km); (5) 2,700 miles (4345km).
Armament: (-1) one 0·5in Browning in nose turret, two in dorsal turret and two manually aimed from waist windows, one 0·30in in extreme tail (manually aimed over small cone of fire); (3B, 3C) twin-0·5in dorsal, nose and tail turrets; (3S) four manually aimed 0·5in in nose, tail and two waist windows; (5) eight 0·5in in three power turrets and two waist windows; weapon bays in engine nacelles with capacity of 2,000lb (907kg) in (-1) 4,000lb (1814kg) in all later versions (with provision for two externally hung torpedoes).
History: First flight (XPBM-1) 18 February 1939; service delivery (-1) September 1940; first flight (-5) May 1943; final delivery (5A) April 1949.
Users: Brazil, UK (RAF), US (Navy).

Development: Had it not been for the Catalina the PBM would have been by far the most important Allied patrol flying boat of World War II. It was designed in 1936 and proved by flying a quarter-scale model (Martin 162A). The full-size prototype was ordered on 3 June 1937, followed by 20 production -1 in December 1937. These were advanced and challenging boats, with high wing and power loading and stabilising floats which retracted inwards into the wing. Only one XPBM-2 was built, with long-range tanks and stressed for catapulting. Hundreds followed of the -3, -3C (which sank the U-boat which sank *Ark Royal*), -3R transport and -3S long-range anti-submarine versions, followed by the turreted -3D used throughout the South West Pacific. A small number of -3B served with RAF Coastal Command in 1943. The more powerful -5 had improved dorsal ASV radar (usually APS-15), the -5A was an amphibian and the post-war 5E had later equipment. Total deliveries were 1,235, and over 500 were in front-line service in the Korean war in 1950–53.

Left: This PBM-3S has two manually-aimed 0·5in nose guns and the usual search radar. All turrets were omitted from this ASW version.

Below: The PBM-5 was the last major production version, with powerful Double Wasp engines.

Martin 123,139 and 166 Bomber

Model 123, 139 and 166, B-10, -12 and -14

Origin: The Glenn L. Martin Company.
Type: 4/5-seat medium bomber.
Engines: (YB-10) two 775hp Wright R-1820-25 Cyclone nine-cylinder radials; (YB-12) two 665hp Pratt & Whitney R-1690-11 Hornet nine-cylinder radials; (XB-14) two 850hp P&W R-1830-9 Twin Wasp 14-cylinder two-row radials; (most export 139) 750hp Cyclone SGR-1820-F3S; (export 166) usually 850hp Cyclone R-1820-G2, but some 900hp Twin Wasp R-1830-SC3-G.
Dimensions: Span 70ft 6in (21·48m); length 44ft 8¾in (13·63m); (XB-10) 45ft; (B-12A) 45ft 3in; (export 166) 44ft 2in; height 11ft (3·35m); (XB-10) 10ft 4in; (B-10B) 15ft 5in; (export 166) 11ft 7in.
Weights: Empty (typical B-10, 139) 8,870—9,000lb; (166) 10,900lb (4944kg); maximum loaded (XB-10) 12,560lb; (B-10B) 14,600lb (6622kg); (B-12A) 14,200lb; (139) 14,192lb; (166) 15,624lb (Cyclone) or 16,100lb (Twin Wasp).
Performance: Maximum speed (all B-10, 139, B-12) 207—213mph (340km/h); (166) 255mph (W) or 268mph (P&W); initial climb (all) 1,290—1,455ft (about 410m)/min; service ceiling (all) 24,200—25,200ft (about 500m); range with bomb load (typical) 700 miles (1125km); maximum range with extra fuel (early models) 1,240 miles, (166) 2,080 miles.
Armament: (All) three rifle-calibre (usually 0·3in) machine guns manually aimed from nose turret, rear cockpit and rear ventral hatch; bomb load of 1,000lb (454kg) in internal bay beneath centre section in fuselage.
History: First flight (Model 123) January 1932; service delivery (123) 20 March 1932; (YB-10) June 1934; (export 139) late 1935; (166) January 1938.
Users: (WWII) Argentina, Netherlands East Indies, Turkey.

Development: The Glenn L. Martin Company, of Baltimore, was one of the earliest important suppliers of US Army and Navy aircraft, and "Billy" Mitchell used Martin MB-2 bombers to demonstrate, in 1922, that battle-

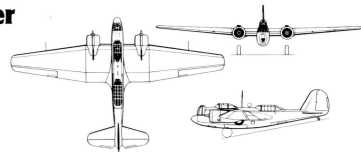

Above: Three-view of Martin B-10B (except for Model 166, others similar apart from engine installations).

ships could be sunk from the air. After many historic heavy bombers, torpedo bombers, dive bombers and flying boats, Martin built the Model 123 as a company venture. Several recent observers have judged "the Martin Bomber" one of the most significant single advances in the history of military aircraft. For the first time it introduced cantilever monoplane wings, flaps, stressed-skin construction, retractable landing gear, advanced engine cowls, variable-pitch propellers and an internal bomb bay with power-driven doors. Despite only 600hp Cyclone engines the prototype walked away from every pursuit (fighter) in the US Army and the Model 139 went into production as the YB-10, followed by the 12 and 14, total delivery being 152 by 1936. Export sales were inevitable and once these were permitted, in 1935, a further 189 were built. By far the largest user was the Dutch East Indies, which bought 120 Martin 139W and 18 of the improved 166 with single "glasshouse" canopy. All the Netherlands Indies machines were in constant action from December 1941 as the only bombers available until late January 1942, fighting fiercely and with much success against Japanese sea and land forces. Other major users were Argentina (25) and Turkey (20).

Right: A Martin 139W-H2 exported to the Netherlands East Indies and used by the Luchtvaartdienst Army Air Division. A total of 117 of these bombers were bought by that service, and though obsolescent when the Japanese attacked in December 1941 they fought courageously. Most were of a slightly later design with long "greenhouse" canopy.

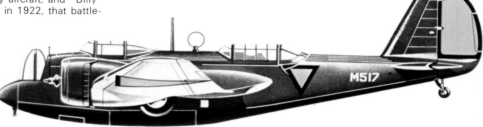

North American NA-16 (T-6 Texan, Harvard) family

AT-6/BC-1/SNJ series (Texan) and Harvard; (data for post-war T-6G)

Origin: North American Aviation Inc, Inglewood, Downey and Dallas; built under licence by Noorduyn Aviation and (post-war) Canadian Car & Foundry, Canada; Commonwealth Aircraft Corporation, Australia; ASJA (later Saab), Sweden; KK Watanabe and Nippon Hikoki KK, Japan; and Construcoes Aeronauticas SA, Brazil.
Type: Two-seat (some, single-seat) basic or advanced trainer, and attack.
Engine: Typically one 550hp Pratt & Whitney R-1340-AN1 nine-cylinder radial (see text).
Dimensions: Span 42ft 0¼in (12·8m); length 29ft 6in (8·99m); height 11ft 8½in (3·56m).
Weights: Empty 4,271lb (1938kg); loaded 5,617lb (2546kg).
Performance: Maximum speed 212mph (341km/h); initial climb 1,640ft (500m)/min; service ceiling 24,750ft (7338m); range 870 miles (1400km);
Armament: Normally provision for machine gun in either or both wing

roots and manually aimed in rear cockpit; light series wing bomb racks.
History: First flight (NA-16 prototype) April 1935; (production BT-9) April 1936; (NA-26) 1937; (Wirraway) 27 March 1939.
Users: (Wartime) Argentina, Australia, Bolivia, Brazil, Chile, China, Colombia, Cuba, Dominica, Ecuador, France, Honduras, Italy (Co-Belligerent), Japan, Mexico, Netherlands, New Zealand, Paraguay, South Africa, Southern Rhodesia, Soviet Union, Sweden, UK, USA (AAC/AAF, Navy, Marines), Uruguay, Venezuela.

Development: Perhaps the most varied family of aircraft in history began as a little monoplane trainer, with fixed gear and two open cockpits but all-metal stressed-skin construction, flown as a US civil machine in 1935. Its first offspring was the BT-9 basic trainer, supplied to many countries and made in many more (Yale was the RCAF name), powered by Wright R-975 Whirlwind, P&W Wasp Junior or Wasp engine. About 970 were built by North American. A second family were combat warplanes. Biggest family were the T-6 Harvard/Texan trainers derived from the NA-26, of which 15,109 were made by NAA in 1938—45, 755 in Australia as CAC Wirraways, 2,610 by Noorduyn in Canada, 176 by Japan (even receiving an Allied code-name: "Oak") and 136 by Saab in Sweden. By far the most important Allied training machine in World War II, thousands were re-furbished or remanufactured (2,068 by the original maker) in 1946—59 for 54 nations. Cancar built 555 T-6G in 1951—54.

Left: A large group of Harvard IIAs, from a training school in Canada. The IIA was a mass-produced version containing almost no aluminium alloys, steel and wood taking their place. Later came the AT-6D (Harvard III) with the original structure.

Below: The original Harvard I, as introduced to the RAF at Grantham in December 1938.

North American NA-62 B-25 Mitchell

B-25 to TB-25N, PBJ series, F-10

Origin: North American Aviation Inc, Inglewood and Kansas City.

Type: Medium bomber and attack with crew from four to six (see text).

Engines: (B-25, A, B), two 1,700hp Wright R-2600-9 Double Cyclone 14-cylinder two-row radials; (C, D, G) two 1,700hp R-2600-13; (H, J, F-10), two 1,850hp (emergency rating) R-2600-29.

Dimensions: Span 67ft 7in (20·6m); length (B-25, A) 54ft 1in; (B, C, J) 52ft 11in (16·1m); (G, H) 51ft (15·54m); height (typical) 15ft 9in (4·80m).

Weights: Empty (J, typical) 21,100lb (9580kg); maximum loaded (A) 27,100lb; (B) 28,640lb; (C) 34,000lb (15,422kg); (G) 35,000lb (15,876kg); (H) 36,047lb (16,350kg); (J) normal 35,000lb, overload 41,800lb (18,960 kg).

Performance: Maximum speed (A) 315mph; (B) 300mph; (C, G) 284mph (459km/h); (H, J) 275mph (443km/h); initial climb (A, typical) 1,500ft (460m)/min; (late models, typical) 1,100ft (338m)/min; service ceiling (A) 27,000ft (8230m); (late models, typical) 24,000ft (7315m); range (all, typical) 1,500 miles (2414km).

Armament: See text.

History: First flight (NA-40 prototype) January 1939; (NA-62, the first production B-25) 19 August 1940; (B-25G) August 1942.

Users: (Wartime) Australia, Brazil, China, France (FFL), Italy (Co-Belligerent), Mexico, Netherlands (1944), Soviet Union, UK (RAF, RN), US (AAC/AAF, Navy).

Development: Named in honour of the fearless US Army Air Corps officer who was court-martialled in 1924 for his tiresome (to officialdom) belief in air power, the B-25 — designed by a company with no previous experience of twins, of bombers or of high performance warplanes — was made in larger quantities than any other American twin-engined combat

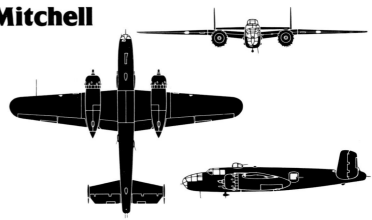

Above: Three-view of B-25J (RAF, Mitchell III).

aircraft and has often been described as the best aircraft in its class in World War II. Led by Lee Atwood and Ray Rice, the design team first created the Twin Wasp-powered NA-40, but had to start again and build a sleeker and more powerful machine to meet revised Army specifications demanding twice the bomb load (2,400lb, 1089kg). The Army ordered 184 off the drawing board, the first 24 being B-25s and the rest B-25A with armour and self-sealing tanks. The defensive armament was a 0·5in manually aimed in the cramped tail and single 0·3in manually aimed from waist windows and the nose; bomb load was 3,000lb (1361kg). The B had twin 0·5in in an electrically driven dorsal turret and a retractable ventral turret, the tail gun being removed. On 18 April 1942 16 B-25Bs led by Lt-Col Jimmy Doolittle made the daring and morale-raising raid on Tokyo, having made free take-offs at gross weight from the carrier *Hornet* 800 miles distant. Extra fuel, external bomb racks and other additions led to the C, supplied to the RAF, China and Soviet Union, and as PBJ-1C to the US Navy. The D was similar but built at the new plant at Kansas City. In 1942 came the G, with solid nose fitted with a 75mm M-4 gun, loaded manually with 21 rounds. At first two 0·5in were also fixed in the nose, for flak suppression and sighting, but in July 1943 tests against Japanese ships showed that more was needed and the answer was four 0·5in "package guns" on the sides of the nose. Next came the B-25H with the fearsome armament of a 75mm, 14 0·5in guns (eight firing ahead, two in waist bulges and four in dorsal and tail turrets) and a 2,000lb (907kg) torpedo or 3,200lb (1451kg) of bombs. Biggest production of all was of the J, with glazed nose, normal bomb load of 4,000lb (1814kg) and 13 0·5in guns supplied with 5,000 rounds. The corresponding attack version had a solid nose with five additional 0·5in guns. Total J output was 4,318, and the last delivery in August 1945 brought total output to 9,816. The F-10 was an unarmed multi-camera reconnaissance version, and the CB-25 was a post-war transport model. The wartime AT-24 trainers were redesignated TB-25 and, after 1947, supplemented by more than 900 bombers rebuilt as the TB-25J, K, L and M. Many ended their days as research hacks or target tugs and one carried the cameras for the early Cinerama films.

Above: First model with the slow-firing but punchy 75mm gun was the B-25G. Then came the hard-hitting B-25H, see text.

Below: This B-25J was one of 870 of various sub-types supplied freely under Lend-Lease to the Soviet Union in 1941-44.

Northrop P-61 Black Widow

P-61A, B and C and F-15 (RF-61C) Reporter

Origin: Northrop Aircraft Inc, Hawthorne, California.
Type: (P-61) three-seat night fighter; (F-15) two-seat strategic reconnaissance.
Engines: Two Pratt & Whitney R-2800 Double Wasp 18-cylinder two-row radials; (P-61A) 2,000hp R-2800-10; (B) 2,000hp R-2800-65; (C and F-15) 2,800hp (wet rating) R-2800-73.
Dimensions: Span 66ft (20·12m); length (A) 48ft 11in (14·92m); (B, C) 49ft 7in (15·1m); (F-15) 50ft 3in (15·3m); height (typical) 14ft 8in (4·49m).
Weights: Empty (typical P-61) 24,000lb (10,886kg); (F-15) 22,000lb (9979kg); maximum loaded (A) 32,400lb (14,696kg); (B) 38,000lb (17,237kg); (C) 40,300lb (18,280kg); (F-15, clean) 28,000lb (12,700kg).
Performance: maximum speed (A, B) 366mph (590km/h); (C) 430mph (692km/h); (F-15) 440mph (708km/h); initial climb (A, B) 2,200ft (670m)/min; (C, F-15) 3,000ft (914m)/min; service ceiling (A, B) 33,000ft (10,060m); (C, F-15) 41,000ft (12,500m); range with maximum fuel (A) 500 miles; (B, C) 2,800 miles (4500km); (F.15) 4,000 miles (6440km).

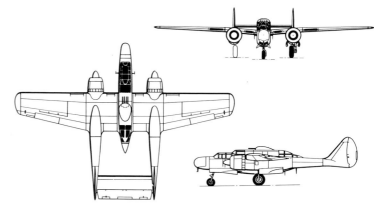

Above: Three-view of P-61A with turret (others similar).

Armament: Four Fixed 20mm M-2 cannon in belly, firing ahead (plus, in first 37 A, last 250 B and all C) electric dorsal turret with four 0·5in remotely controlled from front or rear sight station and fired by pilot; (B and C) underwing racks for 6,400lb load; (F-15A) no armament.
History: First flight (XP-61) 21 May 1942; service delivery (A) May 1944; first flight (F-15A) 1946.
User: USA (AAF).

Development: The first aircraft ever ordered to be designed explicitly as a night fighter, the XP-61 prototypes were ordered in January 1941 on the basis of combat reports from the early radar-equipped fighters of the RAF. A very big aircraft, the P-61 had the new SCR-720 AI radar in the nose, the armament being mounted well back above and below the rather lumpy nacelle housing pilot, radar operator and gunner with front and rear sighting stations. The broad wing had almost full-span double-slotted flaps, very small ailerons and lateral-control spoilers in an arrangement years ahead of its time. Black-painted (hence the name), the P-61A entered service with the 18th Fighter Group in the South Pacifice and soon gained successes there and in Europe. Buffet from the turret led to this soon being deleted, but the B and C had pylons for the very heavy load of four 250 gal tanks or 6,400lb (2900kg) bombs. Total production was 941, followed by 35 slim photo-reconnaissance versions.

Left: Though one of the largest fighters of all time, the P-61 was surprisingly tractable, and its lateral controls (shown off in operation) were exciting.

Below: A P-61A-5, one of the first to reach Europe, with 422 NFS, 9th AAF, Scorton, England.

Below: Another turretless P-61A is seen here at readiness at a 9th AAF dispersal somewhere in England. D-day stripes were worn by all P-61s in the European theatre.

25536

HUSSLIN HUSSEY

Republic P-47 Thunderbolt

P-47B, C, D, M and N

Origin: Republic Aviation Corporation.
Type: Single-seat fighter; (D and N) fighter-bomber.
Engine: One Pratt & Whitney R-2800 Double Wasp 18-cylinder two-row radial; (B) 2,000hp R-2800-21; (C, most D) 2,300hp R-2800-59; (M, N) 2,800hp R-2800-57 or -77 (emergency wet rating).
Dimensions: Span 40ft 9¼in (12·4m); length (B) 34ft 10in; (C, D, M, N) 36ft 1¼in (11·03m); height (B) 12ft 8in; (C, D) 14ft 2in (4·3m); (M, N) 14ft 8in.
Weights: Empty (B) 9,010lb (4087kg); (D) 10,700lb (4853kg); maximum loaded (B) 12,700lb (5760kg); (C) 14,925lb; (D) 19,400lb (8800kg); (M) 14,700lb; (N) 21,200lb (9616kg).
Performance: Maximum speed (B) 412mph; (C) 433mph; (D) 428mph

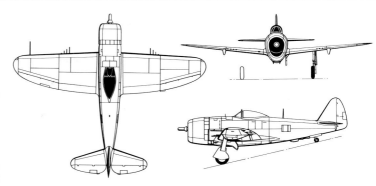

Above: Three view of P-47D-25.

(690km/h); (M) 470mph; (N) 467mph (751km/h); initial climb (typical) 2,800ft (855m)/min; service ceiling (B) 38,000ft; (C-N) 42,000—43,000ft (13,000m); range on internal fuel (B) 575 miles; (D) 1,000 miles (1600km); ultimate range (drop tanks) (D) 1,900 miles (3060km); (N) 2,350 miles (3800km).
Armament: (Except M) eight 0·5in Colt-Browning M-2 in wings, each with 267, 350 or 425 rounds (M) six 0·5in; (D and N) three to five racks for external load of tanks, bombs or rockets to maximum of 2,500lb (1134kg).
History: First flight (XP-47B) 6 May 1941; production delivery (B) 18 March 1942; final delivery (N) September 1945.
Users: Australia, Brazil, France, Soviet Union, UK (RAF), USA (AAF).

Development: Before the United States entered World War II it was eagerly digesting the results of air combats in Europe and, in 1940, existing plans by Republic's chief designer Alexander Kartveli were urgently replaced by sketches for a much bigger fighter with the new R-2800 engine. This appeared to be the only way to meet the Army Air Corps' new targets for fighter performance. Kartveli began by designing the best installation of the big engine and its turbocharger, placed under the rear fuselage. The air duct had to pass under the elliptical wing, and there were problems in achieving ground clearance for the big propeller (12ft diameter, even though it had the exceptional total of four blades) with landing gear able to retract inwards and still leave room in the wing for the formidable armament of eight 0·5in guns. After severe and protracted technical difficulties the P-47B was cleared for production in early 1942 and at the beginning of 1943 two fighter groups equipped with the giant new fighter (one the famed 56th, to become top scorers in Europe) joined the 8th AF in Britain to

continued on page 250 ▶

Above: When first used in Europe the P-47B was given white stripes to distinguish it from a Focke-Wulf 190 (which it in no way resembled). This P-47D-10 is seen later with Group insignia, D-day stripes, 108-gal paper tank and two 500lb bombs.

Left: Colourful P-47D-25 from the 352nd FS of the 353rd FG (same group that later used the P-51 on p. 243) based at Raydon.

Below: Early models became known as "razorbacks". These are probably over Long Island, but a yellow cowl would denote the 361st FG of the 8th AAF. The C introduced a longer fuselage and bomb/tank racks, the D a better engine, the D-25 the bubble hood and the D-30 a dorsal fin.

begin escorting B-17 and B-24 heavies. Their value was dramatically increased when they began to carry drop tanks and fly all the way to the target. The same capability turned the big and formidable fighter into a much-feared bomber and, with devastating firepower, vast numbers of P-47Ds strafed and bombed throughout the European and Pacific theatres until the end of World War II. Republic's output of D models (12,602) is the largest total of one sub-type of any fighter in history, total production of the "Jug" amounting to 15,660. The lightweight M was too late for its role of chasing flying bombs but scored successes against the Me 262 and Ar 234 jets, while the long-range P-47N matched the M fuselage with a bigger wing for the Pacific war. There were numerous experimental versions, one of which reached 504mph. After World War II the "Jug" was popular with many air forces until well into the 1950s.

Left: The ultimate P-47 was the P-47N, designed for the Pacific theatre. The need here was extreme range, and the fuselage and 2,800hp engine of the hot-rod P-47M (designed to catch flying bombs) was married to a new long-span wing which raised total fuel capacity to 954 Imp gal, and carried zero-length launchers.

Right: Pleasing study of an early P-47D of the razorback variety flying with the 8th AAF's 78th FG based at Duxford, Cambridgeshire. When the P-47 reached the Army some wag said the only thing it could do well was dive (while the RAF said pilots could evade enemy shells by running about inside the cockpit). Such feelings soon changed to respect, but the fact that it was undeniably a juggernaut led to its enduring nickname.

Right: The cutaway drawing shows that pilots could not, after all, dodge about inside a "Jug": it was far too full of equipment. Despite believers in small dog-fighters, it did well.

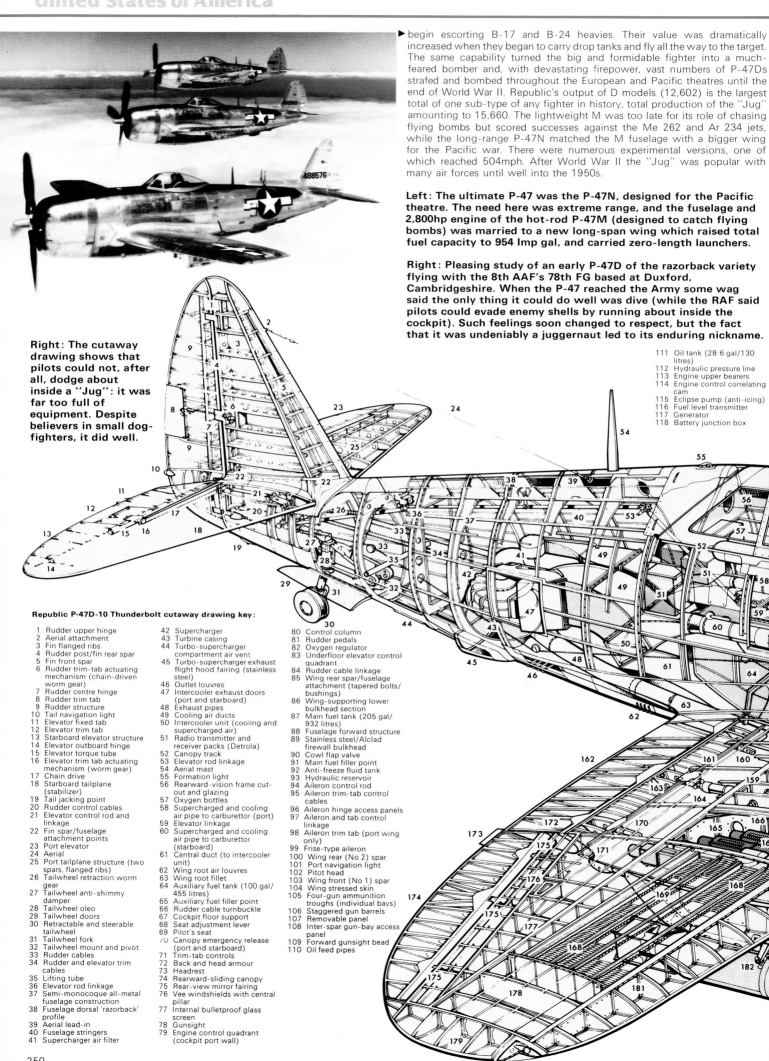

Republic P-47D-10 Thunderbolt cutaway drawing key:

1 Rudder upper hinge
2 Aerial attachment
3 Fin flanged ribs
4 Rudder post/fin rear spar
5 Fin front spar
6 Rudder trim-tab actuating mechanism (chain-driven worm gear)
7 Rudder centre hinge
8 Rudder trim tab
9 Rudder structure
10 Tail navigation light
11 Elevator fixed tab
12 Elevator trim tab
13 Starboard elevator structure
14 Elevator outboard hinge
15 Elevator torque tube
16 Elevator trim tab actuating mechanism (worm gear)
17 Chain drive
18 Starboard tailplane (stabilizer)
19 Tail jacking point
20 Rudder control cables
21 Elevator control rod and linkage
22 Fin spar/fuselage attachment points
23 Port elevator
24 Aerial
25 Port tailplane structure (two spars, flanged ribs)
26 Tailwheel retraction worm gear
27 Tailwheel anti-shimmy damper
28 Tailwheel oleo
29 Tailwheel doors
30 Retractable and steerable tailwheel
31 Tailwheel fork
32 Tailwheel mount and pivot
33 Rudder cables
34 Rudder and elevator trim cables
35 Lifting tube
36 Elevator rod linkage
37 Semi-monocoque all-metal fuselage construction
38 Fuselage dorsal 'razorback' profile
39 Aerial lead-in
40 Fuselage stringers
41 Supercharger air filter
42 Supercharger
43 Turbine casing
44 Turbo-supercharger compartment air vent
45 Turbo-supercharger exhaust flight hood fairing (stainless steel)
46 Outlet louvres
47 Intercooler exhaust doors (port and starboard)
48 Exhaust pipes
49 Cooling air ducts
50 Intercooler unit (cooling and supercharged air)
51 Radio transmitter and receiver packs (Detrola)
52 Canopy track
53 Elevator rod linkage
54 Aerial mast
55 Formation light
56 Rearward-vision frame cut-out and glazing
57 Oxygen bottles
58 Supercharged and cooling air pipe to carburettor (port)
59 Elevator linkage
60 Supercharged and cooling air pipe to carburettor (starboard)
61 Central duct (to intercooler unit)
62 Wing root air louvres
63 Wing root fillet
64 Auxiliary fuel tank (100 gal/455 litres)
65 Auxiliary fuel filler point
66 Rudder cable turnbuckle
67 Cockpit floor support
68 Seat adjustment lever
69 Pilot's seat
70 Canopy emergency release (port and starboard)
71 Trim-tab controls
72 Back and head armour
73 Headrest
74 Rearward-sliding canopy
75 Rear-view mirror fairing
76 Vee windshields with central pillar
77 Internal bulletproof glass screen
78 Gunsight
79 Engine control quadrant (cockpit port wall)
80 Control column
81 Rudder pedals
82 Oxygen regulator
83 Underfloor elevator control quadrant
84 Rudder cable linkage
85 Wing rear spar/fuselage attachment (tapered bolts/bushings)
86 Wing-supporting lower bulkhead section
87 Main fuel tank (205 gal/932 litres)
88 Fuselage forward structure
89 Stainless steel/Alclad firewall bulkhead
90 Cowl flap valve
91 Main fuel filler point
92 Anti-freeze fluid tank
93 Hydraulic reservoir
94 Aileron control rod
95 Aileron trim-tab control cables
96 Aileron hinge access panels
97 Aileron and tab control linkage
98 Aileron trim tab (port wing only)
99 Frise-type aileron
100 Wing rear (No 2) spar
101 Port navigation light
102 Pitot head
103 Wing front (No 1) spar
104 Wing stressed skin
105 Four-gun ammunition troughs (individual bays)
106 Staggered gun barrels
107 Removable panel
108 Inter-spar gun-bay access panel
109 Forward gunsight bead
110 Oil feed pipes
111 Oil tank (28·6 gal/130 litres)
112 Hydraulic pressure line
113 Engine upper bearers
114 Engine control correlating cam
115 Eclipse pump (anti-icing)
116 Fuel level transmitter
117 Generator
118 Battery junction box

119 Storage battery
120 Exhaust collector ring
121 Cowl flap actuating cylinder
122 Exhaust outlets to collector ring
123 Cowl flaps
124 Supercharged and cooling air ducts to carburettor (port and starboard)
125 Exhaust upper outlets
126 Cowling frame

127 2,000 hp Pratt & Whitney Double Wasp R-2800-21 eighteen-cylinder two-row engine
128 Cowling nose panel
129 Magnetos
130 Propeller governor
131 Propeller hub

132 Reduction gear casing
133 Spinner
134 Propeller cuffs
135 Curtiss constant-speed electric propeller (12 ft 2in)

136 Oil cooler intakes (port and starboard)
137 Supercharger intercooler (central) air intake
138 Ducting
139 Oil-cooler feed pipes

140 Starboard oil cooler
141 Engine lower bearers
142 Oil-cooler exhaust variable shutter
143 Fixed deflector
144 Excess exhaust gas gate
145 Belly stores/weapon shackles
146 Metal auxiliary drop tank (75 gal/341 litres)
147 Inboard mainwheel well door
148 Mainwheel well door actuating cylinder
149 Camera gun port
150 Cabin air-conditioning intake (starboard wing only)
151 Wing root fairing
152 Wing front spar/fuselage attachment (tapered bolts/bushings)
153 Wing inboard rib mainwheel well recess
154 Wing front (No 1) spar
155 Undercarriage pivot
156 Hydraulic retraction cylinder
157 Auxiliary (undercarriage mounting) wing spar
158 Gun bay warm air flexible duct
159 Wing rear (No 2) spar
160 Landing flap inboard hinge
161 Auxiliary (No 3) wing spar inboard section (flap mounting)
162 NACA slotted landing flaps
163 Landing flap centre hinge
164 Landing flap hydraulic cylinder
165 Four 0·5 in Browning guns
166 Inter-spar gun bay inboard rib
167 Ammunition feed chutes
168 Individual ammunition troughs (350 rpg)
169 Underwing stores/weapons pylon
170 Landing flap outboard hinge
171 Flap door
172 Landing flap profile
173 Aileron fixed tab (starboard wing only)
174 Frise-type aileron structure
175 Aileron hinge/steel forging spar attachments
176 Auxiliary (No 3) wing spar outboard section (aileron mounting)
177 Multi-cellular wing construction
178 Wing outboard ribs
179 Wingtip structure
180 Starboard navigation light
181 Leading-edge rib sections
182 Bomb shackles
183 500 lb (227 kg) M-43 demolition bomb
184 Undercarriage leg fairing (overlapping upper section)
185 Mainwheel fairing (lower section)
186 Wheel fork
187 Starboard mainwheel
188 Brake lines
189 Landing gear air/oil shock strut
190 Gun barrel blast tubes
191 Staggered gun barrels
192 Rocket-launcher slide bar
193 Centre strap
194 Front mount (attached below front spar between inboard pair of guns)
195 Deflector arms
196 Triple-tube 4·5in rocket-launcher (Type M10)
197 Front retaining band
198 4·5in M8 rocket projectile

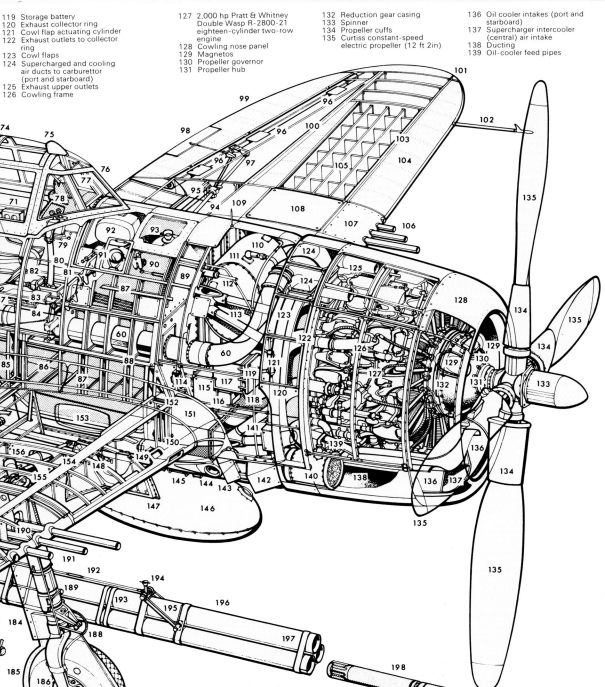

Vought V-166B F4U Corsair

F4U-1 to -7, F3A, FG, F2G and AU

Origin: Chance Vought Division of United Aircraft Corporation; also built by Brewster and Goodyear.
Type: Single-seat carrier-based fighter-bomber (sub-variants, see text).
Engine: (F4U-1) 2,000hp Pratt & Whitney R-2800-8(B) Double Wasp 18-cylinder two-row radial; (-1A) 2,250hp R-2800-8(W) with water injection; (-4) 2,450hp R-2800-18W with water-methanol; (-5) 2,850hp R-2800-32(E) with water-methanol; (F2G) 3,000hp P&W R-4360 Wasp Major 28-cylinder four-row radial.
Dimensions: Span 40ft 11¾in (12·48m), (British, 39ft 7in); length 33ft 8¼in (10·27m); (-1, -3) 33ft 4in; (-5N and -7) 34ft 6in; height 14ft 9¼in (4·49m); (-1, -2) 16ft 1in.
Weights: Empty (-1A) 8,873lb (4025kg); (-5, typical) 9,900lb (4490kg); maximum loaded (-1A) 14,000lb (6350kg); (-5) 15,079lb (6840kg); (AU-1) 19,398lb.
Performance: Maximum speed (-1A) 395mph (635km/h); (-5) 462mph (744km/h); initial climb (-1A) 2,890ft (880m)/min; (-5) 4,800ft (1463m)/min; service ceiling (-1A) 37,000ft (11,280m); (-5) 44,000ft (13,400m); range on internal fuel, typically 1,000 miles (1609km).
Armament: See text.

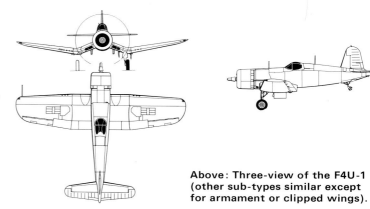

Above: Three-view of the F4U-1 (other sub-types similar except for armament or clipped wings).

History: First flight (XF4U) 29 May 1940; (production -1) June 1942; combat delivery July 1942; final delivery (-7) December 1952.
Users: (Wartime) Mexico, New Zealand, UK (RN), USA (Navy, Marines).

Development: Designed by Rex Beisel and Igor Sikorsky, the inverted-gull-wing Corsair was one of the greatest combat aircraft in history. Planned to use the most powerful engine and biggest propeller ever fitted to a fighter, the prototype was the first US warplane to exceed 400mph and outperformed all other American aircraft. Originally fitted with two fuselage and two wing guns, it was replanned with six 0·5in Browning MG 53-2 in the folding outer wings, each with about 390 rounds. Action with land-based Marine squadrons began in the Solomons in February 1943; from then on the Corsair swiftly gained air supremacy over the previously un-troubled Japanese. The -1C had four 20mm cannon, and the -1D and most subsequent types carried a 160gal drop tank and two 1,000lb (907kg) bombs or eight rockets. Many hundreds of P versions carried cameras, and N variants had an APS-4 or -6 radar in a wing pod for night interceptions. Brewster made 735 F3A, and Goodyear 4,008 FG versions, but only ten of the fearsome F2G. Fabric-skinned wings became metal in the post-war -5, most of which had cannon, while the 110 AU-1 attack bombers carried a 4,000lb load in Korea at speeds seldom exceeding 240mph! In December 1952 the last of 12,571 Corsairs came off the line after a longer production run (in terms of time) than any US fighter prior to the Phantom.

Above: Rejected by the US Navy for carrier operations, the F4U-1 was flown aboard USS Essex in December 1944, by Marine Corps fighter squadron VMF-124.

Left: An F4U-1D, with twin tank/bomb pylons and rails for eight rockets, serving with a squadron aboard USS Essex in 1945.

Below: An F4U-1A, with hook removed, operating with 18 Sqn, RNZAF, over the Solomon Islands and Guadalcanal in early 1945.

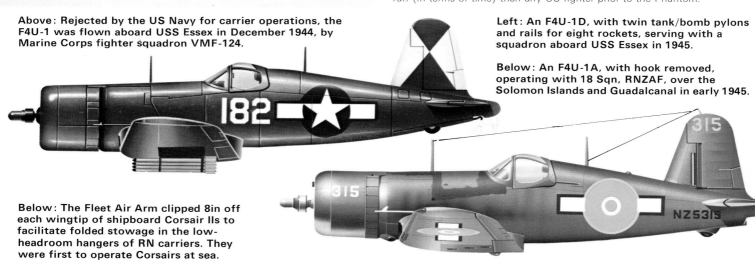

Below: The Fleet Air Arm clipped 8in off each wingtip of shipboard Corsair IIs to facilitate folded stowage in the low-headroom hangers of RN carriers. They were first to operate Corsairs at sea.

Vultee 72 A-31 Vengeance

A-31 and -35, Vengeance I-IV

Origin: Consolidated Vultee Aircraft Corporation, Nashville Division; also built by Northrop Aircraft, Hawthorne.
Type: Two-seat dive bomber.
Engine: One Wright R-2600 Cyclone 14-cylinder two-row radial; (A-31, Vengeance I, II, III) 1,600hp R-2600-19; (A-35, IV) 1,700hp R-2600-13.
Dimensions: Span 48ft (14·63m); length 39ft 9in (12·12m); height 14ft 6in (4·40m).
Weights: Empty (typical) 9,900lb (4490kg); maximum loaded (A-31) 14,300lb (6486kg); (A-35) 15,600lb; (A-35B) 17,100lb (7756kg).
Performance: Maximum speed (all) 273–279mph (440–450km/h); initial climb, typically 1,200ft (366m)/min; service ceiling (typical) 22,000ft (6700m); range (typical) 600 miles (966km).
Armament: (A-31, Vengeance I to III) four 0·303in Brownings in wings, and two manually aimed from rear cockpit; internal bomb load of up to 2,000lb (907kg); (A-35A, Vengeance IV) four 0·50in in wings, one manually aimed from rear, same bomb load; (A-35B) same but six 0·50 in in wings.
History: First flight, July 1941; service delivery (RAF) November 1942; termination of production, September 1944.
Users: Australia, Brazil, India, UK (RAF, RN), US (AAF, Navy).

Development: Designed by a team led by Richard Palmer to a British specification passed to Vultee in July 1940, the Vengeance eventually became combat-ready in a different world. No longer was the dive bomber the unstoppable agent of destruction; by 1943 it was recognised to have value only in conditions of local air superiority, and even then to need fighter cover. Eventually 1,528 of all types were built, of which 1,205 were passed to the

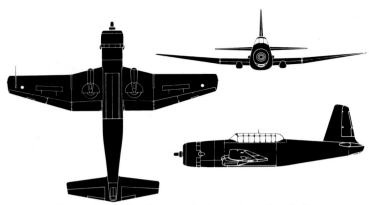

Above: Three-view, all sub-types being externally similar.

RAF (some purchased in 1940, others on Lend-Lease). Many served with the RAF, RAAF and Indian AF in Burma and South East Asia, where they at least saw considerable active duty. In 1940 it had been thought vast numbers would be needed, and a second production line was opened at Northrop, while the US Army adopted the type as the A-31. In 1942 the Americanised A-35 was in production at Convair's Nashville plant, but the US Army soon dropped even this version. Many RAF aircraft were modified as target tugs, and the last batch went to Brazil.

Right: Vultee built 831 aircraft designated A-35B with six wing guns and the R-2600-13 engine. None saw action with the US Army but 562 were allocated to the RAF and RAAF as the Vengeance IV. This one served on the Arakan (Burma) front with 7 Sqn, Indian AF.

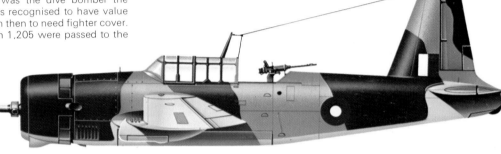

Waco CG-4A Haig, Hadrian

CG-4A Haig; RAF name Hadrian

Origin: The Waco Aircraft Company; also built by 14 other companies.
Type: Assault glider.
Engine: None.
Dimensions: Span 83ft 8in (25·5m); length 48ft 3¾in (14·7m); height 12ft 7½in (3·84m).
Weights: Empty 3,790lb (1721kg); normal loaded 7,500lb (3405kg); overload 9,000lb (4086kg).
Performance: Normal towing speed 125mph (200km/h); typical speed off tow 65mph (105km/h); minimum speed 38mph (61km/h).
Armament: None.
History: First flight, early 1941; (production CG-4A) April 1941; final delivery, December 1944.
Users: Canada, UK (RAF), US (AAF).

Development: Though the vast US aircraft industry produced many types of military glider during World War II, the entire production effort was concentrated upon this one type, which was the only US glider to see combat service. In sharp contrast to Britain's larger, all-wood Horsa, the CG-4A fuselage was constructed of welded steel tube with fabric covering, the entire nose being arranged to hinge upwards for loading/unloading vehicles up to Jeep size, or light artillery. The side-by-side pilot stations hinged with the nose, the two control wheels being suspended from the roof. In the main fuselage were benches for up to 15 fully armed troops or cargo up to 3,710lb (5,210lb as overload). The wing loading was very low; there were no flaps, but spoilers above the wing to steepen the glide. No fewer than 15 companies collaborated to build the CG-4A, and in two years more than 12,393 were delivered. In 1943 an RAF Hadrian was towed in stages from Montreal to Britain in a flight time of 28 hours. A few weeks later hundreds were used in the invasion of Sicily. Several thousand were used in 1944 in Normandy and the Rhine crossing, while large numbers went to the Far East for the planned invasion of Japan.

Right: An armada en route for France on D-day, the tugs being C-47s. The photographer's tug is linked both by the tow-rope and a wrapped-around intercom link, seldom used on operational missions. One snag with the Waco, as with the British Horsa, was that collisions with even small obstructions, such as saplings, could stave in the flimsy nose and injure the pilots. In practice assigned landing areas often did contain both natural and enemy-made obstacles.

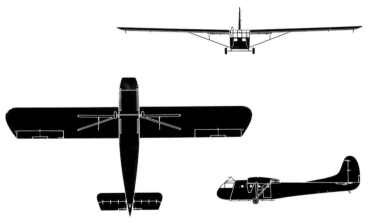

Above: Three-view of CG-4A.

Index

Picture credits

The publishers wish to thank the following organisations and individuals who have supplied photographs for this book. Photographs have been credited by page number.

Jacket: Charles E. Brown. ½ **title:** J. G. Moore Collection. **Title page:** US Navy. **Credits and contents page:** Charles E. Brown. **Foreword page:** Charles E. Brown. page 8: Interinfo.; **11-12:** M. B. Passingham Collection; **13** (top): M. B. Passingham Collection; (bottom) J. Cuny via M. B. Passingham Collection; **16** (top): IWM. **17:** M. B. Passingham Collection. **18-20:** Pilot Press Ltd. **21:** (top) IWM; (bottom) Pilot Press Ltd. **22:** (top) Pilot Press Ltd. **23:** (top and bottom) Pilot Press Ltd.; (centre) J. G. Moore Collection. **24:** J. G. Moore Collection. **25-27:** Pilot Press Ltd. **28:** (top and centre) Pilot Press Ltd.; (bottom) Dornier-Pressestelle. **29:** Pilot Press Ltd. **30:** (top) Pilot Press Ltd; (bottom) Fokker-VFW. **31:** J. G. Moore Collection. **32-34:** Pilot Press Ltd. **35:** J. G. Moore Collection. **36-37:** Pilot Press Ltd. **39:** Bapty and Co. **40:** J. G. Moore Collection. **41:** (top) Pilot Press Ltd; (bottom) IWM. **42-44:** Pilot Press Ltd. **45:** J. G. Moore Collection. **46:** (left) Bapty; (right) Pilot Press Ltd. **47:** J. G. Moore Collection. **48:** Pilot Press Ltd. **58-59:** J. G. Moore Collection; (bottom) Messerschmitt Archiv. **62:** Pilot Press Ltd. **62-63:** J. G. Moore Collection. **65:** Robert Hunt Library. **66:** J. G. Moore Collection. **67:** Pilot Press Ltd. **68:** (top) Pilot Press Ltd.; (bottom) Bapty. **70-71:** Pilot Press Ltd. **72:** Pilot Press Ltd. **73:** (top) IWM; (bottom) Pilot Press Ltd. **74-75:** Pilot Press Ltd. **76-78:** IWM. **79:** (top) Hawker Siddeley Aviation; (bottom) IWM. **80-82:** IWM. **83:** Hawker Siddeley. **84-90:** IWM. **91:** John G. Moore Collection. **92:** Hawker Siddeley. **93:** (top) IWM; (bottom) Paul Popper Ltd. **94:** (top) Hawker Siddeley (Philip Byrtles Collection); (bottom) IWM. **97-102:** IWM. **103:** Charles E. Brown. **104:** IWM. **105-106:** Hawker Siddeley. **107:** IWM. **108:** (top) IWM; (centre) Hawker Siddeley; (bottom) Charles E. Brown. **109:** (top) Hawker Siddeley; (bottom) IWM. **110:** (top) IWM; (bottom) Charles E. Brown. **111:** IWM. **112-113:** IWM. **114:** (top) IWM; (bottom) Pilot Press Ltd. **115:** J. G. Moore Collection. **116:** IWM. **117:** J. MacClancy Collection. **118:** (top) IWM; (bottom) Charles E. Brown. **119:** IWM. **121:** J. Scutts Collection. **122:** (top) IWM; (bottom) J. Scutts Collection. **123:** IWM. **124:** IWM. **125:** (top left) Westland Helicopters Ltd; (top right) US Navy; (bottom) Westland Hellicopters Ltd. **126-127:** VFW-Fokker. **128:** (top) VFW-Fokker; (bottom) M.B. Passingham Collection. **129:** SMA. **130:** Interinfo. **131:** SMA. **132-136:** SMA. **137:** (top) SMA; (bottom) SIAI Marchetti S.p.A. **138:** SMA. **140:** (top right and bottom right)

SMA; (top left and bottom left) SIAI Marchetti S.p.A. **141:** (top) Interinfo; (bottom) US Navy. **142:** M. B. Passingham Collection. **143:** M. B. Passingham Collection; (bottom) US Navy. **144:** US Navy (J. G. Moore Collection). **145:** (top left) IWM; (top right) US Navy (J. G. Moore Collection; (bottom) M. B. Passingham. **146-147:** Pilot Press Ltd.; (bottom) M. B. Passingham Collection. **149:** (bottom left) Fujifotos (J. G. Moore Collection); (bottom right) Interinfo. **150:** (top) Fujifotos (J. G. Moore Collection); (bottom two) Robert Hunt Library. **151-152:** Fujifotos (J. G. Moore Collection). **153:** (top) M. B. Passingham Collection; (bottom) Interinfo. **155:** (top) IWM; (bottom) US Navy. **157:** (top) M. B. Passingham Collection; (bottom) IWM. **158:** Fujifotos (J. G. Moore Collection). **159:** (top) US Navy; (bottom) M. B. Passingham Collection. **160-170:** M. B. Passingham Collection. **171:** (top) M. B. Passingham Collection; (bottom) US Navy. **172-173:** J. B. Cynck (Polish Aircraft Archives). **174:** M. B. Passingham Collection. **175:** Novosti. **177-178:** M. B. Passingham Collection. **181:** IWM. **182-183:** Novosti. **184:** (left) Carson Seeley (M. B. Passingham Collection); (right) Novosti. **185:** (top) Novosti; (bottom) M. B. Passingham Collection. **187:** Novosti. **188:** (top) M. B. Passingham Collection; (bottom) Robert Hunt Library. **189:** M. B. Passingham Collection. **190:** Novosti. **191:** M. B. Passingham Collection. **195-196:** Novosti. **197:** USAF. **198:** (top) J. MacClancy Collection; (bottom) Bell Aerospace Textron. **199:** (top) Bell Aerospace Textron; (bottom) USAF. **201:** USAF (J. MacClancy Collection). **202:** J. G. Moore Collection. **203:** (top) USAF; (bottom) USAF (J. MacClancy Collection). **204:** (top) J. MacClancy Collection; (bottom) USAF. **205:** USAF. **207:** USAF (J. Scutts Collection). **208:** Convair (General Dynamics). **209:** (bottom left) IWM; (bottom right) US Navy (J. MacClancy Collection); (bottom) J. G. Moore Collection. **211:** (top) US Navy (J. MacClancy Collection); (bottom) J. G. Moore Collection. **212-213:** J. MacClancy Collection. **214:** US Navy. **215:** (top) Pilot Press Ltd.; (bottom) US Navy. **216:** (top) J. MacClancy Collection; (bottom) IWM. **217:** (top) J. G. Moore Collection; (bottom) USAF. **218:** McDonnell Douglas. **219:** (top) USAF; (bottom) McDonnell Douglas. **220:** (top) USAF; (bottom) USAF. **221:** (top) USAF; (bottom) US Navy (J. Scutts Collection). **224:** US Navy (J. MacClancy Collection). **225:** (top) Bill Gunston Collection; (centre) US Navy (J. Scutts Collection); (bottom) Paul Popper Ltd. **226:** J. G. Moore Collection. **227:** J. MacClancy Collection. **228:** (top) US Navy; (bottom) Pilot Press Ltd. **229:** (top) US Navy; (bottom) USAF. **236:** J. MacClancy Collection. **238:** J. MacClancy Collection. **239:** Paul Popper Ltd. **243-244:** USAF. **245:** (top) SMA; (bottom) US Navy. **246:** J. G. Moore Collection. **247:** (top) J. MacClancy Collection; (bottom) USAF. **248:** (top) Bill Gunston Collection; (bottom) USAF (J. Scutts Collection). **249:** USAF. **250:** Fairchild Republic Co. **251:** J. MacClancy Collection. **252:** (top) US Navy; (bottom) Jerry Miller. **253:** IWM.